ARTHUI
Parer

M000158364

The purpose of the Cambridge Edition of the Works of Schopenhauer is to offer translations of the best modern German editions of Schopenhauer's work in a uniform format for Schopenhauer scholars, together with philosophical introductions and full editorial apparatus.

With the publication of *Parerga and Paralipomena* in 1851, there finally came some measure of the fame that Schopenhauer thought was his due. Described by Schopenhauer himself as 'incomparably more popular than everything up till now', *Parerga* is a miscellany of essays addressing themes that complement his work *The World as Will and Representation*, along with more divergent, speculative pieces. It includes his Aphorisms on the Wisdom of Life, reflections on fate and clairvoyance, trenchant views on the philosophers and universities of his day, and an enlightening survey of the history of philosophy. The present volume offers a new translation, a substantial introduction explaining the context of the essays, and extensive editorial notes on the different published versions of the work. This readable and scholarly edition will be an essential reference for those studying Schopenhauer, history of philosophy, and nineteenth-century German philosophy.

SABINE ROEHR is Assistant Professor of Philosophy at New Jersey City University. She is the author of *Hubert Fichte: Poetische Erkenntnis. Montage, Synkretismus, Mimesis* (1985) and *A Primer on German Enlightenment* (1995).

CHRISTOPHER JANAWAY is Professor of Philosophy at the University of Southampton. His most recent books include *Schopenhauer: A Very Short Introduction* (2002), and *Beyond Selflessness: Reading Nietzsche's Genealogy* (2007). His most recently edited collections include *The Cambridge Companion to Schopenhauer* (Cambridge, 2000), and *Better Consciousness: Schopenhauer's Philosophy of Value* (2009, co-edited with Alex Neill). He is General Editor of the Cambridge Edition of the Works of Schopenhauer, in which he has translated *The Two Fundamental Problems of Ethics* (2009), and co-translated three other volumes.

THE CAMBRIDGE EDITION OF THE WORKS OF SCHOPENHAUER

GENERAL EDITOR

Christopher Janaway

Titles in this series:

The Two Fundamental Problems of Ethics
translated and edited by Christopher Janaway

The World as Will and Representation: Volume 1
translated and edited by Judith Norman, Alistair Welchman and
Christopher Janaway with an Introduction by Christopher Janaway

On the Fourfold Root of the Principle of Sufficient Reason and Other Writings
translated and edited by David E. Cartwright, Edward E. Erdmann and
Christopher Janaway with an introduction by David E. Cartwright and Edward
E. Erdmann

Parerga and Paralipomena: Volume 1
translated and edited by Sabine Roehr and Christopher Janaway with an
introduction by Christopher Janaway

ARTHUR SCHOPENHAUER

Parerga and Paralipomena

Short Philosophical Essays

Volume I

TRANSLATED AND EDITED BY

SABINE ROEHR

CHRISTOPHER JANAWAY

with an Introduction by

CHRISTOPHER JANAWAY

CAMBRIDGE
UNIVERSITY PRESS

CAMBRIDGE
UNIVERSITY PRESS

University Printing House, Cambridge CB2 8BS, United Kingdom

Cambridge University Press is part of the University of Cambridge.

It furthers the University's mission by disseminating knowledge in the pursuit of education, learning and research at the highest international levels of excellence.

www.cambridge.org
Information on this title: www.cambridge.org/9781316616420

© Sabine Roehr and Christopher Janaway, 2014

First published 2014
First paperback edition 2016

A catalogue record for this publication is available from the British Library

Library of Congress Cataloguing in Publication data
Schopenhauer, Arthur, 1788–1860.
[Parerga und Paralipomena. English]
Parerga and paralipomena : short philosophical essays / Arthur Schopenhauer ; translated and edited by Sabine Roehr, Christopher Janaway ; with an introduction by Christopher Janaway.
pages cm. – (The Cambridge edition of the works of Schopenhauer; Volume 1)
Includes bibliographical references and index.
ISBN 978-0-521-87138-9
1. Philosophy. I. Roehr, Sabine, 1957-, translator. II. Title.
B3118.E5R64 2013
193–dc23
2013026736

ISBN 978-0-521-87138-9 Hardback
ISBN 978-1-316-61642-0 Paperback

Contents

General editor's preface

Schopenhauer is one of the great original writers of the nineteenth century, and a unique voice in the history of thought. His central concept of the will leads him to regard human beings as striving irrationally and suffering in a world that has no purpose, a condition redeemed by the elevation of aesthetic consciousness and finally overcome by the will's self-denial and a mystical vision of the self as one with the world as a whole. He is in some ways the most progressive post-Kantian, an atheist with profound ideas about the human essence and the meaning of existence which point forward to Nietzsche, Freud and existentialism. He was also the first major Western thinker to seek a synthesis with Eastern thought. Yet at the same time he undertakes an ambitious global metaphysics of a conservative, more or less pre-Kantian kind, and is driven by a Platonic vision of escape from empirical reality into a realm of higher knowledge.

Schopenhauer was born in 1788, and by 1809 had gone against his family's expectations of a career as a merchant and embarked on a university career. He completed his doctoral dissertation *On the Fourfold Root of the Principle of Sufficient Reason* in 1813, then spent several years in intensive preparation of what became the major work of his life, *The World as Will and Representation*, which was published at the end of 1818, with 1819 on the title page. Shortly afterwards his academic career suffered a setback when his only attempt at a lecture course ended in failure. Thereafter Schopenhauer adopted a stance of intellectual self-sufficiency and antagonism towards university philosophy, for which he was repaid by a singular lack of reaction to his writings. In 1835 he published *On Will in Nature*, an attempt to corroborate his metaphysics with findings from the sciences, and in 1841 two self-standing essays on free will and moral philosophy, entitled *The Two Fundamental Problems of Ethics*. A large supplementary second volume to *The World as Will and Representation* appeared in 1844, accompanied by a revised version of the original which now appeared as Volume One; then in 1851 another two-volume work, *Parerga and Paralipomena*, a collection of essays and observations. Only in the 1850s did serious interest in Schopenhauer's philosophy begin, with a favourable review appearing in an English journal and a few European universities offering courses on his work. In this final decade before his death in 1860 he published a third edition of *The World as Will and Representation* and a second edition of *The Two Fundamental Problems of Ethics*. After Schopenhauer's death his follower Julius Frauenstädt produced the first six-volume edition of his works in 1873, providing the basis for many subsequent German editions up to the *Sämtliche Werke* edited by Arthur Hübscher, which we use as the basis for our translations in the present edition.

Though Schopenhauer's life and the genesis of his philosophy belong to the early part of the nineteenth century, it is the latter half of the century that provides the context for his widespread reception and influence. In 1877 he was described by Wilhelm Wundt as 'the born leader of non-academic philosophy in Germany', and in that period many artists and intellectuals, prominent among them Richard Wagner, worked under the influence of his works. The single most important philosophical influence was on Nietzsche, who was in critical dialogue throughout his career with his 'great teacher Schopenhauer'. But many aspects of the period resonate with Schopenhauer's aesthetic theory, his pessimism, his championing of the *Upanishads* and Buddhism, and his theory of the self and the world as embodied striving.

Over the last three decades interest in Schopenhauer in the English-speaking world has been growing again, with a good number of monographs, translations and collections of articles appearing, where before there were very few. More general trends in the study of the history of philosophy have played a part here. There has recently been a dramatic rise in philosophical interest in the period that immediately follows Kant (including the German Idealists and Romanticism), and the greater centrality now accorded to Nietzsche's philosophy has provided further motivation for attending to Schopenhauer. Yet until now there has been no complete English edition of his works. The present six-volume series of Schopenhauer's published works aims to provide an up-to-date, reliable English translation that reflects the literary style of the original while maintaining linguistic accuracy and consistency over his philosophical vocabulary.

Almost all the English translations of Schopenhauer in use until now, published though they are by several different publishers, stem from a single translator, the remarkable E. F. J. Payne. These translations, which were done in the 1950s and 1960s, have stood the test of time quite well and performed a fine service in transmitting Schopenhauer to an English-speaking audience. Payne's single-handed achievement is all the greater given that he was not a philosopher or an academic, but a former military man who became a dedicated enthusiast. His translations are readable and lively and convey a distinct authorial voice. However, the case for new translations rests partly on the fact that Payne has a tendency towards circumlocution rather than directness and is often not as scrupulous as we might wish in translating philosophical vocabulary, partly on the fact that recent scholarship has probed many parts of Schopenhauer's thought with far greater precision than was known in Payne's day, and partly on the simple thought that after half a century of reading Schopenhauer almost solely through one translator, and with a wider and more demanding audience established, a change of voice is in order.

In the present edition the translators have striven to keep a tighter rein on philosophical terminology, especially that which is familiar from the study of Kant – though we should be on our guard here, for Schopenhauer's use of a Kantian word does not permit us to infer that he uses it in a sense Kant would have approved of. We have included explanatory introductions to each volume, and other aids to the reader: footnotes explaining some of Schopenhauer's original German vocabulary, a glossary of names to assist with his voluminous literary and philosophical references, a chronology of his life and a bibliography of German texts, existing English translations and selected further reading. We also give a breakdown of all passages that were added or altered by Schopenhauer in different editions of his works, especially noteworthy being the changes made to his earliest publications, *On the Fourfold Root* and the single-volume first edition of *The World as Will and Representation*. A further novel feature of this edition is our treatment of the many extracts Schopenhauer quotes in languages other than German. Our guiding policy here is, as far as possible, to translate material in any language into English. The reader will therefore not be detained by scanning through passages in other languages and having to resort to footnote translations. Nevertheless, the virtuoso manner in which Schopenhauer blends Latin, Greek, French, Italian and Spanish extracts with his own prose style is not entirely lost, since we have used footnotes to give all the original passages in full.

CHRISTOPHER JANAWAY

Editorial notes and references

Three kinds of notes occur in the translation:
(1) Footnotes marked with asterisks (*, ** and so on) are notes original to Schopenhauer's text. In the case of *Parerga and Paralipomena*, some of these notes are from the published text of 1851; others are incorporations by later editors of the German text, using handwritten material by Schopenhauer.
(2) Footnotes marked with small letters (a, b, c) are editorial notes. These either give information about the original wording in Schopenhauer's text (in German or other languages), or provide additional editorial information. All (and only) such *additional* information is enclosed in brackets [ ]. All footnote material *not* in brackets consists of words from the original text.
(3) Endnotes marked with numerals 1, 2, 3. The endnotes are collected at the end of the volume and indicate some variations between the published text of 1851 and the Hübscher text that has been used for this translation.

Schopenhauer's works are referred to by the following abbreviations. We give page references to those Cambridge editions published as of the date of the present volume. *BM* and *FW* are found in *The Two Fundamental Problems of Ethics*. *FR*, *VC* and *WN* appear collected in one volume. The Hübscher page numbers, which appear as marginal numbers in the Cambridge translations, are supplied in all cases, and can be used to locate passages in future volumes of the Cambridge edition.

Hübscher *SW* 1–7   *Sämtliche Werke*, ed. Arthur Hübscher (Mannheim: F. A. Brockhaus, 1988), vols. 1–7.
BM   *On the Basis of Morals* [*Über die Grundlage der Moral*].
FR   *On the Fourfold Root of the Principle of Sufficient Reason* [*Über die vierfache Wurzel des Satzes vom zureichenden Grunde*].

FW	*On the Freedom of the Will* [*Über die Freiheit des Willens*].
PP 1, 2	*Parerga and Paralipomena* [*Parerga und Paralipomena*], vols. 1 and 2.
VC	*On Vision and Colours* [*Über das Sehn und die Farben*].
WN	*On Will in Nature* [*Über den Willen in der Natur*].
WWR 1, 2	*The World as Will and Representation* [*Die Welt als Wille und Vorstellung*], vols. 1 and 2.

Unpublished writings by Schopenhauer are referred to thus:

GB	*Gesammelte Briefe*, ed. Arthur Hübscher (Bonn: Bouvier, 1978).
HN 1–5	*Der handschriftlicher Nachlaß*, ed. Arthur Hübscher (Frankfurt am Main: Kramer, 1970), vols. 1–5.
MR 1–4	*Manuscript Remains*, ed. Arthur Hübscher, trans. E. F. J. Payne (Oxford: Berg, 1988), vols. 1–4 [a translation of *HN* vols. 1–4].

Passages in Kant's *Critique of Pure Reason* are referred by the standard method, using A and B marginal numbers corresponding to the first and second editions of the work. Other writings by Kant are referred to by volume and page number of the monumental '*Akademie*' edition (Berlin: Georg Reimer/Walter de Gruyter, 1900–), in the form Ak. 4: 397. References to works of Plato and Aristotle use the standard marginal annotations.

Introduction

In June 1850 Schopenhauer had completed his two-volume work *Parerga and Paralipomena*, and was looking for a publisher. He sent a letter to F. A. Brockhaus, who had previously published his *The World as Will and Representation*, and explained how he viewed the new offering:

> Now, after six years' work, I have completed my miscellaneous philosophical writings: the preliminary drafts of them stretch back 30 years. For in them I have set down all the thoughts that could find no place in my systematic works. Hence this one is, for the most part, also incomparably more popular than everything up till now, as you can see from the list of contents that I include. After this I do not propose to write anything more; because I want to prevent myself from bringing into the world weak children of old age who accuse their father and vilify his reputation.[1]

Schopenhauer was 62 years old and would live for another decade. But in that final ten years he produced only revised versions of the works that were already behind him in 1850: *The World as Will and Representation*, *On Will in Nature* and *The Two Fundamental Problems of Ethics*. The contents of the new, popular work were already settled, and Schopenhauer requested only a small honorarium, but Brockhaus turned the proposal down, and Schopenhauer asked his friend Julius Frauenstädt for assistance in finding another publisher. As a result of Frauenstädt's efforts *Parerga and Paralipomena* was finally published in 1851 by A. W. Hayn of Berlin. Schopenhauer specified that there was to be a print-run of only 750, and no honorarium at all.[2]

In describing these writings as 'miscellaneous' Schopenhauer used the word *vermischt*, which might also be rendered as 'mixed'. Indeed his Latin phrase for them in his letters is *opera mixta*.[3] But his characteristic love of a learned phrase from an ancient language had led him to choose two Greek words for his title: *parerga* meaning 'subordinate works' or works 'apart

---

[1] Translation from *GB*, 242, letter to F. A. Brockhaus, 26 June 1850.   [2] See *GB*, 250.
[3] E.g. *GB*, 234.

from the main business', *paralipomena* things 'left aside' or 'passed over'. So this suggests a variety of pieces that for one reason or another did not fit into the programme of *The World as Will and Representation*, the work that defined his philosophy, or pursued different tacks that interested him but were not essential to that programme. In the draft of a Preface that was never published (see 438 below) Schopenhauer gave a more precise explanation:

> It can be said on the whole that the first volume contains the Parerga, the second the Paralipomena, the greatest portion of which are to be regarded as supplements to my chief work. – ... Thus these chapters presuppose knowledge of my philosophy, while the rest of the second volume, and the whole of the first, are comprehensible without such knowledge, although those who have become attached to my philosophy will recognize many connections to it everywhere, and indeed elucidations of it.

The essays that cover similar ground to *The World as Will and Representation* are those concerning the nature of philosophy, idealism, the history of philosophy (some of these being in Volume I despite what Schopenhauer says), ethics, aesthetics, religion, and the 'affirmation and negation of the will to life', the central theme of the massive Fourth Book of *The World as Will*. Other pieces are more divergent, speculative pieces on topics such as the apparent fatedness of our lives and the phenomena of clairvoyance and hypnotism, or what was then known as animal magnetism. Some of the writings are decidedly popular in tone, for example the aphorisms on the wisdom of life, and the essays on noise, reading, physiognomy and the notoriously offensive 'On Women'. In the latter case Schopenhauer is for the most part ranting, as he is at greater length in the well-known 'On University Philosophy', an impressive tirade against the careerism of professors making their living in the wake of Hegelianism and toeing the line of religious orthodoxy – favourite targets of Schopenhauer's wrath and well-worked themes in his writings during the 1830s and 1840s.

Parerga and Paralipomena was the first work of Schopenhauer's to gain a relatively wide audience, and with its publication in 1851 there finally came some measure of the fame that Schopenhauer thought his due. There were positive reviews in German journals, followed in April 1852 by one in English in *The Westminster Review*, and historical summaries of German philosophy started to make reference to him. The author of the English review was John Oxenford, who in 1853 wrote a much longer article on Schopenhauer, entitled 'Iconoclasm in German Philosophy' (*The Westminster Review*, April 1853).[4]

---

[4] For publication details, and discussion of the reception and influence of this article, see David E. Cartwright, *Schopenhauer: A Biography* (New York: Cambridge University Press, 2010), 526–9.

This review generally pleased Schopenhauer, with its recognition of his attempt to 'subvert the whole system of German philosophy which has been raised by university professors since the decease of Immanuel Kant', and its fulsome description of

> one of the most ingenious and readable authors in the world, skilful in the art of theory building, universal in attainments, inexhaustible in the power of illustration, terribly logical and unflinching in the pursuit of consequences, and – a most amusing qualification to everyone but the persons 'hit' – a formidable hitter of adversaries.

The translation of Oxenford's article into German played an important role in spreading the news of what it called 'this misanthropic sage of Frankfort', and helped to set in train the increased intensity of his reception during the final years of his life. A number of books and articles on Schopenhauer appeared, as did the revised editions of *The World as Will and Representation*, *On Will in Nature* and *The Two Fundamental Problems of Ethics*.

Oxenford found Schopenhauer 'misanthropic' and referred to his philosophy as 'ultra-pessimism' and the labels seem to have stuck ever since, although Schopenhauer was unhappy with the former epithet, and did not describe his own philosophy even as 'pessimism'. But by the 1870s pessimism was what he was chiefly known for. In a survey of German philosophy in 1877 Wilhelm Wundt called Schopenhauer 'the born leader of Non-Academic Philosophy in Germany', saying that 'the chief attraction of Schopenhauer's philosophy [has been] simply his Pessimism', in which '[he has] completely . . . fallen in with the current of his time'.[5] The view is echoed by Rüdiger Safranski: 'Schopenhauer would at last make his breakthrough – but not by himself and not by his own strength: the changed spirit of the time met him half-way.'[6] Whether it was because of the aftermath of the failed revolutions of 1848, the decline in influence of the Hegelian philosophy he had railed against, or the growth of scientific materialism and the cultural recognition of what Nietzsche would later call the 'death of God', Schopenhauer's work became well known and well received for the first time. The initial fame of his popular writings in *Parerga and Paralipomena* paved the way for a posthumous six-volume edition of Schopenhauer's works, edited by Frauenstädt in 1873, and opened a period in which the systematic philosophy first developed over half a century earlier became more widely read and commented upon.

[5] Wilhelm Wundt, 'Philosophy in Germany', *Mind* 2 (1877), 503–4.
[6] Rüdiger Safranski, *Schopenhauer and the Wild Years of Philosophy*, trans. Ewald Osers (London: Weidenfeld & Nicolson, 1989), 330.

Outline of *The World as Will and Representation*

The writings collected in the two volumes of *Parerga* are avowedly popular, and much that they contain can be approached without a thorough knowledge of Schopenhauer's metaphysics, ethics or aesthetics. However, he is writing against the background of his own systematic thought, and in some parts makes more substantial reference to it. So some awareness of that thought, as presented in *The World as Will and Representation*, will be of assistance to the reader of the present volume.

First published in 1818, then re-issued in 1844 with many textual changes and a large amount of supplementary material placed in a new second volume, *The World as Will and Representation* was always Schopenhauer's major work, and his other publications, *On the Fourfold Root of the Principle of Sufficient Reason*, *On Will in Nature* and *The Two Fundamental Problems of Ethics*, though they contain much that is of independent interest, are intended as elaborations and confirmations of it. Schopenhauer said that it contains a 'single thought'. But the nature of that thought has been the subject of some slightly perplexed debate.[7] If there is a single thought, it must be highly elusive or highly complex, or both. But we can perhaps make an initial approach towards what Schopenhauer means if we examine the framework of four Books into which *The World as Will and Representation* is divided. Their titles and discursive subtitles are as follows:

(1) The world as representation, first consideration. Representation subject to the principle of sufficient reason: the object of experience and science.
(2) The world as will, first consideration. The objectivation of the will.
(3) The world as representation, second consideration. Representation independent of the principle of sufficient reason: the Platonic Idea: the object of art.
(4) The world as will, second consideration. With the achievement of self-knowledge, affirmation and negation of the will to life.

What we first notice here is an oscillation between the two key terms from the book's title. At the core of the single thought, then, is this: one and the same world has two aspects, and we can learn about it by considering it as representation, then as will, then as representation in altered fashion, then as will in altered fashion. The two alterations in question introduce two more vital oppositions. With the world as representation, we can either consider it subject to the principle of sufficient reason, or independently of that principle.

---

[7] For one substantial discussion see John E. Atwell, *Schopenhauer on the Character of the World: The Metaphysics of Will* (Berkeley: University of California Press, 1995), 18–31.

With the world as will, we can consider it either descriptively for what it is, or on an evaluative dimension – with respect to its affirmation or negation. This, however, leaves us with an immense amount to explain. Let us next try to flesh out these bare bones a little, keeping in mind the four-part dynamic structure that any would-be 'single thought' really needs to have if it is to map on to the work as a whole.

Schopenhauer uses 'representation' (German *Vorstellung*) in the same way as his predecessor Kant uses it. It stands for anything that the mind is conscious of in its experience, knowledge or cognition of any form – something that is present to the mind. So we first consider the world as it presents itself to us in our minds. In ordinary human experience, and in the extension of this in the realm of scientific inquiry, we encounter objects, and these are ordered for us, necessarily, by space and time, and by relations of cause and effect. All the ways in which the world is thus ordered for us are species of the single principle 'Nothing is without a ground for its being rather than not being', otherwise known as the principle of sufficient reason. Every object is experienced as related to something else which grounds it. Everything in space and time has a determinate position in relation to other things in space and time, everything that happens has a determinate cause, every action relates back to a motive and to its agent's character, every truth is grounded in some other truth or in the evidence of the senses. So starting, as we must, from the world as we find it in everyday experience and empirical investigation, we see a multiplicity of objects related in necessary ways.

Schopenhauer allies himself with *transcendental idealism*. According to this doctrine, originally developed by Kant in the *Critique of Pure Reason* (1781), the objects that we experience as outside of us constitute a world of *appearance*, and we do not experience them *in themselves*. Empirical objects, the objects of which any subject has conscious experience, are a species of the subject's representations and what this realm of objects can contain is necessarily limited, shaped by the form of the mind itself. So the familiar world of empirical things is a world of objects *for a subject*, which is to say a world consisting of the subject's representations, and not a world that can be regarded as existing in itself, independently of the way it appears and must appear to an experiencing mind.

For Schopenhauer, the human mind, and indeed any conscious mind, receives data through the bodily senses and structures them using what he calls the understanding (*Verstand*) or intellect (*Intellekt*). Without this structuring we would register only a conglomeration of subjective sensations, but with it we attain a picture of material objects persisting in time, occupying space and serving as the casual origins of observed changes and of our sensations themselves. However, Schopenhauer's account of cognition differs quite markedly from Kant's in two principal ways. One is that the understanding or intellect cognizes the world in a manner that is not essentially conceptual. Adopting another technical term of Kant's, Schopenhauer maintains that what the understanding gives us is intuition (*Anschauung*), which essentially means perceptual awareness of particular objects in space and time. For Kant, the senses give us an array of intuitions, and the understanding provides concepts under which it actively orders the intuitions to produce an experience of a world of objects. Only creatures capable of forming concepts and making judgements could have such experience in the full sense. But for Schopenhauer animals such as a dog or a horse, who are incapable of forming concepts, are as much aware of a world of objects as any human subject: they perceive objects in space and time as we do, being simply incapable of making judgements, forming thoughts or carrying out reasoning, and hence being unable to comprehend anything more than what is immediately present in their perception.

The other, related feature that differentiates Schopenhauer from Kant is that the capacity to form and manipulate concepts discursively to frame thoughts and arguments, the capacity which for Schopenhauer is reason (*Vernunft*), though indeed unique to human beings, confers on them no special 'dignity', nor has any special connection with freedom or morality. Reason's concepts are secondary representations abstracted from the primary material given in intuition, and reason itself is merely instrumental in value: it enables us, unlike other animals, to be guided in our actions by a vast range of motives that involve thoughts about what is not present immediately in intuition. But a rationally motivated action is no more free than one motivated by fear, thirst or lust – it is just determined by a more complicated cause. The demotion of reason from any foundational role in characterizing human behaviour or explaining what has moral worth, and the consequent levelling that occurs between human beings and all other animals, are vital distinguishing features of Schopenhauer's ethics and of his philosophy as a whole.

In the Second Book of *The World as Will and Representation*, we find Schopenhauer maintaining that the idealist account of the world as representation, though true, is seriously inadequate. For by definition it does not tell us what we are in ourselves, nor what anything in the world apart from us is in itself. All this remains a 'riddle'. Schopenhauer proposes to solve that riddle by claiming that the essence, the very being in itself of all things is will (*Wille*). The world that appears to us as representation is, in itself, will. Representation gives us the world as it is empirically: diverse, plural, spatio-temporal, law-like and open to investigation. Will is what that same world and we ourselves are metaphysically – one and the same essence underlying all the many empirical appearances. We must make sense of the world and ourselves from within, not merely experience its manifestations in an ordered fashion from a standpoint detached from reality. This is the central message of the Second Book of *The World as Will and Representation*.

A guiding thought here is that there is one single essence that underlies all objects and all phenomena, ourselves included, one single way in which the 'riddle' of all existence can be deciphered. Arguing from our immediate cognition of our own actions, Schopenhauer suggests that whenever we are conscious of ourselves, we are conscious of ourselves as willing something. This unique inner consciousness is to give us the vital clue to our own essence: it is that we strive towards ends. The intrinsic core of our being is will. Schopenhauer uses this term 'will' very widely, including in it not only desires, but actions, emotions and affects, and non-conscious or 'blind' processes that can be described as end-directed. Human rationality and consciousness are extremely useful, and give us an instrumental superiority over other beings, but are really only a froth on the surface, and do not distinguish humanity from the rest of nature at the most fundamental level. Indeed, our advanced capacities for cognition can be explained, for Schopenhauer, as serving the ends of willing: our ability to perceive and investigate the world functions primarily to enable us to manipulate objects that confront us, in order to continue existing and to reproduce ourselves. If we are really to understand the world and our place within it, we must not remain at the surface of the world as representation, but must delve into this deeper and darker aspect of reality, the world as will – darker because everything that wills or strives is necessarily at the mercy of suffering, and because this suffering has neither point nor end. As long as we will, we suffer; but that we will, and ultimately what we will, is a function of our inescapable essence, not something rationally chosen, and not something we have the means to put an end to by willing. Schopenhauer then extends this idea to the whole of nature, claiming that we can make sense of the world as such by seeing its essence as a kind of blind striving manifesting itself in multiple instances within our experience. Thus the one world is both representation and will.

As *The World as Will and Representation* progresses the tone becomes more sombre. The individual's existence is dominated by will: desires and needs are incessant, shaping all our perception and understanding of the world, ends can never finally be fulfilled, suffering is ever-present, but the will drives us on to strive and want more things that can never properly satisfy us even if we attain them. Willing goes on perpetually and without final purpose: it is built into us and into the whole fabric of the world. Throughout nature one being dominates and destroys another, the world-will tearing itself apart, says Schopenhauer, because it is a hungry will and there is nothing for it to feed on but itself.

At the mid-point of *The World as Will and Representation* we return to a new, and brighter, consideration of the world as representation. It can happen, according to Schopenhauer, that we confront objects in a kind of experience that is out of the ordinary. We find all the usual kinds of relation – space, time and cause and effect – suspended, and lose ourselves in contemplation, forgetful of ourselves and of the distinction between ourselves and what we perceive. This is aesthetic experience, an extreme form of disinterestedness, a passive 'mirroring' of the world in which we cease to grapple with the world of objects, cease striving, and find temporary release from pain. While becoming as free as we can from subjectivity, we apprehend nature in a manner that takes our cognition as close as possible to the true essence of things: we perceive timeless features than run throughout nature, which Schopenhauer calls Ideas, intending us to take this notion in a sense close to Plato's (or to what are often called Platonic Forms nowadays). Art provides the best opportunity for this kind of experience because it gives us a view of nature mediated through the exceptionally objective mind of a genius. Art enables in us as spectators a state of calm passivity and enhanced objectivity, and the various art forms allow us to recognize diverse aspects of the will's manifestation in the world, from, as it were, a vantage point where our individual own will is not engaged.

The transition to the Fourth Book of *The World as Will and Representation* takes us back to the world as will, considered now with respect to its 'affirmation and negation', or at any rate the affirmation and negation of the 'will to life' that Schopenhauer finds to be the essence of each individual. This final part – by far the longest and, in Schopenhauer's words, the 'most serious' – is concerned with ethics, in both a narrower and broader sense. Building on the descriptive account of the will from the Second Book, Schopenhauer gives his own answers to conventional ethical questions: What are morally good and bad actions and characters? What is the nature of right and wrong? What constitutes compassion, and the virtues of justice and loving kindness? In what sense, if at all, are our actions free? But the main thrust of the Fourth Book is a broader ethical treatment of the value of human existence as such – a profound and troubling discussion that borders on religious territory while remaining resolutely atheist in its conviction.

Although we exist as empirical individuals separate from one another and so naturally regard the good as consisting in what we can attain through the activity of our own individual wills, this is a mistaken view. When fully understood, the life of a human individual does not and cannot contain anything of true value. Worse, the existence of everything – as a manifestation of the pointlessly self-perpetuating and self-devouring will – is something ultimately to be lamented. To exist as a manifestation of will is to strive without fulfilment, and hence to suffer. Attaining an end through willing brings us nothing of positive value – it just temporarily erases a painful lack or absence. New desires flood in almost immediately to plague us with their non-satisfaction. And if no new desires arrive we are tormented by boredom. Because will is our essence, 'All life is suffering' – and consequently we need 'salvation' or 'redemption' from it. Such redemption can be achieved only by the will within us 'turning' and 'denying itself'.[8] Schopenhauer has argued that the notion of a 'highest good' makes no sense.[9] But, he says, if we wish to bring that expression back from retirement and apply it to anything, then it must be to the denial of the will: cessation of desires and wants that relate to the individual we find ourselves as, detachment of identification from this individual, elimination of one's personality, one's natural self with its in-built attachment to the ends of living and willing, and contemplation of the whole world, with all its strivings and pains, as if from nowhere within in it. Calling on mystical ideas from diverse cultural traditions, Schopenhauer argues that only such a radical transformation, occasioned by a deep and rare knowledge of the ubiquity of suffering and the illusoriness of the individual, can restore any value to our existence. The world in itself, outside of the forms of space and time that govern the world as representation for us, cannot be separated into individuals. The truly wise human being would comprehend this and would cease to be attached to the strivings of the particular individual manifestation of will he or she is. The will that is the human being's essence would recoil from pursuing any of its goals, and the sense of individuality weaken to the point where reality could be contemplated with a serenity that is void of the usual pains of existence because the subject has become void of all striving and void of the usual sense of self.

History of philosophy in *Parerga*, Volume I

The present volume opens with two essays on the history of philosophy, the short 'Sketch of a history of the doctrine of the ideal and the real' and the

---

[8] See *WWR* I, §§56, 69 (Hübscher *SW* 2, 366, 472–3).   [9] Ibid., §65 (Hübscher *SW* 2, 427–8).

more substantial 'Fragments for the history of philosophy'. Throughout both discussions Schopenhauer assumes the philosophical position in *The World as Will and Representation* as true, and traces a course in which earlier thought leads up to it. The 'Sketch' concerns modern philosophy, beginning with Descartes and ending with Fichte, Schelling and Hegel, who are pointedly set apart in an Appendix. The 'Fragments' take a much broader view that goes back to the Presocratics and culminates in some remarks on Schopenhauer's own philosophy.

The 'Sketch' is organized around the view that the central problem in philosophy is 'the problem of the ideal and the real, i.e. the question what in our cognition is objective and what subjective, thus what is to be ascribed to any things distinct from ourselves and what to ourselves' (7). Schopenhauer claims with some plausibility that it is only in modern philosophy, from Descartes onwards, that this problem comes to the fore. Schopenhauer's outline of the post-Cartesian debate encompasses Malebranche, Leibniz, Spinoza, Locke, Berkeley, Hume and Kant – though the latter is not discussed with the thoroughness found elsewhere is Schopenhauer's writings.[10] Descartes posed philosophy's central question because he came to realize what Schopenhauer sees as a straightforward truth, namely the truth – expressed in Kant's terminology, not Descartes' – that the world is given to us only 'as representation'. This reveals a 'chasm' between subjective and objective, between what is ideal and what is real. Schopenhauer interprets the thought of Malebranche, Leibniz and Spinoza, with their various notions of occasional causes, pre-established harmony, and the identity between the order of ideas and the order of things, as centring upon this issue, but as mishandling it by retaining wrong-headed concepts such as 'God', 'substance' and 'perfection'.

It is only with the philosophy of John Locke that the problem of the real and the ideal comes properly into focus, and the route to transcendental idealism is discernible. Schopenhauer puts Berkeley in the same tradition as Malebranche, Leibniz and Spinoza, and gives him credit for being the first true proponent of idealism, meaning

> the recognition that what is extended in space and fills it, thus the intuitive world in general, by all means can exist as such only in our *representation*, and that it is absurd, even contradictory, to attribute to it as such an existence outside of all representation and independent of the cognitive subject. (16)

---

[10] See the following essay 'Fragments for the History of Philosophy', §13, and especially the extended Appendix to *WWR* 1, and ch. 2 of *BM*.

This single idea, for Schopenhauer, was Berkeley's achievement, in response to the realism of Locke. What then is it that Locke gets right? First, he abandons spurious 'hyperphysical hypotheses' about God and immaterial, thinking substances. He relies on 'experience and common understanding' and for him substance is simply matter. Secondly, he marks out certain qualities, which are called secondary qualities, as 'ideal' in Schopenhauer's sense, that is, belonging merely to what is present in subjective consciousness: 'This is the origin of the distinction between thing in itself and appearance, which later became so extremely important in the Kantian philosophy' (19). From his idealist perspective Schopenhauer finds this fundamental distinction of huge significance, but parts company with Locke over his realism concerning the primary qualities, extension, motion and so on. Spatial and temporal qualities are none of them on the 'real' side of the divide that Locke seems to imply: Schopenhauer takes it as established that such determinations of space and time are, as Kant taught, all a priori forms of cognition, not dwelling in things in themselves but rather on the side of the subject's representation. Schopenhauer ends this brief narrative with the suggestion that he himself has 'solved the problem around which all philosophizing has revolved since *Descartes*' (21) with his dual theory of the world as representation and as will. The ideal, the subjective, is the world as representation, and 'the will alone is left as the real'. Schopenhauer believes that there have only been half a dozen real minds at work on the issue in Europe, and seems confident that he has sorted things out for them.

Schopenhauer opens the Appendix to the 'Sketch' by saying that his readers may be surprised to find Fichte, Schelling and Hegel excluded from the preceding discussion, an attitude that could be shared by today's reader, who may be used to the classification of these figures precisely as the German Idealists. Schopenhauer is blunt: these people are not like Descartes, Spinoza, Locke and Kant, they are not even philosophers, but sophists, whose thought never goes beyond advancing their personal interest – lovers of self, not lovers of wisdom. While Schopenhauer proceeds chiefly by impugning the motives of these contemporaries, and mocking their convoluted styles of writing, there are some criticisms of their actual doctrines here. Fichte is accused of solving the problem of the real and the ideal by simply abolishing the former, Schelling of absurdly identifying abstract conceptual thought with reality, Hegel of taking this idea and running with it to the allegedly absurd lengths of positing 'self-movement of the concept' as 'a revelation of all things within and outside of nature' (29). In a handwritten addition to his text Schopenhauer descends to crudity, calling Hegel's writings 'psychically effective vomitive', which should be kept in a pharmacy 'since the disgust they excite is really quite specific' (30). Schelling, by contrast, receives some praise as 'the most talented of the three', but even then only as a useful eclectic and stop-gap until some real philosopher should come along.

Schopenhauer's narrative in the longer essay 'Fragments for the history of philosophy' begins at the beginning, with the Presocratic philosophers, and proceeds through sections on Socrates, Plato, Aristotle, the Stoics, Neoplatonists, Gnostics, Scotus Erigena, Scholasticism, Bacon, then (reprising the previous essay to some extent) the post-Cartesian 'Philosophy of the Moderns', and finally Kant and himself. In his writings on the ancient philosophers Schopenhauer shows his considerable powers as a scholar, priding himself on his direct encounter with the original texts, and giving detailed and penetrating analysis of a wide range of sources. He is especially aware of vagaries of transmission of earlier thinkers through later accounts. Nonetheless he tends to assume that philosophers in different periods of history are in pursuit of timeless truths. He thinks that the fundamental propositions of Anaxagoras, Empedocles or Democritus are to be found 'in the works of the modern philosophers, for example those of Descartes, Spinoza, Leibniz and even Kant, ... repeated countless times' (33). He emphasizes those doctrines which he regards as clear anticipations of what he thinks right – e.g. the Eleatics are given a Kantian-sounding distinction between *phainomena* and *nooumena*, Empedocles' ordering principles of love and hate are glossed as 'a blind drive, i.e. a will without cognition' (34), and so on. He maintains that 'There is also much in the remaining doctrines of these Presocratic philosophers that can be proven true'; and that Socrates exhibits 'quite a few similarities' with Kant (41).

The short section on Plato does not reflect Schopenhauer's debt to this great ancient thinker, which he elsewhere puts on a par with his debt to Kant. In fact, the section focuses less on Plato as such, and more on the notion of a pure rational soul. Schopenhauer uses the term 'dianoiology' for this theoretical view, which for him is as pernicious as it is persistent in the history of philosophy. For Schopenhauer there is no soul separate from the body, and besides, it is intuition, the grasp of an objective world through the senses, that is fundamental to human cognition, not rational, discursive thought. More than half the section entitled 'Plato' returns to the modern arena, arguing that Kant's view of cognition puts paid to the Cartesian version of dianoiology. Schopenhauer's attitude to Aristotle is strikingly different to his attitude to Plato. Throughout his writings he quotes short extracts from Aristotle's works to substantiate a point in his argument, and he recognizes Aristotle as 'a great, even stupendous mind' (48), but he shows only limited respect, finding him superficial rather than profound – 'his view of the world is shallow even if ingeniously elaborated' (45) – and laments how he 'cannot stick to anything but jumps from what he plans to tackle to something else that occurs to him just now, in the way that a child drops a toy in order to seize another one that it has just noticed' (46). Aristotle's empirical approach is valuable, though he does not always practise it consistently, according to Schopenhauer, and it is only from Bacon onwards that true empiricism emerges.

Schopenhauer's disquisitions on writers of later antiquity show wide scholarly reading but often strike a critical, even churlish note. Stobaeus' exposition of the Stoics is 'incredibly dreary' (51), Iamblichus is 'full of crass superstition and crude demonology . . . he is a bad and unpleasant writer: narrow, eccentric, grossly superstitious, muddled, and vague' (53–4), Proclus is an 'insipid chatterer'. Style of writing is of enormous importance to Schopenhauer, as a transparent reflection of the clarity of thought and the character of the writer. We have seen how critical he is of Hegel for his obscure and pompous writing. In this respect he is scarcely less harsh on his great hero, Kant.[11] So it is not surprising that virtually no one in the history of philosophy escapes this kind of complaint, though he finds Plotinus, despite his 'boring verbosity and confusion' (55) an important and insightful thinker. Schopenhauer attempts no comprehensive account of these earlier figures, but rather picks out certain themes of particular interest to him: the realism–nominalism debate, free will, metempsychosis, the world-soul, the ideality of time, in all of which he finds pre-echoes of themes from his own philosophy. He is also keen to postulate Indian origins for certain ideas: he thinks Plotinus must have been influenced by Indian thought via Egyptian religion, and later claims that 'a small drop of Indian wisdom may have reached Erigena' on the grounds that Dionysius, his source for many of his doctrines, probably lived in Alexandria (61).

The later portions of the essay contain more cohesive argument, and indeed more than half of the history is devoted to developments from Kant's critical philosophy of the 1780s up to the 1850s, with some careful, critical exposition of Kant contrasted with more elaborate deprecation of the German Idealists: 'foolish pseudo-demonstrations, whose absurdity was hidden under the mask of obscurity', 'the pap . . . of absolute identity', 'a platitudinous, dull, loathsome-repulsive, ignorant charlatan', and the like.

---

[11] See 'Critique of the Kantian Philosophy', Appendix to *WWR* 1.

The culmination of this essay is once again Schopenhauer's own philosophy. The expositions of Kant are philosophically the most sophisticated passages in this volume. Schopenhauer clearly explains Kant's distinction between the *transcendent* (what purports to be knowledge beyond all experience) and the *transcendental* (knowledge of the a priori formal features of experience). He also gives his major objection to Kant's theoretical philosophy, directed at Kant's assumption of things in themselves lying beyond experience, which had already been criticized by one of Schopenhauer's early teachers, G. E. Schulze. The allegation is that without falling into fatal inconsistency Kant could not account for the thing in itself. Having limited cognition to what falls within possible experience, he could not, or should not, use the principles that apply within experience to try to account for the relation between experience and something wholly outside it:

> However, this transition from the effect to the cause is the only way to arrive at what is external and objectively existing from what is internal and subjectively given. But after Kant had attributed the law of causality to the cognitive form of the subject, this path was no longer open to him. Moreover, he himself warned often enough against making transcendent use of the category of causality, that is, use that goes beyond experience and its possibility. (86–7)

Schopenhauer's view is that this was rightly seen as a difficulty for Kant's exposition of his position, but wrongly taken by Kant's immediate idealist successors to discredit the thing in itself altogether, starting Fichte on the path which he so deplores. Kant is inconsistent over the thing in itself, according to Schopenhauer, but that merely means that we have to look for a different means of arriving at the truth about it, as he claims to do in his theory of the will as inner essence of ourselves and the world.

The other major part of Schopenhauer's discussion of Kant here concerns the 'brilliant' Transcendental Dialectic section of the *Critique of Pure Reason*, in which Kant 'undermined speculative theology and psychology to such an extent that since then for the life of us we have not been able to resurrect them' (90). Schopenhauer does not want to resurrect pre-Kantian metaphysical speculation about a supposed God or immaterial, immortal soul, and, as we see here, he thinks it impossible to do so after Kant's demolition job. But what motivates much of his discussion in this essay and elsewhere is the refusal of much of the contemporary intellectual world (see especially the following essay on university philosophy) to see beyond religion and leave its metaphysics behind. He gives a revised account of Kant's critique of the rationalist doctrine of the soul as immaterial substance, and an exposition of the three arguments for the existence of God which Kant had shown not to prove any such thing. So far he is with Kant, but he is less sympathetic to the 'sop' or 'anodyne' Kant goes on to offer:

> Kant provided, as a substitute for the proofs of God's existence, his postulate of practical reason and ensuing moral theology, which, without any claim to objective validity for knowledge, or theoretical reason, was to have complete validity in respect to acting, or practical reason, whereby a faith without knowledge was grounded – so that people at least could put their hands on something. (102)

In earlier writings Schopenhauer had been contemptuous of what he saw as Kant's conjuring trick:[12] the way in which the idea of God appears to emerge as a consequence of Kant's ethics, when it was already smuggled in among its presuppositions along with the assumption of absolute imperatives. Here Schopenhauer is a little more conciliatory. The idea of a just God who rewards and punishes after death might serve as 'an allegory of truth', though not a terribly good one:

> An analogous schema of the same tendency, but containing much more truth, greater plausibility, and thus more immediate value, is Brahmanism's doctrine of retributive metempsychosis, according to which some day we must be reborn in the shape of every being injured by us in order to suffer the same injury. (102)

Schopenhauer – whom Nietzsche later called 'the first admitted and uncompromising atheist among us Germans'[13] – uses the remainder of this historical essay as an extended critique of theism, and of the inability of Kant's successors to swallow the consequences of his argument that there could be no theoretical proof of God. The notion of 'the absolute' gained currency in German Idealism, and the academic establishment thus found a way of making God self-evident without having to reveal too much of his nature: 'they keep him behind a hill, or rather behind a resounding edifice of words, so that we can see hardly a tip of him' (104). Theistic belief has its origins in egoism, for Schopenhauer, in the need to posit some being whom one could expiate in order to achieve reward and salvation. Theism, he argues, not only faces the traditional problem of evil, but 'is in conflict with morality, because it abolishes freedom and accountability', and can offer finite beings no consolation over their individual deaths. Moreover, it is only out of Judaism, for which Schopenhauer does not disguise his contempt,

---

[12] See *BM*, 129–30 (Hübscher SW 4, 125–6).
[13] *The Gay Science*, ed. Bernard Williams, trans. Josephine Nauckhoff (Cambridge University Press, 2001), 219.

that monotheistic belief has ever developed. He reminds us that the great majority of human beings from other cultures have held no such belief.

University philosophy

'On university philosophy' is an extended polemic against academic philosophy in mid-nineteenth-century German universities, and can be viewed in different lights. It is, on the one hand, a powerful and poignant defence of intellectual freedom against craven, time-serving conformism, a plea for the pursuit of truth over that of livelihood and self-interest, and a devastating attack on the perversion of thought by the influence of regimes and religions. On the other hand, it is the work of a man who had once aspired to a university career and been disappointed, whose books had gone neglected by the establishment, but who was fortunate enough to have a private income that gave him the capacity to live self-sufficiently and write philosophy purely for its own sake. The resulting piece is a blend of high-minded principle and vindictiveness, and, for all that, a vivid and engaging read. The same individual targets from the previous two essays reappear, and Schopenhauer is again in full flow against Hegel for his overwhelming, and allegedly utterly destructive, influence on the German academy. But Schopenhauer goes further and turns 'philosophy professor' into a blanket term of abuse, arguing that to do philosophy for money is *ipso facto* to be corrupt as a thinker – dishonest, unoriginal and liable to produce self-congratulatory nonsense. Schopenhauer also assumes an elitist, aristocratic picture of intellectual life, in which there a few rare geniuses who genuinely advance the subject, but are destined to be ignored by the benighted rabble of their contemporaries. It suits those of modest talent to deny such a hierarchy and at the same time dress up their productions in impenetrable 'expert' verbiage that lends them the appearance of profundity. But whatever does not conform to the jargon of the day is mistrusted and shunned.

In this protracted rant, the same recurring points are cumulatively impressed on the reader using the gamut of rhetorical devices: textual evidence, literary parallel, simile, humour, sarcasm, insult, appeal to history, and appeal to plain common sense. Schopenhauer derides his academic contemporaries as 'comic philosophers', and labels their trade as 'philosophy for hire', invoking Plato's contrast between Socrates and the mercenary Sophists. He argues that philosophizing in order to gain a livelihood is by definition at odds with philosophy proper, which he idealizes as always a disinterested pursuit of truth for its own sake, undertaken at all times in history by a minority of superior minds against whom the mass of mediocrities conspire. He writes at length of the corrupting effect of university philosophy on the minds of its students. On the one hand such teaching is conceived as a utilitarian training for public life, 'ensuring that the future junior barristers, lawyers, doctors, candidates, and teachers receive even in their innermost convictions that orientation which is adequate to the intentions that the state and its government have in regard to them' (132). But at the same time to theorize the state as the purpose of human existence (Hegel again) had the result that 'the barrister and the human being were ... one and the same. It was a true apotheosis of philistinism' (133). Apart from questioning the necessity for academic philosophy as such – 'It is not necessary at all to keep a couple of insipid windbags at every university in order to spoil philosophy for young people for the rest of their lives' – Schopenhauer's one really practical proposal is to limit the teaching of philosophy to logic, which is 'a completed science capable of strict proof' and, so as to acquaint students at least with something great,

> a history of philosophy, succinctly delivered and to be completed within one semester, reaching from Thales to Kant, so that, as a consequence of its brevity and lucidity, it allows as little leeway as possible for the Herr Professor's own views and acts merely as a primer for the student's own future study. (175)

The most serious theme of this essay, connecting with the discussion that closed the 'Fragments', is the relationship between philosophy and theology. Kant's demolition of the proofs of the existence of God was so effective that there was no going back to them as a basis for theology. Instead the philosophers of the nineteenth century were forced to rely on a spurious 'immediate consciousness of God' that bypassed the need for any proof, while happily decorating their ideas with Kantian terms that 'sound erudite':

> since their philosophy has always only the good Lord as its chief subject matter, who for that reason also appears as a familiar old acquaintance needing no introduction, they now discuss whether he is in the world or remains outside, i.e. resides in a space where there is no world. In the first case they dub him *immanent*, in the second case *transcendent*, while acting most serious and scholarly and speaking Hegelian jargon. It is the greatest fun – which reminds us older people of a copper engraving in *Falk's* satirical almanac, which depicts *Kant*, ascending to heaven in a balloon, casting all the articles of his wardrobe, including his hat and wig, down to earth, where monkeys pick them up and adorn themselves with them. (155)

But this God of the philosophers is, in any case, a confusion. For he has to be something like the personal God of Christianity, while also being the pantheistic Absolute, or God as world, that is fashionable in intellectual circles. The confusion then has to be fudged with impenetrable language in order to seem to conform to orthodoxy.

Speculations on fate and spirits

There follow two essays in which Schopenhauer takes phenomena that we might now describe as 'paranormal', fate and spiritual apparitions, and tries to give some rational account of them. About the first account he is hesitant: 'Although the thoughts to be imparted here yield no firm result, indeed, might be called a mere metaphysical fantasy, I have not been able to bring myself to abandon them to oblivion' (177). At issue here is 'The belief in special providence, or else in the supernatural guidance of events in the course of an individual's life' (177). Schopenhauer reiterates the claim he had defended in his *Essay of the Freedom of the Will* in 1841, that everything that happens, happens with strict necessity, and that there is no freedom of the will in respect to individual actions. He now calls that view 'demonstrable fatalism'. But 'transcendent fatalism' would be a much stronger view, that the actions and experiences of each individual life are playing out some overall set purpose, that our lives have a design and integrity, and 'bear the stamp of a moral, or inner, necessity' (180). But what to make of such a view? The language Schopenhauer uses here is, by his standards, wavering and tentative, when he speaks of a thought that 'can be the most absurd or the most profound' (178), says 'it might not be true, but it is as good as true' (189), and begins by admitting: 'Our meditations on this may . . . not be much more than a groping and fumbling in the dark, where we are aware of something being there, yet do not really know where or what it is' (177).

One interesting and positive idea to be found in this essay is that we construe our lives in two ways, one in terms of objective causal necessity, the other in terms of a subjective necessity like that with which the events of a poem or drama unfold, and that the two are not incompatible ways of understanding ourselves. Schopenhauer's speculation is that some metaphysical account of this may be possible. For him there is definitely no intelligent agency that has literally designed our lives. But he toys with the idea that his own metaphysics can supply a rationale for the purposive view of ourselves:

> If we look back from here to the principal result of my entire philosophy, namely that what presents and maintains the phenomenon of the world is the *will* that also lives and strives in each individual, and remind ourselves at the

same time of the generally acknowledged similarity between life and dream, then ... we can quite generally imagine as possible that, just as we are all the secret impresarios of our dreams, so too by analogy the fate that governs the actual course of our lives actually springs somehow from the *will*. (193)

Even here, however, it remains vague what Schopenhauer thinks he has really shown. The upshot of the essay would appear to be that we have a natural and irresistible tendency to construct for ourselves a narrative in which everything that happens to us is a necessary part of an unfolding plan, that to think in this way need not conflict with an explanation of events as contingently caused, and that the idea of some external power that constructs a plan for us can be at least a helpful allegory for understanding the course of our lives.

The 'Essay on spirit-seeing and related issues' is a much weightier affair in terms of length and the extensive documentation Schopenhauer provides, though no amount of evidence is likely to endear many of today's readers to his argument. In his earlier book, *On Will in Nature*, Schopenhauer had devoted a chapter to 'Animal Magnetism', the term originating from Anton Mesmer, who was famous in the late eighteenth and early nineteenth centuries for his hypnotic techniques, which he believed gave evidence of a magnetic force transmissible in and between living beings. Similar practices continued during the first half of the nineteenth century and many studies were made of a range of phenomena that went under the names of 'clairvoyance' (for which Schopenhauer uses the German equivalent *Hellsehen*) and 'somnambulism' (literally 'sleepwalking'). Writing in 1850 Schopenhauer is confident that the evidence shows these to be genuine phenomena: 'whoever nowadays doubts the facts of animal magnetism and the clairvoyance connected with it should not be called incredulous but ignorant' (200). His essay recounts a large number of these facts from eyewitness testimonies and scientific collections of data, which include prophetic dreaming, lucid dreaming (or 'truth-dreaming'), in which one perceives one's real environment, quasi-seeing through the stomach or limbs, second sight, presentiment of the future, thought-control and mind-reading, sympathetic cures, and apparitions of the deceased.

What explanation can be given for all these apparent phenomena? Schopenhauer cannot accept any *spiritualistic* explanation: there are no such things as spirits in his universe, and in the objective world of our experience there are only material things occupying space and time. What he offers instead is an *idealistic* explanation (200). According to Schopenhauer's interpretation of idealism, the world of material things in space and time is not the world as it is in itself, and distinctions of space and time, and therefore distinctions between individuals, are not ultimately real. So why can there not be experiences of what is located remotely in time or space, and of what another is thinking or feeling? The experience may arise not by external causal influence, but from within the subject, and could be seen as a manifestation of the wider reality in itself of which the individual is an expression. Most readers of today are unlikely to accept this explanation, or perhaps even the need of it. But Schopenhauer catalogues a large number of published investigations that describe the clairvoyant and somnambulistic practices and theories of the day, and in doing so provides a potentially rich source for the historian of ideas.

The wisdom of life

Schopenhauer's 'Aphorisms on the wisdom of life' were very influential from the moment they were published: as Rüdiger Safranski puts it, they 'rapidly became the Bible of the educated bourgeoisie'.[14] Ever since then this section of *Parerga* has enjoyed something of an existence apart from the rest of the book, and apart from the central themes of Schopenhauer's original philosophy. This is understandable, given that they are 'philosophical' more in the commonly used sense of 'thoughtfully reflective from a somewhat resigned point of view', rather than in any more technical sense. In his 'Introduction' to the Aphorisms Schopenhauer makes some brief remarks about their status and relation to his philosophy which will bear a little exposition. The aphorisms, he says, constitute eudaemonology, or 'instructions to a happy existence' (*eudaimonia* being the Greek term that is often, if misleadingly, translated as 'happiness'). But according to Schopenhauer's philosophy, especially as expounded in *The World as Will and Representation*, a happy existence is not really possible, not in a human life. Worse still, it is at the same time inborn in us, as living creatures whose essential drive is towards life, that we make the mistake of thinking that we exist in order to be happy.[15] Hence the discussion that follows constitutes 'an accommodation . . . insofar as it retains the ordinary, empirical standpoint and adheres to its error' (274).

Schopenhauer has argued that if we had the choice whether or not to have a human life, we could not reasonably choose it over non-existence, if we understood its nature fully. But given that we find ourselves in such a life, how should we regard it? From his 'higher, metaphysical–ethical standpoint' Schopenhauer has given the answer that we should hope we can come to regard it in detachment from our individuality with all its striving, and all its weals and woes. The wisdom to be imparted here, however, is for

---

[14] Safranski, *Schopenhauer and the Wild Years of Philosophy*, 334.
[15] See *WWR* 2, ch. 49 (Hübscher *SW* 3, 729).

someone who falls short of that ideal and wishes to live as well as possible, and attain at least what passes for happiness in ordinary life. The message of the higher standpoint still rubs off on the advice, however: 'those who have fully absorbed the doctrine of my philosophy ... will not have great expectations of any thing or any condition, will not passionately strive for anything in the world, nor will they greatly lament the failure of some undertaking' (359). Schopenhauer's outlook owes much to Stoicism, and his advice is peppered with quotations from the likes of Seneca and Epictetus.

The first three chapters of the Aphorisms deal with the three kinds of things that make a difference to one's life: 'What one is', 'What one has', and 'What one represents' or what one is in the eyes of others, this last comprising matters such as honour, rank and fame. Schopenhauer makes the preliminary comment that the first category, what one is *by nature* (including 'health, strength, beauty, temperament, moral character, and intelligence' (275)) far outweighs the other two in importance. 'The principal element in the well-being of human beings ... is what exists or happens within themselves' (275–6). After these divisions comes a sequence of 'Counsels and maxims' in 53 numbered sections, subdivided into 'General views', 'Our attitude towards ourselves', 'Our attitude towards others' and 'Our attitude towards the course of the world and fate'. The volume ends with a chapter entitled 'On the different stages of life'.

As with much elsewhere in this volume, the Aphorisms contain a blend of the general and the personal. Schopenhauer begins by stating that 'the sages of all ages have always said the same, and the fools, i.e. the vast majority in all eras, have always done the same, namely the opposite' (274), suggesting that his task is merely to transmit timeless wisdom. He offers good advice on many matters such as not attaching too much value to the opinions of others and on the absurdity of a code of honour so extreme as to lead to a culture of duelling. Yet often his particular perspective thrusts itself forward. For example, the chapter on 'What one is' claims that 'the person richly endowed by nature in an intellectual respect appears to be the happiest' (298). Such people are privileged in that their intellectual life 'becomes their real purpose ... whereas for the rest this stale, empty, and sad existence must itself be regarded as the end' (296). Schopenhauer straightforwardly disparages the 'ordinary' human being who continually relies on external diversions and company to make life bearable, and lauds the solitary, self-sufficient and unsociable life of the mind as superior. Again, when he talks of fame, he seeks to convince us that those, like himself, who go unappreciated by their own age are destined for greater long-term recognition:

the more someone belongs to posterity, i.e. to humanity in general and as a whole, the more alien he is to his own age . . .; therefore, such a person is not tinged with this age's local colour, and as a result it can easily happen that it lets him pass as a stranger. This age rather appreciates those who serve the affairs of its brief day or the mood of the moment and, therefore, belong entirely to *it*, live with it and die with it. (345)

The final chapter 'On the different stages of life' could only have been written by someone of relatively advanced years. It has insightful things to say about ways in which our perceptions of past, present and future, and of the passage of time, alter as we age: 'Seen from the standpoint of youth, life is an infinitely long future; from the standpoint of old age, it is a very short past' (424), and some of the handwritten sentences Schopenhauer added to his own copy of *Parerga* between 1851 and his death in 1860 have a definite poignancy: 'When we are young we imagine that the events and persons important for the course of our life will make their entrance with drums beating and trumpets sounding; in old age retrospective reflection shows that they all slipped in through the back door quietly and hardly noticed' (423). 'In old age every day that we have lived produces a sensation related to the one that a delinquent has at every step on his way to the gallows' (424). 'The older we become, the less consciously we live. Things rush by without leaving an impression, just as the work of art that we have seen a thousand times makes none. We do what we have to do, and afterwards do not know whether we have done it' (427). 'When life draws to a close, we do not know where it has gone' (425).

Notes on text and translation

German edition

The present translation is based on the German edition of Schopenhauer's
works, as edited by Arthur Hübscher, *Sämtliche Werke* (Mannheim:
F. A. Brockhaus, 1988). Volume 1 of *Parerga and Paralipomena* appears
in Hübscher, Volume 5. Page numbers of the Hübscher edition are given
in the margins of the translation. Hübscher's definitive edition follows the
first complete edition compiled by Julius Frauenstädt in 1873, with revisions taking account of numerous later editorial interventions. A paperback edition of the Hübscher edition, but using roman type and fewer
editorial notes, is the so-called *Zürcher Ausgabe, Werke in zehn Bänden*
(Zurich: Diogenes, 1977), in which Volume 1 of *Parerga* appears in
Volumes 7 and 8. (Those wishing to read the German text of these
works that Schopenhauer himself last issued should consult Ludger
Lütkehaus (ed.), *Arthur Schopenhauers Werke in fünf Bänden. Nach den
Ausgaben letzter Hand* (Zurich: Haffmans, 1988).) Arguments for using
Hübscher as the basis for translation are given by Richard Aquila in his
'Introduction' to Arthur Schopenhauer, *The World as Will and
Presentation*, Vol. 1 (New York: Pearson/Longman, 2008), xli–xlii. Long
recognized as the standard German source in the field, the Hübscher
collected works have served Schopenhauer studies for decades. In prepar-
ing this translation, we have consulted both Hübscher's editorial notes
and those of Paul Deussen (ed.), *Arthur Schopenhauers sämtliche Werke*
(Munich: R. Piper, 1911–12).

Vocabulary

The editorial footnotes give terms from the German when these may be
helpful for understanding a particular passage. Here we shall comment on
some of the decisions that have been made about translating frequent items

in Schopenhauer's vocabulary. We translate the term *Vorstellung*, for whatever comes before the mind in consciousness, as 'representation'. This follows the most common rendering of the term in Kant's writings. For discussion of this choice see the Cambridge edition of *The World as Will and Representation*, Vol. I, pp. xlviii–xlix. The second central term in Schopenhauer's philosophy is *Wille*, which can only be translated as 'will'. Some interpreters writing in English impose a distinction between 'will' and 'Will', intending by the latter *the* will, the will that Schopenhauer equates, or appears to equate with the world as a whole in itself. But there is in general no such orthographic differentiation in any of Schopenhauer's texts themselves, and we have not made any such distinction in the translation. (Arguably one would anyway need more variants than just two if one wanted to reflect the many nuanced roles that Schopenhauer gives to the term *Wille*: standing for the individual's will as manifested in his or her actions, for the underlying, non-empirical but individual character that is *my will*, for the one will that is common to all creatures, and so on.) The verb *wollen* is standardly translated as 'to will' (except in non-technical contexts where 'to want' is more appropriate) and *das Wollen* as 'willing'. The vital Schopenhauerian notion *Wille zum Leben* is always rendered as 'will to life'. It is not just a striving for individual survival, but also towards the end of propagating new life.

German has two words that are ordinarily translated as 'knowledge' – *Wissen* and *Erkenntniß* – and Schopenhauer makes a philosophical distinction between the two of them, arguing that *Wissen* is just one form of *Erkenntniß*. We have therefore tended to reserve the term 'knowledge' for *Wissen*, rendering *Erkenntniß* as 'cognition', its cognate verb *erkennen* as 'recognize', 'cognize' or 'have cognition of', and *erkennend* as 'cognitive' or 'cognizing' in contexts where they make a contribution to Schopenhauer's epistemology and theory of mind. One of Schopenhauer's major themes is that *Erkenntniß* is common to human beings and other animals, but that animals have only an 'intuitive', immediate and non-conceptual understanding of the world, and lack the abstract, conceptual or mediate kind of *Erkenntniß* that he calls *Wissen*. The other part of this theme is that the portion of cognition that we do not share with animals, conceptual thought, reasoning, *Vernunft*, is really of far less importance than philosophers have tended to think: it contains only what immediate cognition already contains, but in a more handy, abstract form. Schopenhauer uses the Kantian terms *Sinnlichkeit*, *Verstand*, *Anschauung* and *Begriff* (which we translate conventionally as 'sensibility', 'understanding', 'intuition' and 'concept'), but he does so in order to present a theory of cognition that diverges markedly from Kant's in many ways. 'Intuition' is therefore to be understood as a term of art denoting an awareness of objects in space and time through the senses; and we translate *anschaulich* as 'intuitive' and so on.

In this usage we differ from Payne's well-known translation, which tended to translate *Anschauung* as 'perception'. We, again more standardly, use 'perception' to translate *Wahrnehmung*. A similar case is that of *Erscheinung*, where we normally use the customary 'appearance' (not 'phenomenon', except in cases where to talk of 'appearances' could be misleading in English). Behind the world's aspect as appearance or representation lies the world as thing in itself (*Ding an sich*), and Schopenhauer uses somewhat novel expressions for the relation between thing in itself and appearance, saying that the latter is the *Objektivation*, or the *Objektität* of the former. The world of appearance is the world 'become object'. We coin the equally novel English words 'objectivation' and 'objecthood' for these two terms.

The frequently occurring *Grund* is translated as 'ground'. Sometimes this refers to a cause, at other times to a reason – and in fact there are four basic types of ground, as Schopenhauer had explained in his earlier essay *On the Fourfold Root of the Principle of Sufficient Reason*. In fact the principle referred to in that title, and throughout Schopenhauer's work, is *der Satz vom zureichenden Grunde* which should in strictness be rendered as 'the principle of sufficient ground'. However, in this one instance we have used 'principle of sufficient reason' simply as the more readily recognizable set phrase in English. Everywhere else *Grund* is 'ground'.

In talking of human actions Schopenhauer varies his terminology without any detectable change in basic sense. Thus, often he talks of *handeln* and *Handlung*, 'to act', 'action', then switches to *That, thun* or *Thun* (modern German *Tat, tun, Tun*), which we generally translate as 'deed', 'to do', 'doing' or 'doings' to preserve a similar variation in style. The *th* for *t* here (see also *Theil, Werth*, etc.) is one instance of divergence in spelling from that of the present day. All German words in editorial notes are given in the original orthography that the Hübscher edition preserves (other examples being *aa* for *a, ey* for *ei, ä* for *e*, and *dt* for *t*, thus *Spaaß, Daseyn, Säligkeit, gescheidt*).

The words *Moral* and *Moralität* are translated as 'morals' and 'morality' respectively. An immediate effect is to change the title of Schopenhauer's 1841 essay to *On the Basis of Morals* (when in Payne's version it was *On the Basis of Morality*). Schopenhauer tends to treat 'morals' as a theoretical study or philosophical enterprise for which the term 'ethics' is equivalent, while 'morality' describes people's real life actions and judgements. The adjective *moralisch* is easily translated as 'moral' (and the adverb as 'morally'), *Ethik* and *ethisch* likewise as 'ethics' and 'ethical'.

We translate *Geistersehn*, the subject of the fifth section of this work, fairly straightforwardly as 'spirit-seeing'. Schopenhauer frequently uses *Hellsehn*, which we translate as 'clairvoyance'.

Style, syntax and punctuation

Schopenhauer writes sentences of great variety in length. The general policy has been to reflect the character, pace and flow of the original as much as possible in the English version. Often he uses a direct and punchy statement, or a balanced classical sentence with two or three well-constructed clauses. But the greatest difficulty is presented by those many occasions where Schopenhauer launches into a disproportionately long sentence. On occasion it can become hard to discern fully clear syntax, but generally Schopenhauer is a master of structure. Helped by well-known features that distinguish German from English, notably the ability to frame long subordinate clauses with a verb postponed to the end, and three grammatical genders which allow nouns from earlier in the sentences to be picked up anaphorically without ambiguity, he can produce majestic sentences whose parts fit together perfectly and which have a powerful cumulative effect on the reader. While at times it has been necessary to split these passages into more than one English sentence, we have by and large retained their length, sometimes dividing them with a semicolon or dash.

Schopenhauer's punctuation, as transmitted by way of the Hübscher editions, is unlike standard present-day usage. One feature retained in the translation is his use of a simple dash (–) between sentences to separate out parts within a long paragraph. We have tried to reflect rather than straightforwardly copy his practice of inserting commas, colons and semicolons inside sentences. There is no overall policy here other than that of matching the rhythm and pace of the original while producing something that makes good sense to the contemporary reader of English. Another feature is Schopenhauer's italicization of proper names. We have tended to limit this to occasions when Schopenhauer first mentions someone in a given context, or shifts back to discussing them.

Schopenhauer's use of other languages

Schopenhauer is a master of many languages and delights in quoting extracts from other authors in Greek, Latin, French, Italian and Spanish. These extracts vary in length from the isolated phrase within a sentence to several unbroken pages of quotation which he thinks will substantiate his own view. Very often he will round off his argument with some apt words from Homer, Dante or Voltaire, always in the original language. He also has the scholar's habit of incorporating short tags in Latin or Greek into his own idiom (e.g. he will generally refer to something as a *petitio principii* rather than saying that it begs the question, or as a πρῶτον ψεῦδος rather than 'a false first step' or 'primary error'). Finally, when a substantial passage of Greek occurs Schopenhauer sometimes adds his own Latin translation for the reader's benefit. Hübscher's edition systematically leaves Greek text without accents and some other diacritical marks. In this volume we have inserted diacritics. We have also transliterated single items of Greek vocabulary that appear in the text, indicating the full Greek version in footnotes.

The cumulative effect of Schopenhauer's use of other languages gives his style historical depth and a pan-European literary flavour. The question is how to deal with all of this in an English translation. Earlier versions have taken two different lines. One is simply to reproduce all the non-German passages in their original languages and leave it at that. This was done by R. B. Haldane and J. Kemp in their translation of *The World as Will and Idea* in 1883 and by Madame Karl Hillebrand in *On the Fourfold Root and On the Will in Nature* in 1891. While it may have been a reasonable assumption in those days, as it may have been for Schopenhauer himself, that anyone likely to read his book seriously would have sufficient access to the requisite languages, at the present time of writing such an assumption would appear misplaced. The second expedient is to leave all the original language passages where they stand in the text, but to add footnotes or parentheses giving English equivalents. This is the method, adopted in Payne's translations, that readers of Schopenhauer in English have been most familiar with.

In the present translation, by contrast, we have adopted a third strategy: with a few exceptions, everything in the text is translated into English, and the original language version given in footnotes. This sacrifices some of the richness involved in reading Schopenhauer – but it arguably disadvantages only a reader who is a good linguist in several languages but not German. For all other readers of English, the relevance of Schopenhauer's quotations to his argument, and the overall flow of his writing, are better revealed by following the sense of quotations directly, especially on those many pages where he makes his point by way of a chunk of Greek followed by a chunk of Latin that gives a second version of the same, or where he quotes extensively in French. Nor is anything really lost by our policy, since every word of the original language extracts is given in footnotes on the same page. Some exceptions to this practice occur where Schopenhauer specifically introduces a word in another language for discussion of its sense, or where he offers us a Spanish proverb or a Latin expression from the medieval scholastic tradition as especially apposite. In such cases the original language expression is retained in the text and the English equivalent offered in a footnote.

Chronology

1788	Arthur Schopenhauer born on 22 February in the city of Danzig (now Gdansk), the son of the Hanseatic merchant Heinrich Floris Schopenhauer and Johanna Schopenhauer, née Trosiener
1793	Danzig is annexed by the Prussians. The Schopenhauer family moves to Hamburg
1797	His sister Adele is born. Schopenhauer begins a two-year stay in Le Havre with the family of one of his father's business partners
1799	Returns to Hamburg, and attends a private school for the next four years
1803–4	Agrees to enter a career as a merchant and as a reward is taken by his parents on a tour of Europe (Holland, England, France, Switzerland, Austria). From June to September 1803 is a boarder in Thomas Lancaster's school in Wimbledon
1804	Is apprenticed to two Hanseatic merchants in Hamburg
1805	His father dies, probably by suicide
1806	Johanna Schopenhauer moves with Adele to Weimar, where she establishes herself as a popular novelist and literary hostess
1807	Schopenhauer abandons his commercial career for an academic one. Enters Gotha Gymnasium and then receives private tuition in Weimar
1809	Studies science and then philosophy (especially Plato and Kant) at the University of Göttingen
1811	Studies science and philosophy at the University of Berlin. Attends the lectures of Fichte and Schleiermacher
1813–14	Lives in Rudolstadt, writing his doctoral dissertation, *On the Fourfold Root of the Principle of Sufficient Reason*, which is accepted by the University of Jena and published in 1814. Conversations with Goethe on colour and vision

1814	Begins reading a translation of the *Upanishads*. Stays with his mother in Weimar, but breaks with her permanently after a final quarrel. Lives in Dresden until 1818
1814–18	Works on *The World as Will and Representation*
1816	Publishes *On Vision and Colours*
1818	March: completion of *The World as Will and Representation*, published by Brockhaus at the end of the year, with '1819' on title page
1818–19	Travels in Italy (Florence, Rome, Naples, Venice) and returns to Dresden
1819	Is appointed as unsalaried lecturer (*Privatdozent*) at the University of Berlin
1820	Gives his only course of lectures, which is poorly attended
1822–3	Travels again to Italy (Milan, Florence, Venice). Returns from Italy to live in Munich. Is ill and depressed
1824	Lives in Bad Gastein, Mannheim and Dresden. Proposes to translate Hume's works on religion into German, but does not find a publisher
1826	Returns to Berlin
1829–30	Plans to translate Kant into English, without success; publishes *Commentatio Exponens Theoriam Colorum Physiologicam, Eandemque primariam, Auctore Arthurio Schopenhauero*
1831	Leaves Berlin because of the cholera epidemic. Moves to Frankfurt am Main
1831–2	Lives temporarily in Mannheim
1833	Settles in Frankfurt, where he remains for the rest of his life
1836	Publishes *On Will in Nature*
1838	His mother dies
1839	Enters competition set by the Royal Norwegian Society of Sciences and wins prize with his essay *On the Freedom of the Will*
1840	Submits *On the Basis of Morals* in a competition set by the Royal Danish Society of Sciences, and is not awarded a prize
1841	*On the Freedom of the Will* and *On the Basis of Morals* published under the title *The Two Fundamental Problems of Ethics*
1844	Publishes second, revised edition of *The World as Will and Representation*, adding a second volume consisting of fifty essays elaborating on ideas discussed in the first volume
1847	Publishes second, revised edition of *On the Fourfold Root*
1851	Publishes *Parerga and Paralipomena* in two volumes

1853	An article on his philosophy by J. Oxenford in *Westminster and Foreign Quarterly Review* marks the beginning of his belated recognition
1854	Publishes second editions of *On Will in Nature* and *On Vision and Colours*. Julius Frauenstädt publishes *Letters on Schopenhauer's Philosophy*
1857	Schopenhauer's philosophy taught at Bonn University
1858	Declines invitation to be a member of Berlin Royal Academy
1859	Publishes third edition of *The World as Will and Representation*
1860	Publishes second edition of *The Two Fundamental Problems of Ethics*. Dies on 21 September in Frankfurt am Main

Bibliography

GERMAN EDITIONS OF SCHOPENHAUER'S WRITINGS

Arthur Schopenhauers sämtliche Werke, ed. Paul Deussen, 16 vols. (Munich: R. Piper, 1911–42).

Der handschriftlicher Nachlaß, ed. Arthur Hübscher, 5 vols. (Frankfurt am Main: Kramer, 1970).

Faksimilenachdruck der 1. Auflage der Welt als Wille und Vorstellung, ed. Rudolf Malter (Frankfurt am Main: Insel, 1987).

Gesammelte Briefe, ed. Arthur Hübscher (Bonn: Bouvier, 1978).

Philosophische Vorlesungen, aus dem handschriftlichen Nachlaß, ed. Volker Spierling (Munich: R. Piper, 1984–6).

Sämtliche Werke, ed. Arthur Hübscher, 7 vols. (Mannheim: F. A. Brockhaus, 1988).

Werke in fünf Bänden. Nach den Ausgaben letzter Hand, ed. Ludger Lütkehaus, 5 vols. (Zurich: Haffmans, 1988).

Werke in zehn Bänden (Zürcher Ausgabe), ed. Arthur Hübscher, 10 vols. (Zurich: Diogenes, 1977).

ENGLISH TRANSLATIONS OF SCHOPENHAUER'S WRITINGS

Essay on the Freedom of the Will, trans. Konstantin Kolenda (Indianapolis: Bobbs-Merrill, 1960).

Essays and Aphorisms, trans. R. J. Hollingdale (Harmondsworth: Penguin, 1970).

Manuscript Remains, trans. E. F. J. Payne, 4 vols. (Oxford: Berg, 1988).

On the Basis of Morality, ed. David E. Cartwright, trans. E. F. J. Payne (Oxford: Berghahn Books, 1995).

On the Fourfold Root of the Principle of Sufficient Reason, trans. E. F. J. Payne (La Salle, IL: Open Court, 1974).

On the Fourfold Root of the Principle of Sufficient Reason and On the Will in Nature, trans. Mme Karl Hillebrand (London: George Bell and Sons, 1891).

On the Fourfold Root of the Principle of Sufficient Reason, On Vision and Colours, and On Will in Nature, ed. and trans. David E. Cartwright, Edward E. Erdmann and Christopher Janaway (Cambridge University Press, 2012).

xliii

On the Will in Nature, ed. David E. Cartwright, trans. E. F. J. Payne (New York: Berg, 1992).

On Vision and Colors, ed. David E. Cartwright, trans. E. F. J. Payne (Oxford: Berg, 1994).

On Vision and Colors by Arthur Schopenhauer and Color Sphere by Philipp Otto Runge, trans. Georg Stahl (New York: Princeton Architectural Press, 2010).

Parerga and Paralipomena, trans. E. F. J. Payne, 2 vols. (Oxford: Clarendon Press, 1974).

Prize Essay on the Freedom of the Will, ed. Günter Zöller, trans. E. F. J. Payne (Cambridge University Press, 1999).

Schopenhauer's Early Fourfold Root: Translation and Commentary, F. C. White (Aldershot: Avebury, 1997).

The Two Fundamental Problems of Ethics, ed. and trans. Christopher Janaway (Cambridge University Press, 2009).

The Two Fundamental Problems of Ethics, trans. David E. Cartwright and Edward Erdmann (Oxford University Press, 2010).

The World as Will and Idea, trans. R. B. Haldane and J. Kemp, 3 vols. (London: Routledge & Kegan Paul, 1883).

The World as Will and Idea: abridged in one volume, trans. J. Berman, ed. D. Berman (London: Everyman, 1995).

The World as Will and Presentation, Vol. 1, trans. Richard E. Aquila in collaboration with David Carus (New York: Pearson/Longman, 2008).

The World as Will and Representation, Vol. 1, trans. and ed. Judith Norman, Alistair Welchman and Christopher Janaway (Cambridge University Press, 2010).

The World as Will and Representation, trans. E. F. J. Payne, 2 vols. (New York: Dover, 1969).

SELECTED BOOKS AND EDITED COLLECTIONS IN ENGLISH

App, Urs, 'Arthur Schopenhauer and China: A Sino-Platonic Love Affair'. Sino-Platonic Papers No. 200, April 2010. Available at http://www.sino-platonic.org/complete/spp200_schopenhauer.pdf

Atwell, John E., *Schopenhauer on the Character of the World: The Metaphysics of Will* (Berkeley: University of California Press, 1995).

Schopenhauer: The Human Character (Philadelphia: Temple University Press, 1990).

Ausmus, Harry J., *A Schopenhauerian Critique of Nietzsche's Thought: Toward a Restoration of Metaphysics* (Lewiston, NY: Edwin Mellen Press, 1996).

Barua, Arati, *The Philosophy of Arthur Schopenhauer* (New Delhi: Intellectual Publishing House, 1992).

(ed.), *Schopenhauer & Indian Philosophy: A Dialogue between India and Germany* (New Delhi: Northern Book Centre, 2008).

Bridgewater, Patrick, *Arthur Schopenhauer's English Schooling* (New York: Routledge, 1988).

Bykhovsky, Bernard, *Schopenhauer and the Ground of Existence* (Amsterdam: B. R. Grumer, 1984).

Cartwright, David E., *Historical Dictionary of Schopenhauer's Philosophy* (Lanham, MD: Scarecrow Press, 2005).

Schopenhauer: A Biography (New York: Cambridge University Press, 2010).

Copleston, Frederick, *Arthur Schopenhauer: Philosopher of Pessimism* (1947; repr. London: Search Press, 1975).

Dauer, Dorothea W., *Schopenhauer as Transmitter of Buddhist Ideas* (Berne: Herbert Lang, 1969).

Fox, Michael (ed.), *Schopenhauer: His Philosophical Achievement* (Totowa, NJ: Barnes and Noble, 1980).

Gardiner, Patrick, *Schopenhauer* (Bristol: Thoemmes Press, 1997 (originally pub. Penguin Books in 1963)).

Gonzales, Robert A., *An Approach to the Sacred in the Thought of Schopenhauer* (Lewiston, NY: Edwin Mellen Press, 1992).

Hamlyn, D. W., *Schopenhauer* (London: Routledge & Kegan Paul, 1980).

Hannan, Barbara, *The Riddle of the World: A Reconsideration of Schopenhauer's Philosophy* (Oxford University Press, 2009).

Hübscher, Arthur, *The Philosophy of Schopenhauer in its Intellectual Context,* trans. Joachim T. Baer and David E. Cartwright (Lewiston, NY: Edwin Mellen Press, 1989).

Jacquette, Dale (ed.), *Schopenhauer, Philosophy, and the Arts* (Cambridge University Press, 1996).

The Philosophy of Schopenhauer (London: Acumen, 2005).

Janaway, Christopher (ed.), *The Cambridge Companion to Schopenhauer* (Cambridge University Press, 1999).

Schopenhauer: A Very Short Introduction (Oxford University Press, 2002).

Self and World in Schopenhauer's Philosophy (Oxford: Clarendon Press, 1989).

(ed.), *Willing and Nothingness: Schopenhauer as Nietzsche's Educator* (Oxford: Clarendon Press, 1998).

Janaway, Christopher and Alex Neill (eds.), *Better Consciousness: Schopenhauer's Philosophy of Value* (Oxford: Blackwell, 2009).

Jordan, Neil, *Schopenhauer's Ethics of Patience: Virtue, Salvation and Value* (Lewiston, NY: Edwin Mellen Press, 2009).

Knox, Israel, *The Aesthetic Theories of Kant, Hegel, and Schopenhauer* (1936; repr. New York: Humanities Press, 1958).

Krukowski, Lucian, *Aesthetic Legacies* (Philadelphia: Temple University Press, 1993).

Lauxtermann, P. F. H., *Schopenhauer's Broken World-View: Colours and Ethics Between Kant and Goethe* (Dordrecht: Kluwer Academic Publishers, 2000).

Lewis, Peter B., *Arthur Schopenhauer* (London: Reaktion Books, 2012).

Magee, Bryan, *The Philosophy of Schopenhauer* (Oxford: Clarendon Press, 1997).

Mannion, Gerard, *Schopenhauer, Religion and Morality: The Humble Path to Ethics* (London: Ashgate, 2003).

Marcin, Raymond B., *In Search of Schopenhauer's Cat: Arthur Schopenhauer's Quantum–Mystical Theory of Justice* (Washington, DC: Catholic University of America Press, 2006).

McGill, V. J., *Schopenhauer: Pessimist and Pagan* (New York: Haskell House, 1971).

Neeley, G. Steven, *Schopenhauer: A Consistent Reading* (Lewiston, NY: Edwin Mellen Press, 2003).

Ryan, Christopher, *Schopenhauer's Philosophy of Religion: The Death of God and the Oriental Renaissance* (Leuven: Peeters, 2010).

Safranksi, Rüdiger, *Schopenhauer and the Wild Years of Philosophy*, trans. Ewald Osers (London: Weidenfeld & Nicolson, 1989).

Simmel, Georg, *Schopenhauer and Nietzsche,* trans. Helmut Loikandl, Deena Weinstein and Michael Weinstein (Amherst: University of Massachusetts Press, 1986).

Singh, R. Raj, *Death, Contemplation and Schopenhauer* (Burlington, VT: Ashgate, 2007).

Tanner, Michael, *Schopenhauer: Metaphysics and Art* (London: Phoenix, 1998).

Vandenabeele, Bart (ed.), *A Companion to Schopenhauer* (Oxford: Wiley-Blackwell, 2012).

von der Luft, Eric (ed.), *Schopenhauer: New Essays in Honor of His 200th Birthday* (Lewiston, NY: Edwin Mellen Press, 1988).

Weiner, David Abraham, *Genius and Talent: Schopenhauer's Influence on Wittgenstein's Early Philosophy* (Rutherford, NJ: Fairleigh Dickinson University Press, 1992).

White, F. C., *On Schopenhauer's Fourfold Root of the Principle of Sufficient Reason* (Leiden: E. J. Brill, 1992).

Wicks, Robert, *Schopenhauer* (Malden, MA and Oxford: Blackwell, 2008).

Young, Julian, *Schopenhauer* (London and New York: Routledge, 2005).

Willing and Unwilling: A Study in the Philosophy of Arthur Schopenhauer (Dordrecht: Martinus Nijhoff, 1987).

Parerga and Paralipomena

Short Philosophical Essays

Volume I

ARTHUR SCHOPENHAUER

Vitam impendere vero.
['To devote one's life to truth.'
Juvenal, *Satires*, IV. 91]

Contents

These additional writings, delivered subsequently to my more important and systematic works, consist partly of a few essays on a wide variety of special topics and partly of isolated thoughts on even more diverse subjects, all brought together here because, largely due to their subject matter, they could not find a place within the systematic works; some, however, merely because they came too late to claim their rightful place there.

Above all, I had in mind here those readers who are acquainted with my systematic and more comprehensive work, for perhaps they too will find here some desired elucidation. But on the whole the content of these volumes, with the exception of a few passages, will be intelligible and palatable even to those lacking such acquaintance. Nevertheless, the reader familiar with my philosophy will be at an advantage, because it forever casts its light on everything I think and write, albeit only from afar; as, on the other hand, it itself receives some further illumination from everything that emanates from my mind.

Frankfurt am Main, December 1850.

Sketch of a history of the doctrine of the ideal and the real

Plurimi pertransibunt, et multiplex erit scientia

Daniel 12:4

['Many shall run through it, and knowledge shall be increased']

Descartes is justly considered the father of modern philosophy, primarily and generally because he taught reason to stand on its own feet by instructing people to use their own minds, which had rested until then on the Bible on the one hand and Aristotle on the other. He is the father in a particular and more narrow sense[1] because he was the first to become aware of the problem around which all philosophizing has mainly revolved since then: the problem of the ideal and the real, i.e. the question what in our cognition[a] is objective and what subjective, thus what is to be ascribed to any things distinct from ourselves and what to ourselves. – For in our heads images arise, occasioned not internally – originating from choice or from the association of ideas – but externally. These images alone are what is immediately known to us, what is given. What kind of relation might they have to things that exist completely separately from and independently of us and that would somehow cause these images? Are we certain that such things are even there? And, in case they are, do the images give us any information about their constitution? – This is the problem, and consequently, for the last two hundred years, it has been the main endeavour of the philosophers to separate the ideal, that is, that which belongs exclusively to our cognition, from the real, that is, that which exists independently of our cognition, clearly in a well-executed, clean cut, and thus to determine their relation to one another.

---

[a] *Erkenntniß*

4   In reality, neither the ancient nor the scholastic philosophers seem to
have become distinctly aware of this primordial philosophical problem,
although we find a trace of it, as idealism and even as the doctrine of the
ideality of time, in *Plotinus*, in *Ennead* III, Book 7, ch. 10, where he teaches
that the soul made the world by emerging from eternity into time. It says
there, for example: 'for there is no other place for the universe than soul'[a]
and also: 'Time, however, is not to be conceived as outside of soul, just as
eternity is not outside being';[b] which in fact already pronounces Kant's
ideality of time. And in the following chapter: 'and this life generates time.
This is why it is said that time came into existence simultaneously with this
universe, because soul generated it along with this universe.'[c] Nevertheless,
the distinctly known and distinctly pronounced problem remains the
characteristic theme of *modern* philosophy, after the necessary reflective-
ness[d] had first been awakened in *Descartes*, who was struck by the truth that
we are initially limited to our own consciousness and that the world is given
to us only as *representation*. With the help of his well-known 'I doubt, I
think, therefore I am'[e] he wanted to emphasize the exclusive certainty of the
subjective consciousness, in contrast to the problematic nature of everything else, and to pronounce the great truth that self-consciousness is the
only thing truly and unconditionally *given*. Closely considered, his famous
proposition is the equivalent of the one I started out from: 'The world is my
representation.' The only difference is that his stresses the immediacy of the
subject, mine the mediacy of the object. Both propositions express the same
thing from different angles. They are the reverse of each other and thus
related in the same way as the laws of inertia and causality, according to my
5   explanation in the preface of the *Ethics*.[f] People have indeed repeated his
proposition innumerable times since then, from a mere feeling of its
importance and without a clear understanding of its actual meaning and
purport. (See Descartes, *Meditations*, Med. II,[g] p. 15.)[2] Thus it was he who

---

[a] οὐ γάρ τις αὐτοῦ τούτου τοῦ παντὸς τόπος, ἢ ψυχή (*neque datur alius hujus universi locus, quam
    anima*)
[b] δεῖ δὲ οὐκ ἔξωθεν τῆς ψυχῆς λαμβάνειν τὸν χρόνον, ὥσπερ οὐδὲ τὸν αἰῶνα ἐκεῖ ἔξω τοῦ ὄντος. (*oportet
    autem nequaquam extra animam tempus accipere, quemadmodum neque aeternitatem ibi extra id, quod
    ens appellatur.*) [Schopenhauer refers to III, 7, 10, but the two passages actually are from III, 7, 11]
[c] οὗτος ὁ βίος τὸν χρόνον γεννᾷ· διὸ καὶ εἴρηται ἅμα τῷδε τῷ παντὶ γεγονέναι, ὅτι ψυχὴ αὐτὸν μετὰ τοῦδε τοῦ
    παντὸς ἐγέννησεν (*haec vita nostra tempus gignit: quamobrem dictum est, tempus simul cum hoc universo
    factum esse; quia anima tempus una cum hoc universo progenuit*)
[d] *Besonnenheit*   [e] *dubito, cogito, ergo sum*
[f] [*The Two Fundamental Problems of Ethics*, Preface to the first edition, 17–18 (Hübscher *SW* 4,
    XXIIf.)]
[g] [René Descartes, *Meditations on First Philosophy*; incidentally, Med. II does not contain the exact
    phrasing that Schopenhauer provides above]

uncovered the chasm between the subjective, or ideal, and the objective, or real. He clothed this insight in the form of a doubt concerning the existence of the external world; but through his barely adequate way out of this – namely that the benevolent God Almighty could not possibly betray us – he showed how profound the problem is and how difficult to solve. Meanwhile it was through him that this scruple entered philosophy and was bound to continue to trouble people until it was thoroughly laid to rest. Since then the consciousness has existed that without thorough knowledge and elucidation of the described distinction no certain and satisfactory system was possible, and the question could no longer be dismissed.

In order to answer it, *Malebranche* first invented the system of occasional causes.[a] He grasped the problem itself, in its full extent, more clearly, more seriously, and more deeply than *Descartes*. (*The Search after Truth*,[b] Book III, second part.) The latter had assumed the reality of the external world upon the credit of God; and then it seems strange that, while the other theistic philosophers take pains to demonstrate the existence of God from that of the world, Descartes, on the contrary, proves the existence of the world only on the basis of the existence and truthfulness of God; it is the cosmological proof in reverse. Going a step further here as well, *Malebranche* teaches that we see all things immediately in God himself. Of course this is to explain something unknown with the help of something even more unknown. Moreover, according to him, we not only see all things in God; but He is also the only active element[c] within them, so that the physical causes are only apparently so, but are mere occasional causes.[d] (*The Search after Truth*, Book VI, second part, ch. 3.) So we have here already essentially the pantheism of *Spinoza*, who seems to have learnt more from Malebranche than from Descartes.

Altogether one might be surprised that pantheism did not gain complete victory over theism already in the seventeenth century; since the most original, beautiful and thorough European expositions of it (for compared to the *Upanishads* of the *Vedas* all of that is nothing) all became known during that period, namely through *Bruno, Malebranche, Spinoza*, and *Scotus Erigena*. The latter was rediscovered in Oxford, after having been forgotten and lost for many centuries, and first appeared in print in 1681, four years after Spinoza's death. This seems to prove that the insight of individuals cannot prevail as long as the spirit of the age is not ripe to receive it. In our time, on the other hand, pantheism, even if only in Schelling's eclectic and confused revival, has become the prevalent mode of thought of

___

[a] *gelegentlichen Ursachen*   [b] *Recherches de la vérité*   [c] *Wirkende*   [d] *causes occasionelles*

scholars and even educated people. For Kant had gone before with his
overthrow of theistic dogmatism and had cleared the way for it, whereby the
spirit of the age got prepared, just as a ploughed field for the seed. In
contrast, in the seventeenth century philosophy left that path again, and on
the one hand arrived at *Locke*, for whom Bacon and Hobbes had paved the
way, and on the other hand, by way of *Leibniz*, at *Wolff*; these two then
reigned supreme in Germany in the eighteenth century, even if in the end
only by being absorbed into syncretistic eclecticism.

    The profound thoughts of *Malebranche* first gave rise to *Leibniz's* system of
pre-established harmony,[a] whose widespread fame and high repute in its own
time prove that the absurd most easily succeeds in the world. Although I
cannot claim to possess a distinct grasp of Leibniz's monads, which are
mathematical points, physical atoms, and souls at the same time, it seems to
me beyond doubt that such an assumption, once established, could serve to
avoid all further hypotheses for explaining the connection between the ideal
and the real and to dispatch the question by claiming that both are already
completely identified in the monads. (For that reason in our own day
Schelling, as the originator of the system of identity, has relished this assumption.) However, the famous philosophizing mathematician, polyhistorian, and
politician did not favour using them for this purpose; to this end he formulated
pre-established harmony instead. The latter provides us with two completely
different worlds, each incapable of acting on the other in any way (*Principles of
Philosophy*[b] §84; and 'Examen du sentiment du P. Malebranche,' pp. 500ff. of
Leibniz's *Works*, published by Raspe[c]), each one the completely superfluous
duplicate of the other. Yet the two are supposed to exist once and for all, run
parallel, and be exactly in step with each other to a hair. Therefore the creator
of both, right from the beginning, established the most precise harmony
between them, in which they now most beautifully run side by side.
Incidentally, pre-established harmony might be best made comprehensible
by comparing it to the stage, where very often the physical influence[d] is present
only apparently, as cause and effect are merely connected by means of a
harmony pre-established by the director, for example when one character
shoots and the other falls down in time.[e] In §§62 and 63 of his *Theodicy*,

---

[a] *harmonia praestabilita*

[b] ['*Principia philosophiae, more geometrico demonstrata: cum exceptis ex epistolis philosophi et scholiis
     quibusdam ex historia philosophica*' is the Latin title of Gottfried Wilhelm Leibniz's *Monadology*]

[c] ['*Examen du sentiment du P. Malebranche que nous voyons tout en Dieu, contre J. Locke*', *Oeuvres
     philosophiques, latines et françaises, de feu M. de Leibnitz.* Tirées de ses manuscrits qui se conservent de
     la Bibliothèque royale à Hanovre, ed. Rudolf Erich Raspe, Amsterdam and Leipzig, 1765]

[d] *influxus physicus*   [e] *a tempo*

Leibniz presented this monstrous absurdity at its crassest and with brevity. And yet he does not even possess the merit of originality for this whole dogma, since Spinoza already stated pre-established harmony clearly enough in the second part of his *Ethics*, in the sixth and seventh proposition, together with the corollaries, and again in the fifth part, first proposition, after having expressed in his own way, in proposition five of the second part, the extremely closely related doctrine of *Malebranche* that we see everything in God.* Thus Malebranche alone is the originator of this whole line of thought, which both Spinoza and Leibniz, each in his own way, utilized and adapted. Leibniz could very well have dispensed with the thing, for[3] he had thereby left behind the mere fact that constitutes the problem, namely that the world is immediately given to us only as our representation, in order to substitute the dogma of the corporeal and the spiritual world between which no bridge is possible. He does so by interweaving the question regarding the relation between representations and things in themselves with that regarding the possibility of the movements of the body through the will, and solves both together with the help of his pre-established harmony (see *New System of Nature*,[a] in Leibniz, *Works*, ed. Erdmann, p. 125.[b] – Brucker, *Critical History of Philosophy*, volume IV, pt. II, p. 425[c]). Some of his contemporaries, especially *Bayle*, already threw a bright light on the monstrous absurdity of his presumption by pointing out the consequences that resulted from it. (See in Leibniz's *Shorter Works*, translated by Huth in the year 1740,[d] the note to p. 79, where Leibniz himself

8

---

* *Ethics* II, prop. 7: *Ordo et connexio idearum idem est, ac ordo et connexio rerum.* [The order and connection of ideas is the same as the order and connection of things.] – V, prop. 1: *Prout cogitationes rerumque ideae concatenantur in Mente, ita corporis affectiones, seu rerum imagines ad amussim ordinantur et concatenantur in Corpore.* [Just as the thoughts and the ideas of things are ordered and connected in the mind, so are the affections of the body, or the images of things, precisely in the same way ordered and connected in the body.] – II, prop. 5: *Esse formale idearum Deum, quatenus tantum ut res cogitans consideratur, pro causa agnoscit, et non quatenus alio attributo explicatur. Hoc est, tam Dei attributorum, quam rerum singularium ideae non ipsa ideata, sive res perceptas pro causa efficiente agnoscunt: sed ispum Deum, quatenus est res cogitans.* [The formal being of ideas admits God as a cause, only insofar as he is considered as a thinking thing, not insofar as he is explained by any other attribute; that is, the ideas both of the attributes of God and of particular things admit as their efficient cause not the objects themselves, or the things perceived, but God himself insofar as he is a thinking thing. (English translations of Latin quotes by Benedict de Spinoza closely follow those of Edwin Curley)]

[a] *Système nouveau de la nature* [*Système nouveau de la nature et de la communication des substances, aussi bien que l'union qu'il y a entre l'âme et le corps* (1685) (*New System of the Nature of Substances and their Communication, as well as the Union that Exists between the Soul and the Body*)]

[b] [*God. Guil. Leibnitii Opera philosophica quae exstant Latina, Gallica, Germanica omnia*, ed. J. E. Erdmann, Berlin, 1839–40]

[c] [Johann Jacob Brucker, *Historia Critica Philosophiae a mundi incunabulis ad nostram usque aetatem deducta* (*A Critical History of Philosophy from the Beginning of the World all the Way up to our own Age*), Leipzig: Christoph Breitkopf, 1742–4]

[d] *Kleine Schriften* [*Kleinere philosophische Schriften*, ed. Caspar Jacob Huth, Jena, 1740]

is compelled to expose the shocking consequences of his assertion.) However, the very absurdity of his assumption, to which a thinking mind was driven by the problem in question, proves its magnitude, difficulty, and perplexity and how little we are able to brush it aside through mere denial, and thus to cut the knot, as some have dared to do in our day. –

Spinoza starts again directly from *Descartes*; therefore, acting like a Cartesian, he initially retained even the dualism of his teacher and thus posited a thinking substance[a] and an extended substance,[b] the former as subject, the latter as object of cognition. Later however, when standing on his own feet, he found that both were one and the same substance viewed from different sides, thus at one time conceived as extended substance, at another as thinking substance. This really means that the distinction between what thinks and what is extended, or mind and body, is unfounded and thus inadmissible, and therefore that nothing more should have been said about it. Nevertheless, he retains it since he never tires of repeating that the two are one. He adds to this, connected through a mere 'Thus also', that 'the mode of extension and the idea of that mode are one and the same thing'[c] (*Ethics* II, prop. 7, schol.), which means that our representation of bodies and these bodies themselves are one and the same. The 'thus also', however, provides an insufficient transition for this; for from the fact that the distinction between mind and body or between what represents and what is extended is unfounded it does not follow that the distinction between our representation and something objective and real existing outside of that representation – the fundamental problem raised by Descartes – is unfounded as well. The representing and the represented may very well be homogeneous; yet the question remains whether I can infer with certainty from representations in my head the existence of entities that are distinct from me and exist in themselves,[d] that is, independently. This is not the difficulty that *Leibniz* in particular would like to make it into (e.g. *Theodicy*, pt. I, §59), the difficulty that between the presumed souls and the corporeal world, as two entirely heterogeneous kinds of substances, no acting-on[e] and community can take place, which is why he denied physical influence. For this difficulty is merely a consequence of rational psychology and, as happens in Spinoza, only needs to be discarded as fiction. In addition, as an *ad hominem* argument, one has to uphold against those who hold such a view[f] their dogma that God, who is indeed a spirit, created the corporeal world and continuously rules over it, therefore that a spirit can immediately act on bodies. Rather the difficulty is and remains the

---

[a] *res cogitans*   [b] *res extensa*
[c] *Sic etiam … modus extensionis et idea illius modi una eademque est res*   [d] *an sich selbst*
[e] *Einwirken*   [f] [that there is no interaction between the mind and body]

Cartesian one, that the only world which is immediately given us is an utterly ideal world, i.e. one that consists of mere representations in our head; while we undertake to make judgements about a real world beyond the ideal one, i.e. one that exists independently of our representing. Thus by abolishing the distinction between thinking substance and extended substance *Spinoza* did not yet solve this problem, but at most made a physical influence admissible again. However, this influence does not suffice to solve the difficulty, for the law of causality is demonstrably of subjective origin; but even if, conversely, it originated in external experience, it would still belong to the world that is in question and given to us only ideally. So it can by no means function as a bridge between the absolutely objective and the subjective; on the contrary, it is merely the bond that connects the representations with each other. (See *The World as Will and Representation*, vol. 2, p. 12.[a])

In order to explain in more detail the above-mentioned identity of extension and the representation of it, *Spinoza* lays down something that simultaneously encompasses the views of *Malebranche* and *Leibniz*. In perfect conformity with *Malebranche* we see all things in God: 'The ideas ... of particular things admit as their efficient cause not the objects themselves, or the things perceived, but God himself insofar as he is a thinking thing.'[b] (*Ethics* II, prop. 5.) And this God is simultaneously the real and the active in them, just as in *Malebranche*. However, since Spinoza signifies the world with the name 'God',[c] ultimately this explains nothing. But at the same time, there is an exact parallelism in him between the extended and the represented world, as in Leibniz: 'The order and connection of ideas is the same as the order and connection of things',[d] II, prop. 7, and many similar passages. This is Leibniz's pre-established harmony; only that here the represented world and the objectively existing world do not remain completely separated, as in Leibniz, corresponding to each other merely by means of a harmony that is regulated in advance and from the outside, but are truly one and the same. Thus we have here above all a complete *realism*, insofar as the existence of things corresponds precisely to their representation within us, as both are one.[*,4] Accordingly, we

---

* He demonstrates a decided *realism* in the *Tractatus de intellectus emendatione* [*Treatise on the Emendation of the Intellect*], pp. 414/25 [§33], namely that *idea vera est diversum quid a suo ideato* [the true idea is different from what is thought through it]; etc. However, this treatise is undoubtedly older than his *Ethics*.

[a] [Hübscher *SW* 3, 12–13]
[b] *rerum singularium ideae non ipsa ideata, sive res perceptas, pro causa agnoscunt, sed ipsum Deum, quatenus est res cogitans*
[c] *Deus*   [d] *ordo et connexio idearum idem est, ac ordo et connexio rerum*

11   know the things in themselves: they are in themselves extended,[a] and they also manifest themselves as extended insofar as they appear as being thought,[b] that is, in our representation of them. (Incidentally, here is the origin of Schelling's identity of the real and the ideal.) All of this is really only based on mere assertion. The exposition is already unclear because of the ambiguity of the term 'God', which is used in a figurative sense, and for other reasons as well. Thus he gets lost in obscurity, and in the end he says: 'And for now, I cannot explain this more clearly.'[c] However, obscurity in the exposition always stems from the obscurity of one's own understanding and thinking-through of philosophemes. *Vauvenargues* has said very appropriately: 'Lucidity is the good faith of the philosophers.'[d] (See *Revue des deux Mondes*, 15 August 1853, p. 635.) What in music is the 'pure phrase',[e] in philosophy is perfect clarity, insofar as it is the indispensable condition[f] without whose fulfilment everything loses its value and we have to say: 'Whatever you show me in this way is incredible to me and hateful.'[g] If even in affairs of ordinary, practical life we have to prevent possible misunderstandings carefully, through clarity, how then could it be permissible to express ourselves imprecisely, and indeed enigmatically, when it comes to the most difficult, abstruse, barely accessible subject of thinking, the tasks of philosophy? The admonished obscurity in Spinoza's doctrine stems from the fact that he did not start impartially from the nature of things, but from Cartesianism, and thus from all kinds of traditional concepts, such as 'God', 'substance', 'perfection',[h] and so on, which he now, by way of detours, tried hard to harmonize with his truth. He very often expresses the best ideas only indirectly, especially in the second part of the *Ethics*, by always speaking by way of circumlocutions[i] and almost allegorically. Again on the other hand, Spinoza evinces an unmistakable *transcendental idealism*, namely the recognition, if only in a general way, of the truths clearly expounded by Locke and especially by Kant, that is, a real distinction between appearance and thing in itself and the recognition that only the former is accessible to us. One should consult *Ethics* II, prop. 16 with the second corollary; prop. 17,

12   schol.; prop. 18, schol.; prop. 19; prop. 23, which extends it to self-knowledge; prop. 25, which expresses it clearly, and finally, as a summary,[j] the corollary to prop. 29, which clearly states that we know neither ourselves nor things as they are in themselves, but only as they appear.[5] The

---

[a] *extensa*   [b] *cogitata*   [c] *nec impraesentiarum haec clarius possum explicare*
[d] *La clarté est la bonne foi des philosophes.*   [e] *der 'reine Satz'*   [f] *conditio sine qua non*
[g] *quodcunque ostendis mihi sic incredulus odi* [Horace, *Ars poetica*, 188]   [h] *Deus, substantia, perfectio*
[i] *per ambages*   [j] *résumé*

demonstration of III, prop. 27 expresses the matter most distinctly at the very beginning. In regard to the relationship between Spinoza's and Descartes' doctrines I remind the reader of what I said about it in *The World as Will and Representation*, vol. II, p. 639.[a] Because Spinoza started out from the concepts of the Cartesian philosophy not only have much obscurity and occasion for misunderstanding entered his exposition, but he has fallen into many flagrant paradoxes, obvious falsehoods, and indeed absurdities and contradictions. For this reason, the many true and excellent elements of his doctrine have been unpleasantly intermixed with positively indigestible elements, and the reader is tossed back and forth between admiration and annoyance. However, in regard to the present concern, Spinoza's fundamental error is that he has drawn the line between the ideal and the real, or the subjective and the objective world, from the wrong place. For *extension* is by no means the opposite of *representation*, but lies entirely within it. We represent things as extended, and insofar as they are extended they are our representation. But the question and the original problem is whether, independently of our representing, anything is extended, indeed, whether anything exists at all. *Kant* later solved this problem, undeniably correctly so far, by claiming that extension, or spatiality, lies exclusively in representation, and thus adheres to it, since the whole of space is the mere form of it; which means that nothing extended can exist independently of our representing, and surely nothing does. Thus, the line that Spinoza has drawn has fallen completely on the ideal side, and he stopped at the *represented* world. This world, marked by its form of extension, he takes as the real,[b] that is, as existing in itself, independent of being represented. Consequently he is justified in asserting that what is extended and what is represented – i.e. our representation of bodies and these bodies themselves, – are one and the same (II, prop. 7, schol.). For indeed the things are extended only as represented things and can be represented only as extended: the world as representation and the world in space is one and the same thing;[c] this we can altogether admit. Now if extension were a quality of things in themselves, then our intuition would be cognition of the things in themselves: this is what he assumes and this is what his realism consists in. However, since he does not establish it and does not prove that, corresponding to our intuition of a spatial world, there is a spatial world that is independent of this intuition, the fundamental problem remains unsolved. And this results from the fact that the line between the real and the ideal, the objective and the subjective, the thing in itself and the

13

---

[a] [See Hübscher *SW* 3, 742]   [b] *das Reale*   [c] *una eademque res*

appearance, is not correctly drawn. Rather, as said before, he cuts through the middle of the ideal, subjective, appearing side of the world, that is, through the world of representation, divides it into the extended or spatial world and our representation of it, and then tries hard to demonstrate that the two are one, as in fact they are. Exactly for the reason that Spinoza stays entirely on the ideal side of the world, since he presumed to find the real already in the extended, which belongs to the ideal world, and since according to him the intuitive world is the sole reality *outside of* us and that which cognizes (*thinks*)[a] is the sole reality *within* us, he relocates the only truly real, the will, into the ideal by making it a mere mode of thinking[b] and, indeed, identifying it with *judgement*. See *Ethics* II, the proofs of prop. 48 and 49, where it says: 'by the *will* I understand the faculty of affirming and negating',[c] – and again: 'let us conceive a particular *volition*, namely, the mode of thinking whereby the mind affirms that the three angles of a triangle are equal to two right angles',[d] whereupon the corollary follows: 'The will and the intellect are one and the same.'[e] – In general Spinoza commits the great mistake of misusing words on purpose to designate concepts that for everyone else go by different names, whereas he takes away the meaning they everywhere have. Thus he names 'God' that which everywhere is called 'the world'; 'right'[f] that which everywhere is called 'violence'; and 'the will' that which everywhere is called 'judgement'. We are completely justified to call to mind the hetman of the Cossacks in Kotzebue's 'Benyowsky'.[g] –

Although coming later and already familiar with *Locke*, *Berkeley* consistently went farther on this path of the Cartesians and thus became the creator of the proper and true *idealism*, that is, the recognition[h] that what is extended in space and fills it, thus the intuitive world in general, by all means can exist as such only in our *representation*, and that it is absurd, even contradictory, to attribute to it as such an existence outside of all representation and independent of the cognitive subject, and hence to

14

[a] *Das Erkennende* (cogitans)   [b] *modus cogitandi*
[c] *per* voluntatem *intellego affirmandi et negandi facultatem* [prop. 48, schol.]
[d] *concipiamus singularem aliquam* volitionem, *nempe modum cogitandi, quo mens affirmat, tres angulos trianguli aequales esse duobus rectis* [prop. 49, schol.]
[e] *Voluntas et intellectus unum et idem sunt* [prop. 49, coroll.]
[f] *das Recht* [which can also mean 'law']
[g] [Schopenhauer refers to August von Kotzebue's play *Graf Benjowsky oder die Verschwörung auf Kamtschatka* (1795) (*Count Benyowsky, or the Conspiracy in Kamtchatka*), in which the hetman, that is, the commander of the Cossacks, is a self-important fool who redefines words at a whim ('When I say Nobody, I mean by that a lot of people who, however, have already run away') and reinterprets reality according to the delusions of his imagination, for example, making himself the king of California]
[h] *Erkenntniß*

assume a matter existing in itself.*,6 This is an absolutely correct and deep insight; however, his entire philosophy consists in it. He had hit upon the ideal and clearly distinguished it; but he did not know how to find the real, does not try very hard to do so and explains himself only occasionally, incompletely and in piecemeal fashion. God's will and omnipotence are the immediate causes of all appearances of the intuitive world, i.e. of all our representations. Actual existence belongs only to cognizing and willing beings, such as we ourselves are; these make up the real, besides God. They are spirits, in other words, cognitive and willing beings; for he deems cognizing and willing absolutely inseparable. He also shares with his predecessors the view that God is better known than the given world and that therefore reference to him is an explanation. In general, his clerical, and indeed episcopal, position put him in too heavy chains and confined him to a narrow circle of ideas against which he was not allowed to offend; thus he could not go further, but truth and falsehood had to learn to get along in his head as best they could. This can be said about the works of all these philosophers, with the exception of Spinoza; they all are corrupted by Jewish theism, which is impervious to investigation, dead to all examination, and so appears as a fixed idea and stands in the way of the truth at every step. Thus the harm that it has done in the theoretical realm is a counterpart to that which, for a thousand years, it has done in the practical realm, by which I mean in religious wars, tribunals and conversions of peoples by the sword.

The closest affinity between *Malebranche*, *Spinoza* and *Berkeley* cannot be missed. In addition, we see them all start out from *Descartes*, insofar as they hold on to the fundamental problem as he formulated it in the form of doubt concerning the existence of the external world and tried to solve it by attempting to investigate the distinction and the relation between the ideal, subjective world, which is given in our representation alone, and the real, objective world, which exists independently of it and thus in itself. Consequently, as stated before, this problem is the axis around which all of modern philosophy revolves.

Now *Locke* differs from these philosophers in relying as closely as possible on experience and common understanding and avoiding hyperphysical

---

* One should take away the term 'idealism' from the laypeople in philosophy, which include many doctors of philosophy, since they do not know what it means and do all kinds of nonsense with it; they imagine idealism to be now spiritualism, now roughly the opposite of philistinism, and are supported and confirmed in this view by the vulgar literati. The terms 'idealism and realism' are not unclaimed, but have their fixed philosophical meaning; those who mean something else should just use another term. – The opposition between *idealism* and *realism* refers to *what is cognized* [*das Erkannte*], the *object*, the opposition between *spiritualism* and *materialism* to *that which cognizes* [*das Erkennende*], the *subject*. (Today's ignorant scribblers confuse idealism with spiritualism.)

hypotheses as much as possible, probably because he was influenced by
Hobbes and Bacon. The *real* for him is *matter*, and, without heeding
Leibniz's scruple about the impossibility of a causal connection between
immaterial, thinking substance, and material, extended substance, he assumes
an outright physical influence between matter and cognitive subject. With
rare thoughtfulness and honesty he goes so far as to acknowledge the
16   possibility that that which cognizes and thinks itself could be matter (*On
human understanding*,[a] Book IV, ch. 3, §6), which later earned him the
repeated praise of the great *Voltaire*, but in his own time the malicious attacks
of a wily Anglican priest, the bishop of Worcester.*,[7] For Locke the *real*, that
is, matter, produces through 'impulse', that is, impact, representations, or the
ideal, in that which cognizes (ibid., Book I, ch. 8, §11).[b] We have here a rather
massive realism, which, evoking contradiction precisely through its excessive-
ness, brought about Berkeley's idealism. The latter's specific point of origin is
perhaps what *Locke*, at the end of §2 of chapter 21 of Book II, puts forward
with such conspicuous lack of thoughtfulness when he says, for example:
*solidity, extention, figure, motion and rest, would be really in the world, as they
17   are, whether there were any sensible being to perceive them, or not.*[c] For as soon

---

* There is no church that shuns the light more than the Anglican; because no other has a greater
pecuniary interest at play than this church, whose income amounts to five million Pounds Sterling,
which is said to be 40,000 more than that of the entire remaining Christian clergy of both hemispheres
taken together. On the other hand, there is no nation which it is so painful to see methodically made
stupid by the most degrading blind faith than the English, which in intelligence surpasses all the
others. The root of evil is the lack of a ministry for public education in England, which has therefore
remained entirely in the hands of the clergy, who have made sure that two thirds of the nation cannot
read or write and who even, on occasion, have the audacity, with the most ludicrous presumption, to
grumble against the natural sciences. It is therefore a human duty to smuggle into England, through
every conceivable channel, light, enlightenment and science in order to finally put out of business
those most well-fed of all priests. When the educated English on the continent display their Jewish
Sabbath superstition and other stupid bigotry one should meet them with unconcealed ridicule – *until
they be shamed into common sense* [English in the original]. For things like that are scandalous for
Europe and should not be tolerated any longer. For that reason we should never, even in ordinary life,
make the least concession to English Church superstition, but immediately stand up to it in the most
trenchant manner wherever it shows itself. For no arrogance surpasses the arrogance of English priests;
therefore it must experience so much humiliation on the continent that it carries a portion of it home,
where it is lacking. For the impudence of Anglican priests and their slavish followers is quite incredible
to this day; therefore, it should remain banished to their isle and, if it dares to let itself be seen on the
continent, should immediately be made to play the role of the owl by day.

[a] [John Locke, *An Essay Concerning Human Understanding*]
[b] [Book I of Locke's *Essay* has no chapter 8. Schopenhauer obviously refers to Book II, where in ch. 8,
§11, Locke indeed talks about how bodies produce ideas in us through impulse]
[c] [English in the original. Schopenhauer then provides the German translation in parentheses:
'(*Undurchdringlichkeit, Ausdehnung, Gestalt, Bewegung und Ruhe würden, wie sie sind, wirklich in der
Welt seyn, gleichviel ob es irgend ein empfindendes Wesen, sie wahrzunehmen, gäbe, oder nicht.*)'
Incidentally, this is not a quote from this paragraph, but is a paraphrase of Book II, ch. 31, §2]

as we reflect on this, we have to recognize it as false; but then Berkeleyean idealism stands in front of us and is undeniable. In the meantime, *Locke* does not overlook that fundamental problem, the gulf between the representations within us and the things that exist independently of us, that is, the difference between the ideal and the real. In the main he rebuffs it with the help of arguments of the sound, but crude, understanding and by appealing to the adequacy of our cognition of things for practical purposes (ibid., Book IV, chs. 4 and 9), which obviously misses the point and only demonstrates how inadequate to the problem empiricism remains. But it is exactly his realism that makes him limit that which in our cognition corresponds to the *real* to the qualities inherent in the things *as they are in themselves*, and distinguish these from the qualities that belong to our *cognition*, thus to the *ideal* alone; accordingly he now names these the *secondary*, but the former the *primary* qualities. This is the origin of the distinction between thing in itself and appearance, which later became so extremely important in the Kantian philosophy. Here is the Kantian doctrine's true genetic link to earlier philosophy, namely to *Locke*. This doctrine was advanced and further occasioned by *Hume's* sceptical objections against Locke's doctrine: in contrast, it has only a polemic relation to the Leibnizian–Wolffian philosophy.

Now those *primary* qualities, which are said to be exclusively determinations[a] of things in themselves and thus to belong to them outside and independently of our representation, turn out to be such that one *cannot* imagine them to *be absent* in those things: namely, extension, solidity, figure, motion, or rest, and number. All the others are recognized as *secondary*, namely as products of the action[b] of those primary qualities on our sense organs, hence as mere sensations in these: such as colour, sound, taste, smell, hardness, softness, smoothness, roughness, and so on. Consequently these lack the slightest resemblance with the constitution in the *things in themselves* that produces them, but can be traced back to the primary qualities as their causes, and these alone exist purely objectively and actually in things. (Ibid., Book I, ch. 8, §7ff.)[c] Thus our representations are really faithful copies of these, which precisely reproduce the qualities that exist in the things in themselves (Book I, ch. §15.[d] I congratulate[e] the reader who really perceives here how realism turns quaint). Thus we see that *Locke* abstracts that which is the action of the nerves of the *sense organs* from the quality of the things in themselves, whose

18

---

[a] *Bestimmungen*   [b] *Einwirkung*   [c] [Again, he refers to Book II, not Book I]
[d] [Refers to Book II, ch. 8, §15]
[e] [The verb 'Glück wünschen' is ambiguous here – it could either mean 'to wish luck' or 'to congratulate']

representations we receive from outside: an easy, comprehensible, indisputable view. In the same way *Kant* later took the immeasurably greater step of also abstracting the activity of our *brain* (this incomparably greater mass of nerves), with the result that all those ostensibly primary qualities are reduced to secondary ones and the presumed things in themselves to mere appearances; the actual thing in itself, now stripped of those qualities as well, is left as a completely unknown quantity, a mere x. This required a difficult and deep analysis that for a long time needed to be defended against challenges through misapprehension and want of understanding.

Locke does not deduce his primary qualities of things and gives no further reason why just they and not others are purely objective, except to say that they are ineradicable. Now if we ourselves investigate why he declares as *not* objectively existent those qualities of things that act immediately on sensation and consequently come directly from outside, but grants objective existence to those that (as since recognized) spring from our intellect's own proper functions, then the reason for this is that the objectively intuiting consciousness (the consciousness of other things) necessarily requires a complicated apparatus as whose function it appears. For this reason its most essential fundamental determinations are already fixed from within, which is why the universal form, that is, the manner and mode, of the intuition, from which alone that which can be cognized a priori can arise, presents itself as the basic fabric of the intuited world and therefore emerges as the absolutely necessary which is without exception and cannot be removed, so that it is established in advance as the condition of everything else and its manifold diversity. As is well known, this is space and time together with what follows from and is possible only through them. In themselves space and time are empty; if something is to come into space and time it must come forth as *matter*, that is, as something *active*, thus as causality. For matter is pure causality through and through; its being consists in its activity, and vice versa; it is just the understanding's form of causality itself, grasped objectively.[a] (*On the Fourfold Root of the Principle of Sufficient Reason*, second edn., p. 77,[b] and also *The World as Will and Representation*, vol. 1, p. 9, and vol. 2, pp. 48–9.[c]) It follows that *Locke's* primary qualities are all such that one cannot imagine them to be absent – which shows clearly enough their subjective origin insofar as they immediately arise from the constitution of the intuitive apparatus itself. Thus he deems as absolutely objective that which, as a function of the brain, is much

19

[a] *die objektiv aufgefaßte Verstandesform der Kausalität selbst*   [b] [*FR*, 80 (Hübscher *SW* 1, 82)]
[c] [*WWR* 1, 29–30 (Hübscher *SW* 2, 10), and Hübscher *SW* 3, 52–3]

more subjective than the sensation, which is caused directly from the outside, or at least more closely determined.

Meanwhile it is nice to see how, through all these different conceptions and explanations, the problem of the relation of the ideal and the real, raised by Descartes, is ever more developed and elucidated and thus the truth is advanced. Certainly this happened through the favourable circumstances of the times, or, more correctly, of nature, which within the short period of two centuries allowed over half a dozen thinking minds to be born and mature in Europe. It was an additional gift of fate that these thinkers, in the middle of a vulgar-minded world indulging solely in utility and pleasure, were permitted to follow their sublime calling, unconcerned about the grumbling of priests and the twaddle, or intent-ridden[a] dealings, of the contemporary professors of philosophy.

Since *Locke*, in line with his strict empiricism, let us become acquainted   20 even with the relation of causality only through experience, *Hume* did not dispute this wrong assumption, as would have been proper; on the contrary, by overshooting the mark, he at once denied the reality of the causal relation itself, and did so through the remark, correct in itself, that experience really can never provide more, sensuously and immediately, than a mere succession of things, but not a true ensuing and effecting,[b] a necessary connection. It is all too known how this sceptical objection by *Hume* occasioned *Kant's* incomparably deeper investigations of the matter, which led him to the result that we know causality, and space and time as well, a priori, meaning that they lie within us before all experience and therefore belong to the *subjective* part of cognition. In addition it follows that all those primary, i.e. absolute, qualities of things that *Locke* had established cannot belong to things in themselves, but are inherent in our manner of cognizing them, and thus have to be assigned not to the real, but to the ideal, for the reason that they are all composed of pure determinations of space, time, and causality. It finally follows that in no respect do we know things as they are *in themselves*, but solely in their *appearances*. Accordingly, the real, the thing in itself, remains completely unknown, a mere x, and the entire intuitive world falls into the ideal, as a mere representation, an appearance; however, as such, something real has somehow to correspond to it. –

From this point I have finally taken an additional step and believe that this will be the last one, since I have solved the problem around which all philosophizing has revolved since *Descartes* by ascribing all being and cognition to the two elements of our self-consciousness, and therefore to something in

---

[a] *absichtsvolle*   [b] *Erfolgen und Bewirken*

respect to which no explanatory principle is any longer possible since it is that which is most immediate and thus ultimate.[8] For I have realized that, as follows from the investigations of all my predecessors recounted here, the absolutely real, or the thing in itself, can certainly never be given to us from the outside, by way of mere *representation*, because it inevitably is part of the essence of representation to furnish only the ideal. However, since we ourselves are indisputably real, it must be possible in some way to draw the cognition of the real from within our own essence. Indeed it enters consciousness in an immediate manner, namely as *will*. Therefore my line between the real and the ideal turns out such that the entire intuitive, objectively present world, including everyone's body, space, time and causality, consequently including the extended of Spinoza and the matter of Locke, as *representation*, belongs to the *ideal*. The will alone is left as the real, which all my predecessors, thoughtlessly and without reflection, had thrown in with the ideal as the mere result of representation and thinking and which Descartes and Spinoza even identified with judgement.* Therefore my ethics is immediately connected with metaphysics and much more closely so than in any other system; hence the moral significance of the world and of existence is more firmly established than ever.[9] *Will* and *representation* are fundamentally distinct insofar as they account for the final and fundamental opposition in all things in the world and leave room for nothing else. The represented thing and its representation are the same, but only the *represented* thing, not the thing *in itself*, the latter is always *will*, in whatever shape it may present itself in representation.

Appendix

Readers who are familiar with what has passed for philosophy in the course of this century in Germany might perhaps be surprised, for the period between Kant and me, to see neither Fichtean idealism nor the system of absolute identity of the real and the ideal mentioned, as they seem quite properly to belong to our subject. I have not been able to include them because, according to my judgement, *Fichte*, *Schelling* and *Hegel* are not philosophers, lacking as they do the first requisite for being counted as such, seriousness and honesty in research. They are merely sophists; they want to appear, not be, and have not sought the truth, but their own interest and advancement in the world. Appointment by governments, fees from students and booksellers, and, as means to this end, the greatest possible attention and racket with their sham philosophy – such were the guiding

---

* Spinoza, loc. cit. – Descartes, *Meditations on First Philosophy*, Med. IV, p. 28.

stars and inspiring genii of those disciples of wisdom. Therefore they do not pass the entrance test and cannot be admitted into the venerable company of thinkers for humanity.

Meanwhile they have excelled in one thing, which is the art of charming the audience and passing themselves off for what they are not; which undoubtedly calls for talent, just not philosophical talent. The reason why they were unable to accomplish anything real in philosophy was ultimately that *their intellect had not become free*, but had remained in the service of the *will*. There it can accomplish a whole lot for the will and its ends, but nothing for philosophy or art. For these require as their first condition that the intellect be active on the basis of its own spontaneity and, for the period of this activity, stop serving the will, i.e. having an eye towards one's own personal ends. But the intellect itself, when activated solely by its own drive,[a] does not know any purpose other than just the truth. Therefore, in order to be a philosopher, that is, a lover of wisdom (which is nothing but truth), it is not enough to love wisdom insofar as it accords with one's own interest or the will of the superiors or the articles of the church or the prejudices and tastes of contemporary people: as long as one rests content with that, one is merely a lover of self, not a lover of wisdom.[b] For this honorary title is beautifully and wisely devised in that it proclaims that one loves the truth sincerely and with all one's heart, thus unconditionally, unreservedly, beyond measure, and, if necessary, even in defiance of all else. Now the reason for this is the one previously mentioned, namely that the intellect has become *free*, a state in which it knows and understands no other interest than that of the truth. As a consequence we then develop an implacable hatred of all lies and frauds, however they might dress themselves up. With such an attitude, we will not go far in the world; but in philosophy we will. – In contrast, it is not at all auspicious if, pretending to explore the truth, we start to bid farewell to all veracity, honesty, and sincerity and are only intent on passing ourselves off as something we are not. We then adopt, just like those three sophists, now a false pathos, now an affected lofty earnestness, now the air of infinite superiority, in order to impress where we despair of being able to convince. We write thoughtlessly because, thinking only in order to write, we have reserved the thinking for the writing, and then seek to smuggle in palpable sophisms as proofs and to pass off hollow and meaningless verbiage as deep thoughts. We appeal to intellectual intuition, or to absolute thinking and the self-movement of concepts, reject with horror the standpoint of 'reflection', i.e. of rational deliberation, impartial consid- eration and honest exposition, that is the proper, normal employment of

[a] *bloß aus eigenem Antriebe thätig*   [b] *ein* φίλαυτος, *kein* φιλόσοφος

reason as such. Accordingly, we declare an infinite contempt for the 'philosophy of reflection', a name by which one designates every coherent train of thought that deduces effects from causes, as all earlier philosophizing does. And thus, if one possesses enough audacity encouraged by the baseness of the age, one shall express oneself about it in something like the following manner: 'But it is not difficult to see that the way of asserting a proposition, adducing reasons for it, and in the same way refuting its opposite by reason, is not the form in which truth can appear. Truth is its own self-movement',[a] and so forth (Hegel, preface to *Phenomenology of Spirit*,[b] p. LVII, in *Complete Works*,[c] p. 36). I think it is not difficult to see that whoever puts forward such a thing is a shameless charlatan who wants to fool the simpletons and realizes that he has found his people in the Germans of the nineteenth century.

Hence if, as we ostensibly rush towards the temple of truth, we hand the reins over to our personal interest, which looks sideways and at quite different guiding stars, for example the taste and foibles of contemporary people, the religion of a country, and especially the intentions and beckonings of the rulers – oh how shall we reach the temple of truth up on that steep, precipitous, barren rock! – Certainly we can then bind to ourselves, through the secure bond of interest, a host of quite hopeful disciples, hopeful, that is, for protection and employment, who will seemingly form a sect, but really a faction, whose united stentorian voices will proclaim us to all the four winds as a sage without equal; the interest of the person is satisfied, that of the truth betrayed.

All this explains the embarrassed impression that we get when, after studying the genuine thinkers scrutinized above, we start to read the writings of Fichte and Schelling, or even the nonsense of Hegel, presumptuously scribbled out of boundless but justified confidence in German stupidity.* In regard to the former we found everywhere an *honest* inquiry after the truth

25

---

* Hegel's pseudo-wisdom is really that millstone in the student's head in *Faust*. If one intentionally wants to make a young man stupid and wholly incapable of any thought, then there is no better proven means than the diligent study of Hegel's original works; for these monstrous conjunctions of words, which cancel and contradict each other, so that the spirit torments itself in vain to connect some thought to them, until it finally sinks down exhausted, gradually destroy in him so completely the capacity to think that from then on hollow, empty phrases pass for thoughts for him. Add to this the illusion, attested for the young man by word and example of all persons of respect, that that verbal rubbish is the true, noble wisdom! – If once a guardian should be worried that his ward could become too clever for his plans, then this misfortune could be prevented through the diligent study of Hegel's philosophy.

[a] [Translations of quotes from Hegel's *Phenomenology of Spirit* are taken from A. V. Miller's translation]
[b] *Phänomenologie des Geistes* [1807]
[c] *Gesammtausgabe* [Georg Wilhelm Friedrich Hegel, *Werke, Vollständige Ausgabe* (*Complete Works*), Berlin: Duncker and Humblot, 1832–45; vol. 2, ed. Johann Schulze (1832)]

and an equally *honest* attempt to communicate their ideas to others. Thus those who read Kant, Locke, Hume, Malebranche, Spinoza, Descartes feel elated and filled with joy; this is the effect of communion with a noble mind, which possesses ideas and awakens them, thinks and sets one thinking. The reverse of all this takes place when reading the above-mentioned German sophists. An unbiased reader who opens one of their books and then asks himself whether this is the style of a thinker wanting to instruct or that of a charlatan wanting to deceive, cannot doubt this for five minutes; everything here breathes so much *dishonesty*. The tone of calm investigation, which characterized all previous philosophy, has been exchanged for that of unshakeable certainty, such as belongs to every kind of charlatanry of all ages. Here, however, it claims to rest on immediate, intellectual intuition, or absolute thought, meaning thought that is independent of the subject and thus of its fallibility as well. From every page, every line, speaks the endeavour to bewitch and to deceive the reader, now to disconcert him through impressing upon him, now to stupefy him through incomprehensible phrases and even utter nonsense, now to dumbfound him through the insolence of what is claimed, in short, to throw dust in his eyes and mystify him as much as possible. Therefore, the impression one has when passing from one[a] to the other[b] in a theoretical respect is comparable in a practical respect to the feeling somebody might have who, coming from the company of men of honour, happens on a den of crooks. What a worthy man in comparison with them is *Christian Wolff*, whom those three sophists slight and mock! He entertained and communicated real thoughts, whereas they provide mere verbal creations and empty phrases with the intention to deceive. Hence the true distinguishing character of the philosophy of this whole so-called post-Kantian school is *dishonesty*, its element blue smoke and its aim personal interest. Its chorus leaders[c] try hard to *appear*, not to *be*; thus they are sophists, not philosophers. The ridicule of posterity awaits them, extending to their admirers, and then oblivion. The bickering, chiding tone, by the way, which runs through Schelling's writings everywhere as an obligatory accompaniment, also depends on the stated tendency of these people. – If all this were not the case, if they had proceeded with honesty instead of posturing and windbaggery, then *Schelling*, as definitely the most talented among the three, could fill the subordinate rank of a temporarily useful eclectic in philosophy. The amalgam he has prepared from the doctrines of Plotinus, Spinoza, Jakob Böhme, Kant and modern natural science was able to fill for a time the great vacuum created by the negative results of Kant's philosophy, until one day a

26

[a] [the genuine philosopher]   [b] [the sophists]   [c] *Koryphäen*

really new philosophy should come along and actually grant the satisfaction demanded by the former. In particular, he has used the natural science of our century in order to revive Spinoza's abstract pantheism. For, without any knowledge of nature, Spinoza had philosophized merely from abstract concepts in a random kind of way and erected his system without really knowing the things themselves. It is Schelling's undeniable merit in his philosophy of nature to have invested this scrawny skeleton with flesh and colour and, as best as he could, to have imparted life and movement to it by applying natural science, which had grown to maturity in the meantime, even if he often employed it incorrectly. For this reason, his philosophy of nature is the best among his many different attempts and new departures.[10]

Like children who play with weapons, meant for serious purposes, or other implements belonging to adults, the three sophists considered here have dealt with the subject matter whose treatment I am relating here by delivering the comical counterpart to two hundred years of laborious investigations by ruminating philosophers. For after *Kant* had brought the great problem of the relation between what exists in itself and our representations to a sharper point than ever, and had thus brought it much closer to a solution, *Fichte* came forward with the claim that there was nothing more behind the representations, that they were just products of the cognitive subject, the I. While he was trying to outdo *Kant* in this way, he produced merely a caricature of the latter's philosophy since, by continuously applying the method those three pseudo-philosophers have already been credited with, he abolished the real completely and left nothing but the ideal. Then came *Schelling*, who in his system of the absolute identity of the real and the ideal declared the whole distinction null and void and claimed that the ideal is also the real; that everything is really one. In so doing he tried to throw again into confusion what had been separated painstakingly, by means of a thoughtfulness that developed gradually and step by step, and to mix everything up (Schelling, *On the Relation of the Philosophy of Nature to Fichte's*,[a] pp. 14–21). He boldly denies the difference between the ideal and the real, in imitation of Spinoza's above-censured errors. In doing so he even brings out Leibniz's monads again, solemnly apotheosizes them and makes use of them, this monstrous identification of two impossibilities,[b] that is, atoms and those indivisible, originally and

---

[a] *Vom Verhältniß der Naturphilosophie zur Fichte'schen* [Friedrich Wilhelm Joseph von Schelling, *Darlegung des wahren Verhältnisses der Naturphilosophie zu der verbesserten Fichte'schen Lehre* (1806) (*Exposition of the True Relation of the Philosophy of Nature and the Improved Doctrine of Fichte*)]

[b] *Undinge*

essentially cognitive individuals that are called souls (Schelling, *Ideas for a Philosophy of Nature*,[a] second edn., pp. 38 and 82). Schelling's philosophy of nature bears the name of identity philosophy because, walking in Spinoza's steps, it follows him in abolishing three distinctions that the latter had eliminated, namely that between God and world, that between body and soul, and finally also that between the ideal and the real in the intuited   28 world. However, this last distinction by no means depends on the other two, as shown above in the treatment of Spinoza. It depends so little on them that the more one emphasizes it, the more the other two become subject to doubt. For they are based on dogmatic proofs (overturned by Kant), but the last distinction is based on a simple act of reflection. Accordingly, Schelling identified metaphysics with physics and bestowed the lofty title 'On the world soul'[b] on a merely physico-chemical diatribe. All genuinely metaphysical problems, as they incessantly force themselves on human consciousness, were to be allayed through impudent denial, by peremptory order. Nature is here just because it is, out of itself[c] and through itself. We grant it the title God, with that it is settled, and whoever asks for more is a fool. The distinction between the subjective and the objective is a mere trick of the schools, as is the entire Kantian philosophy, whose distinction between a priori and a posteriori is null and void; our empirical intuition actually delivers the things in themselves, and so on. One should look at *On the Relation of the Philosophy of Nature to Fichte's*,[d] pp. 51 and 67, while on p. 61 there is explicit mockery of those 'who are truly amazed that there is not nothing, and cannot wonder enough that something really exists'. To such an extent everything seems to go without saying for Herr von Schelling. Strictly speaking such talk is an appeal, wrapped in elegant phrases, to the so-called sound, or rather crude, understanding. By the way, I am referring here to what I said at the very beginning of chapter 17 of the second volume of my chief work. Also p. 69 of the aforementioned book by Schelling is characteristic for the subject matter at hand and truly naïve: 'If experience had completely achieved its purpose, then its opposition to philosophy, and with this philosophy itself, would disappear as a proper area or type of science; all abstractions would dissolve into immediate "friendly" intuition; the highest would be a play of desire and naïvety, the

---

[a] [*Ideen zu einer Philosophie der Natur als Einleitung in das Studium dieser Wissenschaft* (1797) (*Ideas for a Philosophy of Nature: as Introduction to the Study of this Science*)]

[b] *von der Weltseele* [*Von der Weltseele: eine Hypothese der höheren Physik zur Erklärung des allgemeinen Organismus* (1798) (*On the World-soul: a Hypothesis of Higher Physics for Explaining the General Organism*)]

[c] *aus sich selbst*   [d] [See p. 26, n. a]

29 most difficult easy, the least sensible sensible, and humans would be allowed
to read joyfully and freely in the book of nature.' – To be sure, that would be
so lovely! But that is not how things stand with us; thinking cannot be
shown the door like that. The stern old sphinx with her riddle lies there
motionless and will not hurl herself from the rock because you declare her to
be a spectre. When, for that reason, Schelling himself later realized that
metaphysical problems cannot be dismissed through peremptory assertions,
he provided a real metaphysical attempt in his treatise on freedom,[a] which
nevertheless is a mere fantasy,[II] a tall tale,[b] which is why his delivery, as soon
as it takes on the demonstrating style (for example pp. 453ff.), has a
decidedly comical effect.

Through his doctrine of the identity of the real and the ideal *Schelling* had
attempted to solve the problem, which, since Descartes had initiated it, all
great thinkers had dealt with and which Kant had brought to a head. He
attempted to solve it by cutting through the knot by means of his denial of
the opposition between the two. Thus he came into direct contradiction
with Kant, from whom he professed to start out. Meanwhile he had at least
held on to the original and proper meaning of the problem, which concerns
the relationship between our *intuition* and the being and essence in itself of
the things that present themselves in it. However, since he drew his doctrine
mainly from *Spinoza*, he adopted from him the expressions *thinking* and
being, which state the problem under discussion very badly and later gave
rise to the most insane monstrosities. With his doctrine that 'thinking
substance and extended substance are one and the same substance, comprehended now under this attribute, now under that'[c] (II, prop. 7, schol.);
or 'obviously, mind and body are one and the same thing, conceived now
under the attribute of thought, now under the attribute of extension'[d] (III,
prop. 2, schol.), *Spinoza* had initially meant to abolish the Cartesian
opposition between body and soul. He also may have recognized that the
empirical object is not distinct from our representation of it. Now *Schelling*
took over from him the expressions *thinking* and *being*, which he gradually
30 substituted for those of *intuiting*,[e] or rather the intuited,[f] and thing in itself.

---

[a] [*Philosophische Untersuchungen über das Wesen der menschlichen Freiheit und die damit
zusammenhängenden Gegenstände* (1809) (*Philosophical Inquiries into the Nature of Human Freedom
and Related Matters*)]
[b] *conte bleu*
[c] *substantia cogitans et substantia extensa una eademque est substantia, quae jam sub hoc jam sub illo
attributo comprehenditur*
[d] *scilicet mens et corpus una eademque est res, quae jam sub cogitationis, jam sub extensionis attributo
concipitur*
[e] *Anschauen*   [f] *Angeschauten*

(*Neue Zeitschrift für spekulative Physik*, vol. I, essay 1: '*Fernere Darstellungen*' and so on.)[a] For the relation of our *intuition* of things and their *being* and *essence in itself* is the great problem whose history I am outlining here; but not that of our *thoughts*, that is, *concepts*, since these are obviously and undeniably mere abstractions of what is intuitively cognized, resulting from arbitrary abstraction from, or dropping of, some qualities and keeping others; to doubt this would not occur to any reasonable human being.[*] These *concepts* and *thoughts*, which make up the class of *non-intuitive* representations, therefore never have an *immediate* relation to the *essence and being in itself* of things, but only a *mediated* one, namely through the mediation of *intuition*. It is the latter which on the one hand provides the material[b] and on the other is related to the things in themselves, i.e. to the unknown, intrinsic[c] essence of things, which objectifies itself in intuition.

The imprecise expression that Schelling had borrowed from Spinoza later provided the occasion for *Hegel*, that spiritless and tasteless charlatan, who in this respect acts as Schelling's buffoon, to distort the matter so that *thinking* itself in the proper sense, or *concepts*, were to be identical with the essence in itself of things. Hence what is as such and immediately thought abstractly[d] was to be identical with that which objectively exists in itself; accordingly logic was to be at the same time the true metaphysics. Therefore we only needed to think, or let concepts rule, in order to know how the world outside is absolutely constituted. Accordingly, everything haunting a skull would at once be true and real. Moreover, since the motto of the philosophasters of this period was 'the crazier, the better', this absurdity was supported by a second one, that it is not *we* who are thinking, but that the concepts, alone and without our help, perform the process of thinking, which was therefore called the dialectical self-movement of the concept and was supposed to be a revelation of all things within and outside of nature.[e] However, this caricature was really based on another one that also depended on a misuse of words and is, even if it was never clearly stated, without doubt behind it. Following the precedent of Spinoza, *Schelling* had bestowed the title of *God* on the world. *Hegel* took this literally. Since the word properly means a personal being that, among other qualities completely incompatible with the world, also possesses that of *omniscience*, he

31

---

[*] *On the Fourfold Root of the Principle of Sufficient Reason*, 2nd edn., §26. [*FR*, 93–6 (Hübscher *SW* I, 97–100)]

[a] [*Neue Zeitschrift für speculative Physik*, I. Band, erstes Stück 'Fernere Darstellungen aus dem System der Philosophie' (1802) (*New Journal for Speculative Physics*, vol. I, essay 1: 'Further Expositions from the System of Philosophy']

[b] *Stoff*   [c] *Selbsteigenen*   [d] *in abstracto*   [e] *in et extra naturam*

transferred *this quality* as well onto the *world*, where it could find no place other than beneath the foolish brow of human beings, who now only had to give free play to their thoughts (dialectical self-movement) in order to reveal all mysteries of heaven and earth, namely in the absolute nonsense[a] of Hegel's dialectic. *One* art this Hegel has really mastered, namely to lead the Germans by the nose. But that is not a great art. For we see the kinds of antics with which he has been able to command the respect of the German academic world for thirty years. The only reason why the professors of philosophy still take these three sophists seriously and make a big show of granting them a place in the history of philosophy is because it provides their livelihood,[b] furnishing them with the material for extensive, oral and written lectures about the history of the so-called post-Kantian philosophy which present the tenets of these sophists in detail and consider them in earnest. – However, it would be sensible not to concern oneself with what these people, in order to appear as something, have brought to market, unless one wanted to declare Hegel's writings as officinal and stock them in pharmacies as psychically effective vomitive, since the disgust that they excite is really quite specific.[12] But enough of them and their creator, whose adoration we will leave to the Danish Academy of Sciences, which has recognized in him a 'distinguished philosopher'[c] to its liking. Thus it demands respect for him in its judgement, appended as a lasting memorial to my prize essay *On the Basis of Morals*.[d] That judgement merited rescue from oblivion because of its sagacity as well as its memorable honesty, and also because it provides striking confirmation of Labruyère's beautiful remark: 'for the same reason that we neglect a man of merit, we can also admire a fool'.[e]

---

[a] *Gallimathias*   [b] *gagne-pain*   [c] *summus philosophus*   [d] [See *BM*, 258 (Hübscher *SW* 4, 276)]
[e] *du même fonds, dont on néglige un homme de mérite, l'on sait encore admirer un sot* [Jean de La Bruyère, *Les Caractères ou Les mœurs de ce siècle* (1688), ch. 'Des jugements' (On judgements), 43 (I)]

§1.   About such a history

To read all kinds of expositions of the doctrines of the philosophers, or in general the history of philosophy, instead of reading their own original works is like letting somebody else chew our food. Would anyone read world history if we were free to watch with our own eyes the events of former times that interest us? Now in respect to the history of philosophy such an autopsy[a] of the subject is actually available, namely in the original writings of the philosophers. At any rate, we can then limit ourselves, for the sake of brevity, to well-chosen principal chapters, the more so as they all abound in repetitions, which we can spare ourselves. In this way we will get to know the essence of their doctrines in authentic and unadulterated form, whereas from the half dozen histories of philosophy that now appear every year we merely receive what entered the head of a philosophy professor, and in the form in which it there appears at that. It goes without saying that the thoughts of a great mind are bound to shrink considerably in order to fit into the three-pound-brain of such a parasite of philosophy, out of which they are then to emerge again, clothed in the respective jargon of the day, accompanied by his precocious judgement. – Moreover, we can reckon that   36 such a salaried historian of philosophy can scarcely have read a tenth of the writings of which he gives an account. Their real study requires all of a long and industrious life, such as formerly the brave *Brucker* invested in them in the old, studious times. On the other hand, what could such small people[b] have thoroughly researched, while being detained by constant lectures, official business, vacation travels and dissipations, to come out with histories of philosophy in their early years? Moreover, they claim to be pragmatic, to have fathomed and to expound the necessity of the origin and sequence of

---

[a] *Autopsie* [literally: 'self-gaze' or 'seeing for oneself', the close examination of an object; in library science the compilation of documents by means of extant originals]
[b] *Leutchen*

systems, and even want to judge, reprimand and master those serious, genuine philosophers of the past. How can it fail to happen that they copy the older ones and one another, but then, in order to conceal this, spoil things more and more by trying to impart on them the modern spin[a] of the current quinquennium,[b] just as they also judge them in this spirit? – In contrast, a collection of important passages and essential chapters of all the principal philosophers, compiled jointly and conscientiously by honest and insightful scholars, would be very useful, put together in chronological–pragmatic order, more or less in the manner in which first *Gedicke* and later *Ritter* and *Preller* have done with ancient philosophy, but much more extensive; thus a great and general anthology, prepared with care and expert knowledge.

The fragments that I am providing here are at least not traditional, i.e. copied; rather they are thoughts occasioned by my own study of the original works.

§2. Presocratic philosophy

The *Eleatic philosophers* are probably the first who became aware of the opposition between what is intuited and what is thought, *phainomena* and *nooumena*.[c] The latter alone was for them true being, the *ontôs on*.[d] – Of this they then asserted that it is One, unchangeable and immovable. They did not claim the same of the *phainomena*, i.e. of what is intuited, appearing, empirically given, which would have been outright ridiculous. For that reason Diogenes refuted that proposition, thus misunderstood, in the well-known manner. Thus they really distinguished already between *appearance, phainomenon*, and *thing in itself, ontôs on*. The latter could not be sensibly intuited, but only grasped through thinking and was therefore *nooumenon*. (Aristotle, *Metaphysics* I, 5, 986 and *Scholia*, Berlin edition,[e] pp. 429, 430 and 509.) The *Scholia to Aristotle* (pp. 460, 536, 544 and 798) mention Parmenides' text 'On Opinion';[f] which would have been the doctrine of *appearance*, physics. Doubtlessly another work corresponded to it, 'On Truth',[g] the doctrine of the *thing in itself*, thus metaphysics. A scholium of Philoponus explicitly says of *Melissus*: 'Whereas in regard to truth he says that what exists is one, in regard to opinion there are two (it

---

[a] *Tournüre*   [b] [period of five years]   [c] φαινόμενα *und* νοούμενα   [d] *das* ὄντως ὄν

[e] [*Aristotelis Opera*, Deutsche Akademie der Wissenschaften zu Berlin, vol. 4, *Scholia in Aristotelem*, ed. Christian August Brandis, Berlin: Georg Reimer, 1836]

[f] τὰ κατὰ δόξαν

[g] τὰ κατ᾽ ἀλήθειαν [These are indeed the two main parts of Parmenides' poem *On Nature*]

should be "many")'.'ᵃ – *Heraclitus* is the opposite of the Eleatics, and was probably provoked by them insofar as he taught the ceaseless motion of all things, whereas *they* taught absolute motionlessness; thus he confined himself to the phenomenon (Aristotle, *On the Heavens* III, 1, 298,ᵇ Berlin edition). Because of that he provoked, as *his* antithesis, *Plato's* doctrine of ideas, as is revealed in Aristotle's exposition (*Metaphysics*, 1078ᶜ).

It is remarkable that we find the easily enumerated principal propositions of the Presocratic philosophers, which have been preserved, repeated innumerable times in the ancient writings, but beyond that very little. Thus we have, for example, Anaxagoras' doctrines of mindᵈ and homoeomeries;ᵉ Empedocles' doctrines of love and hateᶠ and the four elements; those of Democritus and Leucippus of the atoms and the likenesses;ᵍ those of Heraclitus of the continuous flux of things; those of the Eleatics as explained above; those of the Pythagoreans of numbers, metempsychosis, and so on. However, it may be the case that this was the sum of all their philosophizing, for we also find in the works of the modern philosophers, for example those of Descartes, Spinoza, Leibniz and even Kant, the few fundamental propositions of their philosophies repeated countless times. Thus these philosophers all seem to have adopted the motto of Empedocles, who may have already been a lover of the repeat sign,ʰ 'the good can be said twice or thrice'.ⁱ (See Sturz, *Empedocles of Acragas*,ʲ p. 504.)ᴵ

Incidentally, the two theories of *Anaxagoras* just mentioned are closely connected. – For 'In everything there is a share of everything'ᵏ is his symbolic description of the theory of homoeomeries. Accordingly, the homogeneous partsᴵ (in the physiological sense) of all things were present and complete in the chaotic primal mass. In order to separate them and to combine, order and form them into specifically diverse things (heterogeneous partsᵐ), a mindⁿ was needed that, by means of selecting the constituents, would bring order to the confusion, since the chaos, indeed, contained the most complete mixture of all substances (*Scholia to*

38

ᵃ ἐν τοῖς πρὸς ἀλήθειαν ἓν εἶναι λέγων τὸ ὄν, ἐν τοῖς πρὸς δόξαν δύο (*müßte heißen πολλὰ*) φησὶν εἶναι [*Scholium to Aristotle, Physics* II]

ᵇ *de coelo* [*De caelo* III, 1, 298b]   ᶜ [*Metaphysics* XIII, 4, 1078b]   ᵈ νοῦς   ᵉ ὁμοιομερίαι

ᶠ φιλία καὶ νεῖκος   ᵍ εἴδωλα   ʰ *Repetitionszeichen* [musical term]

ⁱ δὶς καὶ τρὶς τὰ καλά [cf. Plato, *Philebus* 59e]

ʲ [Friedrich Wilhelm Sturz, *Empedocles Agrigentinus. De vita et philosophia eius exposuit, carminum reliquias ex antiquis scriptoribus collegit, recensuit, illustravit, praefationem et indices adiecit Fr. W. S.* (*Empedocles of Acragas. His life and philosophy expounded, his sayings collected from ancient authors, revised, explained, with a preface and index added*, by Friedrich Wilhelm Sturz), Lipsiae (Leipzig), 1805]

ᵏ πάντα ἐν πᾶσιν   ᴵ *partes similares*   ᵐ *partes dissimilares*   ⁿ νοῦς

Aristotle, p. 337). However, the mind had not completely accomplished this first separation; for that reason one could find in every thing the elements of all the others, although to a lesser degree: 'For, again, everything is mixed with everything'[a] (ibid.). –

On the other hand, *Empedocles* had, instead of innumerable homoeomeries, only four elements, from which the things were now to emerge as products, not, as for Anaxagoras, as educts.[b] The role of mind in uniting and separating, and thus in ordering, is played for him by *philia* and *neikos*,[c] love and hate. Both views are much more sensible. He assigns the ordering of things not to the *intellect* (*nous*) but to the *will* (*philia* and *neikos*), and the different kinds of substances are not mere educts, as in Anaxagoras, but real products. Whereas Anaxagoras had them be produced through a separating understanding, Empedocles lets them be produced through a blind drive, i.e. a will without cognition.

Altogether, *Empedocles* is a true man[d] and, underlying his *philia* and *neikos* there is a profound and true insight.[e] Already in inorganic nature we see the materials seek or flee each other, combine or separate, in accordance with the laws of elective affinity. However, those that have the strongest tendency to combine chemically, a tendency which can only be satisfied in the state of fluidity, enter into the most determined electrical opposition when they come into contact with each other in the solid state; they now separate inimically[f] into opposite polarities in order subsequently to seek and embrace one another again. And what else is that polar opposition, occurring in all of nature everywhere under the most varied forms, but a constantly renewed division followed by a fervently desired reconciliation? Thus *philia* and *neikos* really is present everywhere and only according to the circumstances will one or the other step forward at a time. Thus we ourselves can instantly become friends, or foes, with any human being who comes near us; the disposition for both is there and awaits the right conditions. Only prudence bids us to cling to the neutral point of indifference, although it is simultaneously the freezing point. In the same way the strange dog whom we approach is instantly ready to adopt either a friendly or a hostile tone and easily changes from barking and growling to wagging its tail, and also in the opposite direction. What is at the bottom of this universal phenomenon of love and hate is ultimately the great primal opposition between the unity of all beings, according to their being in itself,[g] and their complete diversity in

39

---

[a] πάλιν γὰρ πᾶν ἐν παντὶ μέμικται   [b] *Edukte* [discharge]   [c] φιλία καὶ νεῖκος   [d] *ein ganzer Mann*
[e] *apperçu* [*aperçu*]   [f] *feindlich*   [g] *Seyn an sich*

appearance, whose form is the principle of individuation.[a] Equally, Empedocles recognized the falsity of the doctrine of atoms that was already known to him and instead taught the infinite divisibility of bodies, as Lucretius tells us in Book I, v. 749ff.[b]

But above all, the resolute pessimism in the teachings of Empedocles is remarkable. He fully recognized the misery of our existence and, for him, as for the true Christian, the world is a vale of tears – a meadow of delusions.[c] He already compares it, as Plato did later, with a dark cave in which we are imprisoned. He sees in our earthly existence a state of exile and misery, and the body is the prison of the soul. These souls were once in a state of infinite bliss and have fallen into present ruin through their own fault and sin, ensnaring themselves in it further and further through their sinful conduct and falling into the cycle of metempsychosis. On the other hand, through virtue and moral purity, which also includes the abstention from an animal-based diet, and by turning away from the earthly pleasures and desires, they can return to their former state. – Thus this ancient Greek was aware of the same original wisdom that makes up the fundamental idea of Brahmanism and Buddhism, and even true Christianity (not to be understood as the optimistic, Jewish–Protestant rationalism), whereby the agreement of peoples[d] about it is made complete. It is probable that Empedocles, whom the ancients consistently call a Pythagorean, took over this view from Pythagoras, especially since at bottom Plato, who is also influenced by Pythagoras, shares it as well. Empedocles decidedly professes to the doctrine of metempsychosis, which is connected to this worldview. – The ancient passages that testify to that conception of the world by Empedocles, together with his own verses, are found compiled with great diligence in Sturz's *Empedocles of Acragas*, pp. 448–58. – Egyptians, Pythagoreans, and Empedocles share with Hindus and Buddhists the view that the body is a prison and life a state of suffering and purification, from which death redeems us when we escape the transmigration of souls. With the exception of metempsychosis it is also part of Christianity. Diodorus Siculus, Cicero, and others attest to that view of the ancients. (See Wernsdorf, *De metempsychosi Veterum*,[e] p. 31, and Cicero, *Fragmenta*,[f]

40

---

[a] *principium individuationis*   [b] [*De rerum natura (On the Nature of Things)*]
[c] Ἄτης λειμών [Empedocles, Fragment 31 B 121 DK]
[d] *consensus gentium* [proof of a belief based on its widespread dissemination; originally a Stoic concept]
[e] [Gottlieb Wernsdorf, *Disputatio de Metempsychosi Veterum non figurate sed proprie intelligenda (On the metempsychosis of the ancients, understood not in the figurative but in the literal sense)*, Vitembergæ (Wittenberg), 1741]
[f] [Marcus Tullius Cicero, *Fragmenta Philosophicorum*]

p. 299 (*Somnium Scipionis*),[a] 316,[b] 319,[c] Editiones Bipontinae.[d]) Cicero does not indicate in these passages to which school of philosophy they belong, but they appear to be remnants of Pythagorean wisdom.[2]

There is also much in the remaining doctrines of these Presocratic philosophers that can be proven true, and I will give a few examples of this.

According to the cosmogony of *Kant* and *Laplace*, which has received factual confirmation a posteriori through *Herschel's* observations and which Lord *Rosse* now attempts, for the consolation of the English clergy, to render doubtful again with the help of his giant telescope, planetary systems form through condensation from slowly coagulating and subsequently revolving luminous nebulae. Thus after thousands of years *Anaximenes*, who declared air and vapour the fundamental matter of all things, is right in the end (*Scholia to Aristotle*, p. 514). But at the same time, *Empedocles* and *Democritus* are confirmed since, like *Laplace*, they explained the origin and permanence of the world from a vortex, *dínē*[e] (*Aristotelis Opera*, Berlin edn., p. 295, and *Scholia*, p. 351). *Aristophanes* (*The Clouds*,[f] v. 820) had already mocked this as godlessness, just as nowadays the English parsons, who, as with all truth coming to light, feel ill at ease, meaning afraid for their benefices,[g] ridicule Laplace's theory. – Even our chemical stoichiometry to a certain extent leads back to the Pythagorean philosophy of numbers: 'For the affections and states of numbers are the reason for the affections and states of being, as, for example, in the double, one and a third, and one and a half'[h] (*Scholia to Aristotle*, pp. 543 and 829). – It is well known that the Copernican system had been anticipated by the *Pythagoreans*; indeed, it was known to Copernicus, who drew his fundamental idea straight from the famous passage about *Hicetas* in Cicero's *Academica* (II, 39)[i] and about *Philolaus* in Plutarch, *The Doctrines of the Philosophers*,[j] Book III, ch. 13 (after MacLaurin, *On Newton*,[k] p. 45). Aristotle afterwards rejected this old and important knowledge in order to put in its place his own humbug, about which more below, §5. (See *The World as Will and Representation*, vol. 2,

---

[a] ['*Somnium Scipionis*' (The Dream of Scipio), Part VI of *De republica*]

[b] [*De Philosophia sive Hortensius*]   [c] [*De consolatione liber*]

[d] [Series of editions of Greek and Latin classical authors, published in Zweibrücken from 1779; from now on quoted as 'Bipont edition']

[e] δίνη   [f] *Nubes*

[g] *Pfründe* [religious term, referring to rights to revenue streams from the Church]

[h] τὰ γὰρ πάθη καὶ αἱ ἕξεις τῶν ἀριθμῶν τῶν ἐν τοῖς οὖσι παθῶν τε καὶ ἕξεων αἴτια, οἷον τὸ διπλάσιον, τὸ ἐπίτριτον, καὶ ἡμιόλιον

[i] *quaestionibus acad.* [*Academicae quaestiones* II, 39, 123]

[j] *de placitis philosophorum* [pseudo-Plutarch]

[k] [Colin MacLaurin, *Sir Isaac Newton's Philosophical Discoveries* (1748)]

p. 342.)[a] But even *Fourier's* and *Cordier's* discoveries concerning the heat in the interior of the earth are confirmations of the doctrines of the ancients: 'The Pythagoreans said that a burning fire was found near the middle or centre of the earth, giving warmth and life to the earth.'[b] *Scholia to Aristotle*, p. 504. And if, as a consequence of those discoveries, the earth's crust is nowadays regarded as a thin layer between two media (atmosphere and hot, molten metals and metalloids), contact between which must cause a fire that destroys that crust, then this confirms the opinion that the world will in the end be consumed by fire, an opinion which all ancient philosophers agree upon and which is also shared by the *Hindus* ('Lettres édifiantes',[c] edition of 1819, vol. 7, p. 114). – It is also worth noting that, as can be seen in Aristotle (*Metaphysics* I, 5, 986), the Pythagoreans had correctly conceived of the *Yin* and *Yang* of the Chinese under the name of the ten principles.[d]　42

　　That the metaphysics of music, as I have presented it in my chief work[e] (vol. 1, §52, and vol. 2, ch. 39), can be interpreted as an exposition of the Pythagorean philosophy of numbers, I have already briefly alluded to in that work and will explain here in a little bit more detail; however, I presume that the passages just mentioned are familiar to the reader. – According to the metaphysics of music, *melody* expresses all the movements of the will as it makes itself known in human self-consciousness, i.e. all affects, feelings, and so on. *Harmony*, on the other hand, indicates the scale of the will's objectivation in the rest of nature. In this sense music is a second reality which perfectly parallels the first but incidentally is of a completely different kind and constitution; thus it is in complete analogy with nature but bears absolutely no resemblance to it. However, music *as such* is present only in our auditory nerve and brain. Outside of that, or *in itself* (understood in the *Lockean* sense), it consists of nothing but numerical relations: namely first, in accordance with its quantity, in respect to measure;[f] and then, in accordance with its quality, in respect to the intervals of the scale, which are based on the arithmetical relations of vibrations; or, in other words, music consists of numerical relations in its rhythmic as well as in its harmonic element. Accordingly, the whole essence of the world, as microcosm and macrocosm, can be expressed by means of mere numerical relations and thus in a way can be traced back to it. In this sense

---

[a] [Of the second edn. (Hübscher *SW* 3, 389)]

[b] Ἔλεγον δὲ Πυθαγόρειοι πῦρ εἶναι δημιουργικὸν περὶ τὸ μέσον καὶ κέντρον τῆς γῆς, τὸ ἀναθαλποῦν τὴν γῆν καὶ ζωοποιοῦν

[c] [*Lettres édifiantes et curieuses, écrites des missions étrangères. 'Mémoires des Indes'*, Lyon: Vernarel, 1819; rather, p. 116]

[d] δέκα ἀρχαί　　[e] [*The World as Will and Representation*]　　[f] *Takt*

Pythagoras would be right to ascribe the proper essence of things to numbers. – But what are numbers? – Relations of succession whose possibility is based on *time*.

If one reads what is said about the Pythagorean philosophy of numbers in the *Scholia to Aristotle* (p. 829, Berlin edn.), one can be led to surmise that the strange and mysterious use of the term *logos*,[a] verging on the absurd, at the beginning of the gospel ascribed to John, as also its earlier analogues in Philo, stems from the Pythagorean philosophy of numbers, namely from the meaning of the term *logos* in the arithmetical sense, as a relation of numbers, *ratio numerica*. For according to the Pythagoreans such a relation constitutes the innermost and indestructible essence of every being, thus its prime and original principle, *archê*;[b] consequently it would be true of every thing that 'In the beginning was the *logos*'.[c] One should consider here that Aristotle said (*On the Soul*[d] I, 1): 'The affections are *logoi* embedded in matter', and shortly after, 'For the *logos* is the form of things'.[e] This also reminds one of the seminal *logos*[f] of the Stoics, to which I shall return shortly.

According to the biography of *Pythagoras* by Iamblichus, he received his education mostly in Egypt, where he lived between his twenty-second and fifty-sixth year, and namely from the priests there. Returning in his fifty-sixth year he in fact intended to found a kind of priestly state in imitation of the Egyptian temple hierarchies, although with the modifications necessary for the Greeks; however, he did not succeed in his native Samos, but did to some extent in Croton. Now since, without doubt, Egyptian culture and religion came from India, as proven by the holiness of the cow (Herodotus II, 41[g]) together with a hundred other things, this explains Pythagoras' prescription of abstinence from an animal diet, namely the prohibition of slaughtering cows (Iamblichus, *On the Pythagorean Life*,[h] ch. 28, §150), as also the prescribed careful treatment of all animals; similarly his doctrine of metempsychosis, his white robes, his endless mystery-mongering, giving rise to symbolic aphorisms and even extending to mathematical theorems; furthermore the founding of a kind of priestly caste, with strict discipline and lots of ceremonial, the worship of the sun (ch. 35, §256), and much else.

---

[a] λόγος [word, speech, story, account, reason]   [b] ἀρχή

[c] ἐν ἀρχῇ ἦν ὁ λόγος [John 1:1; usually translated as 'In the beginning was the word', although Schopenhauer would probably translate *logos* as 'number']

[d] *De anima* [403a–b]

[e] τὰ πάθη λόγοι ἔνυλοί εἰσι, *et mox:* ὁ μὲν γὰρ λόγος εἶδος [original has ὅδε] τοῦ πράγματος [Since it is far from clear that Aristotle understands *logos* in the Pythagorean sense described here and *logos* has many different meanings, it has not been translated here]

[f] λόγος σπερματικός [Usually rendered as 'seminal reason']   [g] [*Histories*]

[h] *vit. Pyth.* [*De vita Pythagorica*]

He also took over his more important basic astronomical concepts from the Egyptians. For that reason *Oenopides*, who had been with him in Egypt, disputed his prior claim to the doctrine of the obliquity of the ecliptic. (See the end of ch. 24 of Book I of the *Eclogues* of Stobaeus with Heeren's note from Diodorus.[a]) In general, if we look through the elementary astronomical concepts[b] of all Greek philosophers compiled by Stobaeus (especially I, 25ff.), we find that they consistently brought absurdities to market, with the exception of the Pythagoreans, who usually get it exactly right. That this came about not through their own means but from Egypt cannot be doubted.

44

Pythagoras' well-known prohibition of beans is of pure Egyptian origin and merely a superstition taken over from there, since Herodotus reports (II, 37) that in Egypt the bean is considered unclean and abhorred, so that the priests cannot even bear the sight of it.

By the way, that the Pythagorean doctrine was a decided pantheism is attested, conclusively and concisely, by an aphorism of the Pythagoreans, preserved for us by Clement of Alexandria in the *Exhortation of the Peoples*,[c] whose Dorian dialect points to its genuineness. It runs as follows: 'Nor must we lose sight of the followers of the Pythagoreans, who say that God is One; and he is not, as some suspect, outside the universal order and separated, but within it, being wholly present in the whole circle, the guardian of all coming-into-being, mixing the whole, forever existing, wielder of his own powers, light-giver of all his works in heaven and the father of all things, mind and living principle of the whole circle, movement of all things.'[d] (See Clement of Alexandria, *Opera*, vol. I,[e] p. 118 in Sanctorum Patrum, *Opera Polemica*, vol. IV, Würzburg, 1778.[f]) For it is a good thing to convince ourselves at every opportunity that theism proper and Judaism are interchangeable concepts.

According to Apuleius, Pythagoras is supposed to have reached even as far as India and been instructed by the Brahmans themselves.[3] (See Apuleius, *Florida*, p. 130, Bipont edition.[g]) Consequently I believe that

---

[a] [*Ioannis Stobaei Eclogarum physicarum et ethicarum libri duo* (Johannes Stobaeus, *Eclogues*), ed. A. H. L. Heeren, Göttingen: Vandenhoek and Ruprecht, 1792–1801]

[b] *astronomische Elementarbegriffe* ['*elementar*' in the sense of 'fundamental']   [c] *Cohortatio ad gentes*

[d] Οὐκ ἀποκρυπτέον οὐδὲ τοὺς ἀμφὶ τὸν Πυθαγόραν, οἵ φασιν· Ὁ μὲν θεὸς εἷς· χ᾽οὗτος δὲ οὐχ, ὥς τινες ὑπονοοῦσιν, ἐκτὸς τᾶς διακοσμήσιος, ἀλλ᾽ ἐν αὐτᾷ, ὅλος ἐν ὅλῳ τῷ κύκλῳ, ἐπίσκοπος πάσας γενέσιος, κρᾶσις τῶν ὅλων· ἀεὶ ὤν, καὶ ἐργάτας τῶν αὐτοῦ δυνάμιων καὶ ἔργων ἁπάντων ἐν οὐρανῷ φωστήρ, καὶ πάντων πατήρ, νοῦς καὶ ψύχωσις τῷ ὅλῳ κύκλῳ, πάντων κίνασις

[e] [Clemens Alexandrinus, *Opera quae exstant*, tome 1, *Cohortatio ad gentes*]

[f] [*Opera Polemica, de veritate Religionis Christianæ, contra Gentiles et Judæos*, Wirceburgi, 1777–85]

[g] [*Lucii Apuleji Madaurensis Philosophi Platonici Opera*, vol. 2, *Florida* (1788)]

the wisdom and knowledge of Pythagoras, which indeed must be highly rated, did not consist so much in what he thought but in what he had learnt, and so was less his own than that of others. This is confirmed by something Heraclitus said about him (Diogenes Laertius, VIII, 1, 5[a]). Otherwise he would have written them down in order to save his ideas from extinction; in contrast, what he had learnt from others remained secure at the source.

§3. Socrates

The wisdom of *Socrates* is a philosophical article of faith. It is clear that Plato's Socrates is an ideal, or poetical figure that expresses Platonic thoughts; on the other hand, there is not exactly much wisdom to be found in Xenophon's Socrates. According to Lucian (*Philopseudes*,[b] 24), Socrates had a fat belly, which is not exactly a mark of genius. – Yet the same doubt in regard to high intellectual faculties applies to all those who did not write, thus also to Pythagoras. For a great mind must gradually recognize its vocation and position in regard to humanity and consequently become conscious that it does not belong to the herd but to the shepherds, I mean to the educators of humankind; this will clarify for it the duty not to limit its immediate and assured influence to the few whom chance brings close to it, but to extend it to humanity in order to be able to reach among it its exceptions, the superior and hence rare individuals. However, the organ by means of which one speaks *to humanity* is solely writing; verbally one speaks only to a number of individuals, so that what is said in that way remains a private matter in relation to humankind. For such individuals are mostly a poor soil for the noble seed, in which it either does not thrive at all or quickly degenerates in its products; thus the seed itself must be preserved. Yet this does not happen through tradition, which is adulterated at every step, but through writing alone, this sole faithful preserver of thoughts. Moreover, every profound thinker necessarily has the impulse, for his own satisfaction, to record his thoughts and bring them to the greatest possible clarity and distinctness, and consequently to embody them in words. This, however, happens completely only through writing; for the written delivery is essentially a different one from the oral one, since it alone allows for the highest precision, conciseness, and exact brevity, thus becoming the pure ectype[c] of thought. As a result of all this, it would be a strange presumption in a thinker to want to leave unused the most important invention of

---

[a] [*Lives and Opinions of Eminent Philosophers*; rather VIII, 1, 6]
[b] [*Philopseudes sive Incredulus* (*The Lover of Lies, or the Doubter*)]   [c] *Ektypos* [exact copy]

humankind. Accordingly, it is hard for me to believe in the truly great intellect of those who have not written; rather I am inclined to regard them as mainly practical heroes who effected more through their character than through their brain. The sublime authors of the *Upanishads* of the *Vedas* did write; however, the *Sanhita* of the *Vedas*, consisting of mere prayers, may have been propagated only orally in the beginning.

Quite a few similarities can be detected between *Socrates* and *Kant*. Both reject all dogmatism; both profess a complete ignorance in matters of metaphysics and place their characteristic feature in the clear consciousness of this ignorance. Both maintain that in contrast the practical, that which human beings ought and ought not to do, is completely certain and is so by itself, without further theoretical justification. Both shared the fate that, nevertheless, their immediate successors and declared disciples deviated from them in respect to those foundations and, in their work on metaphysics, established completely dogmatic systems; furthermore, that these systems turned out utterly different, but yet all agreed in maintaining that they had started from the doctrine of Socrates, or Kant, respectively. – Since I am myself a Kantian I wish to say a word here to characterize my relation to him. Kant teaches that we cannot know anything beyond experience and its possibility; I concede this but maintain that experience itself, in its totality, is capable of an explanation, and I have attempted to provide this by deciphering experience like a written text, but not, like all previous philosophers, by undertaking to go beyond it by means of its mere forms, which Kant indeed had demonstrated to be inadmissible. –

The advantage of the *Socratic method*, as we come to know it from Plato, consists in having the grounds for the propositions that we intend to demonstrate be admitted by the collocutor[a] or opponent one at a time, before he has surveyed their consequences. For with a didactic, continuously delivered speech, he would have the opportunity to immediately recognize consequences and grounds as such and would attack the latter if he did not like the former. – Meanwhile, among the things that Plato wants us to believe is this, that by means of this method the sophists and other fools, with utter patience, let Socrates show them that this is what they are. That is inconceivable; on the contrary, at about the last quarter of the way or, at any rate, as soon as they realized where this was supposed to lead, they would have spoiled Socrates' artificially constructed game for him and torn his net, by digressing or denying what had been said before or intentionally misunderstanding, and by whatever else obstinate dishonesty instinctively

46

47

---

[a] *Kollokutor* [dialogue partner]

applies as its tricks and chicaneries. Or they would have become so rude and insulting that he would have found it advisable to save his skin in good time. For how could the sophists not also have known the means by which anyone can make himself equal to anyone else and instantly level the greatest intellectual inequality, namely insult. Base nature, therefore, feels, even instinctively, an invitation to use the latter as soon as it starts to sense intellectual superiority. –

§4. Plato

Already in *Plato* we find the origin of a certain false dianoiology,[a] established with a secretly metaphysical intention, namely for the sake of a rational psychology and attached doctrine of immortality. This has subsequently proved to be a deceptive doctrine clinging to life with the greatest tenacity, prolonging its existence throughout the whole of ancient, medieval,[b] and modern philosophy, until *Kant*, the destroyer of everything, finally did it in. The doctrine here alluded to is rationalism in the theory of knowledge, with a metaphysical final purpose. It can be briefly summarized as follows. That which cognizes within us is an immaterial substance, fundamentally distinct from the body and called soul; the body, in contrast, is an obstacle to cognition. Therefore, all cognition mediated through the senses is deceptive; in contrast, the sole true, correct and certain cognition is that which is free of and removed from all sensibility (thus all intuition), consequently *pure thought*, i.e. operating with abstract concepts alone. For this is done by the *soul* entirely through its own resources; consequently this operation succeeds best after the soul has separated from the body, in other words when we are dead. – In this way dianoiology plays into the hands of rational psychology for the sake of the latter's doctrine of immortality. One finds this doctrine, as I have summed it up here, explicitly and distinctly in the *Phaedo*, ch. 10. It is conceived somewhat differently in the *Timaeus*, based on which Sextus Empiricus presents it precisely and clearly in the following words: 'An ancient opinion is circulated by the natural philosophers, that the homogeneous can be known by the homogeneous.' Shortly after: 'But Plato, in the *Timaeus*, in order to prove that the soul is without body, makes use of the same method of proof. For he says, if the sense of sight, because it is susceptible to light, is plainly light-like, and the sense of hearing, because it can distinguish the concussions of the air and hear the sound, is immediately known as air-like, and also smell, discerning all vapours, is

48

---

[a] *Dianoiologie* [doctrine of thought or intellect]   [b] *mittlere*

vapour-like, and taste, tasting juices, is liquid-like, then it is necessary that also the soul, receiving incorporeal ideas, for example those of numbers and of the limits of bodies (that is, pure mathematics),[a] be incorporeal.'[b] (*Against the Mathematicians*[c] VII, 116 and 119.)

Even Aristotle admits this argumentation, at least hypothetically, since he says in the first book of *On the Soul*[d] (ch. 1) that the separate existence of the soul would depend on whether any expression accrued to it in which the body had no part. Such an expression seemed to be thinking above all else. However, should even *this* not be possible without intuition and imagination, then it could not happen without the body ('But if thinking is a kind of imagination, or is not possible without imagination, then it cannot happen without a body.'[e]). However, Aristotle does not admit the condition[f] made above, and thus does not admit the premise of the argumentation, insofar as he teaches what has been formulated later in the proposition 'Nothing is in the intellect that has not been previously in the senses';[g] on this one should see *On the Soul* III, 8. Thus he already understood that everything purely and abstractly conceived nevertheless must borrow its entire material and content from what is intuited. This alarmed the scholastic philosophers as well. Therefore, an effort was made already during the Middle Ages to prove that *pure rational cogni-tions*[h] existed, i.e. thoughts that did not refer to images, or a kind of thinking that derived all material from itself. One finds the efforts and controversy over this point collected in Pomponatius, *On the Immortality*

49

---

[a] [Schopenhauer's addition]

[b] Παλαιά τις παρὰ τοῖς φυσικοῖς κυλίεται δόξα περὶ τοῦ τὰ ὅμοια τῶν ὁμοίων εἶναι γνωριστικά. *Mox.* Πλάτων δέ, ἐν τῷ Τιμαίῳ, πρὸς παράστασιν τοῦ ἀσώματον εἶναι τὴν ψυχήν, τῷ αὐτῷ γένει τῆς ἀποδείξεως κέχρηται. Εἰ γὰρ ἡ μὲν ὅρασις, φησί, φωτὸς ἀντιλαμβανομένη, εὐθύς ἐστι φωτοειδής, ἡ δὲ ἀκοὴ ἀέρα πεπληγμένον κρίνουσα, ὅπερ ἐστὶ τὴν φωνήν, εὐθὺς ἀεροειδὴς θεωρεῖται, ἡ δὲ ὄσφρησις ἀτμοὺς γνωρίζουσα πάντως ἐστὶ ἀτμοειδής, καὶ ἡ γεῦσις, χυλούς, χυλοειδής· κατ᾽ ἀνάγκην καὶ ἡ ψυχὴ τὰς ἀσωμάτους ἰδέας λαμβάνουσα, καθάπερ τὰς ἐν τοῖς ἀριθμοῖς καὶ τὰς ἐν τοῖς πέρασι τῶν σωμάτων γίνεται τις ἀσώματος. [quotation slightly changed] (*vetus quaedam, a physicis usque probata, versatur opinio, quod similia similibus cognoscantur. – – Mox. Plato, in Timaeo, ad probandum, animam esse incorpoream, usus est eodem genere demonstrationis: 'nam si visio', inquit, 'apprehendens lucem statim est luminosa, auditus autem aërem percussum judicans, nempe vocem, protinus cernitur ad aëris accedens speciem, odoratus autem cognoscens vapores, est omnino vaporis aliquam habens formam, et gustus, qui humores, humoris habens speciem; necessario et anima, ideas suscipiens incorporeas, ut quae sunt in numeris et in finibus corporum, est incorporea.'*)

[c] [*Adversus mathematicos*; *Against the Mathematicians* VII and VIII equals *Against the Logicians* I and II]

[d] *De anima*

[e] εἰ δ᾽ ἐστὶ καὶ τὸ νοεῖν φαντασία τις, ἢ μὴ ἄνευ φαντασίας, οὐκ ἐνδέχοιτ᾽ ἂν οὐδὲ τοῦτο ἄνευ σώματος εἶναι

[f] [the condition that expressions of the soul exist in which the body has no part]

[g] *nihil est in intellectu, quod non prius fuerit in sensibus* [See Thomas Aquinas, *Disputed Questions on Truth* (*Quaestiones disputatae de veritate*), quaest. II, article III, 19]

[h] *reine Vernunfterkenntnisse*

of the Soul,[a] since he takes his main argument from there.[b] – Universals[c] and cognitions a priori, conceived as eternal truths,[d] were meant to satisfy the aforesaid requirement. I have already discussed the execution that the matter then received from *Descartes* and his school in the extensive note to §6 of my prize essay *On the Basis of Morals*, where I also quoted the Cartesian *de la Forge* in his own words, which are worth reading. For, as a rule, one finds especially the false doctrines of every philosopher expressed most clearly by his disciples, since they do not attempt, as does the master himself, to keep in the dark those aspects of his system which might betray its weakness, as they do not suspect it yet. *Spinoza*, however, already set against the whole Cartesian dualism his own doctrine, that 'Thinking substance and extended substance are one and the same substance, comprehended now through one attribute, now through the other',[e] thereby showing his great superiority. In contrast, *Leibniz*, like a good boy, remained on the path of Descartes and orthodoxy. This then, in turn, brought about the great *Locke's* endeavour, so exceedingly beneficial for philosophy, who finally insisted on examining the *origin of concepts* and made the proposition 'no innate ideas',[f] after expounding it in detail, the foundation of his philosophy. The French, for whom his philosophy was elaborated by *Condillac*, went too far, although for the same reason, by putting forward and insisting on the proposition 'to think is to perceive'.[g] Taken absolutely, this proposition is false; but the truth lies in the fact that all thinking in part presupposes sensation, which, as an ingredient of intuition, provides its material, and in part is itself conditioned by bodily organs, just like sensation: the latter by the sensory nerves, the former by the brain; and both are an activity of the nerves. Now the French school did not hold on to that proposition for its own sake either, but for a metaphysical, namely materialist, purpose, just as the Platonic–Cartesian– Leibnizian opponents clung to the false proposition that the only correct cognition of things consists of pure thinking also for a metaphysical purpose, in order to prove on its basis the immateriality of the soul. – *Kant* alone leads to the truth away from these two erroneous paths and from a controversy in which both parties really do not act honestly, since

---

[a] *de immortalitate animi* [Petrus Pomponatius (Pietro Pomponazzi), *Tractatus de immortalite animae*, 1516]
[b] [From the medieval debate]   [c] *Universalia*   [d] *aeternae veritates*
[e] *Substantia cogitans et substantia extensa una eademque est substantia, quae jam sub hoc, jam sub illo attributo conprehenditur* [*Ethics* II, prop. 7, schol.]
[f] [English in the original, followed by Schopenhauer's German translation '*keine angeborene Begriffe*']
[g] *penser est sentir*

they pretend dianoiology but aim at metaphysics and thus falsify dianoiology. *Kant* says: indeed there is pure rational cognition, that is, cognitions a priori that precede all experience, and consequently thinking that owes its material not to any cognition mediated through the senses. However, this cognition a priori, although not borrowed *from* experience, has value and validity only *for the sake of* experience; for it is nothing else but the awareness of our own *cognitive apparatus* and its mechanism (brain function), or, as Kant puts it, the *form* of cognitive consciousness itself, which obtains its *material* only through the additional empirical cognition, by means of sensation, and is empty and useless without it. For that reason his philosophy is called the *critique of pure reason*. Through this, all metaphysical psychology collapses and together with it all of Plato's pure activity of the soul. For we see that cognition without intuition, which the body brings about, has no material and that, therefore, the cognitive[a] as such, without the presupposition of the body, is nothing but an empty form; not to mention that all thinking is a physiological function of the brain, just as digestion is of the stomach.

Now if *Plato's* instruction to abstract cognition and keep it pure of the community with the body, the senses and intuition turns out to be inappropriate, wrong, and indeed impossible, then we can nevertheless regard my doctrine as its corrected analogue, that only that cognition which is kept pure of all community with the *will*, but which is intuitive all the same, reaches the highest objectivity and thus perfection – in regard to which I refer to the Third Book of my chief work. 51

§5. Aristotle

Aristotle's main characteristic could be described as the greatest sagacity, combined with circumspection, talent for observation, versatility, and lack of profundity. His view of the world is shallow even if ingeniously elaborated. Depth of thought finds its material within ourselves; sagacity has to receive it from outside in order to have data. However, in those times the empirical data were in part scanty and in part even false. Therefore, the study of Aristotle is nowadays not very rewarding, while that of Plato remains so to the highest degree. The lack of profundity reprimanded in Aristotle of course becomes most visible in metaphysics, where mere sagacity does not suffice, as it does elsewhere; so that in this he satisfies least. His *Metaphysics* is for the most part talking back and forth about the

[a] *das Erkennende*

philosophemes of his predecessors, whom he criticizes and refutes from his point of view, mostly in reference to isolated utterances by them, without really penetrating their meaning, rather like someone who breaks the windows from the outside.[a] He advances only a few, or none, of his own dogmas, at least not in systematic fashion. That we owe a large part of our knowledge of the older philosophemes to his polemics is an accidental achievement. He is hostile towards Plato mostly where the latter is completely right. Plato's 'Ideas' continue coming back up into his mouth, like something that he cannot digest; he is determined not to admit their validity. – Sagacity suffices in the empirical sciences; consequently Aristotle has a predominantly empirical direction. But as empirical science[b] since that time has made so much progress that it compares to its past state as the manly[c] age compares to infancy, today's empirical sciences cannot be much advanced directly through the study of his philosophy, but indirectly they can through the method and the properly scientific attitude that characterizes him and was brought into the world by him. However, in zoology he is of direct use even to this day, at least in some individual matters. Now in general his empirical direction creates the tendency in him always to go for breadth, which means that he digresses so easily and often from his train of thought that he is almost unable to follow the whole length of it to the end; however, that is just what *profound* thinking consists in. Instead he raises the problems everywhere but only touches on them and, without solving them or even discussing them thoroughly, moves on to something else. For this reason his reader so often thinks 'now it is coming', but nothing comes. And for this reason, when he has raised a problem and pursued it for a short distance, the truth seems to be at the tip of his tongue; but suddenly he is on to something else and leaves us mired in doubt. For he cannot stick to anything but jumps from what he plans to tackle to something else that occurs to him just now, in the way that a child drops a toy in order to seize another one that it has just noticed. This is the weak side of his intellect; it is the liveliness of superficiality. It explains why Aristotle's exposition generally lacks systematic order and why we miss methodical progress in it, even separation of the dissimilar and juxtaposition of the similar, although he was a highly systematic mind, for he originated the separation and classification of the sciences. He discusses things as they occur to him, without having first thought them through and without having drawn up a clear plan for himself. He thinks with the pen in his hand, which is a great relief for the author but a great burden for the reader.

[a] [Presumably without entering the building]   [b] *Empirie*   [c] *männliche*

That explains the haphazardness and insufficiency of his presentation; hence he comes to talk a hundred times about the same thing, because something foreign had intervened; hence he cannot stick to the same subject but jumps from one to another. Hence, as described above, he leads the reader, who anxiously awaits the solution of the problems raised, by the nose; hence he begins his inquiry into a matter, after having spent several pages on it, suddenly anew with 'Let us, therefore, take another starting point for our reflection',[a] and that six times in one text. Hence the saying 'What great matter of value might be gained from the pompous announcements of such a braggard?'[b] fits so many introductions[c] of his books and chapters; hence, in one word, he is so often confused and insufficient. Of course, by way of exception he did behave differently, as for example the three books of the *Rhetoric* are a model of scientific method throughout and even show an architectonic symmetry that may have been the model for the Kantian one.

53

The radical antithesis of Aristotle, in the way of thinking as well as in the presentation, is *Plato*. The latter holds on to his main thought as if with an iron hand, follows its thread, even if it becomes ever so thin, in all its ramifications, through the labyrinths of the longest dialogues, and finds it again after all episodes. One can tell, before he started writing, he had thoroughly and entirely thought through his subject and had designed an artful order for its presentation. Thus each dialogue is a carefully planned work of art all of whose parts stand in a well-thought-out connection, often intentionally hidden for a while, and whose frequent episodes, by themselves and often unexpectedly, lead back to the main thought, which is then elucidated by them. Plato always knew, in the full sense of the word, what he wanted and intended, although for the most part he did not bring the problems to a definite solution but was content with their thorough discussion. Therefore, we need not be so much surprised if, as some reports indicate, especially in Aelian (*Historical Miscellany*[d] III, 19; IV, 9; etc.), a major personal disharmony manifested itself between Plato and Aristotle, and Plato may even from time to time have spoken somewhat contemptuously of Aristotle, whose wanderings, vagaries,[e] and digressions relate to his polymathy, but are wholly antipathetic to Plato. Schiller's poem 'Breadth and Depth'[f] can also be applied to the opposition between Aristotle and Plato.

---

[a] λάβωμεν οὖν ἄλλην ἀρχὴν τῆς σκέψεως
[b] *quid feret hic tanto dignum promissor hiatu* [Horace, *Ars poetica* (*The Art of Poetry*), 138]
[c] *Exordien* [in rhetoric, the introduction to a speech]
[d] *var. hist.* [Claudius Aelianus, *Varia historia*]   [e] *Irrlichterliren*   [f] *'Breite und Tiefe'*

54   Despite this empirical intellectual tendency Aristotle nonetheless was
not a consistent and methodical empiricist; consequently he had to be
overthrown and driven out by the true father of empiricism, *Bacon of
Verulam*. Whoever really wants to understand in which sense and for
what reason the latter is the opponent and conqueror of Aristotle and his
method, should read Aristotle's books *On Generation and Corruption*.[a]
There he really will find reasoning[b] a priori about nature, which wants to
understand and explain its processes from mere concepts; a particularly
glaring example is provided in Book II, ch. 4, where a chemistry is constructed a priori. Against that Bacon came up with the advice not to make
the abstract but the intuitive, experience, the source of cognition of nature.
The brilliant success of this lies in the present exalted state of the natural
sciences, from which we look down with a pitiful smile on to those
Aristotelian vexations. In regard to this it is noteworthy that the books by
Aristotle just mentioned clearly reveal even the origin of scholasticism and
that the hair-splitting, quibbling method of the latter can already be found
in the former. – For the same purpose the books *On the Heavens*[c] are very
useful and, therefore, worth reading. Immediately the first chapters are a
true specimen for the method of wanting to know and determine the
essence of nature from mere concepts, and the failure is obvious here. In
ch. 8 it is proved to us from mere concepts and truisms[d] that there are not
several worlds, and in ch. 12 there is a similar speculation about the path of
the stars.[e] It is a consistent subtilizing[f] from false concepts, a quite peculiar
dialectic of nature, undertaking to decide a priori, from certain universal
principles meant to express what is rational and proper, how nature must
exist and function. In seeing such a great, even stupendous mind, as
Aristotle is after all, so deeply ensnared in errors of this kind, which
maintained their validity until just a few hundred years ago, it becomes
clear to us above all how much humanity owes to Copernicus, Kepler,
Galileo, Bacon, Robert Hooke, and Newton. In chs. 7 and 8 of the second
book Aristotle presents to us his wholly absurd arrangement of the heavens:

55   the stars are fixed to the revolving hollow sphere, sun and planets to similar
closer ones; the friction from revolution causes light and heat; and the earth
positively stands still. All that might pass if nothing better had existed
before; but when he himself, in ch. 13, presents the entirely correct views
of the Pythagoreans on the shape, position, and motion of the earth, only to
dismiss them, then this must provoke our indignation. The latter will

---

[a] *de generatione et corruptione*   [b] *Räsonniren*   [c] *de caelo*   [d] *locis communibus*   [e] [Book I]
[f] *Vernünfteln*

increase when we see from his frequent polemics against Empedocles, Heraclitus, and Democritus that they all had much more accurate insights into nature, and also paid better attention to experience than the shallow twaddler whom we have here before us. *Empedocles* indeed had already taught about a tangential force originating in rotation and counteracting gravity (II, 1 and 13,[a] together with *Scholia*, p. 491). Far from being able to estimate the proper value of such things, Aristotle does not even once accept the rightful views of the older thinkers about the true significance of the above and the below, but even here joins the opinion of the common herd, which follows superficial appearance (IV, 2). But now we must consider that these opinions of his found recognition and dissemination, pushed aside everything earlier and better, and later became the foundation of Hipparchus and then Ptolemaic cosmology, a burden which humanity had to carry until the beginning of the sixteenth century. Certainly this system was to the great advantage of the Judaeo–Christian religious doctrines, which are incompatible with the Copernican system of the world; for how should there be a god in heaven when there is no heaven?[4] Sincere *theism* necessarily presupposes that one divide the world into *heaven* and *earth*: human beings stroll about on *the latter*, the God who governs them sits in *the former*. Now if astronomy takes away the heaven, then it takes away the God *together with* it, for it has extended the world such that no room is left for the God. However, a personal being, as every god inevitably is, that has no *place* but is everywhere and nowhere, can merely be spoken of, not imagined, and thus not believed in. Accordingly, to the degree that physical astronomy is popularized, theism must disappear, however firmly it is impressed upon the people through incessant and most solemn prompting,[5] as the Catholic Church correctly recognized at once and consequently persecuted the Copernican system. Therefore, it is foolish to be so very amazed about, and to raise such outcry over, the oppression of Galileo; for 'everything in nature strives to preserve itself'.[b] Who knows whether some quiet insight, or at least presentiment, of this congeniality of Aristotle to the doctrine of the Church, and the danger averted by him, did not add to his excessive adoration in the Middle Ages?[*,6] Who knows whether some, provoked by his reports about the older astronomical systems, had not

56

---

* The older authors who ascribe real *theism* to Aristotle take their evidence from the books *De mundo* [*On the Universe*], which are decidedly not by him, which of course is now generally accepted.

[a] [*On the Heavens*]
[b] *omnis natura vult esse conservatrix sui* [Cicero, *On the Ends of Goods and Evils* (*De finibus bonorum et malorum*) IV, 7, 16]

quietly realized long before Copernicus the truths that the latter finally dared to proclaim, after many years of hesitating and on the brink of parting from the world?

§6. Stoics

A very beautiful and profound concept of the *Stoics* is that of *logos spermatikos*,[a] although we would wish for more extensive accounts of it than have come down to us (Diogenes Laertius, VII, 136.[b] – Plutarch, *The Doctrines of the Philosophers* I, 7.[c] – Stobaeus, *Eclogues* I, p. 372[d]). But this much is clear, that by means of it we conceive that which asserts and preserves the identical form in successive individuals of a species[e] by passing from one to the other; hence, as it were, the concept of the species embodied in the seed. Therefore, *logos spermatikos* is what is indestructible in the individual, what makes it one with the species, representing and preserving the latter. It is what prevents death, which destroys the individual, from attacking the species, by virtue of which the individual exists again and again, in defiance of death. Hence one could translate *logos spermatikos* as the magic formula which at any time calls this form into appearance.[7] – Closely related to it is the scholastic concept of substantial form,[f] by means of which the inner principle of the complex of all the qualities of every natural being is conceived. Its opposite is prime matter,[g] pure matter,[h] without any form and quality. The soul of human beings is precisely their substantial form. What distinguishes both concepts is that seminal reason belongs merely to animate and propagating beings, whereas substantial form also belongs to inorganic ones; similarly, the latter is primarily concerned with the individual, the former with the species; meanwhile, both are obviously related to the Platonic Idea. Explanations of substantial form are found in Scotus Erigena, *On the Division of Nature*, Book III, p. 139 of the Oxford edition;[i] in Giordano Bruno, *Cause, Principle, and Unity*,[j] Dialogue 3, pp. 252ff., and at length in Suarez's *Metaphysical Disputations*[k] (Disputatio 15, sect. 1), that true compendium of the whole of scholastic wisdom. That is where one should seek its acquaintance, but not in the broad twaddle of mindless German philosophy professors, this quintessence of insipidness and tedium. –

57

---

[a] λόγος σπερματικός [seminal reason]   [b] [*Lives and Opinions of Eminent Philosophers*]
[c] *De placitis philosophorum* [Pseudo-Plutarch]   [d] *ecl.* [*Eclogae physicae et ethicae* I, 17, 1]
[e] *Gattung*   [f] *forma substantialis*   [g] *materia prima*   [h] *Materie*
[i] *de divisione naturae* [*Joannis Scoti Erigenæ De divisione naturae libri quinque* (*Periphyseon: On the Division of Nature*), ed. Thomas Gale, Oxford: Oxon, 1681; III, 28–9]
[j] *della causa* [*De la causa, principio ed uno*, 1584]
[k] *disputationibus metaphysicis* [*Disputationes metaphysicae*]

A principal source of our knowledge of Stoic ethics is the very detailed exposition preserved for us by Stobaeus (*Eclogues* II, 7),[a] in which we possess mostly literal excerpts from Zeno and Chrysippus, as we like to believe; if such is the case then it is not suited to give us a high opinion of the minds of these philosophers. On the contrary, it is a pedantic, schoolmasterly, exceedingly broad, incredibly dreary, flat, and insipid exposition of Stoic ethics, without force or life, and without valuable, pertinent, subtle ideas. Everything in there is derived from mere concepts; nothing is drawn from reality and experience. Accordingly humanity is divided into *spoudaioi* and *phauloi*,[b] the virtuous and the wicked, everything good being attributed to the former, everything bad to the latter, whereby everything proves black and white, like a Prussian sentry box. Hence these shallow school exercises[c] do not stand comparison with the highly energetic, ingenious, and well-thought-out writings of Seneca.[8] –

The *Discourses* by *Arrian* about the *philosophy of Epictetus*,[d] written some four hundred years after the origin of the Stoa, do not give us thorough information either about the true spirit and genuine prinicples of *Stoic morals*; on the contrary, this book is unsatisfactory in form and content. First of all, in regard to form, we miss any trace of method, of systematic treatment, even of orderly progression in it. Chapters that are arranged side by side without order or connection repeat incessantly that we ought to reckon as nothing whatever is not an expression of our own will, accordingly that we should view with complete indifference everything that usually moves people. That is Stoic *ataraxia*.[e] Namely, what is not under our control[f] is not of concern to us[g] either. This huge paradox, however, is not derived from any principles; but the most peculiar disposition in the world is imposed on us without providing a reason for it. Instead, we find endless declamations related through relentlessly recurring expressions and turns of phrase. For the propositions following from those curious maxims are presented most fully and vividly; and hence it is variously described how the Stoic does not attach importance to anything in the world. Meanwhile, anybody who thinks otherwise is reviled as a slave and fool. In vain do we hope for a clear and cogent reason to be stated for adopting such a strange mentality; for such a reason would be so much more effective than all the declamations and invectives of the entire voluminous book. Yet with its hyperbolic descriptions of Stoic equanimity, its tirelessly repeated praises of the patron saints Cleanthes, Chrysippus, Zeno, Crates, Diogenes, and

---

[a] *Eclogae ethicae*   [b] σπουδαῖοι *und* φαῦλοι   [c] *Schulexercitien*
[d] *Dissertationen Arrian's zur Epiktetischen Philosophie* [*Epictetus: The Discourses as reported by Arrian*]
[e] ἀταραξία [peace of mind]   [f] ἐφ' ἡμῖν   [g] πρός ἡμᾶς

Socrates, and its tirades against all who think differently, this book is a veritable capuchin sermon.[a] Of course, then the aimlessness and desultoriness of the whole exposition is in keeping with such a sermon. What the title of a chapter provides is only the subject matter of the beginning; at the first opportunity a digression occurs and, according to the connection of ideas,[b] we jump from one subject to another. So much for the *form*.

Now as to the *content*, it is not at all genuinely and purely Stoic, even apart from the fact that the foundation is completely lacking, but has a strong foreign admixture that smacks of a Christian–Jewish origin. The most undeniable proof of this is the theism that is found on every page and also supports the morals. The Cynics and Stoics act on the command of God, whose will is their guidance, they acquiesce in Him, hope for Him, and so forth. That is quite alien to the genuine, original Stoa; God and the world are one for them, and they do not know of such a thinking, willing, commanding, provident human being of a God at all. However, not only in Arrian, but in most pagan philosophical authors of the first Christian century, we see the Jewish theism, which soon after, as Christianity, was to become popular creed, already shining through, just as nowadays in the writings of scholars the pantheism native to India shines through, which is also destined to turn into popular faith only later. 'Out of the east comes the light.'[c]

For the reason stated the morals here expounded is not itself purely Stoic; some of its precepts cannot even be reconciled with each other; and so, of course, no common fundamental principles could be laid down for it. Equally, Cynicism is completely falsified through the doctrine that the Cynic should be such mainly for the sake of others, namely, in order to influence them through his own example, as a messenger of God, and to guide them by interfering in their affairs. Hence it is said: 'In a city of no one but sages, no Cynic would be needed'; likewise, that he should be healthy, strong and cleanly in order not to disgust people. How far removed this is from the self-sufficiency of the old genuine Cynics! Certainly Diogenes and Crates were the friends and advisers of many families; but that was secondary and accidental and by no means the purpose of Cynicism.

Thus *Arrian* completely missed the real fundamental ideas of Cynicism, as well as those of Stoic ethics;[d] he does not even seem to have felt the need for it. He preaches self-renunciation just because it pleases him, and possibly it only pleases him because it is difficult and contrary to human

---

[a] *Kapuzinerpredigt* [drastic but folksy exhortation]   [b] *nexus idearum*   [c] *Ex oriente lux*
[d] *Ethik* [Schopenhauer does not seem to distinguish between '*Moral*' and '*Ethik*' here]

nature, whereas preaching is easy. He has not searched for the grounds of self-renunciation; thus we think we hear now a Christian ascetic and now again a Stoic. For the maxims of both often coincide; however, the princi- 60 ples which they rely on are completely different. In this respect, I refer to my chief work, vol. 1, §16, and vol. 2, ch. 16 – where, probably for the first time, the true spirit of Cynicism and the Stoa is thoroughly discussed.

Arrian's inconsistency becomes apparent even in a ridiculous manner in the following characteristic: that in the description of the perfect Stoic, repeated innumerable times, he always also says: 'he reproaches no one, complains neither about the gods nor human beings, rebukes no one', – yet his entire book is written in a predominantly scolding tone, often descending into abuse.

In spite of all this we can find genuinely Stoic ideas here and there in the book, which Arrian, or Epictetus, drew from the ancient Stoics; and similarly, Cynicism is described fittingly and vividly in some of its features. Also in places it contains much common sense, as well as striking descriptions of human beings and their actions that are drawn from life. The style is facile and fluent but very broad.

I do not believe that Epictetus' *Enchiridion* was written by Arrian as well, as F. A. Wolf assured us in his lectures. It possesses much more spirit in fewer words than the *Discourses*, throughout shows common sense, no empty declamations, no ostentation, is concise and to the point and written in the tone of a friend giving well-meaning advice; in contrast the *Discourses* speak mostly in a scolding and reproachful tone. The content of both books is overall the same; only that the *Enchiridion* shares very little of the theism of the *Discourses*. – Maybe the *Enchiridion* was Epictetus' own compendium that he dictated to his listeners, while the *Discourses* was the notebook jotted down by Arrian as a commentary to the former's free lectures.

§7. Neoplatonists

Reading the *Neoplatonists* requires much patience since they all lack form and presentation. Yet in this respect, *Porphyry* is by far better than the 61 others; he is the only one who writes clearly and coherently, so that one reads him without aversion.

On the other hand, the worst is *Iamblichus* in his book *On the Mysteries of the Egyptians*;[a] he is full of crass superstition and crude demonology and also

---

[a] *de mysteriis Aegyptiorum*

obstinate. To be sure, he has another, as it were, esoteric view of magic and theurgy, but his explanations of them are merely shallow and insignificant. On the whole, he is a bad and unpleasant writer: narrow, eccentric, grossly superstitious, muddled, and vague. One sees clearly that what he teaches has not at all sprung from his own reflection. On the contrary, it consists in alien dogmas, often only half understood but defended all the more doggedly; and so he is full of contradictions. However, people now want to dispute that the book mentioned is by him, and I am inclined to agree with this opinion when reading the long excerpts from his lost works that Stobaeus has preserved for us and which are by far better than that book, *On the Mysteries*, and contain quite a few good ideas of the Neoplatonist school.[9]

Proclus, on the other hand, is a shallow, diffuse, and insipid chatterer. His commentary on Plato's *Alcibiades*, one of the worst Platonic dialogues, which also might not be genuine, is the most diffuse and verbose drivel in the world. It endlessly goes on about Plato's every word, even the most insignificant, seeking a deeper meaning in it. What Plato expressed mythically and allegorically is interpreted literally and strictly dogmatically, and everything is distorted into something superstitious and theosophical. Nevertheless, it cannot be denied that some very good ideas can be found in the first half of the commentary, which, however, may belong to the school rather than to Proclus. It is a most important proposition that concludes the first section of the first part:[a] 'The desires of souls (before their birth) have the greatest influence on the chosen course of life, and we do not seem to have been formed from without, but bring forth from within ourselves the choices according to which we lead our lives.'[b] This, of course, has its root in Plato, but also comes close to Kant's doctrine of intelligible character. It is far superior to the flat and narrow-minded doctrines of the freedom of individual will that in each case can act this way and also differently,[c] with which our philosophy professors, their eyes always fixed on the catechism, have been encumbered to this day. Augustine and Luther, for their part, availed themselves of predestination.[d] That was good enough for those pious times, when one was still ready to go in God's name to the

62

---

[a] *fasciculum primum [fasciculus prior] partis primae*

[b] αἱ τῶν ψυχῶν ἐφέσεις τὰ μέγιστα συντελοῦσι πρὸς τοὺς βίους, καὶ οὐ πλαττομένοις ἔξωθεν ἐοίκαμεν, ἀλλ' ἐφ' ἑαυτῶν προβάλλομεν τὰς αἱρέσεις, καθ' ἃς διαζῶμεν (*animorum appetitus [ante hanc vitam concepti] plurimam vim habent in vitas eligendas, nec extrinsecus fictis similes sumus, sed nostra sponte facimus electiones, secundum qua deinde vitas transigimus) [Proclus Diadochus, Initiae Philosophiae ac Theologiae ex Platonicis Fontibus Ducta sive Procli Diadochi et Olympiodori in Platonicis Alcibiadem Commentarii (Commentary on Alcibiades*), ed. Friedrich Creuzer, Frankfurt: Moen, 1820; Part I, 1, 4, p. 144]

[c] *jedesmal so und auch anders kann*　　[d] *Gnadenwahl*

devil, if it so pleased God. However, in our times we can only find refuge in the aseity[a] of the will and must recognize that, as Proclus has it, 'we do not seem to have been formed from without'.[b]

Finally *Plotinus*, the most important of them all, is extremely inconsistent, and the individual *Enneads* are of very different value and content: the fourth one is excellent. However, in his case too presentation and style are for the most part poor; his thoughts are not organized, not reflected upon in advance, but written down at random, the way they occurred. Porphyry writes in his biography about the slovenly, careless manner in which he set to work. Hence his diffuse, boring verbosity and confusion often make us lose all patience, so that we wonder how this jumble could have come down to posterity. For the most part, he has the style of a pulpit orator, and in the way the latter talks the gospel to death, so the former does with the Platonic doctrines, whereby he drags down to an explicitly prosaic earnestness what Plato has said mythically, and indeed half metaphorically, chewing for hours on the same idea without adding anything from his own resources. At the same time, he proceeds in a manner of revelation, not demonstration, speaking throughout from the tripod[c] and relating things as he imagines them without engaging in justification at all. Nevertheless, great, important, and profound truths are to be found in him, which he himself has certainly understood. For he is not at all without insight, so that he deserves by all means to be read and richly rewards the patience required for doing so.

I find the explanation for these contradictory qualities of Plotinus in the fact that he, and the Neoplatonists in general, are not genuine philosophers or independent thinkers; on the contrary, what they present is an alien doctrine that was handed down to them, but which they have for the most part digested and assimilated well. For it is Indo–Egyptian wisdom that they intended to incorporate into Greek philosophy; and as an appropriate connecting link, or means of transmission, or solvent,[d] they use Platonic philosophy, especially the part that tends to the mystical. The entire doctrine of the One in Plotinus, as we find it particularly in the fourth *Ennead*, primarily and undeniably bears witness to the Indian origin of the Neoplatonic dogmas, mediated through Egypt. The very first chapter of its first book, 'On the Essence of the Soul',[e] provides, in great brevity, the fundamental doctrine of his entire philosophy, of a soul[f] that is originally one and is only split into many by means of the corporeal world.

63

---

[a] *Aseität* [absolute independence of other things]   [b] οὐ πλαττομένοις ἔξωθεν ἐοίκαμεν
[c] *ex tripode* [an allusion to the Pythia, the seer at the oracle at Delphi]   [d] *menstruum*
[e] περὶ οὐσίας ψυχῆς   [f] ψυχή

Especially interesting is the eighth book of this *Ennead*, which explains how that soul has fallen into this state of plurality through sinful striving. Consequently, it bears a twofold guilt, first, of having descended into this world, and second, of its sinful deeds in the same; for the first it atones through its temporal existence in general; for the second, lesser, guilt through the transmigration of the soul (ch. 5). Obviously this is the same idea as that of Christian original sin and particular sin. But worthy of reading above all is the ninth book, 'Whether all Souls are One',[a] where in ch. 3 the miracles of animal magnetism are explained from the unity of that world-soul, particularly the phenomenon, which occurs even nowadays, where the sleepwalker hears a softly spoken word from the greatest distance – which of course must be conveyed through a chain of persons who are in contact with her. – And probably for the first time in Western philosophy, even *idealism* makes an appearance in Plotinus, which at that time had long been current in the East, since it is taught (*Ennead* III, 7, 10) that the soul has made the world by stepping from eternity into time; with the explanation: 'for there is no other place for the universe than soul',[b] indeed, the ideality of time is expressed in the words: 'Time, however, is not to be conceived as outside of soul, just as eternity is not outside of being.'[c] That *ekei* (the life to come)[d] is the opposite of *enthade* (this life)[e] is a concept very familiar to him, which he explains more fully by 'the intelligible world' and 'the sensible world'[f], and also through 'the above and the below'.[g] And also, in chs. 11 and 12, the ideality of time is given very good elucidations. Connected to that is the fine explanation that in our temporal state we are not what we ought to be and wish to be, so that we always expect something better from the future and anticipate compensatiion for our shortcoming, out of which then the future and its condition, time, arise (chs. 2 and 3). Further proof of the Indian origin is given to us in the doctrine of metempsychosis expounded by *Iamblichus* (*On the Mysteries of the Egyptians*, sect. 4, chs. 4 and 5), as well as, in the same work (sect. 5, ch. 6), the doctrine of the ultimate liberation and salvation from the bonds of birth and death, 'the purification and perfection of the soul, and the liberation from becoming',[h] and (ch. 12)

64

---

[a] εἰ πᾶσαι αἱ ψυχαὶ μία

[b] οὐ γάρ τις αὐτοῦ τοῦδε τοῦ παντὸς τόπος, ἢ ψυχή (*neque est alter hujus universi locus, quam anima*) [compare p. 8, where Schopenhauer gives a slightly different Latin translation of the Greek]

[c] δεῖ δὲ οὐκ ἔξωθεν τῆς ψυχῆς λαμβάνειν τὸν χρόνον, ὥσπερ οὐδὲ τὸν αἰῶνα ἐκεῖ ἔξω τοῦ ὄντος (*oportet autem nequaquam extra animam tempus accipere*) [second part of Latin translation of quote missing; see p. 8; both quotes are from III, 7, 11]

[d] ἐκεῖ (*jenseits*)   [e] ἐνθάδε (*diesseits*)

[f] κόσμος νοητός und κόσμος αἰσθητός, *mundus intelligibilis et sensibilis*   [g] τὰ ἄνω καὶ τὰ κάτω

[h] ψυχῆς κάθαρσις, καὶ τελείωσις, καὶ ἡ ἀπὸ τῆς γενέσεως ἀπαλλαγή

'the fire in the sacrifices releases us from the claims of becoming',[a] and hence that promise stated in all Indian religious books, which in English is expressed as 'final emancipation',[b] or salvation. Finally, there is in addition (ibid. sect. 7, ch. 2) the account of an Egyptian symbol depicting a creating god sitting on the lotus: obviously the world-creating Brahma, sitting on the lotus blossom, which springs from the navel of Vishnu, the way he is often portrayed, for example in Langlès, *Monuments de l'Hindoustan*,[c] vol. 1, at p. 175; in Coleman's *Mythology of the Hindus*,[d] plate 5, and others. This symbol is most important as certain proof of the Indian origin of the Egyptian religion, as is also, in the same regard, the account given by *Porphyry, On Abstinence*,[e] Book II, that in Egypt the cow was holy and was not allowed to be slaughtered. – Even the circumstance related by Porphyry in his life of Plotinus, that he was for several years the disciple of Ammonius Saccus and wanted to go to Persia and India with Gordian's army, which was prevented by the defeat and death of Gordian, points to the fact that the doctrine of Ammonius was of Indian origin and Plotinus now intended to draw it in purer form from its source. The same Porphyry has provided a detailed theory of metempsychosis entirely in the Indian sense, although dressed up in Platonic psychology; it is found in the *Eclogues* of Stobaeus, I, 52, 54.

65

§8. Gnostics

The *Cabbalistic* and the *Gnostic philosophies*, for whose founders, Jews and Christians, monotheism was a foregone conclusion, are attempts to remove the flagrant contradiction between the creation of the world by an all-powerful, infinitely benevolent, and all-knowing being, and the sad, defective state of this world. Consequently they introduce, between the world and that cause of the world, a series of intermediate entities,[f] through whose fault an apostasy[g] occurred through which the world first came into being. Thus they take the blame away from the sovereign and assign it to the ministers. Of course this procedure was already hinted at in the myth of the fall, which is altogether the culminating point of Judaism. Those entities now, in the Gnostics, are fullness,[h] aeons, matter,[i] the demiurge, etc. The series was lengthened at the discretion of every Gnostic.

---

[a] τὸ ἐν ταῖς θυσίαις πῦρ ἡμᾶς ἀπολύει τῶν τῆς γενέσεως δεσμῶν   [b] [English in the original]
[c] [Louis Mathieu Langlès, *Monuments anciens et modernes de l'Hindoustan*, Paris: P. Didot, 1821]
[d] [Charles Coleman, *The Mythology of the Hindus*, London, 1832]
[e] *de abstinentia* [II, 11, 2 (141) and II, 61, 7 (186)]   [f] *Mittelwesen*   [g] *Abfall*   [h] πλήρωμα   [i] ὕλη

The whole procedure is analogous to the one in which, in order to mitigate the contradiction entailed by the assumed connection and mutual influence of material and immaterial substance in human beings, physiological philosophers sought to interpose intermediate entities, such as nervous fluid, nerve ether, animal spirits, and the like. Both cover up what they are unable to abolish.

§9.   Scotus Erigena

This admirable man affords us the interesting spectacle of the struggle between the truth that he has independently recognized and seen for himself and local dogmas, fixed through early inoculation and grown beyond all doubt, at least beyond all direct attack, together with the ensuing striving of a noble nature to somehow restore to harmony the dissonance thus generated. This, however, can only happen if the dogmas are turned, twisted, and, if necessary, distorted, until, willingly or unwillingly,[a] they fit the truth that he has recognized independently. This truth remains the dominant principle, but is forced to walk along in a strange and even cumbersome garment. Throughout his major work, *On the Division of Nature*,[b] Erigena knows how to carry out this method with success until he finally wants to apply it to the origin of evil[c] and sin as well, together with the threatened torments of hell. Here it fails, and exactly because of the optimism that is a consequence of Jewish monotheism. He teaches, in Book Five, the return of all things in God and the metaphysical unity and indivisibility of all humankind and even of all nature. Now the question arises: What happens to sin? It cannot be part of God. – Where is hell with its endless torment, such as was promised? – Who is supposed to enter? For humankind is redeemed, in fact, in its entirety. – Here the dogma remains insurmountable. Erigena wriggles miserably through lengthy sophisms that amount to nothing but words and is finally forced into contradictions and absurdities, especially since the question of the origin of sin inevitably had to come in. However, this origin can lie neither in God nor in the will created by him, because otherwise God would be the author of sin. He understands that perfectly, see p. 287 of the Oxford first edition[d] of 1681. Now he is driven into absurdities; sin is supposed to have neither a cause nor a subject: 'Evil is without cause, ... it is completely without cause and substance', ibid.[e] – The deeper reason for these defects is that the doctrine of the *redemption* of humanity and the

66

---

[a] *nolentes volentes*   [b] *de divisione naturae*   [c] *Uebel*   [d] *editio princeps* [See p. 194, n. b]
[e] *malum incausale est, ... penitus incausale et insubstantiale est*; ibid. [V, 36]

world, which obviously is of Indian origin, also presupposes the Indian doctrine according to which the origin of the world (this *samsara*[a] of the Buddhists) itself is already wickedness, namely a sinful deed of Brahma. We ourselves really are this Brahma; for the Indian mythology is everywhere transparent. In Christianity, on the other hand, the doctrine of the redemption of the world had to be grafted on to Jewish theism, where the Lord not only made the world but afterwards also found it to be excellent: 'Everything was very good'.[b] 'Hence those tears':[c] from here arise those difficulties which Erigena perfectly recognized, although, in his age, he could not dare to attack the evil at its root. Meanwhile, possessing Hindustani gentleness, he rejects the eternal damnation and punishment posited by Christianity; all creatures, rational, animal, vegetable, and inanimate, must, according to their inner essence, themselves reach eternal bliss through the necessary course of nature; for they originated in eternal benevolence.[d] But the saints and the righteous alone achieve complete unity with God, deification.[e] By the way, Erigena is so honest as not to hide the great embarrassment that the origin of evil leaves him in; he lays it clearly open in the passage quoted from Book Five. Indeed, the origin of wickedness is the cliff upon which theism, just as much as pantheism, is wrecked; for both imply optimism. However, evil and sin, both in their terrible magnitude, cannot be disavowed; indeed, because of the promised punishments for the latter, the former is only further increased. Whence all this, in a world that is either itself a God or the well-intentioned work of a God? When the theistic opponents of pantheism cry out against this: 'What? All these evil, terrible, abominable beings are supposed to be God?' – then the pantheists can counter: 'What? All those evil, terrible, abominable beings are supposed to have been, with a happy heart,[f] created by a God?' – We find Erigena in the same distress in another of his works come down to us, the book *On Predestination*,[g] which, however, is far inferior to *On the Division of Nature*; as he acts in it not as a philosopher but as a theologian. Here too he struggles pitifully with the same contradictions, which have their ultimate ground in the fact that Christianity is grafted onto Judaism. But his efforts only put them into an even brighter light. God is supposed to have made all, everything and everything in everything,[h] that much is certain: – 'consequently evil and wickedness as well'. This inescapable consequence must be removed and Erigena sees

---

[a] *Sansara* [alternate spelling of '*samsara*'; cycle of rebirths]　　[b] πάντα καλὰ λίαν [Gen. 1:31]
[c] *Hinc illae lacrimae* [Horace, *Epistles* I, 19, 41]　　[d] *Güte*　　[e] *Deificatio*　　[f] *de gaieté de coeur*
[g] *de praedestinatione* [*De divina praedestinatione* (*Treatise on Divine Predestination*) (*c*.851)]
[h] *Alles, Alles und in Allem Alles*

himself necessitated to utter miserable quibbles. Thus wickedness and evil are not supposed *to be*, thus supposed to be nothing. – Deuce! – Or the *free will* is supposed to be at fault; for God has created it, yet he created it *free*; thus it does not concern him what it carries out afterwards; for certainly it was *free*, that is, it could be such and also otherwise, could be good as well as bad. – Well done! – The truth, however, is that being free and being created are two qualities that cancel and thus contradict one another. So the claim that God has created beings and at the same time given them freedom of the will really means that he created them and at the same time did not create them. For acting follows from being,[a] that is, the effects, or actions, of any possible thing can never be anything else but the consequence of its constitution,[b] which itself is known only through the effects. Therefore, in order to be *free* in the sense here demanded, a being would have to have no constitution at all, in other words, be *nothing* at all, thus be and at the same time not be. For what *is* must be *something*; an existence without essence cannot even be thought. If a being is *created*, then it is created in the way it is *constituted*; thus it is *created* badly if it is *constituted* badly, and *constituted* badly if it acts badly, meaning, having bad effects. Consequently the world's *guilt*, as well as its *wickedness*, which is just as undeniable, is laid onto the shoulders of its author, to exonerate whom Scotus Erigena here labours piteously, as Augustine did earlier.

If, on the other hand, a being is to be morally *free*, then it cannot be created, but must possess aseity,[c] that is, must exist originally, through its own original force and absolute power, and not refer to another. Then its existence is its own act of creation that unfolds and extends in time. To be sure, this act exhibits a once and for all decided constitution of this being, which, however, is of its own making; thus responsibility for all of the manifestations of this constitution belongs to itself. – Furthermore, if a being is to be *responsible* for its own doings, in other words if it is to be *accountable*, then it must be *free*. Thus from the responsibility and imputability which our conscience attests to it follows with utmost certainty that our will is free, and from this that the will is the original thing itself, and that not just acting but already the existence and essence of human beings are their own doing. Concerning all this I refer to my essay on the freedom of the will,[d] where one finds it fully and irrefutably discussed; which is why the professors of philosophy have tried to hide[e] this winning prize-essay through the most unbreakable silence. – The guilt of sin and wickedness

---

[a] *operari sequitur esse*   [b] *Beschaffenheit*   [c] *Aseität*   [d] [*Prize Essay on the Freedom of the Will*]
[e] *sekretiren*

always falls back from nature onto its author. Now if that author is the *will* presenting itself in all of nature's appearances, then this guilt has come to the right place. If, on the contrary, it is supposed to be a god, then the authorship of sin and wickedness contradicts his divinity. –

When reading *Dionysius the Areopagite*, to whom Erigena so often refers, I have found him to have been in every respect his model. Erigena's pantheism as well as his theory of evil and wickedness are, in their main features, found already in Dionysius; of course, what Erigena develops, pronounces with audacity and presents with fervour, is only hinted at in the former. Erigena has infinitely more spirit than Dionysius; but Dionysius gave him the material and the direction and very much prepared the ground for him. The fact that Dionysius is said to be inauthentic is irrelevant; it does not matter what the name was of the author of the book *On the Divine Names*.[a] However, since he probably lived in Alexandria, I believe that, in some other way unknown to us, he also was the channel through which a small drop of Indian wisdom may have reached Erigena, since, as *Colebrooke* has noted in his exposition of the philosophy of the Hindus (in Colebrooke's *Miscellaneous Essays*, vol. I,[b] p. 244), the proposition III of the *Karika*[c] of *Kapila* is found in Erigena.

§10. Scholasticism

I want to place the characteristic quality of *scholasticism* in the fact that its supreme criterion of truth is holy scripture, to which we can consequently appeal from every rational conclusion. – One of its peculiarities is the consistently polemical character of its delivery: every inquiry is soon turned into a controversy whose pro and contra[d] produce new pro and contra and 70 thus provide it with the content that otherwise would soon run short. However, the hidden, ultimate root of this peculiarity lies in the conflict between reason and revelation. –

The mutual justification of *realism* and *nominalism* and thus the possibility of such a long and tenacious dispute over them can be made intelligible in the following manner.

I call the most heterogeneous things *red* if they have this colour. Obviously *red* is a mere name by means of which I signify this phenomenon, no matter where it occurs. Similarly, all general concepts are mere

---

[a] *de divinis nominibus* [The author of that work is now commonly referred to as Pseudo-Dionysius]
[b] [Henry Thomas Colebrooke, *Miscellaneous Essays*, vol. I, London: Allen and Co., 1837]
[c] [Colebrooke spells '*cáricá*']   [d] *pro et contra*

names for signifying qualities that occur in different things; these things, on the other hand, are actual and real. Thus *nominalism* is obviously right.

In contrast, if we consider that all those actual things, to which alone we just attributed reality, are temporal and consequently soon will perish, while the qualities, such as red, hard, soft, alive, plant, horse, human being, which are signified by those names, continue to exist unhampered by that and thus are always present, then we find that these qualities, which we think by means of general concepts signified by those names, have much more reality on the strength of their ineradicable existence. Thus reality must be attributed to these *concepts*, not to the individual entities; therefore, *realism* is right.

Nominalism really leads to materialism; for in the end, after eliminating all qualities, only matter remains. Now, if concepts are mere names, but individual things are what is real, and if their qualities, as individual in them, are transient, then matter alone remains as permanent and thus real.

Now, strictly speaking, the above-given justification of realism accrues not really to it, but to the Platonic theory of Ideas, whose extension it is. The eternal forms and qualities of the natural things, *eidê*,[a] are the ones that subsist through all change and to which, therefore, must be attributed a reality of a higher kind than the individuals in which they manifest themselves. In contrast, the same cannot be said about mere abstractions,[b] which cannot be verified in an intuitive way; for example, what is real in such concepts as 'relation, difference, separation, disadvantage, indeterminateness', and the like?

A certain affinity, or at least a parallelism of opposites, becomes evident when one contrasts Plato with Aristotle, Augustine with Pelagius, and the realists with the nominalists. One could claim that, in a way, a polar divergence in the human way of thinking manifests itself in this – which, strangely enough, expressed itself for the first time and most emphatically in two eminently great men who lived simultaneously and side by side.

§11. Bacon of Verulam

In another and more specifically determined sense than the one just described, the explicit and deliberate antithesis to Aristotle was *Bacon of Verulam*. For the former was the first to thoroughly expound the correct method for arriving at particular truths from universal truths, or the descending path; that is the doctrine of syllogisms, the *Organon* of

---

[a] εἴδη   [b] *Abstraktis*

Aristotle.[a] In contrast, Bacon demonstrated the ascending path by stating the method for reaching universal through particular truths: this is induction, as opposed to deduction, and its exposition is the *new organon*,[b] a term, chosen in opposition to Aristotle, meant to express: 'a quite different manner of approaching it'. – The error of Aristotle, but even more so of the Aristotelians, lay in the assumption that they really possessed all truth already, namely that it was contained in their axioms, that is, in certain propositions a priori, or ones considered as such, and that, in order to gain particular truths, only deduction from those propositions was needed. An Aristotelian example of this was given by his books *On the Heavens*.[c] In contrast, Bacon showed quite rightly that those axioms did not possess such content at all, that the truth did not already lie in the system of human knowledge at that time, but rather outside of it, and so could not be generated from within this knowledge, but first had to be brought into it. Consequently, universal and true propositions, with large and rich content, had to be gained first through *induction*.

The scholastics, guided by Aristotle, thought: First we want to establish the universal; the particular will follow from it, or will find a place under it afterwards as best it can. Accordingly we want first to find out what belongs to being,[d] the *thing in general*. What is specific to the individual things can be gradually added later, if need be through experience; what is universal cannot be changed by that. – Bacon, on the other hand, said: We want first to get to know the particular things as completely as possible; then we will in the end come to know what the thing in general is.

Meanwhile *Bacon* is inferior to Aristotle in that his method of the ascending path is by no means as regular, certain and infallible as Aristotle's method of the descending path. Indeed, in his physical investigations, Bacon himself put aside the rules of his method provided in the *New Organon*.

Bacon focused mainly on physics. What he did for it, namely to start from the beginning, *Descartes* did immediately afterwards for metaphysics.

§12.   The philosophy of the moderns

In books on arithmetic the correctness of the solution of an example will usually make itself known through the balancing of the result, the fact that no remainder is left. The case of the solution to the riddle of the world is

---

[a] *Organum Aristotelis*   [b] *novum organum* [Francis Bacon, *Novum Organum*, 1620]   [c] *de caelo*
[d] *ens*

similar. All systems are sums that do not balance out; they leave a remainder or, if one prefers a chemical analogy, an insoluble precipitate. This consists in the fact that when we draw conclusions from their propositions, the results do not match the present actual world, do not harmonize with it; rather, some of its aspects remain utterly inexplicable. Thus, for example, the universal and admirable purposiveness of nature does not harmonize with materialist systems, which have the world arising from, and according to the laws of, matter endowed with mere mechanical qualities. Neither does the existence of cognition, through which that matter, after all, first presents itself. Hence, this is its remainder. – On the other hand, the preponderant physical evils and the moral corruption of the world cannot be brought into harmony with theistic systems, but neither with pantheistic ones; these then are left as the remainder, or the insoluble precipitate. – To be sure, in such cases we do not fail to cover up such remainders with sophisms, and if necessary with mere words and fine-sounding sentences; however, in the long run that does not hold water. Since the sum does not balance out, we might then search for individual errors in the calculation, until in the end we have to admit to ourselves that the starting point itself was wrong. If, on the other hand, the universal consistency and harmony of all propositions of a system are accompanied at every step by the equally universal harmony with the world of experience without an audible dissonance between the two – then this is the criterion of its truth, the required balancing out of the arithmetical problem. Similarly, the fact that already the starting point was wrong means that from the beginning we did not approach the thing from the right end, so that afterwards we are led from error to error. For it is with philosophy as it is with so many things: everything depends on tackling it from the right end. Now the phenomenon[a] of the world, which is to be explained, offers innumerable ends, of which only one can be the right one; it resembles a tangled mass of threads, with many wrong ends hanging from it; only the person who can find the right one can disentangle the whole thing. But then one thing easily follows from another, and from that we know that it was the right end. It can also be compared to a labyrinth that offers a hundred entrances opening into corridors all of which, after long and variously twisted turns, lead outside again, with the exception of a single one, whose turns really lead to the centre, where the idol stands. If we have found this entrance, then we will not miss the path; through no other path can we ever reach the goal. – I will

73

[a] *Phänomen*

not hide the view that only the will within us is the right end of the tangle of threads, the true entrance to the labyrinth.

On the other hand, *Descartes*, following the precedent of Aristotle's   74
metaphysics, started out from the concept of *substance*, with which we see all his successors still encumbered. However, he assumed two kinds of substance: thinking and extended. These were supposed to act on each other through physical influence,[a] which soon, however, proved to be his remainder. For this took place not only from the outside to the inside, in representing the corporeal world, but also from the inside to the outside, between the will (which without hesitation was attributed to thinking) and the actions of the body. The details of this relation between these two kinds of substance now became the main problem, giving rise to such great difficulties that as a consequence people were driven to the system of occasional causes[b] and pre-established harmony,[c] after the animal spirits,[d] which had mediated the thing for Descartes himself, would be of no further use.[*,10] *Malebranche* thought physical influence[e] inconceivable; however, he did not take into consideration that the same is assumed without hesitation in the creation and guidance of the corporeal world by a God who is a spirit. Thus he put in its place occasional causes and 'we see everything in God';[f] here lies his remainder. – And also *Spinoza*, following in the footsteps of his teacher, started out from that concept of *substance*, just as if it were a given. But he declared both kinds of substance, thinking and extended, to be one and the same, whereby the above-mentioned difficulty was avoided. However, for that reason his philosophy became mainly negative, for it amounted to a mere negation of the two great Cartesian oppositions, since he extended his identification also to the other antithesis stipulated by Descartes, that of God and world. This latter identification was really a mere method of teaching, or form of exposition. For it would have been much too shocking to say directly: 'It is not true that a God has made this world, but it exists by   75
its own absolute power.' Hence, he chose an indirect phrase and said: 'The world itself is God' – which it would never have occurred to him to assert if,

---

* By the way, the animal spirits already occur as a known fact in Vanini, *de naturae arcanis* [Lucilio Giulio Cesare Vanini, *De Admirandis Naturae Reginae Deaeque Mortalium Arcanis* (1616) (*Of the Admirable Secrets of Nature, the Queen and Goddess of the Mortals*)], dial. 49. Maybe their author is [Thomas] Willisius [Willis] (*de anatome cerebri* [*Cerebri Anatome* (*Of the Anatomy of the Brain*), 1664]; *de anima brutorum* [*Of the Soul of Brutes*, 1672], Geneva, 1680, pp. 35f.). [Jean Pierre] Flourens, *de la vie et de l'intelligence* [1858] [*On Life and Intelligence*], vol. 2, p. 72, attributes them to *Galen*. Even Iamblichus, in Stobaeus (*Eclogues* I, 52, 29), already mentions them rather clearly as a doctrine of the Stoics.

[a] *influxus physicus*   [b] *causes occasionelles*   [c] *harmonia praestabilita*   [d] *spiritus animales*
[e] *influxus physicus*   [f] *Nous voyons tout en Dieu*

instead of from Judaism, he could have impartially started out from nature itself. This phrase at the same time serves to impart the semblance of positivity to his theorems, while they are at bottom merely negative. Thus he really leaves the world unexplained, since his doctrine amounts to saying: 'The world is because it is; and it is the way it is because it is such.' (With this phrase Fichte used to mystify his students.)[11] Now the deification of the world, arising in the way explained above, did not allow for a true ethic and in addition was in flagrant contradiction to the physical evils and the moral wickedness of this world. Here, then, is his remainder.

As already mentioned, *Spinoza* takes the concept of *substance*, from which he also starts out, as a given. To be sure, he defines it according to his purposes; but he does not care about its origin. For it was only *Locke* who, soon after him, laid down the great doctrine that a philosopher who intends to derive or demonstrate anything from concepts first must investigate the *origin* of each such concept, since its content, and what may follow from it, is entirely determined by its origin as the source of all knowledge attainable through it. However, if *Spinoza* had inquired into the origin of that concept of substance, he ultimately would have had to find that this is *matter* alone and that, therefore, the true content of the concept is nothing but its essential qualities, which can be stated a priori. Indeed, everything with which Spinoza credits substance finds its proof in matter, and only there: it is not generated, thus without cause, eternal, unique and singular, and its modifications are extension and cognition, the latter, namely, as exclusive quality of the brain, which is material. Accordingly, Spinoza is an unconscious materialist. However, matter, if one expounds it,[a] and realizes its concept and empirically substantiates it, is not the wrongly conceived and atomistic matter of Democritus and the later French materialists, which has no other than mechanical qualities, but correctly conceived matter, endowed with all its inexplicable qualities. For this difference I refer to my chief work, vol. 2, ch. 24, pp. 315ff.[b] – We already find this method of admitting the concept of *substance* unexamined in order to make it the starting point in the *Eleatics*, as can be seen especially in the Aristotelian book *On Xenophanes*, etc.[c] Xenophanes also starts out from being,[d] that is, from substance, and its qualities are demonstrated without first asking or stating from where he has knowledge of such a thing. If that

76

---

[a] [In the orginal 'es', which as a neutral personal pronoun does not correspond with matter, which is a feminine noun in German]
[b] [Hübscher *SW* 3, 357ff.]
[c] *de Xenophane etc* [*De Xenophane, Zenone et Gorgia*; the text is no longer attributed to Aristotle; in addition, the authenticity of the title is in doubt]
[d] ὄν

happened it would become clear what he is really talking about, meaning, which intuition is ultimately the basis for his concept and provides it with reality; so in the end it would turn out to be only matter, of which everything that he says is valid. In the following chapters, on *Zeno*, the agreement with Spinoza extends to exposition and expressions. Thus we cannot help assuming that Spinoza knew and made use of this work; for during his time Aristotle was still held in high esteem, even if attacked by Bacon, and good editions, with Latin versions, existed. Thus Spinoza was a mere reviver of the Eleatics, as Gassendi was of Epicurus. And we experience once again how exceedingly rare the genuinely new and wholly original is in all branches of thought and knowledge.

Besides, and especially in a formal respect, Spinoza's starting out from the concept of *substance* rests on the false fundamental idea, taken over from his teacher Descartes, who got it from Anselm of Canterbury, to the effect that existence[a] could ever arise out of essence,[b] that is, that from a mere concept there could be inferred an existence which consequently would be necessary. Or, in other words, that by virtue of the nature, or definition, of a merely *thought* object,[c] it could become necessary that it is no longer a merely thought object, but an actually existing one. Descartes applied this false fundamental idea to the concept of the most perfect being;[d] Spinoza, however, took that of substance[e] or cause of itself[f] (the latter expressing a contradiction in terms;[g] see his first definition, which is his first falsehood,[h] at the beginning of the *Ethics*, and then prop. 7 of the First Book).[i] The difference between the fundamental concepts of both philosophers consists almost entirely in their expression alone. However, the use of these concepts as starting points, thus as given, is grounded for the one as for the other in the mistake of letting intuitive representation originate in abstract representation, whereas in truth all abstract representation springs from intuitive representation and is thus grounded in it. We have here a fundamental confusion of ground and consequent.[j]

Spinoza burdened himself with a difficulty of a special kind by calling his sole substance God.[k] For this word had already been taken to designate a completely different concept, so that now he has to continuously battle the misunderstandings that arise from the fact that the reader still associates the word with the concept that it usually designates, instead of the one that it is

77

---

[a] *existentia*   [b] *essentia*   [c] gedachten *Sache*   [d] *ens perfectissimum*   [e] *substantia*   [f] *causa sui*
[g] *contradictio in adjecto*   [h] πρῶτον ψεῦδος
[i] [Second parenthesis missing in 1972 Brockhaus edition, but supplied in 1977 Diogenes edition; the sentence, starting with 'Spinoza, however, . . .' is incomplete]
[j] ὕστερον πρότερον   [k] *Deus*

supposed to designate according to Spinoza's initial explanations. Had he not used the word, he would have been spared long and painful discussions in the First Book. However, he did it so that his doctrine would give less offence, a purpose he missed nevertheless. So now a certain ambiguity runs through his entire delivery, which one could, therefore, call an allegorical one, so to speak, all the more since he does the same with a few other concepts – as was mentioned above (in the first essay). How much clearer, and thus better, would his so-called *Ethics* have turned out if he had spoken candidly, according to his intention, and called things by their proper name, and if in general he had presented his ideas, together with their reasons, honestly and naturally, instead of letting them appear laced up in the Spanish boots of propositions, demonstrations, scholia, and corollaries, in this garb borrowed from geometry, which, instead of conferring the certainty of geometry to philosophy, rather loses all significance as soon as geometry itself with its construction of concepts is not involved in it. Thus here too the point is: 'The cowl does not make the monk.'[a,12]

In the Second Book he presents the two modes of his sole substance as extension and representation (*extensio et cogitatio*), which is obviously a false division, since extension exists solely for and in representation, thus should not be opposed but subordinated to it.

The fact that Spinoza everywhere explicitly and emphatically praises joyfulness[b] and stipulates it as condition and sign of every praiseworthy act, but completely dismisses all sorrow[c] – although his Old Testament told him: 'Sorrow is better than laughter; for through sadness the heart is made better' (Qohel. 7:4)[d] – all this he does only out of love for consistency. For if this world is a god, then it is an end in itself and must rejoice in its existence and praise it, so 'Jump, Marquis!'[e] Always merry, never sad!'[f] Pantheism is essentially and necessarily optimism. This obligatory optimism forces quite a few other false conclusions on Spinoza, the most conspicuous being the absurd and very often revolting propositions of his moral philosophy, which in the sixteenth chapter of his *Tractatus theologico-politicus* rise to true infamies. On the other hand, he sometimes loses sight of a conclusion where it would have led to correct views, for example in his unworthy as well

---

[a] *cucullus non facit monachum* [William Shakespeare, *Twelfth Night*, Act I, scene 5]   [b] *laetitia*
[c] *tristitia*   [d] (Kohel[eth] 7:4) [Ecclesiastes (Qoheleth) 7:3 in King James Bible]
[e] *saute, Marquis!* [A reference to the line 'Allons, saute, marquis!' in Pierre Carlet de Chamblain de Marivaux's play *Le Jeu de l'amour et du hasard* (*The Game of Love and Chance*), which takes it from Jean-François Regnard's *Le Joueur* (*The Gamester*), where in Act IV, scene 10, the marquis repeats the phrase several times, referring to his happiness]
[f] *Semper lustig, nunquam traurig!*

as false propositions regarding animals. (*Ethics* IV, appendix, ch. 26, and in the same part, prop. 37, scholium.) Here he speaks the way a Jew understands it, in accordance with chs. 1 and 9 of Genesis, so that we others, who are accustomed to more pure and worthy doctrines, are overpowered by the 'Jewish stench'.[a] Dogs he does not seem to have known at all. The shocking sentence with which ch. 26 begins: 'Besides men, we know of no particular thing in nature in whose mind we may rejoice, and whom we can associate with ourselves in friendship or any sort of fellowship',[b] is best answered by a Spanish man of letters of our day (Larra, pseudonym Figaro, in *El doncel*, ch. 33)[c]: 'El que no ha tenido un perro, no sabe lo que es querer y ser querido.' (He who has never kept a dog does not know what it is to love and be loved.) The torture of animals that, according to Colerus,[d] Spinoza used to perform on spiders and flies, for his amusement and while laughing heartily, corresponds only too closely to his statements here criticized, as also to the above-mentioned chapters of Genesis. Because of all this then Spinoza's *Ethics* is throughout a mixture of the false and the true, the admirable and the bad. Towards the end, in the second half of the last part, we see him trying in vain to reach clarity for himself; he is not able to, so there is nothing left for him but to become *mystical*, as happens here. Thus in order not to treat this truly great mind unjustly, we must consider that not enough came before him, really only Descartes, Malebranche, Hobbes, and Giordano Bruno. The fundamental philosophical concepts had not yet been worked through enough, the problems not properly ventilated.[13]

79

Leibniz also started out from the concept of *substance* as given, but focused mainly on the fact that it had to be *indestructible*. For this purpose it had to be *simple*, because everything extended was divisible and thus destructible; consequently it was without extension, hence immaterial. Therefore, no other predicates were left for his substance but the mental ones, hence perception, thought, and desire. Now of such simple mental substances he assumed innumerably many. Although they themselves were not extended, they were nevertheless to be at the basis of the phenomenon of extension; for that reason he defines them as *formal atoms* and *simple substances* (*Works*, ed. Erdmann, pp. 124, 676)[e] and gives them the name

---

[a] *foetor judaicus* [medieval anti-Semitic concept]

[b] *Praeter homines nihil singulare in natura novimus, cujus mente gaudere et quod nobis amicitia, aut aliquo consuetudinis genere jungere possumus.*

[c] [Mariano José de Larra, *El doncel de Don Enrique el Doliente* (1834)]

[d] [Johann Colerus, *The Life of Spinoza* (1705)]

[e] [*God. Guil. Leibnitii Opera philosophica quae exstant Latina, Gallica, Germanica omnia*, ed. Johann Eduard Erdmann, Berlin, 1839–40]

monads. These are supposed to be at the basis of the phenomenon of the corporeal world, which is thus a mere appearance without actual and immediate reality; the latter accrues only to the monads, which are found in and behind reality. Now this phenomenon of the corporeal world, on the other hand, is brought about in the perception of the monads (that is, of those that really perceive, which are just a few, the majority being perpetually asleep) by means of pre-established harmony, which the central monad produces all alone and at its own expense. Here we encounter some obscurity. However, be that as it may:[14] the mediation between the mere thoughts of these substances and what is actually and in itself extended is brought about by a harmony pre-established by the central monad. – Here, one wants to say, all is remainder. However, in order to do justice to *Leibniz*, we must call to mind the manner of reflection on *matter*, claimed back then by Locke and Newton, in which it exists as absolutely dead, purely passive and without will, endowed merely with mechanical forces and subject only to mathematical laws. Leibniz, on the other hand, rejects *atoms* and purely *mechanical* physics in order to put a *dynamic* physics in its place, preparing the way for *Kant* with all this. (See *Works*, ed. Erdmann, p. 694.)[a] In doing so, he recalled[15] first of all the substantial forms[b] of the scholastics and subsequently arrived at the view that even the merely mechanical forces of matter, besides which scarcely any other were known or admitted at that time, must have something mental as their foundation. This he did not know how to make clear to himself except by means of the most awkward fiction that matter consisted of nothing but little souls that at the same time were formal atoms and existed most of the time in a state of insensibility, yet possessing an analogue of perception[c] and of appetite.[d] In this he was misled, as everybody else, each and all, by making cognition the basis and indispensable condition[e] of everything mental, instead of the will, whose proper primacy I first advocated, whereby everything in philosophy is transformed. Nevertheless, Leibniz's endeavour to ground spirit and matter in one and the same principle deserves recognition. We could even see in this a premonition of Kant's as well as my own doctrine,[16] but 'as if one saw it through a mist'.[f] For already underlying his monadology is the idea that matter is not a thing in itself, but mere appearance. Therefore, we

80

---

[a] [See n. e above]   [b] *formas substantiales*   [c] *perceptio*   [d] *appetitus*   [e] *conditio sine qua non*
[f] *quas velut trans nebulam vidit* [Schopenhauer might be paraphrasing here a half-sentence from Descartes, *Regulae ad directionem ingenii* (*Rules for the Direction of the Mind*): *quas prorsus ignorant, obscuras eaque veritates quasi per nebulam se videre praesagiunt* (in matters about which they are completely ignorant they pronounce that they see, as if through a mist, truths which are often obscure). (*Regula* XII, 25, AT X, p. 428)]

must seek the ultimate ground of its action, which in itself is only mechanical, not in the purely geometrical, that is, in that which belongs to appearance, like extension, motion, form; consequently, impenetrability already is not a solely *negative* quality, but the manifestation of a positive *force.*[17] – Leibniz's fundamental view, which is praised here, is most clearly expressed in a few shorter French writings, as in *New System of Nature*[a] and others, which were taken, from the *Journal des Scavans*[b] and from the edition by Dutens,[c] into the Erdmann edition and into the letters, etc., Erdmann, *Works,*[d] pp. 681–95. In addition, a well-selected compilation of passages by Leibniz relevant here is located on pp. 335–40 of his *Short Works,*   81 translated by Köhler and revised by Huth, Jena, 1740.[e]

But in general we see in this whole concatenation of strange dogmatic teachings *one* fiction always drawing on another for its support, just as in practical life *one* lie necessitates many others. At the root is Descartes' division of all that exists into God and world, and of the human being into spirit and matter; everything else falls under the latter division. Added to this is the error, common to these and all past philosophers, of placing our fundamental essence in cognition, instead of the will, and thus of letting the will be secondary and cognition primary. These then were the original errors,[f] against which the nature and reality of things protested at every step and for whose rescue animal spirits,[g] materiality of animals, occasional cause, seeing-all-in-God, pre-established harmony, monads, optimism and all the rest of it then had to be invented. With me, on the other hand, where things are tackled at the right end, everything happens by itself, each thing shows itself in its proper light, no fictions are required, and 'simplicity is the seal of truth'.[h,18]

Kant was not directly affected by the problem of substance; he is beyond it. With him, the concept of substance is a category, thus a mere form of

---

[a] *systême nouveau de la nature* [*Système nouveau de la nature et de la communication des substances*, 1695 (*New System of the Nature of Substances and their Communication*)]

[b] *Journal des savans* [*Journal des Scavans . . . par le Sieur de Hedouville (et al.)*]

[c] [*Gothofredi Guillelmi Leibnitii Opera Omnia. Nunc primum collecta . . .* ed. Louis Dutens, 6 vols., Geneva, 1768]

[d] [See above p. 69, n. e]

[e] [*Des Freyherrn von Leibni*[?]*z Kleinere philosophische Schriften . . . ehedem von dem Jenaischen Philosophen Herrn Heinrich Köhler Teutsch übersetzt nun auf das neue übersehen von M. Caspar Jacob Huth der teutschen Gesellschaft in Jena Senior*, Jena: Mayerische Buchhandlung, 1740; the reference is to *Merckwürdige Schriften welche . . . zwischen dem Herrn Baron von Leibniz und dem Herrn D. Clarke über besondere Materien der natürlichen Religion in Französ(ischer) und Englischer Sprache gewechselt und . . . in teutscher Sprache herausgegeben worden von Heinrich Köhler*, Frankfurt and Leipzig (Jena), 1720]

[f] *Ur-Irrthümer*   [g] *spiritus animales*   [h] *simplex sigillum veri*

thinking a priori. Now, by means of it, through its necessary application to sensible intuition, nothing is known as it is in itself; thus the essence that lies at the basis of bodies as well as of souls might in itself be one and the same. That is his doctrine. It paved the way for my insight that everyone's own body is nothing but the intuition of his will, generated in his brain, which relation subsequently, extended to all bodies, resulted in the resolution[a] of the world into will and representation.

Now that concept of *substance* that *Descartes*, true to Aristotle, had made the principal concept of philosophy, and with whose definition *Spinoza* also begins (although in the manner of the Eleatics) amounts on close and honest examination to a higher, but unjustified, abstraction[b] of the concept of *matter*. For, besides matter, it was also supposed to include the substituted[c] child *immaterial substance*, as I have explained in detail in my *Critique of the Kantian Philosophy*, pp. 550ff. of the second edition.[d] However, apart from this, the concept of *substance* is of no use as the starting point of philosophy already for the reason that, in any case, it is an *objective* concept. For everything objective is always *mediated* for us; the subjective alone is immediate. Therefore, we may not pass over the subjective, but must make it the absolute starting point. To be sure, Descartes did so; indeed, he was the first to recognize and act on it, on account of which a new major period of philosophy starts with him. However, he does so only in a preliminary way, in the very first attempt, after which he at once assumes the objective, absolute reality of the world on the credit of God's veracity and from then on philosophizes further in a completely objective manner. Moreover, he becomes guilty here of a vicious circle.[e] For he proves the objective reality of the objects of all our intuitive representations on the basis of the existence of God, as their author, whose veracity does not allow him to deceive us. However, he proves God's existence by means of the representation innate in us, which we supposedly have of him as the most-perfect being. 'He starts out doubting everything and ends up believing everything',[f] one of his compatriots says about him.

Berkeley first put into genuine practice the subjective starting point and irrefutably demonstrated its absolute necessity. He is the father of idealism.

---

[a] *Auflösung*   [b] *Abstraktum*   [c] *untergeschobene*   [d] [*WWR* I, 520–1 (Hübscher *SW* 2, 582f.)]
[e] *circulus vitiosus*
[f] *Il commence par douter de tout, et finit par tout croire.* [A somewhat distorted paraphrase of Jean Le Rond d'Alembert, *Discours préliminaire de l'Encyclopédie* (1751) (*Preliminary Discourse to the Encyclopedia of Diderot*), where he says about Descartes: 'S'il a fini par croire tout expliquer, il a du moins commencé par douter de tout . . .' ('If he finished by believing he could explain everything, at least he started out doubting everything . . .')]

But this is the basis of all true philosophy and, since then, has always been held, at least as a starting point, although every successive philosopher has attempted different modulations and evasions of it. For *Locke* already started out from the subjective by attributing a large part of the qualities of bodies to our sensation.[a] It must be noted, however, that his reduction of all *qualitative* differences, as secondary qualities, to merely *quantitative* ones, namely size, shape, position, etc., as the only primary, that is, objective qualities, in truth is still the doctrine of *Democritus*, who also reduced all qualities to shape, composition, and position of atoms. This can be seen with special clarity in Aristotle's *Metaphysics* I, 4, and in Theophrastus' *On Sensation*,[b] chs. 61–5. – To this extent, Locke was a reviver of the philosophy of Democritus, as Spinoza was of the Eleatic philosophy. In addition, he truly paved the way for subsequent French materialism. Directly though, through this preliminary distinction of the subjective from the objective in intuition, he prepared the ground for *Kant*, who then, following Locke's direction and path in a much more elevated sense, arrived at the pure separation of the subjective from the objective, a process in which so much now falls to the subjective that the objective is left as an entirely obscure point, a something that cannot be known any further[c] – the thing in itself. I in turn have traced the latter to the essence which we find in our self-consciousness as the will; thus here I have also returned once more to the subjective source of knowledge. It could not have turned out otherwise since everything objective is always merely secondary, that is to say, representation. Consequently we are to seek the innermost core of beings, the thing in itself, by no means outside of us, but solely within ourselves, thus in the subjective as that which alone is immediate. In addition, with the objective we can never reach a resting point, something ultimate and original, since we are there in the realm of *representations*. These, however, altogether and essentially, have the principle of sufficient reason, in its four aspects, as their form, according to which every object falls under and is subject to its demand. For example, the questions Whence? and Why? at once destructively press upon an assumed objective absolute,[d] which must retreat and fall in their wake. The case is different when we immerse ourselves in the quiet, though obscure depth of the subject. However, here we are threatened by the danger of falling into mysticism. Thus we are to draw from this source only what is in fact true, accessible to each and all, and consequently absolutely undeniable.

83

---

[a] *Sinnesempfindung*   [b] *de sensu* [*De sensibus*]   [c] *ein nicht weiter erkennbares Etwas*   [d] *Absolutum*

The *dianoiology* which, as a result of the inquiries since Descartes, was current until Kant, is found summarized and explained with naïve clarity in *Muratori, On imagination*,[a] chs. 1–4 and 13. Locke appears there as a heretic. The whole thing is a nest of errors, which show how completely differently I have conceived and presented it after having had Kant and Cabanis as predecessors. That whole dianoiology and psychology is built upon the false Cartesian dualism; now everything in the entire work, by hook or by crook,[b] must be traced back to it, even many correct and interesting facts that he relates. The whole procedure is interesting as a type.[19]

§13. Some further elucidations on the Kantian philosophy

As the motto for the *Critique of Pure Reason* a passage from *Pope* would be very fitting (*Works*, vol. 6, p. 374, Basel edition[c]), which he wrote down roughly 80 years ago: 'Since 'tis reasonable to doubt most things, we should most of all *doubt that reason of ours* which would *demonstrate* all things.'[d,20]

The true spirit of the Kantian philosophy, its fundamental idea and proper meaning, can be grasped and presented in many different ways. However, such different phrases and expressions of the subject will be suited, some more than others in accordance with the diversity of minds, to reveal the right understanding of that very profound and hence difficult doctrine to one person rather than another. The following is one more attempt of this kind, in which I undertake to shed my own clear light on Kant's profundity.*

At the basis of mathematics are *intuitions*, which support its proofs; however, because these intuitions are not empirical, but a priori, its doctrines are apodictic. Philosophy, on the other hand, has mere *concepts* as the given from which to start out, providing necessity (apodicticity) to its proofs. For it cannot rest on mere *empirical* intuition, since it undertakes to explain the universal in things, not the particular, with the intention to lead beyond what is empirically given. So nothing remains but universal

---

* I note here, once and for all, that the pagination of the first edition of the *Critique of Pure Reason*, in accordance with which I usually quote, has also been appended to the Rosenkranz edition. [See *WWR* 1, 462–3 (Hübscher *SW* 2, 515–16) for Schopenhauer's account of his correspondence with Johann Karl Friedrich Rosenkranz, concerning the then little-known first edition of the *Critique*, which was subsequently included in Rosenkranz's edition of Kant's works in 1838]

[a] *della fantasia* [Lodovico Antonio Muratori, *Della forza della fantasia umana* (1740) (*On the Power of Human Imagination*)]
[b] *per fas et nefas*   [c] [Alexander Pope, *The Works*, 9 vols., Basel: J. J. Tourneisen, 1803]
[d] [original English]

concepts, since these are not intuitive, or purely empirical. Such concepts, therefore, must be the foundation of its doctrines and proofs, and they, as something existing and given, must be the starting point. Accordingly, philosophy is a science from mere *concepts*, whereas mathematics is a science based on the *construction* (intuitive presentation) of its concepts. Strictly speaking, however, it is only demonstration[a] in philosophy that starts from mere *concepts*. For it cannot, like mathematics, start from an *intuition*, since that would have to be either purely a priori or empirical; the latter yields no apodicticity, the former only mathematics. Thus, if philosophy wants in some way to support its doctrines through demonstration, this must consist in correct logical inference from the concepts taken as the basis. – This had worked out well throughout the entire long period of scholasticism and even during the modern period established by Descartes; so that we still see *Spinoza* and *Leibniz* follow this method. Finally, however, it occurred to *Locke* to investigate the *origin* of concepts, and the result was that all universal concepts, as broad as they might be conceived, are drawn from experience, that is, from the actually existing, sensibly intuitive, empirically real world, or else from inner experience, which is provided for all of us by empirical self-observation. Consequently, the entire content of universal concepts stems from these two; they cannot deliver more than what outer or inner experience have put into them. From this it should have been strictly concluded that they can never lead beyond experience, that is, can never lead to the goal. But *Locke* went beyond experience with principles drawn from experience.

In further opposition to and correction of the Lockean doctrine, *Kant* showed that there are some concepts that form an exception to the above rule, and do *not* arise from experience, but at the same time that these are partly derived from pure, that is, a priori given intuition of space and time, and partly make up the peculiar functions of our understanding itself, for the purpose of guiding experience in their application. Hence the validity of these concepts extends only to possible experience, which is always mediated through the senses, in that the concepts themselves are merely destined to produce experience, together with its lawful occurrences, on the initiation of sensation; thus they are themselves without content and expect to receive all material and content solely from *sensibility* in order then, together with it, to produce experience. Apart from sensibility, they have neither content nor meaning since they are only valid on condition of intuition grounded in sensation and essentially relate to intuition. It

86

[a] *Beweisführung*

follows from this that they cannot act as guides in leading us beyond all possibility of experience; and from this again that *metaphysics*, as a science of what lies beyond nature, that is, beyond the possibility of experience, is *impossible*.

Now since one part of experience, namely the universal, formal, and lawful part, can be known a priori, but for that reason depends on the essential and lawful functions of our own intellect, whereas the other, namely the particular, material and contingent part, originates from sensation, both are of *subjective* origin. From this it follows that all of experience, including the world presenting itself in it, is mere *appearance*, that is, something that exists primarily and immediately only for the cognitive subject; yet this appearance points to some *thing in itself* as its ground, which as such, however, is utterly unknowable. – These then are the negative results of the Kantian philosophy.

I must mention here that Kant acts as if we were merely cognitive beings and were not aware of anything given apart from *representation*, whereas in reality we possess something else in the *will* within us, which is of a completely different kind[a] from representation. To be sure, he took the will also into consideration, though not in theoretical, but merely in practical philosophy, which for him is completely separate, solely in order to assert the fact of the purely moral significance of our actions and to establish on that basis a moral doctrine of faith, as a counterweight to the theoretical ignorance (and thus also the impossibility of theology) to which we are subject according to the above. –

Kant's philosophy, in contrast and even in opposition to all others, is also called *transcendental philosophy*, or, more precisely, *transcendental idealism*. The expression 'transcendent' is not of mathematical, but of philosophical origin, for it was already familiar to the scholastics. Leibniz first introduced it into mathematics in order to signify 'what transcends the powers of algebra',[b] thus all operations that general arithmetic and algebra are not sufficient to perform, as, for example, finding the logarithm of a number, or vice versa, or, purely arithmetically, the trigonometrical functions of an arc, or vice versa; and, in general, all problems that can only be solved by means of an infinite calculus. The scholastics, however, called *transcendent* the very highest concepts, namely those that were even more universal than Aristotle's ten categories; *Spinoza* still uses the word in this sense. *Giordano Bruno* (*Cause, Principle and Unity*,[c] Dialogue 4) calls *transcendent*

---

[a] toto genere *verschieden*　　[b] *quod Algebrae vires transscendit*
[c] *della causa etc.* [*De la causa, principio ed uno*, 1584]

those predicates that are more universal than the distinction between corporeal and incorporeal substance and which, therefore, belong to substance in general; according to him, they refer to that common root in which the corporeal is one with the incorporeal and which is the true, original substance; indeed, he sees in this a proof that such a substance must exist. Finally then *Kant* understands by *transcendental* first the acknowledgement of what is a priori and thus merely formal in our cognition *as such*, i.e. the realization that such cognition is independent of experience and even prescribes the unchangeable rule to it which experience must accord with. Such insight is connected with an understanding of why such cognition is and has this power, namely because it makes up the *form* of our intellect; in other words, as a consequence of its subjective origin. Therefore, actually only the critique of pure reason is *transcendental*. In   88 contrast to this he calls *transcendent* the use, or rather misuse, of what is purely formal in our cognition beyond the possibility of experience. This he also calls hyperphysical. Consequently, *transcendental*, put briefly, means 'prior to all experience',[a] *transcendent* 'beyond all experience'.[b] Thus Kant accepts metaphysics only as transcendental philosophy, that is, as a doctrine of the formal *as such*, contained in our cognitive consciousness, by virtue of which cognition of things in themselves is impossible for us, since experience can provide nothing but mere appearances. However, the term '*metaphysical*' is for him not completely synonymous with 'transcendental'; for he calls *metaphysical* everything that is a priori certain but refers to experience; in contrast, he calls *transcendental* solely the explanation that what is a priori certain is so only because of its subjective origin and as something purely formal. *Transcendental* is that philosophy which becomes aware that the first and essential laws of this world that presents itself to us are rooted in our brain and, therefore, can be known a priori. It is called *transcendental* because it *goes beyond* the whole given phantasmagoria[c] towards its origin.[21] For that reason, as mentioned, only the *Critique of Pure Reason*, and in general the critical (that is, Kantian) philosophy is transcendental.[*,22] In contrast, the *Foundations of Natural Science*[d] and those of the 'Doctrine of Virtue',[e] and so on, are *metaphysical*. –

---

* The *Critique of Pure Reason* has transformed ontology into dianoiology.

[a] *vor aller Erfahrung*   [b] *über alle Erfahrung hinaus*   [c] *Phantasmagorie*
[d] *Anfangsgründe der Naturwissenschaft* [*Metaphysische Anfangsgründe der Naturwissenschaft* (*Metaphysical Foundations of Natural Science*)]
[e] *Tugendlehre* [*Metaphysische Anfangsgründe der Tugendlehre* (*Metaphysical First Principles of the Doctrine of Virtue*), part II of *The Metaphysics of Morals*]

In the meantime, the concept of a transcendental philosophy can be conceived in an even more profound sense if we attempt to concentrate in it the innermost spirit of the Kantian philosophy, perhaps in the following way. That the whole world is given to us only in a *secondary* manner, as representation, image in our mind, phenomenon of the brain, whereas our own will is given to us immediately in self-consciousness; hence that a
89 division, indeed an opposition, occurs between our own existence and that of the world – this is a mere consequence of our individual and animal existence, with whose discontinuation it thus ceases. But until then it is impossible for us to repeal in thought this fundamental and original form of our consciousness, which is what we call separation of subject and object, since all thinking and representing presupposes it. Therefore, we always let it stand and accept its validity as primordially essential,[a] as the fundamental constitution[b] of the world, while in fact it is only the form of our animal consciousness and the appearances it mediates. Now from this all those questions arise, concerning the beginning, end, limits, and origin of the world, our own continued existence after death, and so on. They are thus all based on the false assumption that attributes to the thing in itself, and consequently passes off as original and fundamental nature of the world, what is only the form of *appearance*, that is, *representations* mediated by an animal, cerebral consciousness. This is the meaning of the Kantian expression: All such questions are *transcendent*. They are, therefore, not only *subjectively*, but in and for themselves, that is, *objectively*, incapable of any answer. For they are problems that disappear entirely with the discontinuation of our cerebral consciousness and the opposition based on it, but nonetheless seem as if they had been posed independently of that. For example, whoever asks whether he will continue to exist after his death hypothetically[c] abrogates his animal brain consciousness, yet asks about something that exists only under its presupposition by depending on its form, namely subject, object, space and time; that is, he asks about his individual existence. Now a philosophy that brings to distinct consciousness all these conditions and limitations *as such* is *transcendental* and, insofar as it attributes the universal fundamental determinations of the objective world to the subject, it is *transcendental idealism*. – Little by little we shall realize that the problems of metaphysics are insoluble only insofar as the questions themselves already contain a contradiction.

Meanwhile, transcendental idealism does not dispute the *empirical reality*
90 of the actually existing world, but only says that it is not unconditioned,

---

[a] *das Urwesentliche*   [b] *Grundbeschaffenheit*   [c] *in hypothesi*

since it depends on our brain functions, from which the forms of intuitions, that is, time, space, and causality, ensue, and that, therefore, empirical reality itself is only the reality of an appearance. Now if within this reality a plurality of beings presents itself to us, one of which is always perishing and another one coming into existence, yet we know that plurality is only possible by means of the intuitive form of space, and perishing and coming-into-existence are possible only by means of that of time, then we realize that such events have no *absolute* reality, meaning that they do not belong to the essence in itself that presents itself in that appearance. If it were possible to remove those forms of cognition like the glass from the kaleidoscope, we would, to our amazement, have in front of us this essence as something single and enduring, as imperishable, unchangeable, and, underneath all apparent change, perhaps even down to the wholly individual determinations, identical. In accordance with this view the following three propositions can be laid down:

(1) The sole form of reality is the present; in it alone the real is capable of immediately being found and always entirely and completely contained.

(2) The truly real is independent of time, thus one and the same at every point in time.

(3) Time is the intuitive form of our intellect and thus alien to the thing in itself.

These three propositions are at bottom identical. Whoever clearly comprehends their identity as well as their truth has made great progress in philosophy in having grasped the spirit of transcendental idealism.

Altogether, how momentous is Kant's doctrine of the ideality of space and time, which he presented in such dry and unadorned fashion – while exactly nothing results from the pompous, pretentious, and intentionally incomprehensible chatter of the three notorious sophists,[a] who drew the attention of an audience unworthy of Kant away from him on to themselves. Before Kant, it may be said, we were in time; now time is in us. In the first case, time is *real*, and, like everything that lies in time, we are consumed by it. In the second case, time is *ideal*; it lies within us. First of all then the question concerning a future after death falls away. For if I do not exist, then time no longer exists either. It is only a deceptive appearance, showing me time that would continue without me after my death; all three parts of time, past, present, and future, alike are my product, belong to me, but I do not belong to any one of them in preference to another. – Again,

91

---

[a] [Fichte, Schelling and Hegel; see the first essay in this volume, *Sketch of a history of the doctrine of the ideal and the real*]

another conclusion that might be drawn from the proposition that time does not accrue to the essence in itself of things would be that, in some sense, the past is *not* past, but that everything that ever really and truly was, at bottom must still be, since time really only resembles a waterfall in the theatre, which appears to stream downwards, while, as a mere wheel, it does not get anywhere. – Analogously, already in my chief work, I have compared space with a glass cut into facets, which lets us see what simply exists in countless replication. Indeed, if at the risk of skirting enthusiasm[a] we engage even more deeply in the matter, it can seem to us as though, when vividly bringing to mind our own remote past, we were immediately convinced that time does not touch the true essence of things but is only inserted between this essence and ourselves, as a mere medium of perception, after whose removal all would be there again. As, on the other hand, our faithful and vivid faculty of memory, within which what is long past maintains an unfading existence, testifies to the fact that equally within us there is something that does not age and consequently does not lie within the realm of time. –

The main tendency of the Kantian philosophy is to demonstrate the complete *difference between the real and the ideal*, after Locke had already paved the way for this. – Perfunctorily we can say: The *ideal* is the intuitive form that presents itself spatially, with all its perceivable qualities; the *real*, on the other hand, is the thing in, by and for itself,[b] independent of being represented in the head of another or in our own. But to draw the boundary between the two is difficult and yet is exactly what matters most. *Locke* had shown that everything in that form that is colour, sound, smoothness, roughness, hardness, softness, cold, heat, etc. (secondary qualities) is merely *ideal*, and so does not belong to the thing in itself, because in those qualities it is not the being and essence, but only the action of the thing, that is given to us, and rather an action determined in a very one-sided manner, namely action upon the very specifically determined receptivity of our five sense organs, by virtue of which, for example, sound does not affect the eye, and light does not affect the ear. Indeed, the action of bodies on the sense organs consists in putting them into the state of their characteristic activity, almost in the same way as when I pull the thread that makes a musical clock play. On the other hand, Locke left extension, shape, impenetrability, motion or rest, and number as the real pertaining to the thing itself – therefore he called these primary qualities. Now Kant, with infinitely superior thoughtfulness, subsequently showed that even these qualities do

---

[a] *Schwärmerei*   [b] *in, an und für sich selbst*

not belong to the purely objective essence of things, or the thing in itself, and therefore simply cannot be *real*, since they are conditioned by space, time, and causality. The latter, in accordance with their entire lawfulness and constitution, are given to us *prior to* all experience and are known precisely; thus they must lie within us preformed, as does the specific kind of receptivity and activity of each of our senses. Accordingly I have stated straightforwardly that those forms are the brain's share in intuition, as the specific sensations are those of the respective sense organs.[*,23] Already according to Kant, the purely objective essence of things, which is independent of our representing and its apparatus and which he calls the thing in itself, thus the actual real, is, in contrast to the ideal, something completely different from the form[a] that presents itself to us intuitively. 93 Actually, neither extension nor duration can be attributed to this essence, since it is supposed to be independent of space and time, although it imparts the power to exist to everything that has extension and duration. Even Spinoza generally has understood the matter, as can be seen from *Ethics* II, prop. 16 with the second corollary, and also prop. 18, scholium.

The real for Locke, as opposed to the ideal, is basically *matter*, stripped, to be sure, of all the qualities that he removes as secondary ones, that is, as conditioned by our sense organs; but nonetheless, in and for itself, as extended, etc., it is something existing, whose mere reflex, or image, is the representation within us. Here I remind the reader that I have explained (*On the Fourfold Root*, second edn., p. 77,[b] and, in less detail, in *The World as Will and Representation*, vol. 1, p. 9, and vol. 2, p. 48[c]) that the essence of matter consists solely in its *action*, hence that matter is causality through and through, and that, since in regard to matter conceived as such we abstract from all particular quality and thus from all specific manner of action, it is action or pure causality, lacking all specific determinations, causality in abstraction.[d] A more thorough understanding can be found in the passages quoted above. Although I was the first to provide the correct proof of it, *Kant* had already taught that all causality is only a form of our understanding, and hence exists only for and in the understanding. Consequently we now see Locke's alleged real, matter, in this way retreating altogether into the ideal and thus into the subject, that is, existing solely in and for

---

* Just as it is our eye that produces green, red, and blue, so it is *our brain* that produces *time*, *space*, and *causality* (whose objectified abstraction is *matter*). – My *intuition* of a body in space is the product of my sense- and brain-function together with *x*.

[a] *Gestalt* [b] [*FR*, 80 (Hübscher *SW* 1, 82)]
[c] [*WWR* 1, 29 (Hübscher *SW* 2, 10), and Hübscher *SW* 3, 52–3] [d] *Kausalität* in abstracto

representation. – In his exposition, Kant already surely took away the materiality of the real, or the thing in itself; but for him it remained only as a completely unknown *x*. However, I have at last established the truly *real*, or the thing in itself, which alone has real existence, independent of the representation and its forms, to be the *will* within us, which until then had unhesitatingly been attributed to the *ideal*. It can thus be seen that Locke, Kant, and I stand in close connection, in that we present, within the space of nearly two centuries, the gradual development of a coherent, indeed uniform train of thought. *David Hume* as well can be seen as a connecting link within this chain, although, properly speaking, only in respect to the law of *causality*. In reference to him and his influence I now must add the following to the above exposition.

94

Locke, as well as *Condillac*, following in his footsteps, and Condillac's disciples, show and explain that a cause outside of our body must correspond to the sensation occurring in a sense organ, and that, consequently, differences of the causes must correspond to differences of that effect (sensation), and finally, what these differences can possibly be; from this results the above-mentioned distinction between primary and secondary qualities. With that they have done enough and now an objective world exists for them in space, consisting of nothing but things in themselves, which may be without colour, without smell, without sound, neither warm nor cold, and so on, but nonetheless are extended, have shape, are impenetrable, movable, and countable. However, the axiom itself in virtue of which that transition from inner to outer and thus that whole derivation and establishment of things in themselves have happened, namely *the law of causality*, they have assumed to be self-evident, as had all previous philosophers, and have not subjected its validity to an examination. Now *Hume* directed his sceptical attack on to this by casting doubt on the validity of that law, because experience, from which, according to that very philosophy,[a] all our knowledge is supposed to derive, can never provide the causal connection itself, but always only the mere succession of states in time, thus never a consequence, but a mere sequence, which, precisely as such, always turns out to be only contingent, never necessary. This argument, repugnant to common sense, but not easily refuted, prompted *Kant* to investigate the true *origin* of the concept of causality. He found it to lie in the essential and innate form of our understanding itself, thus in the subject, but not in the object, since it was not taught to us from the outside. Now because of this that whole objective world of *Locke* and *Condillac* was drawn into the

95

[a] [Of Locke and followers]

subject again, since Kant had shown the key to it to be of subjective origin. For just as sensation is subjective, so now also the rule is subjective, according to which it is to be understood as the effect of a cause, since it is that cause alone that is intuited as the objective world. For the subject assumes an outside object only due to the peculiar feature of its intellect of presupposing a cause for every change, thus really projecting it from within itself, into a space ready for that purpose, which is itself also a product of the intellect's own and original constitution, just as the specific sensation in the sense organs, which initiates the entire process. Accordingly, Locke's objective world of things in themselves was transformed by *Kant* into a world of mere appearances in our cognitive apparatus, and this the more completely in that the space in which they present themselves, as well as the time in which they pass, were shown by him to be of undeniably subjective origin.

Despite all this *Kant*, just like *Locke*, still let the thing in itself persist, that is, something that existed independently of our representations, which provide us with mere appearances, and that lay at the basis of these very appearances. Now, as much as here too Kant was basically right, still no justification for it could be derived from the principles that he had put forward. Here therefore was the Achilles' heel of his philosophy; and, because of the proof of this inconsistency, it had to forfeit again the recognition of absolute validity and truth it had achieved. Nevertheless, on the whole, it was treated unjustly in this. For certainly the assumption of a thing in itself behind the appearances, of a real core under so many layers, is by no means untrue, since, on the contrary, its denial would be absurd. Only the manner in which Kant introduced such a thing in itself and tried to unite it with his principles was faulty. At bottom, therefore, it is only his exposition (taking this term in the broadest sense) of the matter, not the matter itself, which succumbed to the opponents. In this sense it could be claimed that the arguments used against him really were only directed at the man,[a] not the matter.[b] In any case, the Indian proverb again finds application here: 'No lotus without a stem.' Kant was guided by the truth, felt to be certain, that behind every appearance lies a being in itself from which it receives its existence, or that behind the representation lies a represented. However, he undertook to derive this from the given representation itself by including its laws, of which we are a priori conscious, yet which, exactly because they are a priori, cannot lead to something independent of, and different from, the appearance or representation, which is why we must take an altogether different route towards it. The inconsistencies in which Kant

96

<hr/>

[a] *ad hominem*   [b] *ad rem*

had entangled himself due to the faulty course he had chosen in this respect, were pointed out to him by G. E. Schulze, who in his ponderous and rambling manner discussed the matter, first anonymously in the *Aenesidemus*[a] (especially pp. 374–81) and later in his *Critique of Theoretical Philosophy*[b] (vol. 2, pp. 205ff.); against which Reinhold conducted Kant's defence, yet without any particular success, so that the matter had to end with 'This could be asserted and could not be refuted.'[c]

At this point I want to clearly highlight in my own way the real essence of the matter itself that lies at the basis of the entire controversy, independently of Schulze's conception of it. – *Kant* never provided a strict deduction of the thing in itself; on the contrary, he took it over from his predecessors, especially *Locke*, and retained it as something whose existence cannot be doubted since it is essentially self-evident; indeed, in a certain sense he was allowed to do so. For according to Kant's discoveries our empirical cognition contains one element that is demonstrably of subjective origin, and another for which this is not the case; the latter remains objective because there is no reason to think of it as subjective.* Accordingly, Kant's transcendental idealism denies the objective essence of things, or their reality independent of our comprehension of them, as far as the a priori[d] in our cognition extends, but no farther, because the reason for denial does not go farther; accordingly he allows what lies beyond to remain, that is, all those qualities of things that cannot be constructed a priori. For in no way can the entire essence of given appearances, that is, of the corporeal world, be a priori determined by us; on the contrary, only the universal form of its appearance can be thus determined, and this form can be derived from space, time, and causality, together with the entire lawfulness of these three forms. In contrast, what is left undetermined by all those a priori existing forms, thus what is contingent in respect to them, is precisely the manifestation of the thing in itself. Now the *empirical* content of the appearances,

97

---

* Each thing has *two kinds of qualities*: those that are a priori and those that can only be known a posteriori; the former spring from the intellect that comprehends them, the latter from the essence in itself of the thing, which is what we find in ourselves as the will.

[a] [Gottlob Ernst Schulze, *Aenesidemus, oder über die Fundamente der von dem Herrn Prof[essor] Reinhold in Jena gelieferten Elementar-Philosophie. Nebst einer Vertheidigung des Skepticismus gegen die Anmaaßungen der Vernunftkritik* (*Aenesidemus, or On the Foundations of the Elementary Philosophy offered by Professor Reinhold in Jena, Including a Defense of Skepticism against the Presumptuousness of the Critique of Reason*), Helmstedt, 1792 (originally published anonymously without author, place and publisher)]

[b] *Kritik der theoretischen Philosophie* [vol. 2, Hamburg: Carl Ernst Bohn, 1801]

[c] *haec potuisse dici, et non potuisse refelli* [Ovid, *Metamorphoses* I, 759; wording slightly changed]

[d] *das Apriori*

that is, every further determination of them, every physical quality present in them, cannot be known other than a posteriori; therefore, these empirical qualities (or rather their common source) remain in the thing in itself, as expressions of its very own essence, through the medium of all those a priori forms. Accordingly this a posteriori,[a] which comes forward in every appearance, covered as it were in the a priori, but which nonetheless imparts to every being its particular and individual character, is the *material*[b] of the world of appearance, in contrast to its *form*. Now this material can in no way be derived from the *forms* of appearance that adhere to the subject, the forms which Kant so thoroughly searched for and, by means of the mark of apriority, established with certainty. Rather it is left over after subtracting all that flows from these forms; thus it is found as a second, completely distinct element of empirical appearance and as an ingredient alien to those forms. On the other hand, it by no means originates in the free choice of the cognitive subject, but, on the contrary, often stands in opposition to it. In light of all this, Kant did not hesitate to leave this *material* of the appearance to the thing in itself, thus to regard it as entirely coming from the outside. For it must come from somewhere or, as Kant expresses himself, it must have some ground. For since we can by no means isolate such qualities that are knowable solely a posteriori and comprehend them as separate from and purified of the a priori certain qualities, since they always come forward as enveloped in these, Kant teaches that, indeed, we know the *existence* of things in themselves, but nothing beyond that, thus we only know *that* they are, but not *what* they are. Thus with him, the essence of things in themselves remains an unknown quantity, an x. For the *form* of appearance everywhere covers and conceals the essence of the thing in itself. At best this much can be said: Since those a priori forms, without distinction, accrue to all things as appearances, because they originate in our intellect, while things at the same time show significant differences, that which determines these differences, namely the specific diversity of things, is the thing in itself.

Viewed in this light, Kant's assumption and presupposition of things in themselves, notwithstanding the subjectivity of all our forms of cognition, seems perfectly legitimate and well founded. Nevertheless, it proves to be untenable if one closely examines its sole argument, namely the empirical content in all appearances, and traces it to its origin. For, indeed, empirical cognition and its source, intuitive representation, contain *material*, which is independent of the form of this cognition, of which we are a priori conscious. The next question is whether this matter is of objective or

[a] *dieses Aposteriori*   [b] *Stoff*

subjective origin, because only in the first case can it guarantee the thing in itself. Thus, if we follow it to its origin, we find it nowhere else but in our *sensation*; for it is an alteration occurring on the retina of the eye, or in the auditory nerve, or in the tips of the fingers that initiates the intuitive representation, that is, first puts into play the whole apparatus of our a priori ready forms of cognition, the result of which is the perception of an external object. For the *law of causality* initially is applied to that sensed alteration in the sense organ by means of a necessary and inevitable a priori function of the understanding; this law, with its a priori assurance and certainty, leads to a *cause* of that alteration, which, since it does not depend on the choice of the subject, now presents itself as something *external* to it.

99   This quality first receives its meaning[a] by virtue of the form of *space*, which, however, is likewise superimposed by our own intellect for this purpose. In this way, that necessarily assumed *cause* at once presents itself in intuition, as an *object* in space, which carries the alterations, effected in our sense organs by that cause, as its qualities. The reader will find this whole process presented thoroughly and in detail in the second edition of my treatise on the principle of sufficient reason, §21.[b] However, sensation, which provides the starting point and indisputably the whole *material* for empirical intuition, is something entirely subjective. And now, since all *forms* of cognition, by means of which objective, intuitive representation arises from that material and is projected outward, in accordance with Kant's absolutely correct proof, are of subjective origin as well, it is clear that the material as well as the form of intuitive representation originate in the subject. Accordingly, our entire empirical cognition is resolved into two components, both of which have their origin *within ourselves*, namely sensation and the forms, time, space, and causality, which are a priori given, and thus lie in the functions of our intellect, or brain. Kant had added yet another eleven categories of the understanding, which I have demonstrated to be superfluous and inadmissible. Consequently, intuitive representation and our empirical cognition, which is based on the former, in truth provide no data for inferring things in themselves and Kant, in accordance with his principles, was not entitled to assume such things. Like all previous philosophies, Locke's too had taken the law of causality as absolute and was, therefore, justified to infer from sensation to external objects that actually exist independently of us. However, this transition from the effect to the cause is the only way to arrive at what is external and objectively existing from what is internal and subjectively given. But after Kant had attributed

---

[a] *Bedeutung*   [b] [*FR*, 52ff. (Hübscher *SW* 1, 51ff.)]

the law of causality to the cognitive form of the subject, this path was no longer open to him. Moreover, he himself warned often enough against making transcendent use of the category of causality, that is, use that goes beyond experience and its possibility.

In fact, the thing in itself can never be reached in this way, and not at all on the path of purely *objective* cognition, which always remains representation, but as such is rooted in the subject and can never provide anything really different from representation. But we can only get to the thing in itself by *shifting the standpoint*, meaning, instead of, as has happened until now, always starting out from that which *represents*, for once starting out from what is *represented*. However, this is possible for all of us in regard to one thing alone, which is accessible to us also from within and thus is given to us in a twofold way. It is our own body, which in the objective world is present as representation in space, but at the same time makes itself known to our own *self-consciousness* as *will*. In that way the body provides the key, first for understanding all its actions and movements caused by external causes (here motives), which without this internal and immediate insight into their essence would remain as incomprehensible and inexplicable as the alterations, occurring in accordance with natural laws and as expressions of natural forces, in all other bodies given to us in objective intuition alone. Furthermore, it is pivotal for understanding the permanent *substratum* of all these actions in which their powers are rooted – that is, the body itself. This immediate cognition that all people have of the essence of their own given appearance, which is otherwise also given to them, like all others, only in objective intuition, must afterwards be transferred by analogy on to all other appearances given in the latter manner alone; and it then becomes the key to recognizing the inner essence of things, that is, the things in themselves. We can only reach such cognition in a way entirely different from purely *objective* cognition, which remains mere representation, by making use of the *self-consciousness* of the subject of cognition, that always occurs only as an animal individual, and making it the interpreter of the *consciousness of other things*, that is, of the intuiting intellect. This is the path I have taken and it is the only correct one, the narrow gateway to truth.

Instead of taking this path, people confused Kant's presentation with the essence of the matter, believed that refuting the former meant also refuting the latter, took what really were arguments against a person[a] for arguments against a subject matter,[b] and therefore, as a result of the attacks by Schulze, declared Kant's philosophy to be untenable. – As a result, the field was now

---

[a] *argumenta ad hominem*   [b] *argumenta ad rem*

open for sophists and windbags. The first of this class to appear on the scene was *Fichte*, who, since the thing in itself had been discredited, quickly fabricated a system without any thing in itself, and hence repudiated the assumption of anything that was not representation through and through, thus letting the cognitive subject be everything, or at least create everything from its own resources. For this purpose he at once abolished what was essential and most deserving in Kant's doctrine, the distinction between the a priori and the a posteriori, and thus between appearance and thing in itself, by declaring everything as a priori, naturally without any proofs for such an egregious assertion. Instead of these, he partly gave sophistical and, indeed, foolish pseudo-demonstrations, whose absurdity was hidden under the mask of profundity and of the incomprehensibility allegedly arising from it. And partly he appealed, openly and impudently, to intellectual intuition, that is, effectively to inspiration. This was certainly sufficient for a public lacking all power of judgement and unworthy of Kant; it took outbidding for outperforming and accordingly declared *Fichte* a far greater philosopher than Kant. Indeed, to this day there is no lack of philosophical authors who take pains to foist on to the new generation as well that false fame of Fichte, which has become a tradition, and quite seriously assure us that what *Kant* had only attempted was accomplished by *Fichte*: *he* was really the right one. Through their Midas judgement in the second instance, these gentlemen clearly show their utter inability to understand Kant at all and, in general, their deplorable lack of understanding in such a palpable way that hopefully the next generation, finally disappointed, will know better than to waste its time and corrupt its minds with their numerous histories of philosophy and other scribblings. – I want to take this oppor-

102   tunity to call to mind a short writing from which we can see what kind of impression Fichte's personal appearance and conduct had on unprejudiced contemporaries. It is called 'Cabinet of Berlin Characters'[a] and appeared in 1808 without place of publication; supposedly it is by *Buchholz*, but I am not sure about that. We should compare this with what the jurist *Anselm von Feuerbach* says about *Fichte* in his letters edited by his son in 1852;[b] also with *Schiller's and Fichte's Correspondence*,[c] 1847; and one will get a better idea of this pseudo-philosopher.[24]

---

[a] *Kabinet Berliner Charaktere* [*Kabinet Berlinischer Karaktere*, 1808; an anonymous publication without place or publisher, providing critical portraits of contemporary public characters in Berlin]
[b] [Ludwig Feuerbach, *Leben und Wirken Anselm von Feuerbachs*, Leipzig: Wigand, 1852]
[c] [*Schiller's und Fichte's Briefwechsel*, ed. J. G. Fichte, Berlin: Veit and Co., 1847]

Soon *Schelling*, worthy of his predecessor, followed in Fichte's footsteps, which, however, he abandoned in order to pronounce his own invention, the absolute identity of the subjective and the objective, or the ideal and the real, which implies that everything that rare minds such as Locke or Kant had separated by means of an unbelievable effort of ingenuity and reflection, had to be poured together again into the pap of that absolute identity. For the doctrine of these two thinkers can fittingly be called that of the *absolute diversity*[a] *of the ideal and the real, or the subjective and the objective.* But now aberrations followed on aberrations. Once incomprehensibility of speech was introduced by Fichte and semblance of profundity was put in place of thought, the seed was spread from which one corruption after the other, and ultimately the utter demoralization of philosophy that has come to pass in our day, was to arise, and through it that of the whole of literature.*,[25]

By now *Schelling* was followed by a philosophical ministerial creature,[b] namely *Hegel*, who, for political purposes, and through a blunder at that, was dubbed a great philosopher from above, a platitudinous, dull, loathsome-repulsive, ignorant charlatan, who, with unprecedented impudence, scribbled together folly and nonsense that was trumpeted by his 103
venal followers as immortal wisdom and accepted as such by dunces, whereby such a complete chorus of admiration arose as had never before been heard.**
The extended spiritual effect procured by force for this person has resulted in the intellectual ruin of a whole educated generation. The scorn of posterity awaits the admirers of that pseudo-philosophy, and the ridicule of the *neighbours* – so lovely to listen to – is already a prelude to that. – Or should it not sound sweet to my ears when the nation whose educated caste for thirty years has deemed my achievements nothing and less than nothing, worth not even a glance – earns from the neighbours the reputation of having revered, indeed, deified, for thirty years as highest and unprecedented wisdom what is utterly bad, absurd, nonsensical, but at the same time serves material interests? Without doubt, as a good patriot, I am also supposed to gush with praise for the Germans and Germanity, and rejoice in having belonged to this and no other nation? But it is as the Spanish proverb says: *Cada uno cuenta de la*

---

* Nowadays the study of the Kantian philosophy is still particularly useful for teaching how low the philosophical literature in Germany has sunk since the *Critique of Pure Reason*; so much are his profound inquiries in striking contrast with today's crude gibberish, at which we feel we are hearing hopeful candidates from one side and barbers' assistants from the other.

** See the preface to my 'Fundamental Problems of Ethics'. [*The Two Fundamental Problems of Ethics*, Preface to the first edition, 5–27]

[a] *Unterschiedlichkeit*   [b] *Ministerkreatur*

feria, como le va en ella. (Everybody reports about the fair depending on how he fared.) Go to the people's sycophants[a] and let yourself be praised. Efficient, coarse charlatans, puffed up by ministers and obediently scribbling nonsense, without mind and without merit, that is what belongs to the Germans, not men like myself. – This is the testimony that I must give them on parting. Wieland (*Letters to Merck*, p. 239)[b] calls it a misfortune to have been born a German; Bürger, Mozart, Beethoven, and many others would certainly have agreed with him; I do too. It depends on the fact that 'One must be a sage to recognize a sage',[c] or 'Only the mind understands the mind'.[d]

Among the most brilliant and meritorious sides of the Kantian philosophy is indisputably the Transcendental Dialectic, by means of which he undermined speculative theology and psychology to such an extent that since then for the life of us we have not been able to resurrect them. What a blessing for the human spirit! Or do we not see, during the entire period since the revival of the sciences down to Kant, the thoughts of even the greatest men go awry, indeed, often become completely distorted, as a result of those two absolutely unassailable presuppositions that paralyse the whole mind and that are first withdrawn from, and afterwards are dead to, all examination? Do the primary and essential fundamental views of ourselves and of all things not become wrongheaded and adulterated if we start out with the presupposition that everything is produced and arranged from the outside, according to concepts and well-thought-out designs, by a personal, and thus an individual being? Similarly, that the fundamental essence of a human being should be thinking and that he consisted of two completely heterogeneous parts that had come together and were soldered together without knowing how and now had to get along with each other as best they could in order soon to separate again from each other forever, whether they wanted to or not?[e] How strongly Kant's criticism of these ideas and their grounds has influenced all the sciences is obvious from the fact that since then those presuppositions, at least in higher German literature, occur at most in a figurative sense, but are no longer put forward seriously; instead one leaves them to the writings for the common people and the professors of philosophy, who earn their living with their help. In particular, our works in

---

[a] *Demokolaken*

[b] *Briefe an Merck* [*Briefe an Johann Heinrich Merck von Göthe, Herder, Wieland und anderen bedeutenden Zeitgenossen* (*Letters to Merck by Goethe, Herder, Wieland, and other important contemporaries*), ed. Karl Wagner, Darmstadt: Johann Philipp Diehl, 1835]

[c] σοφὸν εἶναι δεῖ τὸν ἐπιγνωσόμενον τὸν σοφόν [Diogenes Laertius, *Lives and Opinions of Eminent Philosophers* IX (Life of Xenophanes), 20]

[d] *il n'y a que l'esprit qui sente l'esprit* [Claude Adrien Helvétius, *De l'esprit* (*On Mind*) II, 3)]

[e] *nolentes volentes*

the natural sciences keep themselves free of such things, whereas the English ones degrade themselves in our view through idioms and diatribes aiming at them, or through apologies.*,26 Just before Kant, matters of course still 105 stood quite differently in this respect; thus we see the eminent *Lichtenberg*, whose education as a youth had been pre-Kantian, hold on to that opposition between soul and body seriously and with conviction in his essay on physiognomy, and thereby ruin his case.

Whoever considers the high value of the *Transcendental Dialectic* will not find it superfluous that I enter here into the particulars of it. Therefore, I first submit to the connoisseurs and enthusiasts of the critique of reason[a] the following attempt, namely to conceive the argument in the critique of rational theology quite differently and to criticize it accordingly – in the first edition, as it is only there included in full, whereas in the following ones it is castrated. The argument is criticized there on pp. 361ff. under the title 'paralogism of personality'.[b] For Kant's admittedly profound presentation of it is not only exceedingly subtle and difficult to understand, but it can also be charged with taking the object of self-consciousness, or, in Kant's language, of inner sense, all of a sudden and without any further warrant, as the object of a foreign consciousness, even of an external intuition, in order then to judge it in accordance with the laws and analogies of the corporeal world; it even ventures (p. 363)[c] to assume two different times, one in the consciousness of the judged subject, the other in that of the judging subject, that do not harmonize. – Thus I would give said argument concerning personality a quite different turn and present it accordingly in the following two propositions:

(1) In regard to all movement in general, whatever its nature, we can ascertain a priori that it first becomes perceivable by comparison with something at rest; from which it follows that the course of time, with everything in it, also could not be perceived unless there were something having no part in it and with whose rest we compare the movement.

---

* Since the above was written, things have changed here. As a result of the resurrection of the ancient and ten-times-exploded materialism philosophers from the pharmacy and the hospital have showed up, people who have not learnt anything but what belongs to their trade and who now, quite innocently and respectably, as if Kant were yet to be born, deliver their old-women's-speculation, argue about 'body and soul' and their relation to each other, indeed (believe it, posterity! [*credite posteri!*]), demonstrate the seat of aforesaid soul in the brain. Their presumption deserves the reprimand that you have to have learnt something in order to be allowed to join in the discussion and that they would act wisely not to expose themselves to unpleasant allusions to plaster ointment [*Pflasterschmieren*] and catechism.

[a] *Vernunftkritik*   [b] [*Critique of Pure Reason*, A361ff.]   [c] [A363]

Of course, we judge here in analogy with movement in space; but space and time must always serve to mutually elucidate each other, which is why we must represent time as well by means of the image of a straight line in order

106 to construct it a priori by comprehending it intuitively. For that reason, we cannot imagine that, if everything in our consciousness moved forward, simultaneously and jointly, in the flux of time simultaneously and together, this forward movement would nevertheless be perceivable; for this we must rather assume something fixed past which time flows with its content. Matter, as permanent substance underneath the change of accidents, achieves this for the intuition of outer sense, as indeed Kant outlines in the proof of the 'First Analogy of Experience', p. 183 of the first edition.[a] However, it is precisely in this passage that he makes the intolerable mistake, which I have admonished already elsewhere and which indeed contradicts his own doctrines, of claiming that time itself does not flow, but only the appearances within it. That this is fundamentally incorrect is proven by the utter certainty, innate in all of us, that even if all things in heaven and on earth suddenly stood still, time, undisturbed by that, would continue its course; so that if later nature once again would be set in motion, the question regarding the length of the pause that had occurred would in itself be capable of a perfectly precise answer. If it were otherwise, time would have to stop together with the clock or, if it ran, run with it. It is precisely this state of affairs, together with our certainty a priori about it, that irrefutably proves that time runs its course, and thus has its essence, in our head and not outside. – In the realm of external intuition, as I have said, it is matter that is permanent; in our argument about personality, on the other hand, we talk only about perception of *inner* sense, into which also that of outer sense is first taken up. For that reason I have said that if our consciousness, with its entire content, moved uniformly within the stream of time, we would not be able to notice this movement. Therefore, there must be something immovable in consciousness itself. However, this cannot be anything but the cognitive subject itself, which, unmoved and unchanged, watches the course of time and the change of its content. Before its gaze life runs its course to the end, like a drama. How little it itself takes part in this course becomes palpable for us when, in old age, we vividly imagine scenes from youth and childhood.

107   (2) Internally, in self-consciousness, or, to speak with Kant, through inner sense, I know myself solely in *time*. However, *objectively* considered,

[a] [A183]

there can be nothing persistent in mere time alone, because it presupposes duration, which in turn presupposes simultaneous existence, which again presupposes *space*. (The justification for this proposition is found in my treatise on the principle of sufficient reason, second edn., §18,[a] and also in *The World as Will and Representation*, second edn., vol. 1, §4, pp. 10, 11 and 531.)[b] In spite of this I actually find myself as the persistent substratum of my representations, remaining the same through all their change, which relates to these representations in the same way that matter relates to its changing accidents. As a consequence, it deserves, just like matter, the name of *substance* and, since it is not spatial, hence not extended, that of *simple substance*. However, since, as mentioned before, nothing persistent can occur on its own, yet the substance in question, on the other hand, is not perceived through outer sense and hence not in space, we must, in order to think ourselves nonetheless as something persistent in the face of the course of time, assume it to lie outside of time and thus say: Every object is in time, whereas the cognitive subject proper is not. Since outside of time there is also no cessation, or end, we would have in the cognitive subject in us a persisting substance that is neither spatial nor temporal, hence indestructible.

In order to demonstrate the argument about personality thus conceived to be a paralogism, we would have to say that its second proposition uses an empirical fact that can be contrasted with another fact, namely that the cognitive subject is bound up with life and even wakefulness and that, therefore, its persistence during both in no way proves that it could also exist apart from them. For this factual persistence for the duration of the conscious state is far removed, indeed, completely different[c] from the persistence of matter (this origin and sole realization of the concept of *substance*), which we know in intuition and of which we not only comprehend a priori its factual duration, but its necessary indestructibility and impossibility of annihilation. Yet it is in analogy with this truly indestructible substance that we wish to assume a *thinking*   108 *substance* within us that would then be certain of an endless continuation. Apart from the fact that the latter would be an analogy with a mere appearance (matter), the error committed by dialectical reason in the above proof consists in treating the persistence of the subject during the change in time of all its representations in the same way as the persistence

---

[a] [*FR*, 33–5 (Hübscher *SW* 1, 28–30)]   [b] [*WWR* 1, 30–2, 501–2 (Hübscher *SW* 2, 11–12, 559–60)]
[c] toto genere *verschieden*

of matter given to us in intuition. Thus reason combines both under the concept of substance in order now to attribute everything that it can say about matter a priori, albeit under the conditions of intuition, namely continuation through all time, to that supposedly immaterial substance. It does so despite the fact that the persistence of this immaterial substance is based only on the assumption that it itself does not lie in time at all, let alone in all of time, so that the conditions of intuition, as a result of which the indestructibility of matter is declared a priori, here are explicitly removed, namely spatiality. On this, however, the persistence of immaterial substance is founded (according to the aforementioned passages in my writings).

In regard to the proofs of the immortality of the soul from its assumed *simplicity* and ensuing *indissolubility*, through which the only possible way of extinction, the dissolution of the parts, is excluded, it can generally be said that all laws of coming-into-existence, passing-out-of-existence, alteration, persistence, etc., which we know, be it a priori or a posteriori, apply solely to the *corporeal world*, which is objectively given to us and in addition conditioned by our intellect. As soon as we leave that world behind and talk about *immaterial* beings, we are no longer justified in applying those laws and rules for the purpose of asserting how the coming-into-existence and passing-out-of-existence of such beings is possible or not, but are lacking any guiding principle. For this reason all such proofs of the immortality from the simplicity of the thinking substance are cut off. For the amphiboly lies in the fact that we speak about an immaterial substance and then insinuate the laws of material substance in order to apply them to the former.[27]

109   Meanwhile, the paralogism of personality, as I have conceived it, provides in its first argument the a priori proof that something persistent must exist in our consciousness; in the second argument it demonstrates it a posteriori. On the whole it seems that the truth usually found at the bottom of each error, and thus also that of rational psychology, has its root here. This truth is that, indeed, even in our empirical consciousness an eternal point can be demonstrated, but really only a point, and really just demonstrated without providing material for further proof. Here I refer to my own doctrine, in accordance with which the cognitive subject[a] is that which has all cognition, but is not cognized; nonetheless, we conceive it as the fixed point past which time flows with all representations, although this flow can

---

[a] *das erkennende Subjekt*

only be recognized in contrast to something permanent. I have called this the point of contact between the object and the subject. With me the subject of cognition, like the body, as whose brain function it presents itself objectively, is an appearance of the will. The latter, as the sole thing in itself, here is the substratum of the correlate of all appearances, that is, of the subject of cognition. –

If we now turn to rational cosmology, we find in its antinomies incisive expressions of the perplexity that springs from the principle of sufficient reason and from times immemorial has driven people to philosophize. The purpose of the following account is to emphasize such perplexity in a slightly different manner from Kant's, more distinctly and more plainly; it will not operate, as the Kantian account does, merely dialectically with abstract concepts, but will directly address itself to intuitive consciousness.

Time cannot have a beginning, and no *cause* can be the first. Both are a priori certain, and so indisputable; for all beginning is in time, thus presupposes it; and every cause must have an earlier one behind it whose effect it is. Then how could a first beginning of the world and of things have occurred? (Admittedly, the first verse of the Pentateuch then appears to be begging the question[a] and, to be sure, in the most literal sense of the word.) But, on the other hand, if there had *not* been a first beginning, then the current actual present could not be *only just now*, but would have *already* existed *long ago*. For between the present and the first beginning we must assume some interval, yet a definite and limited one, which, however, will move back with it if we deny the beginning, that is, move it back into infinity. But even *if* we posit a first beginning, that does not effectively help us; for, even if we have arbitrarily cut off the causal chain, then mere time will straight away prove itself troublesome to us. That is to say, the continuously renewed question 'Why did that first beginning not occur already earlier?' will step by step push it back in beginningless time, so that the chain of causes lying between such a beginning and us is drawn to such length that it will never be capable of growing long enough to reach down to the current present, and accordingly it would *still not* have reached it. But that is contradicted by the fact that the present now really *exists* and even constitutes our only given[b] in the calculation. However, the justification for that uncomfortable question above arises from the fact that the first begin-ning as such does not presuppose a previous cause and for that reason could just as well have occurred trillions[c] of years earlier. For if it needed no cause for its occurrence, then it did not have to wait for one and accordingly was

110

---

[a] *petitio principii*   [b] *Datum*   [c] *Trillionen*

bound to have occurred already infinitely earlier, since nothing was there to stop it. For just as nothing may precede the first beginning as its cause, so nothing may precede it as its hindrance; thus it has absolutely nothing to wait for and never comes early enough. Therefore, at whatever point in time we might posit it, we can never comprehend why it should not have existed much earlier. This, therefore, pushes it ever farther backwards. However, since time itself can never have a beginning, an infinite time, an eternity, has elapsed down to the present moment; thus, pushing back the beginning of the world is without end, so that every causal chain turns out too short, as a result of which we then never get from the first beginning to the present. This results from the lack of a given and fixed starting point (*point d'at-tache*); therefore, we must arbitrarily assume such a point somewhere, which, however, perpetually retreats before our hands, upwards into infinity. – Such is the result if we posit a *first beginning* and start from it; we never get *down* from it *to the present*.

III

If, conversely, we start from the actually given *present*, we never arrive at the *first beginning*, as already stated, because every cause to which we ascend must always have been the effect of a previous one, which itself is in the same position in turn; and this can never reach an end. Therefore, now the world becomes beginningless for us, like infinite time itself, and then our power of imagination tires and our understanding finds no satisfaction.

These two antithetical views can thus be compared to a stick whose one end, whichever one, we can conveniently grasp while the other one always extends itself into infinity. The essence of the matter can be summed up in the proposition that time, as absolutely infinite, always turns out to be much too great for a world within it that is assumed to be *finite*. At bottom, the truth of the 'antithesis' in the Kantian antinomy here proves itself again, because, if we start out from what alone is certain and actually given, the really present, then beginninglessness[a] results. On the other hand, the first beginning is merely an arbitrary assumption that as such cannot be made to harmonize with that which has alone been said to be certain and actual, the present. – Incidentally, we must look at these considerations as uncovering the inconsistencies that arise from the assumption of the absolute reality of time and consequently as confirmations of Kant's fundamental doctrine.

The question whether the world is limited or unlimited in regard to *space* is not transcendent as such, but rather empirical in itself, since the matter still lies within the realm of possible experience, which only our own physical constitution prevents us from making actual. A priori there is no

[a] *Anfangslosigkeit*

demonstrably certain argument here, neither for one nor for the other alternative; thus the matter really resembles an antinomy insofar as significant disadvantages arise with the first as with the second assumption. For a limited world in an infinite space, and be it ever so large, shrinks to an infinitely small size, and we ask, For what purpose does the rest of the space exist? On the other hand, we cannot conceive that no fixed star would be the outermost in space. – By the way, the planets of such a star would have a starry heaven only during one half of their year, but during the other half a heaven without stars – which would have to make an eerie impression on the inhabitants. Correspondingly, that question can also be expressed as follows: Is there a fixed star whose planets are in this predicament or not? Here the question proves to be evidently empirical.

In my 'Critique of the Kantian Philosophy'[a] I have demonstrated the whole assumption of the antinomies to be false and illusory. On proper reflection, everyone will recognize in advance that it is impossible that concepts that are correctly derived from appearances and their a priori certain laws should lead to contradictions when they are, in accordance with the laws of logic, combined in judgements and conclusions. For then there would have to be contradictions in the intuitively given appearance itself or in the lawful connection of its elements, which is an impossible assumption. For the intuitive as such knows no contradiction; in reference to it, contradiction has neither meaning nor significance. For contradiction exists only in abstract cognition of reflection; we might be able, openly or covertly, to posit something and simultaneously not to posit it, that is, to contradict ourselves; but nothing actual can be and not be at the same time. Of course, Zeno the Eleatic, with his well-known sophisms, wanted to prove the opposite of the above, as did Kant with his antinomies. Hence I refer to my critique of the latter.

I have already touched in general upon Kant's service to *speculative theology*. In order to emphasize it still more, I will now, in the greatest brevity, attempt to make the essence of the matter comprehensible in my own way.

In the Christian religion the existence of God is an established fact elevated beyond all investigation. That is as it should be, for there it belongs and is established through revelation. Therefore, I regard it as a blunder of the rationalists when they try in their dogmatic theories to demonstrate God's existence other than from Scripture; in their innocence they do not know how dangerous this pastime is. Philosophy, on the other hand, is a

112

113

---

[a] [i.e. the Appendix to *WWR* I]

science and as such possesses no articles of faith; therefore, nothing in philosophy can be assumed as existing except what is either empirically immediately given or demonstrated through indubitable conclusions. These, of course, people believed they already possessed when Kant disappointed the world in this respect and explained the impossibility of such proofs with such certainty that since then no philosopher in Germany has tried again to establish them. He was absolutely justified in doing so; indeed, he did something highly meritorious; for a theoretical dogma that sometimes ventures to brand everybody as a rogue who does not accept it surely deserves that we seriously put it to the test once and for all.

The case now with those alleged proofs is the following. Since the *actuality* of God's existence cannot be shown by empirical evidence, the next step really would have been to account for its *possibility*, in the course of which we would already have encountered difficulties enough. Instead, people attempted to prove its *necessity*, thus to establish God as a *necessary being*. Now *necessity*, as I have demonstrated often enough, is nothing but the dependence of an effect on its cause, thus the occurrence or positing of an effect because the cause is given. For this people had the choice between the four forms of the principle of sufficient reason demonstrated by me, of which they found only the first two to be useful. Therefore, two theological proofs emerged, the cosmological and the ontological proof, the one in accordance with the principle of sufficient reason of becoming (cause), the other in accordance with that of the sufficient reason of knowing. The first one, according to the law of *causality*, will present the *necessity* in question as a *physical* one by conceiving of the world as an *effect* that must have a *cause*. This cosmological proof is then joined for support by the physico-theological one. The cosmological argument becomes strongest in Wolff's version of it, as a result expressed in the following manner: 'If something exists, then an absolutely necessary being also exists'[a] – to be understood either as the given itself or as the first of the causes through which it comes into being. The latter is then assumed. This proof, first of all, shows its weak point by being an inference from the consequent to the ground, a type of conclusion for which logic already denies all claims to certainty. Next it ignores that we can think something as *necessary* only if it is the consequent, not insofar as it is the ground of something else given. Furthermore, applied in this way, the law of causality proves too much;

114

---

[a] [Paraphrase of Christian Wolff, *Theologia naturalis* (*Natural Theology*), Part I, ch. 1, §58: '*Mundus existere hic non potest, nisi existat ens aliud necessarium ab ipso diversum.*' (The world cannot exist, if another, necessary being does not exist.)]

for if it had to guide us from the world to its cause, then it does not allow us to stop at this, but leads us further back to the cause of that, and so on remorselessly into infinity.[a] Its essence implies this. And we are in the same position as Goethe's magician's apprentice, whose creature, it is true, starts on command but does not stop again. In addition, the force and validity of the law of causality extends only to the *form* of things, not their matter. It is the guiding principle of the change of forms and nothing more; matter remains untouched by all their coming-into-existence and passing-out-of-existence, which we understand prior to all experience and thus know with certainty. Finally, the cosmological proof is subject to the transcendental argument that the law of causality demonstrably is of subjective origin and thus is applicable only to *appearances* for our intellect, not to the essence of *things in themselves.*[*][,28] – As mentioned before, the *physico-theological* proof is added for support to the cosmological one, aiming to furnish the latter's assumption with proof, confirmation, plausibility, colour, and shape at the same time. However, it can only act under the condition of that first proof, whose elucidation and amplification it is. Its method consists in enhancing that presupposed first cause of the world into a being that knows and wills by attempting to establish this ground by means of induction from the many consequents that can be explained through such a ground. However, induction can provide at most strong probability, never certainty; moreover, as mentioned, the whole proof is dependent on the first one. However, if we dwell more closely and seriously on this ever so popular physico-theology and examine it in the light of my philosophy, it turns out to be the explication of a false basic view of nature, which reduces the *immediate* appearance, or objectivation, of the will to a mere *mediate* one; thus, instead of recognizing in natural beings the original,

115

---

* Taking things realistically and objectively, it is clear as daylight that the world *sustains itself*; organic beings persist and propagate by virtue of their inner, intrinsic [*selbsteigenen*] vital force; inorganic bodies have within them the forces of which physics and chemistry are merely the description; and the planets proceed in their course from inner forces by virtue of inertia and gravitation. Thus for its subsistence the world needs no one outside itself. For this is *Vishnu*.

But now to say that at one point in time this world, with all its inherent forces, did not exist but was created out of nothing by an alien force lying outside of it – that is a wholly idle notion incapable of proof, the more so as all its forces are bound up with matter, whose coming-into-being or passing-out-of-being we cannot even think.

This conception of the world lasts until *Spinozism*. That human beings in their anguish have thought up beings everywhere that rule the forces of nature and their course in order to be able to invoke them – is completely natural. The Greeks and Romans, however, were content to let the matter rest with the ruling of each being in its own domain; it did not occur to them to say that one of them had made the world and the forces of nature.

[a] *in infinitum*

primordially powerful, cognitionless and for that reason unfailingly certain action of the will, it interprets it as merely secondary, occurring only in the light of cognition and guided by motives; accordingly, what is driven from the inside out is conceived as framed, modelled, and carved from the outside. For if the will, as the thing in itself, which is *not* at all representation, in the act of its objectivation, enters from its original nature into representation, and we approach what presents itself in representation under the condition that it has been produced in the world of representation, and thus as a result of *cognition*, then it presents itself as possible only by means of an excessively perfect cognition that takes in all objects and their connections at a glance, that is, as the work of supreme wisdom. Here I refer to my treatise *On Will in Nature*, especially pp. 43–62,[a] under the rubric 'Comparative Anatomy', and to my chief work, vol. 2, beginning of ch. 26.

116

As mentioned before, the second theological proof, the *ontological* one, does not take the law of causality as its guiding principle, but the principle of sufficient reason of knowing, making the necessity of God's existence a *logical* one. For here God's existence is supposed to arise as the result of merely analytical reasoning[b] from the concept of *God*, so that this concept could not be made the subject of a proposition that denied his existence, since that would contradict the subject of the proposition. That is logically correct, but is also very natural and a conjuror's trick easy to see through. For after introducing the predicate of existence into the subject by means of manipulating the concept of 'perfection' or 'actuality', needed as the middle term,[c] we cannot fail to find it there again subsequently and to expose[d] it through an analytical judgement. However, this in no way demonstrates the justification for asserting the whole concept; rather, it either was completely arbitrarily invented or introduced by the cosmological proof, in which everything is reduced to physical necessity. Christian Wolff seems to have recognized this since in his metaphysics he makes use of the cosmological argument alone and explicitly says so. One can find the ontological proof closely examined and assessed in the second edition of my treatise *On the Fourfold Root of the Principle of Sufficient Reason*, §7, which therefore I refer to here.[29]

To be sure, both theological proofs support each other, but nonetheless they cannot stand up. The cosmological proof has the advantage of justifying how it has arrived at the concept of a God and now makes this concept plausible with the help of its adjunct, the physico-theological proof. The ontological proof, on the other hand, cannot show at all how it arrived at its concept of a most real being, thus either pretends that it is innate or borrows it

---

[a] [*WN*, 351–70 (Hübscher *SW* 4, 36–58)]　　[b] *Urtheilen*　　[c] *terminus medius*　　[d] *exponirt*

from the cosmological proof and then tries to hold it up through lofty 117
sounding propositions about a being that cannot be thought except as
existing, whose existence is already contained in its concept, and so on.
Meanwhile, we shall not deny the glory of sagacity and subtlety to the
invention of the ontological proof when considering the following. In order
to explain a given existence we demonstrate its cause, in relation to which it
then presents itself as necessary, which counts as explanation. However, this
path, as has been sufficiently shown, leads to an infinite regress[a] and can
therefore never reach anything final that would provide a fundamental
ground of explanation. Now things would be different if the *existence* of
any being could actually be deduced from its *essence*, hence its mere concept
or definition. For then it would be recognized as a *necessary* one (which here,
as everywhere else, simply says 'something following from its *ground*') without being bound to anything other than its own concept, hence without its
necessity being merely transitory and momentary, or a necessity itself conditioned and thus leading to endless series, as *causal* necessity always is.
Rather, the mere cognitive ground[b] would then transform itself into a real
ground,[c] that is, a cause, and thus be perfectly suited to provide the ultimate
and hence fixed starting point for all causal series; we would then have what
we are looking for. However, we have seen above that all this is illusory; and it
is really as if Aristotle had already wanted to avoid such a sophism when he
said: 'Existence pertains in no way to essence.'[d] (*Posterior Analytics* II, 7.)
Unconcerned about this, *Descartes* later established the concept of God as one
that achieved what was required, after Anselm of Canterbury had paved the
way for such a line of thought. However, *Spinoza* established the concept of
world as the solely existing substance, which thus would be the cause of itself,[e]
that is, 'what exists through itself and is conceived through itself, therefore
needs no other thing in order to exist'.[f] To such an established world he then
awards, honorarily,[g] the title God[h] – in order to satisfy all people. However, it
is still the same sleight of hand[i] that tries to show the logically necessary as the 118
actually necessary and that, together with other similar deceptions, finally
caused Locke's great investigation into the origin of concepts, with the help of
which the foundation of the critical philosophy was laid. A more detailed
presentation of the method of those two dogmatists is contained in my
treatise on the principle of sufficient reason,[j] in the second edition, §§7 and 8.

---

[a] *regressus in infinitum*   [b] *Erkenntnißgrund*   [c] *Realgrund*
[d] τὸ δὲ εἶναι οὐκ οὐσία οὐδενί; *ad nullius rei essentiam pertinet existentia*   [e] *causa sui*
[f] *quae per se est et per se concipitur, quamobrem nulla alia re eget ad existendum* [partial quote from *Ethics* I,
    definition 3]
[g] *honoris causa*   [h] *Deus*   [i] *tour de passe-passe*   [j] [*FR*, 14–22 (Hübscher *SW* I, 9–17)]

Now after Kant, by means of his critique of speculative theology, had sounded the death-knell to this method, he had to try to soften its impression, thus to administer a sop[a] to it as an anodyne,[b] analogous to the method of Hume, who, in the last of his *Dialogues on Natural Religion*, which are as worth reading as they are inexorable, informs us that everything had been just a joke, a mere logical exercise.[c] In accordance with that, Kant provided, as a substitute for the proofs of God's existence, his postulate of practical reason and ensuing moral theology, which, without any claim to objective validity for knowledge, or theoretical reason, was to have complete validity in respect to acting, or practical reason, whereby a faith without knowledge was grounded – so that people at least could put their hands on something. If well understood, his account says nothing other than that the assumption of a just God who rewards and punishes after death is a useful and adequate *regulative schema*[d] for the purpose of interpreting the serious, deeply felt ethical significance of our conduct and also of guiding this conduct itself; thus in a sense it is an allegory of truth, so that, in this respect, which is the only one that ultimately matters, that assumption could represent the place of truth, even if theoretically, or objectively, it is not justifiable. – An analogous schema of the same tendency, but containing much more truth, greater plausibility, and thus more immediate value, is Brahmanism's doctrine of retributive metempsychosis, according to which some day we must be reborn in the shape of every being injured by us in order then to suffer the same injury. – Therefore, Kant's moral theology has to be taken in the specified sense by considering that he himself was not allowed to express himself in such outright terms about the actual matter as happens here, but, by establishing the monstrosity of a *theoretical* doctrine of mere *practical* validity, counted on the more judicious people to take it with a grain of salt.[e] Hence the theoretical and philosophical writers of the recent period, which is alienated from the Kantian philosophy, have mostly tried to make it appear as if Kant's moral theology were an actual dogmatic theism, a new proof of the existence of God. However, that is not at all what it is; rather it is valid solely within morality, merely for the purpose of morality, and not a straw's breadth further.[30]

Not even the professors of philosophy remained content with this for long, although they were greatly embarrassed by Kant's critique of speculative theology. For from time immemorial they had recognized their particular vocation in demonstrating the existence and qualities of God and making him the main subject of their philosophizing. Thus, when Scripture teaches that

---

[a] *Besänftigungsmittel*   [b] *Anodynon* [painkiller, soothing agent]   [c] *exercitium logicum*
[d] *regulatives Schema*   [e] *granum salis*

God feeds the ravens in the field, I must add: and the professors of philosophy at their lecterns. Indeed, to this day they assert quite brazenly that the absolute[a] (as is well known, the newfangled title for the good Lord) and its relation to the world is the real subject matter of philosophy; and they are still occupied with determining it more closely, picturing it, and fantasizing about it. For the governments, which provide the money for such philosophizing, certainly want to see good Christians and keen churchgoers emerge from the philosophical lecture-halls. How then must those gentlemen of lucrative philosophy have felt when Kant had moved their conception so far out of place, through the proof that all proofs of speculative theology are untenable and that all knowledge pertaining to their chosen subject is absolutely inaccessible to our intellect? Initially they had tried to help themselves through the well-known household remedy of ignoring, but then also of denying; but that did not stand the test in the long run. Thus they applied themselves to the assertion that although God's existence was not capable of any proof, it did not need one either; for it was self-evident, the most settled matter in the world, we could not doubt it at all, we had a 'consciousness of God',[*,31] our reason was the organ for immediate cognitions of other-worldly[b] things, reason immediately *discerned* the teachings about such things, and that was precisely why it was called *reason* or *discernment!*[c] (I kindly ask the reader to consult my treatise on the principle of sufficient reason[d] in the second edn., §34, and my *Fundamental Problems of Ethics*, pp. 148–54,[e] and finally my *Critique of the Kantian Philosophy*, pp. 574–5.[f]) However, according to others, reason provided mere presentiments; and still others even had intellectual intuitions! Yet again others invented absolute thought, that is, thinking that does not require people to look at things but, with divine omniscience, determine once and for all how they are. This is unquestionably the most convenient among all those inventions. But all of them resorted to the word 'absolute', which is nothing but precisely the cosmological proof in a nutshell, or rather so heavily contracted that, having become microscopic, it escapes the

120

---

* Recently we have received a curious figurative presentation of the *genesis* of this consciousness of God, namely a copper engraving showing us a mother who drills her three-year-old child, kneeling on the bed with its little hands folded, into praying – certainly a frequent occurrence that precisely constitutes the genesis of the consciousness of God. For it cannot be doubted that, after the brain has been moulded in this way during its most tender age, the stage of its first growth, the consciousness of God has become embedded as firmly as if it were actually inborn.

[a] *das Absolutum*   [b] *überweltlichen*
[c] [There is a play on words here that cannot be rendered in English, namely the similarity of the words *vernehmen* (to hear, perceive, discern) and *Vernunft*]
[d] [*FR*, 105–22 (Hübscher *SW* 1, 110–29)]   [e] [*BM*,149–50 (Hübscher *SW* 4, 147–8)]
[f] [*WWR* 1, 550–2 (Hübscher *SW* 2, 617–18)]

eye, slips through unnoticed and is passed off as something self-evident. For since Kant's rigorous examination[a] it dares not be seen in its true form, as I have explained more closely in the second edition of my treatise on the principle of sufficient reason, pp. 36ff.[b] and also in my *Critique of the Kantian Philosophy*, second edition, p. 544.[c] I can no longer tell who was the first, roughly fifty years ago, to use the trick of smuggling in *incognito* the exploded and proscribed cosmological proof under the exclusive name of the *absolute*; but the trick was wholly appropriate for the capabilities of the public, for to this day the absolute is taken at face value. In short, the professors of philosophy, despite the critique of reason and its proofs, have never lacked authentic news about God's existence and his relation to the world; and to impart such news at length is what philosophizing should properly consist in, according to them. Yet, as we say, 'you get what you pay for';[d] and that is what this God is like who for them is self-evident: he does not hold water.[e] For that reason they keep him behind a hill, or rather behind a resounding edifice of words, so that we can see hardly a tip of him. If we could only force them to explain themselves clearly as to how the word God is to be understood, then we would see whether he is self-evident. Not even naturing nature[f] (which their God often is in danger of merging into) is self-evident, since we see Leucippus, Democritus, Epicurus, and Lucretius construct the world without it. But these men, despite all their errors, were worth more than a legion of weathervanes, whose philosophy-for-a-living[g] turns with the wind. However, naturing nature is still far from being God. Rather, its concept contains the realization that behind the ever so fleeting and restlessly changing appearances of natured nature[h] an everlasting and indefatigable power must be hidden, in virtue of which those appearances constantly renew themselves, while this power itself would not be affected by their extinction. Just as natured nature is the subject of physics, so is naturing nature that of metaphysics. The latter will lead us to realize that we ourselves too belong to nature and, therefore, possess in ourselves not only the closest and most distinct specimen of natured nature as well as naturing nature, but also the only one accessible *from within*. Since serious and careful reflection about ourselves lets us then recognize the *will* as the core of our being, we have in that an immediate

---

[a] *examen rigorosum*   [b] [*FR*, 41–3 (Hübscher *SW* 1, 38–40)]
[c] [*WWR* 1, 513–14 (Hübscher *SW* 2, 574)]
[d] 'kupfernes Geld, kupferne Waare' ['copper money, copper ware'; version of old German proverb with Latin origin, mostly in the form 'kupfernes Geld, kupferne Seelmess' (requiem)]
[e] [literally: He has neither hand nor foot (he makes no sense)]   [f] *natura naturans* [creating nature]
[g] *Erwerbs-Philosophie*   [h] *natura naturata* [created nature]

revelation of naturing nature, which afterwards we are justified in transferring on to all other beings, known to us only from one side. Thus we then arrive at the great truth that naturing nature, or the thing in itself, is the will in our heart, and natured nature, or the appearance, is the representation in our head. But apart from this result this much is obvious, that the mere distinction between naturing nature and natured nature is far from being theism; indeed, it is not even pantheism since for this (if it is not to be mere empty talk) certain moral qualities would have to be added that obviously do not belong to the world, for example, benevolence, wisdom, blessedness, and so on. Moreover, pantheism is a self-defeating concept, because the concept of a God presupposes a world different from him as an essential correlate. If, on the other hand, the world is supposed to take over his role, then an absolute world without God remains; hence pantheism is only a euphemism for atheism. However, the expression of pantheism for its part works under false pretences by assuming in advance that theism is self-evident, thereby cleverly evading the point that 'Proof is incumbent upon the person who makes a claim',[a] whereas the so-called atheism possesses the right of first occupancy[b] and first has to be driven from the field by theism. I venture here the remark that human beings come into the world uncircumcised and consequently not as Jews. – However, even the assumption of a cause different from the world is still not theism. This requires not only a cause different from the world, but an intelligent, that is, knowing and willing, thus personal, and hence individual cause of the world; only such a cause is designated by the word God. An impersonal God is no God at all, but merely a misused word, a non-concept,[c] a contradiction in terms,[d] a shibboleth for professors of philosophy, who, after having had to give up the thing, try hard to slip in the word. On the other hand, the personality, that is, the self-conscious individuality, which first *knows* and then *wills* according to what is known, is a phenomenon that is familiar to us exclusively from the animal nature that exists on our small planet and is so intimately connected with it that we are not only not justified, but also not even capable of thinking it as separate from and independent of this nature. Yet to assume a being of this kind as the origin of nature itself, indeed, of all existence in general, is a fantastic and enormously daring idea that would amaze us if we heard about it for the first time and if it had not, through earliest inculcation and constant repetition, become familiar to us, indeed, second nature, and I almost want to say, a fixed idea. And so I want to mention incidentally that nothing has attested for me

122

123

---

[a] *affirmanti incumbit probatio*   [b] *jus primi occupantis*   [c] *Unbegriff*   [d] *contradictio in adjecto*

to the authenticity of *Caspar Hauser*[a] as much as the statement that the so-called natural theology, as presented to him, was not particularly evident to him, as one should have expected. Moreover (according to the 'Letters of Lord Stanhope to the school teacher Meyer'[b]), he professed a strange veneration for the sun. – Thus to teach in philosophy that this fundamental theological idea is self-evident and reason is just the capability to immediately conceive it and recognize it as true, is an impertinent pretence. Not only must such an idea not be assumed without the most fully valid proof in philosophy, but even for religion it is not at all essential. This is attested by the religion that has the greatest number of followers on earth – now numbering three hundred and seventy million[32] – ancient, deeply moral, indeed ascetic Buddhism, which even feeds the most numerous clergy. Buddhism does not allow for such an idea, on the contrary, it expressly abominates it and is, most avowedly,[c] after our expression, atheistic.*

---

* 'The Zaradobura, Supreme Rahan (high priest) of the Buddhists in Ava, in his essay about his religion that he gave to a Catholic bishop, counts among the six damnable heresies also the doctrine that a being exists that created the world and all things in the world and that alone is worthy of being worshipped.' Francis Buchanan, 'On the Religion [and Literature] of the Burmas', *Asiatic Researches*, vol. 6 [1809], p. 268. It is also worth citing what is mentioned in the same collection, vol. 15 [1825], p. 148 [Kishen Kant Bose, 'Some Account of the Country of Bhútán'], namely that the Buddhists do not bow their head in front of any divine image, citing as a reason that the primal being penetrates all of nature and hence is also in their heads. Similarly worth mentioning is that the erudite orientalist and Petersburg academic J. J. Schmidt, in his *Forschungen im Gebiete der älteren Bildungsgeschichte Mittelasiens*, Petersburg 1824 [Isaac Jacob Schmidt, *Forschungen im Gebiete der älteren religiösen, politischen und literärischen Bildungsgeschichte der Völker Mittel-Asiens, vorzüglich der Mongolen und Tibeter* (*Research in the Area of the Older Religious, Political, and Literary Educational History of the Peoples of Central Asia, in particular of the Mongols and the Tibetans*)], p. 180, says: 'The system of Buddhism knows no eternal, uncreated, single divine being that existed before all times and created everything visible and invisible. This idea is quite foreign to it, and one finds not the slightest trace of it in the Buddhist books. Similarly there is no creation', and so on. – Where is now the 'consciousness of God' of the philosophy professors, pressed hard by Kant and the truth? How can this be brought into agreement with the fact that the language of the Chinese, who make up roughly two fifths of the whole human race, has no expressions for *God* and *creating*? So that already the first verse of the Pentateuch cannot be translated into it, to the great perplexity of the missionaries, whom *Sir George Staunton* intended to help with a special book, called: *An Inquiry into the Proper Mode of Rendering the Word God in Translating the Sacred Scriptures into the Chinese Language*, London 1848. [Here Schopenhauer's German rendering of the English title follows. Schopenhauer is mistaken about the author of this book. It is not the orientalist George Staunton (1781–1859), but the British missionary in China, Walter Henry Medhurst (1796–1857). The book was published in Shanghai: London Missionary Society Press, 1848]

[a] [Caspar Hauser (1812?–33), a foundling who claimed to have grown up in a dark cell without access to the outside world; as the prototype of a feral child, he was and still is an object of fascination. Schopenhauer compares himself to Hauser at the end of this essay. See also *WN*, Preface, 307 (Hübscher SW 4, xii)]

[b] *Briefe des Grafen Stanhope an den Schullehrer Meyer* [Philip Henry, Earl of Stanhope adopted Caspar Hauser and eventually had a friend, Johann Georg Meyer in Ansbach, look after him.]

[c] *ex professo*

According to the above, anthropomorphism is an absolutely essential 124 characteristic of theism. And that consists not only in the human form, and not even solely in the human affects and passions, but in the basic phenomenon itself, namely in that of a will equipped with an intellect for guidance, a phenomenon known to us, as mentioned, merely from animal nature, and most perfectly from human nature, and which can be conceived solely as individuality which, when it is rational, is called personality. This is also confirmed by the expression 'as God liveth';[a] for he is a living being, that is, one that wills with cognition.[b,33] And for that very reason a heaven belongs to God, where he sits enthroned and rules. Precisely for this reason, rather than because of the expression in the book of Joshua,[c] the Church immediately greeted the Copernican cosmological system with such rage; and, accordingly, a hundred years later we find Giordano Bruno the advocate of that system along with pantheism. Attempts to purify theism of anthropomorphism, while imagining that they touch only the shell, in reality strike at its innermost essence; by trying to conceive their object in the abstract, they sublimate it into a vague hazy form whose contour, in the attempt to avoid the human form, gradually dissolves completely, whereby the infantile fundamental idea itself finally evaporates into nothing. The rationalist theologians, for whom such attempts are characteristic, can be accused of flatly contradicting Holy Writ, which says: 'So God created man in His own image; in the image of God created He him.'[d] Thus 125 let us get rid of the jargon of the philosophy professors! There is no other God than God, and the Old Testament is his revelation, especially the Book of Joshua.[*,34]

In a certain sense we could, with *Kant*, call theism a practical postulate, but in a quite different sense than meant by him. For theism, indeed, is not a product of *cognition*, but of the *will*. If it were originally *theoretical*, then how could all its proofs be so untenable? However, it springs from the will in the following manner. The constant need that now heavily frightens, now violently moves the heart (will) of human beings and keeps them in a state of fear and hope, while the things *about* which they hope and fear are not in their power and the connection of the causal chains that bring about these things can be traced by their cognition only for a short distance – this

---

* Philosophers and theologians have stripped the God who was originally Jehovah of one layer after the other, until in the end nothing but the word was left.

[a] *So wahr Gott lebt* [Job 27:2, Luther's translation]   [b] *mit Erkenntniß Wollendes*
[c] [See Joshua 2:11 and 10:11]   [d] [Genesis 1:27]

need, this constant fear and hope, cause them to hypostatize[a] personal beings on whom everything depends. Such beings can be assumed, like other persons, to be receptive to entreaty and adulation, service and offering, thus to be more tractable than rigid necessity, the inexorable, unfeeling forces of nature and the obscure powers of the course of the world. Whereas in the beginning there were several gods according to the diversity in affairs, as is natural and was very appropriately implemented by the ancients, later, through the desire to bring consistency, order, and unity to knowledge, these gods were subordinated or even reduced to one – who, however, is very undramatic, as Goethe once remarked to me, because we cannot imagine what to do with just one person. But what is essential is the urge of anguished human beings to prostate themselves and cry out for help, in their frequent, miserable and great distress and also in regard to their eternal salvation. Human beings prefer to depend on foreign grace rather than on their own merit; that is one of the main pillars of theism.[35] The intellect must create a God for them, so that their hearts (wills) enjoy the relief of praying and the comfort of hope; but not conversely, meaning they do not pray because their intellect has logically correctly deduced a God. Let them be without need, desires, and wants, merely intellectual beings without a will; then they do not need a God and thus do not create one. The heart, that is, the will, in its great distress has the need to call upon all-powerful, and thus supernatural assistance; therefore, a God is hypostatized because a prayer is to be offered, not the other way around. Hence the theoretical part of the theology of all the peoples is very different as regards the number and nature of the gods; but that they can and do help if we serve and worship them – this they all have in common, because it is what is important. At the same time this is the birthmark whereby we recognize the origin of all theology, namely, that it has sprung from the *will*, from the heart, not from the head or from cognition, as is claimed. In accordance with this, the true reason why Constantine the Great or even Chlodowig, King of the Franks, changed their religion was that they hoped for better support in war from the new God.[36] There are a few peoples who, preferring the minor to the major key, so to speak, merely have evil spirits instead of the gods, whom, through sacrifices and prayers, they entreat not to do harm. On the whole, there is not much difference in regard to the result. The indigenous inhabitants of the Indian peninsula and Ceylon also seem to have been such peoples before the introduction of Brahmanism and Buddhism, and

126

---

[a] *die Hypostase ... macht* ['*hypostasieren*' = 'to symbolize in material form'; 'hypostasis' also refers to the person of Christ]

their descendants are still said to have in part such a cacodemonological[a] religion, as do some savage peoples. Kapuism,[b] which is mixed in with Singhalese Buddhism, comes from it. – Similarly the devil-worshippers in Mesopotamia belong here, who were visited by *Layard*.[c]

Closely related to the true origin of all theism we have described and likewise originating in human nature is the impulse to make *sacrifices* to the gods in order to purchase their favour or, if they have already shown such favour, its continuance, or to bribe them to ward off evils. (See Sanchoniathon's *Fragments*,[d] ed. Orelli, Leipzig 1826, p. 42.) This is the meaning of every sacrifice and thus the origin and support of the existence of all gods; so that it can be truly said that the gods live off sacrifice. For since the impulse to invoke and buy the assistance of supernatural beings, though the offspring of want and intellectual limitation, is natural to human beings and its satisfaction is a need, they create gods for themselves. Hence the universality of sacrifice, during all ages and among the most diverse peoples, and the identity of the matter despite the greatest difference of circumstances and levels of education. Thus, for instance, Herodotus reports (IV, 152)[e] that a ship from Samos made an unprecedented fortune through the extremely favourable sale of its cargo in Tartessus, after which these Samians spent a tenth of this, amounting to six talents, on a large brazen and very artfully worked vase and presented it to Hera in her temple. And nowadays we see as a counterpart to these Greeks the miserable, nomadic, reindeer-raising Laplander, shrunk to the form of a dwarf, hide his saved money in different secret places among the rocks and in the glens, which he does not divulge to anyone except his heir in the hour of death – save one that he conceals even from him, because he has sacrificed the money laid

127

---

[a] *kakodämonologische* [believing in evil spirits]

[b] *Kappuismus* [rather: *Kapuismus*, referring to the *Kapurala*, Buddhist priests who conducted rites asking for this-worldly goods]

[c] [Austen Henry Layard, *Nineveh and Its Remains: with an Account of a Visit to the Chaldaean Christians of Kurdistan, and the Yezidis or Devil-worshippers; and an Inquiry into the Manners and Arts of the Ancient Assyrians* (1848–9)]

[d] *Sanchoniathonis fragmenta* [Johann Konrad Orelli, *Sanchoniathonis Berytii quae feruntur Fragmenta de Cosmogonia et Theologia Phoenicum, Graece versa a Philon Byblio, servata ab Eusebio Caesariensi, Praeparationis Evangelicae Libro I, cap. VI. et VII., Graece et Latine, recognovit, emendavit, notis selectis Scaligeri, G. I. Vossii, Cumberlandi, aliorumque permultorum suisque animadversionibus illustravit Ioh. Conradus Orellius*, Lipsiae MDCCCXXVI (*Fragments on the Cosmogony and Theology of the Phoenicians, related by Sanchoniathon of Beirut, edited by Philo of Byblos, preserved by Eusebius of Caesarea, Book I of Preparation for the Gospel, Greek and Latin, revised, corrected, with selected notes by Scaliger, Bochart, G. I. Voss, Cumberland, and many others, and elucidated with his own commentaries by Johann Konrad Orelli*, Leipzig, 1826). It is controversial whether Sanchoniathon actually existed or was invented by Philo to promote his own views on cosmogony, which is more likely]

[e] [*Histories*]

down there for the spirit of the place,[a] the tutelary god of his area. (See Albrecht Pancritius, *Hägringar: A Journey through Sweden, Lapland, Norway, and Denmark in the Year 1850*,[b] Königsberg, 1852, p. 162.) – Thus the belief in gods is rooted in egoism. Solely in Christianity has the sacrifice proper disappeared, although it is still there in the form of the masses for the dead and the buildings of cloisters, churches, and chapels. But otherwise, and especially with the Protestants, praise, glory, and thanks must serve as substitute for sacrifice, which, therefore, are carried to the utmost superlatives, even on occasions that seem to the impartial person little suited for them. By the way, this is analogous to the state not always rewarding merit with gifts, but also with mere marks of esteem, thus maintaining its continued effectiveness. In regard to this it deserves to be recalled what the great *David Hume* has said about this: 'Whether his god, therefore, be considered as their peculiar patron, or as the general sovereign of heaven, his votaries will endeavour, by every art, to insinuate themselves into his favour; and supposing him to be pleased, like themselves, with praise and flattery, there is no eulogy or exaggeration, which will be spared in their addresses to him. In proportion as men's fears or distresses become more urgent, they still invent new strains of adulation; and even he who outdoes his predecessor in swelling up the titles of his divinity, is sure to be outdone by his successor in newer and more pompous epithets of praise. Thus they proceed; till at last they arrive at infinity itself, beyond which there is no farther progress.' (*Essays and Treatises on Several Subjects*, London, 1777, vol. 2, p. 429.[c]) And further: 'It appears certain that, though the original notions of the vulgar represent the Divinity as a limited being, and consider him only as the particular cause of health or sickness; plenty or want; prosperity or adversity; yet when more magnificent ideas are urged upon them, they esteem it *dangerous to refuse their assent*. Will you say, that your deity is finite and bounded in his perfections; may be overcome by a greater force; is subject to human passions, pains and infirmities; has a beginning and may have an end? This they dare not affirm; but thinking it *safest to comply with the higher encomiums, they endeavour, by an affected ravishment and devotion, to ingratiate themselves* with him. As a confirmation of this, we may observe, that the assent of the vulgar is, in this case, merely verbal, and that they are incapable of conceiving those sublime qualities which they seemingly

128

---

[a] *genio loci*
[b] *Hägringar, Reise durch Schweden, Lappland, Norwegen und Dänemark im Jahre 1850* [published by Bornträger]
[c] [*The Natural History of Religion*]

attribute to the Deity. Their real idea of him, notwithstanding their pompous language, is still as poor and frivolous as ever.' (Ibid., p. 432.)[a,37]

In order to mitigate the offensive character of his critique of all speculative theology, *Kant* not only added moral theology, but also the assurance that, even if the existence of God had to remain unproven, it was equally impossible to prove its opposite, and many people acquiesced in this, because they did not notice that, with feigned naïvety, he ignored that 'Proof is incumbent upon the person who makes the claim',[b] and also that the number of things whose non-existence cannot be proved is infinite. Of course, he was even more careful not to prove the arguments that could serve as apagogical[c] counterproof, if one no longer wished to maintain a merely defensive attitude, but wanted to proceed aggressively. The following, for example, would be of this nature:

(1) First of all, the sad constitution of a world whose living beings subsist by devouring each other, the consequent distress and dread of all that is alive, the quantity and colossal magnitude of evils, the variety and inevitablity of sufferings often growing close to the horrible, the burden of life itself and its rush towards bitter death, can honestly not be reconciled with being the supposed result of infinite goodness, wisdom, and power working together. To raise an outcry against this is as easy as it is difficult to counter the case with convincing reasons.

(2) There are two points that not only are of concern to every thinking human being, but also which the followers of every religion have most at heart, so that the strength and survival of religions rest upon them: first of all the transcendent moral significance of our conduct, and second our continued existence after death. If a religion has well taken care of both points, everything else is secondary. Therefore, I shall here examine theism in respect to the first point and under the following number in respect to the second.

Theism has a twofold connection with the morality of our conduct, namely one in regard to the past[d] and one in regard to the future,[e] that is, in regard to the grounds and in regard to the consequences of our actions. To take up the last point first, theism may provide support for morals, but support of the crudest kind, indeed, one through which the true and pure

129

---

[a] [Both quotes given by Schopenhauer in the original English]
[b] *affirmanti incumbit probatio* [goes back to Justinian's *Corpus iuris civilis*, whose Digest (Pandect) 22.3.2 says: '*Ei incumbit probatio qui dicit, non qui negat*' (Proof is incumbent upon the person who affirms, not the one who negates)]
[c] [indirect proof by demonstrating the incorrectness or impossibility of the contrary]
[d] *a parte ante* 　　[e] *a parte post*

morality of conduct basically is abolished, since because of it every unselfish action is immediately transformed into a selfish one by means of a very long-sighted, but secure bill of exchange that we receive as payment for it. For God, who in the beginning was the creator, appears in the end as revenger and rewarder. Deference to such a God admittedly can produce virtuous

130 actions; however, because fear of punishment or hope for reward are their motive, these actions will not be purely moral; on the contrary, the inner essence[a] of such virtue will amount to prudent and carefully calculating egoism. Ultimately the firmness of the belief in indemonstrable things is what alone counts; if this is present, then we shall certainly not hesitate to accept a short period of suffering for an eternity of joy, and the actual guiding principle of morals will be: 'to be able to wait'. However, everyone who seeks a reward for his deeds, be it in this world or a future one, is an egoist; if he misses the hoped-for reward, it does not matter whether it happens through chance, which rules this world, or through the emptiness of the delusion that built the future world for him. For this reason, Kant's moral theology also undermines morality.

On the other hand, theism in regard to the past is also in conflict with morality, because it abolishes freedom and accountability. For neither guilt nor merit can be conceived in a being that, in regard to its existence[b] and essence,[c] is the work of another. Already Vauvenargues says very correctly: 'A being that has received everything can act only according to what has been given to it; and all the divine power that is infinite could not make it independent.'[d] (*Discourse on Liberty*.[e] See *Complete Works*,[f] Paris 1823, vol. 2, p. 331.)[38] For, as any other conceivable being, it cannot act except *in accordance with its constitution* and thereby make the latter known; but it is created here the way it is constituted. If it acts badly, that is a result of its *being* bad, and then the guilt does not belong to it but to him who made it. It is inevitable that the author of its existence and its constitution, as well as the circumstances in which it has been placed, is also the author of its actions and its deeds, which are determined by all this with such certainty as a triangle by two angles and a line. St Augustine, Hume, and Kant have clearly seen and understood the correctness of this reasoning, while others have ignored it in shrewd and cowardly fashion; about which I have written

---

[a] *das Innere*　　[b] *existentia*　　[c] *essentia*
[d] *Un être, qui a tout reçu, ne peut agir que par ce qui lui a été donné; et toute la puissance divine, qui est infinie, ne saurait le rendre indépendant.*
[e] *Discours sur la liberté*
[f] *Œuvres complètes [de Vauvenargues précédées d'une notice sur sa vie et ses ouvrages et accompagnées des notes de Voltaire, Morellet, Fortia, Suard*, Paris: J. L. J. Brière, 1823]

extensively in my *Prize Essay on the Freedom of the Will*, pp. 67ff.[a] Precisely 131
in order to elude this terrible and crushing difficulty, people have invented
the freedom of the will, the liberty of indifference,[b] which contains an
utterly egregious fiction and has always been disputed by all thinking minds
and rejected long ago, but perhaps nowhere as systematically and thoroughly as in the work just mentioned. Let the rabble continue to lug around
freedom of the will, even the literary and the philosophical mob: What does
it matter to us? The assertion that a given being is *free*, i.e. can under given
circumstances act this and also another way, says that it possesses existence[c]
without all essence,[d] which means that it merely *is* without being *something*;
therefore that it is *nothing*, yet still *is*; thus that it is and is not at the same
time. Hence this is the height of absurdity, but nonetheless good for people
who seek not the truth but their fodder and thus will never admit anything
as valid that does not suit their purposes, the convenient story[e] by which
they live; their impotence is served by ignoring rather than refuting. And
should we attach any importance to the opinions of such 'herd of cattle who
are bent down toward the ground and obedient to their bellies'?![f] –
Everything that *is* also is *something*, has an essence, a constitution, a
character; it must be active, must act (which means to be active according
to motives) when the external occasions arise that call forth its individual
manifestations. The source of its existence is also the source of its What, its
constitution, its essence, since both differ conceptually, but in reality cannot
be separated. However, what has an essence, that is, a nature, a character, a
constitution, can only be active in accordance with it and not in any other
way; merely the point in time and the particular form and constitution of
the individual actions are each time determined by the occurring motives.
That the creator created human beings free implies an impossibility, namely
that he endowed them with an existence without essence, thus had given
them existence merely in the abstract by leaving it up to them *what* they
wanted to exist as. On this point I ask the reader to consult §20 of my
treatise *On the Basis of Morals*.[g] – Moral freedom and responsibility, or 132
accountability, absolutely presuppose *aseity*. Actions will always result with
necessity from character, that is, from the specific and thus unalterable
constitution of a being under the influence and in accordance with motives;

---

[a] [*FW*, 83ff. (Hübscher *SW* 4, 66ff.)]   [b] *liberum arbitrium indifferentiae*   [c] *existentia*
[d] *essentia*   [e] *fable convenue*
[f] βοσκήματα, *in terra prona et ventri obedientia* [*pecora, quae natura prona atque ventri oboedientia finxit* (a
herd of cattle that nature has shaped in such a way that they bend to the ground and are obedient to
their bellies), Sallust, *Bellum Catilinae* (*The Catilinarian War*), ch. 1]
[g] [*BM*, 235–44 (Hübscher *SW* 4, 249–59)]

therefore, if the being is to be responsible, it must exist originally[a] and by virtue of its own absolute power; it must, in regard to its existence and essence, be its own doing and the author of itself if it is to be the true author of its *deeds*. Or, as I have expressed in my two prize-essays, freedom cannot lie in acting,[b] it must lie in being;[c] for exist it does.

Since all this is not only a priori demonstrable, but since even daily experience teaches us clearly that we all bring our finished moral character with us into the world and remain unalterably loyal to it until the end; and further, since this truth is tacitly but confidently presumed in actual, practical life in that we all forever fix our trust, or mistrust, in another person in accordance with that person's once and for all demonstrated character traits, we could wonder how, incidentally for one thousand six hundred years, the opposite could ever have been theoretically asserted and accordingly taught, namely that all human beings, from a moral point of view, are originally exactly equal, and the great disparity in their acting did not spring from the original, inborn difference of predisposition and character, and just as little from actual circumstances and occasions, but really from nothing, such absolute nothing then receiving the name 'free will'. – However, this absurd doctrine is made necessary by another assumption, also purely theoretical, with which it is closely connected, namely this, that the birth of a human being is the absolute beginning of his existence in that he is *created* out of nothing (an expression referring to an idea that is valid only for a particular case[d]). Now if on this assumption life is still to retain moral significance and propensity, these must surely first originate during the course of this life, and from nothing at that, just as this whole human being thus conceived is from nothing. For any relation to a preceding condition, an earlier existence, or an atemporal deed is here excluded for good, although the immeasurable, original and inborn diversity of moral characters clearly refers back to these. Hence the absurd fiction of a free will. – As is well known, truths are all connected; but also errors render one another necessary – just as *one* lie requires a second one, or as two cards on edge mutually support each other – as long as nothing knocks them over.

(3) On the assumption of theism, things are not much better with our continued existence after death than with freedom of the will. What has been created by another has had a beginning to its existence. Now that the same being, after having not existed at all for an infinite time, is supposed to continue existing through all eternity, is an exceedingly bold assumption. If

---

[a] *ursprünglich*   [b] *operari*   [c] *esse*   [d] *terminus ad hoc*

at birth I first came to be and was created out of nothing, then it is highly probable that I will become nothing again in death. Infinite duration in the future[a] and non-existence[b] in the past[c] do not go together. Only what is itself orginal, eternal, and ungenerated, can be indestructible. (See Aristotle, *On the Heavens*[d] I, 12, 281–3, and Priestley, *On Matter and Spirit*, Birmingham, 1782, vol. I, p. 234.[e]) Therefore, those people at best can despair in death who believe in having been a pure nothing thirty or sixty years ago and in having arisen from this as the work of another, since now they have the difficult task of assuming that an existence thus arisen, irrespective of its late beginning, having occurred only after the lapse of an infinite time, shall still be of endless duration. In contrast, how should anyone fear death who recognizes himself as original and eternal essence, the source of all existence, and knows that outside of himself nothing really exists, he who ends his individual existence with the dictum of the sacred *Upanishads* on his lips, or at least in his heart: 'I am, altogether, all these creatures, and beside me no other being exists.'[f] Therefore, it is only he who, thinking consistently, can die calmly. For, as said before, *aseity* is the condition of accountability as well as of immortality. Accordingly, the disdain for death and the most perfect equanimity and even joy in dying are effectively at home in India. Judaism, on the other hand, which originally was the sole purely monotheistic religion, teaching an actual God-creator of heaven and earth, has, perfectly consistently, no doctrine of immortality, thus also no retribution after death, but merely temporal punishments and rewards, whereby it distinguishes itself from all other religions, even if not to its advantage. The two religions that have arisen from Judaism have effectively turned inconsistent by adding immortality, from better doctrines of faith otherwise known to them, but keeping the God-creator.*,[39]

134

---

* The true *Jewish religion*, as it is presented and taught in Genesis and all the historical books up until the end of the Chronicles, is the crudest of all religions, because it is the only one that has no doctrine of immortality at all, not even a trace of it. Every king and hero, or prophet, when he dies, is buried with his fathers, and with that everything is over: no trace of any existence after death; rather, any idea of this kind seems to have been erased as if intentionally. For example, Jehovah delivers a long eulogy for King Josiah; it ends with the promise of a reward, which says: ἰδοὺ προστίθημί σε πρὸς τοὺς πατέρας σου, καὶ προστεθήσῃ πρὸς τὰ μνήματά σου ἐν εἰρήνῃ ['Behold, I will gather thee to thy fathers, and thou shalt be

[a] *a parte post* [b] *Nichts* [c] *a parte ante* [d] *de coelo* [*De caelo*]
[e] [Joseph Priestley, *Disquisitions Relating to Matter and Spirit. To which is added, The History of the Philosophical Doctrine concerning the Soul and the Nature of Matter; with its Influence on Christianity, especially with respect to the Doctrine of the Pre-existence of Christ*, Birmingham: Pearson and Rollason, 1782]
[f] *hae omnes creaturae in totum ego sum, et praeter me aliud ens non est* [Schopenhauer quotes from the Latin translation by Abraham Hyacinthe Anquetil Duperron, which the latter made from a Persian translation of the Sanskrit original (1801–2)]

135   As just mentioned, the fact that Judaism is the sole purely monotheistic
136 religion, i.e. teaches a God-creator as the origin of all things, is a merit that,
incomprehensibly, people have tried hard to conceal by maintaining and
teaching that all peoples worshipped the true God, even if under different
names. But this is not only lacking a lot, but lacking everything. Through
the agreement of all authentic testimonies and original documents, it is
proven beyond doubt that Buddhism, that religion that is the foremost on
earth in virtue of the overwhelming number of followers, is absolutely and
expressly atheistic. The Vedas as well teach no God-creator, but a world soul
called *Brahm* (in the neuter), of which *Brahma*, sprung from the navel of
Vishnu, with the four faces and as part of the *Trimurti*,[a] is merely a popular
personification in the highly transparent Indian mythology. Obviously he
portrays procreation, the coming-into-existence of beings, as Vishnu portrays their acme, and Shiva their demise.[40] Moreover, his generation of the
world is a sinful act, just as the incarnation of the world by the Brahm.

gathered to thy grave in peace'] (2 Chronicles 34:28), and that, therefore, he shall not live to see
Nebuchadnezzar. However, no thought of another existence after death and thus of a positive reward,
instead of the negative one of dying and experiencing no further sufferings. On the contrary, when the
Lord Jehovah has worn out and tormented his handiwork and plaything, he throws it away onto the
dung-hill; that is the reward for it. Precisely because the Jewish religion knows no immortality and
consequently no punishments after death either, Jehovah can threaten the sinner who prospers on earth
with nothing but punishing his misdeeds in his children and children's children unto the fourth
generation, as can be seen in Exodus 34:7 and Numbers 14:18. – This proves the absence of any doctrine
of immortality. In addition, there is the passage in Tobias 3:6, where he begs Jehovah for his death, ὅπως
ἀπολυθῶ καὶ γένωμαι γῆ ['so that I be set free and return to dust'], nothing more, no notion of an
existence after death. – In the Old Testament the reward promised for virtue is to live a really long life on
earth (e.g. Moses 5:16 and 33), whereas in the *Vedas* the reward is not to be born again. – The contempt in
which the Jews were always held by all contemporary peoples may have been based for the most part on
the wretched nature of their religion. What Qoheleth [Ecclesiastes] 3:19 and 20 pronounces is the true
conviction of the *Jewish religion*. When, as in Daniel 12:2, there is an allusion to immortality, it is an
imported foreign doctrine, as follows from Daniel 1:4 and 6. In 2 Maccabees 7, the doctrine of
immortality clearly appears and is of Babylonian origin. All other religions, that of the Indians,
Brahmans as well as Buddhists, Egyptians, Persians, even the Druids, teach immortality and also,
with the exception of the Persians in the *Zendavesta* [*Zend-Avesta*] metempsychosis. That the *Edda*, in
particular the *Völuspa* [*Völuspá*, one of the Eddic poems], teaches transmigration of the soul, is verified by
D[aniel] G[eorg] von Ekendahl in his review of *Svenska Siare och Skalder* [*Swedish Prophets and Poets*
(1841–55)] by [Per Daniel Amadeus] Atterbom – in the *Blätter für litter. Unterhaltung* [*Blätter für
literarische Unterhaltung*, ed. Heinrich Brockhaus and others], 25 August 1843. Even the Greeks and
Romans had something *post letum* [after death], Tartarus and Elysium, and said:

Sunt aliquid manes, letum non omnia finit:
Luridaque evictos effugit umbra rogos.

(Propertius, *Elegies* IV, 7)

[The souls of the dead are something, death does not end it all: a pale shadow escapes from the
vanquished pyres.]

[a] [triad of the three main Hindu gods, Brahma, Vishnu and Shiva]

Furthermore, as we know, Ahriman is the equal of Ormuzd[a] of the *Zend-Avesta*, and both have emerged from immeasurable time, *Zervane Akerene* (if that is correct). We also find no trace of theism or world creation by a personal being in the very beautiful and highly readable 'Cosmogony of the Phoenicians', written down by *Sanchoniathon* and preserved for us by Philo of Byblos, which is perhaps the prototype of the Mosaic cosmogony. For here we see as well how in the Mosaic Genesis the original chaos submerged into night; but no God appears, commanding that there be light and there be this and there be that: oh no! rather 'The spirit fell in love with its own origin'.[b] The spirit, fermenting in the mass, falls in love with its own essence, whereby a mixture of those primary constituents of the world comes into being, out of which, and indeed very appropriately and meaningfully, as a result of the longing, *pothos*[c] – which, as the commentator   137 correctly observes, is the *eros* of the Greeks – the primeval slime arises, and from that ultimately originate plants and, in a final step, cognitive beings, that is, animals. For up to here, as is expressly observed, everything happened without cognition: 'But it did not itself recognize its own creation.'[d] (It can be found like this, Sanchoniathon adds, in the cosmogony written by *Taautos*, the Egyptian.) His *cosmogony* is then followed by the more detailed *zoogony*. Certain atmospheric and terrestrial processes are described that really remind us of the logically consistent assumptions of our contemporary geology. In the end, heavy rainstorms are followed by thunder and lightening, startled by whose claps the cognitive animals awake to their existence, 'and now, on the earth and in the ocean, move *the male and the female*'. Eusebius, to whom we owe these fragments of Philo of Byblos (see *Preparation of the Gospel*, Book II, ch. 10[e]), rightfully accuses this cosmogony of atheism; that it is indisputably, as is every doctrine of the genesis of the world, with the sole exception of the Jewish one. For sure, we find gods as fathers of gods and incidentally of human beings (although these are originally the potter's work of Prometheus) in the mythology of the Greeks and Romans, but no God-creator. For the fact that later a couple of philosophers, having become acquainted with Judaism, tried to reinterpret Father Zeus as such a God-creator does not matter to him; and it matters just as little that Dante, in his *Inferno*, without having sought his

---

[a] [Ahriman is the evil, destructive deity and Ormuzd the good, creative one]
[b] ἡράσθη τὸ πνεῦμα τῶν ἰδίων ἀρχῶν [*Sanchoniathonis Fragmenta* (ed. Orelli) (see above p. 109, n. d), pp. 8–10 (chapter on the Phoenician theology according to Sanchoniathon)]
[c] πόθος   [d] αὐτὸ δὲ οὐκ ἐγίγνωσκε τὴν ἑαυτοῦ κτίσιν [p. 10]
[e] *Preparat*[*io*] *Evangel*[*ica*] (actually, he refers to Book I, ch. 10)]

permission, wants to identify him, without further ado, with *Domeneddio*,[a] whose egregious thirst for vengeance and cruelty are celebrated and depicted there, for example, Canto XIV, line 70 and Canto XXXI, line 92. Finally (for people grasped at anything) the report, repeated countless times, that the North American savages worshipped God, the creator of heaven and earth, under the name of the *Great Spirit*, and hence were pure theists, is completely incorrect. This error has recently been refuted in a treatise about the North American savages, which *John Scouler* read at a meeting of the London Ethnographical Society in 1846[b] and of which *L'Institut, Journal des sociétés savantes*,[c] sect. 2, July 1847, provides an excerpt. It says: 'In like manner, when we hear the term Great Spirit so often used in speaking of Indian superstitions, we are ready to suppose that such an expression conveys an idea that corresponds to the idea we attach to it, and that their faith is a simple natural theism. This, however, is very far from being the case. The religion of the Indian is merely a kind of fetishism, consisting in charms and incantations. In the narrative of Tanner, who lived from his childhood among the Indians, and whose faithful and detailed narrative is so different from the speculations of certain writers, we find that the religion of the Indian is merely a system of fetishism similar to that which once prevailed among the Finns, and is found at the present day among the people of Siberia. Among the Indians east of the Mountains, the fetish, under the name of medicine bag, is well known, and consists merely of some object supposed to be possessed of mysterious powers etc.'[d]

As a result of all this, the opinion here discussed must give way to its opposite, namely that only a single, certainly very small, insignificant people, despised by all contemporary peoples, being alone among all others in lacking belief in a continued existence after death,[41] but nevertheless a people chosen for such destiny, have had a pure monotheism, or knowledge of the true God; and this not with the help of philosophy, but solely through revelation, as is appropriate for it; for what value would a revelation have that only taught what one already knew without it? – Therefore it should contribute to our appreciation of revelation that no other people has ever conceived of such an idea.

---

[a] [God]   [b] [Presented on 29 April 1846]
[c] [published in Paris (*Mémoires de la Société des antiquaires de Picardie*)]
[d] ['On the Indian Tribes Inhabiting the North-West Coast of America', *Journal of the Ethnological Society of London* (1848), pp. 228–52]

§14. Some remarks on my own philosophy

There is hardly another philosophical system so simple and composed of so few elements as my own; hence it can be taken in and summed up at a glance. This is based on the complete unity and agreement of its fundamental ideas and generally is a favourable indication of its truth, which certainly is related to simplicity: 'Whoever has truth to tell does so simply';[a] 'Simplicity is the seal of truth'.[b] One could call my system an *immanent dogmatism*, for its theorems are indeed dogmatic, yet do not go beyond the world given in experience; rather they explain *what this world is* by analysing it into its ultimate components. For the old dogmatism, overthrown by *Kant* (and likewise the windbaggeries of the three modern university sophists) is *transcendent*, because it transcends the world in order to explain it on the basis of something else; it makes it the effect of a cause that it infers from this effect. On the other hand, my philosophy starts out from the proposition that causes and effects exist only *within* the world and on the assumption[c] of this world, since the principle of sufficient reason, in its four aspects, is merely the most general form of the intellect, while the objective world exists in this intellect alone, as the true place of the world.[d] –

In other philosophical systems consistency is brought about by inferring proposition from proposition. However, for this it is necessary that the proper content of the system is already present in the very highest propositions, so that what remains, as inferred from them, can hardly turn out other than monotonous, poor, empty, and boring, since it just develops and repeats what was already asserted in the fundamental principles. This dismal outcome of demonstrative deduction is most noticeable in Christian Wolff; but even Spinoza, who strictly followed that method, was not quite able to avoid this disadvantage, although he knew how to compensate for it by means of his intellect. – My propositions, on the other hand, for the most part do not rely on chains of reasoning but immediately on the intuitive world itself, and the strict logical consistency, which exists in my system as much as in any other, is generally not achieved in a merely logical manner. It is rather the natural agreement of propositions that inevitably occurs because these are based on the same intuitive cognition, that is, intuitive comprehension of the same object, only viewed successively from different perspectives, in

---

[a] ἁπλοῦς ὁ τῆς ἀληθείας λόγος ἔφυ [paraphrase of Euripides, *The Phoenician Women*, 469]
[b] *simplex sigillum veri*   [c] *unter Voraussetzung*   [d] *locus mundi*

140 other words the real world in all its phenomena, whilst taking into consideration the consciousness in which it presents itself. For that reason I have been able never to worry about the agreement of my propositions, even when individual ones seemed incompatible to me, as was occasionally the case for a while; for the agreement later correctly happened by itself, as all propositions came together, being for me nothing but the agreement of reality with itself, which surely can never be amiss. Analogously, we sometimes fail to comprehend the connection of the parts of a building when seeing it for the first time and only from one side; yet we are certain that this connection is not wanting and will become apparent as soon as we walk all the way around. This manner of agreement indeed is completely certain by virtue of its primary nature[a] and of its being under the constant control of experience. On the other hand, the deduced agreement, brought about solely through syllogism, can easily be found false at times, namely as soon as any part of the long chain is not genuine, loosely fitted, or otherwise of a faulty nature. Accordingly, my philosophy has a broad basis on which everything stands immediately and thus securely, whereas other systems resemble towers built up tall; if *one* support beam breaks, everything collapses. – Everything said here can be summed up in the proposition that my philosophy has arisen and is presented in the analytic, not the synthetic way.

As the particular character of my philosophy I may mention that I attempt everywhere *to get to the bottom* of things in that I do not desist from pursuing them to the ultimate, actual given. This happens by virtue of a natural tendency that makes it almost impossible for me to acquiesce in some yet more general and abstract, and hence yet more indeterminate cognition, in mere concepts, let alone in words, but that drives me on until I have plainly in front of me the ultimate foundation[b] of all concepts and propositions, which is always intuitive. This I then either let stand as a primary phenomenon[c] or, where possible, dissolve it further into its elements, in any case pursuing the essence of the thing to the limit. For 141 this reason people will eventually (of course not as long as I live) recognize that any previous philosopher's treatment of the same subject appears shallow when compared with mine. Thus humanity has learnt a few things from me that will never be forgotten, and my writings will not perish. –

---

[a] *Ursprünglichkeit*   [b] *Grundlage*   [c] *Urphänomen*

Theism also has the world proceed from a *will* and has the planets guided by a will in their orbits and a nature generated by it on their surface. It is just that theism naïvely shifts this will to the outside and lets it affect things only in a mediate way, that is, by having cognition and matter come in between, in the human manner, while with me the will acts not so much on the things as within them; indeed, the things are nothing but the will's very visibleness.[a] However, we see from this agreement that none of us are able to conceive what is primary[b] except as a *will*. *Pantheism* calls the will that acts in things a God, the absurdity of which I have often and strongly reprimanded. I call it the *will to life*,[c] because this expresses what can ultimately be known in it. – This same relation between mediateness and immediacy also appears again in morals. The theists want proportionality[d] between what someone does and what he suffers; so do I. However, they assume such balance only by means of time and a judge and revenger; I, in contrast, assume it immediately by proving the same essence in the one who acts and the one who suffers. The moral results of Christianity up to the most extreme asceticism are found with me grounded rationally and in the connection of things, whereas in Christianity they are grounded in mere fables. The belief in these disappears further every day; thus people will have to turn to my philosophy.[42] The *pantheists* cannot have seriously conceived morals – since with them everything is divine and excellent. –

I have received much blame for presenting life, in a philosophizing and thus theoretical manner, as wretched and not at all desirable; yet whoever shows in a practical way the most determined contempt for life is praised, indeed admired, and whoever carefully strives to preserve it is despised. –

Scarcely had my writings attracted the attention of even a few people when the complaint, in regard to my fundamental idea and its priority, could be heard and was cited, namely that *Schelling* had once said 'Willing is primal being'[e] and whatever else of this kind they could find. – In regard to the matter itself, it may be said about this that the root of my philosophy already lies in the Kantian philosophy, especially in the doctrine of empirical and intelligible character, but generally that, as soon as Kant throws more light on the thing in itself, it looks out through its veil as *will*, to which I have explicitly drawn attention in my *Critique of the Kantian Philosophy* and consequently have said that my philosophy is only the

142

---

[a] *Sichtbarkeit*   [b] *das Ursprüngliche*   [c] *Willen zum Leben*   [d] *Ausgleich*
[e] *Wollen ist Urseyn* [Friedrich Wilhelm Joseph von Schelling, *Philosophical Investigations into the Essence of Human Freedom and Related Matters* (*Philosophische Untersuchungen über das Wesen der menschlichen Freiheit und die damit zusammenhängenden Gegenstände*, 1809; *Schellings sämmtliche Werke* (*Complete Works*), Part I, vol. 7, 350)]

thinking-through-to-the-end of his.[a] Thus we should not be surprised when traces of the same fundamental thought can be found in the philosophemes of *Fichte* and *Schelling*, which also start out from Kant, although there they occur without consistency, connection, and completion, and are thus to be seen as a mere foreshadowing of my doctrine. In general it needs to be said about this point that of every great truth, before it has been discovered, an anticipation makes itself known, a presentiment, a faint image, as in a fog, and a futile attempt to grasp it, because the progress of time has prepared for it. Accordingly, isolated expressions then precede it. However, only that person is the author of a truth who has recognized it from its grounds, thought it through in its consequences, developed its entire content, surveyed the extent of its domain, and then expounded it clearly and coherently, with the full consciousness of its value and importance. However, that at one time or another, in ancient or modern times, it has been uttered half-consciously and almost as if speaking in one's sleep, and thus can be found there if we look for it afterwards, means not much more than if it were written in just so many letters,[b] even if it is written in just so many words[c] – in the same way that the finder of a thing is only that person who, in recognizing its value, picked it up and kept it, but not the one who accidentally took it in his hand and dropped it again; or, in the way that Columbus is the discoverer of America, but not the first shipwrecked person washed up there by the waves. This is precisely the meaning of the saying by Donatus: 'May those perish who have pronounced our truths before us.'[d] However, if one wanted to hold such accidental utterances against me as priorities, one could have reached back much further and quoted what Clement of Alexandria says (*Stromata*, Book II, ch. 17): 'Therefore, willing precedes everything; for the intellectual faculties are the servants of the will.'[e] See *Sanctorum Patrum Opera polemica*,[f] vol. 5. Würzburg, 1779; *Clementis Alexandrini Opera*, vol. 2, p. 304. And also Spinoza says: 'Desire is each man's nature and essence'[g] (*Ethics* III, prop. 57, proof), and before: 'This impulse, when it is referred solely to the mind, is called will; but when it is referred to the mind and the body at the same time, it is called appetite; it is, therefore, nothing else but the essence itself of a human

143

---

[a] [See *WWR* I, 531 (Hübscher *SW* 2, 595)]   [b] *totidem litteris*   [c] *totidem verbis*

[d] *pereant qui ante nos nostra dixerunt* [St Jerome, *Commentaries on Ecclesiastes* (Hieronymus, *Commentarius In Ecclesiasten*), 1019A; St Jerome attributes this sentence to his teacher Aelius Donatus]

[e] προηγεῖται τοίνυν πάντων τὸ βούλεσθαι, αἱ γὰρ λογικαὶ δυνάμεις τοῦ βούλεσθαι διάκονοι πεφύκασι (*Velle ergo omnia antecedit: rationales enim facultates sunt voluntatis ministrae*)]

[f] [*Sanctorum Patrum Opera polemica de veritate religionis Christianæ contra gentiles, et judæos*]

[g] *Cupiditas est ipsa unius cujusque natura seu essentia*

being'[a] (III, prop. 9, scholium, and finally III, definition I, explication). – Helvétius remarks absolutely correctly: 'There are no means that the envious person, in the guise of justice, does not employ to degrade merit . . . It is mere envy that makes us find in the ancients all the modern discoveries. A phrase devoid of meaning, or at least unintelligible before the discoveries, suffices for bringing about shouts of plagiarism.'[b] (*On Mind* IV, 7[c].)[43] And I ask for permission to recall yet another passage from Helvétius in regard to this point, whose citation I beg not to interpret as vanity and presumption, but only to bear in mind the correctness of the idea expressed in it, leaving it open whether anything contained in it could be applied to me or not. 'Whoever takes pleasure in observing the human mind sees, in every century, five or six persons of intellect circle around the discovery made by a person of genius. If the honour rests on the latter, that is because this discovery is much more fertile in his hands than in those of all the others, because he expresses his ideas with greater force and precision; and finally we can always see from the different ways in which people make use of a principle or discovery to whom this principle or this discovery belong'[d] (*On Mind* IV, 1). –

As a result of the old, irreconcilable war, fought everywhere and always   144
by incompetency and stupidity against spirit and understanding – the former represented by legions, the latter by a few individuals – everyone who produces something valuable and genuine has to fight a heavy battle against folly, obtuseness, spoiled taste, private interests, and envy, all part of a worthy alliance, namely the one of which *Chamfort* says: 'When examining the league of blockheads against people of intelligence, one could believe we are witnessing a conspiracy of servants to overthrow their masters.'[e] For me there was in addition an unusual enemy: a majority of those in my discipline who held the profession and the opportunity to guide the

---

[a] *Hic conatus, cum ad mentem solam refertur, Voluntas appellatur; sed cum ad mentem et corpus simul refertur, vocatur Appetitus, qui proinde nihil aliud est, quam ipsa hominis essentia.*

[b] *Il n'est point de moyens que l'envieux, sous l'apparence de la justice, n'emploie pour dégrader le mérite . . . C'est l'envie seule qui nous fait trouver dans les ancients toutes les découvertes modernes. Une phrase vide de sens, ou du moins inintelligible avant ces découvertes, suffit pour faire crier au plagiat.*

[c] *De l'esprit* [IV, 7, main text and note]

[d] *Quiconque se plaît à considérer l'esprit humain voit, dans chaque siècle, cinq ou six hommes d'esprit tourner autour de la découverte que fait l'homme de génie. Si l'honneur en reste à ce dernier, c'est que cette découverte est, dans ses mains, plus féconde que dans les mains de tout autre; c'est qu'il rend ses idées avec plus de force et de netteté; et qu'enfin on voit toujours à la manière différente, dont les hommes tirent parti d'un principe ou d'une découverte, à qui ce principe ou cette découverte appartient.*

[e] *En examinant la ligue des sots contre les gens d'esprit, on croirait voir une conjuration de valets pour écarter les maîtres.* [Sébastien-Roch Nicolas Chamfort, *Maximes et pensées* (*Maxims and Considerations*) (1796), ch. 3 (*De la société, des grands, des riches, des gens du monde*)]

judgement of the public, were employed and paid to disseminate, to praise, indeed, to praise to the skies, the worst of all philosophies, namely Hegelry.[a] However, this cannot succeed if at the same time one wants to affirm the good, if only to a certain extent. This might explain to the subsequent reader the otherwise mysterious fact that to my proper contemporaries I have remained as alien as the man in the moon. However, a system of thought that, even without the participation of others, was capable of engaging its author incessantly and vividly and spurring him on to unremitting, unrewarded labour, finds in this testimony as to its value and truth. Without any encouragement from the outside the love of my subject alone sustained my efforts and prevented me from growing weary through the many days of my life; with contempt I looked down upon the noisy glorification of the bad.[b] For when I entered life my genius offered me the choice either to recognize the truth, but to please no one with it, or together with the others to teach the false, with followers and applause; to me the choice was not difficult. Accordingly, the fate of my philosophy became so completely the counterpart of the fate of Hegelry that both can be seen as reverse sides of the same sheet, corresponding to the constitution of both philosophies. Hegelry, without truth, clarity, intelligence, indeed, without common sense, appearing moreover in the garb of the most repulsive Gallimathias[c] ever heard until then, became an academic philosophy,[d] privileged and forced upon

145   people, thus a nonsense that fed its man. Appearing simultaneously with it, my own philosophy certainly had all the qualities which that one lacked; but it was not cut out for any higher purposes, was not at all suited for the lectern[e] of that time, and hence, as we say, it was good for nothing. It then followed, as day follows night, that Hegelry became the banner to which everybody flocked, whereas my philosophy found neither approbation nor followers, rather, with unanimous intent, it was completely ignored, glossed over, and, where possible, smothered, since through its presence that very profitable game would have been disturbed, as is the shadow-play on the wall by the entering daylight. As a result I became the iron mask,[f] or, as the noble *Dorguth* says, the Caspar Hauser[g] of the philosophy professors: barred from air and light, so that no one would see me and my inborn claims could not be made valid. But now the man who was suppressed by the silence of the philosophy professors has again risen from the dead to their great consternation, for they do not know at all which face now to put on.[44]

---

[a] *Hegelei*   [b] *Ruhm des Schlechten*   [c] [nonsense]   [d] *Kathederphilosophie*   [e] *Katheder*
[f] [Famous political prisoner under Louis XIV]   [g] See above p. 106, n. a.

Ἡ ἀτιμία φιλοσοφίᾳ διὰ ταῦτα προσπέπτωκεν,
ὅτι οὐ κατ᾽ ἀξίαν αὐτῆς ἅπτονται· οὐ γὰρ
νόθους ἔδει ἅπτεσθαι, ἀλλὰ γνησίους.

[Philosophy has fallen into disgrace, because people do not engage in it
in accordance with its own worth; not spurious, but genuine philosophers should undertake it.] Plato, *Republic* VII [535c]

That philosophy is taught at universities certainly benefits it in many
respects. In this way it obtains official existence and its standard is planted
before the eyes of people, so that its presence is always freshly brought to
mind and attracts attention. However, the main benefit might be that
many a young and capable mind will be introduced to and inspired to
study philosophy. Meanwhile it must be admitted that whoever has a
talent for it and thus is in need of it, might very well encounter and get to
know it in other ways. For things that love and are born for one another
converge easily; kindred souls greet each other already from afar. Any
book of a genuine philosopher that falls into the hands of such people
will excite them more strongly and more effectively than is possible
through the lecture of an academic philosopher[a] of the garden-variety.
In addition, Plato should be diligently read in the high schools, for he is
the most effective stimulant for the philosophical mind. But in general I
have gradually formed the opinion that the benefit of academic philosophy[b] just mentioned is outweighed by the disadvantage that philosophy
as a profession produces for philosophy as the free search for truth, and
that philosophy by government order imposes on philosophy practised on
behalf of nature and humanity.

[a] *Kathederphilosophen*   [b] *Kathederphilosophie*

First of all, a government will not pay people to contradict directly, or even just indirectly, what it has proclaimed from all the pulpits by a thousand priests, or teachers of religion, in its employ, since this, to the degree that it were effective, would have to render the former arrangement ineffective. For it is well-known that judgements cancel each other not only through contradictory, but also through merely contrary opposition; for example, the judgement 'The rose is red' is not only gainsaid by 'It is not red', but also by 'It is yellow', which achieves as much or, indeed, more. Hence the principle: 'We will reject whoever teaches otherwise.'[a] However, on account of this, the university philosophers get into a quite peculiar position whose open secret may here for once find expression. For in all other sciences professors only have the duty to teach, according to their strength and capability, what is true and appropriate. Only in the case of the philosophy professors must we take this matter with a grain of salt. For the case of philosophy is unique since the subject matter of its science is the same as that on which religion sheds light in its own manner, for which reason I have called the latter the metaphysics of the people. In accordance with this, the professors of philosophy are also to teach what is true and appropriate; however, this must essentially be the same as what established religion teaches too, since that is true and appropriate as well. From this arose that naïve remark by a quite reputable philosophy professor, already referred to in my *Critique of the Kantian Philosophy*, in the year 1840: 'If a philosophy denies the fundamental ideas of Christianity, it is either wrong or, *even if true, still useless.*'[b] We can see here that in university philosophy truth takes only a back seat and, if required, must get up to make way for another quality. – This, therefore, distinguishes philosophy at universities from all other established[c] sciences taught there.

As a result of this, as long as the Church exists, the only philosophy that will ever be taught at universities is one that is formulated with consistent respect for established religion, runs parallel to it and hence always is essentially and in the main nothing but a paraphrase and apology for the religion of the land – at best confusedly composed, strangely dressed up and thus made difficult to comprehend. Nothing then remains for those who teach under these constraints than to look for new phrases and forms by means of which to compile the content of established religion, dressed up in

---

[a] *improbant secus docentes* [from Art. 10 of the *Augsburg Confession*, the Lutheran confession of faith]
[b] [In a note in *WWR* 1 (Hübscher *SW* 2, 607), Schopenhauer identifies the author of this passage as (Karl Friedrich) Bachmann, writing in the *Jenaische Allgemeine Literatur-Zeitung*, July 1840, no. 126)]
[c] *kathedersässigen*

abstract expressions and thereby made trite, which afterwards is called philosophy. However, if this or that person wants to do more, he will either stray into neighbouring disciplines or resort to all sorts of innocent drolleries, like, for example, carrying out difficult analytic calculations about the equilibrium of representations in the human brain and similar jokes. Meanwhile the university philosophers who are thus constrained remain quite cheerful about the matter, since their real concern is to earn with honour a fair livelihood for themselves, their wives and their children and also to enjoy a certain prestige in the eyes of the people. On the other hand, they count among mythological beings the profoundly moved mind of a true philosopher, whose entire and great seriousness consists in seeking a key to our – as enigmatic as it is precarious – existence. If indeed the person thus afflicted, should he ever present himself to them, should not appear obsessed by monomania. For normally a teacher of philosophy would be the last person to whom it would occur that philosophy could in effect be dead earnest, just as the most irreligious Christian usually is the Pope. Hence it is among the rarest of cases that a genuine philosopher is at the same time a lecturer in philosophy.*,1 In the second volume of my main work, ch. 17, p. 162,a I have already discussed the fact that *Kant* represented this excep- 152 tional case, together with the grounds and consequences of this. Incidentally, the well-known fate of *Fichte* provides proof for the conditional existence of all university philosophy, uncovered above, even if in the end he was a mere sophist, not a genuine philosopher. For he had dared to omit the doctrines of established religion from his philosophizing, with the result that he was dismissed and, in addition, insulted by the rabble. Moreover, his punishment was effective in that, after his subsequent appointment in Berlin, the absolute I quite obediently transformed itself into the good Lord and the whole doctrine generally assumed a greatly Christian coating, in particular attested to by the *Guide to the Blessed Life.*b It is also noteworthy in his case that what counted as his chief crime was the

---

* It is quite natural that the more godliness [*Gottseligkeit*], the less erudition is required of a professor – just as in Altenstein's time it was enough that somebody confessed to the Hegelian nonsense. However, since godliness can substitute for erudition in the appointment to professorships, the gentlemen do not break their backs in regard to the latter. – The *Tartuffes* should rather take it easy and ask themselves: 'Who is going to believe that we believe this?' – That *these gentlemen* are professors concerns those who made them such; I know them merely as bad writers whose influence I work against. – I have sought truth, not a professorship; this is at bottom the basis of the distinction between me and the so-called post-Kantian philosophers. People will recognize this more and more with time.

a [Third edn., p. 179 (Hübscher *SW* 3, 179)]
b *Anweisung zum seligen Leben* [*Anweisung zum seligen Leben oder auch die Religionslehre*, 1806 (*Guide to the Blessed Life, or the Doctrine of Religion*)]

proposition that God is nothing other than the moral world order itself, whereas this is really not very different from the dictum of St John: 'God is love'. The private lecturer *Fischer* in Heidelberg experienced the same fate in 1853, being stripped of his right to lecture,[a] because he taught pantheism. Thus the password is: 'Eat your pudding, slave, and pass off Jewish mythology as philosophy!'[b] – However, the joke in the matter is that these people call themselves philosophers and as such pass judgement on me, and with an air of superiority at that; indeed, they put on airs against me and for forty years did not even deign to look down on me, not deeming me worthy of their attention. – But the state must also protect its own and thus should pass a law forbidding making fun of philosophy professors.[2]

Hence it is easy to foresee that under such circumstances academic philosophy can scarcely fail to act

> Like one of those grasshoppers in the garden
> That leg it skip-a-skimming all day long
> And in the grass chirp out the same old song.[c]

153   The alarming aspect of this matter is merely the possibility, at least to be conceded, that the ultimate insight attainable by human beings into the nature of things, into their own essence and that of the world, might not exactly coincide with the doctrines that in part were revealed to the ancient small people of the Jews and in part emerged one thousand eight hundred years ago in Jerusalem. In order to defeat such doubt, the philosophy professor *Hegel* invented the expression 'absolute religion', with the help of which he surely achieved his purpose, for he knew his audience. Moreover, academic philosophy actually is really absolute, that is, of such a kind that absolutely and simply should and must be true, or else . . .! – Again other seekers of truth fuse philosophy and religion into a centaur, which they call philosophy of religion; they are also in the habit of teaching that religion and philosophy are really the same, a statement, however, that seems to be true only in the sense in which Francis I is supposed to have said in regard to Charles V in a very conciliatory way: 'What my brother Charles wants, that I want too' – namely Milan. Others again do not trouble themselves so much, but speak directly of a Christian philosophy, which is much the same as if we

---

[a] *jus legendi*
[b] [A variation on the line *'Isz deinen Pudding, Sklav, und halt das Maul!'* (Eat your pudding, slave, and shut up!) in Johann Gottwerth Müller's *Siegfried von Lindenberg: Ein komischer Roman* (1779)]
[c] *'Wie eine der langbeinigen Cikaden, / Die immer fliegt und fliegend springt – / Und gleich im Gras ihr altes Liedchen singt.'* [Johann Wolfgang von Goethe, *Faust* I, 288–90; translations of passages from Goethe's *Faust* follow those by Walter Arndt]

were to speak of a Christian arithmetic, that makes five be an even number.[a] Moreover, such epithets taken from religious doctrines are obviously improper for philosophy, since it presents itself as the attempt of reason to solve the problem of existence from its own resources and independently of all authority. As a science it has nothing at all to do with what may or ought or must be *believed*; rather it deals with what can be *known*. Should this turn out to be something completely different from what we are to believe, then even that would not compromise faith; for it is faith for the reason that it contains what one can *not* know. If we could also know it, faith would look completely useless and even ridiculous, just as if a doctrine of faith about objects of mathematics would be construed in addition. However, if one is convinced that the entire and full truth is contained and expressed in established religion, then one should abide by it and give up all philosophizing. But one should not aspire to appear as something that one is not. The pretence of an impartial search for truth with the determination to make the religion of the country its result, indeed, its criterion and control, is intolerable, and such a philosophy, bound to established religion as the chained dog is to the wall, is only the exasperating caricature of the highest and noblest endeavour of humankind. In the meantime, philosophy of religion, called a centaur above, is a principal article offered for sale by the university philosopher; it actually amounts to a kind of gnosis, and also to philosophizing under certain favoured presuppositions that are not at all substantiated. Also programme titles like 'On the piety of true philosophy as compared with religion',[b] a fitting inscription over such a philosophical sheep stall, indicate quite clearly the bias and the motive of academic philosophy. To be sure, these gentle philosophers sometimes take a run-up that looks dangerous; but we can quietly wait out the matter, convinced that they will still reach the goal set once and for all. Indeed, at times we feel tempted to believe that they had finished their seriously meant philosophical investigations before their twelfth year and had already back then established forever their opinion of the essence of the world and what is connected to it. This is because, after all philosophical discussions and breakneck detours under adventurous guides, they always come back to what is ordinarily made plausible to us at that age and even seem to accept it as the criterion of truth. All the heterodox philosophical doctrines with which they had to occupy themselves meanwhile during the course of

154

---

[a] *die fünf grade seyn ließe*

[b] *de verae philosophiae erga religionem pietate* [Probably a reference to Georg Andreas Gabler (Professor of Philosophy at the University of Berlin), *De Verae Philosophiae erga Religionem Christianam Pietate*, Berlin: Duncker and Humblot, 1836]

their lives only seem to exist in order to be refuted and, thereby, to establish those first ones the more firmly. We should indeed admire how they knew to preserve their inner philosophical innocence, spending their lives with so many wicked heresies.

Whoever, after all this, still has doubts about the spirit and purpose of university philosophy should contemplate the fate of the Hegelian pseudo-wisdom. After all, has it been harmed by the fact that its fundamental idea was the most absurd notion, a world turned upside down, a philosophical buffoonery,* that its content is the most shallow, meaningless verbal rubbish of which blockheads have had their fill, and that its delivery in the works of the author himself is the most repulsive and nonsensical gibberish, indeed reminding us of the rantings of madmen? Oh no, not in the slighest! On the contrary, for twenty years it flourished and grew fat as the brightest academic philosophy that ever provided salaries and fees. For it has been praised to the skies in the whole of Germany, through hundreds of books, as the finally achieved pinnacle of human wisdom and the philosophy of philosophies; students were examined in it and professors appointed on its basis; whoever did not want to go along was declared a 'blockhead by his own hand'[a] by some impudent tutor[b] for its author, who is as docile as he is dull. Even the few who risked feeble opposition against this nonsense came forward only timidly, while acknowledging the 'great mind and exalted genius' – of that insipid philosophaster. The proof of what has been said here can be found in the entire literature of these fine goings-on, which, now as closed files, proceeds through the forecourt of derisively laughing neighbours to that seat of judgement where we all meet again, the tribunal of posterity, which, among other implements, also has a bell of infamy that can be rung through entire ages. – But what was it finally that brought such sudden end to that glory, precipitated the fall of this triumphant beast,[c] and scattered the entire great army of its mercenaries and simpletons, except for a few leftovers, who, still banded together as stragglers and marauders under the banner of the *Hallische Jahrbücher*,[d] were permitted to do mischief for a while, resulting in a public scandal; and a few miserable simpletons,

---

* See my *Critique of the Kantian Philosophy*, second edn., p. 572 [*WWR* 1, 538–9 (Hübscher *SW* 2, 603)].

[a] *'Narrn auf eigene Hand'* [Goethe, 'Den Originalen']

[b] *Repetent* [Literally: 'repetitor'; at German universities of the time a tutor who helped students with their studies]

[c] *bestia trionfante* [After Giordano Bruno, *Spaccio de la bestia trionfante*, 1584 (*The Expulsion of the Triumphant Beast*)]

[d] [*Hallische Jahrbücher für Wissenschaft und Kunst*, a literary and political magazine edited by Arnold Ruge and Theodor Echtermeyer; organ of the Young Hegelians]

who believe to this day what they were made to believe in their youth and which they still peddle? – Nothing else than that someone has had the mischievous idea to prove that this is a university philosophy that agrees with established religion only apparently and in the letter, but not actually and in the proper sense. In and of itself this accusation was justified, since this was later proved by *neo-Catholicism*. For *German* or *neo-Catholicism* is   156 nothing but popularized *Hegelry*. Like the latter, it leaves the world unexplained, it is just there, without further information. It simply receives the name *God*, and humanity the name *Christ*. Both are 'ends in themselves', i.e. are just there to enjoy themselves as long as the short life lasts. Therefore let us rejoice![a] And the Hegelian apotheosis of the state is pursued further into communism. A very thorough exposition of neo-Catholicism in this sense is provided by F. Kampe, *History of the Religious Movement of Modern Times*, vol. 3, 1856.[b,3]

However, that such an accusation could be the Achilles' heel of a dominant philosophical system reveals to us

> what qualities avail
> To mark that man and turn the scale,[c]

or what the actual criterion of the truth and validity of a philosophy at German universities is, and what it depends on. Furthermore, such an accusation should have been dispatched succinctly with 'nothing to do with Dionysus',[d] apart from the contemptible nature of all charges of heresy.

Whoever needs yet further proofs for this very insight, should consider the sequel to the great Hegel-farce, namely the immediately following, indeed very timely conversion of Herr von Schelling from Spinozism to bigotry and his subsequent transfer from Munich to Berlin, accompanied by the trumpet blasts of all newspapers, according to whose insinuations one could have believed that he brought along the personal God, for whom there was such a great desire, in his pocket; whereupon the throng of students became so great that they even climbed through the windows into the auditorium. Then, at the end of his tenure, there

---

[a] *Gaudeamus igitur!*
[b] *Geschichte der religiösen Bewegung der neuern Zeit* [Friedrich Ferdinand Kampe, 4 vols., Leipzig: Wigand, 1852–60]
[c] *welch eine Qualität/ Den Ausschlag giebt, den Mann erhöht* [Goethe, *Faust* I, 2099f.]
[d] οὐδὲν πρὸς Διόνυσον [Greek proverb originating in a joke by audiences, after the customary dithyrambs sung in honour of Dionysus at the beginning of plays were abandoned and other songs were substituted]

was the 'megalo-man's-diploma',[a] which a number of professors of the
university who had been his listeners most subserviently bestowed upon
him, and in general his whole, extremely illustrious and no less lucrative role
in Berlin, which he played to the end without blushing, and this in his old
age, when in noble natures the concern about the memory that one leaves
behind outweighs any other. One could become duly depressed about
something like this; indeed, one could even think the philosophy professors
themselves would have to blush about this; but that is a pipe dream.
However, anyone whose eyes are not yet opened about academic philosophy and its heroes after contemplating such a tab[b] cannot be helped.

157

Meanwhile, fairness demands that we judge university philosophy not
only, as has happened here, from the standpoint of its alleged purpose, but
rather from that of its true and proper purpose. For this purpose is
tantamount to ensuring that the future junior barristers, lawyers, doctors,
candidates,[c] and teachers receive even in their innermost convictions that
orientation which is adequate to the intentions that the state and its government have in regard to them. I have no objection to this and shall thus
content myself with it. For I do not feel competent to judge the necessity, or
dispensability, of such a measure of the state. Rather I leave this judgement
up to those people who have the difficult task of ruling *human beings*, i.e. to
maintain law, order, peace and quiet among the many million members of a
species that, with respect to its great majority, is boundlessly egoistic,
unjust, unfair, dishonest, envious, malicious, and at the same time parochial
and wrong-headed, and to protect the few who have been given some
property from the host of those who have nothing but their bodily strength.
The task is so difficult that I truly do not presume to argue with them about
the means to be employed in this. For 'I praise God for each day's bliss, that
the Roman Empire's not my business'[d] – has always been my motto. But it
was these purposes of state on the part of university philosophy that
procured such unprecedented ministerial favour for *Hegelry*. For the *state*
was for Hegelry 'the absolutely perfected ethical organism'; for it, the whole
purpose of human existence was realized in the *state*. Could there be a better

---

[a] *Groß-Mannsdiplom* [A play on words like: '*Großmannssucht*' (megalomania); '*Großmaul*' (loud-
mouth); '*Großtuer*' (braggart), and many others with the negative connotation of 'boasting']
[b] *Konsummation* [*Konsumation*]
[c] *Kandidaten* [In general, students who have passed their first, theoretical exam, but still have to take the
final exam; they could be candidates in any field, such as *theologiae candidatus, medicinae candidatus,
philosophiae candidatus*, etc.]
[d] *ich danke Gott an jedem Morgen, daß ich nicht brauch' für's Röm'sche Reich zu sorgen* [Goethe, *Faust* I,
2093f.; quotation changed by Schopenhauer from second person plural imperative to first person
singular indicative]

preparation for future barristers and soon-to-be civil servants than this, as a result of which their whole essence and being, with body and soul, was completely forfeited to the state, like that of the bee in the beehive, and they had to work towards nothing, neither in this world or the next, but to become efficient wheels by contributing to keeping the great machine of the state running, this ultimate end of everything good?[a] The barrister and the   158 human being were thus one and the same. It was a true apotheosis of philistinism.[4]

But the relation of such university philosophy and the state is one thing, and its relation to philosophy proper, in itself, is another; the latter might in this respect be distinguished as *pure* philosophy from the former as *applied* philosophy. For pure philosophy knows no other purpose than the truth, and thus it may come about that every other purpose pursued by means of it spoils this. Its lofty goal is to satisfy that noble necessity, which I call the *metaphysical*, which makes itself profoundly and vividly felt by humankind at all times, but in particular when, as at the present time, the esteem of religious doctrine has been declining more and more. This doctrine, intended and adequate for the great mass of humanity, can only comprise *allegorical* truth, which, however, it must pass off as true in the literal sense.[b] For that reason, with the ever wider dissemination of all sorts of historical, physical, and even philosophical *knowledge*,[c] the number of people for whom this kind of truth does not suffice any longer grows ever larger, and they will increasingly insist on truth in the proper sense. What then can an academic puppet, moved by alien strings,[d] achieve? How far shall we proceed with this imposed spinning-wheel philosophy, or with hollow verbal edifices, with clichés that are bland or which obfuscate even the most common and comprehensible truths through verboseness, or even with Hegelian absolute nonsense? – And on the other hand, even if the righteous John were to come out of the desert, dressed in hides and nourished by locusts, untouched by all this confusion, and all the while, with a pure heart and utter seriousness, apply himself to the search for truth and offer its fruits – what kind of reception would he have to expect from those businessmen of the lectern?[e] They are hired for the purposes of the state, and with wife and child have to live off philosophy and hence their motto is 'first live, then philosophize',[f] and accordingly they have cornered the market and made sure that nothing counts but what they accept, so that   159 merit exists only if it suits them and their mediocrity to acknowledge it. For

---

[a] *ultimus finis bonorum*   [b] *sensu proprio*   [c] *Kenntnisse*
[d] *nervis alienis mobile* [Horace, *Satires* II, 7, 82]   [e] *Katheder*   [f] *primum vivere, deinde philosophari*

they have on the leash the attention of the public, small as it is, that concerns itself with philosophy, since this public surely will not spend its time, labour, and effort on things that promise not amusements, like poetic productions, but instruction, and financially unfruitful instruction at that, without having complete assurance in advance that such efforts will be richly rewarded. Now this public expects instruction from the experts, because of its inherited faith that someone who lives off a thing also understands it, experts who, sure enough, behind lecterns and in compendiums, journals, and literary periodicals comport themselves as the true masters of the subject; hence it lets these experts sample and select for it what is worthy of note and, conversely, what is not. – Oh, how would you fare, my poor John from the desert if, as is to be expected, what you offer is not composed according to the tacit convention of the gentlemen of this lucrative philosophy! They will look upon you as someone who does not comprehend the spirit of the game and, therefore, threatens to spoil it for all of them; thus they will look upon you as their common enemy and adversary. Even if what you bring were the greatest masterpiece of the human spirit, it could never find favour in their eyes. For it would not be composed according to conventional norm,[a] and consequently would not be of the right sort for them to be able to make it the subject of their academic lecture in order to make a living *off it*. It never occurs to a philosophy professor to study an emerging new system in regard to its truth; on the contrary, he immediately checks only whether it can be reconciled with the doctrines of established religion, the interests of the government, and the dominant views of the time. Afterwards he decides its fate.[5] However, if such a new system prevailed nonetheless, if it attracted the attention of the public as instructive and informative and were found to be worthy of study, then it would to this extent have to deprive philosophy that is suited for academia[b] of its attention, indeed, of its reputation and, worse still, of its sales. God forbid![c] Therefore, such a thing is not to happen and all must resist it, standing together as one. A happy instinct provides the method and tactics for this, as it is readily given to every being for its self-preservation. For the denial and refutation of a philosophy running counter to conventional norm[d] is often a precarious matter, especially where one smells merit and certain qualities that cannot be imparted by a professor's diploma. In the latter case, one should definitely not venture on such a matter, since by doing so the work may be placed on the index of forbidden books and would obtain notoriety; the inquisitive would come running;

160

---

[a] *ad normam conventionis*   [b] *kathederfähige*   [c] *Di meliora!*   [d] *norma conventionis*

and then highly inconvenient comparisons could be drawn and the result might be disagreeable. On the contrary, as like-minded and equally capable brothers, to regard such inopportune achievement as null and void,[a] to receive with the most impartial countenance the most significant as completely insignificant; what is profoundly thought through and destined for the ages as not worth mentioning in order to smother it; derisively to purse one's lips and keep silent about it, being silent in that kind of 'silence' already denounced by old Seneca, 'which is imposed by envy' (*Epistles*, 79);[b] and at times to crow the more loudly about the abortive intellectual offspring and freaks of the confraternity, in the reassuring consciousness that what nobody knows about might as well not exist, and that the issues in the world amount to what they appear as and are named, not according to what they are; – this is the safest and least dangerous method against merit, which, consequently, I would recommend to all numbskulls who seek their livelihood in things for which a greater aptitude is needed. Yet I do not vouch for later consequences.

However, we should by no means invoke the gods here, as over an egregious sacrilege;[c] for all this is nothing but a scene from the drama playing out before our eyes at all times, in all the arts and sciences, namely the ancient battle between those who live *for* a cause and those who live *off* it, or between those who *are* the cause and those who *represent* it. For the former it is the end to which their life is the mere means; for the latter it is the means, indeed the burdensome condition for living, for well-being, for enjoyment, for domestic happiness, in which alone lies their true earnest-   161
ness, since it is here that nature has drawn the boundary of their sphere of action. Whoever wants to see examples of this drama and come to know it more closely, should study the history of literature and read the biographies of great masters of every kind and art. We will then see that it has always been like this and understand that it will remain this way as well. Everybody recognizes it in the past, but hardly anybody does so in the present. The brilliant pages of the history of literature are at the same time almost universally the tragic ones. In all disciplines they show us how merit usually had to wait until the fools had finished fooling, the feast had ended, and everybody had gone to bed; then it rose, like a ghost in the dead of night, in order to claim at last, yet as a shadow, its place of honour that was withheld from it.

Meanwhile we are concerned here solely with philosophy and its representatives. There we initially find that very few philosophers have ever been

---

[a] *non avenue*   [b] *silentium, quod livor indixerit* [Seneca, *Epistles*, 79, 17]   [c] *inauditum nefas*

professors of philosophy, and proportionately even fewer philosophy professors were philosophers; thus it could be claimed that, just as idioelectric[a] bodies are no conductors of electricity, so the philosophers are no professors of philosophy. Indeed, this appointment stands in the way of the independent thinker almost more than any other. For the philosophical lectern is in a way a public confessional box, where people make their confessions of faith before the public.[b] Furthermore, there is almost nothing as obstructive to the actual attainment of thorough, or even profound insights, thus to truly becoming wise, as the constant necessity to appear wise, the exhibition of ostensible knowledge in front of students eager to learn, and the readiness to answer all imaginable questions. Worst of all, however, is that a man in such a position, with each thought that may still occur to him, will be worried how such a thought will fit in with the interests of his superiors; this paralyses his thinking so much that the thoughts themselves no longer dare to form. The atmosphere of freedom is indispensable to truth. What needs to be said concerning the exception that confirms the rule,[c] that *Kant* was a professor, I have already mentioned above and shall only add that Kant's philosophy as well would have become more magnificent, more decisive, more pure, and more beautiful if he had not held that professorship, although, very wisely, he kept the philosopher separate from the professor by not lecturing about his own doctrine from the lectern. (See Rosenkranz, *History of the Kantian Philosophy*, p. 148.[d])

162

However, if I look back at the supposed philosophers who have appeared in the half century that has elapsed since *Kant's* influential work, I sadly see no one whom I could credit with seeking truth with true and complete seriousness; on the contrary, I find them all, even if not always clearly conscious of this, intent on the mere semblance of a matter, on having an effect, impressing, indeed, mystifying and trying hard to obtain the approbation of their superiors and subsequently of their students, and in all this the ultimate goal always remains to feast comfortably with their wife and child on the income from the matter. But this is also really in keeping with human nature, which, like every animal nature, knows as its immediate ends only eating, drinking, and caring for the brood, but as its particular inheritance has received only the passion for glittering and showing off. In contrast, the first condition for real and genuine achievements in philosophy, as in poetry and the fine arts, is a completely abnormal propensity, contrary to the usual norm of human nature, to substitute *subjective* striving

---

[a] *idioelektrischen*   [b] *coram populo*   [c] *exceptio, quae firmat regulam*
[d] *Geschichte der Kant'schen Philosophie* [Karl Rosenkranz, Leipzig: Voss, 1840]

for the well-being of one's own person with a completely *objective* striving aimed at an *achievement* alien to the person, which therefore very fittingly is called *eccentric* and occasionally is even ridiculed as quixotic. However, Aristotle already said it: 'We must not follow those who advise us to have human thoughts, since we are human, and mortal thoughts, as mortals should; on the contrary, we should try to become immortal as far as is possible and do our utmost to live in accordance with what is highest in us.'[a] Such an intellectual tendency certainly is an extremely rare anomaly; yet for this reason its fruits benefit the whole of humanity in the course of time, since luckily they are of the kind that can be preserved. And further: thinkers can be divided into those who think *for themselves* and those who think *for others*; the latter are the rule, the former the exception. Accordingly, the former are independent thinkers in a twofold sense and egoists in the most noble sense of the word; from them alone does the world receive instruction. For only the light that someone kindles for himself also shines for others afterwards, so that the converse of what Seneca asserts in a moral respect, 'You must live for others if you wish to live for yourself',[b] is true in an intellectual respect: 'You must think for yourself if you wish to have thought for all.'[c] But this is precisely the rare anomaly, which cannot be forced through by any premeditation and good will, yet without which no actual progress in philosophy is possible. For a mind never undergoes the highest exertion, required for such progress, for the sake of others or, in general, for mediate goals, an exertion which precisely calls for forgetting oneself and all purposes; instead, what remains is the semblance and pretence of the matter. To be sure, some found concepts are combined in various ways and, as it were, a house of cards is built in this way; but nothing new and genuine comes into the world through this. Add to this that people whose own well-being is the true end and for whom thinking is only a means to this end merely have to keep an eye on the temporary needs and inclinations of their contemporaries, the interests of those in authority, and so forth. That does not allow for aiming at the truth, which, even if faced honestly, is extremely difficult to come upon.

163

---

[a] οὐ χρὴ δέ, κατὰ τοὺς παραινοῦντας, ἀνθρώπινα φρονεῖν ἄνθρωπον ὄντα, οὐδὲ θνητὰ τὸν θνητόν, ἀλλ', ἐφ' ὅσον ἐνδέχεται, ἀθανατίζειν, καὶ πάντα ποιεῖν πρὸς τὸ ζῆν κατὰ τὸ κράτιστον τῶν ἐν αὐτῷ (*neque vero nos oportet humana sapere ac sentire, ut quidam monent, quum simus homines; neque mortalia, quum mortales; sed nos ipsos, quoad ejus fieri potest, a mortalitate vindicare, atque omnia facere, ut ei nostri parti, qua in nobis est optima, convenienter vivamus.* (*Nicomachean Ethics* X, 7 [1177b; following, with minor changes, Martin Ostwald's translation])

[b] *alteri vivas oportet, si vis tibi vivere* ([Seneca] *Epistles*, 48 [2])

[c] *tibi cogites oportet, si omnibus cogitasse volueris*

In general, how should someone who seeks an honest living for himself and wife and child devote himself to the *truth*? The truth that at all times has been a dangerous companion, a guest unwelcome everywhere – that probably is depicted naked also for the reason that it brings nothing with it, has nothing to bestow, but only wants to be sought for its own sake. Two masters as different as the world and the truth, which have nothing else in common than the initial letter,[a] cannot be served at the same time; such an enterprise leads to hypocrisy, eye-service,[b] and double-dealing.[c] Then it can happen that a priest of the truth turns into a champion of deception, who eagerly teaches what he himself does not believe, thereby wasting the time and the minds of trusting young people, and who, renouncing all literary conscience, even is a party to eulogizing influential bunglers, e.g. sanctimonious blockheads; or that, paid by the state and for state purposes, he now concerns himself with deifying the state, making it the pinnacle of all human striving and all things, and thereby not only transforms the philosophical lecture-hall into a school of the most shallow philistinism, but in the end, as for example Hegel, arrives at the scandalous doctrine that the destiny of human beings merges with the *state* – like, for instance, that of the bee with the beehive; whereby the lofty end of our existence is completely removed from view.

That philosophy is not suited for gaining a livelihood Plato had already shown in his portrayals of the Sophists, whom he contrasts with Socrates, but most delightfully described the activities and the success of these people with unmatched humour at the beginning of the *Protagoras*. For the ancients, earning money by means of philosophy was and remained the mark that distinguished the Sophist from the philosopher. Accordingly, the relation between Sophists and philosophers was completely analogous to that between girls who abandon themselves for love and paid prostitutes.[6] I have already proved in my chief work, vol. 2, ch. 17, p. 162[d] that for this reason Socrates relegated Aristippus to the Sophists and Aristotle too counted him among them. Stobaeus reports that the Stoics also thought so (*Eclogae ethicae* II, 7): 'A difference must be drawn between those who declare that they act as sophists and impart the doctrines of philosophy for money, and those who think that to embrace teaching as a sophist is worthless, as if hawking ideas, and who believe that it is wrong to earn

---

[a] ['*Welt*' and '*Wahrheit*']
[b] *Augendienerei* [from the Greek ὀφθαλμοδουλεία (see Colossians 3:22), meaning 'adulation', 'sycophancy']
[c] *Achselträgerei*   [d] [Third edn., p. 179 (Hübscher *SW* 3, 179)]

money for the education of those who seek it, since this kind of money-making devalues the dignity of philosophy.'ᵃ (See Stobaeus, *Eclogae physicae et ethicae*, ed. Heeren, Part 2, vol. 1, p. 226.) Also the passage in Xenophon, 165 which Stobaeus quotes in *Florilegium* I, p. 57, reads in the original (*Memorabilia* I, 6, 17): 'Those who sell wisdom for money to those who want it are called sophists.'ᵇ Also *Ulpian* raises the question: 'Are philosophers to be counted among the *professors*? I do not think so, not because the subject matter is not conscientiously pursued, but because they must above all *confess publicly* that they *despise paid work*'ᶜ (Lex I, §4, *Digesta de extraordinaria cognitione* 50, 13).⁷ Opinion on this point was so unshakable that we even find it fully accepted among the later emperors; even in *Philostratus* Apollonius of Tyana chiefly reproaches his opponent Euphrates for 'hawking wisdom';ᵈ and also in his fifty-first epistle he writes to the same: 'There are those who rebuke you for having accepted money from the emperor, which would not be odd if you had not made it clear that you had accepted it as wages for philosophy, and so many times, and so much, and from someone who was bound to believe you to be a philosopher.'ᵉ In accordance with this he says of himself in the forty-second epistle that in case of need he would accept alms, but never wages for his philosophy, not even when destitute: 'If anyone offers money to Apollonius and is judged by him to be worthy, he will accept it if he needs it. But for philosophy he will not accept wages, not even if he needs them.'ᶠ This ancient opinion is well foundedᵍ and grounded in the fact that philosophy has many points of contact with human life, public as well as individual life. For that reason, when philosophy is done for gain, intent will soon prevail

---

ᵃ τῶν μὲν αὐτὸ τοῦτο λεγόντων σοφιστεύειν, τὸ ἐπὶ μισθῷ μεταδιδόναι τῶν τῆς φιλοσοφίας δογμάτων· τῶν δ' ὑποτοπησάντων ἐν τῷ σοφιστεύειν περιέχεσθαί τι φαῦλον, οἱονεὶ λόγους καπηλεύειν, οὐ φαμένων δεῖν ἀπὸ παιδείας παρὰ τῶν ἐπιτυχόντων χρηματίζεσθαι, καταδεέστερον γὰρ εἶναι τὸν τρόπον τοῦτον τοῦ χρηματισμοῦ τοῦ τῆς φιλοσοφίας ἀξιώματος.

ᵇ τοὺς μὲν τὴν σοφίαν ἀργυρίου τῷ βουλομένῳ πωλοῦντας, σοφιστὰς ἀποκαλοῦσιν [Rather: I, 6, 13]

ᶜ *an et philosophi* professorum *numero sint? Et non putem, non quia non religiosa res est, sed quia hoc primum* profiteri *eos oportet,* mercenariam operam spernere

ᵈ τὴν σοφίαν καπηλεύειν (*sapientiam cauponari*) (I, 13) [Flavius Philostratus, *The Life of Apollonius of Tyana*]

ᵉ ἐπιτιμῶσί σοί τινες, ὡς εἰληφότι χρήματα παρὰ τοῦ βασιλέως· ὅπερ οὐκ ἄτοπον, εἰ μὴ φαίνοιο φιλοσοφίας εἰληφέναι μισθόν, καὶ τοσαυτάκις, καὶ ἐπὶ τοσοῦτον, καὶ παρὰ τοῦ πεπιστευκότος εἶναί σε φιλόσοφον. (*Reprehendunt te quidam, quod pecuniam ab imperatore acceperis: quod absonum non esset, nisi videreris philosophiae mercedem accepisse, et toties, et tam magnam, et ab illo, qui te philosophum esse putabat.*) [Philostratus, *Apollonius of Tyana. Letters of Apollonius, Ancient Testimonia, Eusebius's Reply to Hierocles*, Epistle 51]

ᶠ Ἐάν τις Ἀπολλωνίῳ χρήματα διδῷ, καὶ ὁ διδοὺς ἄξιος νομίζηται, λήψεται δεόμενος· φιλοσοφίας δὲ μισθὸν οὐ λήψεται, κἂν δέηται. (*Si quis Apollonio pecunias dederit et qui dat dignus judicatus fuerit ab eo; si opus habuerit, accipiet. Philosophiae vero mercedem, ne si indigeat quidem, accipiet.*) [Epistle 42]

ᵍ *hat guten Grund*

over insight[a] and supposed philosophers turn into mere parasites of philosophy; however, such parasites will oppose genuine philosophy in an obstructing and hostile manner, indeed, they will conspire against it in order to assert only what advances their cause. For as soon as profit is at stake it can easily happen that, where advantage demands it, all sorts of base means, connivances, coalitions, etc. are employed in order, for material purposes, to gain entry and validity for the false and the bad, and then it becomes necessary to suppress the opposing true, genuine, and valuable. But no one is less equal to such tricks than a genuine philosopher who might have become mixed up with his work in the doings of these tradespeople. – The fine arts, even poetry, are scarcely harmed by also serving for gain; for each of their works has a separate existence for itself, and the bad can no more supplant the good than it can obscure it. However, philosophy is a whole, a unity, and aims at truth, not beauty; there are many kinds of beauty, but only *one* truth; so many Muses, but only *one* Minerva. For that reason, the poet can confidently disdain to castigate the bad; but the philosopher can find himself in the situation where he must do so. For here the bad that has gained acceptance opposes the good in a downright hostile manner, and the proliferating weeds crowd out the useful plant. Philosophy, by its nature, is exclusive, for it grounds the manner of thinking of the age; therefore, the governing system, like the sons of a sultan, will not tolerate another beside it. In addition, the judgement here is extremely difficult; indeed, already obtaining the data for it is laborious. If, through artifice, the false is brought into circulation and everywhere is loudly proclaimed as the true and genuine by paid stentorian voices, then the spirit of the times is poisoned, all branches of literature are corrupted, all elevation of the mind comes to a standstill, and a long-lasting bulwark is erected against what is actually good and genuine of every kind. These are the fruits of 'philosophy for hire'.[b] For elucidation, one should behold the mischief that has been done with philosophy since Kant and what, consequently, has become of it. But only the true history of the Hegelian charlatanry and the path of its dissemination will eventually provide the right illustration of what I have said.

As a result of all this, someone who is concerned not with state-philosophy and comic philosophy,[c] but with knowledge and thus with seriously meant and consequently uncompromising search for truth, must

---

[a] [Schopenhauer plays on the similarity of the terms *Absicht* (interest, intention, intent) and *Einsicht* (insight)]
[b] φιλοσοφία μισθοφόρος   [c] *Spaaßphilosophie*

seek them anywhere but at the universities, where their sister, philosophy according to conventional norm,[a] reigns and writes the menu. Indeed, I am increasingly inclined to the view that it would be more beneficial for philosophy if it stopped being a trade and no longer appeared in civil life, represented by professors. It is a plant that, like alpine rose and edelweiss,[b] thrives only in free mountain air, but gets out of control with artificial cultivation. Those representatives of philosophy in civil life represent it mostly in the same way that an actor represents the king. For instance, were the Sophists, whom Socrates fought so tirelessly and Plato made the subject of his ridicule, anything but professors of philosophy and rhetoric? Is it not really that ancient feud, never extinguished since then, that is still carried on by me in the present? The highest aspirations of the human spirit are simply not compatible with profit; its noble nature cannot be closely associated with it. – University philosophy might still pass muster if the salaried teachers tried to meet the requirements of their profession by passing to the next generation, after the manner of other professors, the existing knowledge of their discipline, accepted as true for the time being, thus faithfully and precisely explaining to their audience the system of the last existing real philosopher, and hashing and rehashing the subjects for them. – I say that would work if they possessed only so much judgement, or at least discretion, not to regard as philosophers mere sophists, as e.g. a Fichte, a Schelling, not to mention a Hegel. However, not only do they normally lack such qualities, but they are trapped in the unfortunate delusion that it is part of their duty to play philosophers themselves and present the world with the fruits of their profundity. Out of this delusion those productions, as miserable as they are numerous, come forth, in which humdrum minds, even sometimes those that are not even humdrum, deal with *those* problems towards whose solution the greatest efforts of the rarest   168 minds have been directed for thousands of years, minds equipped with the most extraordinary abilities, forgetting their own person over the love for truth, sometimes driven into the dungeon by the passion of striving for light, even on to the scaffold, minds whose rarity is so great that the history of philosophy, which for two thousand five hundred years has been running parallel to the history of nations, cannot boast even one hundredth as many renowned philosophers as the history of nations can show off famous monarchs; for it is none other than the completely solitary minds in whom nature had come to a clearer consciousness of itself than in others. But these are so far removed from ordinariness and the masses that most

[a] *ad normam conventionis*   [b] *Fluenblume*

receive just acknowledgement only after their death, or at most in their old age. For example, the real, great fame of *Aristotle*, which later spread farther than any other, began, by all appearances, only two hundred years after his death. *Epicurus*, whose name is still known nowadays to the crowd, lived in Athens completely unknown until his death. (Seneca, *Epistles*, 79.[a]) *Bruno* and *Spinoza* achieved influence and honour only in the second century after their death. Even *David Hume*, who wrote with such clarity and in such a popular manner, was fifty years old when people started to pay attention to him, although he had long ago delivered his works. *Kant* became famous only after his sixtieth year. However, things are faster with the academic philosophers of our day, since they have no time to lose. One professor proclaims the doctrine of his colleague who thrives at a neighbouring university as the finally attained pinnacle of human wisdom; and at once that one is a great philosopher, who promptly takes up his place in the history of philosophy, namely in the history that a third colleague works on for the next fair, who, without embarrassment, now adds to the immortal names of the martyrs of truth from all centuries the worthy names of his duly appointed colleagues who are flourishing just then, as so many philosophers who can also join the ranks, since they have filled so much paper and found universal recognition among colleagues. So then it is, for example, 'Aristotle and Herbart', or 'Spinoza and Hegel', 'Plato and Schleiermacher', and the astonished world must witness that philosophers, whom austere nature formerly only managed to produce few and far between over the course of centuries, have during these recent decades shot up like mushrooms among the Germans, well-known to be so highly gifted. Of course, this glory of the age is helped along in every way; thus, whether in learned journals or else in his own works, one philosophy professor will not fail to take into close consideration, with important countenance and official gravity, the preposterous ideas of another; and so it looks precisely as if we were dealing here with actual progress in human knowledge. In return, his stillborn efforts[b] will very soon experience the same honour, and, of course, we know that 'Nothing looks more dignified than two mules scratching each other.'[c] So many ordinary heads who believe themselves officially and professionally obligated to represent what nature least intended for them and to bear burdens requiring the shoulders of intellectual giants in all earnestness provide a miserable spectacle. For to hear the

169

---

[a] [79, 15]   [b] *Abortus*

[c] *nihil officiosius, quam cum mutuum muli scabunt* [See Marcus Terentius Varro, *Saturae Menippeae* (*Menippean Satires*) 55 (*Mutuum muli scabunt, peri chorismou*)]

hoarse sing and to see the lame dance is embarrassing; but to listen to the limited mind philosophize is unbearable. In order to hide the lack of real thought, some devise an imposing apparatus of long, composite terms, intricate phrases, immeasurable periods, new and unheard-of expressions, which all together then make for a jargon as difficult and scholarly sounding as possible. However, with all of this they say – nothing; we receive no thoughts and do not feel our insight increased, but must only sigh: 'I may hear the clapper of the mill, but I do not see the flour';[a] or we see all too clearly what meagre, vulgar, insipid, and crude views are behind the high-sounding bombast. Oh! That it were possible to teach such comic philosophers the concept of the true and terrible seriousness with which the problem of existence grips the thinker and stirs his innermost being! Then they could no longer be comic philosophers, no longer dispassionately   170 concoct idle fibs about absolute thought, or the contradiction supposedly contained in all fundamental concepts, nor could they relish with enviable satisfaction such hollow nuts as 'the world is the existence of the infinite in the finite', and 'the spirit is the reflection of the infinite in the finite', etc. That would be bad for them, for they really want to be philosophers and quite original thinkers. However, it is as likely that an ordinary mind should have extraordinary thoughts as that an oak tree should bear apricots. On the other hand, everyone for himself already has *ordinary* thoughts and has no need to read them; hence, since in philosophy it is thoughts, not experiences and facts that count, nothing will ever be achieved here by ordinary minds. Some, conscious of the drawback, have saved a store of alien thoughts, mostly incompletely, always superficially conceived, which nonetheless in their heads are in danger of evaporating into mere phrases and words. They shift these around and at the most seek to fit them together like dominoes; for they compare what this one has said, and that one, and again another, and still another, and try to make sense of it. With such people we would seek in vain some firm fundamental conception of things and the world, resting on an intuitive basis and thus uniformly coherent. Just for that reason they have no completely decided opinion or determinate, firm judgement on anything; instead, they grope about, as in a fog, with their acquired thoughts, views, and exceptions.[b] They have really only worked towards knowledge[c] and erudition for the purpose of imparting it. So be it: But then they should not play the philosopher, but understand how to separate the wheat from the chaff.

---

[a] *das Klappern der Mühle höre ich wohl, aber das Mehl sehe ich nicht* [German proverb]
[b] *Exceptionen*   [c] *Wissen*

The real thinkers have worked towards *insight*, that is, insight for its own sake, because they fervently desired to make the world in which they live somehow comprehensible to themselves, but not to teach and twaddle. Therefore, slowly and gradually a firm, coherent fundamental belief grows in them, as the result of continuous meditation, which is always based on the intuitive comprehension of the world and from which paths proceed to all particular truths, which themselves again throw light on that fundamental belief. As a result of this they have at least a definite, well understood opinion, coherent with the whole, about every problem of life and the world and thus need not satisfy anybody with empty phrases, as those other thinkers do, who are always found occupied with comparing and weighing alien opinions instead of the things themselves, so that we might believe that it was a question of far-away countries of which we had to critically compare the reports of the few travellers who managed to get there, but not of the actual world lying also before them, spread out and distinct. For them it is a case of:

> In regard to ourselves, gentlemen, our habit is
> To revise at length, from point for point,
> another's thought, for we have none.   Voltaire[a]

However, the worst in all this business, which otherwise might continue at least for the curious enthusiast, is the following: it is in the interest of the thinkers just discussed for the shallow and mindless to pass for something. But this it cannot do if justice is done to anything genuine, great, and profound that might appear. Therefore, in order to stifle the latter and bring the bad into circulation unopposed, they band together, like all the weak, form cliques and parties, and take over the literary magazines, where, as in their own books, they talk with deep veneration and important countenance about their respective masterpieces and in that way lead the short-sighted public by the nose. Their relation to the real philosophers is somewhat like that of the former meistersinger to the poets. To elucidate what has been said one should consult the scribblings of the academic philosophers, published in time for the fairs, and the literary magazines, that play their tune. Whoever is skilled at this, should observe the cunning by means of which, if the occasion arises, they take pains to hush up the significant as

---

[a] *Pour nous, Messieurs, nous avons l'habitude / De rédiger au long, de point au point, / Ce qu'on pensa, mais nous ne pensons point.* [Voltaire, *Le temple du goût* (1733); addition of the first three words by Schopenhauer]

insignificant, and the tricks they use to deprive it of the attention of the public, reminiscent of the maxim by Publilius Syrus: 'Powerless is all virtue, if its fame does not extend widely.' (See *Sententiae of Publilius Syrus and other ancients*, edition by J. Gruter, Meißen: Erbstein, 1790, l. 280.)[a] But now we should go back farther on this path and with these considerations, to the beginning of this[b] century and see what the Schellingites, but then in a much worse manner the Hegelians, have carelessly sinned;[c] we should bring ourselves to leaf through the repulsive jumble! for no one can be expected to read it. Then we should consider and calculate the invaluable time, together with the paper and the money, that the public must have wasted on these charlatanries over half a century. To be sure, the patience of the public, which reads this rubbish of mindless philosophasters, is incomprehensible as well, continuing year in and year out, regardless of the agonizing tedium brooding like a thick fog over it, just because one reads and reads without ever getting hold of a thought, since the writer, who himself has nothing distinct and determinate in mind, heaps words upon words, phrases upon phrases and still says nothing, because he has nothing to say, knows nothing, thinks nothing, but nonetheless wants to talk. Therefore, he chooses his words not according to the aptness with which they express his thoughts and insights, but according to the greater skill with which they conceal his lack of them. Nonetheless, stuff like that is printed, bought, and read; and half a century has passed without readers realizing that, as the Spanish say, '*papan viento*', i.e. they gulp down mere air. Meanwhile, to be fair, I have to mention that, in order to keep this clattering mill going, often a quite peculiar device is employed, whose invention can be traced to Messrs Fichte and Schelling. I mean the canny trick of writing enigmatically, i.e. incomprehensibly, the real refinement being to arrange the gibberish so that readers must believe it is their fault if they do not understand it; while the writer knows very well that it is due to himself in that he in fact has nothing intelligible, i.e. nothing clearly thought out, to say. Without this artifice Messrs Fichte and Schelling could not have achieved their pseudo-glory. However, as is well known, no one has employed the same gimmick so impudently and to such high degree as *Hegel*. If the latter, from the beginning, had clearly explained the absurd fundamental thought of his pseudo-philosophy – namely to turn the true

172

173

---

[a] *Jacet omnis virtus, fama nisi late patet (Publii Syri et Aliorum Veterum Sententiae: in usum scholarum adspersis notulis ex rec[ensione] J. Gruteri* [Jean Gruter], *Misenae: Erbstein, 1970, v.280)*
[b] [nineteenth]
[c] *in den Tag hineingesündigt* [Schopenhauer's variation on the common phrase 'in den Tag hineinleben', which means 'to live from day to day, without care']

and natural course of things outright on its head to make the universal concepts, which we abstract from empirical intuition and which hence arise through imagining determinations as absent[a] and which, consequently, are the emptier the more general they are, into the primary, the original, the truly real (into the thing in itself, in Kantian language), as a result of which the empirically real world is first supposed to come into existence – I say, if he had, in clear, intelligible words, distinctly explained this monstrous inversion of the logical order,[b] indeed this effectively ludicrous idea, together with the admixture that such concepts think and move themselves without our assistance, then everyone would have laughed in his face or shrugged his shoulders, and would have deemed the buffoonery not worthy of attention. But then even venality and perfidy would have sounded the trumpet in vain in order to impose on the world as highest wisdom the most absurd thing that it has ever seen and to compromise forever the German world of letters with its judgement. In contrast, under the veil of unintelligible nonsense, it worked and the madness succeeded:

> For fools admire and love much more everything
> That they perceive hidden under twisted words.   Lucretius I, 642[c]

Encouraged by such examples, almost every pathetic scribbler has sought to write with affected obscurity, so that it looks as if no words could express his lofty, or deep, thoughts. Instead of trying in every way to make himself clear to his readers, he often seems to call out to them teasingly: 'You cannot guess what I am thinking here, right!' Now if the readers, instead of answering, 'I do not give a toss about it', and throwing away the book, struggle with it in vain, in the end they think that it had to be something extremely clever, exceeding their mental capacity, and now, with raised eyebrows, call its author a profound thinker. One result of this whole fine method is, amongst other things, that if in England one wants to describe something as very obscure, indeed completely incomprehensible, one says 'it is like German metaphysics';[d] as one similarly says in France: 'That is as clear as a bottle of ink'.[e]

It is surely superfluous to mention here, yet it cannot be said too often, that, in contrast, good writers always take great pains to urge their reader to

---

[a] *Wegdenken von Bestimmungen*   [b] ὕστερον πρότερον
[c] *Omnia enim stolidi magis admirantur amantque,/ Inversis quae sub verbis latitantia cernunt.* Lucretius [*De rerum natura*] I, [641–]642.
[d] [English in the original]   [e] *c'est clair comme la bouteille à l'encre*

think exactly what they themselves have thought; for whoever has something important[a] to communicate will be anxious that it not be lost. Therefore, good style rests mainly on the fact that one really has something to say; it is just this small detail that is lacking in most contemporary writers and thus is to blame for their bad delivery. In particular, the generic character of the *philosophical* writings of this century is writing without really having anything to say; this is common to all and can thus be studied alike in Salat as in Hegel, in Herbart as in Schleiermacher. Following the homoeopathic method, the weak minimum of a thought is diluted with a fifty-page torrent of words and now, with limitless confidence in the truly German patience of the reader, quite unperturbedly, it prattles on page after page. In vain the mind, condemned to reading this, hopes for proper, solid, and substantial thoughts; it languishes, indeed, it pines after any thought, as the traveller in the Arabian desert after water – and must die of thirst. In contrast, let us take any *genuine* philosopher, no matter from what period or country, be it Plato or Aristotle, Descartes or Hume, Malebranche or Locke, Spinoza or Kant; we always encounter a beautiful and thoughtful mind that possesses and effects knowledge, but in particular always honestly strives to communicate itself; hence it immediately rewards the receptive reader in every line for the effort of reading. Now what makes the scribblings of our philosophasters so acutely void of thought and thus torturously boring is ultimately, to be sure, the poverty of their intellect, but in the first instance the fact that their delivery consistently happens through highly abstract, general and exceedingly broad concepts and, therefore, proceeds mostly 175 through indeterminate, ambiguous, and vague expressions. However, they are forced into this tightrope walk,[b] because they have to beware of touching the earth where, coming across something real, determinate, individual, and clear, they would run on to nothing but dangerous cliffs upon which their verbal barque[c] might be shipwrecked. For instead of focusing senses and understanding firmly and steadfastly on the intuitively existing world as that which is properly and truly given, undistorted, and in itself not exposed to error, through which we thus can penetrate the essence of things, they know nothing but the highest abstractions, like being, essence, becoming, absolute, infinite, and so forth, start out from them and build systems whose content ultimately amounts to mere words, which are really only soap

---

[a] *etwas Rechtes*
[b] *aerobatischen Gang* [from ἀεροβάτης, Greek for 'tightrope walker', used by German writers of this time in the sense of 'dreamer', 'enthusiast', 'brooding person']
[c] *Wort-Dreimaster*

bubbles, to play with for a while, but which cannot come down to earth without bursting.

If, with all this, the harm done to the sciences by the uncalled[a] and incompetent were only that they achieved nothing, as is the case in the fine arts, we could console ourselves with this and disregard it. However, here they do positive harm, first of all by forming a natural alliance against the good in order to preserve the reputation of the bad, and trying with all their might to prevent the good from developing. For we should not deceive ourselves about this, that at all times, all over the globe, and under all circumstances there exists a conspiracy, hatched by nature itself, of all the mediocre, wretched, and stupid minds against intellect and understanding. They all are loyal and numerous allies against the latter. Or are we really so innocent as to believe that they only wait for superiority in order to acknowledge, revere, and proclaim it, afterwards only to see themselves duly reduced to nothing? – Your obedient servant![b] Rather: 'Everyone praises as much as he hopes he can achieve.'[c] 'There shall be bunglers and nothing but bunglers in the world so that we may also be something!' This is their real motto; and it is as natural an instinct for them not to let the talented rise, as it is for a cat to catch mice. We should also recall here the fine passage by *Chamfort*, quoted at the end of the previous essay.[d] Let the open secret once be expressed, let the mooncalf be pulled to light, as strange as it may look there; at all times and in all places, in all situations and circumstances, imbecility and asininity hate nothing in the world as whole-heartedly and wrathfully as understanding, intellect, and talent. The fact that in this respect they always remain true to themselves, is obvious in all spheres, affairs, and relations of life in that they try hard to suppress, indeed, exterminate and destroy those qualities everywhere in order to exist completely *by themselves*. No kindness, no gentleness can reconcile them with the superiority of intellectual power. This is what they are like, they cannot be altered and will always remain like this. And what formidable majority they have on their side! This is a chief obstacle to any kind of progress of humanity. However, under such circumstances, how can there be progress in that sphere where not even a

---

[a] *Unberufenen* [a term that usually means 'unbidden', but here used to signify those lacking a calling (*Berufung*)]

[b] *Gehorsamer Diener* [most probably a sarcastic play on a common greeting used by people rendering services, like shopkeepers, towards their customers]

[c] *tantum quisque laudat, quantum se posse sperat imitari* [Marcus Tullius Cicero, *Orator ad M. Brutum* 7, 24]

[d] [See p. 123, n. e]

good mind, together with diligence and perseverance, suffices as it does in other sciences, but rather quite peculiar talents are required, which exist only at the expense of personal happiness? For truly, the most disinterested sincerity of striving, the most irresistible urge to solve the riddle of existence, gravity of profundity, the struggle to penetrate the innermost core of being, and genuine enthusiasm for truth – these are the primary and indispensable conditions for the daring deed of stepping anew in front of the ancient sphinx, with a renewed attempt at solving her eternal riddle, with the danger of tumbling down into the dark abyss of oblivion, joining the many who have gone before.

A further disadvantage that the doings of the uncalled bring about in all sciences is that they build the temple of error, at whose subsequent levelling good brains and honest minds will have to work sometimes throughout their lives. And in philosophy, it is the most universal, important, and difficult knowledge! If we want specific proofs of this we should think of the abominable example of Hegelry, that impudent pseudo-wisdom, which substituted for independent, sound, and honest thought and investigation the dialectical self-movement of concepts as philosophical method, that is, an objective *thought-automaton*[a] that gambols on its own freely in the air, or the empyrean, but whose traces, tracks, or fossilized footprints would be the manuscripts of Hegel and the Hegelians, which are rather something concocted under very flat and thick-hulled foreheads and, far from being absolutely objective, are something highly subjective and invented by very mediocre subjects at that. After that we should look at the height and duration of this Babel-structure and consider the incalculable damage that such absolute nonsense-philosophy, forced upon the studying youth by extraneous and outlandish means, must have inflicted on the generation growing up on it and, therefore, on the whole age. Are not innumerable minds of the current generation of scholars radically eccentric and ruined because of it? Are they not full of corrupt views and give out hollow phrases, vacuous drivel, and repulsive Hegel-jargon where we expect thoughts? Is their entire view of life not deranged and has not the most shallow, philistine, indeed, most vulgar attitude taken the place of the noble and lofty thoughts that still inspired their immediate predecessors?[b] In a word, are not the youths matured in the incubator of Hegelry like men intellectually castrated, unable to think, and full of the most ridiculous presumption? Truly, their minds are constituted like the bodies of certain heirs to the throne, who people tried in the past, through debaucheries or drugs, to

177

---

[a] *Gedankenautomaton*   [b] *Vorfahren* [literally: 'ancestors']

render incapable of governing, or at least of propagating their line: intellectually enervated, robbed of the proper use of their reason, a subject of pity,
and a persistent object of paternal tears. – But now let us hear from the other
side, what scandalous judgements about philosophy itself and, in general,
what unjustified accusations are publicized against it. On closer examination we will find that these detractors understand by philosophy precisely
nothing but the mindless and deliberate drivel of that miserable charlatan
178   and its echo in the hollow heads of his insipid admirers; they really believe
this to be philosophy! For they do not know any other. In fact, almost the
entire younger contemporary generation has been infected with Hegelry, as
with the French disease.[a] And just as this latter evil poisons all bodily
humours, the former has ruined all their intellectual powers; for which
reason the younger scholars nowadays are mostly no longer capable of any
healthy thought, nor of any natural expression. Not only does no single
correct concept exist in their heads, but neither does a single distinct and
determinate concept of anything; the desolate, empty jumble of words has
dissolved and swept away their power of thinking.[b] Moreover, it is just as
difficult to eradicate the evil of Hegelry as the disease just compared to it,
once it has really penetrated the humours and the blood.[c] On the other
hand, it was fairly easy to bring it into the world and spread it, since insights
are soon enough defeated if one arrays interests against them, i.e. uses
material means and ways of disseminating opinions and stipulating judgements. Guileless young people attend university full of naïve trust and gaze
with awe at the alleged possessors of all knowledge, and now even at the
presumptive explorer of our existence, the man whose glory they have heard
proclaimed enthusiastically by a thousand tongues and to whose lecture
they have seen elder statesmen listen. So they enter ready to learn, to believe,
and to revere. But if once there they are presented, under the name of
philosophy, with a completely topsy-turvy jumble of thoughts, a doctrine
about the identity of being and nothingness, a conjunction of words that
makes all thought evaporate from a healthy mind, a featureless mess that
reminds one of the madhouse, and on top of that is equipped with features
of crass ignorance and enormous lack of understanding – as I have, incon-
trovertibly and uncontradicted, demonstrated of Hegel's student compendium in the preface to my *Ethics*,[d] namely in order to thoroughly rub the
nose of the Danish Academy, this happily inoculated eulogist of bunglers

[a] [Syphilis]   [b] *Denkkraft*   [c] *in succum et sanguinem*
[d] [*The Two Fundamental Problems of Ethics*, Preface to the first edition, 16–20 (Hübscher *SW* 4,
xx–xxv)]

and 'matron saint'[a] of philosophical charlatans, in their 'distinguished philosopher';[b] – then young people, without guile and critical judgement, will also revere such stuff, will think that philosophy must consist in such 179 abracadabra, and will walk away with a paralysed head in which from then on mere words count as thoughts, who are thus forever incapable of producing actual thoughts and hence are intellectually castrated. Out of this grows up a generation of impotent and strange, but absolutely exacting minds, overflowing with plans, anaemic in regard to insights, such as we have now before us. That is the intellectual history of thousands whose youth and finest powers have been poisoned by that pseudo-wisdom, while they too should have partaken in the blessing that nature provided for many generations when it succeeded in producing a mind like *Kant*. – Genuine philosophy, done by free people for its own sake and without any other support than its arguments, could not have been abused like that; this could only have happened to university philosophy, which by its nature is a tool of the state, which is why we see the state intervening in the philosophical disputes of universities and taking sides, be it in the case of realists and nominalists, Aristotelians and Ramists, Cartesians and Aristotelians, of Christian Wolff, or Kant, or Fichte, or Hegel, or anything else.

Among the disadvantages that university philosophy has created for genuine and seriously intentioned philosophy is in particular, as just mentioned, the displacement of the Kantian philosophy by the windbaggeries of the three trumpeted sophists. For at first Fichte and then Schelling, both of whom were actually not without talent, and finally the crude and nauseating charlatan Hegel, this pernicious person, who has disorganized and corrupted the minds of an entire generation, were loudly proclaimed as the men who had further developed *Kant's* philosophy, had gone beyond it and had thus, by effectively climbing over his body, reached an incomparably higher level of knowledge and insight, from where they now, almost pityingly, looked down on Kant's arduous preparatory work to their magnificence; hence only they were supposed to be genuinely great philosophers. No wonder that young people – without their own judgement and without that distrust in teachers that 180 is often so wholesome, which only the exceptional mind, i.e. one furnished with power of judgement[c] and hence with the feeling for judgement, already brings to the university – believed what they heard and

---

[a] *Schutzmatrone* [a play on the word '*Schutzpatron*', which means 'patron saint'; a 'Matrone' is a 'matron']
[b] *summus philosophus*   [c] *Urtheilskraft*

thus thought that they should not dwell too long on the cumbersome preparatory works for the new lofty wisdom, on the old, stiff Kant, but hasten with quick steps towards the new temple of wisdom, where now accordingly, under the paean of stultified adepts, those three windbags successively sat on the altar. However, there is unfortunately nothing to learn from these three idols[a] of university philosophy; their writings, most of all those by Hegel, are a waste of time, indeed a waste of minds.[b] The result of this course of events has been that the real experts on the Kantian philosophy have died out and hence, to the disgrace of the age, this most important of all philosophical doctrines ever postulated has not been able to continue its existence as a vivid one, sustained in the minds, but only exists in the dead letter, in the works of its author, in order to wait for a wiser generation, or rather one that is not infatuated and mystified. Accordingly, we will hardly find any thorough understanding of the Kantian philosophy even among a few, older scholars. In contrast, the philosophical writers of our day have shown the most scandalous ignorance of it, which comes to light most shockingly in their presenta-tions of this doctrine, but also stands out clearly when they otherwise come to speak of the Kantian philosophy and affect to know something about it; one is filled with indignation when seeing that people who live off philosophy do not actually and properly know the most important doctrine advanced during the last two thousand years and almost con-temporaneous with them. Indeed, it goes so far that they incorrectly quote the titles of Kant's writings, also let Kant sometimes say the exact opposite of what he actually said, garble his technical terms[c] to the point of meaninglessness, and use them without the slightest clue about what is signified by them. For certainly it is impossible and, indeed, a ridiculous undertaking to get to know the doctrine of that profound mind by means of a cursory browsing of the Kantian works, as only these prolific scribblers and philosophical business people are entitled to claim, who furthermore believe they have left all that 'behind them'. Indeed, *Reinhold*, Kant's first apostle, said that only after intensely studying the *Critique of Pure Reason* five times had he penetrated its proper meaning. An indolent public, led around by the nose, then thinks that it can appropriate Kant's philosophy from the presentations provided by those people within the shortest time and without any effort. But that is completely impossible. Without one's own diligent and often repeated study of Kant's chief works one will never get an idea of this most

181

---

[a] *Götzen*   [b] *Kopfverderb*   [c] *termini technici*

important of all philosophical phenomena ever to have existed. For Kant is probably the most original mind ever produced by nature. To think with him and in his manner is something incomparable to anything else, since he possessed a degree of clear and quite particular soundness of mind as has never been granted to another mortal. We partake of this enjoyment when, inducted by diligent and serious study, we succeed in actually thinking with Kant's mind by reading the truly profound chapters of the *Critique of Pure Reason* and completely abandoning ourselves to the subject. Thereby we are elevated far above ourselves, for example, when rereading the 'Principles of Pure Understanding', and especially when considering the 'Analogies of Experience' and fathoming the profound thought of the *synthetic unity of apperception*. Then we feel wondrously removed and estranged from the whole dream-like existence which engulfs us by holding in hand each of its primary elements separately and realizing how time, space, and causality, connected through the synthetic unity of apperception of all appearances, make possible this empirical[a] complex of the whole and its course that our world consists in, which is conditioned so much through the intellect, and hence is mere appearance. For the synthetic unity of apperception is that connection of the world as a whole that rests on the laws of our intellect and is, therefore, inviolable. In the exposition of this unity, Kant   182
proves the primary fundamental laws of the world, at the point where they converge into one with those of our intellect, and presents them to us strung up on a thread. This approach, which is exclusively Kant's own, can be described as the most alienated gaze that has ever been cast upon the world and as the highest degree of objectivity. To follow it affords an intellectual pleasure unequalled by any other. For it is of a higher order than the one which poets grant, who of course are accessible to everyone, whereas the pleasure here described must be preceded by effort and exertion. But what do our present-day professional philosophers[b] know about this? Truly nothing. Recently I read a psychological diatribe by one of them that talks a lot about Kant's 'synthetic apperception' (*sic*); for they love to employ Kant's technical terms, even if only half caught and thus rendered meaningless, as here. This one thought it should be understood as concentrated attention! This and other little things make up the favourite topics of their elementary-school philosophy. In fact, the gentlemen have no time at all, nor the inclination or the drive, to study *Kant* – they are as little concerned with him as they are with me. Quite

[a] *erfahrungsmäßigen*   [b] *Professionsphilosophen*

different people are needed for their refined taste; namely, what the acute Herbart or the great Schleiermacher or even 'Hegel himself' have said – that is stuff for their meditation and suitable for them. Moreover, they love to see the 'all-crushing[a] Kant' sink into oblivion and hasten to make him a dead, historical phenomenon, a corpse, a mummy, whom they can then face without fear. For with the greatest sincerity he has put an end to Jewish theism in philosophy – a fact they like to gloss over, hide, and ignore, since without it they cannot *live*, meaning, they cannot eat and drink.

After such a regress from the greatest progress ever made in philosophy we need not be surprised that the alleged philosophizing of our time has fallen victim to a completely uncritical method, an unbelievable rudeness, hiding behind bombastic phrases, and a naturalistic groping-in-the-dark, much worse than it ever was before Kant. For example, with a brazenness conferred by raw ignorance, people speak everywhere and without hesitation of *moral freedom* as an agreed-upon, and indeed immediately certain matter; similarly of God's existence and essence as self-evident matters; and also of the 'soul' as of a universally known person. Even the expression 'innate ideas', which since Locke's time had to go into hiding, again ventures forth. And also the crude insolence must be mentioned here with which the Hegelians, in all their writings, without further ado and introduction, talk at great length and breadth about the so-called 'spirit', trusting that others will be too dumbfounded by their gibberish to tackle the Herr Professor, as would be justified, with the question: 'Spirit? Who is that fellow? And where do you know him from? Is he perhaps not merely an arbitrary and convenient hypostasis that you have not even defined, let alone deduced or proved? Do you think you have an audience of old women in front of you?' – That would be the appropriate language for such a philosophaster.

In connection with 'synthetic apperception' I have already shown above an amusing feature of the philosophizing of these tradespeople, namely that, although they have no use for Kant's philosophy, which is inconvenient for them and, besides, much too serious, and which they cannot really understand any longer, they still like to throw around expressions belonging to it in order to give their tattle a scientific appearance, more or less like children who play with daddy's hat, stick, and sword. This is what, for example, the Hegelians do with the term 'categories', with which they signify all kinds of

183

[a] *Alleszermalmer* [The origin of this description of Kant is Moses Mendelssohn, *Vorlesungen über das Daseyn Gottes* (*Lectures on the existence of God*), 1785]

broad general concepts, unconcerned about Aristotle and Kant, and blissfully innocent. Further, the Kantian philosophy often speaks of the *immanent and transcendent* usage, together with the validity, of our cognitions; but to get mixed up with such dangerous distinctions would not be advisable for our comic philosophers. However, they would love to have the expressions anyway, since they sound so erudite. Thus they employ them in such a way that, since their philosophy has always only the good Lord as its chief subject matter, who for that reason also appears as a familiar old acquaintance needing no introduction, they now discuss whether he is in the world or remains outside, i.e. resides in a space where there is no world. In the first case they dub him *immanent*, in the second case *transcendent*, while acting most serious and scholarly and speaking Hegelian jargon. It is the greatest fun – which reminds us older people of a copper engraving in *Falk's* satirical almanac,[a] which depicts *Kant*, ascending to heaven in a balloon, casting all the articles of his wardrobe, including his hat and wig, down to earth, where monkeys pick them up and adorn themselves with them.

184

Now it cannot be doubted that the displacement of Kant's serious, profound, and honest philosophy by the windbaggeries of mere sophists guided by personal interests has had the most detrimental effect on the education[b] of the age. In addition, the praise of such an utterly worthless, indeed quite pernicious, mind like that of Hegel's as the foremost philosopher of this and every age has surely been the cause of the whole degradation of philosophy and, as its result, the decline of higher literature in general during the last thirty years. Woe to the times when impertinence and nonsense replace insight and understanding in philosophy! For the fruits assume the taste of the soil in which they have grown. What is noisily, publicly, universally praised, is read and consequently is the intellectual nourishment of the developing generation; and this has the most decided influence on its humours and afterwards on its productions. Hence the dominant philosophy of a time determines its spirit. Thus, if the philosophy of absolute nonsense reigns; if absurdities plucked out of thin air and advanced in the form of the babble of a madman count for great thoughts – then the result of such sowing is this fine generation that we see before us, without intellect, without love of truth, without honesty, without taste, without the upward impulse

---

[a] [*Taschenbuch für Freunde des Scherzes und der Satire* (*Pocketbook for Friends of Humour and Satire*), ed. Johann Daniel Falk, Leipzig: Sommer, 7 vols., 1797–1803]

[b] *Bildung*

towards something noble, something beyond the material interests, to
185   which also belong the political ones. This explains how the age when
Kant philosophized, Goethe wrote poetry, and Mozart composed, could
be followed by the present one, that of the political poets, the even more
political philosophers, the hungry literati, carving out their existence by
means of the lies and deceptions of literature, and the various ink-slingers
who wantonly ruin the language. – It calls itself, by means of one of its
home-made words, as characteristic as it is euphonic, the 'present time':[a]
doubtlessly present time, since one only thinks of the Now and does not
dare glance at the coming time that will judge. I wished I could show this
'present time' in a magic mirror what it will look like in the eyes of
posterity. Meanwhile it calls the past we have just praised the 'age of
pigtails'. But there were heads attached to those tails;[b] now, on the other
hand, it seems as if the fruit has vanished with the stalk.

Thus Hegel's adherents are quite right when they claim that the influence
of their master on his contemporaries has been incalculable. An entire
generation of scholars intellectually completely paralysed, made incapable
of any thought, indeed driven so far as not knowing any longer what
thinking is, but taking for philosophical thought the most wilful and at
the same time most absurd play of words and concepts or the thoughtless
preaching about conventional subjects of philosophy, with claims taken out
of thin air, or completely meaningless sentences, or ones consisting in
contradictions – that has been the lauded influence of Hegel. We should
only compare the textbooks of the Hegelians, as they still nowadays dare to
publish them, with those of a period disparaged, but especially regarded
with infinite contempt by them and all post-Kantian philosophers, namely
the so-called eclectic period just prior to Kant; and we will find that the
latter compares to the former like gold – not to copper, but to dung. For in
those books by *Feder*, *Platner*, and others, we still find a rich store of real
thoughts, in part true, even valuable, and relevant remarks, a fair discussion[c]
of philosophical problems, a stimulation to independent reflection, a guide
186   to philosophizing, but especially an honest treatment throughout.
However, in a textbook of the Hegelian school we search in vain for any

---

[a] *Jetztzeit* [An expression that Schopenhauer employs in his 'Concerning the Recent Methodical
Practice of Mangling of the German Language' ('Ueber die, seit einigen Jahren, methodisch betrie-
bende Verhunzung der deutschen Sprache', in *HN* 4, II, 36ff.), and 'Sporadic Yet Systematically
Ordered Thoughts on Multifarious Topics' ('Vereinzelte, jedoch systematisch geordnete Gedanken
über vielerlei Gegenstände', see *PP* 2) to indicate the spoiling of the German language and of
contemporary society in general, in particular as a result of Hegel's philosophy]
[b] [Schopenhauer plays on the words *Zopf* ('pigtail') and *Kopf* ('head')]   [c] *Ventiliren*

actual thought – it contains not a single one – or for any trace of serious and honest reflection – that is alien to the thing; we find nothing but audacious combinations of words that are supposed to seem to have a meaning, indeed a profound meaning, but are exposed, when examined, as completely hollow, absolutely meaningless clichés and verbal shells, with which the writer certainly seeks not to instruct his readers, but merely to mislead them so that they believe they have a thinker in front of them, whereas it is somebody who does not know at all what thinking is, a sinner without any insight and, on top of that, no knowledge. That is the result of Hegel's having ruined even the *organ* of cognition, understanding itself, whereas other sophists, charlatans, and obscurantists only distorted and ruined *cognition*. For by forcing misguided students to cram into their head as rational cognition a gibberish consisting of the crudest nonsense, a web of contradictions in terms,[a] a drivel as if from the madhouse, the brains of the poor young people who read such stuff with faithful devotion and sought to appropriate it to themselves as supreme wisdom were thrown so much out of joint that they have remained forever incapable of genuine thought. Consequently, we see them walk around to this day speaking in the nauseating Hegelian jargon, praising the master, and seriously believing that sentences like 'Nature is the idea in its otherness' actually say something. To disorganize a young, fresh brain in such a way is truly a sin deserving neither forgiveness nor mercy. This, therefore, has been Hegel's famous influence on his contemporaries; and unfortunately it has really extended and spread out far and wide, since the effect here too was commensurate with the cause. – For just as it is the worst that can happen to a state for the most depraved class, the scum of society, to come to power, nothing worse can happen to philosophy and everything that depends on it, that is, the whole knowledge and intellectual life of humanity, than for an ordinary mind who distinguishes himself on the one hand by his obsequiousness and on the other by his impudence in writing nonsense, hence for a *Hegel*, to be proclaimed, with the greatest, indeed unprecedented emphasis, the greatest genius and the man in whom philosophy has finally reached its long-pursued goal. For the consequence of such high treason against what is most noble in humanity eventually is a state of affairs such as that of philosophy, and as a result of literature in general, in Germany right now: ignorance and insolence fraternizing at the top, camaraderie instead of merit, complete confusion of all fundamental concepts, total disorientation and disorganization of philosophy, dullards as reformers of religion, brazen

187

---

[a] *contradictionibus in adjecto*

appearance of materialism and barbarism,[a] ignorance of the ancient languages and ruining of our own through brainless clipping of words
and perfidious counting of letters at the discretion of ignoramuses and
blockheads, and so on, and so on – just look around you! Even as an
external symptom of the coarseness that is becoming rampant you see its
constant companion – the long beard, this mark of sex in the middle of the
face, saying that one prefers masculinity, which one shares with the animals,
over *humanity*, by first being a *male, mas,*[b] and only afterwards *a human
being*. The shaving of beards in all highly educated ages and countries arose
from the correct feeling of the opposite, by virtue of which one wants to be
first of all a *human being*, in a sense a human being in the abstract,
disregarding the animal sex difference. On the other hand, the length of
the beard has always kept equal pace with barbarity, as already the names
suggests.[c] For that reason, beards flourished during the *Middle Ages*, that
millennium of coarseness and ignorance, whose dress and architecture our
noble present-timers[d] are at pains to imitate.*,[8] – The additional and secondary
effect of the treason to philosophy discussed here cannot fail to materialize: it is
the contempt for the nation by the neighbours, and for the age by posterity.
For as we make our bed, so we must lie in it, and we shall not be spared.

188

    Above I have spoken about the powerful influence of intellectual nour-
ishment on the age. This is based on the fact that it determines the material
as well as the form of thought. Hence a lot depends on what is praised and
accordingly read. For thinking with a truly great intellect strengthens our

---

* The beard, it is said, is natural to humans; indeed and, therefore, it is quite suited to them in the state
of nature, just as shaving is suited to them in the civilized state, by showing that here the raw animal
power, whose mark, immediately palpable for everybody, is that outgrowth characteristic of the male
sex, had to give way to law, order, and civilized behaviour. –
    The beard enlarges the animal part of the face and accentuates it; thereby it gives it this
conspicuously brutal appearance – one should only watch such a bearded man in profile while he is
eating!
    They want to pass the beard off as an *adornment*. For two hundred years we have been accustomed
to see this only in Jews, Cossacks, Capuchins, prisoners, and bandits. –
    The ferocity and atrocity that the beard bestows on the physiognomy rests on the fact that an always
inanimate mass occupies half of the face, namely the half that expresses what is moral. Moreover, all
hairiness is animal-like. Shaving is the symbol (military badge, mark) of higher civilization.
Furthermore, the police are authorized to prohibit beards for the reason that they are semi-masks
that make it difficult to recognize their man again, so that they encourage all kinds of mischief.

[a] *Bestialismus* [The degradation of human life, characterized as the reduction to its physiological
  functions; Schopenhauer also uses the term in connection with socialism and the Young Hegelians]
[b] [Latin for 'man']
[c] [A play on the similarity of the words *barba* (Latin for 'beard') and *Barbarei* ('barbarity'). Perhaps also
  German *Bart* ('beard')]
[d] *Jetztzeitler*

own, imparts real movement to it, and gives it buoyancy; it works in analogy to the hand of the writing-master that leads that of the child. In contrast, thinking with people who are really after mere appearance, hence deception of the reader, like Fichte, Schelling, and Hegel, ruins the mind to an equal extent; no less thinking with cranks or with those who have put on their understanding back to front, of whom Herbart is an example. In general, it is an utter waste of one's time and energy to read even the writings of mere ordinary minds in disciplines not dealing with facts or their determination, but where merely the author's own thoughts make up the material. For what such people think, everyone else can think too; that they have literally sat down comfortably and made thinking their subject does not improve the matter at all, since it does not enhance their powers, and people for the most part think least when they have expressly set out to do so. In addition, their   189
intellect remains true to its natural destiny of working in the service of the will, as is normal. For that reason, there is always an *intent*[a] at the bottom of their doings and thinking; they always have *purposes* and recognize only what relates and thus corresponds to these. Intellectual activity free of the will, which is the condition of pure objectivity and thus of all great achievements, remains forever alien to them, is a fable for their heart. For them, only purposes are of interest, only purposes are real, since willing prevails in them. Hence it is doubly foolhardy to waste one's time with their productions. However, what the public never recognizes and comprehends, because it has good reasons for not wanting to do so, is the *aristocracy of nature*. That is why they so soon put aside the rare and few whom, over the course of centuries, nature had given the noble calling of reflecting on it[b] or of presenting the spirit of its works, in order to make themselves familiar with the productions of the newest bungler. Has there been once a hero, the public will soon put up a thief next to him – as someone more or less like him. Has nature, in a most favourable mood, for once let the rarest of its products, a mind genuinely talented beyond the ordinary measure, originate from its hands; has fate, in a gentle mood, allowed his education, indeed, have his works finally 'overcome the opposition of a stupid world'[c] and been recognized as models and recommended – it will not take long then for people to come dragging a creature made of mud[d] of their own stamp to place him next to that talented mind on the altar, because they do not comprehend, or even suspect, how *aristocratic nature is*; it is so aristocratic that not even one truly great mind is to be found in three hundred

[a] *Absicht*   [b] [nature]   [c] [From Goethe's 'Epilog zu Schiller's Glocke']
[d] *Erdenkloß* [literally 'clod']

million of its manufactured goods.[a] Thus we must become thoroughly acquainted with such a mind, consider its works as a kind of revelation, read them tirelessly and use them day and night;[b] on the other hand, we should leave untouched all the ordinary minds as what they are, namely something so common and ordinary as the flies on the wall.

190   The course of events described above has occurred in philosophy in the most disconsolate way; next to *Kant*, *Fichte* is mentioned consistently and ubiquitously as someone on a par with him: 'Kant and Fichte' has become a standing phrase. 'Look how we apples swim', said the –.[c] An equal honour is conferred on Schelling, indeed – what shame![d] – even on *Hegel*, that scribbler of nonsense and destroyer of minds! For the summit of this Parnassus has been trodden ever more wide. – 'Have you eyes? have you eyes?' one wants to call out to such a public, as Hamlet did to his infamous mother.[e] Alas, they have none! For it is still the same people who everywhere and all the time let genuine merit go to waste in order to pay their homage to apers and mannerists of every genre. Thus they imagine that they study philosophy when reading the monstrous offspring, ready for all the fairs, of minds in whose dull consciousness even the mere problems of philosophy sound as little as the bell in a receptacle void of air, indeed of minds that, strictly speaking, have been produced and equipped by nature for nothing but quietly plying an honest trade, just like the rest, or cultivating a field and providing for the propagation of humanity, yet who believe that they must be 'fools with jangling bells'.[f] Their constant meddling and desire to have a say resembles that of deaf people who join in a conversation. Thus the effect on those who appear only few and far between in all ages and who by nature have the calling and, therefore, the genuine drive to apply themselves to investigate the loftiest truths is only that of a distracting and confusing noise; that is, if the latter does not intentionally stifle their voice, which is often the case, because what they put forward does not suit the purposes of those people who can be serious about nothing but interests and material goals and who, by virtue of their considerable number, soon raise such a clamour that others can no longer hear their own words. Nowadays they have set themselves the task, in defiance of the Kantian philosophy as well as the truth, to teach speculative theology, rational psychology, freedom of the will, total and absolute

---

[a] *Fabrikwaare*   [b] *diurna nocturnaque manu*

[c] '*Seht, wie wir Aepfel schwimmen?*' *sagte der –* [*sagte der Rossapfel und schwamm mit den echten* (German proverb: 'Look how we apples swim, said the horse apple [dung] and swam with the real apples', having its origin in the Latin proverb 'Ut nos poma natamus')]

[d] *proh pudor*   [e] [Shakespeare, *Hamlet*, Act III, scene 4]

[f] *schellenlaute Thoren* [Goethe, *Faust* I, 549; singular in the original]

dissimilarity between humans and animals by ignoring the gradual shades of intellect in the series of animals, with the result that they only act to delay[a] the honest search for truth. If a man like me speaks, they act as if they did not hear. The trick is good, although it is not new. However, I want to see whether I can drag these badgers out of their holes.[b]

Now the universities obviously are the centre of all those games that intent plays with philosophy. Only through such intent could Kant's world-wide epoch-making achievements be supplanted by the windbaggeries of a Fichte, soon afterwards in turn supplanted by fellows just like him. This could never have happened before a genuine philosophical public, i.e. a public that seeks philosophy, without any other intent, merely for its own sake, that is before the extremely small public of genuinely thinking minds, earnestly moved by the mysterious nature of our existence. The scandal of these last fifty years has been possible only with the aid of the universities, before a public of students who faithfully accept everything that Herr Professor sees fit to say. For the fundamental error lies in the fact that the universities assume the last word and decisive voice also in matters of philosophy, a voice which at most belongs to the three principal faculties, each in their area. However, the fact that matters are different in philosophy, a science that first has to be found, is overlooked, as is also the fact that when it comes to the appointment to philosophy chairs, it is not solely the abilities of the candidates that are taken into consideration, as in other disciplines, but even more so their views and attitudes.[c] Accordingly, students think that, just as the professor of theology possesses his dogmas, the professor of law his pandects,[d] and that of medicine his pathology, so the professor of metaphysics, hired in the highest place, should also be a master of his field. Therefore, they attend his lectures with childlike trust, since they find there a man who, with an air of conscious superiority, condescendingly criticizes all philosophers who have ever existed. Thus the students do not doubt that they have come to the right place and memorize all the wisdom gushing forth so faithfully as if they sat in front of the tripod of the Pythia. Of course, from now on there exists no other philosophy for them than that of their professor. They leave unread the real philosophers as obsolete and refuted, the teachers of centuries, indeed millennia, silently and solemnly waiting in the bookcases for those who desire them; like their

191

192

---

[a] *als remora . . . wirken*

[b] [In a letter to Julius Frauenstädt (12 July 1852) Schopenhauer compares the behaviour of philosophy professors defending the masters who pay them to that of badgers not wanting to leave their dens (*GB*, 285–6)]

[c] *Gesinnungen*　　[d] *Pandekten*

professor, they have left them 'behind'. On the other hand, they buy their professor's intellectual offspring, which are published in time for every fair and whose often repeated editions can only be explained from such a course of events. For even after their university years, they all normally retain a faithful attachment to their professor, to whose intellectual tendency they have adapted early and with whose manner they have become familiar. As a result such philosophical monstrosities receive an otherwise impossible dissemination, and their authors lucrative fame. How could it otherwise have happened that, for example, such a complex of follies as Herbart's *Introduction to Philosophy*[a] could run through five editions? That again explains the foolish presumption with which (e.g. pp. 234–5 of the fourth edition) this decided crank loftily looks down upon Kant and patiently puts him right. –

Considerations of this kind, and especially the look back at all the goings-on with philosophy at universities since Kant's departure, have more and more hardened my view that, if there is to be philosophy at all, i.e. if the human intellect is to be allowed to turn its highest and noblest powers towards the incomparably most important of all problems, this can only successfully happen if philosophy remains independent of all influence of the state, and that the state does a great service to philosophy and proves its humanity and noble-mindedness sufficiently, if it does not persecute it but lets it be and allows it to exist as a free art, which after all must be its own reward. At the same time the state can see itself relieved from the expenditure for professorships of philosophy, because the people who want to live *off* philosophy will very seldom be the same ones who indeed live *for the sake of* it, but sometimes can be the ones who covertly plot *against* it.

Public academic chairs belong solely to those sciences that are already 193   created and actually exist, and which one only needs to have learnt in order to be able to teach them, which, therefore, on the whole are just to be passed on, as implied by the *tradere*[b] used on blackboards, while the more capable minds are at liberty to enrich, correct, and perfect them. However, a science that does not yet exist, has not reached its goal, does not even know its path with certainty, indeed whose very possibility is still disputed – to let such a science be taught by professors is surely absurd. The natural consequence of this is that every one of these professors believes that it is his vocation to create the science that is still lacking, failing to consider that such a calling

---

[a] *Einleitung in die Philosophie* [Johann Friedrich Herbart, *Lehrbuch zur Einleitung in die Philosophie* (*Textbook for an Introduction to Philosophy*), fourth edn., Königsberg: August Wilhelm Unzer, 1837]
[b] [Latin for 'to pass on', 'to deliver to posterity']

can only be issued by nature, not the ministry of public education. Thus he tries as best he can, soon gives birth to his monstrosity, and pretends it to be the long-desired Sophia;[a] and an obliging colleague who will act as god-father at her christening will certainly not be wanting. Hereafter the gentlemen, because they live off philosophy, will be so brazen as to call themselves *philosophers*, and think, accordingly, that the last word and the decision in matters of philosophy belong to them, indeed that in the end they even announce conferences of philosophers (a contradiction in terms since philosophers rarely exist simultaneously in twos and almost never in the plural in the world) and then come together in droves to discuss the advancement[b] of philosophy!*,[9]

Above all, such university professors will strive to give philosophy that direction that corresponds to the interests close to their hearts, or rather those suggested to them, and, for that purpose, they will, if need be, even mould and distort the doctrines of earlier genuine philosophers and, if necessary, falsify them, only to achieve the desired result. Now, since the public is so childish as to reach always for the newest authors, and since their writings are titled 'philosophy', it is a consequence that, due to the authors' ineptitude, or absurdity, or at least tormenting tedium, good minds that feel an inclination towards philosophy will shy away from it, so that it gradually becomes discredited, which has already happened.

However, not only are the gentlemen's own creations in bad shape, but the period since Kant shows that they are not even capable of holding on to and preserving the achievements of great minds that are accepted as such and correspondingly entrusted to their care. Have they not let Kant's philosophy slip away because of Fichte and Schelling? Do they not constantly, in the most scandalous and defamatory manner, name the windbag *Fichte* next to *Kant* as roughly his equal? After the two above-mentioned philosophasters had ousted and declared obsolete Kant's doctrine, did not the most rampant fantasy take the place of the strict control imposed by Kant on all metaphysics? Have these gentlemen not in part dutifully participated in this fantasy and in part neglected to firmly oppose it, the

194

---

* 'No solely true [*alleinseligmachende*, lit. 'claiming the monopoly of all means of grace'] philosophy!' the *conference of philosophasters in Gotha* announces, i.e. in plain language: 'no striving for objective truth! Long live mediocrity! No intellectual aristocracy, no autocracy of those favoured by nature! Instead rule by the rabble! No one mince his words, everyone count as much as the next one!' Then the rascals have an easy task. For they want to banish from the history of philosophy the monarchical constitution, which has existed until now, and introduce a proletarian republic; but nature protests, it is strictly aristocratic!

[a] *Sophia* [Wisdom; since capitalized, rather suggesting a common girl's name]   [b] *Wohl*

Critique of Reason in hand? namely because they found it more advisable to use the present lax observance either to bring to market the little things concocted by themselves, e.g. Herbart's buffooneries and Fries' old-women's gossip, and in general everyone his own foibles, or to be able to smuggle in doctrines of established religion as philosophical findings. Has all this not paved the way for the most scandalous philosophical charlatanry that the world has ever had to be ashamed of, for the activities of Hegel and his miserable companions? Have not even those who opposed this mischief, while constantly bowing deeply, talked about the great genius and monumental intellect of that charlatan and nonsense-scribbler, thereby showing themselves to be dunces? Are not the only ones to be exempted from this (in the interest of truth this should be said) *Krug* and *Fries*, who, opposing that twister of minds outright, have afforded him merely that forbearance that every philosophy professor irrevocably shows another? Have not the noise and clamour raised by the German university philosophers in admiration of those three sophists finally attracted general attention also in England and France, which, however, after closer inspection of the matter, resolved into laughter? – But in particular they show themselves as unfaithful custodians and keepers of the truths that were acquired with great difficulty in the course of centuries and finally entrusted to their care, especially if they are such as do not suit their purposes, i.e. do not agree with the results of an insipid, rationalistic, optimistic, in truth merely Jewish theology, which is the quietly predetermined goal of their entire philosophizing and its lofty phrases. Therefore, those doctrines that seriously intentioned philosophy, not without great exertion, has brought to light, they will try to obliterate, gloss over, distort, and drag down to the level that suits their plan for educating students and their above-mentioned spinning-wheel philosophy. A shocking instance of this is the doctrine of the *freedom of the will*. After the strict necessity of all human acts of will had been conclusively demonstrated through the united and successive efforts of great minds like Hobbes, Spinoza, Priestley, and Hume – and Kant too had accepted the matter as already completely established* – they suddenly act as if nothing had happened, and relying on the ignorance of their public, in the name of God, even in this day and age, they take freedom of the will as an established and, indeed, immediately certain thing in almost all of their textbooks. What sort of name does such a procedure merit? If this doctrine of the

---

* His postulate of freedom, grounded in the categorical imperative, is of merely practical, *not theoretical* validity. See my *The Two Fundamental Problems of Ethics*, pp. 80 and 146 [*FW*, 96; *BM*, 146 (Hübscher *SW* 4, 81; 144)]

necessity of our actions, whose ground has been proved as firmly as can be by all the philosophers just mentioned, is nevertheless hidden or denied by the professors to make students swallow the decided absurdity of free will,　196 because it is a necessary ingredient of their spinning-wheel philosophy, are these gentlemen not really the enemies of philosophy? And because (for 'the best condition is that of the last person'[a] Seneca, *Epistles*, 79) the doctrine of the strict necessitation of all acts of will is presented nowhere as thoroughly, clearly, coherently, and completely as in my prize essay, rightly crowned by the Norwegian Society of Sciences, one will find that, in accordance with their old policy of meeting me everywhere with passive resistance, this essay is mentioned neither in their books nor in their scholarly journals and literary magazines; it is kept strictly secret and seen as 'not having happened',[b] like everything that does not serve their miserable purposes, as my ethics in general, indeed as all my works. My philosophy just does not interest the gentlemen, because they have no interest in getting to the bottom of the truth. On the other hand, what does interest them are their salaries, the louis d'or which they charge, and their privy councillor titles. Of course, they are also interested in philosophy, namely insofar as they earn their bread by it; this far they are interested in philosophy. They are the ones who Giordano Bruno already characterizes as 'sordid and mercenary fellows who pay little or no heed to the truth and are content to know what is commonly seen as knowledge; they have little love for true wisdom but crave the fame and reputation that come with it; they want to appear as something but are little concerned about being something' (see *Opere di Giordano Bruno*, Leipzig: Wagner, 1830, vol. 2, p. 83).[c,10] So what would my *Prize Essay on the Freedom of the Will* be to them, even if it had been crowned by ten academies? However, on the contrary, the drivel that the dullards from this crowd have written about this subject since then is made out to be important and recommended. Do I need to qualify such conduct? Are these people who represent philosophy, the rights of reason, freedom of thought? – Another example is provided by *speculative theology*. After *Kant* removed all the proofs that made up its supports and thus has radically overthrown it, this does not at all deter my gentlemen of the lucrative philosophy even sixty years later from claiming speculative theology as the proper and essential subject matter of philosophy and, because they do not

---

[a]　*conditio optima est ultimi* [79, 6]　　[b]　*comme non avenue*

[c]　*Sordidi e mercenarii ingegni, che, poco o niente solleciti circa la verità, si contentano saper, secondo che comunemente èstimato il sapere, amici poco di vera sapienza, bramosi di fama e reputazione di quella, vaghi d'apparire, poco curiosi d'essere. [De l'infinito, universo e mondi (On the Infinite, the Universe, and the Worlds), 1584]*

197   dare to adopt those exploded proofs again, from now constantly talking
about the *absolute*, a word which is nothing but an enthymeme, a conclusion with premises not stated, for the purpose of cowardly disguising and
surreptitiously obtaining the cosmological proof, which since Kant is not
allowed to show itself in its proper form and thus must be smuggled in in
this disguise. As if Kant had had a premonition of this latter trick, he says
expressly: 'In all ages one has talked about the *absolutely necessary* being, but
has taken trouble not so much to understand whether and how one could so
much as think of a thing of this kind as rather to prove its existence. . . . For
by means of the word *unconditional* to reject all the conditions that the
understanding always needs in order to regard something as necessary, is far
from enough to make intelligible to myself whether through a concept of an
unconditionally necessary being I am still thinking something or perhaps
nothing at all.' (*Critique of Pure Reason*, first edn., p. 592, fifth edn., p. 620.)[a]
I recall here once again *my* doctrine that being necessary entirely and in all
cases implies nothing but following from an existing and given ground, such
ground thus being the very *condition* of all necessity; so the unconditionally
necessary is a contradiction in terms, hence not at all a thought but a hollow
expression – but certainly a material often used in the construction of
professorial philosophy. – It must also be mentioned here that, despite
Locke's great, epoch-making fundamental doctrine of the *non-existence
of innate ideas* and all advances in philosophy made since and on that
ground, namely by Kant, the gentlemen of the philosophy for hire,[b] quite
unashamed, make their students believe in a 'consciousness of God', and in
general an immediate cognition, or discerning,[c] of metaphysical objects
through reason. It does not help that Kant, exerting the rarest acumen and
depth of thought, showed that theoretical reason could never arrive at
objects beyond the possibility of all experience; the gentlemen do not care
198   about anything of the sort, but have summarily taught for fifty years that
reason has completely immediate, absolute cognitions, that it really is
primarily a faculty designed for metaphysics that, beyond the possibility
of experience, immediately cognizes and comprehends with certainty the
so-called supernatural, the absolute, the good Lord, and whatever else there
is supposed to be. However, that our *reason* is a faculty whose cognition is
not *mediated through inferences*, but *immediately* cognizes the sought-after
objects of metaphysics, is obviously a fairy tale or, more bluntly, a palpable
lie. For it needs only an honest, but otherwise not difficult self-examination
in order to become convinced of the groundlessness of such a pretence,

---

[a] [A592–3/B620–1; original emphasis]   [b] φιλοσοφία μισθοφόρος   [c] *Vernehmen*

especially since otherwise metaphysics would be in quite different shape. It belongs to the worst consequences of university philosophy that, nonetheless, such a lie, lacking any ground except for the perplexity and the cunning designs of its propagators and for being ruinous to philosophy, has become the established dogma of the lecterns, repeated thousands of times, and is imposed upon the studying youth despite the attestation of the greatest thinkers.

In keeping with such preparation, however, the actual and essential subject of metaphysics for academic philosophers is the discussion of God's relation to the world; the most lengthy explanations of this fill their textbooks. They believe themselves to be called upon and paid to settle this point; and it is amusing to watch how precociously and learnedly they talk about the absolute, or God, conducting themselves quite earnestly, as if they actually knew something about it; it reminds us of the seriousness with which children play their games. Thus at every fair a new metaphysics appears, which consists of a detailed report about the good Lord and explains how matters stand with him and how he came to make or give birth to or otherwise bring about the world, so that it appears as if they received the latest news about him every half year. However, some of them get into a predicament whose effect is most comical. For they are to teach a proper, personal God, as described in the Old Testament; that they know. On the other hand, for the last forty years Spinoza's pantheism, according to which the word God is synonymous with world, has been definitely predominant and the universal fashion among scholars and even the merely educated; they do not want to give this up entirely, but are really not allowed to stretch out their hand for this forbidden jar. So they attempt to extricate themselves from this predicament by way of their usual means, of obscure, confused, and muddled phrases and hollow verbiage, whereby they squirm and writhe woefully as they do so; thus we see some of them assert in the same breath that God is totally, infinitely, and widely different from the world, literally worlds apart,[a] but at the same time wholly united and one with it, indeed, up to his ears within it; so that they remind me each time of Bottom, the weaver, in *A Midsummer Night's Dream*, who promises to roar like a terrifying lion, but at the same time as softly as only a nightingale can sing. In executing this, they get into the oddest predicament; for they claim that there is no place for God outside of the world, but afterwards they have no use for him inside of it either, and change his

199

---

[a] *himmelweit* [a play on words: '*himmelweit*', meaning 'very wide', is composed of 'Himmel' ('heaven') and 'weit' ('wide')]

position back and forth[a] until they fall together with him between two stools.[*],[II]

In contrast, the *Critique of Pure Reason*, with its proofs a priori of the impossibility of all cognition of God, is tittle-tattle for them by which they will not let themselves be confused; they know what they are there for. To object that nothing more unphilosophical can be thought than constantly talking about something of whose existence we have no knowledge, as has been proved, and of whose essence we have no concept – is impudent interference; they know what they are there for. – It is well known that for them I am someone who is far beneath their notice and attention, and by means of the complete disregard of my works they have tried to bring to light what I am (although they actually have shown what *they* are); thus I will be talking in vain, as is the case with everything I have advanced during the last thirty-five years, when I tell them that Kant was not joking, that actually, in dead earnest, philosophy is not theology, nor can it ever be, but on the contrary is something else than and very different from theology. Indeed, as it is well known that every other science is ruined by the meddling of theology, so philosophy is too and indeed the most of all, as is attested by history. That this is even the case with morals I have very clearly shown in my essay about its basis,[b] which is why the gentlemen have been quiet as a mouse about it, true to their tactics of passive resistance. For theology covers all the problems of philosophy with its veil and, consequently, not only makes their solution impossible, but even their comprehension. Thus, as said before, the *Critique of Pure Reason* is in all seriousness the letter of notice by the former maid of theology,[c] which in it has once and for all quit its service to its strict master. Since then the latter has made do with a hireling, who occasionally puts on the left-behind livery of the former servant for the sake of appearance, as in Italy, where such substitutes are often to be seen, especially on Sundays, which is why they are known under the name 'Sunday servants'.[d]

But of course Kant's critiques and arguments had to fail in regard to university philosophy. For there it says: 'I will it, I order it, let the will stand

200

---

* From an analogous predicament comes the praise that some of them bestow on me now that my light is not hidden under a bushel any longer – namely in order to save the honour of their good taste. However, they quickly add the assurance that with regard to the main point I am wrong; for they will take care not to agree with a philosophy that is something completely different from Jewish mythology shrouded in high-sounding verbiage and fantastically dressed up – as is *de rigueur* [required by fashion] for them.

[a] *roren* [*rockiren* (Deussen edition), a chess term indicating the double move of castle and king]
[b] [*Prize Essay on the Basis of Morals*]   [c] *ancilla theologiae*   [d] *Domenichini*

for reason';[a] philosophy is *supposed* to be theology, even if the impossibility
of the matter were proved by twenty Kants; we know what we are there for:
We exist for the greater glory of God.[b] Every professor of philosophy is a
defender of the faith,[c] just like Henry VIII, and recognizes in this his
principal and chief profession.[12] Therefore, after Kant had so clearly severed
the nerve of all possible proofs of speculative theology that since then no one
wanted to deal with them any longer, philosophical endeavour has consisted
for almost fifty years of all sorts of attempts to obtain theology quietly by   201
stealth, and philosophical writings are for the most part nothing but fruitless
resuscitation attempts on a lifeless corpse. Thus for instance the gentlemen
of the lucrative philosophy have discovered a consciousness of God in
human beings that until then had escaped the notice of the whole world
and, emboldened by the mutual agreement and innocence of their immediate public, jauntily and defiantly throw it around, so that in the end they
have even seduced the honest Dutch people at the university of Leiden,
who, assuming the shady tricks of the philosophy professors really to be
advances in science, quite ingeniously on 15 February 1844 asked the prize
question: 'What can be asserted regarding the consciousness of God, which
is said to be innate in the human mind',[d] etc. That which all philosophers
until Kant worked so hard to prove would then, in virtue of such a
'consciousness of God', be something *immediately conscious*. What simpletons must all those previous philosophers have been who struggled their
entire lives to furnish proofs for a matter of which we are directly *conscious*,
meaning that we know it even more immediately than that two and two
make four, which already requires deliberation. Wanting to prove such a
matter would have to be like wanting to prove that the eyes see, the ears
hear, and the nose smells. And what irrational brutes would the followers of
that religion have to be that is the foremost on earth in regard to the number
of its adherents, the Buddhists, whose religious fervour is so great that in
Tibet almost one in six belongs to the holy order and thus is subject to
celibacy. Their doctrine of faith may support a supremely pure, sublime,
loving, indeed strictly ascetic morals (which has not, like the Christian one,
forgotten the animals), yet it is not only decidedly atheistic but explicitly
rejects theism. For personality is a phenomenon that we know only through
our animal nature and that, therefore, separated from this nature, cannot be
clearly conceived. To make such a phenomenon the origin and principle of

---

[a] *sic volo, sic jubeo, sit pro ratione voluntas* [Juvenal, *Satires* IV, 223; wording slightly different]
[b] *in majorem Dei gloriam* [usually '*ad majorem* . . .']   [c] *defensor fidei*
[d] *quid statuendum de Sensu Dei, qui dicitur, menti humanae indito*

202   the world is invariably a proposition that not everyone is readily able to grasp; much less can such a proposition be rooted and live in everyone's mind naturally. On the other hand, an impersonal God is a mere philosophy professor's fib, a contradiction in terms, an empty word to satisfy the unreflecting or to appease the police spies.[a]

To be sure, the writings of our university philosophers breathe the most vivid enthusiasm for theology, but very little zeal for truth. For without any respect for truth sophisms, trickeries, distortions, and false assertions are being employed, and indeed amassed, with incredible impudence; even immediate, supernatural cognitions – that is, innate ideas – are imputed to reason, or more correctly, attributed by means of lies, as explained above; all solely to emphasize theology: only theology! only theology! theology at all cost! – Without being presumptuous, I would like to ask the gentlemen to consider that even though theology may be very valuable, I still know something that in any case is more valuable, and that is honesty: honesty, as in trade and traffic, so also in thought and instruction; that should not be up for sale for the sake of theology.

However, the way matters now stand, whoever is serious about the *Critique of Pure Reason* and in general is honest and offers no theology for sale must come off badly compared to those gentlemen. Even if he offered the most excellent thing the world has ever seen and served up all wisdom of heaven and earth, they will nonetheless avert their eyes and ears if it is not theology; indeed, the more merit his case has, the more it will arouse, not their admiration, but their resentment, the more determined will be their passive resistance to it, the more derisive the silence with which they try to stifle it; at the same time they will intone more loudly encomiums on the lovely intellectual offspring of their fellowship so rich in ideas, only so that the voice of insight and truthfulness, hateful to them, does not prevail. For, in this age of sceptical theologians and orthodox philosophers, this is required by the politics of the gentlemen, who sustain themselves with wife and children by means of *that* science for which someone like me sacrifices all his powers throughout his life. For they are concerned only with theology, in accordance with the hints of their

203   superiors; everything else is secondary. And from the beginning, they define philosophy, each in their language, phrase, and disguise, as speculative theology and quite innocently declare the hunt for theology to be the essential purpose of philosophy. They know nothing about the fact that we should approach the problem of existence freely and impartially

[a] *Vigilanten* [criminals hired as spies by the police]

and consider the world, together with consciousness, in which it represents itself, as that which alone is given, as the problem, the riddle of the old sphinx, in front of whom we have boldly stepped. They prudently ignore the fact that theology, if it demands to be admitted into philosophy, like all other doctrines must first show its credentials, which then are examined in the office of the *Critique of Pure Reason*, which among all thinking people still enjoys the fullest respect, not in the least impaired by the comical grimaces that the academic philosophers of the day attempt to pull against it. Without credentials that pass before the *Critique* theology finds no admission and is neither to extort it, nor obtain it by trickery or begging, appealing to the fact that academic philosophers are not allowed to sell anything else – let them close up shop. For philosophy is no church and no religion. It is that tiny spot in the world, accessible only to the extremely few, where the *truth*, always and everywhere hated and persecuted, is for once to be free of all pressure and coercion, to celebrate its Saturnalia, so to speak, which allow free speech even to the slave, where indeed it is to have the prerogative and the final word, and is to rule alone and accept nothing else beside itself. For the entire world, and everything within it, is full of *intent*, and most of the time common, low, and bad intent; only a small spot, as agreed upon, should remain free of this and be open to *insight* alone, and insight into the most important affairs of concern to all: – That is philosophy. Or might we understand it differently? Then everything is fun and comedy – 'As I am told from time to time befalls.'[a] – Of course, judging from the compendiums of the academic philosophers, we would rather think that philosophy is a guide to piety or an institute to train churchgoers, since in fact speculative theology is often unashamedly assumed to be the essential purpose and goal of the matter and is pursued with the greatest diligence and effort. But it is certain that each and every article of faith brings about decisive ruin for philosophy, be such articles openly and unashamedly introduced into philosophy, as happened with scholasticism, or smuggled in through circular reasoning,[b] false axioms, fabricated inner sources of cognition, consciousnesses of God, pseudo-proofs, high-sounding phrases, and absolute nonsense, as is customary in our time; for they render impossible the clear, impartial, purely objective comprehension of the world and our existence, this first condition of all search for truth.

It might be a rather useful thing to teach, under the name and signature of philosophy and in a strange guise, the fundamental dogmas of established

204

---

[a] *wie das denn wohl zu Zeiten kommen mag* [Goethe, *Faust* I, 529]   [b] *petitio principii*

religion, which are then called 'absolute religion', an expression worthy of Hegel, insofar as this serves to adapt students better to the purposes of the state and also to strengthen the reading public in its faith. But to pass this off as *philosophy* really means selling something for what it is not. For this and all the above to continue their course undisturbed, university philosophy must more and more turn into an obstacle[a] to truth. Philosophy is done for, if the measure of its evaluation, or even the guiding principle of its propositions, are something other than truth alone – the truth that is so difficult to obtain even with all the honesty of investigation and the effort of superior intellectual power; it ends up becoming a mere story agreed upon as true,[b] as *Fontenelle* calls history. We will never come even one step closer to solving the problems with which our infinitely mysterious existence confronts us from all sides, if we philosophize in accordance with a goal set in advance. However, no one will deny that this is the generic character of the various species of present university philosophy, for it is obvious enough that all its systems and propositions converge[c] on one goal.

Moreover, this is not even the proper Christianity of the New Testament, or its spirit, which is too high-minded, too ethereal, too eccentric for them, too much not of this world, too pessimistic and for this reason completely unsuitable for the apotheosis of the '*state*'; instead, it is merely Judaism, the doctrine that the world derives its existence from a supremely eminent, personal being and, therefore, is a most delightful thing and 'every thing was very good'.[d] This is for them the core of wisdom, and here philosophy is supposed to lead, or, if it balks, be led. Hence the war that, since the downfall of Hegelry, all the professors wage against the so-called pantheism, in whose rejection they try to outdo one another, unanimous in their condemnation of it. Has this zeal maybe arisen from the discovery of reasonable and conclusive grounds against it? Or, on the contrary, do we not observe the helplessness and fear with which they look for grounds against that opponent, standing there quietly in its original power and sneering? Can we thus still doubt that it is merely because of the incompatibility of that doctrine with 'absolute religion' that it is not to be true, shall not be true even if the whole of nature proclaimed it with thousands and thousands of throats? Nature is supposed to be silent so that Judaism can speak. And further, if aside from 'absolute religion' they consider anything else, then it is understood to be the remaining wishes of an important ministry that has the power to grant or take away professorships. That is the Muse that inspires them and guides their nightly scholarly

---

[a] *remora*   [b] *fable convenue*   [c] *kollimiren*   [d] πάντα καλὰ λίαν [Genesis 1:31 (Septuagint)]

investigations,[a] for which reason it is invoked at the beginning in the form of a dedication. Those are just the people to pull the truth from a well, tear apart the veil of deception, and mock all obscurity.

No other academic discipline, by its nature, would so strongly require people of outstanding ability and imbued with love for science and zeal for truth, than the one that, through the living word, passes on the results of the greatest efforts of the human spirit in the most important of its affairs to the flower of a new generation, indeed awakens the spirit of investigation in it. On the other hand, the ministries make sure that no discipline has such great influence on the innermost views of the future educated class, which actually controls state and society, as precisely this one; and that is why it must be staffed only with the most devout men who tailor their teaching in complete accordance with the will and the respective views of the ministry. Of course, it is then the first of these two requirements that must take second place. Now to anyone unacquainted with this state of affairs, it could seem at times as though, strangely, the most decided sheepsheads had dedicated themselves to the science of Plato and Aristotle.

206

I cannot refrain here from remarking incidentally that the positions of private tutor are a very harmful preparatory school for professorships in philosophy; almost all of those who ever were professors worked in such positions for several years after their university studies. For such positions are a real training ground for submissiveness and docility. In particular, a person becomes accustomed to subjecting his teachings completely to the will of the employer and knowing no other than his purposes. This early-on acquired habit takes root and becomes second nature, so that later, as a philosophy professor, the person finds nothing more natural than also tailoring and moulding philosophy according to the wishes of the ministry that fills the professorships, from which in the end philosophical views, or even systems, emerge as though made to order. Hence truth has an easy task! – However, it transpires here that, in order to devote ourselves unconditionally to truth, really to philosophize, to the many conditions another one is added almost inevitably, namely to stand on our own two feet and to recognize no master; accordingly the saying 'Give me a place where I may stand'[b] is in a certain sense also valid here. At least, most of those who have achieved something great in philosophy were in that situation. *Spinoza* was so clearly aware of this that he declined the professorship offered to him just for this reason.

[a] *Lukubrationen*   [b] δός μοι ποῦ στῶ [Archimedes; the quote continues 'and I will move the earth']

Zeus, the Old Thunderer, robs a man of half his virtue
the day the yoke clamps down around his neck.[a]

Genuine philosophizing requires independence:

For the man subdued by poverty can neither speak
Nor do anything, because his tongue is tied.   Theognis[b]

207   There is also a passage in Sadi's *Gulistan* (translated by Graf, Leipzig,
1846,[c] p. 185) which says that whoever has to struggle for his livelihood can
achieve nothing.[13] For that reason, the genuine philosopher is, by nature,
a frugal being and does not need much to live independently. For his
motto will always be *Shenstone's* dictum: 'Liberty is a more invigorating
cordial than Tokay.'[d]

Therefore, if this were a question of nothing but advancing philosophy
and progressing on the path to truth, then I would recommend it best to
stop the shadow-boxing carried out in its name at the universities. For
these are really not the environment for philosophy done with serious and
honest intention, whose place is all too often taken by a spruced-up wire
puppet dressed in the clothes of a philosopher having to parade and
gesticulate like a wooden marionette moved by alien wires.[e] However,
if such an academic philosophy wants to supplant real thoughts with
incomprehensible, brain-numbing phrases, newly coined words, and
egregious ideas, whose absurdities are called speculative and transcendental, then it turns into a parody of philosophy that brings the real
philosophy into disrepute, which has happened in our time. How can
even the possibility of the profound seriousness that attaches little value
to anything but truth and is the primary condition of philosophy persist
with such goings-on? – The path of truth is steep and long; no one will
walk it with a block tied to his foot; rather, wings would be necessary.
Therefore, I would be in favour of philosophy ceasing to be a trade; the
sublimity of its aspiration is not compatible with that, as the ancients
already realized. It is not necessary at all to keep a couple of insipid

---

[a] Ἥμισυ γάρ τ' ἀρετῆς ἀποαίνυται εὐρύοπα Ζεύς / Ἀνέρος, εὖτ' ἄν μιν κατὰ δούλιον ἦμαρ ἕλησιν. [Homer, *Odyssey* XVII, 322f.]

[b] Πᾶς γὰρ ἀνὴρ πενίῃ δεδμημένος οὔτε τι εἰπεῖν, / Οὔθ' ἔρξαι δύναται, γλῶσσα δέ /οἱ δέδεται. [Theognis, *Elegies*, v. 177–8]

[c] [Musharrif-uddin Sa'di, *Moslicheddin Sadi's Rosengarten* (*Rosegarden*), trans. Karl Heinrich Graf, Leipzig: Brockhaus, 1846]

[d] [William Shenstone, *Essays on Men and Manners*, 'Of Men and Manners' 86; English in the original, followed by Schopenhauer's German translation]

[e] *nervis alienis mobile lignum* [Horace, *Satires* II, 7, 82]

windbags at every university in order to spoil philosophy for young people for the rest of their lives.[14] Also *Voltaire* says quite rightly: 'Those writers who have rendered the greatest services to the small number of thinking beings recognized in the world, are the isolated educated ones, the true scholars, cloistered in their studies, who have neither expounded their arguments from university lecterns nor half-truths at academies; and it is they who have almost always been persecuted.'[a] – All assistance offered to philosophy from the outside is, by its nature, suspect; for its interest is of too lofty a kind to be able to enter an honest alliance with the doings of this vulgar-minded world. On the contrary, it has its own guiding star that never sets. For that reason, we should let it do as it likes, without assistance, but also without hindrances, and should not attach a companion to that serious pilgrim, anointed and furnished by nature, as it heads for the elevated temple of truth, since that companion is really only concerned with a good night's lodging and an evening meal. For it is to be feared that he will put an obstacle in the pilgrim's path to make him head for these instead.

As a result of all this, disregarding the purposes of the state, as mentioned, and considering only the interest of philosophy, I regard it as desirable to limit all teaching of it at universities strictly to lecturing on logic, as a completed science capable of strict proof, and to a history of philosophy, succinctly delivered and to be completed within one semester, reaching from Thales to Kant, so that, as a consequence of its brevity and lucidity, it allows as little leeway as possible for the Herr Professor's own views and acts merely as a primer for the student's own future study. For we can only become properly acquainted with the philosophers through their own works and certainly not through second-hand accounts – the reasons for which I have already expounded in the preface to the second edition of my chief work. Moreover, reading the original works of genuine philosophers has in any case a beneficial and conducive influence on the mind by bringing it into immediate communion with such an independent and superior intellect, instead of, as in those histories of philosophy, receiving only that movement that the wooden train of thought of an ordinary head[b] can impart which has worked out things in its own way.[15] For that reason, I want to limit academic lectures to the purposes of a general orientation in the field of previous philosophical achievements, eliminating

208

---

[a] *les gens de lettres, qui ont rendu le plus de service au petit nombre d'êtres pensans répandus dans le monde, sont les lettrés isolés, les vrais savans, renfermées dans leur cabinet, qui n'ont ni argumenté sur les bancs de l'université, ni dit les choses à moitié dans les académies: et ceux-là ont presque toujours été persécutés* [*Dictionnaire philosophique*, article 'Lettres, gens de Lettres']

[b] *Alltagskopfs*

209 all explanations as well as all pragmatism of delivery that tries to go further than demonstrating the unmistakable links between successively occurring systems and previous ones. This is in complete contrast to the presumption of Hegelian historians of philosophy, who present every system as necessarily occurring and, constructing the history of philosophy a priori, prove to us that every philosopher had to think exactly what he did think and nothing else, whereby the Herr Professor comfortably looks at all of them with condescension, if he does not sneer at them. The sinner! as if everything has not been the work of individual and unique minds that had to grapple with the bad society of this world for a while in order to save and deliver it from the bonds of barbarism and stultification; minds that are as individual as they are rare, so that Ariosto's 'nature made him and then broke the mould'[a] applies to every one of them to the fullest extent – as though another would have written the *Critique of Pure Reason* if Kant had died of smallpox – surely one of those manufactured goods produced by nature and with its trade-mark on the forehead, one with a normal ration of three pounds coarse brain, pretty firm texture, well preserved in a skull an inch thick, with a visual angle of seventy degrees, feeble heartbeat, blurred, squinting eyes, strongly developed feeding organs, faltering speech, and the clumsy, sluggish gait in keeping with the toad-agility[b] of his thoughts – yes, yes, only wait, they will produce *Critiques of Pure Reason* and systems too as soon as the moment, calculated by the professor, has arrived and it is their turn – which is when the oak trees bear apricots. – Of course, the gentlemen have good reasons for attributing as much as possible to upbringing and education, and indeed, as actually some do, for completely denying inborn talents and fortifying themselves in every way against the truth that everything depends on the way in which someone emerged from the hands of nature, which father begot and which mother conceived him, indeed even at which hour; therefore, no one will write *Iliads* if his mother was a goose and his father a sleepyhead, even if he studies at six universities. For this is how it is: Nature is

210 aristocratic, more aristocratic than any feudal or caste system. Accordingly, its pyramid rises from a very broad base to a very sharp apex. And even if the rabble and ragtag, which will tolerate nothing above them, succeeded in overthrowing all other aristocracies, this one they would still have to have left untouched – and should receive no gratitude for it, for it is really 'by the grace of God'.[c]

---

[a] *natura il fece, e poi ruppe la stampa* [Ludovico Ariosto, *Orlando Furioso* X, 84]   [b] *Krötenagilität*
[c] *von Gottes Gnaden* [referring to the divine right of kings]

Transcendent speculation on the apparent deliberateness in the fate of the individual

Τὸ εἰκῆ οὔκ ἐστι ἐν τῇ ζωῇ, ἀλλὰ
μία ἁρμονία καὶ τάξις.

[Chance does not exist in life, but a single harmony and order]
Plotinus, *Ennead* IV, 4, 35

Although the thoughts to be imparted here yield no firm result, indeed, might be called a mere metaphysical fantasy, I have not been able to bring myself to abandon them to oblivion, since by some they will be welcomed, at the very least as a comparison with their own thoughts nurtured on the same matter. Yet they too have to be reminded that everything about these thoughts is doubtful, not only the solution but indeed the problem. Accordingly, we can expect anything but definite explanations, rather the mere airing of a very obscure state of affairs, which nevertheless, from time to time, may have forced itself on every one of us during the course of our own life, or looking back on it. Our meditations on this may even not be much more than a groping and fumbling in the dark, where we are aware of something being there, yet do not really know where or what it is. If I should nevertheless adopt a positive or even dogmatic tone at times, let it be said here once and for all that this happens only in order not to become dull and redundant through the constant repetition of formulas of doubt and conjecture, and that the following is not to be taken seriously.

The belief in special providence, or else in the supernatural guidance of events in the course of an individual's life, has been universally popular at all times, and occasionally is even found, firmly and unshakably, in **214** thinking minds averse to all superstition, even without any connection to any definite dogmas. – First of all, we can object to this belief that, in the manner of all belief in gods, it does not have its source in *cognition*, but in the *will*, and is primarily the child of our neediness. For the data provided merely by *cognition* might be ascribed to the fact that chance, which plays us a hundred cruel tricks that seem intentional in their maliciousness, once in a while turns out to be particularly favourable, or indirectly provides very well for us. In all such cases we recognize the hand of providence in chance, and the most distinctly when, against our own insight, indeed in ways abhorred by us, it has led us to an exhilarating goal, where we then say: 'Back then I had a good voyage, even though I was shipwrecked',[a] and the contrast between choice and guidance becomes unmistakably palpable, but at the same time to the advantage of the latter. Just for that reason we comfort ourselves, in the face of adverse accidents, with that little adage, tried and tested, 'Who knows what it is good for', – which actually has sprung from the insight that, although *chance* rules the world, nevertheless *error* is its co-regent, since we are as much subject to the latter as to the former, and what now seems like a misfortune to us might actually be good luck. Thus we flee from the pranks of one world tyrant towards the other by turning from chance and appealing to error. Apart from this, to attribute a purpose to mere, pure, obvious chance is a thought unparalleled in its audacity. Nevertheless, I think that we all, at least once in our life, have vividly entertained it. It is found among all peoples and alongside all doctrines of faith, albeit most decidedly among the Muslims. It is a thought that, depending on the way we understand it, can be the most absurd or the most profound. The standing objection against the examples by means of which we want to prove it, as striking as they might sometimes be, remains that it would be the greatest miracle if it never happened that chance managed our affairs well, indeed, even better than our understanding and our insight could have done.

215   That everything that happens, without exception, takes place with *strict necessity* is a truth to be understood a priori and hence is incontrovertible; I want to call it here demonstrable fatalism. In my *Prize Essay on the Freedom of the Will* (p. 62),[b] this truth follows as the result of all prior investigations. It is confirmed empirically and a posteriori, through the no longer doubtful fact that magnetic somnambulists and people endowed with second sight, and sometimes even dreams during ordinary

---

[a] *tunc [nunc] bene navigavi, cum naufragium feci* [Desiderius Erasmus of Rotterdam, *Adagia* (*Adages*, 1515) II, 9, 78]
[b] [*FW*, 178–9 (Hübscher *SW* 4, 60)]

sleep, directly and accurately predict the future.[*,1] This empirical confirmation of my theory of the strict necessity of everything that happens is most conspicuous in regard to *second sight*. For what was predicted by virtue of this long before, we see happen afterwards exactly and in all attendant circumstances as indicated, even when we had deliberately tried to thwart it in all kinds of ways or to make the incident, at least in some minor detail, differ from the imparted vision. This has always been in vain, insofar as the very thing that was meant to foil what was predicted, served to bring it to pass for good, in the same way that in tragedies, as well as in the history of the ancients, the calamity announced by oracles or dreams is precipitated by the very measures meant to prevent it. Out of   216
the many examples I merely want to mention Oedipus the King and the fine story about Croesus with Adrastus in the first book of Herodotus, chs. 35–43.[a,2] We find corresponding cases of second sight reported by the thoroughly honest Bende Bendsen, *Archiv für thierischen Magnetismus*, vol. 8, no. 3, by Kieser[b] (especially examples 4, 12, 14, and 16), and also in Jung-Stilling's *Theory of Pneumatology*,[c] §155. Now if the gift of second sight were as frequent as it is rare, innumerable incidents would be proclaimed in advance, occur exactly as predicted, and the undeniable factual proof of the strict necessity of all that happens would be universally available, accessible to everybody. Then no doubt would remain that the course of events, as much as it appears to be purely accidental, at root is not accidental at all, rather that all these accidents themselves, random occurrences,[d] are encompassed by a deeply hidden necessity, fate,[e] whose mere tool is chance itself. To cast a glance at this has from time immemorial been the desire of all *divination*.[f] From factual divination, called to mind here, it follows not only

---

[*] The following judicial declaration is found in *The Times* of 2 December 1852: The coroner in Newent, Gloucestershire, Mr Lovegrove, undertook a judicial investigation about the body of Mark Lane, found in the water. The brother of the drowned man testified that, on first hearing that his brother Mark was missing, he at once replied: 'Then he is drowned; for I dreamt last night that he was drowned, and that I was up to my armpits in water, endeavouring to get him out.' During the following night he again dreamt that his brother had drowned near the sluice at Oxenhall and that *a trout was swimming next to him*. The following morning, accompanied by his other brother, he went to Oxenhall; there he saw *a trout in the water*. He was immediately convinced that his brother had to be lying there, and, in fact, the body was found in that spot. – Hence something as fleeting as a trout gliding past is predicted several hours in advance, exactly to the second!

[a] [*Histories* I, 35–43]
[b] [Dietrich Georg Kieser, *Archiv für den thierischen Magnetismus* (*Archive for Animal Magnetism*), 12 vols. (1817–24), Bendsen, 'Beiträge zu den Erscheinungen des zweiten Gesichts' (Contributions to the Phenomena of Second Sight), vol. 8 (1820)]
[c] [Johann Heinrich Jung (assumed name: Heinrich Stilling, known as Jung-Stilling), *Theorie der Geisterkunde*, Nuremberg: Raw, 1808]
[d] τὰ εἰκῇ φερόμενα   [e] εἱμαρμένη   [f] *Mantik*

that all events occur with absolute necessity, but also that they are somehow determined in advance and objectively fixed, insofar as they express themselves as present to the eye of a soothsayer. However, this might be ascribed to the mere necessity of their occurrence as a result of the progression of the causal chain. In any case, the realization, or rather the view, that the necessity of everything happening is *not blind*, thus the belief in an orderly and necessary course of our lives, is fatalism of a higher order, which cannot be demonstrated, as can simple fatalism, but upon which perhaps all of us, sooner or later, will stumble someday and which, according to our manner of thinking, will take hold of us, either for a while or forever. We can call this, in contrast to the ordinary and demonstrable kind, *transcendent fatalism*. It does not arise, as does the other, from actual theoretical cognition, nor from the investigation necessary for it, for which few would be qualified, but is gradually deposited by experiences during the course of our own lives. For among these experiences certain instances make themselves known to us that, on the one hand, due to their particular and great usefulness for us, bear the stamp of a moral, or inner, necessity, but, on the other, bear the distinct mark of external, complete randomness. Their frequent occurrence gradually leads to the view, often turning into conviction, that the course of the individual's life, as confused as it may seem, is a whole, consistent within itself and possessing a determinate tendency and edifying meaning, just as the most well-conceived epic.[*,3] However, the instruction we receive from it would refer solely to our individual will – which, at bottom, is our individual error. For it is not in world history that design and integrity reside, as professorial philosophy wrongly believes, but in the life of the individual. Peoples only exist in abstraction; individuals are what is real. Therefore, world history lacks direct metaphysical significance; it is really only an accidental configuration; I remind the reader here of what I have said about this in *The World as Will and Representation*, vol. 1, §35. – Hence in regard to our own individual fate *transcendent fatalism* arises in many, perhaps occasioned in all of us some time through the thoughtful observation of our own life, after its thread has been spun to considerable length. Indeed, reflecting on details in the course of our life, the latter can at times present itself as if everything in it were pre-arranged, and the people who appear in it seem to us like mere actors. This transcendent fatalism has[4]

---

* When we carefully reflect on some scenes from our past, everything in it appears to be as well pre-arranged as in a well-planned novel.

not only much that is comforting, but maybe much that is true as well; hence it has been affirmed at all times, even as dogma.*,5 The testimony   218 of an experienced courtier and man of the world, relayed, moreover, at a Nestorian age, merits mentioning here as completely impartial, namely that of the ninety-year-old *Knebel*, who writes in a letter: 'On close observation, we will find that in the life of most people a certain plan can be found that, through their own nature or the circumstances that guide them, is, as it were, preordained for them. The conditions of their lives may be ever so varied and changeable, in the end there exists a whole that enables us to become aware of a certain consistency. . . . The hand of a particular fate, as much as its operations are hidden, shows itself clearly; it may be moved through external effects or internal feeling; indeed, contradictory grounds are often at work in its direction. As confused as the course might be, ground and direction always shine through.' (*Knebel's Literary Remains*, second edn., 1840, vol. 3,ᵃ p. 452.)

To be sure, the planned orderliness in the course of everyone's life can in part be explained through the invariability and rigid consistency of the inborn character, which always brings the human being back on to the same track. What is most appropriate for the character of each individual, he recognizes with such immediacy and certainty that he does not include it in clear, reflected consciousness, but immediately and, as if from instinct, acts in accordance with it. This type of knowledge, insofar as it passes into acting without having entered distinct consciousness, can be compared to the 'reflex motions'ᵇ of *Marshall Hall*. By virtue of these, everyone not being forced from the outside or by his own false concepts and prejudices, pursues and takes hold of what is appropriate for him as an individual without being able to account for this to himself, just as the turtle in the sand, incubated by the sun and hatched from the egg, without being able to see it, immediately goes straight for the water. So this is the inner compass, the secret pull that   219

---

* Neither our *doings* nor our *course of life* are *our own achievement*; rather *our essence and being* are our work, which nobody sees as such. For, on the basis of this and the circumstances and external events occurring in accordance with strict causal connection, our doings and course of life happen with complete necessity. Consequently, the entire course of life of human beings is already at birth irreversibly determined down to the smallest details, so that a somnambulist of the highest power could accurately predict it. We should keep this great and certain truth in mind when contemplating and judging the course of our life, our deeds and sufferings.

ᵃ [*Karl Ludwig von Knebel's literarischer Nachlaß und Briefwechsel* (*K. L. von Knebel's Literary Remains and Letters*), ed. K. A. Varnhagen von Ense and T. Mundt, 3 vols., Leipzig: Reichenbach, 1835; two minor deviations]

ᵇ [Original English] [Marshall Hall (1790–1857), English physician who studied the physiology of the nervous system] brings everyone correctly on to *that* path which alone is suitable for him and whose steady direction he only becomes aware of after having travelled it. – Nevertheless, this does seem insufficient in comparison with the powerful influence and great force of external circumstances. At the same time, it is not very believable that what is most important in the world, the course of a human life, purchased at the price of so much doing, toil, and suffering, should receive even the other half of its guidance, namely the part that comes from the outside, effectively and solely from the hand of a real blind chance which is absolutely nothing in itself and lacks all structure. On the contrary, we are tempted to believe that – as there are certain images, called anamorphoses (Pouillet II,[a] 171), which provide for the naked eye only distorted, mutilated, and misshapen forms,[b] whereas, when seen in a conical mirror, they show regular human figures — the purely empirical view of the course of the world resembles looking at the image with the naked eye, whereas tracing the intention of fate corresponds to looking at them in the conical mirror, which connects and orders what was cast asunder. However, this view can still be contrasted with the other one, that the systematic connection that we believe to perceive in the events of our life is only the unconscious effect of our ordering and schematizing imagination, similar to that whereby we clearly and nicely see human figures and groups on a speckled wall by creating systematic connections between stains that the most blind chance has scattered. Meanwhile we must assume that what, in the highest and truest sense of the word, is right and beneficial for us, cannot be that which was merely projected, never executed, hence never came to exist other than in our thoughts – the 'vain designs that never have reality' of Ariosto[c] – and whose frustration by chance we would have to lament for the rest of our lives. Rather it is that which finds its actual expression in the great picture of reality and of which, having recognized its expediency, we say with conviction 'thus it was decreed by fate',[d] this is how it was bound to happen. Therefore, there would have to be some kind of provision, a unity of randomness and necessity lying at the very root of things, for realizing what is purposeful in this sense. In virtue of this unity, inner necessity, expressing itself as an instinctive drive,[e] rational deliberation, and finally external influence of circumstances would have to work closely hand in hand in the course of a human life in such a way that in the end, life having run its course, they would make it appear to be a well-rounded, complete

220

---

[a] [Claude Servais Mathias Pouillet, *Eléments de physique expérimentale et de météorologie* (1827)]
[b] *Ungestalten*   [c] *vani disegni, che non han' mai loco* [*Orlando furioso* XXXIV, 75]
[d] *sic erat in fatis* [Ovid, *Fasti* (*On the Roman Calendar*) I, 481]   [e] *instinktartiger Trieb*

work of art, although previously, when it was still in the making, often neither plan nor purpose could be recognized, as in every newly laid out work of art. But whoever approached and closely examined it only after its completion, would have to marvel at such a course of life as the work of the most deliberate foresight, wisdom, and persistence. Its significance as a whole would be, in accordance with its subject, an ordinary or an extra-ordinary one. From this point of view we might conceive the very tran-scendent thought that at the root of this phenomenal world,[a] ruled by chance, there is consistently and universally an intelligible world,[b] which rules chance itself.[6] – Of course, nature does everything for the species and nothing merely for the individual, because the former is everything for it and the latter nothing. However, what we assume here as effective[c] is not nature but the metaphysical, lying beyond nature and existing wholly and undividedly in each individual, so that for the metaphysical the individual means everything.

To be sure, in order to come to terms with these things, we should really answer the following questions: Is a complete disparity possible between a human being's character and fate? – Or does every fate in principle conform to its character? – Or, finally, does a secret, incomprehensible necessity, like the author of a drama, really join them fittingly together each time? – But precisely on this very point we are not clear.

In the meantime, we believe that at every moment we are masters of our deeds. However, when looking back at the completed part of the course of   221 our life, and especially when focusing on our unfortunate steps together with their consequences, we often do not comprehend how we could have done this and neglected to do that; so that it looks as if a foreign power had guided our steps. Thus Shakespeare says:

> Fate, show thy force: ourselves we do not owe;
> What is decreed must be, and be this so!   *Twelfth Night*, Act I, scene 5[d]

The ancients do not tire of stressing the omnipotence of fate in verse and prose, pointing to human powerlessness as a contrast. We see everywhere that this is a conviction with which they are imbued, in that they suspect a mysterious connection of things that is more profound than the clearly empirical one. (See Lucian's *Dialogues of the Dead* XIX and XXX; Herodotus I, 91, and IX, 16.[e]) Hence all the expressions for this concept

---

[a] *mundus phaenomenon*   [b] *mundus intelligibilis*   [c] *wirkend*
[d] [Original English, followed by Schopenhauer's German translation]   [e] [*Histories*]

in the Greek language: *potmos, aisa, heimarmenê, peprômenê, moira*,[a] and perhaps some others. The term *pronoia*,[b] on the other hand, shifts the concept of the matter by starting out from *nous*,[c] which is secondary, thereby becoming plain and comprehensible, but also superficial and false.[*,7] Goethe as well says in *Götz von Berlichingen* (Act V): 'We human beings do not direct ourselves; power over us is given to evil spirits which practise their mischievous tricks to our undoing.' Also in *Egmont* (Act V, last scene): 'Man thinks he guides his life and directs himself; and his innermost being is irresistibly drawn to his fate.' Indeed, the prophet Jeremiah already said it: 'The way of man is not in himself: it is not in man that walketh to direct his steps' (10:23). All this is based on the fact that our deeds are the necessary product of two factors, one of which, our character, is immutably fixed, but becomes known to us only a posteriori, thus gradually; the other is the motives; these lie outside, are brought about necessarily by the course of the world, and determine the given character, under the condition of its fixed constitution, with a necessity that equals a mechanical one. The I that judges the course of events is the subject of cognition; as such, it is a stranger to these two actors and merely the critical observer of their actions. Hence it may very well feel surprised at times.

Once we grasp the point of view of transcendent fatalism and consider an individual life from its perspective, we have at times the strangest of all spectacles before our eyes, in the contrast between the obvious, physical contingency of an event and its moral–metaphysical necessity, of which the latter, however, can never be demonstrated, but rather can always be merely imagined. In order to illustrate this with the help of a well-known example – which at the same time, because of its stridency, is suited to serve as a model of the matter – let us consider Schiller's 'The Walk to the Iron Factory'.[d] For here we see Fridolin's delay, due to the service during mass, brought about completely accidentally, while it is, on the other hand, of the utmost importance and necessity for himself. Maybe everyone, on proper reflection, will find analogous cases in his own course of life, albeit not so important nor so clearly pronounced. Quite a few people will be driven

---

* It is extraordinary how much the ancients were prepossessed and infused by the concept of a sovereign destiny (εἱμαρμένη, *fatum*); not only the poets, especially in tragedy, but also the philosophers and historians bear witness to this. In Christian times the concept has taken a backseat and is emphasized less, because it has been supplanted by that of providence, πρόνοια, which presupposes an intellectual origin and, as coming from a personal being, is not so rigid and unalterable, and also not so deeply conceived and mysterious, and thus cannot replace the former, rather accuses it of unbelief.

[a] πότμος, αἶσα, εἱρμαρμένη, πεπρωμένη, μοῖρα, Ἀδράστεια   [b] πρόνοια   [c] νοῦς [mind, intellect]
[d] *Gang nach dem Eisenhammer*

by this to make the assumption that *a secret and inexplicable power* guides all the turns and twists in the course of our lives, to be sure, often contrary to our temporary motive, but in such a way as to be appropriate to its objective integrity and subjective purposiveness, hence to be conducive to our actual true benefit, so that we often afterwards recognize the foolishness of our desires leading in the opposite direction. 'Fate leads the willing, but drags along the unwilling' – Seneca, *Epistles*, 107.[a] Such a power, running an invisible thread through all things, would have to link even those which the causal chain leaves without any mutual connection so that they would meet at the required moment. Hence it would control the events of real life as completely as the poet controls those of his drama. However, chance and error, which initially and immediately interfere with and disturb the regular, causal course of events, would be mere instruments of its invisible hand.

223

What propels us more than anything to make the bold assumption of such an unfathomable power, sprung from the unity of the deep-lying root of necessity and chance, is the consideration that the determinate, highly unique *individuality* of each human being in physical, moral and intellectual respects, which is everything about him and, consequently, must have sprung from the highest metaphysical necessity, arises, on the other hand (as I have explained in my chief work, vol. 2, ch. 43), as the necessary result of the moral character of the father, the intellectual ability of the mother, and the overall corporization[b] of both; whereas the union of the parents was normally brought about by ostensibly accidental circumstances. Hence the claim, or the metaphysical–moral postulate, of an ultimate unity of necessity and chance here forces itself upon us. However, I regard it as impossible to arrive at a distinct concept of this uniform root of both. Only this can be said, that it would at the same time be what the ancients called destiny, *heimarmenê, peprômenê, fatum*, which they conceived as the guiding genius of each individual, but no less that which Christians revere as providence, *pronoia*. These three differ in that fate is conceived as blind and the other two as seeing; but this anthropomorphistic difference disappears and loses all significance in regard to the innermost, metaphysical essence of things, in which alone we must seek the root of that inexplicable unity of the contingent and the necessary, which constitutes the secret controller of all things human.

---

[a] *Ducunt volentem fata, nolentem trahunt* [*Epistles*, 107, 11]
[b] *Korporisation* ['embodiment'; a technical term that appears in Schelling's *Philosophical Investigations into the Essence of Human Freedom*]

The notion of a *genius*[a] attached to all individuals and presiding over their courses of life is said to be of Etruscan origin, but was already widespread
224　among the ancients. Its essential idea is contained in a verse of Menander, preserved for us by Plutarch (*On Tranquillity of Mind*,[b] ch. 15; also Stobaeus, *Eclogues* I, 6, 4;[c] and Clement of Alexandria, *Stromata* V, 14[d]):

> A spirit is joined to every human being
> immediately at birth, as a guide, to pronounce an omen,
> a good spirit of course.[e]

At the end of the *Republic*, *Plato* describes how each soul, prior to its renewed rebirth, chooses a lot in life,[f] together with the personality appropriate to it, and then says: 'After all the souls had chosen their lives, they went forward to Lachesis in the same order in which they had made their choices, and she assigned to each the *daimôn* it had chosen as guardian of its life and fulfiller of its choice' (X, 621).[g] Porphyry has provided a commentary on this passage that is very much worth reading and Stobaeus has preserved it in his *Eclogues*[h] II, 8, 37 (vol. 3,[i] pp. 368ff., especially p. 376). Plato had said earlier (X, 618), in reference to this: 'Your *daimôn* or guardian spirit will not be assigned to you by lot; you will choose him. The one who has the first lot (the lot that determines merely the order of choice) will be the first to choose a life to which he will then be bound by necessity.'[j],8 – Horace expresses the matter beautifully:

> The Genius knows, companion who tempers destiny fated by our star,
> A god of human nature, mortal, in every
> Human being, of changeable form, now bright and now sombre.[k]
>
> (*Epistles* II, 2, 187)

---

[a]　*Genius*　　[b]　*de tranquillitate animi* [part of Plutarch's *Moralia*; ch. 15, 474b]
[c]　[*Ioannis Stobaei Eclogarum physicarum et ethicarum libri duo* (Johann Stobaeus, *Eclogues*), ed. A. H. L. Heeren, Göttingen: Vandenhoeck & Ruprecht, 1792–1801]
[d]　[*Stromata* V, 14, 131]
[e]　Ἅπαντι δαίμων ἀνδρὶ συμπαραστατεῖ / Εὐθὺς γενομένῳ, μυσταγωγὸς τοῦ βίου / Ἀγαθός. (*Hominem unumque, simul lucem est editus, sectatur Genius, vitae qui auspicium facit, bonus nimirum.*)
[f]　*Lebensloos*
[g]　Ἐπειδὴ δ' οὖν πάσας τὰς ψυχὰς τοὺς βίους ᾑρῆσθαι, ὥσπερ ἔλαχον, ἐν τάξει προσιέναι πρὸς τὴν Λάχεσιν, ἐκείνην δ' ἑκάστῳ ὃν εἵλετο δαίμονα, τοῦτον φύλακα ξυμπέμπειν τοῦ βίου καὶ ἀποπληρωτὴν τῶν αἱρεθέντων. [X, 620d, trans. G. M. A. Grube]
[h]　*Eclogae ethicae*　　[i]　[actually, vol. 2]
[j]　οὐχ ὑμᾶς δαίμων λήξεται, ἀλλ' ὑμεῖς δαίμονα αἱρήσεσθε. πρῶτος δὲ ὁ λαχὼν (*das Loos, was bloß die Ordnung der Wahl bestimmt* [Schopenhauer's comment]) πρῶτος αἱρείσθω βίον, ᾧ συνέσται ἐξ ἀνάγκης. [X, 617d–e]
[k]　*Scit Genius, natale comes qui temperat astrum, / Naturae deus humanae, mortalis in unum- / Quodque caput, vultu mutabilis, albus et ater.*

A passage worth reading is found in Apuleius, *On the God of Socrates*,[a] p. 236, 38, Bipont edition. Iamblichus has a short but important chapter in *On the Mysteries of the Egyptians*,[b] sect. IX, ch. 6, 'On the Personal Demon'.[c] Still more remarkable is the passage in Proclus in his commentary on Plato's *Alcibiades*, p. 77, Creuzer's edition: 'For he who guides our whole life and fulfils the choices made before we were born, and allots the gifts of fate and of the gods fated from birth, and supplies and apportions the sunshine of providence, that is the genius, etc.'[d] Theophrastus Paracelsus has expressed the same thought most profoundly: 'In order for *fate* to be understood, every human being has a spirit that dwells outside of him and has its seat in the outer stars. It uses the bosses*,[9] of its master. It is this spirit   225 that produces predictions, before and after; for these continue to exist after it. These spirits are called *fate*.' (Theophrastus, *Works*, Strasburg, 1603,[e] folio, vol. 2, p. 36.) It is also noteworthy that this thought can already be found in *Plutarch*, since he says that, aside from the part of the soul that is engulfed in the earthly[f] body, another purer part remains outside, hovering above the head of a human, which presents itself as a star and which is rightly called his demon or genius, who guides him and whom the wiser person follows willingly. The passage is too long to quote, it is found in *On the Sign of Socrates*. The main sentence is: 'That which circulates in the body underneath the surface is called Soul, but what cannot perish is called Mind by the many, who customarily think it to be within themselves. Those, however, who guess correctly think that it is outside of them and call it Genius.'[g] Incidentally I note that Christianity, which, as is well known, likes to transform the gods and demons of all the pagans into devils, seems to

---

* Types, protuberances, lumps, from Italian *bozza, abbozzare, abbozzo*; from that comes *Bossiren* [to boss, to create images from soft materials, like gypsum], and French *bosse*.

[a] *de deo Socratis* [*L. Apuleji Madaurensis Philosophi Platonici Opera*, vol. 2, 1788; '38' probably refers to p. 238]

[b] *de mysteriis Aegyptiorum*   [c] *de proprio daemone*

[d] ὁ γὰρ πᾶσαν ἡμῶν τὴν ζωὴν ἰθύνων καὶ τάς τε αἱρέσεις ἡμῶν ἀποπληρῶν, τὰς πρὸ τῆς γενέσεως, καὶ τὰς τῆς εἱμαρμένης δόσεις καὶ τῶν μοιρηγενετῶν θεῶν, ἔτι δὲ τὰς ἐκ τῆς προνοίας ἐλλάμψεις χορηγῶν καὶ παραμετρῶν, οὗτος ὁ δαίμων ἐστί κ.τ.λ. [*Initia Philosophiae ac Theologiae ex Platonicis Fontibus Ducta sive Procli Diadochi et Olympiodori in Platonis Alcibiadem Commentarii (Commentary on Alcibiades I)*, ed. Friedrich Creuzer, Frankfurt: Moen, 1820; I, 1]

[e] [Aureoli Philippi Theophrasti Bombastus von Hohenheim Paracelsi (Theophrastus von Hohenheim, called Paracelsus), *Opera, Bücher, Schrifften (Works)*, ed. Johann Huser, Strasburg: Zetzner, 1603]

[f] *irdischen*

[g] τὸ μὲν οὖν ὑποβρύχιον ἐν τῷ σώματι φερόμενον Ψυχὴ λέγεται· τὸ δὲ φθορᾶς λειφθέν, οἱ πολλοὶ Νοῦν καλοῦντες, ἐντὸς εἶναι νομίζουσιν αὐτόν· οἱ δὲ ὀρθῶς ὑπονοοῦντες, ὡς ἐκτὸς ὄντα, Δαίμονα προσαγορεύουσι [Plutarch, *Moralia* VII, 46, 22 (passage shortened)]

have made this genius of the ancients into the domestic spirit[a] of the scholars and magicians. – The Christian concept of providence is known well enough to make it unnecessary to dwell on it. – However, all these are only figurative, allegorical conceptions of the matter being discussed, since it is not granted to us to grasp the most profound and hidden truths other than through image and simile.

In truth that hidden power which governs even external influences can ultimately have its root only in our own mysterious inner being; for in the end the alpha and omega of all existence lies within ourselves. But even in the luckiest case, we will be able to see the mere possibility of this only to some extent and from far away, and again only by means of analogies and similes.

The closest analogy to the workings of that power can be seen in the *teleology of nature*, by showing us the purposive as occurring without knowledge of the purpose, especially where external purposiveness, i.e. that which happens between different, indeed diverse[b] beings and even within the unorganic, becomes evident. A striking example of this kind is driftwood, which the ocean supplies in abundance especially in the treeless polar regions; another is the fact that the main land mass of our planet lies towards the North Pole, whose winter, for astronomical reasons, is eight days shorter and hence much milder than that of the South Pole. But also internal purposiveness, pronounced unambiguously in a self-contained organism, mediated through the surprising harmony between nature's technique and its mere mechanism, or between purposive causality[c] and efficient causality[d] (in connection with this I refer to my chief work, vol. 2, ch. 26, pp. 334–9[e]), lets us see by analogy how that which starts out from different points far apart, seemingly alien to one another,[f] nevertheless conspires to an ultimate end where it duly comes together, not led by cognition, but by means of a necessity of a higher order preceding all possibility of cognition. – Furthermore, when bringing to mind the theory, established by *Kant* and later by *Laplace*, about the origin of our planetary system, whose probability is close to certainty, and when encountering speculations of the kind which I introduced in my chief work, vol. 2, ch. 25, p. 324,[g] thus reflecting on how ultimately this well-ordered, wondrous planetary world had to emerge from the play of blind natural forces

---

[a] *spiritus familiaris* [magically produced servant spirit, factotum]   [b] *verschiedenartigen*
[c] *nexus finalis*   [d] *nexus effectivus*   [e] [Third edn., pp. 379–87 (Hübscher *SW* 3, 379–87)]
[f] *sich anscheinend Fremde* [in the sense of being unrelated]
[g] [Third edn., p. 368 (Hübscher *SW* 3, 368)]

following their immutable laws, then we have here also an analogy that can serve, in general and from afar, to portend the possibility that even the course of an individual life is governed by events that are the capricious play of blind chance – albeit planned, as it were – in such a way as is suited to the true and ultimate good of the person.*,[10] On this assumption, the dogma of *providence*, as being thoroughly anthropomorphic, could not be deemed true in an immediate and proper sense;[a] but it would be the mediate, allegorical and mythical expression of a truth and consequently, like all religious myths, completely adequate for practical purposes and subjective reassurance, as, for example, Kant's moral theology, which is also to be understood merely as a schema[b] for orientation, hence allegorically – in other words, it might not be true, but it is as good as true. The will to life, which subsequently acts in the most perfect appearances of the world, already is the internally active and guiding principle in those deep, blind, primordial forces of nature from whose interplay the planetary system arises, and it is there that this will, by means of strict laws of nature working towards its purposes, already prepares the foundations for constructing the world and its order, in that, for example, the most accidental thrust, or momentum, the inclination of the ecliptic, and the velocity of the rotation must be determined forever, and the end result must be the expression of its entire essence, just because this itself is already active in the primordial forces. – Just in the same way, all events determining the actions of a human being, together with the causal connection that brings them about, are only the objectivation of the same will that also expresses itself in this human being; which makes it possible to foresee, albeit only as though through a mist, that these events must harmonize and agree with even the most specific purposes of each human being, in which sense they then form the hidden power that guides the fate of the individual and is allegorized as the individual's genius or providence. Considered purely objectively, it is and remains the consistent, all-encompassing, exceptionless causal connection – by virtue of which everything that happens occurs with absolute and strict necessity – that represents the place of the merely mythical world government and, indeed, has the right to bear that name.

The following general reflection can make this clearer. 'Accidental'[c] means the coincidence in time of that which is causally not connected.

227

---

* Αὐτόματα γὰρ τὰ πράγματ᾽ ἐπὶ τὸ συμφέρον/Ῥεῖ κἂν καθεύδῃς ἢ πάλιν τἀναντία [For things somehow by themselves turn out expedient, even when you sleep, or turn back in the opposite direction], Menander in Stob[aeus], *Floril[egium]*, vol. I, p. 363 [*'Peri hyperopsias'* 9, 417].

a *sensu proprio*   b *Schema*   c *zufällig*

However, nothing is *absolutely* accidental; on the contrary, even what is most accidental is only something necessary that has come about on a more distant path, in that definite causes high in the causal chain have long ago determined with necessity that it had to happen just now, simultaneously with another thing. For every event is the individual link in a chain of causes and effects that progresses in the direction of time. But, by virtue of space, there are innumerable such chains side by side. However, these are not entirely alien to one another or without connection among themselves; on the contrary, they are entwined in multiple ways; for example, several causes now acting simultaneously, each of which produces a different effect, have sprung from a common cause higher up and are, therefore, related to one another as are great-grandchildren to their ancestor. On the other hand, an individual effect occurring just now often requires the concurrence of many different causes that, each as a link in its own chain, come from the past. Accordingly, all those causal chains, progressing in the direction of time, form a large, common, much-entwined net, which also moves in the direction of time in its entire breadth and thereby constitutes the course of the world. Now if we make sensible[a] those individual causal chains with the help of meridians that run in the direction of time, then that which is simultaneous and, therefore, not directly causally connected, can everywhere be indicated through parallel circles. Although those things that lie underneath the same parallel circle do not immediately depend on one another, they still stand mediately in some, albeit only remote, connection, in virtue of the interconnectedness of the entire net, or of the totality of all causes and effects rolling forward in the direction of time; their present concurrence is, therefore, necessary. On this rests the accidental coincidence, necessary in a higher sense, of all conditions of an event; the occurrence of what fate has willed. This explains, for example, the fact that, when in the wake of the migration of peoples a flood of barbarism poured into Europe, the finest masterpieces of Greek sculpture, the Laocoön, the Vatican Apollo, and others disappeared at once, as if through a trap-door in the theatre, by finding their way down into the womb of the earth, in order to await there, unscathed through a thousand years, a gentler, nobler era that understood and appreciated the arts. When that time finally arrived, at the end of the fifteenth century under Pope Julius II, those masterpieces re-emerged into the light, as the well-preserved models of art and true type of the human form.[11] Likewise, the arrival at the right moment of the occasions and circumstances important and decisive in the course of

228

229

---

[a] *Versinnlichen*

an individual's life rests on this, ultimately even the occurrence of omens, belief in which is so common and ineradicable that it has frequently found a place even in the most superior minds. For since nothing is *absolutely* accidental, but rather everything occurs with necessity, and since even the very coincidence of the causally *not* connected, which we call chance, is necessary, in that what is now simultaneous was determined *as such* by causes in the remotest past, everything is reflected and echoed in everything else; and that well-known dictum by Hippocrates (*On Nourishment, Works,* ed. Kühn, vol. 2,[a] p. 20), referring to interaction within the organism, can be applied to the totality of things: 'Only one flowing together, one breathing together, all in sympathy.'[b] – The ineradicable tendency of humans to heed omens, their extispicy[c] and auspice,[d] their random opening of the Bible, their cartomancy,[e] pouring of lead,[f] reading of coffee-grounds,[g] and so forth, bear witness to their assumption, defying rational justification, that it is somehow possible to discern, on the basis of what is present to them and clearly before their eyes, what is hidden by space or time, thus is distant or in the future; so that they could read the latter from the former, if they only had the true key to the secret code.[12]

A second analogy that, from an entirely different angle, can contribute to an indirect understanding of the transcendent fatalism we have been considering is provided by *dreams*, to which life in general bears a resemblance that has long been recognized and often expressed; so much so that even Kant's transcendental idealism can be conceived as the most distinct exposition of this dream-like nature of our conscious existence, as I have stated in my critique of his philosophy. – In fact, it is this analogy with dreams that enables us to see, even if only in the misty distance, how the mysterious power that controls and guides the external events that affect us on behalf of the purposes it has in store for us might still have its root in the depths of our own unfathomable essence. For even in dreams the circumstances that become the motives of our actions coincide by pure chance, circumstances   230 that are external and independent of us and often even abhorrent. Yet a secret and purposive connection exists between them, in that a hidden power, which all accidents in dreams obey, governs and ordains these

---

[a] *de alimento* [Vol. 2 of *Magni Hippocratis Opera Omnia* (Greek and Latin), ed. Karl Gottlob Kühn, Leipzig: Knobloch, 1825–7]
[b] Χύρροια μία, σύμπνοια μία, πάντα συμπαθέα.   [c] *extispicia* [divination from entrails]
[d] ὀρνιθοσκοπία [divination from bird flight]   [e] *Kartenlegen*
[f] *Bleigießen* [divination by pouring molten lead into cold water]
[g] *Kaffeesatzbeschauen* [similar to reading tea leaves]

circumstances as well, and solely in relation to us. But the strangest thing of all is that this power can ultimately be none other than our own will, yet from a point of view that does not belong to our dreaming consciousness; and so it happens that events in a dream often turn out quite contrary to our wishes in it, confound and irritate us, even scare us and cause us mortal fear, without fate, which we ourselves secretly control, coming to our rescue. Similarly, that we eagerly ask about something and receive an answer that astonishes us. Or again, that we ourselves are being asked something during an exam and are unable to give the answer, whereupon someone else, to our shame, answers it perfectly, while in one case as in the other, the answer can only come from our own resources. In order to make this mysterious control of events in a dream, coming from ourselves, even clearer and bring its operation closer to understanding, there is yet another explanation that alone can achieve this, but is inevitably of an obscene nature. Therefore, I expect from readers who are worth speaking to that they will neither take offence nor treat the matter as a joke. It is well known that there are dreams which nature uses for a material purpose, namely for emptying the overfilled seminal gland. Dreams of this type of course show salacious scenes; however, other dreams that do not have that goal nor achieve it sometimes do so as well. Now here there is a difference that in dreams of the first kind the beauties and the occasion soon prove to be favourable to us, whereby nature achieves its purpose. By contrast, in dreams of the second kind the path to the thing that we most ardently desire continues to be blocked by fresh obstacles that we try to overcome in vain, so that in the end we do not reach our goal after all. What creates these obstacles and again and again frustrates our vivid desire, is but our own will, yet from a region that lies far beyond the representing consciousness in dreaming and thus appears in it as inexorable fate. – Now, might the case of fate in reality, with the orderliness noticed possibly by all people in the course of their own lives, not be analogous to that described in dreams?*,[13] Once in a while it happens that we have drawn up a plan and enthusiastically adopted it, but it later becomes apparent that it was not truly beneficial to us; in the meantime we eagerly pursue it, but in regard to it we experience a conspiracy of fate

231

---

* Objectively considered, the course of an individual's life is of consistent and strict necessity; for all his actions happen as necessarily as the motions of a machine, and all external events occur on the leading line of a causal chain whose links possess a strictly necessary connection. If we adhere to this, we need not be surprised so much when we see the course of his life turn out as if it were systematically laid out and appropriate for him.

against it, which sets in motion its whole machinery to thwart it, pushing us against our will back on to the path truly appropriate for us. In the face of such seemingly deliberate resistance, some people use the phrase: 'I realize that it is not *meant to* be';[a] others call it ominous, and again others speak of it as a hint from God. However, all share the view that, if fate opposes a plan with such obvious tenacity, we should abandon it, since, as unsuitable for the destiny of which we are unconscious, it will not be realized anyhow and, by doggedly pursuing it, we bring upon ourselves only harder blows of fate, until we finally are back on the right track; or, if we succeeded in forcing the matter, it would only cause us harm and misery. Here the saying 'Fate leads the willing, but drags along the unwilling',[b] mentioned above, finds its complete confirmation. In some cases it is actually revealed afterwards that the frustration of such a plan was definitely conducive to our true welfare. This could also be the case where it does not become known to us, especially if we consider the metaphysical–moral as our true good. – If we look back   232
from here to the principal result of my entire philosophy, namely that what presents and maintains the phenomenon[c] of the world is the *will* that also lives and strives in each individual, and remind ourselves at the same time of the generally acknowledged similarity between life and dream, then, summing up everything so far, we can quite generally imagine as possible that, just as we all are the secret impresarios of our dreams, so too by analogy the fate that governs the actual course of our lives ultimately springs somehow from the *will*. This will is our own, but here, appearing as fate, it operates from a realm that lies far beyond our representing, individual consciousness, whereas the latter provides the motives that guide our empirically knowable, individual will, which, therefore, has often to fight hard with the will that presents itself as fate, our guiding genius, our 'spirit that dwells outside of us and has its seat in the upper stars', that looks far beyond individual consciousness and, consequently, adamantly arranges and determines through external compulsion what it could not leave for consciousness to find out and yet does not want to see being missed.

For now, a passage in *Scotus Erigena* might serve to lessen the alienating, indeed, excessive aspect of this daring proposition, in regard to which we must be reminded that his God,[d] who is without cognition and of whom time and space, along with the ten Aristotelian categories, cannot be predicated, who really only has one predicate, *will* – obviously is nothing but what I call the will to life: 'There is still another kind of ignorance in

---

[a] *ich merke, es* soll *nicht seyn*   [b] *ducunt volentem fata, nolentem trahunt* [See p. 185, n. a]
[c] *Phänomen*   [d] *Deus*

God, insofar as he is said to be ignorant of what he has foreknown and preordained, as long as it has not, in the course of factual events, shown itself in experience.'[a] (*On the Division of Nature*, ed. Oxon, p. 83.[b]) And shortly after: 'There is a third kind of divine ignorance, by which God is said to be ignorant of those events which do not yet manifest themselves in effects in the experience of acts and works, although he possesses the invisible grounds of those in himself, which he himself has created and himself knows.'[c] –

Now if, in order to make the view expounded here somewhat comprehensible to us, we have made use of the acknowledged similarity between individual life and a dream, we must, on the other hand, draw attention to the difference, that in a mere dream the relationship is one-sided, that is to say, only *one* I actually wills and senses, whereas the rest are nothing but phantoms. In the great dream of life, by contrast, a mutual relationship takes place, in that the one not only figures in the dream of another, just as it is needed, but the other in his as well; so that, in virtue of an actual pre-established harmony,[d] each only dreams what suits him, in accordance with his own metaphysical guidance, and all the dreams of life are so ingeniously interwoven that each experiences what is beneficial to him and at the same time achieves what is necessary for others; and consequently some great world event conforms to the fates of many thousands, to each in an individual manner. Therefore, all events in a human being's life are connected in two fundamentally different ways: first, in the objective, causal connection of the course of nature; and second, in the subjective connection, which exists solely in reference to the individual that experiences these events and is as subjective as his own dreams, yet within which their succession and content is necessarily determined, but in the manner of the succession of scenes determined according to the poet's design. The fact that these two kinds of connection exist simultaneously and that the same event, as a link in two completely different chains, exactly fits into both, as a result of which one person's fate matches the fate of another and everybody is the hero of his own drama, but at the same time also a character in that of another – this, admittedly, is something that transcends all our capacity for

---

[a] *est etiam alia species ignorantiae in Deo, quando ea, quae praescivit et praedestinavit, ignorare dicitur, dum adhuc in rerum factarum cursibus experimento non apparuerint [apparuit].*

[b] *De divisione naturae [Joannis Scoti Erigenæ De divisione naturae libri quinque (Periphyseon: On the Division of Nature),* ed. Thomas Gale, Oxford: Oxon, 1681; II, 28]

[c] *tertia species divinae ignorantiae est, per quam Deus dicitur ignorare ea, quae nondum experimento actionis et operationis in effectibus manifeste apparent; quorum tamen invisibiles rationes in seipso, a seipso creatas et sibi ipsi cognitas possidet.*

[d] *harmonia praestabilita*

comprehension[a] and can only be conceived as possible thanks to the wondrous pre-established harmony.[b] But would it not be narrow-minded pusillanimity to think it impossible that the courses of life of all human beings in their intertwining should have as much accord[c] and harmony as the composer is able to create between the many, seemingly chaotic parts of his symphony? Our reserve towards that enormous thought will be lessened if we remember that in a certain sense the subject of the great dream of life is only one, the will to life, and that all the plurality of appearances is determined by space and time. It is a big dream that this one being[d] dreams, but such that all its persons dream it together. Therefore, all things are intertwined and compatible with one another.[14] Now if we accept this and assume that double chain of all events, in virtue of which every being, on the one hand, exists for its own sake and behaves and acts with necessity according to its nature and follows its own path, yet, on the other, is also so thoroughly determined and suited for the apprehension of an alien being and for affecting it as are the images in its dreams, then we will have to extend this to the whole of nature, hence also to animals and beings without cognition.[e] That opens again the prospect of the possibility of omens,[f] forebodings,[g] and miraculous signs,[h] in that something which occurs *necessarily* according to the course of nature can be looked at alternatively as mere image for me and decoration for *my* dream of life, happening and existing merely in reference to *me*, or as mere reflection and reverberation of *my* doing and experience. Accordingly, what is natural and causally demonstrable as necessary in an event by no means eliminates the ominous within it, as, conversely, the latter does not eliminate the former. Hence those people are entirely on the wrong track who imagine that they remove the ominous in an event by explaining the inevitability of its occurrence, in that they demonstrate its natural and necessarily acting causes[i] clearly and, if it is a natural event, also physically with an air of learning. For no rational human being doubts these, and nobody wants to pass off an omen as a miracle.[15] However, the ominous arises precisely from the fact that the infinite chain of causes and effects, with its characteristic strict necessity and immemorial predestination, has inevitably fixed the occurrence of this event at such a significant moment, so that above all we should remind those precocious people, especially when they turn physical, that 'there are more things in heaven and earth, than are dreamt of in your philosophy' (*Hamlet*, Act I, scene 5).[16] On the other hand, with the belief in omens we

234

---

[a] *Fassungskraft*   [b] *harmonia praestabilita*   [c] *concentus*   [d] *Wesen*   [e] *Erkenntnißlose Wesen*
[f] *omina*   [g] *praesagia*   [h] *portenta*   [i] *nothwendig wirkenden Ursachen*

see the door to astrology opened again, since the most minor event that is
235 seen as ominous, the flight of a bird, the encounter with a person, and the
like, is determined by a chain of causes just as infinitely long and strictly
necessary as is the calculable position of the stars at a given time. Of course,
the constellation is high enough for half of the inhabitants of earth to see it
simultaneously, while the omen only appears in the sphere of the individual
concerned. Incidentally, if we want to render sensible to ourselves the
possibility of the ominous with the help of an image, we can compare the
person who, at an important step in his life whose results are still hidden in
the future, sees a good or bad omen and is warned by it or encouraged, to a
string[a] which, when struck, does not hear itself, but which would hear
another string that resonates as a result of its vibration. –

Kant's distinction between the thing in itself and its appearance, together
with my attribution of the former to the will and the latter to representation,
gives us the possibility of anticipating the compatibility of *three oppositions*,
albeit only imperfectly and from afar.

These are:

(1) The compatibility between the freedom of the will in itself and the
universal necessity of all actions of the individual.

(2) That between the mechanics and the technique of nature, or efficient
causality[b] and final causality,[c] or between purely causal and teleological
explicability. (See Kant's *Critique of Judgement*, §78, and my chief work,
vol. 2, ch. 26, pp. 334–9.[d])

(3) That between the obvious contingency of all events in the course of an
individual life and their moral necessity for shaping that life in accordance with a transcendent purposiveness for the individual – or, in
popular language, between the course of nature and providence.

The clarity of our insight into the compatibility of each of these three
oppositions, though in none of them perfect, is more sufficient in the first
than in the second, and least so in the third. At the same time, the understanding, even if imperfect, of the compatibility of one of these oppositions
throws light on the other two by serving as their image and simile. –

236 What the ultimate purpose is of all this mysterious control of the course
of an individual life considered here can only be stated in a very general way.
If we stop at individual cases, it often seems that it aims only at our
temporary, provisional welfare. However, this welfare cannot be its ultimate
goal in earnest because of its insignificance, imperfection, futility, and
impermanence; hence we must seek this goal in our eternal existence,

---

[a] *Saite*   [b] *nexus effectivus*   [c] *nexus finalis*   [d] [Third edn., pp. 379–85 (Hübscher *SW* 3, 379–85)]

which goes beyond the individual life. And there we can say in general that the course of our life is controlled by means of this guidance in such a way that, from the totality of knowledge we acquire during that course, the metaphysically most expedient impression on the *will* arises, as the core and the essence in itself of a human being. For even though the will to life is answered by the course of the world in general, as the appearance of its striving, every human being is that will to life in a wholly individual and unique way, so to speak, an individualized act of it, whose sufficient answer can thus be only a quite definite shaping of the course of the world, given in experiences that are characteristic of that act. Now since we have concluded from the results of my serious philosophy (in contrast to mere professorial or comic philosophy) that the will's turning away from life is the ultimate aim of temporal existence, we must assume that we shall all be gradually guided *in that direction* in a way individually suited to us, thus often through long detours. Further, since happiness and pleasure really work against this purpose, we see, accordingly, misfortune and suffering entwined in the course of every life, although in very unequal measure and only rarely to excess, namely in tragic outcomes, where it looks as if the will is driven to turn away from life by violent means, as it were, and achieve rebirth as if by Caesarian section.

In this way this invisible control, making itself known only in doubtful semblance, accompanies us to our death, the actual result and insofar the purpose of life. At that hour, all the mysterious powers (although rooted within ourselves) that determine the eternal fate of the human being converge and move into action. From their conflict results the path that he has to follow now, that is, his rebirth is prepared together with all weal and woe that is contained in it and irrevocably determined from that moment. – Upon this rests the profoundly serious, important, solemn, and terrible character of the hour of death. It is a crisis[a] in the strongest sense of the word – a last judgement of the world.

237

---

[a] *Krisis*

Und laß dir rathen, habe
Die Sonne nicht zu lieb und die Sterne.
Komm, folge mir ins dunkle Reich hinab.

Goethe

[And you, priestess, take my advice:
Don't love the sun, don't love the stars too much.
Come! Follow me below to the dark kingdom!
(*Iphigenia in Tauris*, Act III, scene 1; trans. Frank G. Ryder)]

The spectres that were not only banned but ostracized everywhere in the all-too-clever past century, in defiance of all previous ages, have been rehabilitated in Germany during these past twenty-five years, as magic was already. Perhaps not without good reason. For the proofs against their existence were in part metaphysical, based as such on uncertain ground; and in part empirical, merely demonstrating that in those cases where no accidental or intentionally arranged deception had been uncovered, neither had anything existed that could have acted on the retina by means of reflection of light rays, or on the eardrum by means of vibrations of the air. However, this merely speaks against the presence of *bodies*, which nobody had actually claimed, indeed whose manifestation in the aforesaid physical manner would nullify the truth of a spirit apparition.[a] For it is already part of the concept of a spirit that its presence manifests itself to us in another way than that of a body. What a spirit-seer who understood and could express himself quite well would assert is merely the presence of an image in his intuitive intellect, completely indistinguishable from that image which, upon mediation of light and his eyes, is caused by bodies, yet 242   without actual presence of such bodies. The same goes for what is audibly present – noises, tones, and sounds – identical to those produced in his ear

---

[a] *Geistererscheinung*

by vibrating bodies and air, but without the presence or motion of such bodies. This is the source of the misunderstanding that pervades all that is said for and against the reality of spirit apparitions. For a spirit apparition presents itself just like a bodily appearance;[a] but it is not a bodily appearance and is not supposed to be one either. This distinction is difficult and calls for expert knowledge, indeed philosophical and physiological knowledge. For it is crucial to understand that an effect similar to that of a body does not necessarily presuppose the presence of a body.

Above all we have to recall and keep in mind in everything that follows what I have often expounded in detail (especially in the second edition of my treatise *On the Principle of Sufficient Reason*, §21,[b] and also *On Seeing and Colours*, §1.[c] – *Theoria colorum*,[d] II. – *The World as Will and Representation*, vol. 1, pp. 12–14. – Vol. 2, ch. 2[e]), namely that our intuition of the external world is not simply *sensuous* but mainly *intellectual*, i.e. (objectively speaking) *cerebral*. – The senses never provide more than a mere *sensation* in their organ, which is therefore in itself quite a tenuous *material*, out of which the *understanding* first constructs the corporeal world by means of applying the law of causality, of which it is conscious a priori, and the forms of space and time, which are also a priori inherent in it. The stimulation of this intuitive act, in a waking and normal state, certainly starts from sensation, which is the effect that the understanding supplies with a cause. But why should it not be possible at times for a stimulus that comes from another direction, that is, from within, from the organism itself, to reach the brain and be processed by the latter, just like that other sensation, by means of the brain's characteristic function and in accordance with the mechanism of the stimulation? Of course, *after* the processing the dissimilarity of the original material could not be recognized any longer, just as it is no longer possible to recognize in chyle[f] the food from which it was prepared. In any actual case of this kind the question would arise whether the even more remote   243 cause of the apparition thus produced could never be sought farther away than within the organism; or whether this cause, in excluding all sensation, nevertheless could be an *external* one, which of course in that case could not have acted physically or corporeally; and, if the latter were the case, what kind of relation the given apparition could have to the nature of such a

---

[a] *Körpererscheinung*   [b] [*FR*, 52ff. (Hübscher *SW* 1, 51ff.)]   [c] [*VC*, 213ff. (Hübscher *SW* 1, 7ff.)]
[d] [Schopenhauer's Latin version of *VC*: *Commentatio exponens theoriam colorum physiologicam* (1830), which can be found in Hübscher, *SW* 1]
[e] [Third edn., pp. 13–15 (Hübscher *SW* 2, 13–15)]
[f] *Chylus* [milky nutritional mixture in lymph vessels of small intestines]

remote external cause, that is, whether the apparition would contain evidence[a] of the cause or even whether its essence would be expressed in it. Accordingly, we would be led to the question of the relation between appearance and thing in itself just as we are in regard to the corporeal world. This, however, is the transcendental perspective, the result of which might possibly be that neither more nor less ideality attaches to a spirit apparition than to a bodily appearance, which, as we know, is inevitably subject to idealism and can only be attributed to the thing in itself, i.e. the truly real, in a roundabout way. Since we have recognized the *will* as this thing in itself, we are led to speculate that perhaps the will lies at the basis of spirit apparitions, as it does in the case of bodily appearances. All previous explanations of spirit apparitions have been *spiritualistic*; and as such they are subject to Kant's critique in the first part of his *Dreams of a Spirit-seer*.[b] I will attempt here an *idealistic* explanation. –

After this introduction, providing an overview of and anticipation of the following investigations, I am now assuming a slower pace appropriate to them. But I must note that I assume the reader to be familiar with the facts to which they refer. For, first of all, my subject is not to narrate, hence not to present the facts but their theory; and second, I would have to write a thick volume if I were to repeat all the stories of magnetic disease, dream visions, spirit apparitions, and so on, which form the basic material of our topic and have been already told in many books. Also I have no wish to fight the scepticism of ignorance, whose all-too-clever airs depreciate daily in value and soon will be current just in England. Whoever nowadays doubts the facts of animal magnetism and the clairvoyance[c] connected with it should not be called incredulous but ignorant. However, I have to assume more, I must assume acquaintance with at least some of the numerous books about spirit apparitions or knowledge of them acquired in some other way. I will even provide quotations referring to such books only when they concern specific statements or controversial points. Apart from that, I expect the reader, who, I imagine, already knows me otherwise, to trust that in cases where I assume something to be factually certain it is known to me from reliable sources or my own experience.

First of all the question arises whether intuitive images can actually originate in our intuitive intellect, or brain, images that are complete and indistinguishable from those which are caused there by the presence of bodies acting on the external senses, but without this influence. Fortunately a very familiar appearance dissolves any doubt in us about this, namely *the dream*.

---

[a] *Indicia*
[b] *Träume eines Geistersehers* [*Träume eines Geistersehers, erläutert durch Träume der Metaphysik* (*Dreams of a Spirit-seer Explained by Dreams of Metaphysics*), 1766]
[c] *Hellsehns*

244

The wish to pass off dreams as mere thought-play,[a] mere images of the imagination, testifies to a lack of reflection or honesty; for obviously they are different from these in specific ways. Images of the imagination are faint, dull, incomplete, one-sided and so fleeting that we are barely able to retain for a few seconds the image of an absent person; and even the most vivid play of the imagination bears no comparison to the palpable reality that dreams present to us. Our ability to represent *in a dream* by far surpasses that of our power of imagination;[b] each intuitive object in a dream has a truth, perfection, and consistent universality[c] down to the most accidental qualities, just as reality itself possesses, and from which the imagination remains worlds apart. Hence the former would furnish us with the most wonderful spectacles if only we could choose the object of our dreams.[1] It is quite wrong to try to explain this with the fact that the images of the imagination are disturbed and weakened by the simultaneous impression of the actual external world; for even in the deepest silence of the darkest night the imagination is incapable of producing anything that would come even close to the objective distinctness   245 and vivid reality[d] of the dream. Moreover, images of the imagination are always caused by association of ideas or by motives and are accompanied by the consciousness of their arbitrariness. The dream, on the other hand, stands out as something utterly foreign, something that, like the external world, forces itself on us without our agency, even against our will. The totally unexpected quality of its events, even the most insignificant, marks them with the stamp of objectivity and reality.[2] All its objects appear definite and distinct, like reality, not merely with respect to us, in other words one-sided like a plane, or merely provided in the main and in general outline, but executed with precision, down to the smallest and most random particulars and the minor details that often hinder us and stand in the way. In a dream, each body casts its shadow, each falls with the gravity appropriate to its specific weight, and each obstacle must first be cleared, just as in reality. Its quite objective nature further manifests itself in that its events most often turn out contrary to our expectations and often contrary to our wishes. At times they even astonish us, in that the actors behave with shocking ruthlessness towards us. And generally, its objective nature shows itself in the purely objective, dramatic accuracy of the characters and actions, which has led to the fitting remark that while dreaming everyone is a Shakespeare. The same omniscience in us that in a dream makes every natural body act exactly according to its essential characteristics, also causes human beings to act and speak in complete accordance with their character.[3] As a result of all this the

---

[a] *Gedankenspiel*   [b] *Einbildungskraft*   [c] *Allseitigkeit*   [d] *Leibhaftigkeit*

illusion that the dream produces is so strong that reality itself, confronting us when waking up, often has to struggle and needs time before it can have its say in order to convince us of the deceptiveness of the dream, which no longer exists but in the past. Also in regard to memory, when it comes to unimportant events, we are at times in doubt whether they were dreamed or actually happened. But when we doubt whether something actually took place or whether we merely *imagined* it, we will be suspected of madness. All this proves that the dream is a quite peculiar function of our brain and

246 definitely different from the mere power of imagination and its rumination. – Aristotle too says: 'In a certain sense, the dream image is a sense-impression', *On Sleep and Waking*, ch. 2.[a] He also offers the subtle and accurate observation that, within the dream itself, we represent absent things in the imagination. From this it may be inferred that during dreaming the imagination is still available, and hence that it is not itself the medium or organ of dreaming.

On the other hand, dreams bear an undeniable resemblance to madness. For what mainly distinguishes dreaming from waking consciousness is the lack of memory, or rather coherent, sober-minded recollection. In dreams we see ourselves in fantastical, even impossible situations and circumstances without it occurring to us to examine their relation to what is absent and the causes of their advent; we perform nonsensical actions, because we are not mindful of the obstacles to them. People long dead still figure in our dreams as living, because in the dream we do not remember that they are dead. Often we see ourselves in circumstances during our early youth, surrounded by the people back then, everything as it was, because all changes and transformations having occurred since then have been forgotten. It seems true that in a dream, with all mental powers active, memory alone is not quite available. On this rests its resemblance to madness, which basically can be ascribed to a certain disruption of the faculty of recollection, as I have shown (*The World as Will and Representation*, vol. 1, §36, and vol. 2, ch. 32). From this point of view, the dream can be described as a brief madness, and madness as a long dream. On the whole, the intuition of *present reality* in a dream is quite complete and even meticulous; on the other hand, our scope of view is very limited, insofar as *the absent* and *the past*, even if fictitious, become conscious only to a small degree.[4]

Just as each change in the real world can occur only as the consequence of
247 another change preceding it as its cause, so too is the advent of all thoughts and representations in our consciousness subject to the principle of

---

[a] τὸ [γὰρ] ἐνύπνιόν ἐστιν αἴσθημα, τρόπον τινά (*somnium quodammodo sensum est*), *De somno et vigilia* II [part of *Parva Naturalia*; 456a26]

sufficient reason[a] in general. Therefore, those thoughts and representations have to be provoked every time either by an external impression on the senses or, according to the laws of association (see ch. 14 of vol. 2 of my chief work), by a thought preceding them; otherwise they cannot occur. Dreams as well, in respect to their occurrence, must be somehow subject to the principle of sufficient reason, as the unfailing principle of the dependence and conditionality of all objects existing for us in some way or other; yet in which way they are subject to it is difficult to detect. For the characteristic nature of dreaming is the condition of sleep, which is essential to it, i.e. the suspended normal activity of the brain and the senses; only when this activity is at rest can the dream occur, just as the pictures of the magic lantern[b] can only appear after the lights in a room have been extinguished. Accordingly the advent, and thus also the material, of the dream are not caused first and foremost by external impressions of the senses; individual cases where, during light slumber, external sounds and also odours have penetrated the sensory centre[c] and influenced the dream are specific exceptions, which I disregard here. But now it is utterly remarkable that dreams are not caused by association of ideas either. For they arise either in the middle of deep sleep, this real repose of the brain which we have every reason to assume as perfect and thus completely unconscious, whereby even the possibility of association of ideas disappears. Or dreams arise during the transition from waking consciousness to sleeping, hence when falling asleep. During that period they never fail to appear and thus afford us an opportunity to become fully convinced that they are not linked by any association of ideas to waking representations,[d] but leave the thread of these untouched in order to take their material and occasion[e] from somewhere completely different, we know not where. For these first dream images of people falling asleep, as is easily observed, are always without any relation to the thoughts they had while falling asleep; indeed, they are so strikingly different that it looks as if they had intentionally chosen exactly that thing among all the things in the world of which they were thinking least. Therefore[5] anyone reflecting on all this is forced to ask what might determine its selection and nature. Moreover, these first dream images (as Burdach remarks keenly and correctly in the third volume of his *Physiologie*[f]) have the distinctive quality of not presenting any coherent episode, and often we ourselves do not appear in them as actors, as we do in other dreams; on the contrary, they are a purely objective spectacle consisting of isolated images

248

---

[a] *Satze vom Grunde*   [b] *Laterna magika*   [c] *Sensorium*   [d] *wachen Vorstellungen*   [e] *Anlaß*
[f] [Karl Friedrich Burdach, *Die Physiologie als Erfahrungswissenschaft* (*Physiology as Empirical Science*), 6 vols., Leipzig: Voß, 1826–40]

that suddenly arise when we fall asleep, or very simple events. Since we often immediately wake up again, we can completely satisfy ourselves that they never have the slightest resemblance, remotest analogy, or other relation with the thoughts present just a moment before; rather, they surprise us by their completely unexpected content, which is as foreign to our preceding train of thought as any object in reality that suddenly enters our perception while we are awake through the merest chance, indeed an object that often is so far-fetched, so strangely and blindly chosen as if it had been determined by lot or dice.[6] – Therefore, the thread that the principle of sufficient reason hands us seems to us cut off at both ends, the inner and the outer. However, that is impossible, inconceivable. There must necessarily be some cause that brings about and thoroughly determines those phantasms;[a] so that from this cause it would have to be possible to explain exactly why, for instance, there suddenly appears to me, who until the moment of falling asleep was occupied with quite different thoughts, a blossoming tree, gently swaying in the breeze, and not something else, another time a maid with a basket on her head, and again another time a line of soldiers, and so forth.

Since during the generation of dreams, be it when we are falling or have already fallen asleep, the brain, this sole seat and organ of all representations, is cut off from outer stimulation through the senses as well as from inner stimulation through thoughts, we are left with no other assumption than that the brain receives some purely physiological stimulation from within the organism. Two paths are open to its influence on the brain: through the nerves and through the blood vessels. During sleep, i.e. during the cessation of all *animal* functions, the vital force concentrates itself entirely on *organic* life and, while to some extent reducing breathing, pulse, body heat,[b] and almost all secretions, is mainly occupied with slow reproduction, restoration of everything depleted, healing of everything injured, and elimination of all disorders that have spread. Hence sleep is the time when the healing power of nature[c] induces beneficial crises in all illnesses, in which it then wins the decisive victory over the present malady, and after which the sick person, with the sure feeling of the approaching recovery, wakes up with relief and joy. However, it produces the same in healthy people, only to a much lesser degree, in all places where it is necessary; so that they too have the feeling of restoration and renewal on waking up. Especially the brain has received its nutrition during sleep, which is not feasible during waking, resulting in restored clarity of consciousness. All these operations are under the guidance and control of the malleable[d] nervous system, that is, all the

---

[a] *Traumgestalten*   [b] *Wärme*   [c] *vis naturae medicatrix*   [d] *plastischen*

large ganglia,[a] which, linked by conducting nerve-cords through the entire length of the torso, make up the *great sympathetic nerve* or *internal* nerve-centre. This is completely separate and isolated from the *external* nerve-centre, the brain, which applies itself exclusively to controlling external relations and which, therefore, has a nervous apparatus directed towards the outside and representations occasioned by it. Therefore, in a normal state, the operations of the internal nerve-centre do not reach consciousness and are not felt.[b] Meanwhile, it still has a mediate and weak connection with the cerebral system through thin and also anastomosing[c] nerves; by way of these the isolation is broken down to a certain degree during abnormal states or even injuries of inner parts, after which these nerves, either in a duller or more distinct manner, enter consciousness in the form of pain. However, in a normal, healthy state, only an extremely faint and feeble echo of the processes and movements in the extremely complicated and active work-shop of organic life, of its easier or exacerbated progress, reaches the sensory centre in this way; such an echo is not perceived at all during waking, when the brain is completely busy with its own operations, receiving external impressions, intuiting, which is induced by the latter, and thinking. At most it has a secret and unconscious influence, from which those changes in mood arise for which no justification can be given based on objective grounds. However, while falling asleep, when external impressions cease to act and also the activity of thoughts within the sensory centre gradually dies down, those faint impressions, arising in a mediate way out of the internal nerve-centre of organic life, and likewise every small modification of the blood-circulation, when making itself known to the brain vessels, become capable of being felt – just as the candle starts to glow when dusk falls; or the way we hear the murmuring of the spring at night, which was rendered inaudible by the bustle of day. Impressions that are much too weak to be able to affect the waking, i.e. active, brain can, when its own activity has been completely suspended, produce a faint excitation of its individual parts and their powers of representation – just as a harp does not resonate from a foreign note while itself being played, but does so when not being played. This must be the cause of the generation and also, by means of this, the continuous, closer determination of those phantasms that arise when we fall asleep, no less than the dreams that possess dramatic coherence, which arise from the absolute mental calm of deep sleep; only

250

---

[a] *Ganglien* [Schopenhauer adds '*oder Nervenknoten*', '*Nervenknoten*' being the German term for 'ganglia']
[b] *empfunden*
[c] *anastomosirende* [Anastomosis: connection of normally separate parts, like veins and arteries]

that for the latter, since they occur when the brain is already in a state of deep repose and completely occupied with its own nutrition, a significantly stronger excitation from within must be required. Thus it is only these dreams that, in individual, exceedingly rare cases, possess predictive or prophetic[a] significance, and Horace says quite rightly:

After midnight, when dreams are true.[b]

251   For in this regard the last dreams in the morning behave like those during falling asleep, insofar as the rested and satiated brain is easily excitable once again.

Therefore, it is the faint echoes from the workshop of organic life that penetrate the sensory activity of the brain that is lapsing into or already in a state of apathy and slightly stimulate it, moreover in an unusual way and from another side than during waking. Since all other stimuli are barred access, this brain activity must take occasion and material for its phantasms from these echoes, as heterogeneous as the phantasms may be from such impressions. For in the same way that the eye, through mechanical concussion or internal nervous convulsion, can receive sensations of brightness and radiance completely identical to those caused by external light; in the same way that sometimes the ear, as a consequence of abnormal occurrences within it, hears sounds of every kind; in the same way that the olfactory nerve smells quite specifically determined odours without any external cause; in the same way that also the gustatory nerves are affected analogously; hence in the same way that all sensory nerves, both from the inside and the outside, can be stimulated to their characteristic sensations, so also can the brain, through stimuli from inside the organism, be determined to execute its function of intuiting space-filling figures. The appearances generated in such a way cannot be distinguished at all from those occasioned by sensations in the sense organs produced by external causes. For just as the stomach prepares chyme[c] from everything that it can master, and the intestines make chyle from this, whose primal material we cannot guess, so the brain too reacts to all stimuli that reach it by means of executing the function proper *to it*. This initially consists in projecting images in space, which is its form of intuition, in all three dimensions; then in moving these in time and following the guiding thread of causality, which are also functions of its proper activity. For it will always speak only its own language; through this it interprets those weak impressions that reach it
252   from the inside during sleep, just like the strong and determinate ones that come in the normal way from the outside during waking. Hence those weak

---

[a] *fatidike* [prophetic, divinatory]
[b] *post mediam noctem* [*visus*], *cum somnia vera* [Horace, *Satires* I, 10, 33]   [c] *Chymus*

impressions from the inside also provide it with the material for *images*, which are completely identical to those originating in excitation from the external senses, although hardly any similarity might exist between the two kinds of impressions that prompt the images. The brain's behaviour in this can be compared to that of deaf people who, from a few vowels that reach their ear, construct for themselves whole, though incorrect, sentences. Or it may be compared to that of mad people in whom the chance use of a word induces wild fantasies in line with their fixed ideas. In any event, it is those faint echoes of certain processes within the organism, petering out on their way to the brain, that serve as occasions for its dreams. These dreams are more specifically determined by the type of these impressions in that they have received at least a cue from them; indeed, as completely different as they may be from them, they will correspond to them somehow analogously, or at least symbolically, and most accurately to those impressions that manage to stimulate the brain during *deep* sleep, since they must already be significantly stronger, as mentioned before. Furthermore, since these inner processes of organic life act upon the sensory centre, designed for apprehending the external world, also in the manner of something foreign and external *to it*, the intuitions arising in it on such an occasion will assume quite *unexpected* forms, completely heterogeneous and foreign to some train of thought that perhaps was present shortly before, as we have occasion to observe when falling asleep and soon after waking up again.

For now, this whole debate teaches us nothing but recognition of the immediate cause or occasion of a dream, which, to be sure, also influences its content, but in itself is bound to be so very different from it that the nature of their relation remains a mystery to us. Even more mysterious is the physiological process in the brain itself, of which dreaming actually consists. For sleep is the repose of the brain, yet the dream is a certain activity of it; consequently, in order to avoid contradiction, we must declare the repose to be ²⁵³ merely relative and the activity to be somehow limited and only partial. In what sense the activity is limited and partial, whether in parts of the brain, or in the degree of its stimulation, or the manner of its internal movement, and what really distinguishes it from the waking state, again we do not know. – There is no mental power that never proved active in a dream; nevertheless, the course of the dream, just as our own behaviour in it, often shows extraordinary lack of judgement[a] and likewise, as already discussed above, of memory.

In respect of our main subject matter the fact remains that we have a faculty[b] for the intuitive representation of space-filling objects and for hearing and comprehending sounds and voices of every kind, both without

---

[a] *Urtheilskraft*   [b] *Vermögen*

external excitation of sensations, which, by contrast, provide the occasion, the material, or the empirical basis for our *waking* intuitions, but are by no means identical with them; for such intuition is definitely *intellectual* and not merely sensuous, as I have frequently explained and for which I have already provided the relevant main passages above. Now we must hold on to this indubitable fact, for it is the *primary phenomenon*,[a] to which all our additional explanations refer back, in that they will merely expound the still further extended activity of the faculty indicated. To name it, the most distinctive expression would be the one that the Scottish have very sensibly chosen for a particular form of its manifestation or application, guided by the fine sense of judgement[b] bestowed by one's own experience; it is called *second sight*.[c] For the ability to dream, under discussion here, is indeed a second intuitive faculty, which is not, as the first one, mediated through the external senses, yet whose objects are the same as those of the first with regard to type and form; from which we can conclude that it is a function of the *brain*, just as the first faculty is. That Scottish name would thus be the most suitable for describing the whole genus[d] of phenomena belonging here and for attributing them to a fundamental faculty.[e] However, since its authors have used it for denoting a particular, rare, and highly curious manifestation of that faculty, I am not allowed to make use of it, as much as I would like, to denote the entire genus of those intuitions, or more precisely, the subjective faculty that makes itself known in all of them. And so for this I am left with no more suitable term than that of *dream-organ*,[f] which describes the entire mode of intuition discussed here by that manifestation of it which is well known and familiar to everyone. I will use it to denote the faculty of intuition just described that is independent of external impression on the senses.

We are used to regarding the objects that this faculty presents to us in ordinary dreams as completely illusory, since they vanish when we wake up. However, that is not always the case, and it is very important in view of our topic to become acquainted with the exception to this through our own experience, something that perhaps we would all be able to do if we paid enough attention to the matter. For there is a state during which we are admittedly asleep and dreaming, but only dream the reality itself that surrounds us. Accordingly, we then see our bedroom with everything in it, also become aware of people who might enter, know that we ourselves

---

[a] *das Urphänomen*   [b] *Takt*
[c] [English in the original, followed by the German rendering '*das zweite Gesicht*'. The phenomenon of being able to foresee the future was associated with the Scottish Highlands, and studied by seventeenth-century scientists including Robert Boyle]
[d] *Gattung*   [e] *Grundvermögen*   [f] *Traumorgans*

lie in bed, and that everything is correct and accurate. And yet we are asleep with our eyes firmly shut, we are dreaming; only what we dream is true and real. It is just as if our skull had become transparent, so that the external world, instead of entering through the detour and narrow gate of the senses, came directly and immediately into the brain. This state is much more difficult to distinguish from wakefulness than the ordinary dream, because when awaking no transformation of the surroundings, hence no *objective* change at all takes place. However, (see *The World as Will and Representation*, vol. 1, §5, p. 19[a]) awaking is the sole criterion of distinguishing between waking and dream, which thus disappears here with regard to its objective and principal half. For when we wake up from a dream of the kind discussed here, only a *subjective* change happens to us consisting in our sudden feeling of a transformation of the organ of our perception; yet this is only barely palpable and, since it is accompanied by no objective change, can easily go unnoticed. Therefore, for the most part we will become acquainted with these dreams that present reality only when figures intrude that do not belong to reality and, consequently, disappear when we wake up, and also when such a dream has been raised to a higher power,[b] of which I shall speak presently. The type of dreaming just described is that which has been called *sleep-waking*,[c] not because it is an intermediate state between sleeping and waking, but because it can be described as becoming awake in sleep itself. Therefore, I would prefer to call it truth-dreaming.[d] To be sure, we will mostly notice it only early in the morning, as well as in the evening some time after falling asleep; but this is merely due to the fact that it is only when the sleep was not deep that awakening occurs easily enough to leave behind the memory of what was dreamed. Certainly this type of dreaming happens much more often during deep sleep, according to the rule that the somnambulist becomes the more clairvoyant the more deeply she sleeps; but then no recollection of this is left. In contrast, that such recollection sometimes occurs when dreaming has happened during lighter sleep, can be explained from the fact that a recollection can enter waking consciousness exceptionally even from magnetic sleep,[e] if it was very light. An example of this is to be found in Kieser's *Archiv für thierischen Magnetismus*, vol. 3, no. 2, p. 139.[f] According to this

255

---

[a] [*WWR* 1, 38 (Hübscher *SW* 2, 19f.)]   [b] *höhere Potenzierung erhalten*   [c] *Schlafwachen*
[d] *Wahrträumen*   [e] *magnetischen Schlaf*
[f] [Dietrich Georg Kieser, *Archiv für den thierischen Magnetismus* (*Archive for Animal Magnetism*), 12 vols., 1817–23; vol. 3, no. 2 (1818), p. 139 refers to an article by Kieser, '*Das magnetische Behältniß (Baquet) und der durch dasselbe erzeugte Somnambulismus. Nach Theorie und Erfahrung*' (*The Magnetic Tub [Baquet] and the Somnambulism produced by it, according to Theory and Experience*)]

the recollection of such immediately and objectively true dreams remains only if they have occurred during light sleep, for example in the morning, when we can immediately wake up from them.

Further, this type of dream, whose particular character consists in our dreaming the most immediately present reality, is at times enhanced in its mysterious essence by the fact that the scope of view of the dreaming person is somewhat extended, namely such that it reaches beyond the bed chamber, and the curtains or shutters cease to be obstacles to seeing and we can perceive quite distinctly what lies behind them – the yard, the garden, or the street, with the houses on the opposite side. Our astonishment at this will lessen if we are mindful that no physical vision takes place but mere dreaming. However, it is a dreaming of that which actually exists at this moment, consequently truth-dreaming, that is, a perception[a] by the dream-organ, which as such is naturally not bound to the condition of uninterrupted passage of the rays of light. The skull itself was, as mentioned before, the first partition wall by which this peculiar type of perception initially remained unimpeded. Now, if this perception is further enhanced, curtains, doors, and walls also no longer act as barriers. Yet how this is possible is a deep mystery; we know no more than that *truth* is *dreamed* here, hence that perception by the dream-organ takes place. This is how far this fact, fundamental for our reflection, goes. What we can do for its illumination, insofar as that may be possible, consists first of all in the compiling and appropriate ordering of all phenomena tied to it, with the intention of recognizing the connection between them, and with the hope of perhaps gaining a deeper insight into it in the future.

Meanwhile, even for those who lack their own experience of this, the above-described perception by the dream-organ is irrefutably substantiated by spontaneous somnambulism proper, or sleepwalking. The fact that those who are stricken by this affliction are fast asleep and cannot see at all with their eyes is absolutely certain; yet they perceive everything in their immediate vicinity, avoid every obstacle, walk long distances, climb along the most dangerous precipices on the narrowest paths, and perform long jumps without missing their target; some of them also perform their daily domestic tasks precisely and properly while asleep; others prepare drafts and write without mistakes. In the same way, somnambulists who have been artificially sent into a magnetic sleep perceive their surroundings and, if they turn clairvoyant, even the remotest objects. Furthermore, the perception that

---

[a] [The close association between the terms '*Wahrträumen*' ('truth-dreaming') and '*Wahrnehmen*' ('perceiving') cannot be rendered in English]

certain people who are seemingly dead[a] have of everything happening around them while lying there rigid and unable to move a limb is undoubt- 257 edly of the same nature; they too dream their present surroundings, hence become conscious of them through a path different from that of the senses. Great efforts have been made to find a clue to the physiological organ or the seat of this perception, but so far without success. That the external senses have entirely suspended their function when the somnambulist state is perfectly present is incontestable, since even the most subjective among them, awareness of the body,[b] has disappeared so completely that the most painful surgeries have been performed during magnetic sleep without the patient betraying any sensation of them. During these operations, the brain seems to be in the state of deepest sleep, hence complete inactivity. This fact, together with certain remarks and statements of somnambulists, has led to the hypothesis that the somnambulist state consists in the complete suspension of the brain's power[c] and the accumulation of the vital force[d] in the sympathetic nerve, whose larger plexuses, and specifically the solar plexus,[e] would be transformed into a sensorium[f] and thus, acting as a substitute, would take over the functions of the brain, which they then perform without the help of the external sense organs and yet with incomparably greater perfection than the brain. This hypothesis, first advanced by Reil I believe, is not without plausibility and has since then been held in high esteem. Its main support remains in the statements by almost all clairvoyant somnambulists that their consciousness now has its seat entirely in the pit of the stomach,[g] where their thought and perception now occurs, as it usually does in the head. In addition, most of them have the objects that they wish to examine closely placed onto the stomach region. Nevertheless, I consider the matter impossible. We only have to observe the solar plexus, this so-called abdominal brain;[h] how small is its mass and how extremely simple its structure, consisting of rings of nerve substance together with a few slight tumefactions! If such an organ were capable of fulfilling the functions of intuiting and thinking, then the law that 'Nature does nothing in vain',[i] confirmed everywhere else, would be overturned. For what would be the purpose then of the highly precious and well-protected bulk of the brain, weighing usually three pounds and in a few individuals more than 258 five, with the exceedingly elaborate structure of its parts, whose intricate complexity is so great that several entirely different methods of dissection

[a] *Scheintodte*   [b] *das körperliche Gefühl*   [c] *Depotenziren des Gehirns*   [d] *Lebenskraft*
[e] *plexus solaris*   [f] *zu einem Sensorio*   [g] *Herzgrube* [epigastrium]   [h] *cerebrum abdominale*
[i] *natura nihil facit frustra*

and their frequent repetition are required in order to understand to even a limited degree the systematic construction of this organ and to be able to form a tolerably clear image of the wondrous shape and interconnectedness of its many parts. Secondly, we have to consider that the steps and movements of a sleepwalker adapt themselves with the greatest speed and precision to the immediate surroundings perceived only through the dream-organ; so that he immediately avoids every obstacle with the greatest agility and in a manner that no one who is awake could imitate, and, with similar dexterity, hurries towards his preliminary goal. However, the motor nerves spring from the spinal cord, which is connected through the *medulla oblongata*[a] with the cerebellum,[b] which regulates movements, and this in turn with the cerebrum,[c] the place of motives, which are the representations by means of which it becomes possible for the movements to adapt themselves with great promptness to even the most cursory perceptions. However, if the representations which, as motives, must determine movements were relocated in the abdominal ganglionic plexus,[d] for which, by means of detours, only difficult, weak, and indirect communication with the brain is possible (so that when healthy we feel nothing of all the intensely and restlessly active doings and workings of our organic life), how should the representations originating in it instantaneously guide the dangerous steps of the sleepwalker?[*,7] – Incidentally, that the sleepwalker traverses the most dangerous paths without mistake and without fear, as he could never do when awake, can be explained by the fact that his intellect is not completely and generally active, but only partially active, namely only as far as required for guiding his steps, so that reflection, and with it all hesitation and vacillation, is eliminated. – Finally, the following fact by *Treviranus (Die Erscheinungen und Gesetze des organischen Lebens*, vol. 2,[e] Part 2, p. 117), according to Pierquin, provides factual certainty that at least *dreams* are a function of the brain: 'In a girl whose cranial bone was in

259

---

* It is remarkable with regard to the hypothesis discussed here that the LXX [Septuagint] calls seers and soothsayers consistently ἐγγαστριμύθους [ventriloquists, referring to ancient oracles where a spirit or god took over a priest's voice], in particular the Witch of Endor – whether this happens on the basis of the Hebrew original or in accordance with concepts and their terms at that time dominant in Alexandria. Obviously, the Witch of Endor is a clairvoyante and that is what ἐγγαστριμύθος means. Saul does not himself see and speak to Samuel, but through the mediation of the woman; she describes to Saul what Samuel looks like. (See [Joseph Philippe François] Deleuze, *de la prévision* [*Mémoire sur la faculté de prévision*, Paris: Crochard, 1834], pp. 147–8.)

[a] *medulla oblongata* [extended spinal marrow]   [b] *kleinen Gehirn* [*Kleinhirn*]
[c] *großen Gehirne* [*Großhirn*]   [d] [referring again to the solar plexus]
[e] [Gottfried Reinhold Treviranus, *Die Erscheinungen und Gesetze des organischen Lebens* (*The Phenomena and Laws of Organic Life*), Bremen: Heyse, vol. 2, Part 2, 1833]

part so destroyed through caries that the brain was completely exposed, it swelled up when she awoke and decreased when she fell asleep. During calm sleep the decrease was strongest. During vivid dreaming swelling occurred.' Yet it is obvious that somnambulism is different from dreaming only by degrees; *its* perceptions too happen through the dream-organ; it is, as stated, an immediate truth-dreaming.*,8

However, it might be possible to modify the hypothesis here in dispute in such a way that the abdominal ganglionic plexus would not itself become the sensorium, but would only assume the role of its external instruments, that is, of the *sense organs*, which here are also entirely decreased in power, so that it would receive impressions from outside that it would transmit to the brain; the latter, processing them in accordance with its function, now would schematize[a] and construct from them the forms of the external world just in the way it does from the sensations of the sense organs. But here too the difficulty recurs of the lightning-fast transmission of the impressions to the brain, which is definitely isolated from this inner nerve centre.   260 Furthermore, the solar plexus, according to its structure, is as unsuited to be the organ of sight and hearing as it is to be that of thought; in addition, it is completely blocked off from the impression of light through a thick partition of skin, fat, muscle, peritoneum, and intestines. Therefore, even if most somnambulists (like van Helmont, in a passage quoted by several people, in *Ortus medicinae*, Leiden, 1667,[b] *demens idea* §12, p. 171) state that their seeing and thinking arises from the region of the stomach, we are not allowed to immediately assume that this is objectively valid, the less so as some somnambulists explicitly deny it; for example, the famous Auguste Müller in Karlsruhe claims (in the report about her, pp. 53ff.)[c] that she does not see with the pit of the stomach but with her eyes, but says that most other somnambulists see with the pit of the stomach. And to the question: 'Can the power of thought also be transplanted into the pit of the stomach?'

---

* That in a dream we often try in vain to shout or to move our limbs must depend on the fact that the dream, as a matter of mere representation, is an activity of the cerebrum alone, which does not extend to the cerebellum; the latter remains suspended in the rigidity of sleep, absolutely inactive, and cannot fulfil its function of acting, as the regulator of limb movement, on the medulla, which is why the most urgent commands of the cerebrum are not executed: hence the anxiety. If the cerebrum breaks through the isolation and takes over the cerebellum, *somnambulism* arises.

[a] *schematisirte*
[b] [Johannes Baptiste van Helmont, *Ortus medicinae* (*Origin of Medicine*), 8 vols. (1648), Leiden: Huguetan & Barbier, 1667]
[c] [Wilhelm Meier, *Höchst merkwürdige Geschichte der magnetisch-hellsehenden Auguste Müller in Karlsruhe* (*Highly Curious Story of the Magnetic-clairvoyant Auguste Müller in Karlsruhe*), ed. Carl Christian von Klein, Stuttgart: Metzler, 1818]

she responds: 'No, but the powers of sight and hearing can.' This corresponds to the statement of another somnambulist, in Kieser's *Archiv*,[a] vol. 10, no. 2, p. 154, who is asked: 'Do you think with the entire brain or only part of it?' and answers: 'With the entire brain, and I get very tired.' The true conclusion from all somnambulists' statements seems to be that the excitation and the material for the intuitive activity of their brain does not come from outside and through the senses, as it does during waking, but, as explained above with respect to dreams, from inside the organism, whose director and ruler are, as is known, the great plexuses of the sympathetic nerve, which consequently, with regard to nervous activity, act for and represent the whole organism with the exception of the cerebral system. These statements can be compared to the fact that we believe we feel the pain in the foot, but actually feel it only in the brain, so that it ceases as soon as the nervous conduction is interrupted. Hence it is an illusion when somnambulists imagine that they see or even read with the region of the stomach, or, in rare cases, claim to perform this function with the fingers, toes, or the tip of the nose (for example the boy *Arst* in Kieser's *Archiv*, vol. 3, no. 2; also the somnambulist *Koch*, ibid. vol. 10, no. 3, pp. 8–21, and also the girl in Justinus Kerner's *Geschichte zweyer Somnambülen*, 1824,[b] pp. 323–30, who adds, however, 'the location of this sight is the brain, as it is in the waking state'). For, even if we should imagine the nervous sensibility of such parts ever so greatly enhanced, seeing in the proper sense, i.e. through the mediation of rays of light, remains absolutely impossible in organs that lack any optical apparatus, even if they were not, as is the case here, covered with thick layers but open to the light. Surely, it is not merely the sensitivity of the retina that enables it to see, but just as much the exceedingly elaborate and complex optical apparatus in the eyeball. For physical vision initially requires a surface sensitive to light, but requires also that the externally dispersed rays of light are collected and concentrated again with the help of the pupil and the light-refracting, transparent media, which are integrated with infinite artfulness, so that an image – more correctly, a nerve impression exactly corresponding to the external object – is generated through which alone the sense[c] data are supplied for the understanding. From these data the understanding then produces intuition in space and time through

261

---

[a] [See p. 179, n. b]
[b] [Justinus Andreas Christian Kerner, *Geschichte zweyer Somnambülen. Nebst einigen andern Denkwürdigkeiten aus dem Gebiete der magischen Heilkunde und der Psychologie (Story of two Somnambulists, together with a few other Memorabilities from the Sphere of Magic Healing Arts and Psychology)*, Karlsruhe: G. Braun, 1824]
[c] *subtilen*

an intellectual process that applies the law of causality. In contrast, even if skin, muscles, etc. were transparent, solar plexuses and finger tips could always only receive isolated light reflections; hence it is just as impossible to see with them as it is to produce a daguerreotype in an open *camera obscura* without a convex lens. Further proof that these supposed sensory functions of paradoxical parts do not really exist and no seeing takes place by means of the physical effect of light rays is provided by the fact that the boy in Kieser, mentioned above, read with his toes even when wearing thick woollen socks and only saw with his finger tips when he explicitly *willed* it, and otherwise groped around in a room with his hands stretched out in front. This is also confirmed by his own statement about these abnormal perceptions (ibid., p. 128): 'He never called this seeing, but replied to the question how he knew what was going on that he just knew and that was exactly what was novel.' In the same way, in Kieser's *Archiv*, vol. 7, no. 1, p. 52, a somnam-   262
bulist describes her perception as 'a seeing that is not seeing, an immediate seeing'. In the story of the clairvoyant Auguste Müller, Stuttgart 1818,[a] it is reported on p. 36: 'She sees completely clearly and recognizes all persons and objects in the most impenetrable darkness, when we would be unable to see our hand in front of us.' The same is attested with regard to the hearing of somnambulists by Kieser's assertion (*Tellurismus*, vol. 2, p. 172, first edi-tion[b]) that woollen strings are excellent conductors of sound – whereas wool is known as the worst conductor of sound. The following passage from the book on Auguste Müller just mentioned is especially instructive on this point: 'It is curious, yet is also observed in other somnambulists, that she hears nothing at all of anything said by people in the same room, even close to her, if the speech is not immediately directed toward her; on the other hand, she definitely understands and replies to every word addressed to her, however softly, even when several people talk at the same time. The same is true when she is being read to; if the person reading aloud thinks about something other than the reading matter, she does not hear that person', p. 40. – In addition it says on p. 89: 'Her hearing is not hearing in the ordinary way through the ear; for it can be tightly squeezed shut without impeding her hearing.' – Similarly in the *Mittheilungen aus dem Schlafleben der Somnambule Auguste K. in Dresden*, 1843,[c] it is repeatedly stated that at

---

[a] [See above, p. 213, n. c]

[b] [Kieser, *System des Tellurismus oder Thierischen Magnetismus* (*System of Tellurism or Animal Magnetism*), 2 vols., Leipzig: Herbig, 1822]

[c] [*Mittheilungen aus dem magnetischen Schlafleben der Somnambüle Auguste K[achler] in Dresden* (*Communications from the Magnetic Sleep-life of the Somnambulist Auguste K[achler] in Dresden*), ed. Johann Karl Bähr and Rudolf Kohlschütter, Dresden and Leipzig: Arnold, 1843]

times she heard solely through the palm of the hand what was spoken inaudibly, through mere movement of the lips; on p. 32 she herself warns us not to take this for hearing in the literal sense.

Accordingly, there is no question at all in any type of somnambulist of sensuous perceptions in the proper sense of the word; but their perceiving is an immediate *truth-dreaming* and thus happens through the deeply mysterious dream-organ. The fact that the objects to be perceived are placed on her forehead or her solar plexus or that the somnambulist, in the above-mentioned individual cases, directs her finger tips towards them, is merely a means of directing the dream-organ on to these objects, through contact with them, so that they become the subject matter of its truth-dreaming. Hence this only happens in order to direct the somnambulist's attention emphatically towards them or, in technical language,[a] to bring her into closer rapport[b] with these objects, whereupon she dreams these objects, and indeed not only their visibility, but also their audibility, their language, even their odour; for many clairvoyants claim that *all their senses* are relocated in the solar plexus. (Dupotet, *Traité complet du magnétisme animal,*[c] pp. 449–52.)[9] Consequently, it is analogous to the use of the hands in magnetizing, which do not really act physically; rather, it is the *will* of the magnetizer that acts, receiving its direction and determination through the use of hands. For only the insight drawn from my philosophy can lead to an understanding of the whole influence of the magnetizer through all kinds of gestures, with and without touch, even from a distance and through partitions, namely the insight that the body is completely identical with the will and is nothing but the image of the will generated in the brain. The fact that the seeing of somnambulists is not seeing in our sense, is not physically mediated through light, already follows from the fact that, when increased to clairvoyance, it is not impeded by walls and in fact at times extends to distant countries. We are afforded a special elucidation of this in internally directed self-intuition[d] that occurs at higher levels of clairvoyance, in virtue of which such somnambulists perceive all parts of their own organism clearly and accurately, although here, because of the absence of any light and because of the many partitions between the intuited part and the brain, all conditions for physical vision are completely lacking. From this we can infer the nature of all somnambulist perception,

---

[a] *Kunstsprache*　　[b] *Rapport* ['relation'; technical term in psychology and psychiatry]

[c] [Jules Denis Dupotet de Sennevoy (le Baron du Potet), *Traité complet du magnétisme animal. Cours en douze leçons* (*Complete Treatise on Animal Magnetism. Course of Twelve Lectures*), third edn., Paris: Germer Baillière, 1856]

[d] *Selbstanschauung nach innen*

even that directed outward and into the distance, and so all intuition by means of the dream-organ, hence all somnambulist vision of external objects, also all dreaming, all visions in a waking state, second sight, the vivid[a] apparition of those who are absent, especially of those who are dying, and so on. For the above-mentioned seeing of internal parts of our own body obviously arises only from an internal effect on the brain, probably through the mediation of the ganglionic system. The brain, true to its 264 nature, processes these internal impressions just like those coming from the outside, as if pouring a foreign material into its intrinsic and customary forms, out of which intuitions arise just like those that come from impressions of the external senses and which therefore correspond to the intuited objects to the same degree and in the same sense as the latter. Consequently, all seeing through the dream-organ is an activity of the intuitive brain function, induced by *internal* instead of, as happens normally, external impressions.*,[10] That such activity, even if it relates to *external*, indeed remote things, can have objective reality and truth is a fact whose explanation can only be attempted by way of metaphysics, that is, through the limitation of all individuation and separation to appearance, as opposed to the thing in itself, something which we will come back to. However, the fact that in general the connection between somnambulists and the external world is fundamentally different from ours in the waking state is proved most distinctly by the circumstance, often occurring at the higher levels, that while the clairvoyant's own senses are inaccessible to any impression, she senses with those of the magnetizer, for example, sneezes when he takes a pinch of snuff, tastes and exactly determines what he eats, and even hears the music playing to his ears in a room of the house far away from her. (Kieser's *Archiv*, vol. I, no. I, p. 117.[b])

The physiological details of somnambulist perceptions are a difficult riddle. However, the first step towards its solution would be a genuine physiology of dreaming, i.e. clear and certain recognition[c] of the kind of brain activity in dreams, of the way in which it differs from the activity during waking, and finally of the origin of the excitation, hence also of the

---

* According to the description by physicians, *catalepsy* appears to be the complete paralysis of the *motor* nerves, while *somnambulism* is that of the *sensory* nerves, for which then the dream-organ substitutes.

[a] *leibhafte*
[b] [1817; Trischler, '*Sonderbare, mit glücklichem Erfolg animal. Magnetisch-behandelte Entwickelungskrankheit eines dreizehnjährigen Knaben*' (Curious Developmental Illness of a Thirteen-year-old Boy, Successfully Treated with Animal Magnetism)]
[c] *Erkenntniß*

closer determination of its course. So far only this much can be assumed with certainty in regard to the entire activity of intuition and thinking during sleep: first, that its material organ, notwithstanding the brain's relative repose, can be no other than this brain; and second, that the stimulation of such dream-intuition[a] occurs from the inside of the organism, since it cannot come from outside through the senses. As regards the correct and precise relationship of the dream-intuition to the external world, which is unmistakable in somnambulism, this remains a mystery whose solution I do not undertake, but about which I shall provide some general remarks below. However, as a basis for the aforementioned physiology, and so as an explanation of our entire dream-intuition, I have come up with the following hypothesis, which in my view is highly probable.

　　Since during sleep the brain receives its excitation for the intuition of spatial figures in the way we stated, from inside instead of from outside, as during waking, this action must affect it from a direction opposite to the ordinary one that comes from the senses. As a result, all of the brain's activity, that is, the inner vibration or agitation of its fibres, happens in an opposite direction and starts to move as if anti-peristaltically.[b] For instead of occurring, as usual, in the direction of the sense impressions, thus from the sensory nerves to the interior of the brain, it now occurs in the opposite direction and order, and for that reason is sometimes executed by different parts, so that it may not be the lower cerebral surface that has to function instead of the upper, but perhaps the white instead of the grey cortical matter, and vice versa. Therefore, the brain now works as if in reverse. First of all, this explains why no recollection of the somnambulistic activity passes into the waking state, namely because the latter is induced through the vibration of brain fibres in the opposite direction, which, consequently, erases any trace of the previous activity. Incidentally, as a special confirmation of this assumption, the very common but strange fact might be mentioned that, when we wake up again immediately after first falling asleep, we often experience complete spatial disorientation, such that we are now forced to look at everything in reverse, that is, imagine what is on the right side of the bed to be on the left, and what is behind to be in front, and with such definition that in the darkness even the rational reflection that it is actually the other way around is incapable of obliterating that false imagination, for which purpose touch is needed. In particular, our hypothesis can make comprehensible the very curious vividness of dream-intuition,

---

[a] *Traum-Anschauung*
[b] *antiperistaltische* [referring to the reversal of the normal peristalsis of the colon]

the seeming reality and corporeality[a] of all objects perceived in a dream. This is made comprehensible by the fact that the excitation of brain activity coming from inside the organism and arising from the centre, following a direction opposite from the ordinary one, finally comes through completely, and extends at last to the nerves of the sense organs, which now, stimulated from the inside instead of the outside, as is usual, begin real activity. Accordingly, when dreaming we actually have sensations of light, colour, sound, smell, and taste, only without the external causes that stimulate them otherwise, merely in virtue of internal excitation and as a consequence of an influence in the opposite direction and chronological order. Therefore, this explains the vivid reality of dreams that makes them so powerfully different from mere fantasies. The picture of the imagination[b] (during wakefulness) is always merely in the brain; for it is the reminiscence, albeit modified, of a previous, material excitation of intuitive brain activity happening through the senses. The dream-apparition,[c] on the other hand, is not only in the brain, but also in the sensory nerves, and has arisen as the consequence of an excitation of them that is material, presently effective, comes from the inside and permeates the brain. Since we actually see in a dream, what Apuleius has Charite say as she is about to gouge both eyes of the sleeping Thrasyllus, is extremely apt, fine, indeed, profoundly conceived: 'Your eyes will be dead for you for the rest of your life, you will see no more than what you see when dreaming.'[d] (*Metamorphoses* VIII, p. 172, Bipont edition.)[11] Hence the dream-organ is the same as the organ of wakeful consciousness and intuition of the external world, only grasped, as it were, from the other end and applied in reverse order, and the sensory nerves, which function in both, can be activated from their internal as well as their external end – roughly in the way that a hollow iron globe can be rendered red-hot from the inside as well as the outside. Since when activated from the inside the sensory nerves are the last to become active, it can happen that this activity has just started and is still in progress when the brain is already waking up, i.e. exchanges the dream-intuition with the ordinary one. In that case, having just woken up, we will discern possible sounds, for example, voices, knocks on the door, gun shots, and so on, with a distinctness and objectivity *perfectly* emulating reality and then firmly believe that we were first awoken as a result of sounds from reality, from the outside, or, more rarely, we will see figures possessing complete empirical

267

---

[a] *Leibhaftigkeit*   [b] *Phantasiebild*   [c] *Traumgesicht*
[d] *vivo tibi morientur oculi, nec quidquam [quicquam] videbis, nisi dormiens* [L. Apuleji Madaurensis Platonici Philosophi Opera, vol. i, Bipont edn.; VIII, 12]

reality, as Aristotle already mentions, *On Dreams* III, towards the end.[a] – It is through the dream-organ described here that somnambulistic intuition, clairvoyance, second sight, and apparitions of every kind are effected. –

From these physiological observations I now return to the previously described phenomenon of truth-dreaming, which can already occur during ordinary sleep at night, where it is then at once confirmed by merely awakening, namely when, as in most cases, it was immediate, i.e. extended only to the present immediate surroundings – although in rarer cases it extends a little bit further, beyond the nearest partitions. But this extension of the scope of view can go much further, not only with respect to space, but also to time. We are given proof of this by the clairvoyant somnambulists who, during the period of the greatest enhancement of their condition, instantly include in their intuitive dream perception any place whatsoever towards which we lead them and are able to give an accurate account of what is happening there. Sometimes they are even able to predict what does not yet exist but still lies hidden in the future and will only come to be realized in the course of time by means of innumerable intermediate causes coinciding by chance. For all clairvoyance, during artificially induced as well as naturally occurring somnambulistic sleep-waking,[b] all perception of what is hidden, absent, far away, or indeed lies in the future, that is made possible by such clairvoyance, is nothing but its *truth-dreaming*, whose objects present themselves intuitively and physically, like our dreams, which is why the somnambulists speak of a *seeing*. Meanwhile, we have certain proof in these phenomena, as also in spontaneous sleepwalking, that this mysterious intuition, not effected by any impression from without and known to us through dreams, can stand in a relation of *perception* to the actual external world, although the connection with the latter that mediates this relation remains a mystery to us. What distinguishes the ordinary, nocturnal dream from clairvoyance, or sleep-waking in general, is first of all the absence of a relation to the external world, thus to reality; and second, the fact that very often a memory of the dream passes into wakefulness, whereas such recollection does not take place from somnambulistic sleep. But these two qualities may very well be connected and reducible to one another. For the ordinary dream too leaves a memory behind only when we have immediately woken up from it; probably this is due to the fact that waking up from natural sleep happens so easily, because it is not nearly as deep as the somnambulistic kind, which is why an immediate or quick awakening cannot occur from the latter, but the return to waking

---

[a] *de insomnis c. 3 ad finem*   [b] *Schlafwachen*

consciousness is only granted by means of a slow and mediated transition. For somnambulistic sleep is only an incomparably deeper, more strongly affecting, more perfect sleep, in which, therefore, the dream-organ comes to develop its fullest capacity, so that the accurate[a] relation to the external world, and hence sustained and coherent truth-dreaming becomes possible for it. Probably this also sometimes happens during ordinary sleep, but not unless it is so deep that we do not immediately awaken from it. On the other hand, the dreams from which we wake up are those of lighter sleep;   269 ultimately, they have sprung from merely somatic causes belonging to our own organism and hence have no relation to the external world. Yet we have already recognized that there are exceptions to this in those dreams that present the immediate surroundings of the sleeping person. But there is also, in exceptional cases, recollection of dreams that announce what happens far away or even in the future; this mainly depends on the fact that we immediately awaken from such a dream. For this reason it has been assumed during all time periods and by all peoples that there are dreams of real, objective significance, and in the whole of ancient history dreams are taken very seriously, so that they play an important role. Nevertheless, prophetic[b] dreams have always been considered rare exceptions[12] among the vast number of empty, merely deceptive dreams. Accordingly, Homer tells (*Odyssey* XIX, 560[c]) of two portals to dreams, one of ivory by which the meaningless ones enter, and one of horn by which the prophetic ones enter. An anatomist might feel tempted to explain this in terms of white and grey brain matter. Most often those dreams prove to be prophetic that relate to the dreamer's state of health; in fact, they will predict mostly illnesses and also deadly attacks (Fabius, *Specimen psychologico-medicum de somniis*, Amsterdam, 1836,[d] pp. 195ff., has collected examples of this), which is analogous to the fact that clairvoyant somnambulists also predict most often and with the greatest certainty the course of their own illness together with its crises, etc. Next, external accidents such as conflagrations, powder explosions, shipwrecks, and especially cases of death, are sometimes predicted through dreams. Finally, some people occasionally dream in advance other, sometimes rather trivial events down to the last detail, of which I have been convinced myself by an unambiguous experience. I shall record it here, since it simultaneously casts a bright light on the *strict necessity of everything that happens*, even the most random events. One morning I was eagerly

[a] *richtige*   [b] *fatidiken*   [c] [See *Odyssey* XIX, 562–7]
[d] [Everardus Fabius, *Specimen psychologico–medicum de somniis* (*A Psychological–medical Example in regard to Dreams*), Amsterdam: Müller, 1836]

writing a long English business letter of great importance to me; when I was
270 finished with the third page, I picked up the inkwell instead of the blotting
sand and poured it over the letter: the ink flowed from the desk on to the
floor. The maid called by my ringing the bell fetched a bucket of water and
scrubbed the floor so that the stains would not soak in. During this work she
told me: 'I dreamed last night that I was here rubbing ink stains from the
floor.' Whereupon I replied: 'That is not true.' And she again: 'It is true, and
after waking up I told the other maid about it, who sleeps together with
me.' – Now, by chance, the other maid comes in, about seventeen years old,
in order to call the one who is scrubbing. I walk up to her and ask: 'What did
this woman dream last night?' – Answer: 'I do not know.' – I again: 'Yes you
do, she told you about it when she woke up.' – The young maid: 'Oh yes,
she dreamed that she would rub ink stains here from the floor.' – This story,
which proves theorematic dreams beyond doubt, since I vouch for its
absolute truth, is no less remarkable for the fact that what was dreamed
beforehand was the effect of an action that might be called involuntary,
insofar as I performed it entirely *against* my intention and it depended on a
slight mistake of my hand; yet this action was predetermined with such
strict necessity and inevitability that its effect appeared as a dream in another
person's consciousness several hours earlier. Here we see most clearly the
truth of my proposition: Everything that happens, happens necessarily (*The
Two Fundamental Problems of Ethics*, p. 62[a]).[13] – In order to derive prophetic
dreams from their immediate cause we face the fact that no recollection,
either of natural or of magnetic somnambulism and its processes, occurs in
waking consciousness, but that sometimes such recollection passes into the
dreams of natural, ordinary sleep, which we afterwards remember when
awake, so that the dream then becomes the connecting link, the bridge,
between somnambulistic and waking consciousness. According to this, we
271 must attribute prophetic dreams foremost to the fact that during deep sleep
dreaming increases to somnambulistic clairvoyance. However, since normally no immediate awakening and thus no recollection from these dreams
take place, those dreams that form exceptions to this and prefigure the
future *immediately* and in the literal sense,[b] and which are called the
theorematic ones, are the most rare. On the other hand, if its content is of
great importance to the dreaming person, the dreamer will be able to retain
the memory of a dream of this kind by transferring it into a dream during
lighter sleep, from which it is possible to wake up immediately. However,
this cannot happen immediately, but only by means of translating the

---

[a] [*FW*, 79 (Hübscher *SW* 4, 60)]   [b] *sensu proprio*

content into an allegory, wrapped in whose guise the original, prophetic dream now enters waking consciousness, where it then still requires reading and interpretation. This then is the other and more frequent kind of prophetic dream, the *allegorical* one. Already *Artemidorus* distinguished both kinds in *The Interpretation of Dreams*,[a] the oldest of books on dreams, and called the first kind *theorematic*. The tendency of human beings to ponder the meaning of their dreams is by no means accidental or affected, but natural and has its ground in our consciousness of the ever-present possibility of the process described above; from this tendency, if it is cultivated and methodically developed, arises oneiromancy.[b] This adds the condition that events in a dream have a fixed meaning[c] that holds once and for all about which a dictionary could be composed. But that is not the case; on the contrary, the allegory is specifically and individually suited to the particular object and subject of the theorematic dream that forms the basis of the allegorical dream. For that reason the interpretation of allegorical, prophetic dreams is often so difficult that most of the time we only understand them after their predictions have come true. But then we have to admire the utterly strange, demonic cunning of the wit, otherwise quite alien to the dreamer, with which the allegory has been constructed and implemented. However, that we retain these dreams so long in our memory can be attributed to the fact that through their singular vividness, indeed corporeality, they impress themselves more deeply into memory than the others. However, practice and experience will be conducive to the art of interpreting them. It is not Schubert's[d] well-known book, however, which contains nothing useful except for the title, but old Artemidorus, from whom we can really learn the 'symbolism of dreams', especially from his last two books, where, with the help of hundreds of examples, he renders comprehensible the manner, the method, and the humour employed by our dreaming omniscience in order to impart, where possible, a few things to our waking ignorance. For this can be learned much better from his examples than from his previous theoremes and rules about them.*,[14] That Shakespeare too had completely grasped the above-mentioned humour of the matter he demonstrates in *Henry VI*, Part II, Act III, scene 2, where, following the quite unexpected news of the death of the Duke of

272

---

* In his *Aus meinem Leben* [*Aus meinem Leben: Dichtung und Wahrheit*, 1811–33 (*Poetry and Truth: From my Life*)], Book I, towards the end, Goethe tells us about the allegorical truth-dreams of mayor Textor [Goethe's grandfather].

[a] *Oneirokritikon* [*Oneirocritica*]   [b] *Oneiromantik* [interpretation of dreams]   [c] *Bedeutung*
[d] [Gotthilf Heinrich von Schubert, *Die Symbolik des Traumes* (*The Symbolism of Dreams*), 1814]

Gloucester, the villainous Cardinal Beaufort, who knows best about this matter, exclaims: 'God's secret judgement: – I did dream tonight / The duke was dumb, and could not speak a word.'

Here then it is important to remark that, in the utterances of ancient Greek oracles, we find the relation between the theorematic and the allegorical prophetic dream, which reproduces it, exactly as discussed. For, just like the prophetic dreams, these too rarely state their message directly and literally,[a] but veil it in an allegory that requires interpretation and is, in fact, often understood only after the oracle has come true, just like allegorical dreams. From numerous instances, merely in order to indicate the matter, I refer to the example in Herodotus III, 57,[b] where the prophecy of the Pythia warns the Siphnians of the wooden host and the red herald, which were to be understood as a Samian ship carrying a messenger and painted red, but which the Siphnians neither understood straight away nor when the ship arrived, but only afterwards. Furthermore, in IV, 163, the oracle of the Pythia warns King Arcesilaus of Cyrene that, if he should find the kiln full of amphoras, he should not fire these, but send them away. But only after he had burnt the rebels together with the tower where they had sought refuge did he understand the meaning of the oracle and became frightened. The many instances of this kind decidedly point to the fact that the prophecies of the Delphic oracle were based on artificially induced fatidical dreams. The story of Croesus (Herodotus I, 47–8) testifies that these could at times be enhanced to the most distinct clairvoyance, upon which a direct, literal utterance followed; Croesus put the Pythia to the test by having his envoys ask her what he was doing far from her in Lydia just then, on the hundredth day after their departure, whereupon she stated accurately and correctly what no one but the king himself knew, that with his own hands he was cooking turtle and mutton meat together in a brazen cauldron with a brazen lid. – According to the stated source of the prophecies of the Pythia, she was also medically consulted for physical ailments; an example of this is found in Herodotus IV, 155.[15]

In accordance with what was said above, the *theorematic* prophetic dreams are the highest and rarest degree of prophetic vision in natural sleep, the *allegorical* ones are the second, lesser degree. This is followed by mere *presentiment*,[c] anticipation,[d] as the final and weakest emanation from the same source. This is more often of a sad than cheerful nature, because there is more sorrow in life than joy. Without any apparent cause, a gloomy mood, an anxious expectation of what is to come has taken possession of us

[a] *sensu proprio*   [b] [*Histories*]   [c] *Ahndung*   [d] *Vorgefühl*

after sleeping. According to our discussion above, this can be explained by the fact that the translation of the theorematic, true dream that occurred during the deepest sleep and announced disaster, into an allegorical dream of lighter sleep has not been successful and, therefore, nothing of the former remains in consciousness, except its impression on the mind,[a] i.e. the *will* itself, this true and ultimate core of the human being. This impression now lingers as prophesying anticipation, gloomy foreboding. Yet sometimes this presentiment will take hold of us only when the former circumstances, connected to the misfortune seen in the theorematic dream, occur in reality, for example when someone is about to embark on a ship that will sink, or when he approaches the powder magazine that is due to blow up; quite a few people have been saved by obeying the fearful presentiment that suddenly arises of the inner dread that afflicts them. We have to explain this through the fact that a faint reminiscence is left from the theorematic dream, although it is forgotten, a dull recollection that may be unable to enter clear consciousness, but a trace of which is refreshed by the sight of the exact things in reality that had affected us in such a terrible manner in the forgotten dream. Also of this nature was Socrates' *daimonion*,[b] that inner voice of warning, which cautioned him as soon as he resolved to undertake something detrimental to him; yet it always advised against, never in favour. An immediate confirmation of the theory of presentiment here discussed is only possible by means of magnetic somnambulism, which divulges the secrets of sleep. Accordingly, we find such confirmation in the well-known 'Geschichte der Auguste Müller zu Karlruhe',[c] p. 78. 'On 15 December the somnambulist, in her nocturnal (magnetic) sleep, became aware of an unpleasant incident concerning her, which greatly depressed her. She noticed immediately that she would feel anxious and uneasy the entire next day without knowing why.' – Further, a confirmation of this matter is provided by the impression, reported in *Die Seherin von Prevorst* (first edn., vol. 2, p. 73; third edn., p. 325),[d] that was made on a clairvoyant while awake by certain verses referring to somnambulistic events of which she knew nothing at that moment. We also find facts that shed light on this point in *Kieser's Tellurismus*, §271.[e]

274

---

[a] *Gemüth*   [b] [genius, little spirit]   [c] [See p. 213, n. c]
[d] [Justinus A. C. Kerner, *Die Seherin von Prevorst. Eröffnungen über das innere Leben des Menschen und über das Hereinragen einer Geisterwelt in die unsere* (*The Seer of Prevorst. Disclosures about the Inner Life of Human Beings and the Projection of a Spiritworld into Ours*), Stuttgart and Tübingen: Cotta, 1829 (first edn.); 1838 (third edn.)]
[e] [D. G. Kieser, *System des Tellurismus oder Thierischen Magnetismus*; §271 is found in vol. 2 (see p. 215, n. b)]

In regard to everything said so far it is very important to grasp and retain the following fundamental truth:[a] Magnetic sleep is only an intensification of natural sleep, a higher degree, if you will; it is an incomparably deeper sleep. Accordingly, clairvoyance is only an intensification of dreaming; it is a continuous *truth-dreaming*, which, however, can be controlled here from the outside and directed towards anything we want. Third, the immediately healing influence of magnetism, proven in so many cases of illness, is nothing but an intensification of the natural healing power of sleep in everybody. For sleep is the true great universal remedy,[b] since, by means of it, the vital force, relieved of the animal functions, now becomes completely free to emerge with all its might as the healing power of nature[c] and in this capacity to straighten out all the disorders that have spread in the organism; which is why everywhere the complete absence of sleep allows for no recovery. However, the incomparably deeper magnetic sleep brings about recovery to a much higher degree. For that reason, when occurring spontaneously in order to remedy grave and already chronic illnesses, it sometimes lasts for several days, as, for example, in the case published by Count Szapáry (*Ein Wort über animalischen Magnetismus*, Leipzig, 1840);[d] indeed, once in Russia a consumptive somnambulist, during the omniscient crisis, ordered her physician to put her into a state of suspended animation for nine days, during which time her lung enjoyed complete rest and thus was cured, so that she woke up fully recovered. Since the essence of sleep consists in the inactivity of the cerebral system and, indeed, its wholesomeness springs precisely from the fact that during that time this system does not engage and consume any vital force with its animal life, and the vital force can now completely devote itself to organic life, it may seem to contradict the main purpose of this essence that especially during magnetic sleep excessively enhanced power of cognition sometimes occurs, which, according to its nature, must somehow be an activity of the brain. Yet we should above all remind ourselves that this case is only a rare exception. Among twenty sick people affected at all by magnetism, only one will become somnambulistic, i.e. hear and speak while asleep, and among five somnambulists hardly even one becomes clairvoyant (according to Deleuze,

---

[a] *Grundwahrheit*   [b] *Panakeion*   [c] *vis naturae medicatrix*
[d] [Franz Graf (Count) von Szapáry, *Ein Wort über animalischen Magnetismus, Seelenkörper und Lebensessenz; nebst Beschreibung des ideo-somnambülen Zustandes des Fräuleins Therese von B͞y zu Vasárhely im Jahre 1838* (*A Word about Animal Magnetism, Spiritual Body, and Life-essence, together with a Description of the Ideo-somnambulistic State of Ms Therese von B͞y of Vasárhely in the Year 1838*), Leipzig: Brockhaus, 1840]

Histoire critique du magnétisme animal, Paris, 1813, vol. 1, p. 138).[a] If magnetism has a healing effect without producing sleep, this happens only for the 276 reason that it awakens the healing power of nature and directs it towards the afflicted part.[16] But apart from that, its effect is primarily just a very deep, dreamless sleep, in fact, with the cerebral system decreased to such an extent that neither sense impression nor injuries are felt at all. Therefore, it has been used most beneficially in surgeries, although chloroform has supplanted its service there. Clairvoyance, whose preliminary stage is somnambulism, or talking in sleep, is allowed by nature actually to occur only when its *blindly operating* healing power does not suffice for eliminating the illness, but auxiliary means from outside are needed, which now, during the clairvoyant state, the patients themselves correctly prescribe. Hence nature brings about clairvoyance[17] for the purpose of self-prescription; for 'nature does nothing in vain'.[b] Its procedure here is analogous and related to that which it followed on a large scale in the production of the first beings when taking the step from the plant to the animal kingdom; for plants, movement in reaction to mere *stimuli* had been sufficient; but now more specific and complicated needs, whose objects had to be sought, selected, and even subdued or outwitted, necessitated movement in response to *motives* and thus to *cognition*, on many different levels, which accordingly is the proper character of animality, what is not accidental, but essential to the animal, that which we necessarily think in the concept of *animal*. For this point I refer the reader to my chief work, vol. 1, pp. 170ff.;[c] also to my *Ethics*, p. 33;[d] and to *On Will in Nature*, pp. 54ff. and 70–8.[e] Hence in the one case as in the other, nature kindles a light for itself in order to seek and procure the assistance that the organism needs *from the outside*. Directing the somnambulist's gift of prophecy, which she has developed anyway, to things other than her own state of health is merely an accidental benefit, indeed, actually a misuse of it. It is also a misuse when we induce somnambulism and clairvoyance arbitrarily through long, continuous magnetizing, contrary to the intention of nature. On the other hand, where these are really necessary, 277 nature produces them after brief magnetization, in fact, sometimes as spontaneous somnambulism. They occur then, as already pointed out, as truth-dreaming, initially of the immediate surroundings, then in ever-widening circles, until, at the highest levels of clairvoyance, such dreaming

---

[a] [Joseph Philippe François Deleuze, *Histoire critique du magnétisme animal* (*Critical History of Animal Magnetism*), Paris: Mame, 1813 (first edn.)]
[b] *natura nihil facit frustra* [c] [*WWR* 1, 174ff. (Hübscher *SW* 2, 178ff.)]
[d] [*FW*, 55–6 (Hübscher *SW* 4, 31f.)] [e] [*WN*, 362ff., 379–84 (Hübscher *SW* 4, 48ff. and 69–75)]

is able to reach all events on earth, wherever attention is directed, sometimes even reaching into the future. The capacity for pathological diagnosis and therapeutic prescription, initially for oneself and then by way of abuse for others, keeps pace with these different levels.

Such truth-dreaming also occurs with somnambulism in the original and proper sense, that is, pathological *sleepwalking*, but here only for immediate use, hence merely extending to the immediate surroundings, since this already fulfils the purpose of nature in this case. For in such a state the vital force, as healing power,[a] has not, as in magnetic sleep, spontaneous somnambulism, and catalepsy, suspended animal life in order to apply its entire might to organic life and to eliminate the disorders that have taken root in it. On the contrary, in virtue of a pathological upset, to which mostly the age of puberty is subject, it occurs as an abnormal excess of irritability, which nature then tries to free itself from and which, as is well known, happens through walking, working, and climbing to the most hazardous heights and the most dangerous leaps, all while asleep. At that moment nature, as the guardian of these perilous steps, at once produces that mysterious truth-dreaming, which here only extends to the immediate vicinity, since that suffices to prevent accidents, which irritability, let loose, must cause if acting blindly. Therefore, such dreaming only has the negative purpose of preventing harm, whereas with clairvoyance it has the positive one of finding assistance from outside; hence the great difference in the range of vision.

As mysterious as the effect of magnetizing may be, it is clear that it consists initially in the suspension of animal functions by diverting the vital force from the brain, a mere pensioner or parasite of the organism, or rather, by forcing it back to organic life, as its primitive function, because its undivided presence and effectiveness as healing power are required there. But within the nervous system, that is, the exclusive seat of all sensible life, organic life is represented by the guide and ruler of its functions, the sympathetic nerve and its ganglia. Therefore, we can view this process also as a forcing-back of the vital force from the brain to the sympathetic nerve, and, in general, understand both as unlike poles: namely the brain, together with the organs of movement attached to it, as the positive and conscious pole; and the sympathetic nerve, with its ganglionic plexuses, as the negative and unconscious pole. In this sense, the following hypothesis about the process of magnetization could be put forward. It is an influence of the magnetizer's brain pole (thus the external nerve pole) on the *like pole*

278

---

[a] *vis medicatrix*

of the patient, and hence acts on it *through repulsion*, in accordance with the universal law of polarity, whereby the nervous force is driven back to the other pole of the nervous system, the internal pole, or the solar plexus. For that reason, men, in whom the brain pole predominates, are most suited for magnetizing; women, on the other hand, in whom the ganglionic system prevails, are more suited for being magnetized and the consequences of that. If it were possible that the female ganglionic system could similarly act on the male one, that is, through repulsion, then through the reverse process an abnormally enhanced cerebral life,[a] a temporary genius, would have to emerge. That is not feasible because the ganglionic system is not capable of acting externally. In contrast, the *baquet*[b] might very well be seen as magnetizing *through attraction*, through the action of *unlike* poles on to each other, so that the sympathetic nerves of all the patients sitting around it, connected with the baquet through iron rods and woollen cords running to the pit of the stomach, acting with united force heightened by the anorganic mass of the baquet, would attract the individual brain pole of each of them, thus decreasing animal life and letting it sink into the magnetic sleep of all of them – comparable to lotus, which is submerged in the flood every night. This accords with the fact that, when in the past the conductors of the bucket had been attached to the head, not the pit of the stomach, heavy congestion and headaches were the result (Kieser, *System des Tellurismus*,[c] first edn., vol. 1, p. 439). That in the *sidereal* baquet[d] the unmagnetized metals exert the same force seems connected to the fact that metal is the most simple, primal being, the lowest level of the will's objectivation and, consequently, diametrically opposed to the brain as the highest progression of this objectivation, hence the farthest removed from it, and in addition presenting the greatest mass in the smallest space. Therefore, metal calls the will back to its primal nature[e] and is related to the ganglionic system just as, conversely, light is related to the brain; for that reason somnambulists shun the contact of metals with the organs of the conscious pole. This also

279

---

[a] *Gehirnleben*

[b] *das Baquet* [magnetizing bucket; a wooden tub filled with magnetized water, glass and iron fillings, designed to facilitate the flow of magnetic fluid among the patients sitting around it]

[c] [See p. 215, n. b]

[d] [Contemporary researchers used the terms *siderisch* ('sidereal') and *Siderismus* instead of 'animal magnetism', the term widely used since Mesmer's experiments. For example, Kieser argues that the latter term is misleading, since it refers to a force that it is also contained in inanimate substances, such as certain metals and water. (See D. G. Kieser, 'Das siderische Baquet und der Siderismus. Neue Beobachtungen, Versuche und Erfahrungen', in *Archiv für den thierischen Magnetismus*, vol. 5, no. 2 (Halle 1819), pp. 1ff. He defines the 'sidereal force' as 'telluric', as the 'inner, organic, living force of the totality of the terrestrial body', ibid., p. 67.)]

[e] *Ursprünglichkeit*

explains the sensitivity to metals and water in those thus disposed. – What is active during the ordinary, magnetized baquet is the ganglionic systems, connected to the baquet, of all the patients gathered around it, which with joined forces draw down the brain poles; in addition, this helps to explain the contagion of somnambulism in general and also the related communication of the activity of second sight, when it is present, by means of mutual touching among those possessing this gift and the communication, and consequently community, of visions in general.

However, if we would allow ourselves an even bolder application of the above hypothesis about the process of actual magnetizing based on the laws of polarity, then we could, even if only schematically, deduce from this how, at the higher levels of somnambulism, the rapport can go as far as the somnambulist coming to share in all the thoughts, knowledge, languages, indeed, all sensations of the magnetizer, hence being present in his brain, while the magnetizer's will has an immediate influence on her and dominates her to such a degree that he can firmly entrance her. For with the now commonly used galvanic apparatus, where the two metals are submerged in two kinds of acids separated by clay walls, the positive current flows through these liquids, from zinc to copper, and then outside of them, along the electrode, from copper back to zinc. Hence by analogy, the positive current of the vital force, as the will of the magnetizer, would flow from his brain to that of the somnambulist, dominating her and driving her vital force, which produces consciousness in the brain, back to the sympathetic nerve, the pit of the stomach, as her negative pole. But then the same current would flow from here back to the magnetizer, to his positive pole, the brain, where it encounters his thoughts and sensations, which as a result are now shared by the somnambulist. Admittedly, these are very bold assumptions; but in the case of such completely unexplained matters like the ones that are our problem here, any hypothesis is admissible that leads to an understanding of them, albeit only a schematic or analogous one.

The exaltedly miraculous and simply unbelievable nature of somnambulistic clairvoyance – unbelievable until it was substantiated by the agreement of hundreds of the most credible testimonies – to which is revealed what is concealed, absent, remote, indeed, what still slumbers in the womb of the future, at least loses its absolute incomprehensibility when we consider that, as I have stated so often, the objective world is a mere phenomenon of the brain; for it is the order and conformity to law[a] of this world, based on space, time and causality (as functions of the brain),

280

---

[a] *Gesetzmäßigkeit*

that to a certain degree are eliminated in somnambulistic clairvoyance. For as a result of the Kantian doctrine of the ideality of space and time we understand that the thing in itself, hence what is alone truly real in all appearances – since free of those two forms of the intellect – does not know the difference between near and far and between past, present, and future; hence the separations based on those intuitive forms prove not to be absolute, and to present no insurmountable barrier to the mode of cognition under discussion, that which is essentially modified through the transformation of its organ. In contrast, if time and space were absolutely real and belonged to the essence in itself of things, then that prophetic gift of somnambulists, as generally all viewing at a distance[a] and foreseeing,[b] would be an incomprehensible miracle. In contrast, Kant's theory even receives factual confirmation in a way through the facts discussed here. For if time is not a determination of the real essence of things, then in respect to the latter, before and after have no meaning; hence an event has to be able to be known before it happens as well as after. Every divination,[c] be it in a dream, in somnambulistic foreseeing, in second sight, or wherever else, consists only in discovering the path to freeing cognition from the condition of time. – This matter can also be illustrated in the following simile.[d] The thing in itself is the prime mover[e] in the mechanism that imparts its movement to the entire, complicated, variegated action[f] of this world. Hence the former must be of a different kind and constitution than the latter. We may very well see the connection of the individual parts of the action in the intentionally exposed levers and wheels (time sequence and causality), but what imparts the *first* movement to all these we do not see. Now when reading how clairvoyant somnambulists predict the future so far in advance and with such accuracy, it seems to me as if they had reached that mechanism hidden back there, from which everything originates and where already at this moment that thing is present which externally, i.e. seen through the optical lens of time, presents itself as something only arriving in the future.

281

Moreover, the same animal magnetism to which we owe these miracles, also confirms in different ways the immediate action of the *will* on others and at a distance; but such an action is exactly the fundamental character of that which the notorious name of *magic* denotes. For magic is the immediate action of our will, freed from the causal conditions of physical action, thus from contact in the widest sense of the word, as I have expounded in a

---

[a] *Fernsehn*   [b] *Vorhersehn*   [c] *Mantik*   [d] *Gleichniß*   [e] *primum mobile*   [f] *Spielwerk*

special chapter in my work *On Will in Nature*.[a] Hence magical action relates to physical action the way divination does to rational conjecture: it is actual and complete action at a distance,[b] just as genuine divination, for example, somnambulistic clairvoyance, means being affected from a distance.[c] Just as in the latter the individual isolation of cognition is lifted, so in the former is the individual isolation of the will. Therefore, in both we achieve independently of the limits imposed by space, time, and causality what we are otherwise and ordinarily only capable of doing under these limits. For our innermost essence, or the thing in itself, has cast off those forms of appearance and emerges free of them. As a result, the credibility of divination is related to that of magic, and the doubt in regard to both has always arisen and vanished simultaneously.

Animal magnetism, sympathetic cures, magic, second sight, truth-dreaming, spirit-seeing and visions of all kinds are related appearances, branches of one stem, and provide certain, irrefutable indication of a nexus of beings that rests on a completely different order of things than nature, which has space, time, and causality as its basis. In contrast, that other order is a deeper, more primal and immediate one; hence the first and most universal laws of *nature*, because they are purely formal, do not apply to it; time and space no longer separate individuals, and their separation and isolation, which is based on those forms, no longer places insurmountable barriers in the way of communication of thoughts and immediate influence of the will. Consequently, changes are effected in a way quite different from that of physical causality and the interconnected chain of its links, that is to say, merely by virtue of an act of the will displayed in a particular way and thereby raised to a level beyond the individual. Accordingly, the peculiar characteristic of all animal phenomena discussed here is seeing at a distance and acting at a distance,[d] both in regard to time and to space.

Incidentally, the true concept of acting at a distance is that the space between that which acts and that which is effected, be it full or empty, has no influence whatsoever on the effect. It makes no difference whether it is an inch or a billion orbits of Uranus. For when the effect is somehow weakened by the distance, it is either because matter already filling the space must transmit it and, therefore, in virtue of its continued counter-action, weakens it in proportion to the distance; or it is because the cause itself consists merely in a material emanation that disperses in space and becomes the more attenuated the larger the space. In contrast, empty space itself

---

[a] ['Animal magnetism and magic']   [b] *actio in distans*   [c] *passio a distante*
[d] *visio in distans et actio in distans*

cannot in any way offer resistance and weaken causality. Hence, where the effect decreases in proportion to the distance from the starting point of the cause, like the effect of light, of gravitation, of magnets, and so on, there is no acting at a distance; neither is there such acting where the effect is only delayed by distance. For only matter can move in space; thus matter would have to be the carrier of such an effect by covering the distance, and would accordingly act only after having arrived, and so not until contact and, consequently, not at a distance.

In contrast, the specific characteristics of the phenomena discussed here and enumerated above as branches of a trunk are precisely, as already mentioned, acting at a distance and being affected from a distance. Through this they initially provide, as also mentioned, *factual* confirmation, as unexpected as it is certain, of the Kantian fundamental doctrine of the opposition of appearance and thing in itself and of the laws applying to both. For nature and its order are, according to Kant, mere appearance; as its opposite we see all the facts considered here, called magical, being rooted in the thing in itself and producing phenomena in the world of appearances that, according to the laws of this world, can never be explained and, therefore, were justifiably denied until hundredfold experience no longer permitted it. But not only the Kantian, but also my own philosophy receives important confirmation through closer inspection of these facts, namely that in all those phenomena the actual agent is the *will* alone, and in this way the latter makes itself known as the thing in itself. Accordingly, struck by this truth while proceeding on his empirical path, a well-known magnetizer, the Hungarian Count *Szapáry*, who apparently knows nothing about my philosophy and possibly not much about any other, calls the very first essay in his book *Ein Wort über animalischen Magnetismus*, Leipzig, 1840:[a] 'Physical proofs that *the will* is the principle of all mental and physical life'.

In addition and apart from this, the phenomena discussed here in any case provide a factual and completely certain refutation not only of materialism, but also of naturalism, which I have described in my chief work, vol. 2, ch. 17, as physics installed on the throne of metaphysics. They do so by establishing that the order of *nature*, which materialism and naturalism want to claim as the absolute and only one, is a purely phenomenal and therefore a merely superficial order which has as its foundation the essence of the things in themselves, an essence that is independent of the laws of that order. However, the phenomena discussed here are, at least from the philosophical point of view, without comparison the most important

284

---

[a] [See p. 226, n. d]

among all the facts presented to us by the whole of experience; hence it is the duty of all scholars to make themselves thoroughly familiar with them.

The following more general remark may serve to elucidate this discussion. Belief in ghosts is innate in human beings; it is found at all times and in all countries, and perhaps no human being is completely free of it.[18] Already the great majority and the ordinary people of all countries and times distinguish between *the natural and the supernatural* as two fundamentally different yet simultaneously existing orders of things. To the supernatural they ascribe, without hesitation, miracles, prophecies, ghosts, and sorcery, but in addition they accept that in general nothing is natural through and through, but nature itself is based on something supernatural. Therefore, the people know this very well when they ask: 'Does this happen naturally or not?' In essence, this popular distinction coincides with the Kantian distinction between appearance and thing in itself; only that the latter determines the thing more precisely and accurately, namely in the sense that the natural and the supernatural are not two different and separate kinds of beings, but one and the same that, taken *in itself,* is to be called supernatural, because only by *appearing,* i.e. entering the perception of our intellect and hence its forms, does it manifest itself as *nature*; it is precisely nature's merely phenomenal lawfulness that we understand as the natural. For my part, I have only clarified *Kant's* expression by calling the 'appearance' simply *representation.* And now, if we take into account that, as soon as Kant's thing in itself, in the *Critique of Pure Reason* and the *Prolegomena,* emerges just a little from the obscurity in which he keeps it, it reveals itself as that which is morally accountable in us, hence as the *will,* then we will also realize that, by showing the *will* to be the thing in itself, I have only elucidated and implemented Kant's thought.

Considered, admittedly, not from the economic and technological, but from the philosophical point of view, animal magnetism is the most momentous of all discoveries ever made, even if for now it creates more riddles than it solves. It is really practical metaphysics, in the way that Francis Bacon already defines magic; it is, so to speak, experimental metaphysics, for it eliminates the primary and most universal laws of nature, which is why it makes possible what even a priori is considered impossible. But if already in mere *physics* experiments and facts fail badly to offer correct insight, and interpretation is required, which is often hard to come by, how much more will this be the case with the mysterious facts of this empirically emerging metaphysics! Rational, or theoretical, metaphysics will have to keep equal pace with it for the treasures here discovered to be unearthed. But then the time will come when philosophy, animal magnetism, and a

285

natural science that has made unparalleled advances in all its branches mutually shed such a bright light on each other that truths will be revealed which we could not otherwise hope to gain. However, we should not think here of the metaphysical statements and theories of the somnambulist: these are mostly pathetic views, originating in the dogmas learnt by the somnam-   286
bulist and mixed up with what she finds in the mind of the magnetizer, and hence not worthy of attention.

In addition, we see magnetism open the path to explanations about *spirit apparitions*, which have at all times been as tenaciously asserted as they have been persistently denied. However, to identify this path correctly will not be easy, although it must lie somewhere in the middle between the credulity of our otherwise very respectable and deserving *Justinus Kerner*[a] and the view, now probably only still prevalent in England, that allows for no other natural order than the mechanical. This is in order to be able to accommodate and concentrate everything that goes beyond that order the more securely in a personal being that is completely different from the world and governs it at its whim.[b] The shady English clergy,[c] defiantly opposing every scientific knowledge with incredible impertinence and thus well-nigh scandalizing our part of the world, is mainly to blame for the injustice that animal magnetism has had to suffer in England, by cosseting all the prejudices favourable to the 'cold superstition that it calls its religion'[d] and by being hostile to the truths that oppose this superstition. Having already been accepted for forty years, in theory and practice, in Germany and France, animal magnetism is still, without proof and with the confidence of ignorance, ridiculed and condemned as crude deception: 'Whoever believes in animal magnetism cannot believe in God', a young English parson told me as recently as 1850; hence those tears!'[e] Nonetheless, animal magnetism has finally planted its banner also on the island of prejudice and priestly deceit,[f] gloriously affirming once again that 'Great is Truth, and mighty above all things',[g] this beautiful verse from the Bible at which every Anglican cleric's heart rightfully trembles for its benefices.[h] Moreover, it is time to send missions of reason, enlightenment, and anticlericalism to England, with von Bohlen's and Strauß's Bible criticism in

[a] [See p. 225, n. d]   [b] *nach Willkür*
[c] *Pfaffenschaft* [The term has intensely negative connations, to which the English translation does no justice]
[d] *kalten Aberglauben, den sie ihre Religion nennt* [inspired by a phrase in Prince Pückler-Muskau's *Briefe eines Verstorbenen*, 4 vols., 1830–1 (*Letters of a Deceased*), where he speaks of the *kalten Glauben* ('cold faith') of the English clergy]
[e] *hinc illae lacrimae* [Horace, *Epistles* I, 19, 41]   [f] *Pfaffenbetrug*
[g] *magna est vis veritatis, et praevalebit* [I Esdras 4:41 (Apocrypha)]   [h] *Pfründen*

one hand and the *Critique of Pure Reason* in the other, in order to put a stop to the activities of these self-styled 'reverend'[a] clerics, the most arrogant and impudent in the world, and put an end to the scandal. In this respect, we may expect the most from steamships and trains, which are as conducive to the exchange of ideas as to the exchange of goods, thereby greatly endangering the uncouth bigotry that is cultivated with such canny care and prevails even in the higher classes. For few read, but all chatter, and for this purpose those institutions[b] provide opportunity and leisure. It should no longer be tolerated that these parsons, through the crudest[19] bigotry, reduce the nation that is most intelligent and, in almost every respect, the first in Europe to the lowest rung and thus make it *contemptible*, at least if we consider the means by which they reach this goal, which is to organize the education of the common people[c] entrusted to them in such a way that two thirds of the English nation are unable to read. In this their foolhardiness goes so far as to attack in public papers even the absolutely certain, universal results of *geology* with fury, scorn, and shallow mockery; for they want in all seriousness to assert the Mosaic fairy tale of creation without noticing that in such attacks they are banging an earthenware pot against an iron one.*,[20] – Incidentally, the real source of the scandalous English obscurantism that deceives the people is the law of primogeniture, which makes it necessary for the aristocracy (taken in the widest sense) to provide for their younger sons; if they are not suited for the Navy or the Army, the 'Church-establishment'[d] (a term that characterizes it), with its revenues of five million pounds, is *the pension institution*. For 'a living'[e] (also a very characteristic name[f]), i.e. a parish, is procured for the squire either through favour or for money; very often parishes are offered for sale in newspapers or even for public auction,**,[21] although, for decency's sake, it is not quite the parish

287

288

---

* The English are such a 'matter of fact nation' [original English] that, when recent historic and geological discoveries (for example, that the Cheops pyramid is a thousand years older than the great flood) deprive them of the factuality and historicity of the Old Testament, their entire religion plunges into an abyss.

** The *Galignani* [*Galignani's Messenger*, English daily newspaper published in Paris] of 12 May 1855 quotes from the *Globe* that the Rectory of Pewsey, Wiltshire, is to be publicly auctioned on 13 June 1855; and the *Galignani* of 12 May 1855 (and since then more frequently) provides from *The Leader* [English weekly] a whole list of parishes that are advertised for auction, including the revenue of each, the local amenities, and the age of the current vicar. For just as commissions in the Army can be bought, so can parishes in the Church; what kind of officers that results in has been brought to light by the campaign in the Crimea, and what kind of parsons experience also teaches.

[a] [Original English] [b] [Referring to Church institutions] [c] *Volkserziehung*
[d] [Original English] [e] [Original English]
[f] [Schopenhauer then provides a German translation (of his own creation), *eine Leberei* (derived from *leben*, 'to live'), whose suffix carries a negative connotation]

itself that is sold, but the right to bestow it this time (the patronage[a]). However, since the deal must be closed before the actual vacancy happens, one adds, in order to give it the right promotion, that the current vicar is already, for example, seventy-seven years old, as one also does not fail to emphasize the fine opportunities for hunting and fishing in the parish and the elegant residence. It is the most impudent simony[b] in the world.[22] This explains why in good, or rather genteel, English society, any ridicule of the Church and its cold superstition is considered in bad taste, indeed, an indecency, in accordance with the maxim 'When good taste appears, common sense retreats'.[c] Therefore, the influence of clerics in England is so great that, to the lasting *disgrace of the English nation*, Thorwaldsen's statue of *Byron*, their greatest poet after the unequalled Shakespeare, was not permitted to join the other great men in the national pantheon of Westminster Abbey,[d] for the very reason that Byron was honourable enough to make no concessions to the Anglican clerics, but followed his own path unhindered, whereas the mediocre poet *Wordsworth*, the most frequent aim of his mockery, had his statue suitably erected there in 1854. The English nation, through such infamy, reveals itself 'as a stultified and priest-ridden nation'.[e] Europe ridicules it with justification. But that will not last. A future, wiser generation will carry Byron's statue with pomp and splendour to Westminster Abbey. In contrast, Voltaire, who wrote a hundred times more against the Church than Byron, rests with glory in the French Panthéon, the Church of St Genevieve, fortunate to belong to a nation that does not allow itself to be led around by the nose and ruled by parsons.[23] As it is, the demoralizing effects of priestly deceit and bigotry cannot fail to show. It has to be demoralizing that the clerics tell the people lies to the effect that half the virtues consist in spending Sundays in idleness and wailing in church, and one of the greatest vices, paving the way to all others, is 'Sabbathbreaking',[f] i.e. not spending Sundays in idleness; that is why they let poor sinners about to be hanged explain in the newspapers that their whole sinful life career had originated in 'Sabbathbreaking', that dreadful vice. Exactly because of the above-mentioned pension institution, unhappy Ireland, whose inhabitants starve to death by the thousands, must still, in addition to its own Catholic clergy, voluntarily paid for from its own resources, also maintain an idle Protestant clergy, including an archbishop, twelve bishops, and an army of deans and rectors,[g] albeit not directly at the expense of the people, but paid for from Church property.

289

---

[a] [Original English] [b] *Simonie* [sale of ministries] [c] *quand le bon ton arrive, le bon sens se retire*
[d] [Poets' Corner] [e] [Original English] [f] [Original English] [g] [Original English]

I have already drawn attention to the fact that dreams, somnambulistic perception, clairvoyance, vision, second sight, and possibly spirit-seeing are closely related phenomena. What they have in common is that, when subject to them, we receive an intuition objectively presenting itself through a completely different organ than during the ordinary waking state, namely not through the external senses, but nevertheless exactly as if by means of them; accordingly, I have called this the *dream-organ*. On the other hand, what distinguishes them from each other is the difference of their relation to the empirically real world perceivable through the senses. For in dreams, as a rule, no such relation to the empirical world exists, and even in the rare prophetic dreams it is mostly an immediate and remote, very seldom a direct relation. On the other hand, in regard to somnambulistic perception and clairvoyance, as well as sleepwalking, the relation is immediate and accurate; in regard to vision and possible spirit-seeing it is problematic. – For the seeing of objects in a dream is admittedly illusory, hence actually just subjective, like that in imagination; but the same kind of intuition becomes completely and actually objective in sleep-waking and somnambulism; in fact, in clairvoyance it acquires a scope of view that is incomparably wider than that of the person who is awake. However, if this intuition extends to the phantoms of the departed, then we want to acknowledge it again merely as subjective seeing. But this does not accord with the analogy of this progression, and we can only claim this much, that now objects are seen whose existence is not substantiated by the ordinary intuition of a person who happens to be awake and present; whereas on the immediately preceding level it was objects that the waking person had to seek out in the distance or await to encounter in the future. For from this level we know clairvoyance as an intuition extending also to that which is not *immediately* accessible to the brain's waking activity, but is nonetheless actually present and real; hence we are not allowed to deny, at least not immediately and readily, the objective reality of those perceptions that waking intuition cannot verify even by means of covering distance or time. Indeed, according to the analogy, we are even allowed to assume that a faculty of intuition which extends to what is actually in the future and does not yet exist, might also be capable of perceiving as actually present what once existed in the past and no longer does. Moreover, it is not settled that the phantoms discussed here cannot also enter waking consciousness. Most frequently they are perceived during the state of sleep-waking, when we actually see the immediate surroundings and presence, although we are dreaming; since here everything that we see is objectively real, the phantoms themselves appearing in this state are initially to be presumed real.

Moreover, experience also teaches that the function of the *dream-organ*, the condition for whose activity normally consists in lighter, ordinary sleep or in deeper, magnetic sleep, can as an exception also become activated while the brain is awake, hence that the eye with which we see dreams might   291 also open while we are awake. Then shapes shall stand before us that so strikingly resemble those which enter the brain through the senses that they are confused with and mistaken for them, until it is shown that these shapes are not links within the cohesion of experience, which connects everything in the causal nexus[a] and is known under the name of corporeal world – a fact that comes to light either at once or only afterwards. A shape thus presenting itself will be called hallucination, vision, second sight, or spirit-apparition, depending on its *more remote* cause. For its *most immediate* cause must always lie within the organism, in that, as shown above, it is an influence[b] arising from within which stimulates the brain to be intuitively active, an activity that, permeating the brain completely, extends as far as the sensory nerves, with the result that the shapes appearing in this way are even endowed with the colour and sheen, and also the sound and voice of reality. However, in case this happens imperfectly, they appear only faintly tinged, pale, grey and almost transparent; or, analogously, if they appear to hearing, their voice will be reduced, hollow, muted, hoarse, or chirping. When the seer directs closer attention to these shapes, they usually vanish, because the senses, which now struggle to turn towards *external* impression, actually receive the latter, which, being stronger and occurring in the opposite direction, overwhelms and pushes back the entire brain activity coming from *within*. Precisely in order to avoid this collision, it happens that, through visions, the inner eye projects the shapes as much as possible where the external eye sees nothing, into dark corners, behind curtains that suddenly turn transparent, and generally into the darkness of night, which is the time of spirits merely because darkness, silence, and seclusion, eliminating external impressions, allow full scope for that activity of the brain that comes from *within*. In this respect, therefore, we can compare it with the phenomenon of phosphorescence, which also depends on darkness. With noisy company and the light of many candles burning, midnight   292 is not the hour of ghosts. But the dark, silent, lonesome midnight is, because during this hour we already instinctively fear the entrance of apparitions that present themselves as entirely external, although their *immediate* cause lies within ourselves; hence we actually fear ourselves. For that reason, whoever is afraid of such appearances will seek company.

[a] *Kausalnexus*   [b] *Einwirkung*

Now, although experience teaches that apparitions of the kind here discussed really occur while being awake, which distinguishes them from dreams, I still doubt that this wakefulness is complete in the strictest sense of the word. For the necessary distribution of the brain's power of representation already seems to require that, when the dream-organ is very active, this cannot happen without subtracting from normal activity, a certain decrease of the waking, externally directed sensory consciousness. So, in accordance with this, I presume that during such an apparition, consciousness, which, to be sure, is awake, nonetheless is veiled as if with a very light gauze, through which it acquires a certain, albeit faint, dreamlike tinge. This would explain, first of all, why those who actually have had such apparitions, have never died of fright, whereas false, artificially arranged spirit apparitions have sometimes had this effect. Indeed, normally real visions of this kind do not cause such fear at all; on the contrary, only afterwards, when thinking about them, do we begin to feel the horror. This might actually be due to the fact that while they lasted they were mistaken for real people, and it only becomes clear afterwards that they could not have been. However, I believe that the absence of fear, which is a characteristic sign even of real visions of this kind, occurs mainly for the reason provided above, namely that, although awake, we are nonetheless lightly veiled by a kind of dream consciousness and, therefore, are in an element to which fear of incorporeal apparitions is essentially alien, precisely for the reason that within it the objective is not as sharply divided from the subjective as it is in respect to the influence of the corporeal world. This is confirmed by the way in which the seer of Prevorst associates with her spirits without inhibition; for instance vol. 2, p. 120 (first edn.), she calmly has a spirit stand and wait until she has finished eating her soup. Also J. Kerner himself states in several passages (e.g. vol. 1, p. 209) that she certainly seemed to be awake, but really never entirely; which might still be reconciled with her own statement (vol. 2, p. 11; third edn., p. 236)[a] that each time she saw spirits she was completely awake.

The *immediate* cause for all these intuitions through the dream-organ which occur during waking and which present us with completely objective intuitions matching those produced by the senses must lie, as we have said, within the organism, where some unusual alteration acts on the brain by means of the vegetative nervous system, which is already akin to the cerebral system, in other words the sympathetic nerve and its ganglia. However, through this action the brain can only be stimulated to its natural and

293

---

[a] [Kerner, *Die Seherin von Prevorst*, see p. 225, n. d]

characteristic activity of objective intuition within the forms of space, time, and causality, in the same way as happens through an effect from outside on the senses, so that now too it exercises its normal function. – But the brain's intuitive activity, stimulated from within, reaches even the sensory nerves, which accordingly, as they are now likewise stimulated from within to have their specific sensations, just as they are otherwise stimulated from outside, furnish the appearing shapes with colour, sound, smell, and so on, and thereby endow them with the complete objectivity and corporeal reality of the sensibly perceived. This theory receives remarkable confirmation through the following statement by a clairvoyante somnambulist, described by Heineken, about the origin of somnambulistic intuition: 'During the night, after a quiet, natural sleep, it suddenly became clear to her that the light was generated in the back of the head, from there flowed into the forehead, then came into the eyes and rendered the surrounding objects visible; with the help of this light, resembling twilight, she saw and recognised everything around her.' (Kieser's *Archiv für den thierischen Magnetismus*, vol. 2, no. 3, p. 43.[a]) As discussed, the *immediate* cause of such an intuition produced in the brain from within must itself again have a cause, which then is the *more remote* cause of this intuition. Now, if we should find out that this cause is not to be sought only within the organism on each occasion, but sometimes also outside of it, we would, if the latter were the case, secure the actual objectivity of that brain phenomenon from a quite different perspective, i.e. the actual causal connection with something existing outside of the subject – a phenomenon that until now has appeared just as subjective as mere dreams, indeed, as a waking dream; its objectivity would, therefore, re-enter through the back door, so to say. Consequently, I shall now enumerate the *more remote* causes of that phenomenon, as far as they are known to us; at which point I must mention, first of all, that, as long as these causes are found solely *within* the organism, the phenomenon is given the name *hallucination*, yet it loses this and acquires other, different names if a cause *outside of* the organism can be shown, or at least must be assumed.

(1) The most frequent cause of the brain phenomenon discussed here are severe and acute illnesses, especially high fevers leading to delirium, during which, under the name fever hallucinations, the aforesaid phenomenon is

294

---

[a] [Vol. 2, no. 3 (1817), Philipp Heineken, 'Geschichte einer merkwürdigen Entzündungskrankheit des Unterleibes mit dem Charakter der Exsudation, welche mit nervösem Leiden von verschiedener Form verbunden war, und im Somnambulismus ihr Heilmittel fand' (Story of a Curious Infectious Disease of the Womb Characterized by Exudation and Connected to Different Forms of Nervous Affliction, which Found its Cure in Somnambulism)]

well known. This cause obviously lies merely in the organism, although the fever itself may have been brought on by external causes.

(2) *Madness* is sometimes, but by no means always, accompanied by hallucinations, whose cause has to be sought in the pathological states – mostly present in the brain, but also in the rest of the organism – which initially produce the madness.

(3) In rare, but fortunately firmly established cases hallucinations arise in the form of appearances of human shapes closely resembling real ones, without fever, or any other acute illness, much less madness, being present. The best-known case of this kind is that of *Nicolai*, who presented it to the Berlin Academy in 1799 and in addition had the lecture printed.[a] A similar one can be found in the *Edinburgh Journal of Science*, by Brewster, vol. 4, no. 8, October–April 1831,[b] and a few others are furnished by Brierre de Boismont, *On Hallucinations*,[c] 1845, second edn., 1852, a book that is very useful for the entire subject matter of our investigation and to which I shall therefore refer frequently. Although it provides no detailed explanation at all of the phenomena relating to this matter and, unfortunately, does not even really have a systematic arrangement, but only one apparently so, it is a copious compilation, carefully and critically assembled, of all the cases that in some way relate to our subject. Especially Observations 7, 13, 15, 29, 65, 108, 110, 112, 114, 115, and 132 pertain to the specific point that we are in the process of investigating. In general, we have to assume and consider that of the facts that belong to the whole subject of present discussion, one that is publicly reported comes with a thousand similar ones, news of which never reaches beyond the narrow circle of their immediate environment. For this reason, the scientific investigation of this subject has dragged on for hundreds, if not thousands of years, with a few isolated cases, truth-dreams, and ghost stories, the like of which have occurred hundreds of thousands of times since then, but which were never made public and for that reason never included in the literature. As an example of those cases, made typical through innumerable repetition, I want to mention only the truth-dream

---

[a] [Christoph Friedrich Nicolai, *Beispiel einer Erscheinung mehrerer Phantasmen, nebst einigen erläuternden Anmerkungen* (*An Example of a Manifestation of Several Phantasms, with Some Explanatory Notes*), read 28 February 1799; also published in *Neue Berlinische Monatsschrift*, no. 1 (May 1799)]

[b] [*Edinburgh Journal of Science*, ed. David Brewster, new series, vol. 4]

[c] *des hallucinations* [Alexandre-Jacques-François Brière (English: Brierre) de Boismont, *Des hallucinations, ou histoire raisonnée des apparitions, des visions, des songes, de l'extase, du magnétisme et du somnambulisme* (*On Hallucinations: A History and Explanation of Apparitions, Visions, Dreams, Ecstasy, Magnetism, and Somnambulism*), Paris: Germer Baillière, 1845 (first edn.); 1852 (second edn.)]

that Cicero relates, *On Divination*[a] I, 27; the ghost in Pliny, in the 'Letter to Sura';[b] and the spirit apparition of Marsilio Ficino, in accordance with the arrangement with his friend Mercatus.[c] – But in regard to the cases considered under the present number, of which Nicolai's illness is typical, they all have been proven to have arisen from purely physiological, abnormal causes entirely located in the organism itself, both by virtue of their meaningless content and their periodical recurrence and by the fact that they were cured through therapeutic means, especially blood-letting. Hence they also belong to mere hallucinations and, indeed, should properly be called that.

(4) These hallucinations are initially followed by certain appearances, incidentally similar to them, of objectively and externally present forms, which, however, distinguish themselves by a character of significance, predominantly sinister, especially directed towards the seer, and whose actual significance is most often shown to be beyond doubt by the shortly ensuing death of the person to whom they appeared. We can consider as a model for this the case that Walter Scott, in his *On Demonology and Witchcraft*,[d] letter 1, recounts – and which Brierre de Boismont repeats as well – of the judicial officer who, continuing for months, saw vividly in front of him first a cat, then a gentleman-usher, and finally a skeleton, whereupon he wasted away and finally died. Also the vision of *Miss Lee* is of exactly the same kind, to whom the apparition of her mother accurately announced the day and hour of her death. It is first told in Beaumont's *Treatise of Spirits*[e] (translated into German in 1721 by Arnold[f]), then in Hibbert's *Sketches of the Philosophy of Apparitions*,[g] 1824, and in Horace Welby's *Signs before Death*,[h] 1825, is also found in J. C. Hennings' *Von Geistern*

296

---

[a] *De div[inatione]*

[b] *epistola ad Suram* [Gaius Plinius Caecilius Secundus (Pliny the Younger), *Epistles* VII, 27]

[c] [Cesare Baronio, in the *Annales ecclesiastici*, recounts the story that, following a promise Marsilio Ficino and his friend Michael Mercatus had made to each other, Ficino's ghost, riding on a horse, appeared to Mercatus on the day of Ficino's death, supposedly proving the truth of the Platonic doctrine of the immortality of the soul. The story is retold, for example, in Welby, *Signs before Death*]

[d] [Sir Walter Scott, *Letters on Demonology and Witchcraft*, addressed to J. G. Lockhart, London: Murray, 1830]

[e] [John Beaumont, *An Historical, Physiological and Theological Treatise of Spirits, Apparitions, Witchcrafts, and Other Magical Practices*, London: Browne, 1705]

[f] [*Historisch-physiologischer und theologischer Traktat von Geistern, Erscheinungen, Hexerei und andern Zauberhändeln* (*Historical-physiological and Theological Treatise of Ghosts, Apparations, Witchcraft, and other Magic Dealings*), trans. Theodor Arnold, Halle, 1721]

[g] [Samuel Hibbert, *Sketches of the Philosophy of Apparitions; or, An Attempt to Trace such Illusions to their Physical Causes*, Edinburgh: Oliver & Boyd, London: Whittaker, 1824]

[h] [Horace Welby, *Signs before Death, and Authenticated Apparitions: In One Hundred Narratives*, London: Simpkin and Marshall, 1825]

und Geistersehern,[a] 1780, and finally also in Brierre de Boismont. A third example is provided in the book by *Welby* just mentioned (p. 156) in the story of Mrs Stephens, who, while awake, saw a dead body lying behind her chair and died a few days later. And also the cases of seeing-oneself,[b] insofar as they sometimes, albeit not always, signal the death of the person seeing himself. The Berlin physician *Formey* has reported a very curious and extraordinarily well attested case of this kind, in his *Der heydnische Philosoph;*[c] it can be found fully reproduced in Horst's *Deuteroskopie,*[d] vol. 1, p. 115, as well as in his *Zauber-Bibliothek,* vol. 1.[e] However, it must be mentioned here that the apparition was not actually seen by the person herself, who died shortly afterwards and unexpectedly, but only by her relatives.[f] *Horst* reports genuine seeing of oneself in a case attested by himself in his *Deuteroskopie,* vol. 2, p. 138. Even *Goethe* relates that he saw himself on a horse and in clothes in which he actually rode in that very same spot eight years later. (*Truth and Poetry,* Book 11.[g]) Incidentally, this apparition really had the purpose of consoling him by letting him see himself riding in the opposite direction again after eight years, visiting the beloved from whom he had just parted in a very painful farewell. Hence for a moment, the apparition lifted the veil of the future in order to announce the reunion to him in his distress. – Apparitions of this kind are no longer mere hallucinations but *visions*. For they either represent something real or refer to actual future events. Therefore, they are during the wakeful state what prophetic dreams are during sleep, which, as mentioned above, relate most often to the dreamer's own state of health, especially when it is adverse, whereas mere hallucinations correspond to ordinary, meaningless dreams.

297

The origin of these *meaningful visions* can be sought in that mysterious cognitive faculty – hidden within us, not limited by spatial and temporal

---

[a] [Justus Christian Hennings, *Von Geistern und Geistersehern* (*Of Spirits and Spirit-seers*), Leipzig: Weygand, 1780]

[b] *Sichselbstsehns*

[c] [Jean Henri Samuel Formey, *Der heydnische Philosoph, oder Gedanken des Plinius* (*The Pagan Philosopher, or Thoughts of Pliny*), Frankfurt and Leipzig: Brönner, 1761 (German translation by Georg Adam Junker of the French *Le philosophe payen, ou pensées de Pline,* 1759)]

[d] [Georg Conrad Horst, *Deuteroskopie, oder merkwürdige psychische und physiologische Erscheinungen und Probleme aus dem Gebiete der Pneumatologie* (*Second Sight, or Curious Psychological and Physiological Phenomena and Problems from the Sphere of Pneumatology*), 2 vols., Frankfurt: Wilmans, 1830]

[e] [G. C. Horst, *Zauber-Bibliothek oder von Zauberei, Theurgie und Mantik, Zauberern, Hexen, und Hexenprocessen, Dämonen, Gespenstern, und Geistererscheinungen* (*Magic Library, or On Magic, Theurgy and Mantic, Witches, Witch Trials, Demons, Ghosts, and Spirit Apparitions*), 6 vols., Mainz: Kupferberg, 1821–6; vol. 1 (1821), pp. 245–7]

[f] [In fact, it was seen by two employees.] [g] *Aus meinem Leben* [See p. 223, n. *]

relations and thus omniscient, not part of ordinary consciousness, veiled to us, but throwing off the veil in magnetic clairvoyance – which for once has spotted something of great interest to the individual, of which now the will, the core of the whole human being, would like to inform cerebral cognition. However, that is only possible through the rarely successful operation of opening the dream-organ during the *wakeful state* and communicating its discovery through intuitive shapes, possessing either direct or allegorical meaning, to cerebral consciousness. In this it was successful in the cases briefly described above. These all referred to the future; but something happening just now can also be revealed in this manner, which then, of course, cannot concern one's own person but only another. For example, the death of my absent friend, happening at this very moment, can make itself known to me through the sudden appearance of his form, as realistically as that of a living person, without the need for the dying person himself to contribute to this by vividly thinking of me, as actually happens in cases of a different kind, to be discussed further below. Moreover, I have only related this for purposes of elucidation, since in this section, in fact, only visions are discussed that relate to the seer himself and that correspond to prophetic dreams, which are analogous to them.

298

(5) On the other hand, certain visions closely related to the ones discussed above correspond to those prophetic dreams concerning not one's own state of health, but completely external events; these announce dangers not arising from within the organism, but threatening us from outside, dangers that often, to be sure, pass over our heads without our noticing them in any way, in which case we cannot establish the external connection of the vision. In order to be *visible*, visions of this kind require various conditions, above all that the respective subject possess the proper susceptibility to them. However, if this exists only to a lesser degree, as is often the case, then the announcement will be merely *audible* and manifest itself through all kinds of sounds, most often through tapping, which usually occurs at night, mostly in the early morning hours, namely in such a way that we wake up and immediately afterwards hear a very loud knocking on the door of the bedroom, possessing all the perfect distinctness of reality. Visible visions, and particular those in allegorically meaningful shapes that are indistinguishable from those of reality, will only happen when a very great danger threatens our lives or after we have safely escaped such danger, often without knowing of it for certain, in which cases they congratulate us, so to speak, and predict that we still have many years to live. Finally, such visions will also occur in order to announce an inescapable misfortune; the well-known vision of Brutus before the battle at Philippi was of this kind,

presenting itself as his evil genius;[a] as was also the very similar vision of Cassius Parmensis after the battle at Actium, which Valerius Maximus relates (I,7,7).[b] In general, I presume that visions of this kind have been a major reason for the ancient myth of the genius adjoined to every person as well as that of the domestic spirit[c] in Christian times. During the Middle Ages people sought to explain them with the help of the astral spirits,[d] as attested in the passage by Theophrastus Paracelsus quoted in the previous essay: 'In order for fate[e] to be understood, every human being has a spirit that dwells outside of him and has its seat in the outer stars. It uses the imprints[f] (fixed types for embossment; 'to boss' derives from this) of its master. It is this spirit that produces predictions, before and after; for these continue to exist after it. These spirits are called *fatum*.'[g] In the seventeenth and eighteenth centuries, in order to explain these phenomena, people used the expression 'vital spirits',[h] which, since concepts were lacking, had arrived just at the right time. The true, more remote causes of visions of this kind, if their connection to external dangers is established, can obviously not merely lie in the organism. I will further investigate how far we can render this kind of connection with the external world comprehensible.

(6) Visions that no longer concern the person having them and, nonetheless, immediately present future events that occur shortly or some time after, accurately and often in all their details, are characteristic of that rare gift that we call *second sight*,[i] or deuteroscopy.[j] An extensive collection of accounts of this is contained in Horst's *Deuteroskopie*, 2 vols., 1830;[k] newer facts of this kind can also be found in various volumes of Kieser's *Archiv für den thierischen Magnetismus*. The strange faculty for visions of this kind is by no means found exclusively in Scotland and Norway, but also occurs in our region, especially in regard to cases of death, about which accounts are to be found in Jung-Stilling's *Theory of Pneumatology*,[l] §§153ff. Also the famous

---

[a] [See Plutarch, *Lives* (or *Parallel Lives*), *Brutus* XXXVI, 6–7]
[b] [Valerius Maximus, *Factorum et dictorum memorabilium libri novem* (*Nine Books of Memorable Deeds and Sayings*)]
[c] *Spiritus familiaris*   [d] *Astralgeister* [referring to the influence of the stars on events and people]
[e] *Fatum*   [f] *Bossen* [Schopenhauer's parenthetical addition explaining the origin of *Bossiren*])
[g] [Theophrastus von Hohenheim, called Paracelsus, *Works*, ed. Johann Huser, Strasburg: Zetzner, 1603, vol. 2, p. 36; see p. 187]
[h] *spiritus vitales*   [i] [English in the original, followed by the German rendering '*das zweite Gesicht*']
[j] *Deuteroskopie*   [k] [See p. 244]
[l] [Johann Heinrich Jung-Stilling, *Theorie der Geisterkunde. In einer Natur-, Vernunft- und Bibelmäßigen Beantwortung der Frage: Was von Ahnungen, Gesichten und Geistererscheinungen geglaubt und nicht geglaubt werden müßte* (*Theory of Pneumatology. In a Response, according to Nature, Reason and the Bible, to the Question What Can and Cannot Be Believed in regard to Forebodings, Visions, and Spirit Apparitions*), Nuremberg: Raw, 1808]

prophecy of *Cazotte* seems to be based on something of this kind.[a] Even among the negroes of the Sahara desert second sight is often found (S. James Richardson, *Narrative of a Mission to Central Africa*, London, 1853[b]).[24] In fact, already in Homer we find (*Odyssey* XX, 351–7) a real deuteroscopy described, which even bears a strange resemblance to the story of Cazotte. Likewise Herodotus tells of a perfect deuteroscopy, VIII, 65.[c] – In second sight the vision, as always arising initially from within the organism, reaches the highest degree of objective, actual reality and betrays through that a kind of connection to the external world completely different from the ordinary, physical one. As a waking state, it parallels the highest degrees of somnambulistic clairvoyance. It is really a perfect *truth-dreaming while awake*, or at least during a state lasting a few moments in the midst of waking. In addition, the vision of second sight, just like truth-dreams, is in many cases not theorematic, but allegorical, or symbolic, but, most curiously, in accordance with fixed symbols carrying the same meaning that arise in all seers, as can be found specified in the book by Horst[d] mentioned above, vol. 1, pp. 63–9, and in Kieser's *Archiv*,[e] vol. 6, no. 3, pp. 105–8.

(7) Visions that render the past, in particular the forms of persons once alive, before the dream-organ that opens during wakefulness, provide the counterpart to those just considered, which are oriented towards the future. It is fairly certain that they can be occasioned by the nearby remains of corpses of these people located nearby. This extremely important experience, to which a lot of spirit apparitions can be traced, has its most solid and highly secure confirmation in a letter by Professor Ehrmann, the son-in-law of the poet *Pfeffel*, which is reproduced at length[f] in Kieser's *Archiv*, vol. 10, no. 3, pp. 151ff.[g] Excerpts from this are found in many books, for example, in

300

---

[a] [The French writer Jacques Cazotte (1719–92), who, according to Jean François Laharpe and quoted by Jung-Stilling, at a dinner party predicted in great detail how many of those present, including himself, would die during the soon-to-come revolution]

[b] [James Richardson, *Narrative of a Mission to Central Africa, Performed in the Years 1850–51*, London: Chapman and Hall, 1853]

[c] [*Histories*]   [d] [*Deuteroskopie*, see p. 244, n. d]

[e] [Vol. 6, no. 3 (1819), Kieser, 'Das zweite Gesicht (second sight) der Einwohner der westlichen Inseln Schottlands, physiologisch gedeutet' (The Second Sight of the Inhabitants of the Western Islands of Scotland, Interpreted Physiologically)]

[f] *in extenso*

[g] [Vol. 10, no. 3 (1821), Ehrmann, 'Über die Erscheinung im Pfeffelschen Garten zu Colmar. An den Herrn Professor von Eschenmayer' (On the Apparition in Pfeffel's Garden in Colmar. In a Letter to Professor von Eschenmayer); the story is about Pfeffel's private secretary, who during walks in the garden had visions of a female form when passing a certain spot; these stopped after human bones dug up there were removed]

F. Fischer's *Somnambulismus*, vol. 1, p. 246.[a] But also apart from this, the experience is confirmed by many cases that can be attributed to it; of these I will mention here only a few. First is the story of pastor Lindner, told in the same letter,[b] and also from a good source, which has been repeated in many books as well, among them *Die Seherin von Prevorst* (vol. 2, p. 98, first edn., and p. 356, third edn.);[c] further, there is a story of a similar kind in the above-mentioned book by Fischer (p. 252), which he tells himself based on eyewitnesses and which he relates as a correction of a short account in *Die Seherin von Prevorst* (p. 358, third edn.). Also we find seven stories of this type about apparitions, all occasioned by remains of dead people nearby, in G. I. Wenzel's *Unterhaltungen über die auffallendsten neuern Geistererscheinungen*,[d] 1800, in the very first chapter. The Pfeffel story is the last of them; but the others too possess the character of truth rather than that of invention. In addition, they all recount the mere apparition of the form of the deceased without any further development or even dramatic context. Therefore, they deserve full consideration in regard to the theory of these phenomena. The rationalistic explanations given by the author can serve to shed a bright light on the utter inadequacy of such solutions. The fourth observation in the above-mentioned book by Brierre de Boismont also belongs here,[e] as do some ghost stories passed down to us by ancient writers; for example a story related by *Pliny* the Younger (Book VII, epistle 27[f]), which is remarkable just because it possesses the same character as innumerable other stories from modern times. One very similar to it, and maybe just another version of it, is the story that Lucian tells in *Philopseudes*, ch. 31. And of the same kind is the story of Damon, in Plutarch's first chapter of *Cimon*;[g] further what Pausanias ('Attica', I, 32[h]) reports of the battlefield at Marathon, with which can be compared what *Brierre* says on p. 590;[i] and finally, the account by Suetonius in *Caligula*,[j] ch. 59. In general,

---

[a] [Friedrich Fischer, *Der Somnambulismus*, vol. 1: *Das Schlafwandeln und die Visionen* (*Somnambulism: Sleepwalking and Visions*), Basel: Schweighauser, 1839]

[b] [By Ehrmann]

[c] [See p. 225, n. d. In this story, a predecessor appears to Lindner together with two children, a pastor who was known to have lived with his maid, with whom he had several illegitimate children; later excavation in the house turned up children's bones]

[d] [Gottfried Immanuel Wenzel, *Unterhaltungen über die auffallendsten neuern Geistererscheinungen, Träume und Ahndungen, nebst Darstellung anderer sonderbaren Beobachtungen am Menschen* (*Discussions of the Most Striking Recent Apparitions, Dreams and Premonitions, with Presentation of other Strange Observations in Humans*) (no place and publisher), 1800]

[e] [See p. 242, n. c]　　[f] [*Epistles*, see p. 243, n. b]　　[g] [Plutarch, *Lives*, *Cimon* I, 478–9]

[h] [Pausanias, *Description of Greece* I, 'Attica', I, 32, 4]

[i] [See p. 242, n. c; Brierre refers directly to Pausanias' *Attica*]

[j] [Suetonius, *The Lives of the Caesars: Caius Caligula*]

almost all cases might be traced to the experience we have described, where spirits always appear in the same place and the spectre is bound to a particular locality, to churches, churchyards, battlefields, murder scenes, places of execution, and the houses which for this reason have fallen into bad repute and which nobody wants to inhabit; one happens across them from time to time, and I myself have been confronted with several in my life. Such localities occasioned the book by the Jesuit Petrus Thyraeus, *de infestis, ob molestantes daemoniorum et defunctorum spiritus, locis*, Cologne, 1598.[a] – But the most curious fact of this kind may be provided by Brierre de Boismont's Observation 77. The vision of a somnambulist, reported in Kerner's *Blätter aus Prevorst*, Collection 10,[b] p. 61, can be considered a noteworthy confirmation of the explanation provided here for so many spirit apparitions, indeed, as a middle term leading to it. For this woman was suddenly confronted with a domestic scene, recounted by her in detail, that may have taken place there more than a hundred years earlier, since the persons described by her resembled existing portraits, except that she had never seen them.

302

The important fundamental experience itself considered here, to which all such incidents can be attributed and which I call 'retrospective second sight',[c] must remain as a primary phenomenon, because we still lack the means to explain it. In the meantime, it can be closely associated with another phenomenon that is just as inexplicable; nonetheless, much would be gained by this association, since then we would have only one unknown variable instead of two, an advantage analogous to the famous one gained by reducing mineral magnetism to electricity. For just as a somnambulist who is clairvoyant to a high degree is not limited by *time* in her perception, but sometimes foresees actual future events occurring completely by chance; just as the same is achieved by people with second sight and those who see corpses;[d] hence just as events that have not yet entered our empirical reality can act on such people and enter their perception out of the night of the future, so events and people that were once real, although they no longer are, can affect certain specially predisposed persons. So while the others can manifest an effect in advance, these manifest an after-effect. The latter is less incomprehensible than the former, in particular when such a perception is

---

[a] [Petrus Thyraeus, *Loca infesta, hoc est: de infestis, ob molestantes daemoniorum et defunctorum hominum spiritus, locis* (*Menacing Places, which is: Places Menacing due to Harrassing Spirits of Demons and of Dead People*), Cologne: Goswin Cholinus, 1598]

[b] [Justinus A. Ch. Kerner (ed.), *Blätter aus Prevorst. Originalien und Lesefrüchte für Freunde des innern Lebens* (*Pages from Prevorst. Originals and Selections for Friends of the Inner Life*), 12 vols., 1831–9; Collection 10, Stuttgart: Brodhag, 1838]

[c] [Original English]   [d] *Leichensehern*

mediated and introduced through something material, such as, for example, the actually existing, physical remains of the perceived person or things that were closely connected with them, their clothes, the room they lived in, or something close to their hearts, a hidden treasure. By analogy, the extremely clairvoyant somnambulist is sometimes brought into rapport with distant people on whose state of health she is to report through some physical link, for example, a piece of cloth worn by the sick person on his bare skin for a few days (Kieser's *Archiv*, vol. 3, p. 24[a]) or a lock of hair cut off, and by means of this receives their image, a case that is closely related to the one in question. According to this view, spirit apparitions that are connected to specific localities or to the physical remains of deceased people lying there would just be the perceptions of a deuteroscopy in reverse, that is, facing the past – a retrospective second sight;[b] accordingly they would actually be what the ancients (whose entire conception of the realm of shades might have arisen from spirit apparitions; see *Odyssey* XXIV) already called them, shadows, *umbrae*, εἴδωλα καμόντων, – νεκύων ἀμενηνὰ κάρηνα[c] – *manes*[d] (from *manere*, remnants, traces, so to speak), thus echoes of past appearances of this our world of appearances that presents itself in space and time, becoming perceptible for the dream-organ, in rare cases during the state of wakefulness but more easily during sleep, as mere dreams, and most easily, of course, during deep magnetic sleep, when dream has intensified to sleep-waking and the latter to clairvoyance; but also in natural sleep-waking, mentioned at the very beginning, which was described as truth-dreaming of the immediate surroundings of the sleeping person and which makes itself known as different from the waking state precisely through the appearance of such alien shapes. For during sleep-waking the forms of people who have just died and whose bodies are still in the house will manifest themselves most often, just as generally, according to the law that this deuteroscopy in reverse is triggered by the bodily remains of the dead, the form of a deceased can appear to the people thus predisposed most easily as long as the body has not been buried, although even then it is perceived only by the dream-organ.

After what has been said it is self-evident that a spectre appearing in this way does not possess the immediate reality of an actually present object, although mediately a reality does lie at its basis; for what we see is by no means the deceased himself, but a mere *eidôlon*,[e] an image of the person

---

[a] [Vol. 3, no. 3 (1818); P. G. van Ghert, 'Sammlung merkwürdiger Erscheinungen des thierischen Magnetismus' (A Collection of Curious Phenomena of Animal Magnetism)]
[b] [Original English] [c] [Shadows of the dead – faint heads of the dead] [d] [Spirits of the dead]
[e] εἴδωλον

who once existed, arising in the dream-organ of a human being disposed for it and caused by some remnant, some trace left behind. Hence it possesses no more reality than the appearance of someone seeing *himself*, or being perceived by others, where he is not present. Cases of this kind are known through reliable reports, several of which we find compiled in Horst's *Deuteroskopie*, vol. 2, sect. 4. Also the case mentioned by Goethe belongs here, and the not so rare fact that sick people who are close to death imagine themselves to be doubly present in their bed. 'How is it going?' a physician recently asked his gravely ill patient: 'Better now that it is the two of us in bed', was the reply. He died soon afterwards. – Accordingly, spirit apparitions of the kind here under consideration may stand in an objective relation to the *former* state of the persons appearing, but in no way to their *present* state; for these people play no active role in the apparitions; hence we cannot deduce their continued individual existence from them. The explanation provided is also in accord with the fact that the deceased appearing in this manner are normally dressed in the clothes they usually wore; also that the murdered person appears with the murderer, the horse with the rider, and so on. Probably most of the spectres seen by the seer of Prevorst are to be counted among visions of this kind; however, the conversations she had with them should be viewed as products of her own imagination, providing from her own resources the text to this silent procession (dumb shew[a]) and thus an explanation for them. For human beings are, by nature, eager to somehow explain everything they see, or at least to introduce some context, indeed, to have the thing talk in their thoughts; which is why children often assign a dialogue even to inanimate things. Accordingly, the seer herself was, without realizing, the prompter of those appearing forms, and her power of imagination performed the kind of unconscious activity with the help of which we guide and join together events in an ordinary, meaningless dream, indeed, sometimes taking the cue from objective, accidental circumstances, for example a pressure felt in bed, a sound reaching us from outside, or a smell, and so forth, in accordance with which we then dream long stories. To explain this dramaturgy of the clairvoyante, one should consult what *Bende Bendsen*, in Kieser's *Archiv*, vol. ii, no. 1, p. 121,[b] relates about his somnambulist, to whom her living

305

---

[a]   [Original English]
[b]   [Vol. ii, no. 1 (1822); Bende Bendsen, 'Nachtrag zu einer Krankheitsgeschichte der Witwe Petersen zu Arröeskjöping [*Archiv*, vols. 9 and 10; both 1821]; nebst Versuchen über die Wirkung der siderischen Substanzen des nichtmagnetisierten Baquets' (Supplement to the History of the Illness of Widow Petersen in Arröeskjöping, together with Approaches to the Influence of Sidereal Substances of the Non-magnetic Baquet)]

acquaintances sometimes appeared during magnetic sleep, upon which she then carried on long conversations with them in a loud voice. It says there: 'Among the many conversations she had with absent persons, the following one is characteristic. During the supposed replies she was silent, seemed to listen to the replies of the others with rapt attention, meanwhile sitting up in bed and turning her head in a certain direction, and then put forward her objections to them. She imagined the old *Karen* to be present, together with her maid, and took turns speaking to one and then the other. ... The apparent split in her own personality into three different personalities, as is common in dreams, went so far that I was unable to convince the sleeping woman back then that she herself made up all three.' In my view, the spirit conversations of the seer of Prevorst are of the same kind, an explanation that finds strong confirmation in the unspeakable insipidness of the text of those dialogues and dramas, which correspond solely to the conceptual horizon of an ignorant girl from the mountains and the folk metaphysic[a] that she was taught; to assign objective reality to these would only be possible on the assumption of an order of the world so infinitely absurd, indeed, outrageously foolish that one would have to be ashamed to be part of it. – If the biased and credulous Justinus Kerner had not had a vague idea about the origin of those spirit conversations provided here, he would not, with such irresponsible carelessness, have neglected everywhere and every time to search sincerely and diligently for the material objects indicated by the spirits, for example, writing implements in church cellars, golden chains in castle vaults, buried children in horse stables, instead of letting himself be deterred from doing so by the slightest impediments. For that would have thrown light on these matters.

306

In general, I am of the opinion that most actually seen apparitions of the deceased belong to this category of visions. Hence a past, but by no means a present, positively objective reality corresponds to them; for example, the apparition of the president of the Berlin Academy, *Maupertuis*, seen in its hall by the botanist *Gleditsch* and cited by *Nicolai* in his already mentioned lecture given to the Academy;[b] likewise Walter Scott's story in the *Edinburgh Review*, repeated by Horst in his *Deuteroskopie*, vol. 1, p. 113, about the magistrate in Switzerland, who, entering the public library, catches sight of his predecessor sitting in the president's chair, in a solemn council meeting, surrounded by nothing but dead people. In addition, it emerges from some reports that belong here that the objective occasion for visions of this kind does not necessarily have to be the skeleton or another

---

[a] *Volksmetaphysik* [b] [See p. 242, n. a]

remnant of a corpse, but that other objects that have been in close contact with the deceased also have this capacity. For example, in G. J. Wenzel's book, mentioned above, we find six out of the seven stories relevant here where the body brings about the apparition, but one where the mere coat of the deceased, which he always wore and was locked away immediately after his death, gives rise to his physical apparition in front of the terrified widow when it is taken out again. Hence it might also be the case that even slighter traces, scarcely perceptible by our senses, such as drops of blood long since soaked into the floor, or perhaps even the mere locality, enclosed by walls, where someone experiencing great dread or despair suffered a violent death, suffice to provoke such a deuteroscopy in reverse in a person predisposed to it. An opinion of the ancients, mentioned by Lucian (*Philopseudes*, ch. 29), that only those who have died a violent death can appear, might be connected to this. Also a treasure, buried and always anxiously guarded by the deceased, towards which his last thoughts were directed, might act as the objective occasion for such a vision, which then might even possibly turn out to be lucrative. In this cognition[a] of the past, mediated through the dream-organ, the aforementioned objective occasions in a sense play the role that the connection of ideas[b] assigns to its objects in ordinary thinking. Incidentally, it is true of the perceptions here discussed – as of all perceptions facilitated by the dream-organ during waking – that they enter consciousness more easily in audible than in visible form. Hence stories of sounds perceived in this or that place are much more frequent than those of visible apparitions.

307

Now if, in regard to some examples of the kind here under consideration, it is reported that the appearing deceased had revealed certain facts, unknown so far, to the person seeing them, then this should be accepted only on the basis of the most secure evidence and be doubted until then; then it might nevertheless best be explained by means of certain analogies with the clairvoyance of somnambulists. For in isolated cases, some somnambulists have told the patients who were presented to them about the entirely accidental occasion through which they had contracted a disease a long time ago and thus had them recall the almost completely forgotten incident. (Examples of this kind are, in Kieser's *Archiv*, vol. 3, no. 3,[c] p. 70, the fright before the fall from the ladder, and in Kerner's *Geschichte zweyer Somnambülen*,[d] p. 189, the remark by the boy that he had slept with an epileptic in the past.) It also belongs here that some clairvoyants have accurately recognized patients and their condition from a lock of hair or a

---

[a] *Erkennen*   [b] *nexus idearum*   [c] [See p. 179, n. b]   [d] [See p. 214, n. b]

piece of cloth worn by them, although they had never seen the patients. Merck's *Travel Reminiscences from London and Paris*,[a] Hamburg 1852, relates how Alexis accurately recognizes from a letter the present state of the writer and from an old needle-case that of the deceased donor.[b,25] – Hence even revelations do not as such prove the presence of a deceased.

308

Likewise, the fact that the appearing form of a deceased is sometimes seen and heard by two people can be ascribed to the well-known contagiousness of somnambulism and of second sight.

Therefore, in this section we have explained at least the majority of attested apparitions of the forms of deceased people insofar as we have traced them back to a common ground, retrospective second sight, which in many such cases cannot be denied, in particular in those cases mentioned at the beginning of this section. – On the other hand, retrospective second sight itself is a highly curious and inexplicable fact. However, we have to be content with an explanation of this kind in regard to many things, as, for example, the entire great edifice of the theory of electricity consists merely in subordinating various phenomena under a primary phenomenon that remains completely unexplained.

(8) Other people's vivid and longing thought about us can stimulate the vision of their form in our brain, not as a mere phantasm, but as something physically[c] standing before us, indistinguishable from reality. In particular, it is dying people who show this capability and thus, in the hour of their death, appear to their absent friends, even to several of them at the same time in different places. This case has been recounted and confirmed so often and from so many sides that I accept it without hesitation as factually grounded. A very fine example, confirmed by distinguished people, is found in Jung-Stilling's *Theory of Pneumatology*, §198. Furthermore, two especially striking cases are the story of Mrs Kahlow, in the above-mentioned book by Wenzel,[d] p. 11, and that of the court chaplain in Hennings' book,[e] also referred to above, p. 329. The following case may be mentioned as a recent one. Not long ago, here in Frankfurt, in a Jewish hospital, a sick maid died during the night. Early the following morning her sister and her niece, one of whom lives here and the other a mile away, arrived at her master and

309

mistress in order to inquire about her, because she had appeared to both of them during the night. The hospital warden, on whose report this fact is

---

[a] *Reise-Erinnerungen aus London und Paris* [Ernst von Merck, Hamburg: Langhoff, 1852 (pp. 97–8 and pp. 101–2)]

[b] [This passage actually relates statements of another somnambulist, not those of Alexis]

[c] *leibhaftig*   [d] [See p. 248, n. d]   [e] [See p. 244, n. a]

based, asserted that such cases happen frequently. That a clairvoyant somnambulist, who during her most intense clairvoyant incidents always fell into a catalepsy resembling a state of apparent death,[a] had physically appeared to her friend, is related in the already mentioned *Geschichte der Auguste Müller in Karlsruhe*,[b] and is repeated in Kieser's *Archiv*, vol. 3, no. 3, p. 118.[c] Another intentional apparition of the same person is reported from a thoroughly reliable source in Kieser's *Archiv*, vol. 6, no. 1, p. 34.[d] – On the other hand, it is much rarer for perfectly healthy people to bring about this effect; but even about this there is no lack of credible accounts. The oldest is given by St Augustine, in *The City of God*[e] XVIII, 18, starting with the words: 'Another man told how, in his own house, etc.'[f] It may be second hand but, he assures us, from a very good source. Here what one person dreams appears to the other as a vision that he takes for reality; an analogous case is reported in the *Spiritual Telegraph*,[g] published in America, 23 September 1854 (apparently without knowing Augustine), of which Dupotet provides the French translation in his *Traité complet de magnétisme*, third edn., p. 561.[h,26] A more recent case of the kind is added to the last mentioned report in Kieser's *Archiv* (vol. 6, no. 1, p. 35). Jung-Stilling relates a wonderful story belonging here in his *Theory of Pneumatology*, §101, but without indicating the source. Several stories are provided by *Horst* in his *Deuteroskopie*, vol. 2, sect. 4. But a highly remarkable instance of the capability for such apparitions, and one passed on from the father to the son and very frequently practised by both without intention, is found in Kieser's *Archiv*, vol. 7, no. 3, p. 158.[i] Yet an older example, very similar to it, is found in Zeibich's *Gedanken von der Erscheinung der Geister*, 1776,[j] p. 29, and repeated in Hennings' *Von Geistern und Geistersehern*, p. 746. Since both were certainly reported independently of each other, they serve to confirm each other in this extremely miraculous

---

[a] *Scheintode*   [b] [See p. 213, n. c]

[c] [Vol. 3, no. 3 (1818); Kieser: 'Meier, Höchst merkwürdige Geschichte der magnetisch-hellsehenden Auguste Müller in Karlsruhe']

[d] [Vol. 6, no. 1 (1819); Meier, 'Erfahrungen und Bemerkungen über den Lebensmagnetismus' (Experiences and Remarks about Animal Magnetism)]

[e] *de civitate Dei*

[f] *Indicavit et alius se domi suae* etc. [The passage tells of a man who sees a philosopher come into his house and explain some problems in Plato, something he had refused to do before. Later asked about this, he claims he only dreamed that he did so]

[g] [American weekly, New York, 1852–60]   [h] [See p. 216, n. c]

[i] [Vol. 7, no. 3 (Eduard Stern, '*Kann man sich auch da wohl zeigen, wo man nicht persönlich ist?*' [Can One Appear Where One is not Personally Present?])]

[j] [Heinrich August Zeibich, *Gedanken von der Erscheinung der Geister* (*Thoughts on Spirit-apparitions*), Philalethopolis (?), 1776]

matter.[a] Also in Nasse's *Zeitschrift für Anthropologie* IV, no. 2, p. 111,[b] such a
310   case is related by Professor Grohmann. And again in Horace Welby's *Signs before Death*, London, 1825,[c] we can find several examples of apparitions of living persons in places where they were present only with their thoughts, for example, pp. 45 and 88. Especially trustworthy are the cases recounted by the thoroughly honest Bende Bendsen, in Kieser's *Archiv*, vol. 8, no. 3, p. 120, under the title 'Doppelgänger'.[d] – Corresponding to the visions discussed here, which take place during wakefulness, are the sympathetic ones during sleep, that is, dreams that communicate themselves at a distance and are dreamt equally by two people at the same time. Examples of these are sufficiently well known; a good compilation is found in E. Fabius, *De somniis*,[e] §21, and among them a particularly good one recounted in Dutch. Further, the extremely curious article by H. M. Wesermann, in Kieser's *Archiv*, vol. 6, no. 2, p. 135,[f] reports five cases, in which he intentionally, by means of his *will*, produced precisely determined dreams in others; but since, in the last case, the person in question had not yet gone to bed, he, as well as another person who happened to be present, experienced the intended apparition during *waking* and just like reality. Consequently, just as in such dreams, so also in waking visions of this category, the *dream-organ* is the medium of intuition. The above-mentioned story related by St Augustine is to be considered the connecting link between both kinds, insofar as what appears to the one person in waking, the other merely dreams. Two very similar cases are found in Horace Welby's *Signs before Death*, pp. 266 and 297; the latter is taken from Sinclair's *Invisible World*.[g] Obviously visions of this kind, however deceptively and vividly the appearing people may present themselves in them, arise not at all by means of influence[h] from outside on the senses, but in virtue of a magical effect of the *will* of the person in whom they originate upon the other, that is, on the essence in itself of an alien organism, which thereby suffers an alteration from within. This alteration, in turn, acting on the person's brain, excites

---

[a] [Actually, in §49 (pp. 746–56) of his book Hennings investigates Zeibich's examples and critically questions their verifiability]

[b] [*Zeitschrift für die Anthropologie*, ed. Friedrich Nasse, 1823–6. This number of the journal has no p. 111; however, Prof. Grohmann contributed several articles to the journal]

[c] [See p. 243, n. h]

[d] [Vol. 8, no. 3 (1820) (Bende Bendsen, 'Beiträge zu den Erscheinungen des zweiten Gesichts' [Contributions to Apparitions of Second Sight])]

[e] [See p. 221, n. d]

[f] [Vol. 6, no. 2 (1819); probably referring to Anonymous, 'Versuche willkührlicher Traumbildung, mitgetheilt in einem Briefe an den Herausgeber' (Attempts at Voluntary Dream-formation, Related in a Letter to the Editor), pp. 136ff.]

[g] [George Sinclair, *Satan's Invisible World Discovered*, Edinburgh: John Reid, 1685]   [h] *Einwirkung*

the image of the first person there as vividly as an effect by way of light rays reflected from his body into the eyes of the other could ever manage to do. 311

The doubles[a] here mentioned, in which the appearing person is obviously alive but absent and normally not aware of his apparition, provide us with the right perspective on the apparitions of dying and deceased people and hence on spirit apparitions proper, by teaching us that an immediately actual presence, such as that of a body acting on the senses, is by no means a necessary condition for them. But precisely this assumption is the fundamental error of all previous interpretations of spirit apparitions, in denying them as well as asserting them. That assumption rests on the adoption of the standpoint of *spiritualism* instead of that of *idealism*.* According to the former, people started out from the completely unjustified assumption that human beings consist of two fundamentally different substances, one material, the body, the other immaterial, the so-called soul. After the separation of the two in death, the soul, albeit immaterial, simple and unextended, was still supposed to exist in space, namely to move, walk, and act on bodies and their senses from outside, just like a body, and accordingly present itself as one; of course, that presupposes the same actual presence in space which a body has that is seen by us. This utterly indefensible, spiritualistic view of spirit apparitions is rightly subject to all the rational disputations of it and also Kant's critical elucidation of the matter, which constitutes the first, or theoretical, part of his *Dreams of a Spirit-seer Explained by Dreams of Metaphysics*. This *spiritualistic* view, this assumption of a substance that is immaterial yet locomotive, acting on bodies and, consequently, on the senses, in the same way that matter does, has to be entirely given up, in order to gain a correct view of all the phenomena that belong here, and in its stead the idealistic standpoint 312
must be achieved, from which we see these matters in a completely different light and attain quite different criteria for their possibility. To lay the foundation for this is the purpose of the present treatise.

(9) The last case to be considered is the possibility of the magical action described under the previous number being continued even after death, so that a spirit apparition proper by means of direct action would take place, in a sense the actual, personal presence of someone already deceased, which would also allow for retroactive influence on him. The denial a priori of any possibility of this kind and the proportionate ridicule of the opposite

---

* See *The World as Will and Representation*, vol. 2, p. 15 [Hübscher *SW* 3, 16].

[a] *Doppelgänger*

assertion cannot rest on anything but the conviction that death is the
absolute annihilation of a human being, unless it is based on the faith of
the Protestant Church. According to this, spirits cannot appear, because
right after death they have forever gone either to heaven, with its eternal
bliss, or to hell, with its eternal torments, corresponding to their faith or lack
thereof during the few years of their earthly existence; and they cannot leave
either place and return to us. Consequently, in accordance with the
Protestant faith, all such apparitions arise from devils, or angels, but not
from human spirits, as expounded at length and in depth by Lavater, *De
spectris*,[a] Geneva, 1580, II, chs. 3 and 4. In contrast, the Catholic Church,
which already in the sixth century, in particular through Gregory the Great,
had very judiciously rectified this absurd and outrageous dogma by inserting
purgatory between these desperate alternatives, allows the apparition of the
spirits dwelling there temporarily and, by way of exception, also of others.
This can be seen in detail in Petrus Thyraeus, *De locis infestis* I, chs. 3ff.,[b] to
which we have already referred. Owing to this dilemma, the Protestants
actually saw themselves compelled to retain the existence of the devil in all
kinds of ways, merely because they could not possibly do without him in
explaining the undeniable spirit apparitions; hence as late as the beginning
of the last[c] century those who denied the devil were called *Adaemonistae*[d]
with almost the same pious horror[e] as atheists[f] today. Accordingly, for
example in C. F. Romanus, *Schediasma polemicum, an dentur spectra, magi
et sagae*, Leipzig, 1703,[g] spirits were immediately defined as 'external apparitions and terrible visions of the devil, in which he assumes a body or
something else perceptible by the senses in order to scare human beings'.[h]
This may also have something to do with the fact that witch trials, which,
as is well known, presupposed a pact with the devil, were much more
common with Protestants than Catholics.[27] – Disregarding such mythological views, however, I mentioned above that the rejection a priori of the

313

---

[a] [Ludwig Lavater, *De spectris, lemuribus et magnis atque insolitis fragoribus variisque præsagitionibus, quæ
plerunque obitum hominum, magnas clades, mutationisque Imperiorum præcedunt* (*Of ghostes and spirites
walking by nyght, and of strange noyses, crackes, and sundry forwarnynges, whiche commonly happen before
the death of menne, great slaughters, and alterations of kyngdoms*), (first edn. 1570), Geneva: Vignon,
1580]
[b] [See p. 249, n. a]   [c] [eighteenth]   [d] [Those not believing in demons]   [e] *pius horror*
[f] *Atheistae*
[g] [Carl Friedrich Romanus, *Schediasma polemicum, expendens quaestionem an dentur spectra, magi, et
sagae, una cum recensione plurimarum hac de re opinionum* (*Polemical Sketch, Investigating the Question
whether Apparitions, Magicians, and Soothsayers Exist, with a Review of Most Opinions of this Matter*),
Leipzig: Fritsch, 1703]
[h] *apparitiones et territiones* Diaboli *externae, quibus corpus, aut aliud quid in sensus incurrens sibi assumit,
ut homines infestet*

possibility of an actual apparition of the deceased can only be based on the conviction that in death the human being becomes altogether nothing. For as long as this conviction is lacking, it is impossible to see why a being still existing in some way should not be able to manifest itself somehow and act on another one that exists, albeit in a different state. Therefore, it is as logical as it is naïve that Lucian, after recounting how Democritus had not let himself be perplexed by a spirit masquerade staged to terrify him, adds: 'So utterly was he convinced that the souls are nothing after being separated from the body.'[a] – But if there is something in human beings, apart from matter, that is indestructible, then it is, at least a priori, hard to see why this something that gave rise to the marvellous phenomenon of life should, after its termination, be incapable of any influence whatsoever on those still living. Consequently, the matter could be determined only a posteriori, through experience. But this is all the more difficult as even the actual vision in which a deceased appears, apart from all intentional and unintentional deceptions of those who report them, can belong to any of the eight types enumerated by me so far; hence this may always be the case. Indeed, even in case such an apparition reveals matters that nobody could have known, this could still, in consequence of the explanation provided at the end of no. 7, be interpreted as the form assumed by the revelation of spontaneous somnam-   314
bulistic clairvoyance, although the occurrence of such an apparition during waking, or even just through complete recollection from the somnambulistic state, can probably not be proved with certainty, since revelations of this kind have in all cases only occurred in dreams, as far as I know. Meanwhile, there may be circumstances that render even such an interpretation impossible. Nowadays, when matters of this kind are looked upon much more frankly than before and, consequently, are also reported and discussed more boldly, we may hope to attain decisive information about this matter.

However, some ghost stories are of such a nature that any other interpretation meets with great difficulties as soon as we deem them not a complete pack of lies. But in many cases, it is partly the character of the persons who initially reported them and partly the mark of honesty and candour of their description that speak against this; yet more than anything else it is the perfect similarity in the quite peculiar course and nature of the alleged apparitions, however far apart the times and countries may be from which the reports originate. This becomes most conspicuous in regard to specific circumstances that have been recognized only in recent times as a

---

[a] οὕτω βεβαίως ἐπίστευε, μηδὲν εἶναι τὰς ψυχὰς ἔτι, ἔξω γενομένας τῶν σωμάτων (*adeo persuasum habebat, nihil adhuc esse animas a corpore separatas*), *Philopseudes*, 32.

result of magnetic somnambulism and the more detailed observation of all
these things that sometimes take place in connection with visions. An
example of this kind can be found in the most captious spirit story of the
year 1697 that Brierre de Boismont recounts in his Observation 120; it is the
fact that only the upper half of his friend's spirit was visible to the young
man, although he spoke with him for three quarters of an hour. This partial
apparition of human forms has been confirmed in our times as a peculiarity
of visions of this kind occurring from time to time, which is why Brierre,
pp. 454 and 473 of his book, without referring to this story, mentions it
as a not infrequent phenomenon. Also Kieser (*Archiv*, vol. 3, no. 2, p. 139[a])
relates the same circumstance about the boy called Arst, but attributes it to
the alleged seeing with the tip of the nose. Accordingly, this factor in the
above-mentioned story provides the proof that this young man had at least
not made up the apparition. But then it would be difficult to explain it other
than through the influence, earlier promised to him and now carried out, by
his friend, who had drowned far away the day before. – Another circumstance of the kind in question here is the vanishing of apparitions as soon as
one intentionally focuses attention on them. This is already the case in the
above-mentioned passage in Pausanias about the audible apparitions on the
battlefield at Marathon, which were heard only by people who happened to
be there by chance, but not by those who had gone there on purpose. We
find analogous observations from most recent times in several passages of
Die Seherin von Prevorst (e.g. vol. 2, pp. 10 and 38), with the explanation that
what was perceived through the ganglionic system was immediately disputed by the brain. According to my hypothesis, it could be explained
through the sudden reversal in the direction of the vibration of the brain
fibres. – In passing, I wish to draw attention to a very striking correlation of
that kind. Photius says in his article *Damascius*: 'There was a holy woman
who had an incomprehensible gift bestowed by the gods. When she poured
pure water into a cup made of glass, she saw at the bottom of the water in the
cup the apparitions of future events; and according to what she had seen,
she perfectly predicted how they were destined to occur. The proof of the
matter has not escaped us.'[b] As inconceivable as it is, the exact same is

315

---

[a] [Vol. 3, no. 2 (1818); Kieser, 'Geschichte eines durch das unmagnetisierte Baquet allein erzeugten
Somnambulismus und hierdurch geheilter Epilepsie' (Story of a Somnambulism Produced solely
through an Unmagnetized Baquet and Epilepsy thereby Cured)]

[b] γυνὴ ἱερά, θεόμοιραν ἔχουσα φύσιν παραλογοτάτην· ὕδωρ γὰρ ἐγχέουσα ἀκραιφνὲς ποτηρίῳ τινὶ τῶν
ὑαλίνων, ἑώρα κατὰ τοῦ ὕδατος εἴσω τοῦ ποτηρίου τὰ φάσματα τῶν ἐσομένων πραγμάτων, καὶ
προὔλεγεν ἀπὸ τῆς ὄψεως αὐτά, ἅπερ ἔμελλεν ἔσεσθαι πάντως· ἡ δὲ πεῖρα τοῦ πράγματος οὐκ ἔλαθεν
ἡμᾶς. [Photius, *Bibliotheca*, 'Damascius' (130)]

reported by the seer of Prevorst, third edn., p. 87. – The character and type of spirit apparitions is so firmly determined and peculiar that anyone with experience, when reading such a story, can judge whether it was made up or based on an optical illusion or was an actual vision. It is to be wished and hoped for that we will soon receive a collection of Chinese ghost stories in order to see whether they too are essentially of the same type and character as ours and even show great correlation in minor circumstances and details, which, given the general fundamental difference of customs and religious doctrines, would provide a strong confirmation of the phenomenon in question. That the Chinese share the same idea as we do about the apparition of the deceased and the messages coming from them, is evident from the spirit apparition, albeit only fictitious, in the Chinese novella *Hing Lo Tou, ou la peinture mystérieuse*, translated by Stanislas Julien and published in his *Orphelin de la Chine, accompagné de Nouvelles et de poésies*, 1834.[a,28] – I also draw attention in this regard to the fact that most of the phenomena that make up the characteristic nature of spectres and ghosts, as they are described in the above-mentioned works by Hennings, Wenzel, Teller, etc., and later by Justinus Kerner, Horst and many others, are already found in very old books, for example in three works from the sixteenth century that I have in front of me just now, Lavater's *De spectris*, Thyraeus' *De locis infestis*, and *De spectris et apparitionibus*, Book 2, Eisleben, 1597, by Anonymous, 500 pages in four volumes.[b] Such phenomena are, for instance, rapping; the apparent attempt to force locked doors, even those that are not locked at all; the crashing of a very heavy weight falling down in the house; the noisy throwing-around of all the kitchen utensils, or the wood on the floor, which afterwards is found completely undisturbed and in order; the slamming of wine casks; the distinct nailing of a coffin, when someone in the house is about to die; the shuffling or faltering footsteps in a dark room; the tugging at the bedcover, the musty smell; the demand of prayers by appearing spirits; and so forth. It cannot be assumed that the authors of modern statements, who are mostly quite illiterate, have read these ancient, rare Latin writings. Among the arguments for the reality of spirit apparitions the tone of incredulity also deserves to be mentioned with which the scholars recount these statements second hand, since it normally

316

---

[a] [*Hing-Lo-Tou, ou la peinture mystérieuse*, trans. Stanislas Julien, in his *Tchao-chi-kou-eul, ou L'orphelin de la Chine, drame en prose et en vers, accompagné des pièces historiques qui on fourni le sujet, de nouvelles et de poésies chinoises* (*The Orphan from China, Drama in Prose and Verse, Accompanied by the Historical Pieces that Inspired it and Chinese News and Poems*), Paris: Montardier, 1834]

[b] [*Magica Seu mirabilium historiarum de Spectris et Apparitionibus Spirituum* (*Magic, or Miraculous Stories of Images and Apparitions of Spirits*), Eisleben: Henning Gross, 1597]

bears the stamp of coercion, affectation, and hypocrisy so very clearly that
the secret belief behind it filters through. – I wish to take this opportunity to
draw attention to a spirit story of recent times that deserves to be examined
more closely and to become better known than through its account, very
317   badly written, in the *Blätter aus Prevorst*, Collection 8, p. 166;[a] in part for the
reason that the statements about it are recorded by a court, and in part
because of the highly curious fact that the spirit that appeared was not seen
for several nights by the person to whom it related and in front of whose bed
it appeared, because that person was asleep, but was merely seen by two
fellow prisoners and only later by herself, who then, however, was so shaken
by this that of her own free will she confessed to seven poisonings. The
report is found in a brochure entitled: '*Verhandlungen des Assisenhofes in
Mainz über die Giftmörderin Margaretha Jäger*',[b] Mainz, 1835. – The verba-
tim protocolled statement is printed in the Frankfurt daily *Didaskalia*,[c]
5 July 1835. –

But now I have to consider the metaphysical aspect of the matter, since
what needs to be said about the physical, in this case physiological side, has
already been said above. – What arouses our interest with all the visions,
that is, intuitions through the opening of the dream-organ during wakefulness, is their possible relation to something empirically objective, i.e. located
outside of and different from us; for only through this relation do they
acquire an analogy and dignity equal to our ordinary sensuous intuitions
during waking. For this reason, of the nine possible causes of such visions
enumerated above, the first three, which amount to mere hallucinations, are
of no interest to us, but the others are. For the perplexity attached to the
consideration of visions and spirit apparitions originates in the fact that with
these perceptions the boundary between subject and object, which is the
first condition of all cognition, becomes doubtful, indistinct, and indeed
blurred. 'Is this outside of me or inside?' everyone will ask who is not robbed
of his sobriety by such a vision, as Macbeth does with the dagger floating in
front of him.[d] If somebody alone has seen a ghost, we wish to explain it as
merely subjective, however objectively it stood right there. However, if two
or more people saw or heard it, we will immediately attribute the reality of a
body to it, since empirically we only know *one* cause in virtue of which
several people must necessarily have the same intuitive representation at the
318   same time, namely that one and the same body, reflecting light to all sides,

---

[a] [(1837); see p. 249, n. b]
[b] [Trial at the Assize Court at Mainz about the Poisoner Margaretha Jäger]
[c] [*Didaskalia, Blätter für Geist, Gemüth und Publicität*]   [d] [Shakespeare, *Macbeth*, Act II, scene 1]

affects the eyes of them all. But apart from this very mechanical cause, there might be other causes of the simultaneous generation of the same intuitive representation in different people. Just as two people sometimes have the same dream at the same time (see above, p. 310[a]), that is, perceive the same matter through the dream-organ while being asleep, the dream-organ of two (or more) people can enter the same activity also during *waking*, whereby a ghost, seen by them simultaneously, presents itself objectively as a body.[29] Generally speaking, the difference between the subjective and the objective is basically not an absolute one, but always still relative; for everything objective is in turn subjective insofar as it is still determined by a subject in general; indeed, it is really only present in the subject, for which reason idealism is proved right in the end. Mostly we believe we have disproved the reality of a spirit apparition if we have demonstrated that it was subjectively conditioned. But what weight can this argument carry for somebody who knows from Kant's doctrine how large the share of subjective conditions is in the appearance of the corporeal world, namely that the latter, including space in which it exists, and time in which it moves, and causality in which the essence of matter consists, that is, in regard to its entire form, is merely a product of brain functions excited through a stimulus in the nerves of the sense organs, so that the only remaining question is the one concerning the thing in itself? – Of course, the *material* reality[b] of bodies acting on our senses from outside belongs as little to the spirit apparition as to the dream, through whose organ it is perceived, which is why we can call it a dream during wakefulness (a waking dream,[c] *insomnium sine somno*;[d] cp. Sonntag, *Sicilimentorum academicorum Fasciculus de Spectris et Ominibus morientium*, Altdorf,[e] 1716, p. 11); but at bottom it does not forfeit its reality[f] because of this. Like a dream, it is a mere representation and only as such present in cognitive consciousness. However, the same can be asserted in regard to our actual[g] external world, since this too is given to us initially and immediately only as representation and, as already pointed out, is a mere brain phenomenon, produced through a nerve stimulus and developed in accordance with the laws of subjective functions (forms of pure sensibility and under-   319 standing). If we require another reality for it, then this is already the question concerning the thing in itself, raised and prematurely settled by *Locke*, then demonstrated by *Kant* in its entire difficulty and indeed given

---

[a] [p. 256 of this edition]   [b] *Wirklichkeit*   [c] [Original English]   [d] [Dream without sleep]
[e] [Johann Michael Sonntag, *Sicilimentorum academicorum fasciculus de spectris et ominibus morientium* (*A Small Bundle of Academic Straw on Apparitions and Portents of the Dying*), Altdorf: Kohles, 1703 (first edn.)]
[f] *Realität*   [g] *realen*

up as insoluble, yet answered by me, albeit under a certain restriction. In any case, just as the thing in itself, which manifests itself in the appearance of an external world, is completely different[a] from it, so what manifests itself in the spirit apparition might be analogous to this, in fact, what makes itself known in both might in the end be the same, namely the *will*. In accordance with this view, in regard to the objective reality of the corporeal world as well as that of spirit apparitions, we find a realism, an idealism, and a scepticism, but ultimately also a criticism, whose interest we pursue right now. Indeed, an explicit confirmation of the same view is provided by the following statement of the most famous and most thoroughly scrutinized spirit-seer, the one from Prevorst (vol. 1, p. 12): 'Whether the spirits are only able to make themselves visible in this form, or whether my eye can only see them and my mind only comprehend them in this form; whether they would not be more spiritual for a more spiritual eye, that I cannot definitely assert, but I almost sense it.' Is this not completely analogous to the Kantian doctrine: 'What the things in themselves might be, we cannot know, but we know only their appearances' – ?

The entire demonology and spirit lore of antiquity and the Middle Ages, and also the views on magic associated with them, were grounded in the still undisputed *realism*, which finally was shaken by *Descartes*. Only *idealism*, which has gradually come to maturity in modern times, leads to the standpoint on the basis of which we can arrive at a correct judgement about all these things, also including visions and spirit apparitions. On the other hand, animal magnetism, proceeding empirically, has simultaneously brought *magic* out into the light of day, which in all previous times was shrouded in obscurity and anxiously concealed, and has also made spirit apparitions the subject of sober-mindedly investigative observation and impartial evaluation. The ultimate in all things always falls to philosophy, and I hope that my own, through the definite surrender of the objective world to *ideality*, has paved the way for the correct view even of visions and spirit apparitions, in the same way that it explained magic as at least conceivable and, if existent, as intelligible on the basis of the sole reality and omnipotence of the *will* in nature.*

The positive disbelief with which, on the one hand, the facts of clairvoyance, and on the other, those of magic, or in plain language,[b] magnetic influence, are at first perceived by every thinking human being – a disbelief

---

* See in *On Will in Nature*, the chapter 'Animal magnetism and magic'.

[a] toto genere *verschieden*   [b] *vulgo*

that only later yields to one's own experience or hundreds of credible testimonies – rests on one and the same ground: namely that both – clairvoyance with its cognition at a distance[a] and magic with its action at a distance – run counter to the laws of space, time, and causality, of which we are a priori conscious and which, in working together,[b] determine the course of possible experience. Hence, when such facts are related, people do not just say 'It is not true', but 'It is not possible' (from impossibility to unreality[c]), while others reply 'But it is' (from reality to possibility[d]). This antagonism rests on the fact, indeed, it even provides proof, that those laws known a priori are not unconditioned, not scholastic eternal truths,[e] not determinations of things in themselves, but spring from mere forms of intuition and understanding, hence from brain functions. The intellect itself, consisting of these, has arisen merely for the purpose of pursuing and achieving the objectives of individual appearances of the will, not for comprehending the absolute nature of things in themselves; for which reason it is, as I have already shown (*The World as Will and Representation*, vol. 2, pp. 177, 273, 285–9[f]), a mere surface force, which essentially relates everywhere to the outer shell, never to the inner core of things. Whoever really wishes to understand my meaning here should read those passages. Yet should we once succeed, since we ourselves too belong to the inner essence of the world, in evading the principle of individuation,[g] and reaching things from quite a different side and on quite a different path, namely directly from within instead of merely from outside, and in this way take possession of them, through cognition in clairvoyance and through action in magic, then we reach a result for cerebral cognition that was actually impossible for it to attain in its own way. Therefore, it insists on denying it; for an achievement of this kind can be understood only metaphysically, physically it is an impossibility. On the other hand, as a result, clairvoyance is a confirmation of the Kantian doctrine of the ideality of space, time, and causality; moreover, magic also confirms my doctrine of the sole reality of the *will* as the core of all things. This, in turn, confirms Bacon's dictum that magic is practical metaphysics.

321

We should now remind ourselves again of the discussions provided above and the physiological hypothesis advanced there, according to which all intuitions accomplished by the dream-organ are distinguished from ordinary perception, which constitutes the state of wakefulness, by the fact that in the case of the latter, the brain is stimulated from the outside, through

---

[a] *in distans*   [b] *in ihrem Komplex*   [c] *a non posse ad non esse*   [d] *ab esse ad posse*
[e] *veritates aeternae*   [f] [Hübscher *SW* 3, 195, 309, 322–6]   [g] *principium individuationis*

physical action on the senses, whereby it receives the data on the basis of which it brings about empirical intuition by means of applying its functions, that is, causality, time, and space. In regard to intuition through the dream-organ, on the other hand, the stimulation starts from within the organism and travels from the malleable[a] nervous system to the brain. This causes the brain to have an intuition very similar to the former one caused from outside, but in regard to which it is to be assumed, since the excitation comes from the opposite side and, therefore, also happens in the opposite direction, that the vibrations, or in general the internal movements of the brain fibres, also occur in reverse direction and, consequently, only in the end extend to the sensuous nerves. These are then the last to be stirred into action, instead of being stimulated first, as in ordinary intuition. Now if, as is assumed in truth-dreams, prophetic visions and spirit apparitions, such an intuition is supposed to refer to something actually external, empirically existent, totally independent of the subject, which accordingly would be recognized through this intuition, then this external object must have somehow communicated with the *interior* of the organism, from where the intuition is caused. However, such communication cannot be empirically proved; in fact, since, according to our assumption, it is not supposed to be spatial, coming from the *outside*, it is not even intelligible empirically, i.e. physically. If it takes place nevertheless, we can understand this communication only metaphysically and think it as occurring independently of appearance and all its laws, in the thing in itself, which, as the inner essence of things, lies everywhere at the basis of an appearance, and as afterwards being perceivable in the appearance. This is what is understood under the name of a magical action.

If we ask what is the path of the magical effect that is given to us in the sympathetic cure as well as in the influence of the distant magnetizer, I say that it is the path covered by the insect that dies here and re-emerges fully alive from every egg that has hibernated. It is the path whereby it happens that in a given population, births will increase after an extraordinary increase in the number of deaths. It is the path that does not pass through time and space led by the string of causality. It is the path through the thing in itself.

Now we know from my philosophy that this thing in itself, and that means also the inner essence of a human being, is the *will*, and that everyone's entire organism, in the way that it manifests itself empirically, is merely the objectivation of the will, or more precisely, the image of this will that arises in the brain. But the will as thing in itself lies outside of the

---

[a] *plastischen*

principle of individuation (time and space), by means of which individuals are *separate*; the boundaries engendered by this principle do not exist for the will. As far as our insight reaches when we enter this region, this explains the possibility of *immediate* action of individuals on each other, independently of their proximity or remoteness in space, which makes itself factually known in some of the above-described nine types of waking intuition by means of the dream-organ, and more often in sleeping intuition. In the same way, the possibility of truth-dreaming, the awareness of the immediate surroundings in somnambulism, and finally clairvoyance, can be explained through this immediate communication, grounded in the essence in itself of things. By virtue of the will of one person, limited by no boundaries of individuation, acting immediately and at a distance on the will of another, this will has acted on the organism of the latter, which is merely his spatially intuited will itself. When such an influence, reaching the inside of the organism through this path, extends to its guide and principal, the ganglionic system, and then from there travels to the brain by breaking through the isolation, it can be processed by the brain only in a brain-like manner, i.e. it will produce intuitions that do not care which ones arise through external stimulation of the senses, hence images in space, according to its three dimensions, with movement in time according to the law of causality, etc.; for both are just the products of intuitive brain function; and the brain can only speak its own language. Meanwhile, such an influence will still bear the character, the mark, of its origin, of that from which it has arisen, and impress this on to the shape that it causes in the brain after such a wide detour, as different as its essence in itself may be from that shape. For example, if a dying person, through intense yearning or some other intention of the will, acts on somebody far away, his form will manifest itself in the brain of the other if the influence is very forceful, i.e. will appear to him like a body in reality. Obviously, such an influence on another brain, occurring from inside of the organism, will happen more easily if that brain is asleep than if it is awake, because in the former case the fibres are not moving, in the latter they are moving in a direction opposite to the one they are to assume. Consequently, a weaker influence of the kind in question will manifest itself merely during sleep, by causing dreams; during waking it will at best stimulate thoughts, sensations, and disquiet; but all according to its origin and its character. Thus such an influence can, for instance, produce an inexplicable, but irresistible drive, or pull, to seek out the one from whom it came; and also, conversely, to drive away the one who wants to enter from the very doorstep of the house by means of the wish not to see him, even if he was summoned and sent for. ('Believe Robert who

323

324

experienced it himself.'[a]) The contagious nature of visions, second sight and spirit-seeing, which is factually attested, is based on this influence, whose ground is the identity of the thing in itself in all appearances; this contagiousness brings about an effect that in its result equals the one that a corporeal object has simultaneously upon the senses of several individuals, so that, consequently, several people see the same object, which is then objectively constituted. The immediate communication of thoughts that is often noticed rests on the same direct action; it is so certain that I advise anyone who has to keep an important and dangerous secret never to discuss the whole affair with the one who is not allowed to know it, because during such discussion he is inevitably bound to have the true state of affairs in mind, and then the other could suddenly see the light, as a kind of communication exists from which neither discretion nor disguise shield. Goethe recounts (in the elucidations to the *West-Eastern Divan*, under the heading 'Exchange of Flowers'[b]) that two loving couples on an excursion set each other charades: 'Soon each one is not only guessed at once as it is uttered, but in the end the word that the other thinks of and wants to make into a word puzzle is recognized and pronounced by the most immediate divination.' – Many years ago, my beautiful landlady in Milan asked me during a very animated conversation at the dinner-table what the three numbers were that she had assigned as a group of three in the lottery. Without thinking I named the first and second correctly, but then, puzzled by her cheers and now awake and reflecting, I named the third one wrongly. As is well known, the highest degree of such influence takes place with very clairvoyant somnambulists, who precisely and accurately describe to their interrogators their distant native countries, their dwellings there, or otherwise far away countries where they have travelled. The thing in itself is the same in all beings, and the state of clairvoyance enables the person in this state to think with my brain instead of his own, which is fast asleep.[30]

On the other hand, since we are certain that the *will*, insofar as it is the thing in itself, is not destroyed and annihilated through death, the possibility cannot outright be denied a priori that a magical effect of the kind described above might not also come from somebody already dead. However, such a possibility can just as little be clearly predicted and thus positively asserted, insofar as, even if it is not inconceivable in general, on

[a] *experto crede Roberto* [after Virgil, *Aeneid* XI, 283; the medieval version of the saying added the name 'Robert']
[b] *Blumenwechsel* [Johann Wolfgang von Goethe, '*Noten und Abhandlungen zum West-Östlichen Diwan*' (Notes and Essays on the West-Eastern Divan, 1827), Rubrik '*Blumen- und Zeichenwechsel*']

closer inspection it is nonetheless subject to great difficulties, which I now wish to state briefly. – Since we must think the inner essence of human beings, which remains intact in death, as existing outside of time and space, its influence on us living could only take place through numerous media-tions, all on our side. For that reason, it would be difficult to detect how much of it had actually come from the deceased. For such an influence would not only first have to enter the forms of intuition of the subject perceiving it, hence manifest itself as something materially acting according to space, time, and the law of causality, but in addition it would also have to enter into association with the subject's conceptual thinking, since other-wise the person would not know what to make of it. However, the ones who appear not only wish to be seen, but also want to be more or less understood in their purposes and corresponding influences; consequently, they would also have to submit to and follow the limited views and prejudices of the subject with respect to the totality of things and the world. But there is even more! It is not just according to my entire exposition so far that spirits are seen through the dream-organ and as a result of an action reaching the brain from within, instead of the usual action from outside through the senses, but J. Kerner, who firmly upholds the objective reality of spirit apparitions, says the same in his frequently repeated assertion that the spirits 'are seen not with the bodily, but with the mind's eye'. Accordingly, although it is produced through an inner influence on the organism, springing from the essence in itself of things, and hence a magical influence, which travels by means of the ganglionic system to the brain, the spirit apparition is never-theless grasped in the manner of objects acting on us from outside through light, air, sound, impact, and smell. What a change would the alleged influence of a deceased have to undergo during such a translation, such a total meta-schematism![a] But how can we then assume that, with such a change and through such detours, a real dialogue could take place, going back and forth, as is often reported? – Incidentally I wish to mention here that the ridiculous aspect, which along with the horrible more or less attaches to every claim to have had an apparition of this kind and on account of which one hesitates to disclose it, stems from the fact that the person reporting it speaks as though about a perception through the external senses, which, however, certainly did not exist, if only for the reason that otherwise a spirit would always be seen and heard by all those present. But to distinguish a merely apparently external perception that has arisen from inner action from mere fantasy is not something everyone is able to do. – Assuming an

326

---

[a] *Metaschematismus*

actual spirit apparition, these are the difficulties on the side of the perceiving subject. Other difficulties exist on the side of the allegedly acting deceased. According to my doctrine, the *will* alone has metaphysical essentiality,[a] in virtue of which it is indestructible through death. The intellect, on the other hand, as function of a bodily organ, is merely physical and perishes together with it. Therefore, the way in which the dead could still attain knowledge of the living in order to act on them accordingly is highly problematic. No less problematic is the manner of this action itself, since together with their corporeality, they have lost all ordinary, i.e. physical, means of acting on others as well as the physical world in general. Nevertheless, if we wanted to allow some truth to the incidents that are reported and maintained from so many and various sides and which definitely show an objective influence of the dead, we would have to explain the matter in such a way that in these cases the will of the deceased was still passionately directed towards earthly affairs and now, lacking all physical means of influence on them, resorted to its *magical* power, that belonged to it in its original and hence metaphysical capacity, consequently in death as in life, which I have touched upon above. I have expounded my thoughts on this in greater detail in *On Will in Nature*, under the heading 'Animal magnetism and magic'. Therefore, only in virtue of this *magical* power might the will be able to do what it could possibly do when still alive, namely perform actual action at a distance,[b] without bodily assistance, and hence directly act on others, without any physical mediation, by affecting their organism in such a way that shapes would have to present themselves to them intuitively, as the organism otherwise produces them only as a result of external action on the senses. Indeed, since this influence is conceivable only as magic, i.e. achieved through the inner essence of things identical in all, hence through naturing nature,[c] so, if the honour of the respected people who report these incidents could be saved only in this way, we could at most venture the awkward step of not limiting it to an influence on human organisms, but also allow it to be not absolutely impossible for inanimate, in other words for inorganic bodies, which consequently could be moved through it. This we could do in order to avoid the necessity of accusing certain stories that are sworn to be true of being outright lies, such as that told by Privy Councillor Hahn in *Die Seherin von Prevorst*, because the latter is by no means an isolated case, but can boast quite a few quite similar equivalent pieces in older writings and, indeed, also in newer reports. However, here the matter borders on the absurd; for even the magical mode of action, insofar as it is legitimately

327

[a] *Wesenheit*   [b] *actio in distans*   [c] *natura naturans*

attested by animal magnetism, until now provides at most *one* weak and, moreover, doubtful analogue for such an action, which is the fact, asserted in the *Mittheilungen aus dem Schlafleben der Auguste K. . . zu Dresden*, 1843,[a] pp. 115 and 318, that this somnambulist had repeatedly succeeded in diverting the magnetic needle through her mere will, without using her hands. The same is recounted by Ennemoser (*Anleitung zur Mesmerischen Praxis*, 328 1852[b]) about a somnambulist, Kachler: 'The clairvoyante Kachler moved the magnetic needle not only by pointing her fingers, but also through her gaze. She directed her gaze to the north point from approximately half a yard away, and after a few seconds the needle turned four degrees to the west; as soon as she pulled back her head and averted her gaze, the needle returned to its former position.'[c] In London too the same happened with the somnambulist Prudence Bernard in a public session and in the presence of selected, competent witnesses.[31]

The view of the problem in question presented here explains first of all why, even if we wish to admit an actual influence of dead people on the world of the living to be possible, such an influence could happen only very rarely and by way of exception, because its possibility would be tied to all the conditions mentioned, which do not easily occur together. Furthermore, this view entails that, if we neither declare the facts reported in *Die Seherin von Prevorst* and the related writings by Kerner, as the most extensive and substantiated reports of spirit-seeing published in print, to be purely subjective, mere dreams of the sick,[d] nor are satisfied with the above-discussed assumption of retrospective second sight,[e] for whose dumb shew[f] (silent procession) the seer had added the dialogue from her own resources, but instead wish to assume an actual influence of the deceased as the ground of the matter, then the flagrantly absurd, indeed infamously stupid world-order emerging from the statements and attitudes of these spirits would still not gain any objectively real ground. On the contrary, it would have to be attributed to the intuitive and cognitive activity of the highly ignorant seer, thoroughly immersed in the beliefs of the catechism, an activity that, albeit stirred by an influence coming from outside of nature, nevertheless remains true to itself.

---

[a] [See p. 215, n. c]

[b] [Joseph Ennemoser, *Anleitung zur Mesmerischen Praxis* (*Manual for Mesmeric Practice*), Stuttgart and Tübingen: Cotta, 1852]

[c] [p. 109; actually, Ennemoser quotes here from *Mittheilungen aus dem Schlafleben der Somnambule Auguste K. in Dresden*; the somnambulist Kachler, therefore, is identical with Auguste K.]

[d] *aegri somnia* [Horace, *The Art of Poetry*, 7]　　[e] [Original English]　　[f] [Original English]

In any case, a spirit apparition is, at first and immediately, nothing but a vision in the brain of the spirit-seer; that somebody dying can trigger such an apparition is confirmed by frequent experience; that a living person could do it as well, is also attested in several cases; the question is just whether also somebody deceased could do it.

Ultimately, in explaining spirit apparitions we could also insist that the distinction between those who lived in the past and those living now is not an absolute one, but that in both one and the same will to life appears, so that a living person, harking back, might bring to light reminiscences that manifest themselves as messages from a deceased.[32]

If in these observations I should have been successful in throwing even a weak light on a very important and interesting matter, in regard to which two parties have faced each other for thousands of years, of which the one persistently assures 'it is!', while the other stubbornly repeats 'it cannot be', then I shall have achieved everything that I was allowed to promise myself and that the reader had the right to expect of me.

*Le bonheur n'est pas chose aisée: il est très difficile de le trouver en nous,
et impossible de le trouver ailleurs.*

[Happiness is no easy matter; it is very difficult to find in ourselves and
impossible to find elsewhere.]

Chamfort
[Nicolas Chamfort, *Maximes, Pensées, Caractères et Anecdotes*,
Part 2, 'Caractères et Anecdotes']

Introduction

I take the concept of wisdom of life entirely in the immanent sense here,
namely that of the art of living life as pleasantly and happily as possible,
instructions to which might also be called eudaemonology. Accordingly,
they are instructions to a happy existence. This, in turn, could at most be
defined as an existence that, considered purely objectively or rather after
cool and careful consideration (since what matters here is a subjective
judgement), would be decidedly preferable to non-existence. It follows
from this concept that we would be attached to it for its own sake and
not merely from the fear of death, and from this that we would like to see it
last forever. Now, whether human life corresponds to such a concept of
existence, or is even capable of doing so, is a question that my philosophy, as
is well known, answers in the negative, whereas eudaemonology presupposes an affirmative answer. For eudaemonology is based upon the innate
error that I rebuke at the beginning of ch. 49 of vol. 2 of my chief work.[a] In
order to be able to develop such a doctrine, I have had to abandon
completely the higher, metaphysical–ethical standpoint to which my philosophy proper leads. Consequently, the entire discussion to be presented

---

[a] [*WWR* 2, Hübscher *SW* 3, 729]

here is in a way an accommodation, namely insofar as it retains the ordinary,
334   empirical standpoint and adheres to its error. Hence its value can only be a
conditional one, since even the term eudaemonology itself is merely a
euphemism. – Furthermore, the discussion makes no claim to completeness, in part because the subject matter is inexhaustible, in part because
otherwise I would have to repeat what has already been said by others.

The only book I can recall that is written with a similar intent as the
present aphorisms is Cardanus' *On the Utility of Adversity*,[a] which is well
worth reading and with the help of which one can complete what is
provided here. Aristotle too included a short eudaemonology in Book I,
ch. 5, of his *Rhetoric*, but it turned out very dry. I have not used these
predecessors, since compiling is not my aim, the less so as the unity of
perspective is lost through it, which is the soul of this kind of work. –
Generally, the sages of all ages have always said the same, and the fools, i.e.
the vast majority in all eras, have always done the same, namely the
opposite; and so it will always be. Therefore, Voltaire says: 'We will leave
this world as stupid and nasty as we found it when we came into it.'[b]

[a] *De utilitate ex adversis capienda* [Hieronymus Cardanus (Girolamo Cardano), 1561]
[b] *nous laisserons* [...] *ce monde-ci aussi sot et aussi méchant que nous l'avons trouvé en y arrivant* [Voltaire,
Letter to Madame la Comtesse de Lutzelbourg, 19 March 1760]

CHAPTER I

Fundamental division

Aristotle (*Nicomachean Ethics* I, 8) divided the goods of human life into three classes – those coming from outside, those of the soul, and those of the body. Retaining nothing but the triad itself, I claim that what makes the difference in the lot of mortals may be reduced to three fundamental stipulations. They are:

(1) What one *is*: that is, personality in the widest sense. Hence this includes health, strength, beauty, temperament, moral character, and intelligence and its cultivation.

(2) What one *has*: that is, property and possessions in every sense.

(3) What one *represents*: By this expression we usually mean what someone is in the eyes of others, thus how he *is represented* by them. Hence it consists in their opinion of him and is divided into honour, rank, and fame.

The differences to be considered under the first category are ones that nature itself has created between human beings, from which we can conclude that their influence on people's happiness or unhappiness will be much more essential and drastic than what is effected by the differences arising merely from human determinations and mentioned under the subsequent two categories. All the advantages of rank, birth, even royal birth, wealth, and so on, relate to *genuine personal merits* – such as a great mind or a great heart – as kings on the stage relate to kings in real life. *Metrodorus*, the first disciple of Epicurus, already titled a chapter: 'The cause of happiness that arises from within ourselves is greater than that which comes from things.' – See Clement of Alexandria, *Stromata* II, 21, p. 362 of the Würzburg edn. of the *Opera Polemica*.[a,1] And the principal element in the well-being of human beings, indeed, in the entire manner of their

336

---

[a] περὶ τοῦ μείζονα εἶναι τὴν παρ ἡμᾶς αἰτίαν πρὸς εὐδαιμονίαν τῆς ἐκ τῶν πραγμάτων (*Majorem esse causam ad felicitatem eam, quae est ex nobis, eâ, quae ex rebus oritur*) [Clement of Alexandria, *Sanctorum Patrum Opera Polemica de veritate religionis Christianae contra Gentiles et Judaeos*]

existence, is what exists or happens within themselves. For it is actually here that our inner satisfaction or dissatisfaction is immediately located, which is primarily the result of our sensing, willing, and thinking, whereas anything external only has an indirect influence on it. Hence the same external events or circumstances affect each one of us completely differently; and even in the same environment, everybody lives in a different world. For we are immediately concerned only with our own representations, feelings, and movements of the will; external things only influence us as far as they cause these. The world in which everybody lives depends first of all on our apprehension[a] of it; therefore, it conforms to the diversity of minds; accordingly, it will turn out poor, dull, and superficial, or rich, interesting, and full of meaning. For example, while many envy another for the interesting events happening to him in his life, they should really envy him for the gift of apprehension that imparted to those events the significance they have in his description; for the same incident that appears so interesting to an ingenious mind would only be an insipid scene from the everyday world when perceived by a shallow ordinary mind. This becomes apparent to the highest degree in some poems by Goethe and Byron, which are obviously based on real events; a foolish reader is able to envy the poet the most delightful incident instead of the powerful imagination that is capable of transforming a rather mundane incident into something great and beautiful.[2] In the same way the melancholic person sees tragedy in a scene, where the sanguine person has only an interesting conflict before him, and the phlegmatic one something without meaning. All this is due to the fact that each reality, i.e. each fulfilled present, consists of two halves, subject and object, albeit necessarily and closely connected, like oxygen and hydrogen in water. Hence with the same objective half, but a different subjective one, the present reality is completely different, just as it is in the converse case: the most beautiful and best objective half combined with a dull, poor subjective one renders only a bad reality and present, like beautiful scenery in bad weather or in the reflection of a bad *camera obscura*. Or to put it more plainly: We all are stuck in our consciousness, as in our skin, and immediately live only inside of it; hence we cannot easily be helped from the outside. On stage, one actor plays the prince, another the councillor, a third the servant, or the soldier, or the general, and so forth. However, these differences exist only externally; internally, at the core of such appearance, the same exists in everyone: a poor comedian with his wants and worries. In life it is the same; the differences of rank and wealth

337

---

[a] *Auffassung*

give everyone his role to play; but no internal difference of happiness and satisfaction corresponds to it. Here too the same poor devil is to be found in everyone, with his needs and troubles that, in regard to their content, are different in everybody, but in regard to form, i.e. their essential nature, are more or less the same in all of us, although with differences of degree which, however, do not depend at all on social position and wealth, i.e., the role we play.[3] Since everything that exists and happens for human beings always exists only in, and happens for, their *consciousness*, obviously the constitution of consciousness itself is first of all essential, and in most cases more depends on this constitution than on the shapes that appear in consciousness. All luxuriance and pleasures, reflected in the dull consciousness of a dunce, are utterly poor when compared with the consciousness of *Cervantes* as he wrote *Don Quixote* in an uncomfortable prison. – The objective half of reality and the present is in the hands of fate and, consequently, is changeable; the subjective half is we ourselves, and so is essentially unchangeable. Accordingly, the life of every human being, despite all changes from the outside, bears the same character throughout and is comparable to a series of variations on *one* theme. No one can escape his individuality. And just as it is with animals, which in all the circum-   338
stances in which we place them remain limited to the narrow sphere that nature has irrevocably drawn around their essential being – which is why, for instance, our attempts to make a beloved animal happy must always remain within narrow bounds due to the limits of its being and consciousness – so it is with human beings: because of their individuality the measure of their possible happiness is determined in advance. In particular, the limits of their mental powers have once and for all established their capacity for higher pleasures. (See *The World as Will and Representation*, vol. 2, p. 73.[a]) If these limits are narrow, all efforts from the outside, everything that people, everything that good luck does for them, will not be able to raise them above ordinary, half-animal human happiness and comfort; they remain dependent on pleasures of the senses, homely and cheerful family life, base company, and vulgar pastimes. Even education, on the whole, cannot do much, just a little, to widen this horizon. For the highest, most diverse, and most permanent pleasures are those of the mind, as much as we may deceive ourselves about this when we are young; but these depend mainly on an inborn capacity.[4] – This makes it clear how much our happiness depends on what we *are*, on our individuality; whereas for the most part we take into account only our fate,[b] only what we *have*, or what

---

[a] [Hübscher *SW* 3, 79]   [b] *Schicksal*

we *represent*. Fate, however, can improve; moreover, we will not ask much of it if we are inwardly rich. A poor wretch, on the other hand, remains a wretch, a dunce remains a dunce to the end of his life, even if he were in paradise surrounded by houris. Hence Goethe says:

> Nations, rulers, slaves subjected
> All on this one point agree:
> Joy of earthlings is perfected
> In the personality. *West-Eastern Divan*[a]

That the subjective is incomparably more essential for our happiness and our pleasure than the objective is confirmed by everything: from the fact that hunger is the best sauce and that the old man looks with indifference at the goddess of the young, to the life of the genius and the saint. Especially health so far outweighs all external goods that a healthy beggar is truly more fortunate than a king in poor health. A calm and cheerful temperament resulting from perfect health and a lucky bodily organization, a clear, lively, penetrating and accurately comprehending understanding, a moderate, gentle will, and consequently a good conscience – these are advantages for which no rank or wealth can compensate. For what somebody is in himself, what accompanies him in solitude, and what nobody can give him or take away from him, is obviously more essential to him than anything that he possesses or that he may be in the eyes of others. A witty person, all alone, has excellent entertainment in his own thoughts and fantasies, whereas in a dullard the continuous diversion of parties, plays, excursions, and amusements cannot fend off the torments of boredom. A good, moderate, gentle character can be contented in meagre circumstances, whereas a greedy, envious, and malicious one is not in spite of all his wealth. Indeed, for the person who continuously enjoys an extraordinary, intellectually eminent personality, most of the generally desired pleasures are entirely superfluous, even just troublesome and annoying. Hence Horace says of himself:

> Gems, marble, ivory, Etruscan figurines, pictures,
> Silver, clothes dyed in Gaetulian purple,
> Many there are who own none, one who does not care to own.[b]

---

[a] [Goethe, *West-Eastern Divan* ('Buch Suleika' [Book of Suleika]): '*Volk und Knecht und Überwinder*' [26 September 1815]. This and all subsequent translations of passages from the *West-Eastern Divan* are by John Whaley (*Poems of the West and East*. Bilingual edn., Frankfurt and New York: Peter Lang, 1998)]

[b] *Gemmas, marmor, ebur, Tyrrhena sigilla, tabellas, / Argentum, vestes Gaetulo murice tinctas, / Sunt qui non habeant, est qui non curat habere* [Horace, *Epistles* II, 2, 180–2]

And Socrates, when looking at luxury articles displayed for sale, says: 'How many things there are I do not need.'[a]

Accordingly, what we *are*, our personality, is primary and essential for our life's happiness, if only because it is active at all times and under all circumstances. Moreover, it is not subject to fate, as the goods in the two other categories, and cannot be taken away from us. Therefore, its value can be called absolute, in contrast with the merely relative value of the other two. From this it follows that people can be much less influenced from the outside than we normally think. Only all-powerful time exercises its right even here; all bodily and intellectual advantages gradually succumb to her; the moral character alone cannot be touched by it. In this respect the goods 340 of the last two categories, of which time does not immediately rob us, have an advantage. We might find a second advantage in that, being objective, they are by their nature achievable and everyone has at least the possibility of coming into their possession; whereas the subjective is not within our power, but, having arisen by divine right,[b] is immutably fixed for our entire life; so that here the saying inexorably applies:

> When you were granted here your brief admission,
> As sun and planets met that day they charted
> For evermore your growing to fruition
> According to the law by which you started.
> Thus must you be, from self there's no remission,
> Thus long have sibyls, prophets this imparted;
> Nor any time nor any power can shatter
> Imprinted form informing living matter.   Goethe[c]

The only thing that is in our power in this respect is to use our given personality to the greatest possible advantage, hence only pursue aspirations that are in accordance with it, strive after the kind of education that is appropriate to it and avoid all others, and consequently choose the position, the occupation, and the way of life suitable for it.

A Herculean person, possessing extraordinary muscle strength, forced by external circumstances to follow a sedentary occupation and perform minute and painstaking manual tasks, or to pursue studies and intellectual tasks that require quite different powers not pronounced in him, and hence to leave exactly those powers untapped in which he excels, this person will be unhappy throughout his life. Even more so will that person be unhappy in whom the intellectual powers predominate and who must leave them

---

[a] [Diogenes Laertius, *Lives and Opinions of Eminent Philosophers* II, 25]   [b] *jure divino*
[c] [Goethe, *Primal Words, Orphic*, 'Daimon' (1817); trans. John Whaley]

undeveloped and unused in order to pursue a common business that has no use for them, or even manual labour, for which his strength is not quite adequate. However, here we must avoid the abyss of presumption, especially in youth, so that we do not attribute to ourselves an excess of powers we do not possess.[5]

341   It follows from the definite prevalence of our first category over the other two that it is wiser to work towards maintaining our health and developing our abilities than acquiring wealth, which, however, must not be misinterpreted as meaning that we should neglect to acquire what is necessary and appropriate. But real wealth, i.e. great affluence, can do little for our happiness, which is why many rich people are unhappy, since they live without proper cultivation of the mind, without knowledge and hence any objective interest that could enable them to engage in intellectual pursuits. For what wealth can accomplish beyond the satisfaction of actual and natural needs has little influence on our real well-being; on the contrary, our comfort is disturbed by the many inevitable worries created by preserving a large estate. Nevertheless, people are a thousand times more anxious to acquire wealth than culture of the mind; whereas what we *are* surely contributes much more to our happiness than what we *have*. Hence we see quite a few people, in restless activity, industrious like ants, trying from morning to night to increase the wealth they already have. Beyond the narrow horizon of the means to this end they know nothing; their minds are empty and hence unreceptive to anything else. The highest pleasures, those of the mind, are inaccessible to them; and in vain do they try to replace them by the fleeting, sensuous ones, costing little time but a lot of money, which they indulge in now and then. At the end of their lives then, as a result, they really have a large pile of money, if they are lucky, which they leave to their heirs either to increase further or to squander. Such a life, though plainly lived with an air of great seriousness and importance, is as foolish as many another that wore a fool's cap as its symbol.

    Hence what somebody *has in himself* is most essential for his life's happiness. Because normally this is not very much, most of those people who have left the fight against want behind them are at bottom just as unhappy as those who are still engaged in it. The emptiness of their inner

342 life, the dullness of their consciousness, the poverty of their mind make them seek company, which, however, consists of people just like them, because 'like takes pleasure in like'.[a] So together they hunt for diversion and entertainment, which they initially seek in sensuous pleasures, in every kind

---

[a] *similis simili gaudet*

of amusement, and finally in excesses. The source of the fatal extravagance with which many a son of a family entering life with riches squanders his large inheritance within an incredibly short period of time, is really nothing but the boredom that has its source in the poverty and emptiness of mind just described. Such a young man was sent into the world outwardly rich, but inwardly poor, and now tried in vain to supplant inner with external wealth by wanting to receive everything *from outside* – like old men who seek to strengthen themselves through the perspiration of young women. And so in the end, inner poverty also led to external poverty.

The importance of the other two categories of goods of human life I do not need to stress. For the value of property is nowadays so universally acknowledged that it has no need for recommendation. The third category, in comparison with the second, even has a quite ethereal nature, since it consists merely in the opinion of others. But everyone must strive for honour, i.e. a good name; those who serve the state must strive for rank; and only very few aspire to fame. Meanwhile, honour is seen as an invaluable good, and fame as the most precious possession that a human being can attain, the Golden Fleece of the chosen; on the other hand, only fools will prefer rank to possessions. The second and third category, by the way, stand in a so-called reciprocal relation, insofar as Petronius' maxim: 'A man is judged by what he has',[a] is true and, conversely, the favourable opinion of others, in all its forms, often helps us obtain possessions.

---

[a] *habes, habeberis* [Petronius, *Satyricon*, 77]

CHAPTER II

What one is

That this contributes much more to a person's happiness than what he *has*, or what he *represents*, we have already recognized in general. All depends on what someone is and, accordingly, has in himself; for his individuality accompanies him at all times and in all places; it colours all that he experiences. In and through everything he initially enjoys only himself; this is true of the bodily, but much more of the intellectual pleasures. Hence the English 'to enjoy one's self' is a very fitting expression, with which, for example, we say 'he enjoys himself at Paris',[a] thus not 'he enjoys Paris', but 'he enjoys *himself* in Paris'. – However, if the individual character is badly constituted, all pleasures are like delicious wines in a mouth full of bile. Accordingly, in good times and bad times, leaving aside great calamities, it is less important what befalls us in life than how we feel about it, hence what is the nature and the degree of our receptivity in every respect. What someone is and has within himself, in short, personality and its worth, is the only thing that immediately counts for his happiness and well-being. Everything else is mediate; consequently, its effects can be frustrated, but those of personality never. For that reason, envy directed towards personal merits is the most unforgiving, as it is also the most carefully concealed. Moreover, the constitution of consciousness alone is persistent and enduring, and individuality acts constantly and incessantly, more or less at every moment; everything else only acts from time to time, occasionally, temporarily, and is also subject to reversal and transformation. Hence Aristotle says: 'Nature is permanent, but wealth is not.'[b] Because of this we bear a misfortune that has befallen us entirely from the outside with more composure than one that is self-inflicted; for fate can change, but one's own nature never. Accordingly, the subjective goods, such as a noble character, a capable

---

[a] [Both phrases in English]

[b] ἡ γὰρ φύσις βεβαία, οὐ τὰ χρήματα, [βέβαιον in original] (*nam natura perennis est, non opes*). *Ethica Eudemia* [*Eudemian Ethics*] VII, 2 [1238a13–14].

mind, a happy temperament, a cheerful spirit, and a perfectly healthy body in good condition, thus in general 'a healthy mind in a healthy body'[a] (Juvenal, *Satires* X, 356), are the primary and most important elements in our happiness; which is why we should be much more concerned about promoting and preserving them than about possessing external goods and external honour.

But of all these goods, what makes us most immediately happy is a cheerful spirit;[b] for this good quality automatically rewards itself. Whoever is cheerful has good reason to be, namely the fact that he is. No other quality can completely replace every other good the way this one can. People may be young, beautiful, rich, and honoured; but if we wish to judge their happiness,[c] we will ask whether they are cheerful. On the other hand, if they are cheerful, it does not matter whether they are young or old, straight or hunchbacked, poor or rich; they are happy. In my early youth I once opened an old book, and there it said: 'Whoever laughs a lot is happy, and whoever cries a lot is unhappy' – a very simple-minded remark, which nonetheless I have not been able to forget because of its plain truth, as much as it is the superlative of a truism.[d] For this reason, whenever it appears we should open wide the door for cheerfulness, since it never comes at the wrong time; instead of having misgivings about letting it in, insofar as we first want to know whether we have every reason to be content, or because we fear being disturbed by it in our serious reflections and important concerns. However, what we improve by means of them is very uncertain; in contrast, cheerfulness is an immediate gain. It alone is, so to speak, the genuine coin[e] of happiness and not, like everything else, merely the paper money, for it makes us immediately happy in the present, which is why it is the highest good for a being whose reality has the form of an indivisible present between two eternities. Therefore, we should have the attainment and promotion of this good precede any other striving. Now it is certain that nothing contributes less to cheerfulness than wealth, and nothing more than health; cheerful and contented faces are found among the low, working classes, especially those who cultivate the land; morose faces are at home among the rich. Consequently, we should above all strive to maintain a high degree of perfect health, whose flourishing entails cheerfulness. The means for this, as is well known, are the avoidance of all excesses and debaucheries, of all violent and disagreeable emotions, also all mental exertion that is too great or too prolonged, two hours daily of brisk movement in fresh air,

345

---

[a] *mens sana in corpore sano*   [b] *die Heiterkeit des Sinnes*   [c] *Glück*   [d] [truism: original English]
[e] *baare Münze*

much cold bathing and similar dietary measures. Without proper daily exercise no one can stay healthy; all vital processes, in order to function properly, require movement of the parts in which they take place as well as of the whole. Hence Aristotle rightly says: 'Life consists in movement.'[a] Life is movement and has its essence within it. The entire inside of the organism consists in constant, rapid movement: the heart, in its complicated double systole and diastole, beats fiercely and untiringly; with its twenty-eight beats it drives the entire volume of blood through the entire large and small circulation; the lungs pump unceasingly like a steam engine; the intestines always writhe in peristaltic movement;[b] all the glands constantly absorb and secrete; even the brain shows a double movement with every pulse and every breath. Now if there is an almost complete lack of external movement, as is the case in regard to the completely sedentary way of life of innumerable people, a glaring and harmful imbalance arises between external calm and internal turmoil. For the constant internal movement must be supported to some extent by an external one; that imbalance is analogous to the one when, as a result of some affect, we are seething internally, but are not allowed to let any of it be seen from the outside. Even trees, in order to thrive, need to be moved by the wind. Here a rule applies that can be expressed most succinctly in Latin: *omnis motus, quo celerior, eo magis motus.*[c,6] – How much our happiness depends on cheerfulness of mood and this, in turn, on the state of our health, is seen when we compare the impression made on us by the same external circumstances or incidents on healthy and vigorous days with that produced when sickliness has made us morose and anxious. Not what things are objectively and actually, but what they are for us, in our apprehension, makes us happy or unhappy. This is exactly what Epictetus says: 'What disturbs human beings is not things, but opinions about things.'[d] In general, nine-tenths of our happiness depends on our health alone. With health, everything becomes a source of pleasure; without it, no external good, whatever kind it may be, can be enjoyed, and even the other subjective goods, the qualities of intellect, mind, and temperament, become depressed and wither away because of ill-health. Consequently, it does not happen without reason that we inquire above all about the other's state of health and wish well-being to each other;

---

[a] ὁ βίος ἐν τῇ κινήσει ἐστί [Apparently a paraphrase of Aristotle. In *De anima* (*On the Soul*) I, 2 (403a25) Aristotle describes the soul, which for him is the principle of life, as having two qualities, movement and sensation]

[b] *motus peristalticus*   [c] [The faster a movement is, the more it is movement.]

[d] ταράσσει τοὺς ἀνθρώπους οὐ τὰ πράγματα ἀλλὰ τὰ περὶ τῶν πραγμάτων δόγματα (*commovent homines non res, sed de rebus opiniones*) [Epictetus, *Enchiridion*, 5]

for this is really by far the most important ingredient in human happiness. From this it follows that it is the greatest of all follies to sacrifice our health, for whatever it may be – for gain, promotion, learning, or fame, not to mention concupiscence and fleeting pleasure; rather we should subordinate everything else to its preservation.

However, as much as health contributes to cheerfulness, which is so essential to our happiness, it does not depend on it alone; for even in a state of perfect health, a melancholic temperament and a predominantly gloomy mood can prevail. The ultimate reason for this lies without doubt in the original and thus irreversible constitution of the organism, and most often in the more or less normal relation of sensibility to irritability and repro- ductive power. An abnormal prevalence of sensibility will lead to uneven moods, periodical bouts of excessive cheerfulness and predominant melan- choly. But since the genius too depends on an excess of nervous power and hence sensibility, Aristotle quite rightly remarked that all excellent and   347 superior human beings are melancholic: 'All men who have distinguished themselves – either in philosophy, or politics, or poetry, or arts – seem to have been melancholic.'[a] Undoubtedly, this is the passage that Cicero had in mind in his often quoted statement: 'Aristotle said that all geniuses are melancholic.'[b] – *Shakespeare* has given a fine description of that great, innate variety in basic mood that we are discussing here:

> Nature has fram'd strange fellows in her time:
> Some that will evermore peep through their eyes,
> And laugh, like parrots, at a bag-piper;
> And others of such vinegar aspect,
> That they'll not show their teeth in way of smile,
> Though Nestor swear the jest be laughable.*
>
> *Merchant of Venice*, scene 1[c]

It is exactly this difference that *Plato* signifies by the expressions 'hard to please' and 'contented'.[d] It can be traced back to the greatly varying degrees of susceptibility in different people for pleasant and unpleasant impressions, as a result of which the one still laughs at the thing that drives the other almost to despair. Indeed, susceptibility for pleasant impressions is usually

---

* [Schopenhauer here provides a German translation of the passage quoted in the original English.]

[a] πάντες ὅσοι περιττοὶ γεγόνασιν ἄνδρες, ἢ κατὰ φιλοσοφίαν, ἢ πολιτικὴν, ἢ ποίησιν, ἢ τέχνας, φαίνονται μελαγχολικοὶ ὄντες (*Problemata* [*Problems*] 30, 1[953a10])

[b] *Aristoteles* [*quidem*] *ait, omnes ingeniosos melancholicos esse* (*Tusculanae disputationes* [*Tusculan Disputations*] I, 33 [80]).

[c] [Act I, scene 1]   [d] δύσκολος *und* εὔκολος

the weaker, the stronger that for unpleasant ones is, and vice versa. In the event that a happy and an unhappy outcome are equally possible, the person that is 'hard-to-please' will be angry or aggrieved over an unhappy outcome, but will not be glad about a happy one; the 'contented' person, on the other hand, will neither be angry nor saddened if an affair goes wrong, but rejoice in a happy ending. If the 'hard-to-please' person succeeds in nine out of ten schemes, he will not be pleased with the nine successes, but annoyed about the one failure; on the other hand, when things are the other way around, the 'contented' person knows how to console and cheer himself up over the one success.[7] – But just as it is not easy to find an evil without some compensation, so it also turns out here that the 'hard-to-please' people, gloomy and anxious characters, on the whole, will have to overcome more imaginary accidents and sufferings, and fewer actual ones, than the cheerful and carefree; for whoever takes a dark view of everything, always fears the worst, and makes preparations accordingly, will not miscalculate as often as the one who always looks at the bright side of things. – However, when a pathological affection of the nervous system, or the digestive organs, plays into the hand of innate 'discontent',[a] then it can reach such a high degree that persistent dissatisfaction produces weariness of life. Consequently, a tendency to suicide develops, which then can be caused by the most trivial annoyances; indeed, at the highest levels of malady there is no need for these, but as a result of continuous discontent, suicide is decided on and committed with such cool deliberation and firm resolve that the sick person, who is often already under observation, is continuously focused on it, and uses the first unguarded moment to seize – without hesitating, fighting, or shrinking back – the means of relief that are now so natural and welcome to him. Detailed descriptions of this state are found in Esquirol, *Mental Maladies*.[b] However, under certain circumstances even the most healthy and perhaps even the most cheerful person can decide to commit suicide, namely if the magnitude of the sufferings or of the inevitably approaching disaster vanquishes the terrors of death. The difference lies solely in the varying magnitude of the necessary inducement, which is inversely proportional to the magnitude of discontent. The greater the latter, the smaller the inducement can be, indeed, in the end it can fall to zero. But the greater the 'contentment'[c] and the health supporting it, the more the cause must

348

---

[a] δυσκολία
[b] *des maladies mentales* [Étienne Esquirol, *Des maladies mentales, considérées sous les rapports médical, hygiénique et médico-légal* (*Mental Maladies: A Treatise on Insanity*), 2 vols., Paris: Baillière, 1838]
[c] εὐκολία

contain. Accordingly, there are innumerable degrees of cases between the two extremes of suicide, one stemming purely from the pathological intensification of innate 'discontent', and the other committed by the healthy and cheerful person entirely for objective reasons.

Beauty is partly related to health. Although this subjective advantage does not really contribute immediately to our happiness, but only mediately, through the impression of others, it is nonetheless of great importance, even in men. Beauty is an open letter of recommendation that wins hearts for us in advance; hence this Homeric verse is especially true of it: 349

> Not to be tossed aside,
> the gifts of the gods, those glories . . .
> whatever the gods give of their own free will –
> How could we ever choose them for ourselves?[a]

The most general overview shows us the two enemies of human happiness to be pain and boredom. In addition, we can observe that to the degree that we succeed in removing ourselves from the one, we come closer to the other, and vice versa, so that our life actually presents a stronger or weaker oscillation between them. This arises from the fact that both stand in a double antagonism to one another, an external or objective, and an internal or subjective antagonism. For externally, want and privation cause pain, but security and abundance cause boredom. Accordingly, we see the lower classes in a perpetual struggle against want, hence pain, and the rich and noble world in a persistent and often really desperate struggle against boredom.[*,8] The inner or subjective antagonism rests on the fact that in the individual, susceptibility to one is inversely proportional to susceptibility to the other, in that this susceptibility is determined by the person's mental powers. For intellectual obtuseness is always associated with dullness of sensation and lack of sensitivity, a constitution which makes one less susceptible to pain and sorrow of whatever sort and magnitude. This intellectual obtuseness gives rise to that *inner emptiness*, pronounced in innumerable faces and betraying itself through the constant lively attention to even the most trivial events in the external world, an emptiness that is the true source of boredom and constantly craves external stimulation in order to stir intellect and mind through anything at all. Hence it is not fastidious 350

---

* The *nomadic life*, which designates the lowest stage of civilization, is found again at the highest in the *life of the tourist*, which has become universal. The former was caused by need, the latter by *boredom*.

[a] Οὔτοι ἀπόβλητ' ἐστὶ θεῶν ἐρικυδέα δῶρα, / Ὅσσα κεν αὐτοὶ δῶσιν, ἑκὼν δ' οὐκ ἄν τις ἕλοιτο [Homer, *Iliad* III, 65ff.]

in its choice, as attested by the pitiful pastimes that people resort to, and also by the nature of their sociability and conversation, and no less so by the people who stand around in doorways or gape out of windows. Mainly from this inner vacuity arises the craving for company, diversion, enjoyment, and luxury of any kind, which leads many to extravagance and then to squalor. Nothing prevents us so reliably from this aberration than *inner* wealth, the wealth of the mind; for the more closely it approaches eminence, the less room it leaves for boredom. The inexhaustible activity of thoughts, their play that constantly renews itself by means of the multifarious appearances of the internal and the external world, the power and the drive to combine them in ever-changing ways, place the great mind, apart from moments of fatigue, completely beyond the reach of boredom. But on the other hand, the immediate condition for increased intelligence is a heightened sensibility, and its root is a greater vehemence of the will, hence of passionateness. Out of their association grows a much greater strength of all affects and an increased sensitivity for mental and even physical pain, also greater impatience with all obstacles or even just disturbances. The vividness of all representations, hence also the repulsive ones, springing from the strength of imagination, greatly contributes to heightening all of this. What has been said applies proportionally at all the intermediate stages that fill the wide space between the dullest blockhead and the greatest genius. Consequently, objectively as well as subjectively, everybody stands the more closely to one source of suffering in human life, the farther away he is from the other. Accordingly, his natural tendency will direct him in this respect to adapt the objective to the subjective as much as possible, in other words, to make the greater provision against that source of suffering to which he is more susceptible. The ingenious person will above all strive for freedom from pain and annoyance, for tranquillity and leisure, and consequently seek a quiet, modest life, as undisturbed as possible, and accordingly, after some acquaintance with so-called human beings, choose seclusion and, if in possession of a great mind, even solitude. For the more somebody has in himself, the less he needs from the outside and the less others can be to him. Therefore, intellectual distinction leads to unsociability. Indeed, if the quality of society could be substituted by quantity, then it would be worth the effort to live in the world at large; but unfortunately a hundred fools in a pile still do not make one intelligent person. – In contrast, the person at the other extreme, as soon as his needs let him regain his breath, will seek diversion and company at any price and readily make do with anything, trying to escape from nothing as much as from himself. For in solitude, where everybody is referred back to himself, it becomes apparent what he has *in himself*, there the dunce in purple garment groans under the inescapable burden of his pathetic individuality, while the highly talented person populates and animates the most dreary surroundings with his thoughts. Therefore, what *Seneca* says is very true: 'All stupidity suffers from weariness with itself',[a] as is Jesus ben Sirach's statement: 'The life of the fool is worse than death.'[b] Accordingly, we will find on the whole that people are sociable to the degree that they are intellectually poor and generally common.[*,9] For in this world we have little more than the choice between solitude and vulgarity. The most sociable of all human beings are said to be the negroes, who indeed are intellectually definitely inferior; according to accounts from North America in French papers (*Le Commerce*,[c] 19 October 1837), black people, free ones and slaves all together, shut themselves up in large numbers in the smallest space, because they cannot look often enough at their black snubnosed faces.

Since the brain appears as the parasite or pensioner[d] of the whole organism, people's hard-won *leisure*, by providing them with the free enjoyment of their consciousness and individuality, is the fruit and gain of their entire existence, which otherwise consists of nothing but effort and labour. But what does leisure yield for most people? Boredom and apathy, as long as sensuous pleasures or follies do not fill the time. How utterly worthless it is becomes apparent through the way in which they spend it – it is Ariosto's 'eternal leisure of ignorant men'.[e] Common people are merely intent on *spending* time – whoever has some talent, on *making use of* it. – That limited minds are so much subject to boredom is due to the fact that their intellect is nothing but the *medium of motives* for their will. Now if for the time being there are no motives to be grasped, the will rests and the intellect takes a holiday, the latter because, like the former, it does not become active by itself; the result is terrible stagnation of all powers in the whole human being – boredom. In order to fight it, people present trivial motives, provisional and arbitrarily adopted, to the will in order to excite it and thereby also to activate the intellect, which has to comprehend them. These motives are related to actual and natural motives as paper money is to silver, since their validity is arbitrarily assumed. Such motives are *games*, with cards etc.,

352

---

* What makes people sociable is their inner poverty.

[a] *omnis stultitia laborat fastidio sui* (*Epistles*, 9 [22])

[b] [*Ecclesiasticus, or The Wisdom of Jesus Son of Sirach* ('Ecclesiasticus' in the *Septuagint*) 22, 12 (the translation follows the *HarperCollins Study Bible*)]

[c] [French newspaper, 1837–48]   [d] *Pensionair*

[e] *ozio lungo d'uomini ignoranti* [Ludovico Ariosto, *Orlando Furioso* (*Orlando Enraged*) XXXIV, 75]

which have been invented for this very purpose. Lacking those, the dull-witted person makes do with rattles and drums, with anything he can lay his hands on. For him, even a cigar is a welcome substitute for thoughts.[10] – Hence in countries everywhere card games have become the main occupation at all social gatherings; they are the measure of their worth and the declared bankruptcy of all thought. For, since they do not exchange ideas, they exchange cards and try to take each other's money. Oh what a pitiful race! However, in order not to be unfair here, I will not suppress the idea that we might excuse card games as a preparatory training for life in the world and in business, insofar as we learn from them the prudent use of irreversible circumstances (cards) dealt by chance in order to make of them whatever we can. For that purpose, we get accustomed to maintaining our composure by making the best of a bad job.[a] But for that very reason, card games have a demoralizing influence. For the spirit of the game is to carry off the other's possessions in every possible manner, through every trick and artifice. But the habit of acting in this way in games takes root, encroaches on practical life, and gradually we come to act in the same way with respect to affairs of mine and thine and to regard every advantage that we have in our hands as permissible as long as it is licit. In fact, bourgeois life provides proof of this every day.[11] – As I have said, since *leisure* is the flower, or rather the fruit, of everyone's existence, because it alone helps us own our own self, those are to be called happy who also receive something substantial in themselves, whereas for most people, free time yields nothing but a chap who is good for nothing, gets terribly bored, and is a burden to himself. Accordingly, let us be glad, 'brethren, that we are not children of the bondwoman, but of the free' (Galatians 4:31).

Furthermore, just as that country is happiest that needs little or no imports, so also human beings are happiest who are content with their inner riches and need little or nothing from the outside for their entertainment, since such influx is expensive, makes us dependent, creates dangers, causes annoyance, and in the end is still an inferior substitute for the products of one's own soil. For from others, from the outside, we cannot expect much in any respect. What one can be to the other is strictly limited; in the end, everyone is alone, and then it all comes down to *who* is alone. Here too what Goethe pronounced in general is true, that in all things everyone is ultimately thrown back onto himself (*Poetry and Truth*, vol. 3, p. 474[b]). Or as *Oliver Goldsmith* says:

---

[a] [The play on words is lost, since the German idiom, 'heitere Miene zum bösen Spiel machen' literally refers to games ('to show a good face during a bad game')]
[b] [*From my Life: Poetry and Truth*, Part 3, Book 15]

Still to ourselves in ev'ry place consign'd,
Our own felicity we make or find.   (*The Traveller*,[a] v. 431f.)[12]

Therefore, we must achieve and be the best and the most to ourselves. The more this is the case and, consequently, the more we find the sources of our enjoyments within ourselves, the happier we will be. Hence Aristotle is quite justified in saying: 'Happiness belongs to those who are independent of others',[b] in other words: Happiness belongs to those who are sufficient in themselves. For all external sources of happiness and pleasure are by their nature utterly uncertain, precarious, transient and subject to chance and might, therefore, even under the most favourable conditions, easily dry up; indeed, this is inevitable, insofar as they cannot always be close at hand. In old age, they all, of necessity, stop almost completely; love, banter, wanderlust, delight in horses, and aptitude for social intercourse desert us; even friends and relatives are carried off by death. Hence what we have in ourselves is more than ever important, since this will hold up the longest. But at every age this is and remains the true and solely permanent source of happiness. There is nothing to be got in the world anywhere; privation and pain pervade it, and boredom lies in wait at every corner for those who have escaped them. Moreover, wickedness usually reigns, and folly does all the talking. Fate is cruel, and human beings are pathetic. In such a world, the people who have much within themselves resemble the bright, warm, merry drawing-room at Christmas in the middle of the snow and ice of a December night. Accordingly, to possess an excellent and a rich individuality, and especially great intellect[c], is without doubt the happiest lot on earth, however differently it might have turned out from the most sparkling. Hence it was a wise statement that the nineteen-year-old Queen Christina of Sweden made about Descartes, whom she only knew through *one* essay and from verbal accounts and who at that point had lived in Holland for twenty years in deepest solitude: 'Mr Descartes is the happiest of all people, and his condition seems to me to deserve envy.' (*Vie de Descartes par Baillet*, Book VII, ch. 10.)[d,13] Of course, as was the case with Descartes, the external circumstances must be favourable to the extent that we can be masters of our lives and be happy with ourselves; for that reason, Qoheleth (7:12)[e] says: 'Wisdom is good with an inheritance: and by it there is profit to them that

354

---

[a] [*The Traveller, or A Prospect of Society* (1764)]
[b] ἡ εὐδαιμονία τῶν αὐτάρκων ἐστί (*Eudemian Ethics* VII, 2 [1238a])   [c] *sehr viel Geist*
[d] *M. Descartes est le plus heureux de tous les hommes, et sa condition me semble digne d'envie* [*La Vie de Monsieur Descartes*, Adrien Baillet, 1691]
[e] [(Ecclesiastes); rather 7:11]

see the sun.' Whoever has been granted this lot through the favour of nature and fate will keep an anxious and careful watch over it, so that the inner source of his happiness remains accessible to him, the conditions for which are independence and leisure. These he will gladly purchase through moderation and thrift, the more so as he does not, like others, depend on external sources of pleasure. Therefore, the prospects of office, money, favour, and the applause of the world will not tempt him to abandon himself in order to conform with the base interests or bad tastes of people.*,[14] When that happens, he will follow *Horace* in the epistle to Maecenas (I, 7).[a] It is a great folly to lose *on the inside* in order to gain *on the outside*, i.e. to give up one's peace, leisure and independence, in its entirety or in part, for the sake of glamour, rank, pomp, title, and honour. This is what *Goethe* did. My genius has drawn me resolutely to the other side.[15]

The truth here discussed, that the main source of human happiness originates within ourselves, is confirmed by the absolutely correct remark by Aristotle in the *Nicomachean Ethics* (I, 7, and VII, 13 and 14), that any pleasure presupposes some activity, the employment of some faculty, and without it cannot persist. This Aristotelan doctrine, that the happiness of a person consists in the unimpeded use of his pre-eminent capability, Stobaeus too provides in his exposition of the peripatetic ethic (*Eclogues* II, 7, pp. 268–78), e.g. 'Happiness is an activity in accordance with virtue, through practices that have the desired effect.'[b] In general, in even shorter expressions, he also explains that virtue[c] is any kind of excellence.[d,16] Now the original purpose of the faculties with which nature has endowed human beings is the fight against want, which presses them hard from all sides. But when this fight stops for once, the idle powers become a burden for them. Therefore, they must now *play* with them, i.e. employ them without a purpose; otherwise they immediately fall prey to the other source of human suffering, boredom. Hence it is mostly the great and rich who are tortured

---

* They achieve their prosperity at the expense of their leisure; but what good is prosperity if I have to give up that which alone makes it desirable, namely my leisure?

[a] [*Epistles* I, 7, where Horace recounts the story of a man who is persuaded by another to exchange his simple, modest life for a richer one, only to come back to him, overworked and miserable, to ask for his old life back]

[b] ἐνέργειαν εἶναι τὴν εὐδαιμονίαν κατ' ἀρετήν, ἐν πράξεσι προηγουμέναις κατ' εὐχήν. (Heeren's version is: *felicitatem esse functionem secundum virtutem, per actiones successus compotes*) [*Ioannis Stobaei Eclogarum physicarum et ethicarum*, ed. Arnold Hermann Ludwig Heeren, Göttingen: Vandenhoeck & Ruprecht, 1792–1801; vol. 2, p. 268]

[c] ἀρετή   [d] *Virtuosität*

by it. Lucretius already gave us a description of their misery, whose aptness we have the chance to recognize to this day in every large city:

Often he leaves his palace and goes outside,
for he is tired of the house, and then suddenly returns,
since he feels that he is no better off in the open.
Or, on the spur of the moment, he races with his Gallic ponies to the villa,
as if bringing urgent help to the burning house;
immediately he yawns when crossing the threshold of the villa,
or falls into a deep sleep, and seeks forgetfulness,
or even desires to hurry back to the city, and returns.   III, 1073[a]

In these gentlemen, muscle strength and reproductive power must bear the brunt during their youth. But later only the intellectual powers remain; if they are lacking, or have not been developed and gathered material for their exercise, then there is much moaning and groaning. Now since the *will* is the only inexhaustible power, it is roused by stirring the passions, for example, by gambling for high stakes, that truly degrading vice. – But in general, every unoccupied individual will choose a game for exercising his powers, in accordance with the kind that is predominant within him, for example, bowling or chess, hunting or painting, racing or music, card games or poetry, heraldry or philosophy, and so on. In fact, we can investigate the matter methodically by tracing the root of all human expressions of power,[b] hence the *three fundamental physiological powers*,[c] which consequently we must consider here in their purposeless[d] play, where they appear as the sources of three kinds of possible pleasures, from which every human being will choose the appropriate ones for himself, depending on whether one or the other predominates in him. First there are the pleasures of the *power of reproduction*: they consist in eating, drinking, digesting, resting, and sleeping. These are actually attributed to whole peoples by others as their national amusements. Second, there are the pleasures of *irritability*: they consist in hiking, jumping, wrestling, dancing, fencing, riding, and athletic games of every kind, also hunting and even fighting and war.   357
Third, we have the pleasures of *sensibility*: they consist in contemplating, thinking, feeling, writing literature, creating,[e] playing music, learning,

---

[a] *Exit saepe foras magnis ex aedibus ille, / Esse domi quem pertaesum est, subitoque reventat; / Quippe foris nihilo melius qui sentiat esse. / Currit, agens mannos, ad villam praecipianter, / Auxilium tectis quasi ferre ardentibus instans: / Oscitat extemplo, tetigit quum limina villae; / Aut abit in somnum gravis, atque oblivia quaerit; / Aut etiam properans urbem petit, atque revisit* [Lucretius, *De Rerum Natura* (*On the Nature of Things*) III, 1060–7]
[b] *Kraftäußerungen*   [c] *physiologischen Grundkräfte*   [d] *zwecklosen*   [e] *Bilden*

reading, meditating, inventing, philosophizing, and so on. – Various observations can be made about the value, degree, and duration of any of these kinds of pleasures, which are left to the readers themselves. But it will be evident to everyone that our enjoyment, always conditioned by the use of our own powers, and hence our happiness, which consists in the frequent repetition of such enjoyment, will be the greater, the nobler the power on which our enjoyment depends. Nor will anybody deny the primacy of sensibility in this respect, whose predominance distinguishes human beings from the other animal species, over the other two fundamental physiological powers, which to an equal or even higher degree inhere in animals. Our powers of cognition belong to sensibility; hence their preponderance enables the pleasures consisting in *cognition*, or the so-called *intellectual* pleasures, which will be the greater, the more

358   decisive that preponderance is.*,[17] A matter can rouse vivid concern in normal, ordinary people only by exciting their *will*, hence by carrying a personal interest for them. But every continuous excitement of the *will* is at least of a mixed nature, and so is associated with pain. An intentional device of exciting it by means of interests so small that they can only cause momentary and light, rather than permanent and serious pain and consequently are to be seen as a mere titillation of the will, is

---

* Nature advances continuously, first from the mechanical and chemical activity of the inorganic kingdom to the vegetable kingdom and its vague enjoyment of self, from there to the animal kingdom with the dawning of intelligence and consciousness, which now from faint beginnings ascend in stages ever higher and finally, by the ultimate and greatest step, rise to *humanity*, in whose intellect nature reaches the pinnacle and the goal of its productions, thus delivering the most perfect and difficult that she is able to bring forth. But even within the human species, the intellect presents us with many and marked gradations and very rarely reaches the highest degree of truly superior intelligence. Intelligence in the narrower and stricter sense is the most difficult and highest product of nature, hence the rarest and most precious thing that the world can boast. In such intelligence, the clearest consciousness occurs and, consequently, the world represents itself more distinctly and more completely than anywhere else. Hence, whoever is endowed with such intelligence possesses the most noble and precious thing on earth and thus a source of pleasures compared to which all others are small. Therefore, he needs nothing from the outside but the leisure to enjoy this possession in peace and to polish his diamond. – For all other, non-intellectual pleasures are of a lower kind; they all amount to movements of the will, hence wishing, hoping, fearing, and achieving, no matter what they are directed at. This can never happen without pain and, in addition, achievement normally brings more or less disappointment in its wake, instead of the truth becoming more and more clear, as is the case with intellectual pleasures. In the realm of intelligence there is no pain, but all is cognition. All intellectual pleasures are accessible to everyone only by means of and in accordance with his own intelligence; for '*tout l'esprit, qui est au monde, est inutile à celui qui n'en a point*' [All the intelligence in the world is useless to the one who has none] [Jean de La Bruyère, *Les Caractères de Théophraste traduits du grec avec Les Caractères, ou les mœurs de ce siècle* (*The Characters, or the Manners of the Age, with The Characters of Theophrastus*), ch. XI, '*De l'homme*' (On Man)]. However, a real disadvantage, accompanying that advantage, is that in the whole of nature the capacity for pain increases together with the degree of intelligence, so that it is precisely here that this capacity reaches its highest level.

the playing of cards, this continuous occupation of 'good society' every-where.*,[18] – People with superior intellectual powers, on the other hand, are capable, and in fact, in need of the most lively interest by way of mere *cognition*, without any interference of the *will*. But this interest then transports them to a region where pain is essentially alien, into the atmosphere of the lightly living gods, 'of the gods who live at ease'.[a] In contrast, the life of the others passes in apathy, in that their thoughts and aspirations are entirely directed towards the petty interests of personal welfare and hence to miseries of all kind, which causes unbearable boredom to befall them as soon as occupation with these purposes comes to an end and they are thrown back onto themselves, since only the fierce fire of passion is able to move the stagnating mass. On the other hand, the existence of people with predominantly intellectual powers is rich in ideas and full of life and meaning; worthy and interesting subject matters occupy them as soon as they can devote themselves to them, and they have within themselves a source of the noblest pleasures. The works of nature and the contemplation of human affairs stimulate them from the outside, also the diverse achievements of the most highly gifted human beings of all times and countries, which really these people alone can thoroughly enjoy, since only they can fully understand and feel them. Hence those highly talented human beings have actually lived for them, have addressed themselves to them, whereas the others only half comprehend this and that as incidental listeners. Because of all this, they naturally have one need more than the others, the need to learn, to see, to study, to meditate, to practise, and thus also the need for leisure. But since, as Voltaire rightly observed, 'there are no real pleasures without real needs',[b] this need is the condition for their

359

---

* *Vulgarity* actually consists in the fact that willing entirely outweighs cognition in consciousness, so that it reaches a degree at which cognition occurs solely in the service of the will and that, consequently, where such service does not need it, when neither great nor small motives are present, cognition ceases entirely, resulting in complete absence of thought. But willing without cognition is the most common thing; every wooden log has it and shows it at least when it falls. Hence this state constitutes vulgarity. Only the sense organs and the minimal activity of the understanding required for the apprehension of sense data remain active, as a result of which vulgar human beings are persistently open for all impressions, and instantly perceive everything that goes on around them, so that the slightest sound and every circumstance, however small, immediately draws their attention, just as in in animals. From this the vulgar appearance arises, whose impression is all the more repulsive when, as is most often the case, the will that alone fills consciousness is base, egoistic, and generally bad.

[a] θεῶν ῥεῖα ζωόντων [Homer, *Iliad* VI, 138, and *Odyssey* IV, 805]
[b] *il n'est de vrais plaisirs qu'avec de vrais besoins* [Voltaire, *Précis de l'Ecclésiaste, et du Cantique des Cantiques* (*Summary of Eccleciastes and the Song of Songs*), line 30]

having access to pleasures that others are denied, for whom beauty of nature and in art and intellectual works of all kinds, even if they accumulate these around them, at bottom are only what mistresses[a] are to an old man. As a result, such privileged people, aside from their personal life, lead a second, namely an intellectual life, which gradually becomes their real purpose and for which they see the first only as a mere means, whereas for the rest this stale, empty, and sad existence must itself be regarded as the end. Consequently, the former are primarily occupied with the intellectual life, which attains, through continuous increase in insight and knowledge, cohesion, steady augmentation, and wholeness and perfection, completing itself more and more, like a slowly maturing work of art. On the other hand, the life of the rest, which is merely practical, merely aimed at personal welfare,

360   merely capable of growing in length, not in depth, stands in sad contrast to it, but must nevertheless count as an end in itself, whereas it is a mere means for the former sort of people.

Our practical, real life, if not moved by passions, is boring and stale; but when moved by them, it soon becomes painful; for that reason only those are lucky who have been meted out some excess of intellect, beyond the measure required for service of the will. For with the help of that, aside from their actual life, they also lead an intellectual life, which occupies and entertains them continuously in a way that is *painless* but still lively. Mere leisure, i.e. intellect *unoccupied* in the service of the will, does not suffice for that, but a real excess of *power* is required; for it alone makes possible a purely intellectual occupation that does not serve the will; in contrast, 'leisure without literature is death and is like being buried alive for a human being'. (Seneca, *Epistles*, 82.)[b] Depending on whether this excess is small or large, there are innumerable degrees of intellectual life, led apart from actual life, from the mere collection and description of insects, birds, minerals, and coins to the highest achievements of poetry and philosophy. And such an intellectual life protects not only against boredom, but also against its pernicious consequences.[19] For it becomes a bulwark against bad company and the many dangers, misadventures, losses, and dissipations into which we stumble when seeking our luck entirely in the actual world. For example, my philosophy has never earned me anything, but it has spared me a lot.

An ordinary human being, on the other hand, depends on things *outside of him* in regard to enjoying life, on property, rank, wife and children,

---

[a] *Hetären*   [b] *otium sine litteris mors est et hominis vivi sepultura* [Seneca, *Epistles*, 82, 3]

friends, society, and the like; these prop up his life's happiness, and this is the reason it is destroyed if he loses these things, or when he sees himself deceived by them. In order to express this relation, we can say that his centre of gravity falls *outside of himself*. Consequently, he has constantly changing desires and whimsies; when his means permit it, he will now buy country-houses, now horses, now give parties, travel, and in general live in great extravagance, since he seeks satisfaction *from the outside* in all kinds of things, just as the debilitated person hopes through broths and medicines to regain the health and strength whose true source lies in his own vital force. Instead of going to the other extreme, let us compare him with a person of intellectual powers that are not quite outstanding, but still exceed the common, narrow measure; we see this person, for example, practise some fine art as a dilettante, or an empirical science,[a] like botany, mineral-ogy, physics, astronomy, history, and such like, and soon find a large part of his enjoyment and relaxation in it when those external sources dry up or do not satisfy him any longer. We can thus say that his centre of gravity already falls in part *within himself*. However, since mere dilettantism in art still is very far from creative ability, and since the mere empirical sciences stop at the relations of appearances among one another, the whole human being cannot lose himself in these, his whole essence cannot be imbued by them to its very roots and, therefore, his existence cannot become so intertwined with them that he would lose all interest in everything else. This is reserved only for the highest intellectual eminence, which we usually describe by the name of genius; for this eminence alone makes the existence and essence of things in their entirety and absoluteness its subject, and will then strive to express its profound comprehension of these in accordance with its indi-vidual tendency, through art, poetry, or philosophy. Hence it is only for this kind of human being that undisturbed occupation with himself, his thoughts and works, is an urgent need, that solitude is welcome, leisure the highest good, and everything else expendable, indeed, when present, often merely a burden. Only of such a human being, therefore, can we say that his centre of gravity falls *entirely within himself*. This explains why the exceedingly rare people of this nature, even when possessing the best character, nonetheless do not show that intimate and unlimited sympathy for friends, family, and community of which some others are capable; for in the end they can console themselves about anything if only they have themselves. Therefore, they possess one more isolating element that is all the more effective, as others never really satisfy them completely. For that

361

362

---

[a] *Realwissenschaft* [a science with an empirical content, as opposed to a formal science like mathematics]

reason, they cannot look at them as quite their equals, and indeed, since they always feel the heterogeneous in everything, they gradually get accustomed to walking among people as different beings and, in their thoughts about them, to using the third, not the first person plural. – Our moral virtues mainly benefit others, whereas the intellectual ones benefit primarily ourselves; consequently, the former make us universally popular, the latter, objects of hate.[20]

From this point of view the person richly endowed by nature in an intellectual respect appears to be the happiest, since it is certain that the subjective is closer to us than the objective, whose effect, of whatever kind it may be, is always first mediated through the subjective and hence is only secondary. This is also attested by the beautiful verse:

> True wealth is wealth of the soul alone,
> the rest of possessions bring more ruin than anything else.
>
> Lucian in *Anthology* I, 67[a]

An inwardly rich person like that needs nothing from the outside but a negative gift, namely undisturbed leisure, in order to be able to cultivate and develop his intellectual abilities and to enjoy his inner wealth, and so actually needs the permission to be entirely himself throughout his whole life, every day and hour. When somebody is destined to impress the trace of his intellect on the whole of humanity, there is for him only one kind of happiness and unhappiness, namely to be able to perfect his talents and to complete his works – or to be prevented from doing so. Everything else is insignificant for him. Accordingly we see the great minds of all times attach the greatest value to leisure. For the leisure of each person is worth as much as he himself is worth.[21] 'Happiness seems to exist in leisure', says Aristotle (*Nicomachean Ethics* X, 7),[b] and Diogenes Laertius (II, 5, 31) reports that 'Socrates praised leisure as the best of all possessions.'[c] In keeping with this, Aristotle (*Nicomachean Ethics* X, 7, 8, 9) declares the philosophical life to be the happiest. Also what he says in the *Politics* (IV, 11) belongs here: 'The happy life is that lived without impediment in accordance with virtue',[d] which, properly translated, means: 'Real happiness is the ability to exercise one's excellence, whatever its nature, without hindrance', which coincides

363

---

[a] Πλοῦτος ὁ τῆς ψυχῆς πλοῦτος μόνος ἐστὶν ἀληθής, / Τἄλλα δ᾽ ἔχει ἄτην πλείονα τῶν κτεάνων [*The Greek Anthology* (in the Loeb edition, vol. IV, Book X, 41 ['The Hortatory and Admonitory Epigrams'])]

[b] Δοκεῖ δὲ ἡ εὐδαιμονία ἐν τῇ σχολῇ εἶναι (*videtur beatitudo in otio esse sita*) [1177b]

[c] Σωκράτης ἐπήνει σχολήν, ὡς κάλλιστον κτημάτων (*Socrates otium ut possessionum omnium pulcherrimam laudabat*) [*Lives and Opinions of Eminent Philosophers*]

[d] τὸν εὐδαίμονα βίον εἶναι τὸν κατ᾽ ἀρετὴν ἀνεμπόδιστον [rather: IV, 9, 2 (1295a35)]

with Goethe's words in *Wilhelm Meister*: 'Whoever is born with a talent and can realize it, finds in it his most beautiful existence.'[a] – However, possessing leisure is alien not only to ordinary fate, but also ordinary human nature; for the natural destiny of a human being is to spend his time procuring what is necessary for his own and his family's existence. He is the son of need, not of free intelligence. Accordingly, leisure soon becomes a burden and indeed ultimately a torment, if he is not able to fill it by means of various artificial and fictitious purposes, through all kinds of play, diversions, and hobbies. It also brings him danger for the same reason, since it is said rightfully: 'Tranquillity is difficult if one has leisure.'[b] On the other hand, an intellect far exceeding the normal measure is also abnormal, hence unnatural. But once it exists nevertheless, what is needed for the happiness of the person so gifted is leisure, sometimes annoying or pernicious to others, since without it he will be a Pegasus under the yoke and hence unhappy. But if both unnatural conditions, external and internal, come together, that is a great stroke of luck; for now the person so favoured will lead a life of a higher order, namely that of someone who is exempt from the two opposing sources of human suffering, want and boredom, or from the anxious activity of securing one's existence and from the inability to endure leisure (i.e. free existence itself), two evils that humans otherwise only avoid because they neutralize and eliminate one other.

On the other hand, we must consider against all this that the great intellectual gifts, as a result of a predominant nervous activity, lead to a greatly enhanced sensitivity for every form of pain and, further, that the passionate temperament that is the condition for these gifts and at the same time the greater vividness and completeness of all representations that is 364 inseparable from them, leads to an incomparably greater intensity of the affects stirred by them – however, in general there are more painful than pleasant affects. Finally, these great intellectual gifts alienate their possessor from other human beings and their activities, since, the more he has in himself, the less he is able to find in others, and a hundred things that greatly please them are to him insipid and unpalatable, so that the law of compensation, which asserts itself everywhere, may perhaps remain in force here too. For it has been maintained often enough, and not without evidence,[c] that the intellectually most limited person is, to all intents and purposes, the happiest, even if no one may envy him this happiness. I will let readers

---

[a] [*Wilhelm Meister's Lehrjahre* (*Wilhelm Meister's Apprenticeship*), Book I, ch. 14]
[b] *difficilis in otio quies*   [c] *Schein*

make their own definite decision in this matter, the more so as even *Sophocles* made two diametrically opposed statements in regard to it:

Understanding is the chief part of happiness. *Antigone*, 1328[a]

And again:

The most pleasant life consists in a lack of understanding. *Ajax*, 550[b]

The philosophers of the Old Testament disagree just as much with one another: 'The life of the fool is worse than death!'[c] And: 'For in much wisdom is much grief.' (Qoheleth, 1:18)[d,22] In the meantime, I want to mention here that it is human beings who have *no intellectual needs* as a result of the strictly and barely normal measure of their intellectual powers whom an expression describes as *philistines,*[e] an expression which is unique to the German language and originated in student life, but afterwards has been used in a higher sense, although still in analogy to the original sense as the opposite of the poet.[f] For the philistine is and remains an 'inartistic man'.[g] Now from a higher point of view, I would define philistines as people who are constantly, in the most serious manner, preoccupied with a reality that is not real. However, such a definition, which is already transcendental, would not be appropriate to the popular point of view I have adopted for this essay, and hence might not be quite comprehensible to every reader. In contrast, the first definition allows more readily for a particular explanation and sufficiently describes the essence of the matter, the root of all qualities that characterize the philistine. According to it, he is a human being *without intellectual needs*. Several things follow from this: first, *in respect of himself,* that he remains without intellectual *pleasures*, according to the already mentioned principle: 'There are no true pleasures without true needs.'[h] No keen urge[i] towards knowledge and insight for their own sake animate his existence, nor one towards actual aesthetic pleasures, which are definitely related to the first urge. Such pleasures as are imposed on him by fashion or authority, he will dispose of as quickly as possible as a kind of forced labour. Real pleasures for him are the sensuous ones alone; in them he finds compensation. Accordingly, oysters and

365

---

[a] Πολλῷ τὸ φρονεῖν εὐδαιμονίας πρῶτον ὑπάρχει [1347] (*Sapere longe prima felicitatis pars est.*)
[b] ἐν τῷ φρονεῖν γὰρ μηδὲν ἥδιστος βίος [554] (*Nihil cogitantium jucundissima vita est.*)
[c] τοῦ γὰρ μωροῦ ὑπὲρ θανάτου ζωὴ πονηρά, Jesus ben Sirach 22, 12 [see p. 289, n. b])
[d] ὁ προστιθεὶς γνῶσιν, προσθήσει ἄλγημα [Ecclesiastes 1:18]   [e] *Philister*
[f] *Musensohn* [literally: 'son of the Muses']   [g] ἄμουσος ἀνήρ [the German term is '*amusisch*']
[h] [See p. 295, n. b]   [i] *Drang*

champagne are the highpoint of his existence, and the purpose of his life is to acquire everything that contributes to bodily well-being. And he is lucky enough if this purpose keeps him busy! For if those goods are already conferred on him in advance, he will inevitably fall prey to boredom, against which all possible means are tried: ballet, theatre, society, card games, gambling, horses, women, drinking, travelling, and so on. But all of these are not sufficient to ward off boredom, when a lack of intellectual needs makes intellectual pleasures impossible. Hence a dull, dry seriousness, close to that of animals, is characteristic of the philistine. Nothing delights him, nothing excites him, nothing rouses his interest. For sensuous pleasures are soon exhausted; a society made up of philistines just like him soon becomes boring; card games finally become tiresome. At most, he is left to enjoy the pleasures of vanity in his own way, consisting in his exceeding others in regard to wealth, or rank, or influence and power, by whom he is then honoured, or in associating with people who excel in such things and thus basking in the reflection of their splendour (a snob[a]). – From the fundamental qualities of a philistine we have described it follows secondly, in respect to others, that, since he has no intellectual, but only physical needs, he will seek out the person who is able to satisfy the latter, not the one who can satisfy the former. Hence among the demands he makes on others, the least will be that of predominant intellectual abilities; on the contrary, if he encounters these, they will arouse his dislike, even his hatred, because in reaction to them he has only an annoying feeling of inferiority and, in addition, one of dull, secret envy. This he carefully hides by trying to conceal it even from himself, which is why it sometimes grows into a secret rage. Therefore, it will never occur to him to measure his appreciation, or deep respect, in accordance with such qualities; this is exclusively reserved for rank and wealth, and power and influence, which in his eyes are the only true merits in which he wishes to excel. – But all this follows from the fact that he is a human being *without intellectual needs.*

A great affliction of all philistines is that *idealities* do not entertain them, but that, instead, they always need *realities* to escape from boredom. The latter in part are soon exhausted when, instead of entertaining, they make us weary; and in part they lead to all kinds of evil. On the other hand, idealities are inexhaustible and in themselves innocent and innocuous.[23] –

366

---

[a] [Original English]

In this entire exposition of the personal qualities that contribute to our happiness I have, besides the physical qualities, mainly considered the intellectual ones. However, in what way moral excellence immediately makes up happy, I have previously described in my *Prize Essay on the Basis of Morals*, §22, p. 275,[a] to which I here refer the reader.

---

[a] [*BM*, 254–5 (Hübscher *SW* 4, 272)]

What one has

Epicurus, the great teacher of happiness, has correctly and beautifully divided human needs into three categories. First, the natural and necessary ones: these are the ones that cause pain when not satisfied. Consequently only food and clothing[a] belong here. They are easy to satisfy. Second, the natural but unnecessary ones: that is the need for sexual satisfaction, although Epicurus does not pronounce this clearly in the account of Laertius (as, in general, I reproduce his doctrine here in a somewhat adjusted and polished form). This need is more difficult to satisfy. Third, the neither natural nor necessary ones: these are the needs for luxury, opulence, pomp, and splendour. They are infinite and their satisfaction is very difficult. (See Diogenes Laertius, Book X, ch. 27, §149 and also §127,[b] and Cicero, *On the Ends of Goods and Evils* I,[c] chs. 14 and 16.)

On the other hand, it is difficult, if not impossible, to determine the limits of our rational desires in regard to possessions. For everyone's satisfaction, in this respect, does not depend on an absolute, but on a merely relative quantity, namely on the relation between his demands and his possessions; hence the latter, considered on their own, are meaningless, just like the numerator of a fraction without the denominator. The goods which it has never occurred to someone to demand, he does not miss at all, but he is perfectly happy even without them; whereas another, who pos- 368 sesses a hundred times more, is unhappy because he lacks a thing that he lays claim to. Everyone has, in this respect too, his own horizon of what he can possibly attain; and his demands extend as far as this. When some object within this horizon presents itself such that he can count on its attainment, he is happy; in contrast, he feels unhappy when difficulties occur that deprive him of the prospect. What lies beyond this horizon has no effect on him at all. Hence the large possessions of the rich do not worry the poor

---

[a] *victus et amictus*   [b] [*Lives and Opinions of Eminent Philosophers* X, sections 127 and 149]
[c] *de finibus*

person; on the other hand, the rich person is not consoled by the many things he already possesses if he misses his goals. Wealth resembles sea water; the more we drink of it, the thirstier we become. – The same is true of fame.[24] – After losing our wealth or prosperity and once the first pain has been overcome, our habitual disposition turns out to be not very different from the earlier one. This arises from the fact that, after fate has decreased the factor of our possessions, we ourselves now equally decrease the factor of our claims. This operation, however, is what is truly painful in the event of misfortune; after it has been performed the pain becomes less and less and in the end is no longer felt; the wound has healed. Conversely, in the case of luck, the compressor of our demands is pushed up, and they expand; this is cause for joy. But this too lasts no longer than it takes to complete the operation fully; we become used to the expanded measure of demands and indifferent towards the possessions that accord with it. This is already conveyed by the passage in Homer, *Odyssey* XVIII, 130–7, which concludes:

> Our lives, our mood and mind as we pass across the earth,
> turn as the days turn ... as the father of men and gods makes each day dawn.[a]

The source of our dissatisfaction lies in our constantly renewed attempts to raise the factor of our claims ever higher, while the other factor's inflexibility prevents this. –

369   Among a race so poor and full of needs as the human, it is not surprising that *wealth* is respected, and indeed worshipped, more highly and more sincerely than anything else, and even power is seen only as a means to wealth; neither does it surprise that for the purpose of acquisition, everything else is pushed or thrown aside, for example, philosophy by the philosophy professors.[25]

Humans are often reproached for the fact that their desires are primarily directed towards money and that they love money more than anything else. But it is natural, even inevitable, to love that which, like an untiring Proteus, is ready at a moment's notice to transform itself into the respective object of our so utterly changeable desire and manifold needs. Every other good can satisfy only *one* desire, *one* need; food is only beneficial for the hungry, wine for the healthy, medicine for the sick, a fur for the winter, women for the young, and so on. Hence they all are only goods for a particular purpose,[b] i.e. only relative goods. Money alone is the absolute

---

[a] Τοῖος γὰρ νόος ἐστὶν ἐπιχθονίων ἀνθρώπων, / Οἷον ἐφ' ἦμαρ ἄγει πατὴρ ἀνδρῶν τε θεῶν τε.
[b] ἀγαθὰ πρός τι

good, because it meets not merely *one* need concretely,[a] but need in general, in the abstract.[b] –

Existing assets should be regarded as a bulwark against the many possible evils and accidents, not as a permission or even obligation to procure the pleasures[c] of the world.[26] People who originally have no assets, but are finally put in the position where they can earn a lot by means of their talents, whatever they may be, almost always imagine that their talent is a permanent capital and what they gain is interest. Accordingly, they do not put aside a part of their earnings in order to accumulate permanent capital, but spend as much as they earn. Afterwards they will very often be reduced to poverty, because their earnings decrease or come to an end, after the talent itself, being finite, is exhausted, as, for example, the talent for almost all the fine arts, or a talent that could only thrive under particular circumstances and economic situations that have ceased to exist. Craftspeople might hold on to their assets, because their capacity to accomplish is not easily lost and can also be replaced by the abilities of their assistants,[d] and because their products are objects that are in demand, hence always find a market, which   370
is why the saying 'A trade in hand finds gold in every land' is true. But that is not the case for artists and virtuosi of every kind; hence they are paid very well. But what they earn should become their capital, whereas they presumptuously consider it as mere interest and for that reason head towards ruin. – On the other hand, people who possess inherited wealth at least immediately know exactly what is capital and what is interest. Most will, therefore, seek to secure the capital and will under no circumstances touch it, and indeed, where possible, will put aside at least one-eighth of the interest in order to prepare for future contingencies. Hence for the most part they remain well-off. – This entire observation does not apply to merchants, since for them money is itself the means to further gain, the tools of the craft, as it were; hence, even if they themselves acquired it, they try to sustain and to increase it by using it. Accordingly, in no class is wealth as much at home as it is in this one.

In general, we normally find that those who have closely experienced real hardship and privation, fear them much less and, therefore, are more inclined to extravagance than those who only know them from hearsay. All those who, by some stroke of luck of any kind, or through some sort of talent, have gone relatively quickly from poverty to wealth belong to the

---

[a] *in concreto*   [b] *in abstracto*   [c] *Plaisirs*
[d] *Gesellen* ['Geselle' in the context of the crafts or trade refers to an apprentice who has completed his training]

former; the latter are those who have been born wealthy and remained so. They are consistently more concerned about the future and hence more parsimonious than the former. We might conclude from this that hardship is not such a bad thing as it seems from afar. But perhaps the true reason might be that to the person who was born into hereditary wealth, this wealth appears indispensable, the element of the only possible life, just like air; therefore, he guards it like his life and is most often orderly, cautious, and thrifty. To the person born into poverty, on the other hand, this appears as the natural state and the wealth that afterwards somehow comes his way seems superfluous, merely fit to be enjoyed and squandered; once it is gone, one again makes do without it, as before, and is rid of one more worry. Then it goes as Shakespeare says:

> The adage must be verified
> That beggars mounted run their horse to death.
>
> *Henry VI*, Part 3, Act I[a]

In addition, these people possess not only in their minds, but also in their hearts a firm and outsized trust partly in their fate and partly in their own resources, which have often rescued them from hardship and poverty already; therefore, they do not take their shallows as fathomless, as would be the case for those born rich, but think that, after hitting bottom, one will be raised again. – This human characteristic also explains why women who were poor girls are often much more demanding and extravagant than those who came with a rich dowry, in that rich girls mostly not only bring with them mere assets, but also more eagerness, indeed, more of an inherited drive to preserve them than the poor ones. Whoever wants to claim the contrary, will find an authority in Ariosto's first satire.[b] On the other hand, Dr Johnson agrees with me: 'A woman of fortune being used to the handling of money, spends it judiciously: but a woman who gets the command of money for the first time upon her marriage, has such a gust in spending it, that she throws it away with great profusion.' (See Boswell, *Life of Johnson*, the year 1776, age 67.[c])[27] In any case, I would like to advise the man who marries a poor girl not to let her inherit capital, but merely an annuity, and, in particular, to make sure that the assets of the children do not fall into her hands.

I certainly do not believe that I am doing anything unworthy of my pen in recommending that one should care for the preservation of acquired and

---

[a] [Scene 4; quoted in the original English followed by Schopenhauer's translation]
[b] [Ludovico Ariosto, *Satire* (1517–25)]   [c] [Ch. 32]

inherited wealth. For to possess by birth so much that one could comfortably live, even if only by oneself without a family, in true independence, i.e.
without working, is an invaluable advantage; for it means exemption and   372
immunity from poverty and toil, hence emancipation from universal compulsory labour, this natural lot of earthlings. Only under such favourable fate
is one born truly free; for only then is one truly one's own master,[a] master of
one's time and powers, and can say every morning: 'The day is mine.' And for
that reason, the difference between the person who has a thousand thaler[b] and
one who has a hundred is infinitely smaller than the difference between the
first person and somebody who has nothing. But inherited wealth achieves its
highest value when it falls to the person who, endowed with intellectual
powers of a higher order, pursues endeavours not quite compatible with
financial gain. For he then is doubly endowed by fate and[28] is now able to
live for his genius; but his debt to humanity he will repay a hundredfold by
achieving what no other could achieve and creating something that benefits
humanity as a whole and even brings honour to it. Again another, being in
such a preferred position, will earn merit for his philanthropic efforts on behalf
of humanity. In contrast, whoever achieves none of all this, not even to some
extent or by way of attempt, and indeed does not even create the possibility for
himself to advance humanity by thoroughly studying some kind of science –
such a person, if possessing inherited wealth, is a mere dawdler and contemptible. What is more, he will not be happy, for the exemption from hardship
delivers him into the hands of the other extreme of human misery, boredom,
which tortures him such that he would be much happier if poverty had
provided him with something to do. But precisely this boredom will easily
lead him to extravagance, which will rob him of the advantage of which he was
not worthy. Innumerable people actually find themselves in a situation of
want for the sole reason that they spent money back when they had it just to
ease momentarily the boredom that oppressed them.[29]

But matters are very different when the goal is to advance in the service
of the state, where consequently favour, friends, and connections must be   373
acquired in order to achieve promotion through them, step by step, perhaps
even to the highest positions; for here it might basically be better to have been
thrust into the world without any wealth. In particular for those who are not
of noble birth but endowed with some talent, it will be advantageous and
serve to recommend them if they are really poor devils. For what everybody
seeks most and loves best, already in mere conversation, but much more in
service, is the inferiority of the other. But only a poor devil is convinced of and

---

[a] *sui juris*   [b] *Thaler* [German coin]

impressed with his own utter, deep, decided and all-round inferiority and total insignificance and worthlessness to the degree that is required here. It is he alone who bows often and long enough, and whose bows reach the full ninety degrees; he alone puts up with everything and smiles on top of it; only he recognizes the utter worthlessness of merits; only he publicly praises as masterpieces – in a loud voice, or in large print – the literary bumblings of those superior to him or otherwise influential; only he knows how to beg. Consequently, he alone can become in good time, that is, in his youth, even an epopt[a] of the secret truth that Goethe unveiled in the words:

> Over this let none lament
> Baseness all perverted;
> That it is omnipotent
> Can't be controverted. *West-Eastern Divan*[b]

In contrast, the one who is born with enough to live will mostly be unruly; he is used to walking with his head held high,[c] has learned none of the arts of the poor devil, boasts perhaps of some possible talents whose inadequacy he ought to realize in the face of the mediocre and servile;[d] in the end he might be able to notice the inferiority of those above him, and when it comes to full-blown indignities, he becomes stubborn and unnerved. This is not the way to curry favour in the world; rather, in the end it can come to the point that he says with cheeky Voltaire: 'We only have two days to live; it is not worth the effort to pass them by grovelling before contemptible scoundrels.'[e] Incidentally, this 'contemptible scoundrel' is a predicate for which, unfortunately, devilishly many subjects exist in the world. Therefore, we see that Juvenal's

> It is not easy to rise for those whose powers are obstructed
> By poverty in the home,[f]

is truer of a career in the arts than of one in the common world. –

Among *what one has*, I have not counted wife and children, since, on the contrary, they have him. Rather, friends might be included; but here the one who owns must equally be owned by the other.

---

[a] [Somebody initiated into the mysteries of a secret system, originally referring to the Eleusian mysteries]
[b] ['*Buch des Unmuts*' (Book of Displeasure): '*Wanderers Gemütsruhe*' (The Wanderer's Peace of Mind)]
[c] *tête levée* [d] *médiocre et rampant*
[e] *nous n'avons que deux jours à vivre: ce n'est pas la peine de les passer à ramper sous des coquins méprisables*
[f] *Haud facile emergunt, quorum virtutibus obstat / Res angusta domi* [Juvenal, *Satires* III, 164–5]

What one represents

This, our existence in the opinion of others, is consistently much overrated as a result of a particular weakness of our nature, although the slightest reflection[a] could teach us that in itself, for our happiness, it is not essential. Accordingly, it is hard to explain how inwardly glad all human beings are as soon as they detect signs of others' favourable opinion and their vanity is somehow flattered. As inevitably as a cat purrs when stroked, sweet bliss is painted on the faces of the people whom we praise, and specifically in the sphere of their pretensions, even if the compliment is a palpable lie.[30] Often signs of the applause of strangers console them for real misfortune or for the scantiness with which the two main sources of happiness flow for them that we have discussed so far; and, conversely, it is astonishing how every injury of their ambition, in any sense, to any degree, or in any relation, every contempt, disregard, or disrespect hurts them without fail and often deeply pains them. Since the feeling of honour is based on this quality, it might have beneficial results for the good conduct of many, as a substitute for their morality. However, its effects on the personal *happiness* of people, and first of all on the tranquillity and independence so essential to it, are more disruptive and detrimental than advantageous. Therefore, it is advisable from our point of view to limit it and, by means of proper deliberation and correct assessment of the value of the goods, to moderate this great susceptibility to the opinions of others as much as possible, not   376 only where it is flattered, but also where it is offended; for both hang from the same thread. Otherwise, we remain the slaves of the opinion and concerns of others:

> So slight, so insignificant is what undermines or restores
> the spirit that thirsts for praise.[b]

---

[a] *Besinnung*
[b] *Sic leve, sic parvum est, animum quod laudis avarum / Subruit ac reficit.* [Horace, *Epistles* II, 1, 179–80]

Accordingly, a correct comparison of the value of what we are in and *for ourselves* with what we are in the eyes of *others*, will greatly contribute to our happiness. To the former belongs all that fills the entire span of our own existence, its inner content, hence all the goods that we have considered under the names of 'what one is' and 'what one has'. For the place where all of this is effective is our own consciousness. In contrast, the place for what we are *for others* is their – alien – consciousness; it is the representation as which we appear in it, together with the concepts that are applied to the representation.*,31 This is something that does not immediately exist for us at all, but merely mediately, insofar as it determines the behaviour of others towards us. And even this behaviour really only comes into question insofar as it influences something by means of which what we are *in and for ourselves* can be modified. Moreover, what happens in the consciousness of others, as such, makes no difference for us, and we will gradually become indifferent towards it when we sufficiently recognize the shallowness and futility of thoughts, the narrowness of concepts, the pettiness of attitudes, the wrongness of opinions and number of errors in most heads, and in addition learn from our own experience how disparagingly everyone is spoken about occasionally as soon as people do not have to fear a person or believe that it would not reach his ears, but especially once we have heard how half a dozen sheepsheads speak dismissively about the greatest man. We will then realize that whoever attaches great importance to the opinions of people pays them too much honour.

377

In any case, those people depend on a scarce resource who seek their happiness not in the two categories of goods already discussed, but in this third one, hence not in what they actually are, but in what they are in the representation of others. For in general the basis of our essential being[a] and, consequently, also our happiness is our animal nature. Therefore, health is what is most essential for our welfare, immediately followed by the means to our preservation, hence a carefree livelihood. Honour, splendour, rank, fame, as much value as some want to place on these, can neither compete with nor replace these essential goods, for which, if necessary, they would be given up without hesitation. Therefore, it will contribute to our happiness if we achieve in good time the simple insight that we all primarily and actually live in our own skin, not in the opinions of others, and that, accordingly,

---

* The highest classes, in all their glamour, magnificence and splendour, their grandeur and representation of every kind can say: 'Our happiness lies outside of ourselves; its place is in the minds of others.'

[a] *Wesens*

our actual and personal state, as it is determined by health, temperament, abilities, income, wife, child, friends, place of residence, and so forth, is a hundred times more important for our happiness than what it pleases others to make of us. The opposite delusion makes us unhappy. If we emphatically exclaim that 'honour is more important than life', then this really says: 'Existence and well-being are nothing; however, what matters is what others think of us.' At most, this motto can count as hyperbole whose basis is the prosaic truth that for our advance and existence among people, honour, i.e. people's opinions about us, is often absolutely necessary; to which I shall return later. On the other hand, if we see how almost everything that human beings untiringly strive for all their lives with indefatigable effort and at the cost of a thousand dangers and hardships, has the ultimate purpose of elevating themselves in the opinion of others, insofar as not only offices, titles, and decorations, but also wealth and even art and science,[*,32] are basically and in the main pursued for this purpose, and the   378 greater respect of others is the ultimate goal towards which we work, then unfortunately this only proves the extent of human folly. Placing too much value on the opinion of others is a false belief that universally prevails, whether it is rooted in our nature itself or has arisen as a result of society and civilization. In any event, it wields an influence on all our doings that is excessive and detrimental to our happiness, an influence that we can trace from where it shows itself in timid and slavish deference to 'What will people say' to the point where it plunges Verginius' dagger[a] into his daughter's heart, or entices a person to sacrifice tranquillity, wealth and health, indeed, even life, for posthumous fame. This delusion offers a convenient means to the person who must govern or otherwise control people, which is why the instruction to keep alive and sharpen the sense of honour takes a prominent place in every kind of art of taming human beings.[b] However, with respect to the personal happiness of people, which is our purpose here, the case is a quite different one; and we must warn people not to place too much value on the opinion of others. If, as daily experience teaches, this happens nonetheless; if most people attach the

---

[*] *Scire tuum nihil est, nisi te scire hoc sciat alter* [What you know is worthless, if others do not know that you know it; Persius, *Satires* I, 27]

[a] [An ancient Roman story, told in Livy's *The History of Rome* III, 44–8, in which Verginius, a high-ranking, respected officer in the army, stabs his daughter Verginia to death, seeing this as the only way to protect her honour against an intrigue by politicians around the Magistrate Appius Claudius, who is determined to possess the young woman, to declare her a slave and remove her from her family and her fiancé]

[b] *Menschendressirungskunst*

greatest importance to the opinion that others have of them and are more concerned about this than what immediately exists for them, because it happens *in their own consciousness*; accordingly, if, by means of inverting the natural order, the former seems to be the real part, whereas the latter seems to be the merely ideal part of their existence; hence if they make what is derivative and secondary the principal thing and the image of their essence in the minds of others is closer to their hearts than this essence itself, then this immediate appreciation of that which does not immediately exist for us at all is a folly that has been called vanity,[a] *vanitas*, in order to indicate the vacuous and worthless character of this striving. It is also easy to see from the above that it is part of forgetting the end over the means, just as is avarice.

379   Indeed, the value that we place on the opinion of others and our constant anxiety in regard to it usually exceeds almost all reasonable aims, so that it can be seen as a kind of universally prevalent, or rather inborn, obsession. In everything we do, the opinion of others is considered almost before everything else, and on closer examination we will see nearly half the grievances and anxieties that we have ever felt to have originated in it. For it is at the root of our entire self-esteem, so often hurt because so pathologically sensitive, of all our vanities and pretensions, and also our flaunting and swaggering. Without this anxiety and addiction, luxury would not be a tenth of what is it. Every form of pride, point of honour[b] and obstinacy,[c] however varied its kind and sphere, rests on it – and what sacrifices it often demands! This concern with the opinion of others already shows itself in the child, and subsequently at every age, but most strongly in old age, since then, when the capacity for sensuous pleasures dries up, vanity and pride have to share their dominance only with avarice. We can see this most distinctly in the French, in whom it is quite endemic and expresses itself often in the most tasteless ambition, most ridiculous national vanity, and insolent swagger; so that their striving then defeats itself, having made them the object of mockery by other nations and the 'great nation'[d] having become a derisive nickname. Now, in order to specifically explain the wrongness of the excessive concern about others' opinion, which is in question here, a quite superlative example of this folly rooted in human

---

[a] *Eitelkeit*
[b] *point d'honneur* [German: 'Ehrenpunct'. In the 'Vorarbeiten zur Rechtslehre' (Preliminary Works for the Doctrine of Right), Kant devotes several pages to the concept, which he defines as '(1) the case of the danger of losing one's honourable reputation, which is based merely on the opinion, or maybe the delusion, of others or, in general, at least of those who belong to the same class'. It is also '(2) the loss of this public opinion that this whole class has to fear due to the behaviour of the first person' (Ak. 23: 363ff., LBl E01 and E04, 'Lose Blätter zum "Ehrenpunct"')]
[c] *puntiglio*   [d] *grande nation*

nature may be given, facilitated to a rare extent by the striking coincidence of the circumstances with the appropriate character, for this example allows us to appreciate fully the strength of this strange incentive. It is the following passage, from *The Times* of 31 March 1846,[a] part of a detailed report of the execution of *Thomas Wix*, a journeyman, who out of revenge had murdered his master. On the appointed morning, 'the rev. ordinary was early in attendance upon him, but Wix, beyond a quiet demeanour, betrayed no interest in his ministrations, appearing to feel anxious only to acquit himself "bravely" before the spectators of his ignominious end.' . . . In this, he was successful. In the courtyard that he had to cross on his way to the scaffold, erected close to the prison, he said: '"Now then, as Dr. Dodd said, I shall soon know the grand secret." On reaching the scaffold the miserable wretch mounted the drop without the slightest assistance despite having his arms tied.[b] On reaching the centre he bowed to the spectators twice, a proceeding which called forth a tremendous cheer from the[c] crowd beneath, etc.' – This is a prime example of the craving for honour, to have no other worry, while facing death in its most terrible form along with eternity, except one's impression on the gathered crowd of gapers and the opinion that one will leave in their minds! – And yet Lecomte, executed in the same year in France for attempted regicide, was likewise mainly annoyed during his trial that he could not appear decently clothed before the Chamber of Peers, and even at his execution he fretted mostly that he had not been allowed to shave. That it was just the same in the past we can see from what Mateo Alemán wrote in the introduction (*declaracion*) to his famous novel, *Guzmán de Alfarache*, namely that many deluded criminals divert their last hours, which they should devote exclusively to the salvation of their soul, to preparing and memorizing a short sermon that they intend to deliver on the ladder of the gallows. – In these features we can see mirror images of ourselves; for extreme cases everywhere provide the clearest explanation. All our concerns, worries, ranklings, annoyances, anxieties, exertions, and the like, perhaps in most cases actually refer to the opinion of others and are as absurd as those of the poor sinners. No less do our envy and hatred spring from the same root.

Obviously hardly anything else could contribute as much to our happiness, which rests mainly on peace of mind and contentment, as the limitation and moderation of this incentive to its reasonably justifiable proportion, which may be one fiftieth of the present one, thus extracting

380

381

---

[a] [*The Times of London*]   [b] [Schopenhauer adds 'despite having his arms tied']
[c] [Schopenhauer leaves out 'degraded']

from our flesh the thorn that constantly gives us pain. But this is very difficult; for we are dealing with a natural, inborn perversity. 'The desire for glory is given up last even by the wise', says Tacitus (*Histories* IV, 6).[a] The only way to get rid of that universal folly would be to recognize it distinctly as such and for this purpose to make it clear to ourselves how completely wrong, perverse, erroneous, and absurd most opinions in the heads of people usually are, making them in themselves not worthy of any attention; also, how little actual influence others' opinion can have on us in regard to most things and cases; further, how unfavourable it is most of the time, so that we all would be extremely angry if we heard all that was said about us and the tone in which people spoke of us; and finally that even honour itself is really only of mediate, not immediate value, and so forth. If we could succeed in such a conversion from universal foolishness, this would lead to an incredibly large increase in peace of mind and cheerfulness and also a more assured manner, a consistently more natural and unaffected conduct. The exceedingly beneficial influence that a seclusive existence has on our peace of mind rests mainly on the fact that it withdraws us from a life continuously lived in front of others, and so from constantly considering the opinions they might have, and thereby returns our selves to us. Equally, we would avoid many real misfortunes into which only this purely ideal striving or, rather, this utter folly draws us; and we would have left much more care for solid goods and enjoy them undisturbed. But, as I said, 'The noble is difficult'.[b]

The foolishness of our nature described here principally grows three offshoots: ambition, vanity, and pride. The difference between the last two rests on the fact that *pride* is the already established conviction of our own superior worth in some particular respect; *vanity*, on the other hand, is the wish to awaken such conviction in others, most of the time accompanied by the secret hope of being able to make it our own conviction as well. Therefore, *pride* is the *internally* arising, and hence direct, esteem of ourselves; in contrast, vanity strives to obtain such esteem *externally*, hence indirectly. Accordingly, vanity makes us talkative, pride taciturn. But vain people should know that the high opinion of others that they seek is much more easily and safely attained by means of continuous silence than by speaking, even if they had the most beautiful things to say.[33] – To be proud cannot be willed; at best those who want to can affect pride, but will soon lose it, as happens with every assumed role. For only the firm, inner, unshakable conviction of superior qualities and special worth makes us

382

---

[a] *Etiam sapientibus cupido gloriae novissima exuitur*   [b] χαλεπὰ τὰ καλά [Plato, *Republic* IV, II (435c)]

really proud. This conviction might be erroneous, or may depend on merely external and conventional qualities – that does not hurt pride, if only the conviction is actually present in earnest. Therefore, since pride is rooted in *conviction*,[a] it is, like cognition, not under the control of our *choice*.[b] Its worst enemy, by which I mean its greatest obstacle, is vanity, which solicits the approval of others in order to ground its own high opinion of itself on it; it is the condition of pride that such opinion is already quite firmly established.

As much as pride is universally condemned and decried, I suspect nonetheless that this comes mainly from those who have nothing of which they might be proud. Faced with the brazenness and impertinence of most people, anyone who has some good qualities does well to keep an eye on himself in order not to have them completely fall into oblivion; for if someone, while good-naturedly ignoring his merits, behaves around others as if they were exactly his equals, the others will at once naïvely regard him as such. But most of all I want to recommend this to those whose qualities are of the highest kind, i.e. actual and hence purely personal, since they are not, like decorations and titles, brought to mind at every moment through sensible effects; for otherwise they will often enough see 'the swine teaching Minerva'.[c] 'Joke with a slave, and he will soon show you his backside' – is an excellent Arab proverb, and Horace's 'Adopt the pride you earned through merit'[d] cannot be dismissed. But the virtue of modesty is a great invention for the scallywags; for according to it, everybody must speak of himself as if he were such a fool, which marvellously levels everything, so that it then looks as if none but fools existed.

The cheapest kind of pride, on the other hand, is national pride. For it betrays in those affected by it the lack of *individual* qualities of which they could be proud, since they would otherwise not grasp at something that they share with so many millions. Rather those who possess significant personal qualities will recognize most clearly the faults of their own nation, since they constantly have them in front of them. But every miserable fool who has nothing to be proud of in the world seizes the last means, to be proud of the nation to which he happens to belong; this compensates him, and he is now gratefully prepared to defend, with tooth and nail,[e] all faults and follies peculiar to it. For example, if we speak with due contempt of the

383

---

[a] *Ueberzeugung*   [b] *Willkür*
[c] *sus Minervam* [an ancient proverb, appearing, among other texts, in Cicero's *Academica* I, 5, 18, in a longer version]
[d] *sume superbiam, quaesitam meritis* [Horace, *Odes* III, 30, 14–15]   [e] πὺξ καὶ λάξ

stupid and degrading bigotry of the English nation, we will find among fifty English people no more than one who agrees; but this one is usually the man of intellect.[a] – The Germans are free of national pride and so provide proof of the honesty with which they have been credited; proof for the contrary is provided by those who pretend such pride and affect it in a ridiculous manner. This is what mostly the 'German brothers'[b] and democrats do, who flatter the people in order to seduce them. Some may claim that the Germans are geniuses,[c] but I cannot share that view. And Lichtenberg asks: 'Why is it that nobody who is not German readily passes himself off as one, but usually pretends to be French or English, if he wants to pass off as something else?'[d] Incidentally, individuality outweighs nationality by far, and in any given human being the former deserves a thousand times more consideration than the latter. National character will honestly not be credited with much good, since it speaks of the masses. Rather, human stupidity, perversity, and depravity appear in every country in a different form, and this is called national character. Disgusted with *one*, we praise another, until we become disgusted with that one too. – Every nation mocks the other, and all are right.

384

The subject matter of this chapter, what we *represent* in the world, i.e. what we are in the eyes of others, can be divided into *honour, rank, and fame*, as we have seen.

Rank, as important as it may be in the eyes of the masses and the philistines, can for our purposes be dealt with in a few words. It is a conventional, i.e. really a simulated value; its effect is a simulated high esteem, and the whole thing is a farce for the masses. – Medals are bills of exchange, based on public opinion; their value rests on the credit of the drawer. Meanwhile, they are a quite useful institution, even apart from the large amount of money that they save the state as a substitute for financial rewards, on the condition that their distribution happens with insight and justice. For the masses have eyes and ears, but not much more, and especially very little judgement, or even memory. Some merits lie completely outside of their sphere of comprehension, others they understand and cheer at their inception, but afterwards soon forget them. Therefore,

---

[a] *Mann von Kopf*
[b] *deutsche Brüder* [A reference to those young Germans, mostly students, in the first half of the nineteenth century, who expressed the desire for national integration]
[c] *die Deutschen hätten das Pulver erfunden* [German idiom]
[d] [Georg Christoph Lichtenberg, *Vermischte Schriften*, Göttingen: Dieterich, 1844; vol. 2 (*Bemerkungen vermischten Inhalts* [*Remarks on Diverse Subject Matters*]), p. 122 ('Nachtrag zu den Urtheilen und Bemerkungen über den Charakter verschiedener Völker' [Supplement to the Judgements and Remarks on the Character of Various Peoples])]

I find it quite fitting, through cross or star,[a] to call out to the masses: 'The man is not one of you; he has merits!' But through unjust, or indiscriminate, or excessive distribution, medals lose their value; therefore, a prince should be as cautious in awarding them as a merchant is in signing bills of exchange. The inscription 'Pour le Mérite'[b] is a pleonasm; every decoration should be for merit – that goes without saying.[c] –

The discussion of *honour* is much more difficult and extensive than that of rank. First we would have to define it. Now if for this end I said that honour is external conscience and conscience is internal honour, then this might please some people, but it would be more of a polished than a clear and thorough explanation. Therefore I say: Honour is, objectively, other people's opinion of our value and, subjectively, our fear of this opinion. In the latter form, it often has a very wholesome, although by no means purely moral effect – in the person of honour.

The root and the origin of the feeling of honour and shame, inherent in everyone who is not completely depraved, and also of the high value accorded to honour, lie in the following. Human beings by themselves are capable of very little and are like Robinson Crusoe on a deserted island; only together with others do they amount to much and are capable of much. They become aware of this circumstance as soon as their consciousness starts to develop to some extent, and at once the desire arises in them to be seen as useful members of human society, that is as people who are capable of contributing their own share,[d] and as a result are entitled to share in the advantages of human society. This they become by accomplishing, first of all, what is required and expected of everybody everywhere, and, secondly, by accomplishing what is required and expected of them in the particular position that they have assumed. They will recognize just as quickly that here it is not important that they are useful in their own opinion, but that they are so in the opinion of others. This is the source of their diligent striving for a favourable *opinion* of others and the high value they attach to it; both show the originality of an inborn feeling, which is called a sense of honour and, depending on the circumstances, a sense of shame (*verecundia*). This is what makes their cheeks blush as soon as they believe they have suddenly sunk in the opinion of others, even when they know themselves to be innocent and even where the fault that reveals itself refers only to a relative obligation,[e] namely one voluntarily assumed. On the other hand, nothing strengthens their vital spirit more than having gained, or renewed,

385

---

[a] [Decorations]   [b] ['For merit'; the highest military and civil order in Prussia]   [c] *ça va sans dire*
[d] *pro parte virili*   [e] *Verpflichtung*

certainty of others' favourable opinion, because it promises them the
386   protection and assistance of the combined forces of all, which are an
infinitely greater bulwark against the evils of life than their own.

Several *kinds of honour* arise from the different relations in which humans
can stand to others and in respect of which the latter must trust them, and so
have a certain good opinion of them. These relations are mainly the 'mine
and thine', then the actions of those who have pledged something, and
finally sexual relationships; to these correspond civic honour, official honour, and sexual honour, each of which again has subspecies.

Civic honour has the widest sphere: it consists in the assumption that we
respect everybody's rights unconditionally and, consequently, will never
employ unjust or unlawful means for our own advantage. It is the condition for participating in all peaceful intercourse. It is lost through a single
action that openly and violently runs counter to this, consequently also
through every criminal punishment, albeit only under the condition that
it is just. At bottom, honour rests on the conviction that moral character is
immutable, in virtue of which a single bad action guarantees the same
moral quality of all subsequent actions as soon as similar circumstances
occur; this is also attested by the English term 'character' for renown,
reputation, and honour. Precisely for this reason, lost honour cannot be
restored, unless the loss was caused by mistake, such as slander or false
appearance. Accordingly, there are laws against slander, written diatribes,[a]
and also insults; for an insult, mere verbal abuse, is a summary slander
without stating the reasons. This could be well expressed in Greek: ἔστι ἡ
λοιδορία διαβολὴ σύντομος[b] – which, however, is nowhere written. Of
course, those who revile others show that they have nothing real or true
to put forward against them, since otherwise they would provide this as the
premises and would safely leave the conclusion to the listeners; instead,
they give the conclusion and fail to provide the premises. But they rely on
the presumption that this is only done for the sake of – much appreciated –
387   brevity. – Civic honour[c] may take its name from the middle class,[d] but it
applies without exception to all classes, even to the highest; nobody can
dispense with it, it is a very serious matter that everybody should beware of
taking lightly. Whoever breaches good faith[e] has also forever lost good
faith, whatever he may do and whoever he may be, and the bitter fruits
borne by this loss will not fail to appear.[34]

---

[a] *Pasquille*   [b] ['An insult is short slander']   [c] *bürgerliche Ehre*   [d] *Bürgerstande*
[e] *Treu und Glauben* [A mostly legal expression]

In a certain sense, *honour* has a *negative* character, namely in contrast to *fame*, which has a *positive* one. For honour is not an opinion about particular qualities, belonging to this subject alone, but only about qualities usually assumed in all, which he too should not lack. Therefore, it only conveys that this subject is no exception, whereas fame says that he is. Consequently, fame has first to be acquired, whereas honour only must not be lost. Accordingly, a lack of fame is obscurity, a negative; lack of honour is disgrace, a positive. – However, this negativity must not be confused with passivity; on the contrary, honour has a thoroughly active character. For it stems solely from the *subject* of honour, depends on all of *his* doings, but not on what others do and what happens to him; hence it is 'what is up to us'.[a] As we shall see in a moment, this is a mark of distinction between true honour and chivalric or pseudo-honour. Only through slander is an attack on honour possible from the outside; the sole antidote is its refutation, with proper publicity and unmasking of the slanderer.

Respect for old age seems to rest on the fact that the honour of young people might be assumed, but has not been proven and, therefore, actually exists on credit. But in older people it had to be proven in the course of their lives whether they could assert their honour through their conduct. For neither the years in themselves, which animals also reach and some even exceed, nor experience, as simple, closer acquaintance with the course of the world, are sufficient ground for the respect that the young are required everywhere to show towards their elders; the mere feebleness of higher age would demand consideration rather than respect. But it is curious that human beings are born with a certain respect for white hair, which, there-fore, is actually instinctive. Wrinkles, an incomparably surer sign of old age, do not inspire this respect at all; we never speak of venerable wrinkles, but always of venerable white hair.

The value of honour is only a mediate one. For, as already explained at the beginning of this chapter, the opinion of others about us can have value for us only insofar as it determines, or can occasionally determine, their actions towards us. But this is the case as long as we live with or among human beings. For, since in the civilized state we owe security and pos-sessions only to society and also need others in all our undertakings, and since they have to trust us in order to have dealings with us, their opinion about us is of high, albeit always mediate, value for us; I cannot afford it an immediate value. *Cicero* agrees with this when he says: 'About a good reputation Chrysippus and Diogenes said that, apart from being useful,

388

---

[a] τῶν ἐφ᾽ ἡμῖν [a Stoic expression]

it was not worth raising a finger for its sake. I strongly agree with this.'
(*On the Ends* III, 17.)[a] Similarly Helvétius provides a detailed discussion of
this truth in his masterwork, *On Mind* (Discourse 3, ch. 13),[b] whose result is:
'We do not love esteem for its own sake, but solely for the advantages that it
brings us.'[c] Hence the slogan[d] 'Honour is more important than life' is
hyperbole, as pointed out before.

So much for civic honour.[35] *Official honour* is the common opinion of
others that a man who holds an office actually has all the qualities required
for it and punctually fulfils his official duties in all cases. The more
important and influential the radius of action of a person is in the state,
and thus the higher and more influential the position that he occupies, the
389 greater the opinion of the intellectual abilities and moral qualities must be
that make him suited for it; therefore, he possesses a correspondingly higher
degree of honour, expressed in his titles, decorations, and so forth, as well as
the deferential attitude of others towards him. – Now by the same measure,
social status universally determines the degree of honour, although this is
modified by the ability of the masses to judge the importance of status. But
we always confer greater honour on the person who has and fulfils special
duties, than on the ordinary citizen, whose honour depends mainly on
negative qualities.

Official honour further demands that whoever holds an office always
respect that office for the sake of his colleagues and successors by strictly
fulfilling his duties and, in addition, by never allowing attacks on the office
and on himself, insofar as he attends to it, to go unpunished – accusations to
the effect that he does not punctually carry out his duties or that the office
itself fails to serve the common good –, but proving by means of legal
punishment that those attacks were unjustified.

Subordinated kinds of honours are the official honour of the civil servant,
the physician, the lawyer, the public teacher, indeed, every graduate, in
brief, of everybody who has been publicly declared to be qualified for a
certain intellectual service and, thereby, has pledged to provide it; thus, in a
word, the honour of all publicly employed people as such. To this belongs
also true *military honour*; it consists of the fact that whoever has pledged to

---

[a] *de bona autem fama Chrysippus quidem et Diogenes, detracta utilitate, ne digitum quidem, ejus causa,
porrigendum esse dicebant. Quibus ego vehementer assentior* [*de finibus bonorum et malorum* (*On the Ends
of Goods and Evils*) III, 17, 57]

[b] *de l'esprit*

[c] *nous n'aimons pas l'estime pour l'estime, mais uniquement pour les avantages qu'elle procure*

[d] *Paradespruch* [No entry in *Grimm's Deutsches Wörterbuch*; among the connotations of '*Parade*' are
'pomp'/'pageantry', 'ostentation', and 'prime/paramount'; the allusion to military honour is obvious]

defend the common fatherland actually possesses the necessary qualities –
above all courage, bravery, and strength – and is sincerely prepared to
defend his fatherland to the death and, in general, not to desert the flag
to which he has sworn allegiance for anything in the world. – I have here
taken official honour in a wider sense than usual, where it signifies the
respect of the citizens that is due to the office itself.

Sexual honour seems to me to require closer examination and derivation
of its principles from its root, which will immediately affirm that all honour
ultimately depends on considerations of utility.

By its nature, *sexual honour* is divided into female and male honour, and   390
from both sides is a well-understood *esprit de corps*.[a] The former is by far the
most important of the two, since in the lives of women, the sexual relation is
most essential. – *Female honour* is the general opinion with respect to a girl
that she has never abandoned herself to a man, and in regard to a woman
that she has given herself only to her husband. The importance of this
opinion is based on the following. The female sex demands and expects
from the male sex everything, namely everything that it desires and needs;
the male sex demands of the female initially and immediately only one
thing. Therefore, it had to be established that the male sex can obtain from
the female this one thing only in exchange for taking over the care of
everything and especially for the children that spring from the union; on
this arrangement rests the welfare of the entire female sex. In order to
enforce it, the female sex must with necessity stick together and show *esprit
de corps*. As a result it faces, as a whole and with closed ranks, the male sex as
the common foe, who by virtue of the superiority of his physical and
intellectual powers is naturally in possession of all earthly goods – a foe
that must be subdued and conquered in order to take over the possession of
these goods by taking possession of the male sex. To this end, it is the
maxim of honour of the entire female sex that the male is absolutely denied
any sexual intercourse outside marriage, so that every single individual
be forced into marriage, as a kind of surrender, and, as a result, the
entire female sex is provided for. But this end can only be achieved by
means of strict observance of the above maxim; therefore, the female sex,
with true *esprit de corps*, guards its preservation among all its members.
Correspondingly, every girl that has betrayed the entire female sex through
illicit intercourse is expelled and shamed, because the welfare of the entire
sex would be undermined if this conduct became universal; this girl has lost
her honour. No woman may have anything to do with her; she is avoided   391

---

[a] ['regard for honour and interests of body one belongs to' (*Concise Oxford Dictionary*)]

like the plague. The adulteress meets the same fate, because she has not adhered to the terms of the capitulation that the man had entered and, through such an example, other men are discouraged from doing so, while the welfare of the entire female sex depends on it. Furthermore, because of the serious breach of faith and betrayal of her deed, the adulteress loses together with her sexual also her civic honour. Consequently, we might speak, with an apologetic expression, of 'a fallen girl', but not 'a fallen wife', and the seducer can restore the girl's honour by marrying her, but not the adulterer the wife after she has been divorced. – Now as a result of this clear insight, if we recognize a wholesome and, indeed, necessary, but calculated and interest-based *esprit de corps* as the basis of the principle of female honour, we might then be able to accord this honour the greatest importance for female existence and, therefore, a great relative value, but not an absolute one that transcends life and its purposes and must accordingly be paid for at the price of life itself. Accordingly, we will not be able to applaud the extravagant deeds of Lucretia[a] and Verginius,[b] which degenerate into tragic farce. For the same reason, the end of *Emilia Galotti*[c] is so outrageous that we leave the theatre completely upset. In contrast, we cannot help but sympathize with Klärchen in *Egmont*,[d] in spite of sexual honour. Carrying the principle of female honour to the extreme is, like so many things, equivalent to forgetting the end over the means; for, through such exaggeration, an absolute value is imputed to sexual honour, whereas, even more than all other kinds of honour, it has only relative value. Indeed, we might say that it has only conventional value when we learn from Thomasius' *De concubinatu*[e] how in almost all countries and during all ages until the Lutheran Reformation concubinage was a legally permitted and recognized relation in which the concubine remained honourable, not to mention the Mylitta in Babylon (Herodotus I, 199[f]), etc. Also there are civil relations that render the external form of marriage impossible, especially in Catholic countries, where no divorce occurs, but everywhere for the ruling sovereigns who, in my opinion, act much more morally when they keep a

---

[a] [A reference to the story of the rape of Lucretia, told in Livy, *The History of Rome* I, 57–8]
[b] [See p. 311, n. a]
[c] [Gotthold Ephraim Lessing, *Emilia Galotti* (1772), a tragedy modelled on the story of Verginius, of a father who kills his daughter to preserve her honour]
[d] [Goethe, *Egmont* (1788), a tragedy in which Count Egmont, the hero of the Dutch people's resistance against Spanish domination, has a love relationship with Klärchen, a young woman from the lower classes, who herself turns into a heroine; Goethe represents this love as transcending social boundaries]
[e] [Christian Thomasius, *De concubinatu* (*On Concubinage*), Halle, 1713]
[f] [*Histories*; in this passage Herodotus describes the Babylonian custom of requiring all women to offer themselves sexually once to a stranger at the temple of Mylitta (Aphrodite)]

mistress than when they enter a morganatic[a] marriage, whose descendants might one day put forward claims in case any legitimate descendants have died, which is why such a marriage creates the possibility of civil war, as remote as that may be. Moreover, such a morganatic marriage, i.e. really a marriage contracted in defiance of all external circumstances, is at bottom a concession made to women and to priests, two classes to which we should be careful not to concede a thing.[36] Furthermore, we should consider that everyone in the country may marry the woman of his choice, except for one, from whom this natural right has been taken away. This poor man is the prince. His hand belongs to the country and is given in marriage for reasons of state, i.e. in accordance with the good of the country. Now in spite of this, he is a human being and also wants to follow the inclination of his heart. Therefore, it is as unjust and ungrateful as it is narrow-minded to prevent the prince from keeping a mistress, or to reproach him for it; naturally, she must not be allowed to have any influence on the government. For her part, such a mistress is in a sense an exceptional person in respect to sexual honour, exempted from the universal rule, for she has given herself merely to a man who could love her and she him, but will never be able to marry him. – But in general, the many bloody sacrifices made to the female principle of honour – in infanticide and suicide of mothers – testify to its origin's not being purely natural. Of course, a girl who surrenders herself illicitly commits a breach of faith against her entire sex; but this faithfulness is only tacitly assumed and not confirmed by oath. And since commonly her own advantage suffers most immediately, her foolishness is infinitely greater than her wickedness.

The sexual honour of men is engendered by that of women; and the corresponding *esprit de corps* requires that everyone who has made the surrender that is so very favourable for the opposite party – marriage – now watches that it is upheld for him, so that this pact should not lose its strength, through laxity of observance becoming common, and the men, in surrendering all, not even be assured the one thing that they have bargained for, exclusive possession of the woman. Accordingly, the honour of the man demands that he avenge his wife's adultery and punish it, at least by separating from her. If he knowingly tolerates it, he is disgraced by the community of men. However, this disgrace is not as radical as that suffered by the woman because of the loss of her sexual honour, but rather merely a lesser kind of stigma,[b] because in a man the sexual relationship is a

393

---

[a] ['*standesungleich*', referring to marriage between people of unequal social rank]
[b] *levioris notae macula*

subordinate one, insofar as he is part of many other and more important relationships. The two great dramatic poets of modern times have both twice made male honour their topic: Shakespeare, in *Othello* and *The Winter's Tale*, and Calderón,[a] in *The Surgeon of His Honour*[b] and *Secret Vengeance for Secret Offence.*[c] By the way, this honour only demands punishment of the woman, not of her lover, which is a mere supererogatory act;[d] this confirms its origin, as mentioned, in men's *esprit de corps.* –

As I have considered it so far in its forms and principles, honour is found to be universally valid in all peoples and ages, although some local and temporary modifications of the principles of female honour can be demonstrated. On the other hand, there still exists another kind of honour, completely different from the universally accepted kind, of which neither the Greeks nor the Romans had any idea, just as the Chinese, Hindus, and Muslims know nothing about it to this day. For it arose only during the Middle Ages and became endemic just in Christian Europe, and even here only among an extremely small section of the population, namely among the upper classes of society and those emulating them. This is *chivalric honour*, or the point of honour.[e] Since its principles are completely different from those of the kind of honour discussed so far, and even partly contradict it, insofar as the former makes an *honourable man* and the latter the *man of honour*, I shall specifically lay down its principles here as a code or mirror of chivalric honour.

394

(1) Honour does *not* consist in the opinion of others, but solely in the *expressions* of such an opinion, irrespective of whether the expressed opinion actually exists or not, much less whether there are grounds for it. Consequently, as a result of our conduct, others may have an ever so bad opinion about us and despise us as much as they want to; as long as no one dares to utter it aloud it does not injure our honour at all. Conversely, even if we compel all others to esteem us highly (for that depends not on their choice[f]), nonetheless it is enough for only one person – and he may be the most evil and stupid – to declare his contempt for us and our honour is immediately violated; indeed, it is lost forever, if it is not restored. – A superfluous proof of the point that what counts is by no means the *opinion* of others, but solely its *expression*, is that slanders can be *taken back* and, if necessary, made subject of an apology, whereby it is then as if they had never

---

[a] [Pedro Calderón de la Barca]
[b] *el medico de su honra* [Followed by Schopenhauer's German translation]
[c] *a secreto agravio secreta venganza* [Followed by Schopenhauer's German translation]
[d] *opus supererogationis*   [e] *point d'honneur*   [f] *Willkür*

happened. Whether the opinion from which they sprung has also changed and why this should have happened does not matter; only the expression is annulled, and then everything is well. Accordingly, the intention here is not to earn respect, but to extort it.

(2) The honour of a man does not depend on what he *does*, but on what he *suffers*, what happens to him. Whereas according to the principles of the universally accepted kind of honour previously discussed this opinion solely depends on what he *himself* says or does, in contrast chivalric honour depends on what another says or does. Consequently, it lies in the hands, in fact, hangs from the tip of the tongue, of everybody, and can be lost forever at every moment, if somebody seizes it, unless the person attacked snatches it back through a restorative process that will be discussed presently, but which can only happen at the risk of his life, health, freedom, possessions, and peace of mind. In accordance with this, the doings of a   395
man may be the most honest and noble, his mind the purest and his intellect the most eminent; nevertheless, his honour can be lost at every moment, namely as soon as it pleases anybody to *insult* him – somebody who has not yet violated these laws of honour, but otherwise can be the most wretched scoundrel, the most stupid brute, an idler, gambler, contractor of debts, in short, a human being who is not worthy for the other to even look at. Most of the time it will indeed be such a person who is fond of doing this, because, as Seneca rightly remarks, 'The more contemptible and ridiculous somebody is, the looser is his tongue' (*On Constancy* XI).[a] Such a person will also be more easily incited against someone like the one first described, because opposites hate each other, and because the sight of superior qualities usually produces the silent rage of a base character. Hence Goethe says:

> At enemies why lament?
> Were they for friends ever meant
> Who find your being, as you be,
> A silent reproach eternally?   *West-Eastern Divan*[b]

We see how much especially people of the kind last described owe to the principle of honour, since it puts them on a par with those who would otherwise be beyond their reach in every respect. – When such a person has insulted the other, i.e. attributed a bad quality to him, then this is, for the

---

[a] *ut quisque contem[p]tissimus et ludibrio [ut ludibrium] est, ita solutissimae linguae est [De constantia sapientis (On the Constancy of the Wise) XI, 3]*
[b] ['*Buch der Sprüche*' (Book of Proverbs)]

time being, considered an objectively true and grounded judgement, a legally valid decree, indeed, it remains true and valid forever, if it is not soon afterwards erased with blood; that means, the insulted person remains (in the eyes of all 'people of honour') what the one insulting him (even if this should be the most worthless of all mortals) has called him; for he has (this is a technical term[a]) 'let it go unchallenged'.[b] Accordingly, the 'people of honour' will now utterly despise him, avoid him like the plague, and, for example, loudly and publicly refuse to attend social gatherings where this person is admitted, and so on. – I think I can trace the origin of this wise fundamental outlook with certainty to the fact that (according to C. G. von Wächter's *Beiträge zur deutschen Geschichte, besonders des deutschen Strafrechts*, 1845[c]) in criminal trials during the Middle Ages, up to the fifteenth century, it was not the accuser who had to prove guilt, but the accused had to prove his innocence. This could happen through an oath of purgation, which still needed the compurgators (*consacramentales*), who swore that they were convinced that the accused was incapable of any perjury. If he did not have these, or if the accuser did not accept them, a judgement of God was introduced, which usually consisted in ordeal by battle. For the accused was now 'disgraced'[d] and had to clear himself. We see here the origin of the concept of being in disgrace and the whole course of things, as it takes place even today among 'people of honour', only that the oath is omitted. Here we also find an explanation for the obligatory deep indignation with which 'people of honour' react to the accusation of lying and demand bloody revenge for it, which, given the ordinariness of lying, seems really odd, but especially in England has grown into a deeply rooted superstition. (Actually, everyone who threatens to punish the accusation of lying with death would have to have never lied in his whole life.) For in the criminal trials of the Middle Ages, the shorter form with which the accused replied to the accuser was: 'You lie', after which an ordeal was declared at once. This is the reason why after an accusation of lying the appeal to arms has to follow immediately.[37] – So much in regard to insults. But now there is something worse than insult, something so terrible that I have to ask the 'people of honour' for forgiveness for even mentioning it in this code of knightly honour, since I realize that the mere thought of it makes their flesh

396

---

[a] *terminus technicus*   [b] *auf sich sitzen lassen*
[c] [Carl Georg von Wächter, *Beiträge zur Deutschen Geschichte, insbesondere zur Geschichte des Deutschen Strafrechts* (*Contributions to German History, in particular the History of German Criminal Law*), Tübingen: Fues, 1845]
[d] *bescholten*

creep and their hair stand on end, insofar as it is the greatest evil[a] in this world and worse than death and damnation. For one person, horrible to say, can slap another, or strike him. This is a dreadful event and leads to such a complete death of honour[b] that, although all other violations of honour can already be healed by blood-letting, this requires a complete death blow 397 to be thoroughly healed.

(3) Honour has nothing at all to do with what human beings may be in and for themselves, with the question whether their moral constitution could ever change, and with all such pedantry. Rather, when it is violated or lost for the time being, it can soon be completely restored, if only one acts speedily, through a single universal remedy, the duel. But if the violator does not belong to the classes that are committed to the code of chivalric honour, or if he has already offended against it, then, in particular if the injury to honour was a physical assault, but also if it was merely verbal, we can operate safely by stabbing him, if we are armed, on the spot or at most an hour later, whereby honour is then made whole again. In addition, or if, out of concern for any inconvenience that might arise, we want to avoid this step, or if we are just uncertain whether the offender submits to the laws of knightly honour or not, we have a palliative in 'Avantage'.[c] This consists in being markedly ruder when he has been rude; when abuse is no longer enough, we resort to blows; and here also there is a climactic progress to the preservation of honour: slaps in the face are cured by beating with a stick; this, in turn, by a hunting-whip; even against the latter some consider spitting as a proven remedy. Only if we do not apply these means in good time, do we have to resort to bloody procedures. This palliative method is actually grounded in the following maxim.

(4) Just as being insulted is a disgrace, insulting another is an honour. For example, let there be truth, right, and reason on the side of my opponent, but I insult him; so all these must surrender, and right and honour are on my side; he, on the other hand, has for now lost his honour – until he restores it, albeit not through right and reason, but through shooting and stabbing. Accordingly, rudeness is a quality that, when it comes to the point of honour, replaces or supersedes all other qualities; the rudest person is 398 always in the right: 'What more does one want?'[d] Whatever stupid, naughty, and evil thing somebody might have done – rudeness will immediately erase and legitimize it.[38] For example, if during a discussion or

---

[a] *summum malum* [b] *Ehrentod*
[c] [The possibility to erase an insult by returning a greater insult] [d] *quid multa*

otherwise during a conversation someone shows more accurate knowledge of the subject, stricter love of truth, sounder judgement, and more understanding than us, or in general demonstrates intellectual virtues that outshine us, we can at once eliminate all such superiority and our own inferiority revealed by it and now, in turn, be superior ourselves by becoming insulting and rude. For rudeness defeats every argument and eclipses all intellect. If the opponent declines to get involved and answer with an even greater rudeness, whereby we would enter the noble contest of Avantage, we remain victorious and honour is on our side; truth, knowledge, understanding, intellect, and wit must retreat and are driven from the field by divine rudeness. Therefore, as soon as someone expresses a different opinion or merely shows more understanding than they can muster, 'people of honour' immediately make as if to mount their charger. And when, for example, during a controversy they lack a counter-argument, they look for some rudeness that will serve the same purpose and is easier to find; then they leave in triumph.[39] We can see here already how much it is justified to credit the principle of honour with ennobling the tone in society. – This maxim, in turn, depends on the following, which is the actual fundamental maxim and soul of the entire code.

(5) The highest seat of rightful judgement that one can appeal to from any other seat, in regard to all differences, insofar as honour is concerned, is that of physical force, i.e. animality.[a] For every rudeness is really an appeal to bestiality, in that it declares the fight of intellectual powers or of moral right to be incompetent, and puts in their place the battle of physical powers, which in the human species, defined by Franklin as the tool-making animal,[b] is executed with the weapons appropriate to it, in a duel, and precipitates an irrevocable decision. – As is well-known, the fundamental maxim is called, in a word, 'law of the fist',[c] which is analogous to the expression 'absurdity', and hence is, like that one, ironic; therefore, chivalric honour should accordingly be called honour of the fist.[d] –

(6) When above we found civic honour to be very scrupulous in regard to mine and thine, obligations entered and promises made, the code considered here shows the most noble liberality in this regard. For it is only *one* word that must not be broken, the word of honour, i.e. the word accompanied by 'on my honour!' – which leads to the presumption that every other word can be broken. Even if this word of honour has been broken,

399

[a] *Thierheit*   [b] [Original English, followed by Schopenhauer's German translation in parentheses]
[c] *Faustrecht [ius manu]*   [d] *Faust-Ehre*

honour can be saved, if necessary, through the universal remedy, the duel, with those who claim that we had given our word of honour. – Further: there is only *one* debt that absolutely needs to be repaid, and that is gambling debt, which accordingly is called by the name 'debt of honour'. In regard to all other debt, we are allowed to cheat the Jew and the Christian; that does not hurt knightly honour at all.*,40 –

The unprejudiced person realizes at first glance that this strange, barbaric, and ridiculous code of honour did not arise from the essence of human nature or a healthy view of human relations. Moreover, this is confirmed by its severely limited sphere of acceptance, which is exclusively in Europe and only since the Middle Ages and also just among the aristocracy, the military, and those who emulate them. For neither the Greeks, nor the Romans, nor the highly educated Asian peoples of ancient and modern times know anything about this honour and its principles. They all know no other honour than the kind first analysed. For them, a person is valued in accordance with what his actions proclaim him to be, not with what it pleases some loose tongue to say about him. For them, what someone says

400

---

* So this is the code. And these principles, to which in Christian Europe in general all those to this day pay homage who belong to the so-called good society and the so-called good tone, when reduced to distinct concepts and clearly pronounced, appear as strange and as grotesque as stated here. Indeed, many of those who have been inoculated with these principles through word and example from the time of their earliest youth, believe in them more firmly than in any catechism, feel the deepest, most unfeigned veneration for them, are at every moment sincerely prepared to sacrifice happiness, peace of mind, health, and life for them, and claim that these principles are rooted in human nature and, consequently, innate, and hence are a priori certain and beyond all scrutiny. I do not wish to offend their hearts, but this is not a credit to their minds. Therefore, there is no social class for which these principles might be least fitting than the one destined to represent intelligence on earth, to become the salt of the earth, which is now supposed to prepare for this great vocation, that is, the studying youths, who in Germany unfortunately indulge in them more than any other class. Once – when I myself still belonged to these youths, who are educated about *Hellas* [Greece] and *Latium* [Rome] – the bad philosophaster J. G. Fichte (whom the educated world in Germany still honestly regards as a philosopher) impressed on them the disadvantages or the immorality of the consequences of these principles in a *Declamatio ex cathedra* [declamation from the lectern]. Instead, I have to say to them just the following. You, whose youth was nursed by the language and wisdom of Hellas and Latium and on behalf of whom such priceless care was taken to direct the beams of light of beautiful antiquity's wise and noble thinkers into your minds at an early age – you wish to begin by making this code of stupidity and brutality the standard of your conduct? Look at how it stands before you, reduced to distinct concepts, in its miserable dullness, and let this be the touchstone not of your heart, but of your understanding. If the latter does not repudiate it, then your mind is not suited to work in the field where the necessary requirements are an energetic power of judgement that easily breaks the chains of prejudice, and an accurately responding understanding that is able clearly to distinguish true from false, even where the difference is deeply concealed and not evident as it is here. In this case, my dear ones, look for another honest way to make it through life, become soldiers, or learn a trade, which finds gold in every land. –

or does can destroy his *own* honour, but never that of others. A blow is just a blow, as every horse and every ass can deal a more dangerous one. According to circumstances, a blow will provoke anger and may also be avenged on the spot; but it has nothing to do with honour, and no accounts are kept about blows, or insults, together with the 'satisfaction' received for them or neglected to be demanded. In terms of bravery and contempt for life, they do not rank behind the peoples of Christian Europe. Greeks and Romans certainly were true heroes; but they knew nothing of the point of honour. For them, the duel was not a matter for noblemen, but for mercenary gladiators, abandoned slaves, and convicted criminals, who, in turn with wild animals, were set to fight one another for the amusement of the people. With the introduction of Christianity, gladiator games were abolished; but during Christian times, mediated through ordeal by battle,[a] the duel took their place. While the former were a cruel sacrifice to common pleasure in spectacles, the latter is a cruel sacrifice to common prejudice, but not, as the former, of criminals, slaves, and prisoners, but of free and noble people.

There are numerous features preserved for us that show that this prejudice was utterly foreign to the ancients. For example, when a Teutonic chief had challenged *Marius* to a duel, this hero had the answer conveyed to him that 'if he were tired of his life, he should hang himself', and offered him instead a worn-out gladiator with whom he could fight (Freinsheim's Supplement to Livy,[b] Book LXVIII, ch. 12). In Plutarch ('Themistocles', 11) we read that the admiral Eurybiades, arguing with Themistocles, had raised a stick in order to hit him, but not that Themistocles drew his sword; instead he said: 'Strike if you will, but listen to me.'[c] How indignant must the reader 'of honour' be when he fails to find the report that the Athenian officers corps immediately declared itself unwilling to serve further under such a Themistocles! – Accordingly, a newer French author says quite rightly: 'If it occurred to anyone to claim that Demosthenes was a man of honour, one would smile indulgently; ... Neither was Cicero a man of honour.' (*Soirées littéraires*, by C. Durand, Rouen, 1828,[d] vol. 2, p. 300.)

---

[a] *Gottesurtheils*
[b] [*T. Livii Patavini Historiarum Libri qui supersunt omnes cum integris Joannis Freinshemii supplementis* (Titus Livius' *Ab urbe condita* [*The History of Rome*] with the Supplement of Johann Freinsheim), vol. 8, Zweibrücken: Bipont, 1785; Freinsheim's ch. XXXIII, pp. 331–2]
[c] πάταξον μὲν οὖν, ἄκουσον δέ [Plutarch, *Parallel Lives*, 'The Life of Themistocles' 11, 3]
[d] *si quelqu'un s'avisait de dire que Démosthène fut un homme d'honneur, on sourirait de pitié; ... Cicéron n'était pas un homme d'honneur non plus* [Charles Durand, *Soirées littéraires, ou cours de littérature. A l'usage des gens du monde* (*Literary Soirees, or a Course on Literature. For the Use of People of the World*), 2 vols., Rouen: E. Frère, 1828]

Furthermore, the passage in Plato (*Laws* IX, last six pages, and also XI, p. 131, Bipont edn.[a]) about *aikia*,[b] i.e. abuse,[c] shows clearly enough that the ancients had no idea of the notion of a chivalric point of honour in such matters. As a result of his frequent disputes, *Socrates* was often physically mistreated, which he suffered calmly. When someone once kicked him, he patiently put up with it and told the person to his amazement this: 'Would I take to court an ass that had pushed me?' – (Diogenes Laertius II,[d] 21.) Another time, when someone said to him: 'Does that person not abuse and taunt you?' his answer was: 'No, for what he says does not apply to me' (ibid., 36). – Stobaeus (*Florilegium*, ed. Gaisford,[e] vol. 1, pp. 327–30) has preserved for us a long passage by *Musonius*, from which we learn how the ancients regarded insults; they knew no other satisfaction than the judicial one, and wise men rejected even that.[41] That the ancients knew no other satisfaction for a received slap in the face than that of the courts can be clearly seen in Plato's *Gorgias* (p. 86, Bipont edn.[f]), where (p. 133) the opinion of Socrates is also found. The same is illustrated through the account by Gellius (XX, 1)[g] of a certain Lucius Veratius, who, without any provocation, was so mischievous as to slap Roman citizens whom he encountered in the street; in order to avoid all complications he arranged to be accompanied by a slave with a purse of copper coins, who immediately paid out the lawful compensation of twenty-five assis[h] to those who had been surprised in this way. *Crates*, the famous Cynic, had received such a strong box on the ear from the musician Nicodromus that his face was swollen and bloody; after which he fastened a slat to his forehead with the inscription 'Nicodromus did this',[i] so that the flute player was greatly shamed, having committed such a brutality (Diogenes Laertius[j] VI, 89) against a man whom all of Athens worshipped like a household god (Apuleius, *Florida*, p. 126, Bipont edn.). – From *Diogenes* of Sinope we have a letter to Melesippus about the fact that the drunken sons of the Athenians had thrashed him, telling him that it means nothing. (Note by Isaac Casaubon on Diogenes Laertius[k] VI, 33.) – Seneca, in his *On*

402

---

[a] *de legibus* [*Platonis philosophi quae extant graece*, ed. H. Stephan, vol. 9, Studiis Societatis Bipontinae, 1786 (879e–882b and 917d–918a)]
[b] αἰκία [Insult, affront]   [c] *Mißhandlung*   [d] [*Lives and Opinions of Eminent Philosophers*]
[e] [Ed. Thomas Gaisford (based on the version of Hugo Grotius), Leipzig: Kuehn, 1823 (*Peri anexikakias* [*On Forbearance*] 16)]
[f] [Vol. 4, 1783 (486b–c and 508b–d)]   [g] [Aulus Gellius, *Noctes Atticae* (*Attic Nights*) XX, 1, 13]
[h] *Aß* [*As*, pl. *Assis*; Roman copper coin of low value]   [i] Νικόδρομος ἐποίει (*Nicodromus fecit*)
[j] [*Lives and Opinions of Eminent Philosophers*]
[k] [*Isaaci Casauboni Notae atque Aegidii Menagii Observationes et Emendationes in Diogenem Laertium* (*Isaac Casaubon's Notes and Aegidius Menagius' Observations and Emendations on Diogenes Laertius*), vol. 2, Leipzig: Koehler, 1833]

Constancy, from ch. 10 to the end, considered insult, *contumelia*, at length, in order to explain that the wise person does not pay attention to it. In ch. 14 he says: "'What should the wise person do if he gets beaten with a fist?" What Cato did when he was struck in the face: He did not become angry or avenge the insult; he also did not forgive it, but denied that it had happened.'[a,42]

403 'Indeed', you cry, 'but those were sages!' – And you are fools? Agreed. – We see, therefore, that the whole principle of chivalric honour was completely unknown to the ancients, because they remained true to the unprejudiced, natural view of things and did not allow themselves to be persuaded of such sinister and unholy pranks.[b] Therefore, they were able not to take a slap in the face for anything other than what it is, a small physical disturbance; whereas for modern people it is a catastrophe and a topic for tragedies, for example in Corneille's *Cid*,[c] and also in a newer German bourgeois tragedy, which is called *The Power of Circumstances*,[d] but should be called 'The Power of Prejudice'.[e] But when a face is slapped in the Paris National Assembly, that echoes in the whole of Europe. To the people 'of honour', who must be disgruntled by the above-mentioned classical recollections and examples from antiquity, I recommend, as an antidote, to read the story of Mr *Desglands* in Diderot's masterpiece, *Jacques the Fatalist*,[f] as an exquisite specimen of modern knightly honour, which they might find enjoyable and edifying.

From what has been said, it becomes clear enough that the principle of chivalric honour is not at all a primary one grounded in human nature itself. Rather it is artificial, and its origin is not difficult to discover. It is obviously an offspring of those times when fists were more exercised than brains and priests kept reason in chains, hence a child of the lauded Middle Ages and its knighthood. For back then, people allowed the good Lord not only to care, but also to judge for them. Consequently, difficult legal cases were decided by ordeals,[g] or judgements of God; these consisted, with few exceptions, of duels, by no means only between knights, but also between ordinary citizens, as shown by a fine example in Shakespeare's *Henry VI* (Part 2, Act II, scene 3). From every judicial verdict, an appeal could still be made to the duel as the appellate court, that is, the judgement of God. By this means physical strength and agility, hence animal nature, instead of reason, were seated on the bench, and not what somebody had done, but what happened

---

[a] *'At sapiens colaphis [colapho] percussus, quid faciet?' quod Cato, cum illi os percussum esset: non excanduit, non vindicavit injuriam; nec remisit quidem, sed factam negavit.* [XIV, 3]
[b] *Fratzen*   [c] [Pierre Corneille, *Le Cid* (1636)]
[d] *Die Macht der Verhältnisse* [by Ludwig Robert (1819)]   [e] *'die Macht des Vorurtheils'*
[f] *Jacques le fataliste* [*Jacques le fataliste et son maître* (1796)]   [g] *Ordalien*

to him decided on right and wrong – completely in accordance with the   404
principle of chivalric honour which is still in effect today. Whoever still doubts
this origin of the institution of duelling, should read the excellent book by
J. G. Millingen, *The History of Duelling*, 1849.[a] Indeed, even to this day we find
among those people who live according to the principle of knightly honour –
usually not the most informed and thoughtful, as is well known – some who
actually regard the outcome of a duel as a divine ruling in the underlying
dispute, certainly in accordance with traditionally inherited opinion.

Apart from this origin of the principle of chivalric honour, its tendency is
primarily to force, through the threat of physical violence, the external
attestations of the kind of respect that is seen as too onerous or superfluous
to be actually earned. This is similar to the person who, by warming the
bulb of a thermometer with his hand, wants to demonstrate from the rising
of the mercury that the room is well heated. Considered more closely, the
heart of the matter is this: whereas civic honour, aiming at peaceful dealings
with others, consists in their opinion of us that we deserve complete *trust*,
because we unconditionally respect everyone's rights, chivalric honour
consists in the opinion of us that we are to be *feared*, because we are inclined
to defend our own rights unconditionally. Since little reliance can be placed
on the justice of human beings, the principle that it is more essential to be
feared than to enjoy trust would not be completely false, if we lived in the
state of nature, where all have to protect themselves and immediately defend
their rights. But in the civilized state, where the state has taken over the
protection of our person and property, this principle is no longer applicable
and stands, like the castles and watch-towers from the times of the law of the
fist, useless and abandoned between well-cultivated fields and busy roads or
even railways. Accordingly, knightly honour, holding on to this principle,
has seized on those interferences with a person that the state only punishes
lightly or not at all, according to the principle 'The law does not concern
itself with trifles',[b] being insignificant slights and in part mere teasing. In   405
regard to these it has risen to an overestimation of the worth of one's own
person* that is wholly inappropriate to the nature, constitution, and destiny
of human beings, raising it to a kind of sanctity; accordingly, chivalric honour
considers the punishment by the state of small slights against it quite
insufficient, therefore taking over their punishment itself and always

---

* What does it really mean to insult somebody? – It means to make him doubt the high opinion he has
of himself.

[a] [John Gideon Millingen, *The History of Duelling* (1841)]
[b] *de minimis lex non curat* [A principle of Roman law]

punishing life and limb of the offender. Obviously, this is grounded in the most excessive arrogance and most flagrant haughtiness, which, by forgetting entirely what human beings really are, claim unconditional inviolability and blamelessness for them.[*,43] However, anyone who is inclined to enforce these and consequently declares 'whoever insults or even hits me shall die', deserves just for this to be banished from the country. All kinds of things are then pretended in order to gloss over this presumptuous arrogance. It is said of two fearless people that none of them will back down, so that the smallest push would lead to insults, then beating, and finally a fatal blow; therefore, it would be better, for decency's sake, to omit the intermediary steps and immediately resort to arms. The more specific procedure then has been developed into a rigid, pedantic system with laws and rules, which is the most sincere farce in the world and stands as a true temple of honour to folly. However, the principle itself is false; in matters of little importance (those of great importance will be left to the courts) of two fearless people one indeed gives in, namely the most prudent, and matters of mere opinion are left to themselves. Proof of this is provided by the people, or rather by all the numerous classes that do not subscribe to the chivalric principle of honour, with whom disputes take their natural course; among these classes killings are a hundred times more rare than in the faction that is devoted to the principle and perhaps makes up a mere one-thousandth of the whole population. Even a brawl is a rare event. – But then it is claimed that the ultimate cornerstone of the good tone and good manners of society is the principle of honour with its duels, which are the bulwark against outbursts of barbarism and bad manners. But without a doubt in Athens, Corinth, and Rome good, and indeed very good, society and also good manners and tone could be found, without that bogey of knightly honour

---

[*] Chivalric honour is an offspring of arrogance and folly. (Its opposite truth is most poignantly expressed by *el principe constante* [the constant prince] with the words '*esa es la herencia de Adan*' [This (neediness) is Adam's inheritance.] [Pedro Calderón de la Barca, *El príncipe constante* (*The Constant Prince*) (1629)].) It is remarkable that this superlative of all arrogance is to be found solely and exclusively among the members of that religion that makes humility the duty of its followers, since neither former ages nor other parts of the world know this principle of knightly honour. Nonetheless, we are not entitled to ascribe it to religion, rather to feudalism, where every nobleman considered himself a small sovereign who recognized no human judge above him and, therefore, learned to attribute complete inviolability and sanctity to his person, so that every attack on it, thus every blow and every swearword, seemed to be a crime deserving death. Accordingly, the principle of honour and the duels were of concern originally only for the nobility and, as a consequence, later for officers, followed afterwards from time to time, although not consistently, by other higher classes in order not to be less worthy. Although the duels arose from the ordeals, the latter are not the ground, but the consequent and application of the principle of honour; whoever does not recognize a human judge, appeals to the divine one. Ordeals themselves, on the other hand, are not unique to Christianity, but are also a strong force in Hinduism, mostly in ancient times; but traces of them still exist.

behind them. Of course, there it was not women who presided over society, as is the case with us, which, since it first of all confers a frivolous and silly character on conversation and prevents any serious discourse, certainly also contributes to the fact that in our good society personal courage claims superiority to all other qualities. However, personal courage is a very subordinate quality, a mere virtue of petty officers, indeed, a quality in which animals surpass us, which is why we say, for example, 'as brave as a lion'. Furthermore, in contrast to the above claim, the principle of knightly honour often is the secure refuge of dishonesty and depravity in large matters and that of rudeness, inconsiderateness, and impertinence in small ones, in that a lot of very annoying bad manners are tacitly tolerated, because no one is inclined to risk his neck for rebuking them. – In   407 accordance with all this, we see the duel flourish and pursued with blood-thirsty zeal, and precisely in that nation that in political and financial affairs has shown a lack of true honourableness; how things stand in private matters we can find out by asking those who have experience with this nation. But as far as its urbanity and social culture are concerned, it is famous as a negative example.

Therefore all those pretexts do not hold up. We have more reason to urge that, as a dog that is growled at growls back and one that is cajoled cajoles in return, it is also in the nature of human beings to answer hostility with hostility and be embittered and aggravated by signs of contempt or hatred. Hence Cicero already says: 'An insult leaves behind a certain sting that prudent and good men find most difficult to suffer',[a] just as nowhere in the world (apart from a few pious sects) are invectives or even blows suffered calmly. But nature does not lead to more than the revenge that is appropriate for a matter, and not at all to the penalty of death for accusations of lying, stupidity, or cowardice; and the old German saying 'Blood for a blow' is a scandalous chivalric superstition. Certainly, the reciprocation or revenge of insults are matters of anger, not not at all of honour and duty, which the principle of chivalric honour makes them out to be. On the contrary, it is quite certain that each reproach can only hurt to the extent that it hits the mark; which is also made evident by the fact that the slightest hint that hits home wounds much more deeply than does the most serious accusation that is baseless. Whoever is actually aware that he does not deserve a reproach is allowed to and will safely disregard it. In contrast, the honour principle

---

[a] *habet* [*enim*] *quendam aculeum contumelia, quem pati prudentes* [*pudentes*] *ac viri boni difficilime possunt* [Cicero, *In Verrem* (*Against Verres*) 2. 3, 95; the original 'pudentes' ('shy', 'sensitive') of course changes the meaning]

requires of him that he show a susceptibility that he does not at all possess and take bloody revenge for insults that do not hurt him. But someone himself must have a poor opinion of his own worth if he rushes to suppress every offensive remark so that it not become public. Accordingly, when

408 insults occur, genuine self-esteem will make us truly indifferent, and where this does not happen, due to a lack of self-esteem, prudence and culture will instruct us to keep up appearances and conceal our anger. If we could only get rid of the superstition of the chivalric honour principle, so that no one would be allowed to believe that he could, through invectives, subtract something from another person's honour or restore something to his own; and also if every wrong, every brutality, every rudeness could no longer be legitimized by readiness to give satisfaction, i.e. to fight a duel; then the insight would soon become universal that when it comes to taunts and insults the one defeated in this battle comes out as victor and that, as *Vincenzo Monti* says, insults are like church processions, which always return to their starting point. Moreover, it would no longer be sufficient, as it is now, for someone to utter something rude in order to be in the right; hence insight and understanding would have much more say than they do now, when they always have to consider first whether they are somehow offending the opinions of stupidity and foolishness, already alarmed and embittered by their mere appearance, and thus make it necessary for the head in which they reside to be gambled against the shallow pate in which those opinions dwell. Consequently, intellectual superiority would attain the appropriate primacy in society, which now, even if covertly, belongs to physical superiority and hussar courage, and as a result the most excellent human beings would have one reason less than now to withdraw from society. Therefore, a change of this kind would lead to the *true* good tone and would pave the way for a genuinely good society, in the form in which it existed, without doubt, in Athens, Corinth, and Rome. Whoever wishes to see an example of such a society should read Xenophon's *Symposium*.

But the last defence of the chivalric code will undoubtedly be: 'God help us, then a person could just strike anybody else!' – to which I might briefly reply that this has happened often enough among the nine hundred and

409 ninety-nine in a thousand in society who do not recognize the code, without anybody ever dying, whereas with the adherents of the code, every blow usually becomes a fatal one. But I wish to go into this in more detail. I have often tried to find a reason, within animal or rational nature, for the conviction, so firmly held by a part of human society, of the dreadful character of a blow – a tenable, or at least plausible, reason, consisting not in mere stale phrases, but deducible from distinct concepts – but in vain.

A blow is and remains a minor physical evil, which one person can inflict on the other, but proves nothing more than that he is stronger, or more agile, or that the other was not on his guard. The analysis yields nothing more. Then I see the same knight to whom being struck by the hand of a human seems the greatest of evils receive a ten times stronger kick from his horse and, doggedly limping away in pain, assure people that it means nothing. So I thought that the human hand must be to blame. But I see our knight receive thrusts with a sword and cuts from the sabre during battle from this hand and claim that it is a trifling matter and not worth mentioning. Furthermore, I hear that even strikes with the flat blade are not nearly as bad as those with a stick and, therefore, not very long ago, cadets were exposed to the former, but not to the latter; and now being dubbed a knight,[a] with a blade, is the greatest honour. Hence I have come to an end with my psychological and moral reasons and there is nothing left to do but look at the matter as an old, deeply-rooted superstition, one more of so many examples showing how people can be talked into believing anything. This is also confirmed by the well-known fact that in China strokes with a bamboo cane are a very frequent civil punishment, even for officials of all classes, by showing us that human nature there, even when highly civilized, does not confirm the same.* As a matter of fact, an unprejudiced look at   410 human nature teaches that beating is as natural to it as biting is to predatory animals and butting to bovines: human beings are simply animals that beat. For that reason we become indignant when we hear, in rare cases, that one person has bitten another; on the other hand, to administer and receive blows is a naturally as well as easily occurring event for them. That higher culture likes to evade it through the exercise of mutual self-constraint is easily explained. But to make a nation, or even merely a class, believe that a given blow is a terrible misfortune that must be followed by blood and slaughter[b] is cruel. There are already too many genuine evils in the world for us to be allowed to multiply them through imaginary ones that entail real evils; but that is what every stupid and malicious superstition does. Therefore, I even have to disapprove that governments and legislative

---

* *Vingt ou trente coups de canne sur le derrière, c'est, pour ainsi dire, le pain quotidien des Chinois. C'est une correction paternelle du mandarin, laquelle n'a rien d'infamant, et qu'ils reçoivent avec action de grâces* [Twenty or thirty strokes with the cane on the behind, that is, so to speak, the daily bread of the Chinese. It is a paternal correction by the mandarin that has nothing shameful about it, and which they receive with grace] – *Lettres édifiantes et curieuses* [*écrites des missions étrangères*, '*Mémoire de la Chine*', Lyon: Vernarel] edition of 1819, vol. ii, p. 454.

[a] *der Ritterschlag*   [b] *Mord und Todtschlag*

bodies abet this by eagerly urging the abolishment of all corporal punishment, civil and military. They believe that they are acting in the interest of humanity, whereas exactly the opposite is the case, because, by doing so, they help to strengthen that perverse and unholy delusion to which so many have already fallen victim. For all offences, with the exception of the worst, beating is the punishment that first occurs to people and, therefore, is the natural one; whoever is not receptive to reasons will be so to a beating. And to punish by moderate flogging those who cannot be fined because they have no possessions and whom we cannot deprive of freedom without hurting ourselves, because we need their services, is as just as it is natural. Moreover, no reasons are given against it, but mere phrases about the 'dignity of human beings', which are not based on clear concepts, but again only on the above-mentioned pernicious superstition. That this superstition lies at the root of this matter finds an almost ludicrous confirmation in the fact that until a short while ago the military in some countries replaced corporal punishment with condemnation to the lath,[a] which altogether means causing physical pain, but is not supposed to be dishonourable and degrading.

411   By promoting this superstition we play into the hands of the principle of chivalric honour and, consequently, the duel, whereas, on the other hand, we are at pains to stop it through laws, or at least pretend to do so.[*,44] As a result, this fragment of the law of the fist, drifted down from the most barbarous medieval times into the nineteenth century, still hovers among us as a public scandal; it is high time that it be kicked out in disgrace. For nowadays methodically setting dogs or cocks at each other is not even permitted (at least in England such baiting is punished); but human beings are, against their will, set at each other for deadly battle because of the

---

* The real reason why governments are apparently keen to suppress the duel and pretend that they are just not successful, whereas this would obviously be very easy, particularly at universities, seems to me to be the following. The state is not able to pay in full for the services of its officers and civil servants; therefore, it lets the other half of their salary consist in honour, represented by titles, uniforms, and medals. Now, in order to keep this ideal compensation at a high value, the sense of honour must in every possible way be nourished, sharpened, and, if necessary, slightly exaggerated. But since civic honour does not suffice for this purpose, if only because we share it with everybody else, then chivalric honour is used as an aid and sustained in the way described. In England, where military and civil renumeration are much higher than on the continent, this assistance is not needed; for that reason it has been almost completely stamped out, especially in the last twenty years, occurs very rarely now, and if it does, is ridiculed as folly. Certainly the Anti-Duelling Society, which counts many lords, admirals, and generals among its members, has contributed much to this, and the juggernaut must do without its victims.

[a] *Lattenstrafe* ['*die latten*' = 'military prison whose floor is covered with nailed-down triangular laths' (*Grimm's Deutsches Wörterbuch*)]

ridiculous superstition of the absurd principle of chivalric honour and its narrow-minded advocates and custodians, who impose on them the obligation to fight each other like gladiators because of some trivial incident. Therefore, I suggest to our German purists in place of the expression 'duel',[a] – which probably does not derive from the Latin *duellum*, but from the Spanish *duelo*, meaning 'sorrow', 'lament', 'complaint'[45] – the term 'chivalric baiting'.[b] The pedantic way in which this folly is carried on certainly affords material for laughter. However, it is scandalous that this principle and its absurd code constitute a state within the state that, not recognizing any other law than that of the fist, tyrannizes the classes under its authority by keeping open a sacred and secret court,[c] before which everyone can arraign everyone else as a henchman by means of easily arranged pretexts, in order for both to submit to a trial for life or death. Of course, this becomes the hiding place from which every completely depraved person, if he only belongs to those classes, can threaten, even dispose of, the most noble and best, who as such has to be hateful to him. After judiciary and police have more or less succeeded in making it impossible in our day for every scoundrel on the road to call out to us 'your money or your life', sound understanding should also finally succeed in preventing scoundrels from being able to shout at us 'your honour or your life' in the middle of peaceful commerce. And the upper classes should be freed from the anxiety that arises from the fact that everybody, at every moment, can become responsible with life and limb for the brutality, rudeness, stupidity, or malice of anybody else who pleases to let them loose against him. It is appalling and shameful that, if two young, inexperienced hotheads verbally clash, they should pay for this with their blood, their health, or their lives. How bad the tyranny of this state within the state and how great the power of this superstition are, can be gauged from the fact that it has happened quite a few times that people whose wounded knightly honour could not possibly be restored because of the offender's superior or inferior rank or an otherwise inappropriate quality, have taken their own life out of despair and thus met a tragicomic end. – Since in the end the false and absurd reveal themselves at their pinnacle by blossoming into a contradiction, this contradiction emerges ultimately in the form of the most blatant antinomy;[d] for an officer is forbidden to take part in a duel, but is punished with dismissal, if he fails to do so when challenged.

But while I am on the subject, I will be even more frank. Considered in the proper light and without prejudice, the fact that the difference between

412

413

---

[a] *Duell*   [b] *Ritterhetze*   [c] *heiliges Vehmgericht*   [d] *Antinomie*

whether one has killed the enemy in an open fight with equal weapons or in an ambush, which is made so important and so highly regarded, merely depends on the fact that, as said before, the state within the state recognizes no other law than that of the jungle, the law of the fist, that it has raised it into a judgement of God and made it the basis for its code. For one has proved nothing more by the former than that one is the stronger or more skilful. The justification that one seeks in prevailing in an open fight presupposes that the *law of the strongest*[a] really is a *right*.[b] But in reality, the circumstance that the other person is inept at defending himself may give me the possibility, but by no means the right, to kill him. The right, hence my *moral* justification, can only depend on the *motives* that I have for taking his life. Now if we assume that these motives really existed and were sufficient, then there is absolutely no reason to have it additionally depend on whether he or I can shoot or fence better; then it does not matter in which manner I take his life, whether from behind or head-on. For morally, the law of the strongest has no more weight than that of the cleverest that is applied in an insidious murder; here the right of the fist and that of the intellect[c] carry equal weight. I should further remark that also in a duel both rights are claimed, in that every feint in fencing is a deceit. If I am morally justified to take somebody's life, then it is stupid to let it also depend on whether he may be better than I am at shooting or fencing; in which case, after already having harmed me, he will on top of that take my life. In *Rousseau's* view, insults should not be avenged by a duel, but through treacherous murder, a view that he cautiously hints at in the very mysterious twenty-first note to the fourth book of *Emile*[d] (p. 173, Bipont edn.). But at the same time he is so caught up in knightly superstition that he considers suffering a reproach for lying justification for murder; whereas he must know that every human being has deserved this reproach innumerous times, indeed, he himself to the highest degree. But the prejudice that has the justification to kill the offender depend on an open fight with equal weapons obviously believes the law of the fist to be a real law and the duel a judgement of God. On the other hand, the Italian who, seized with anger, attacks the offender with a knife wherever he finds him without further ado, at least acts consistently and according to nature; he is smarter, but not worse than the duellist. If one were to say that I am justified in killing my enemy in a duel, because he does his best to kill me, one would have to reply

414

---

[a] *Recht des Stärkeren*   [b] *Recht*   [c] *Kopfrecht*
[d] [Jean-Jacques Rousseau, *Emile, ou, De l'éducation* (*Œuvres complèttes*, 30 vols., Zweibrücken: Societas Bipontina, 1782–83)]

that I have made it necessary for him to defend himself by challenging him. Intentionally making it necessary for each other to defend ourselves, in fact only means seeing a plausible pretext for murder. A better justification would be the principle 'To the willing, no injury is done',[a] insofar as one has put one's life at risk by mutual consent. What stands in the way of this is that the 'willing' is not right, since the tyranny of the principle of chivalric honour and its absurd code is the henchman that has dragged both, or at least one of the two combatants, before this bloody secret court.

I have spoken in great detail about chivalric honour, but with good intention and because philosophy is the sole Hercules against the moral and intellectual monsters of this world. It is mainly two things that distinguish the social conditions of modern times from those of antiquity, to the detriment of the former, by imbuing them with a serious, gloomy, sinister coating, of which antiquity, being free of it, stands before us cheerful and ingenious, like the dawn of life. They are the principle of chivalric honour and venereal disease – a noble pair of brothers![b] Together they have poisoned the hate and love[c] of life. For venereal disease extends its influence much farther than it might appear at first glance, being by no means a merely physical, but also a moral influence. Since Cupid's quiver also contains poisoned arrows, a foreign, hostile, indeed diabolical element has entered the relation between the sexes,[46] as a result of which a sombre and fearful mistrust pervades it. And the mediate influence of such a change in the foundation of all human communion more or less extends also to the remaining social relations, explanation of which would let me stray too far from the subject. – Analogous, although quite different, is the influence of the principle of chivalric honour, this earnest farce, which was alien to the ancients, but renders modern society rigid, stern, and timid, if only because every fleeting utterance is scrutinized and pondered. But this is not all! This principle is a universal minotaur to whom once a year a number of sons from noble houses must be paid in tribute not by one, as was the case with the ancient Minotaur, but by all countries in Europe. Therefore, it is about time that we come to grips with this bogey for once, as has happened here. May both monsters of modern times come to their end in the nineteenth century! We do not want to give up hope that the physicians, with the help of prophylactics, will succeed with the first one after all. But to dismiss the *bogey*, by means of correcting concepts, is the business of philosophers, since governments, by means of legislation, have

415

---

[a] *volenti non fit injuria* [Legal principle]   [b] *par nobile fratrum* [Horace, *Satires* II, 3, 243]
[c] νεῖκος καὶ φιλία [A principle of Empedocles]

so far failed, and since, besides, it is only in this way that we can get down to the root of this evil. Meanwhile, if governments really were serious about abolishing the institution of duelling and the meagre success of their efforts were really due to their incompetence, I wish to suggest to them a law for whose success I vouch, without resorting to bloody operations, scaffold, gallows, or life imprisonment. Rather, it is a small, quite easy, homoeopathic remedy: Whoever challenges another person, or accepts a challenge, receives, in Chinese fashion,[a] in broad daylight, in front of the main station, twelve strokes of the cane from the corporal, and the seconds and the ones who deliver the challenge receive six. In regard to possible effects of duels that have actually taken place ordinary criminal proceedings should take over. Perhaps someone of chivalric disposition would object to me that after the execution of such a penalty some 'men of honour' might be capable of shooting themselves. My response would be: It is better that such fools shoot themselves than others. – To all intents and purposes, I know very well that governments are not serious about abolishing duels. The salaries of civil servants, and even more those of officers, are (apart from the highest positions) far below the value of their services. Therefore, the other half of their remuneration is paid in honour. This is first of all represented through titles and decorations, and in a wider sense through the honour of social rank. For this kind of honour the duel is a useful horse in reserve;[b] hence the universities already offer preparatory training[c] for it. The victims, therefore, pay the shortfall of the salaries with their blood.[47] –

For the sake of completeness, I want to mention *national honour* here as well. This is the honour of an entire people as part of the community of peoples. Since there is no other forum than that of force and, accordingly, every member of this community has to protect its rights itself, the honour of a nation not only consists in the established opinion that it can be trusted (credit), but also in the opinion that it is to be feared; hence it must never allow interference with its rights to go unpunished. Therefore, it combines the civic point of honour with that of chivalric honour. –

Fame was mentioned last among what someone *represents*, i.e. what he is in the eyes of the world; so it is this that we still have to consider. – Fame and honour are siblings, but like the Dioscuri, of whom Pollux was immortal and Castor mortal; fame is the immortal brother of mortal honour. Of course, this can be said only of reputation of the highest order, proper and genuine fame; for there certainly are also all kinds of ephemeral fame. – Furthermore, honour refers only to those qualities that are required of

---

[a] *à la Chinoise* [b] *Handpferd* [c] *Vorschule*

everyone in similar circumstances, fame only to those that we are not permitted to require of anybody; again, honour refers to qualities that we all can attribute to ourselves publicly; fame to those that no one is allowed to attribute to himself. Whereas our honour extends as far as we are known, conversely, fame travels ahead of the tidings about us and carries these as far as it extends itself. Everyone has a claim to honour; but only exceptional people have a claim to fame, for only exceptional accomplishments achieve fame. These consist either in *deeds*[a] or in *works*,[b] accordingly two paths are open to fame. A great heart qualifies primarily for the path through *deeds*, a great mind for that through *works*. Each path has its own advantages and disadvantages. The chief difference is that deeds pass, while works remain. Of deeds, only the memory remains, which becomes increasingly more weak, distorted, and indifferent and must gradually even become extinct, if history does not take it up and hand it down to posterity in a petrified state. Works, on the other hand, are themselves immortal and, especially the written ones, live throughout the ages. The noblest deed still has only a temporary impact; in contrast, the work of genius has a beneficial and elevating effect for all times.[48] Of Alexander the Great name and memory live on; but Plato and Aristotle, Homer and Horace themselves still exist, live, and have an immediate effect. The *Vedas*, with their *Upanishads*, exist; but of all the deeds that happened during their age no knowledge has come down to us.[*,49] – Another disadvantage of deeds is their dependence on opportunity, which first has to make them possible; also connected to this is the fact that their fame is not solely determined by their inner value, but also by the circumstances, which afford them importance and lustre. In addition, if, as in war, the deeds are purely personal, fame depends on the statements of a few eyewitnesses. Such witnesses are not always present and, if they are, not always just and impartial. On the other hand, deeds as

417

418

---

* Accordingly, it is a poor compliment when, as is the fashion nowadays, we think we honour works by calling them deeds; for works are of an essentially higher order. A deed is always merely an action upon a motive, hence something singular, passing, belonging to the universal and original element of the world, the will. A great or beautiful work, on the other hand, is something permanent, because it is of universal significance, and has sprung from intelligence – blameless, pure, rising like a fragrance from this world of will.

One advantage of the fame of deeds is that it usually happens immediately, with a loud bang, which is often so strong that it is heard in the whole of Europe, whereas the fame of works develops slowly and gradually, first quietly, then louder and louder, often reaching its full force only after a hundred years; but then it remains, because the works remain, sometimes for thousands of years. However, that other kind of fame becomes gradually weaker after the first explosion is over, known to fewer and fewer people, until in the end it has only a ghostlike existence left as part of history.

[a] *Thaten*   [b] *Werke*

something practical have the advantage of belonging to the sphere of the
universal human capacity of judgement; therefore, if only the facts[a] are
correctly transmitted, justice is done to them immediately, unless their
motives become correctly known or justly appreciated only later; for in
order to understand any action properly, its motive needs to be known.
With works the opposite is the case; their formation does not depend on
opportunity, but only on their author; and what they are in and for
themselves, they remain as long as they last. With them, the difficulty lies
in the judgement, which is the greater, the more elevated is their genre;
often there is a lack of competent, and often of impartial and honest judges.
On the other hand, their fame is not decided by *one* jurisdiction, but an
appeal takes place. For, as has been mentioned, whereas it is merely the
memory of deeds that comes down to posterity, and in such a manner as
the contemporary world passes it on, the works themselves come down to us
as they are, apart from fragments that might be missing. So here there is
no distortion of the data, and also any detrimental influence of their
environment at the time of their origin later disappears. Often it is rather
time that gradually brings forth the few really competent judges who,
themselves already exceptions, sit in judgement over even greater exceptions. Successively they pass their weighty verdicts and, sometimes it is only
after hundreds of years that a completely just judgement emerges, which no
future age will overthrow. So certain, indeed, so inevitable is the fame of
works. But whether their author lives to enjoy it depends on external
circumstances and chance; it is the rarer, the more elevated and difficult
their genre is. In accordance with this, Seneca says (*Epistles*, 79), in an
incomparably beautiful remark, that merit is followed by fame as unfailingly
as the body is followed by its shadow, but, like the shadow, sometimes walks
in front of it and sometimes behind it, and, after having explained this, adds:
'Even if *envy has imposed silence* on your contemporaries, those will come
who judge without resentment and without favour.'[b] Incidentally, we see
from this that the art of suppressing merit by malicious silence and by
ignoring it in order to hide the good from the public in favour of the bad was
already common among the scoundrels of Seneca's time, as much as among
those of our time, and that in both cases *envy tightened their lips*. – Even
fame will normally appear the later, the longer it will have to last; as indeed
everything excellent slowly matures. Fame that wants to turn into

419

---

[a] *Data*
[b] *etiamsi omnibus tecum viventibus* silentium livor indixerit, *venient qui sine offensa, sine gratia judicent*
[79, 17]

posthumous reputation resembles an oak tree, which grows very slowly from its seed; easy, ephemeral fame resembles that of the annual, fast-growing plant; and false reputation that of quickly sprouting weeds, which will be immediately eradicated. This process is really based on the fact that the more someone belongs to posterity, i.e. to humanity in general and as a whole, the more alien he is to his own age, since what he produces is not particularly dedicated to it, and so does not belong to it as such, but only insofar as it is a part of humanity; therefore, such a person is not tinged with this age's local colour, and as a result it can easily happen that it lets him pass as a stranger. This age rather appreciates those who serve the affairs of its brief day or the mood of the moment and, therefore, belong entirely to *it*, live with it and die with it. Accordingly, the history of art and literature consistently teaches that the highest achievements of the human mind have usually been received with disfavour and have remained out of favour until minds of a higher order arrived who found them appealing and created their reputation, which afterwards they retained by means of the authority they achieved in this way. Ultimately, all this rests on the fact that we can really understand and appreciate only what is like us. Now the dull is like the dullard, the common like the common, the confused like the unclear, nonsense like the brainless, and everyone likes his own works best, since they are completely like him. Hence already the ancient legendary Epicharmus sang:

> It is no wonder that I speak according to my views   420
> And those who are pleased with themselves are under the delusion
> that they were worthy of praise; for a dog to another dog
> appears the fairest being, an ox to an ox,
> an ass to an ass, and a pig to a pig.[a]

As even the strongest arm, when hurling away a light body, cannot impart to it a movement with which it would fly far and hit hard, but instead the body falls down with a dull thud, because it lacked material substance of its own to absorb the alien force – so the same happens to beautiful and great thoughts, indeed the masterpieces of genius, if none but small, feeble, crooked minds exist to receive them. The voices of the sages of all ages have joined in a chorus to lament this. For example, Jesus ben Sirach

---

[a] Θαυμαστὸν οὐδέν ἐστί, με ταῦθ᾽οὕτω λέγειν, /Καὶ ἁνδάνειν αὐτοισιν αὐτους, καὶ δοκεῖν /Καλῶς πεφυκέναι καὶ γὰρ ὁ κύων κυνὶ /Κάλλιστον εἶμεν φαίνεται καὶ βοῦς βοῖ, /Ὄνος δὲ ὄνῳ κάλλιστον, ὑς δὲ ὑΐ. [Diogenes Laertius (*Lives and Opinions of Eminent Philosophers*) III, 16. Schopenhauer makes several changes to the Greek original passage; among others he changes the grammatical person from 'we' to 'I'. Following the Greek passage, he offers his own German translation, which has been rendered into English here instead of the original quote by Diogenes Laertius]

says: 'Whoever tells a story to a fool, tells it to a drowsy man, and at the end he will say, "What is it?"'[a] – And Hamlet: 'a knavish speech sleeps in a fool's ear'.[b] Also Goethe:

> It's always decried, the happiest word,
> When the hearer's ear is bent.[c]

And again:

> Your effect is nought, all remains so dull
> Be cheerful!
> The stone in the swamp makes no waves.[d]

Also Lichtenberg: 'When a head and a book collide and there is a hollow sound, is it always the book?'[e] – and again: 'Such works are mirrors; when an ape looks in, no apostle can look out.'[f] Indeed, father Gellert's beautiful and touching lament is worth remembering here:

> The best of all gifts
> Has often the fewest admirers,
> And most of the world
> Regards the worst as the best;
> We see this evil every day.
> Yet how can we fight back this scourge?
> I doubt that this plague
> Can be removed from our world.
> A sole remedy exists on this earth,
> But it is infinitely difficult:
> The fools would have to become wise;
> And you see! That will never be.
> They never know the worth of things.
> Their eyes judge, not their understanding:
> Eternally they praise the minor,
> Because they have never known the good.[g]

421

---

[a] [See p. 289, n. b; 22, 10]
[b] [*Hamlet*, Act IV, scene 2; followed by Schopenhauer's German translations in parentheses]
[c] [*West-Eastern Divan*, '*Buch der Betrachtungen*' (Book of Observations)]
[d] [From '*Sprichwörtlich*' (Proverbial), series of poems]
[e] [Georg Christoph Lichtenberg, Aphorism D 396 (following the customary numbering by Albert Leitzmann, *Georg Christoph Lichtenbergs Aphorismen, nach den Handschriften*, Berlin: Behr, 1902–8]
[f] [Lichtenberg, Aphorism F 111]
[g] [Christian Fürchtegott Gellert, 'Die beyden Hunde' (The Two Dogs), in his *Sämmtliche Fabeln und Erzählungen*]

This intellectual incapacity of human beings, as a result of which, as Goethe points out, the excellent is even more rarely recognized and appreciated than found,[a] is now joined, here as everywhere, by human moral wickedness,[b] in particular in the form of envy. For as the consequence of the reputation that someone acquires, one more person is elevated above all others of his kind, so that the latter are to the same extent debased. Hence every outstanding merit achieves its fame at the expense of those who have none.

> If to others honour we give
> We are then ourselves demeaning.[c]
>
> Goethe, *West-Eastern Divan*

This explains why, in whatever form excellence may appear, the whole of mediocrity in its great abundance immediately unites and conspires to disallow and, where possible, even smother it. Its secret slogan is: 'Down with merit.'[d] But even those who themselves possess merit and have already acquired the reputation for it will not gladly see the rise of new fame, whose radiance makes theirs the less brilliant. Hence Goethe says:

> Had I lingered at my birth
> Until they granted me life,
> I would still not be on this earth,
> As you may understand when you see,
> How those conduct themselves
> Who, so that something they may appear to be,
> Would gladly negate me.[e]

422

Therefore, whereas *honour* usually finds fair judges and remains unimpugned by envy, and everyone is even credited in advance with it, *fame* must be fought for, in defiance of envy, and a tribunal of decidedly unfavourable judges hands out the laurels. For we are able, and we wish, to share honour with everyone else; fame is diminished or impeded by everyone who achieves it. – Moreover, the difficulty of achieving fame through works is inversely proportional to the number of people who make up the audience for such works, for reasons easily comprehended. Consequently, it is much more difficult to achieve fame with works that promise instruction than with those that promise entertainment. The difficulty is greatest in regard to philosophical works, because the instruction that they promise is, on the one hand, uncertain and, on the other,

---

[a] [See *Wilhelm Meister's Apprenticeship*, Book 7, ch. 9]   [b] *Schlechtigkeit*
[c] ['*Buch des Unmuts*' (Book of Displeasure)]   [d] *à bas le mérite*
[e] [From '*Zahme Xenien*' (Friendly Xenia), 5, a series of poems]

lacking material value; for which reason such works at first appear before a public consisting of none but competitors. – The above-discussed difficulties standing in the way of achieving fame make it clear that, if those who produce works worthy of fame did not do so out of love of those works and their own joy, but needed the encouragement of fame, humankind would have received few if any immortal works. In fact, whoever is to create something good and right and avoid the bad, has to defy the judgements of the masses and their leaders, hence disdain them. On this rests the correctness of the remark, especially emphasized by *Osorius* (*De gloria*),[a] that fame flees those who seek it and follows those who neglect it; for the former adapt to the taste of their contemporaries, the latter defy it.

Accordingly, it is as easy to keep fame as it is difficult to achieve it. This is also in contrast to honour, which is bestowed on everyone, even on credit; people only have to safeguard it. But this is the real task; for it is irretrievably lost by a single wretched act. Fame, on the other hand, can actually never be lost; for the deed or the work by means of which it was acquired stand forever firm, and the reputation for it remains with their author, even if he does not add new fame. However, if fame actually fades away, if it is outlived, then it was not genuine, i.e. undeserved, brought about by temporary overrating, or even of the kind of fame that Hegel possessed and Lichtenberg describes like this, 'broadcast by a junta of friendly candidates and reverberated by empty heads; ... but how will posterity smile, when people shall some day knock on the brightly coloured verbal edifices, the beautiful nests of bygone fashion, the dwellings of extinct conventions, and find everything, everything empty, not even the tiniest thought that could say with confidence: *come in*!'[b] –

Fame really depends on what somebody is in comparison with others. Accordingly, it is essentially relative and, consequently, can have only relative value. It would disappear entirely if all others were to become exactly like the famous person. Absolute value can only belong to that which keeps it under all circumstances, hence what somebody is immediately and for himself; consequently, this is where the value and the happiness of a great heart and a great mind are located. Therefore not fame, but that by means of which we earn it, is what has value. For it is the substance,

---

[a] [*Hieronymi Osorii* (Jerónimo Osório) *Lusitani* (of Lisbon), *De Gloria libri quinque* (*On Fame*, five books)]

[b] [Lichtenberg, *Vermischte Schriften*, Göttingen: Dieterich, 1844, vol. 4, *Über Physiognomik, wider die Physiognomen. Zu Beförderung der Menschenliebe und Menschenkenntniß* (*On Physiognomy, against the Physiognomists. For the Advancement of Human Loving Kindness and Knowledge of Human Nature*), p. 15 (Introduction to the second edition)]

so to speak, and fame is merely the accident of the thing. Fame affects the person who is praised mainly as an external symptom, by means of which he receives the confirmation of his own high opinion about himself. Therefore, we might say that just as light is not visible unless it is reflected by a body, every excellence becomes completely certain of itself only through its reputation. However, fame is not even an infallible symptom, because there is also fame without merit and merit without fame; which is why Lessing's remark is so apt: 'Some people are famous and others deserve to be.' Also it would be a miserable existence whose worth or worthlessness depended on how it appeared in the eyes of others; but such would be the life of the hero or the genius, if their worth consisted in their reputation, i.e. the approval of others. On the contrary, every being lives and exists for its own sake, hence primarily in and for itself. – What somebody is, whatever his mode of existence, he is first and foremost for himself; and if it is not worth much here, then it does not amount to much in general. On the other hand, the reflection of his essence in the minds of others is secondary, derivative, and subject to chance, which refers only very indirectly back to the former. Moreover, the heads of the crowd are too miserable a place for true happiness to have its seat. Rather, only a chimerical happiness can be found there. What a mixed society meets in that temple of universal fame! Generals, ministers, quacks, jugglers, dancers, singers, millionaires, and Jews; indeed, the virtues of all of these are prized there much more honestly, find much more heart-felt esteem[a] than the intellectual ones, especially of the higher order, which with most people attain esteem in name only.[b] Therefore, from the perspective of eudaemonology, fame is nothing but the rarest and most delicious morsel for our pride and vanity. But in most people these exist in excess, although they hide them; perhaps they are strongest in those who are in some way qualified to acquire fame and, therefore, have to carry with them for a long time the uncertain consciousness of their predominant value, before the opportunity arises to put it to the test and then to experience its recognition; until then they felt as though they suffered a secret injustice.[*,50] As explained at the beginning of this chapter, the value that people assign to the opinion of others is generally disproportional and irrational, so that Hobbes expresses the matter rather strongly, but perhaps correctly, with the words: 'And since all the pleasure

* Since our greatest pleasure consists in being *admired*, but the admirers are not keen to do so, even if there is every reason, the happiest people are those who have managed, no matter how, sincerely to admire themselves. Only others must not cause them to doubt themselves.

[a] *estime sentie*   [b] *estime sur parole*

and jollity of the mind consists in this; even to get some, with whom comparing, it may find somewhat wherein to Tryumph, and Vaunt itself' (*The Citizen* I, 5).[a] This explains the great value that is commonly placed on fame and the sacrifices that are made in the mere hope of achieving it some day:

> Fame is the spur, that the clear spirit doth raise
> (That last infirmity of noble minds)
> To scorn delights and live laborious days.[b]

And also:

> how hard it is to climb
> The hights where Fame's proud temple shines afar.[c]

This finally explains why the most vain of all nations constantly talks about glory[d] and considers it without hesitation the main incentive for great deeds and great works. – However, since fame is only secondary, the mere echo, likeness, shadow, symptom of merit, and since what is admired must certainly have more value than the act of admiration, what actually makes us happy cannot lie in fame, but in the means by which we achieve it, hence in merit itself or, more precisely, in the attitude and the abilities from which it has arisen, whether it be of a moral or an intellectual kind. For what is best in people they must necessarily be for themselves; what is reflected in the minds of others and what they are worth in the opinion of others can only be of subordinate interest. Therefore, whoever just *deserves* the fame without actually receiving it possesses by far the most important thing, which can console him about the fame he lacks. For what makes a person enviable is not that he is regarded as a great man by the masses who are so often deluded and lack judgement, but that he is a great man. And it is not the fact that posterity learns about him, but instead that ideas are engendered in him that deserve to be preserved and thought about for centuries, that is a great happiness.[e] Moreover, this cannot be wrested from him; it is 'up to us', and the other is 'not up to us'.[f] In contrast, if admiration itself were the main point, then the thing admired would not be worth the admiration. This is actually the case with false, i.e. undeserved fame. Its owner has to live off the

426

---

[a] *omnis animi voluptas, omnisque alacritas in eo sita est, quod quis habeat quibuscum conferens se, possit magnifice sentire de se ipso* (*de cive* I, 5) [The translation is Hobbes' own, from his English version of *De Cive, The Citizen. Philosophical Rudiments Concerning Government and Society* (1651)]

[b] [John Milton, *Lycidas* (1638), 70–2]

[c] [James Beattie, *The Minstrel, or The Progress of Genius* (1771–4), first two lines of Book I (has 'steep' instead of 'hights')]

[d] *la gloire*   [e] *ein hohes Glück*   [f] τῶν ἐφ' ἡμῖν *und* τῶν οὐκ ἐφ' ἡμῖν [Stoic expressions]

reputation without actually having that of which it is supposed to be the symptom, the mere reflection. But even this reputation must often be spoilt for him, when at times, despite all the self-delusion arising from his self-love, he gets dizzy at a height for which he is not suited or feels as if he were a counterfeit coin;[a] so that he is gripped by fear of being unmasked and rightly humiliated, especially since he already reads the verdict of posterity on the brows of wiser people. Therefore, he resembles one who owns by virtue of a forged last will. – Most genuine fame, posthumous reputation, is never discerned by its subject, but nonetheless we deem the person happy. Therefore, his happiness consisted in the great qualities themselves that achieved fame for him and in his having had the opportunity to develop them, in other words, being allowed to act in a way that was best suited for him, or to do what he loved to do; for only works arising from such a love achieve posthumous fame. Therefore, his happiness consisted in his big heart or in the richness of his mind, whose impression in his works receives the admiration of future centuries; it consisted in the thought itself, and thinking through such thought becomes the occupation and pleasure of the noblest minds of an unbounded future. Therefore, the value of posthumous reputation lies in meriting it, and this is its own reward. Whether the works that achieved it sometimes were also famous among contemporaries depended on accidental circumstances and was not of great importance. For since people in general lack independent judgement and are not at all able to appreciate superior and difficult accomplishments, in this they always follow the authority of someone else; and, in ninety-nine people out of a hundred who praise, fame of a higher order is based on trust and faith. Consequently, even the many-voiced applause of contemporaries can have little value for thinkers, in that they hear in it always only the echo of a few voices, who, moreover, themselves are of the garden variety. Would a virtuoso feel flattered by his audience's loud applause if he knew that, except for one or two, it consisted only of completely deaf people who, in order to hide their defect from one another, vigorously clapped as soon as they saw one person move his hands? And now, if he also knew that those clappers who lead the applause often let themselves be bribed in order to secure the loudest ovation for the most miserable violinist! – This explains why the reputation of contemporaries so seldom experiences the metamorphosis into posthumous fame; which is why *d'Alembert*, in his most beautiful description of the temple of literary fame, says: 'The interior of the temple is inhabited by none but the dead who were not

427

---

[a] *kupferner Dukaten*

there while alive, and a few living most of whom will be thrown out after they die.'[a] And the incidental remark may be permitted here that to build a monument to someone during his lifetime is tantamount to declaring that posterity is not to be trusted with respect to him.[51] – When someone nevertheless lives to experience the reputation that is to become post-humous fame, this will rarely happen before he reaches old age; there may be a few exceptions to this rule among artists and poets, but least of all among philosophers. This is confirmed by the portraits of men made famous by their works, since these are most of the time taken after they had become famous; usually they are depicted old and grey, especially the philosophers. But from a eudaemonological perspective, this is as it should be. Fame and youth all at the same time are too much for a mortal. Our life is so poor that its goods must be allocated more frugally. Youth has more than enough in its own wealth and can be content with that. But when in old age all pleasures and joys, like trees in winter, have died back, then the tree of fame buds most opportunely as a true winter-green; one can also compare it to winter pears, which grow in summer, but are eaten in winter. In old age there is no finer consolation than having incorporated the entire strength of our youth into *works* that will not age *together with* us.[52]

Now if we wish to take a closer look at the ways in which we acquire fame in the sciences, to start with what is close at hand, the following rule can be established. The intellectual superiority indicated by such a reputation is always demonstrated by a new combination of some kind of data.[b] Now such data can be of a very varied nature; but the reputation to be attained through combining the data will be the greater and the more widespread, the more the data themselves are universally known and accessible to everyone. For example, if the data are a few numbers or curves, or some particular physical, zoological, botanical or anatomical fact, or even a few corrupted passages in ancient authors, or half-erased inscriptions, or inscriptions whose alphabet we lack, or obscure points in history, then the fame that can be attained through combining them correctly will not extend much further than knowledge of the data as such, and hence to a small number of people living reclusive lives and envious of the fame of their discipline. – On the other hand, if the whole of humanity is acquainted with

428

---

[a] [Jean le Rond d'Alembert, '*Essai sur la société des gens de lettres et des grands, sur la réputation, sur les mécènes, et sur les récompenses littéraires*' (Essay on the Society of Educated and Great People, on Reputation, on Patrons, and on Literary Rewards). The original quote is: '*Le sanctuaire n'est peuplé que de morts qui n'y ont point été pendant leur vie, ou de vivans qu'on en chasse presque tous après leur mort.*']

[b] *Data*

the data, if, for instance, these data consist in essential qualities common to all of human understanding, mind, or forces of nature whose entire manner of effectiveness is constantly before our eyes, or in the well-known course of nature in general, then the reputation of having shed light on them by means of new, important and evident combination will spread with time to almost all of civilized humanity. For if the data are accessible to everyone, combining them will most often be as well. – Yet the reputation will always correspond only to the difficulty of the outcome. For the more well-known the data, the more difficult it will be to combine them in a new but accurate way, since an enormously large number of minds have tried their hands at it and exhausted the potential combinations. In contrast, data that are not accessible to the larger public and can be reached only in onerous and difficult ways almost always allow for new combinations. Therefore, if we approach the data with the right understanding and sound judgement, and so with a moderate intellectual advantage, then it is easily possible for us to be fortunate enough to come up with a new and correct combination. However, the fame attained by means of this will have approximately the same limits as the knowledge of the data. For the solution of such problems requires much study and work, if only to acquire the knowledge, while with the other kind, in which the greatest and most widespread fame can be achieved, the data are provided for free. But to the degree that this latter kind requires less work, more talent and even genius are necessary, and with these no work or study bears comparison in regard to value and appreciation. 429

As a result, those who are aware of a keen understanding and sound judgement within themselves, without presuming to possess the highest intellectual gifts, are not permitted to shy away from much study and tiring work, in order to work their way out of the great mass of humanity, to whom the well-known data are available, and to reach faraway places that are only accessible to scholarly diligence. For here, where the number of competitors is infinitely smaller, a mind that is to some extent superior will find the opportunity to combine the data in a new and accurate manner; the merit of his discovery will rest in part on the difficulty of gaining access to the data. But the applause thus won by his colleagues in knowledge, who are the sole experts in this field, will only be heard from afar by the crowd. – Now if we wish to pursue the path indicated here to its extreme, a point can be reached where the data alone, because of the great difficulty in obtaining them, are sufficient to establish fame without the need to combine them. This is achieved by travel to remote and rarely visited countries; one becomes famous because of what one has seen, not because of what one has thought. This path also has the great advantage that it is much easier to relate to others what one has seen than what one has thought, and the same is true of others' comprehension; consequently, we will find many more readers for the former than for the latter; For, as Asmus already remarks:

> When someone goes on a journey,
> He has a tale to tell.[a]

430 However, it is also in accordance with all this that we often think of Horace's remark when personally acquainted with famous people of this kind:

> Those who cross the ocean change their climate, not their mind.
> (*Epistles* I, 11, 27)[b,53]

But in regard to the mind that is equipped with superior abilities, which alone may venture the solution of the great problems – referring to the universal and the whole and, therefore, being the most difficult – this mind will do well to extend its horizon as far as possible, but equally in all directions and without losing itself too far in some of the particular regions only known to a few, i.e. without going too deeply into the specialities of some individual science, let alone occupying itself with excessive details.[c] For it is not necessary for it to set to work on subjects that are difficult to access in order to avoid the crowd of competitors; rather, what is generally accessible will provide material for new, important, and true combinations. Accordingly, its merit will be appreciated by all those who are acquainted with the data, hence by the majority of humankind. This explains the great difference between the fame that poets and philosophers achieve, and the fame that physicists, chemists, anatomists, mineralogists, zoologists, philologists, historians, and others like that, can acquire.

---

[a] [Matthias Claudius (pen-name 'Asmus'), '*Urians Reise um die Welt*' (Urian's Journey around the World); first two lines of poem]
[b] *Coelum, non animum, mutant, qui trans mare currunt*   [c] *Mikrologien*

Counsels and maxims

Even less than in other places do I aim here for completeness, for I would otherwise have to repeat the many maxims, some excellent, which have been laid down by thinkers of all ages, from Theognis and Pseudo-Solomon to La Rochefoucauld, and it would be impossible for me to avoid many already well-worn platitudes. But together with completeness, systematic order also falls away for the most part. We can console ourselves about the loss of these two by realizing that, when it comes to matters like this, they would almost inevitably bring boredom in their wake. I only provide what happened to occur to me, seemed to be worth relating, and, as far as I can remember, has not been said before, at least not entirely and in this manner; hence I am providing merely afterthoughts to that which others have already achieved in this vast field.

But in order to introduce some order into the great diversity of the views and counsels that belong here, I will divide them into general ones; those concerning our attitude towards ourselves; towards others; and finally towards the course of the world and fate.

A. General views

(1) I regard as the supreme rule of all wisdom of life a sentence that Aristotle casually pronounced in the *Nicomachean Ethics* (VII, 12): ὁ φρόνιμος τὸ ἄλυπον διώκει, οὐ τὸ ἡδύ[a] (*quod dolore vacat, non quod suave est, persequitur vir prudens*). The Latin version of the sentence is feeble; it translates better into German, for instance: 'It is not pleasure, but painlessness that the sensible person pursues'; or 'The sensible person aims at painlessness, not enjoyment.'[54] Its truth is based on the fact that the nature of all enjoyment and all happiness is negative, whereas that of pain is positive. The exposition and justification of this last sentence are found in my chief work, vol. 1, 432

---

[a] ['The prudent man (*phronimos*) pursues freedom from pain, not pleasure' (1152b15)]

§58.[a] But I wish to explain it here with the help of a fact that can be observed daily. If the entire body is healthy and in one piece except for some small sore, or otherwise painful spot, the health of the whole does not enter consciousness, but attention is focused continuously on the pain of the injured spot and our entire enjoyment of life is lost. – Equally, when all our affairs go well except for *one* that runs counter to our intentions, this one will come to mind again and again, even if it is of little importance; we frequently think about it and think little about all the other more important things that go according to our plans. – In both cases it is the will that is impaired, in one case in the way it objectifies itself in the organism, in the other in the manner in which it does so in human striving; in both we see that its satisfaction acts always merely negatively and hence is not felt directly, but at most becomes conscious by way of reflection. Its inhibition, on the other hand, is something positive and, therefore, makes its presence known. Every enjoyment consists merely in the removal of this inhibition, in liberation from it, and consequently is short-lived.

On this rests the Aristotelian rule, praised above, which instructs us not to direct our attention towards the enjoyments and comfort of life, but to focus on avoiding its numerous evils as far as possible. If this path were not the right one, Voltaire's dictum, 'Happiness is nothing but a dream, and pain is real',[b] would have to be as false as it is in fact true. Accordingly, those who sum up their life from a eudaemonistic perspective calculate not according to the joys they have experienced, but according to the evils they have escaped. In fact, eudaemonology must begin by instructing us that its very name is a euphemism and that 'living happily' is only to be understood as living 'less unhappily', hence in a tolerable way. Certainly life is not meant to be enjoyed, but to be weathered, to be shrugged off; this is signified by some expressions, such as 'Getting through life means overcoming life',[c] the Italian 'One pulls through like this',[d] and the German 'One must try to get through', 'He will surely get through life', and many others. Indeed, it is a consolation of old age to have the labour of living behind us. Accordingly, that person has drawn the happiest lot who lives his life without too much pain, mental and physical; but not the one who was accorded the most vivid delights and the greatest pleasures. Whoever wishes to calculate the happiness of the course of his life according to the latter has

---

[a] [*WWR* 1, 345–9 (Hübscher *SW* 2, 376–81)]
[b] *le bonheur n'est qu'un rêve, et la douleur est réelle* [Voltaire, Letter to the Marquis de Florian, Ferney, 16 March 1774 (see *HN* 3, 708)]
[c] *degere vitam, vita defungi*   [d] *si scampa cosi*

seized upon the wrong criterion. For pleasures are and remain negative; that they make us happy is a delusion entertained by envy for its own punishment. On the other hand, pain is felt positively; therefore, its absence is the criterion of happiness in life. And if a painless state is joined with the absence of boredom, earthly happiness has been essentially achieved; for everything else is a chimera. Now from this it follows that we should never purchase pleasures for the price of pain, indeed, not even for the risk of it, because otherwise we pay with something positive and real for something negative and hence chimerical. In contrast, we remain on the winning side when we sacrifice pleasures in order to avoid pain. In both cases it does not matter whether the pain follows or precedes the pleasures. It is really most absurd to wish to turn this scene of misery into a pleasure spot[a] and set ourselves the goal of achieving pleasures and joys instead of freedom from pain, as so many do. Those who, with too gloomy a gaze, regard this world as a kind of hell and, accordingly, are only concerned with procuring a fireproof room in it, are much less mistaken. The fool runs after the pleasures of life and sees himself cheated; the sage avoids evils. But if even this should fail, then it is the fault of fate, not of his foolishness. However, insofar as he succeeds, he has not been cheated; for the evils that he evades are very real. Even if he should have gone too far in avoiding them and unnecessarily sacrificed enjoyments, nothing is really lost; for all pleasures are chimerical, and to mourn over missing out on them would be petty, indeed ridiculous.

434

The failure to recognize this truth, encouraged by optimism, is the source of much unhappiness. For while we are free from suffering, anxious desires project chimeras of a happiness that does not exist at all, and tempt us to pursue them; in doing so we bring pain down on ourselves, which is undeniably real. Then we lament the loss of the painless state, which, like paradise forfeited, lies behind us, and wish in vain to be able to undo what has been done. Hence it seems as if an evil demon constantly entices us out of the painless state – which is the supreme actual happiness – with the help of the illusions of our desires. – Without hesitation the youth believes that the world is there to be enjoyed, that it is the place of positive happiness, missed only by those who lack the ability to seize it. Novels and poems reinforce him in this, as does the hypocrisy which the world practises consistently and universally in regard to external appearance and to which I shall return shortly. From now on his life is a more or less deliberate hunt for positive happiness, which as such is supposed to consist in positive

[a] *Lustort*

enjoyments. The dangers to which we leave ourselves exposed have to be risked. Therefore, this hunt after a game that does not exist at all usually leads to real, positive unhappiness, which happens in the form of pain, suffering, illness, loss, worry, poverty, disgrace, and a thousand hardships. The disillusionment comes too late. – On the other hand, if by following the rule considered here life's plan is directed towards avoidance of suffering, hence elimination of want, of disease, and of all kinds of distress, then the goal is a real one, is achievable, the more so the less it is marred by striving for the chimera of positive happiness. This is in accord with the passage in *Goethe's Elective Affinities*, where he has *Mittler*, who is always acting for the sake of others' happiness, say: 'Whoever wants to be rid of an evil, always knows what he wants; whoever wants something better than he has, is completely blind.'[a] This reminds us of the fine French saying: *'le mieux est l'ennemi du bien.'*[b] In fact, even the principal idea of Cynicism can be deduced from this, as I have expounded in my chief work, vol. 2, ch. 16. For what induced the Cynics to reject all pleasures if not precisely the thought of the pain more or less closely associated with them, evading which seemed much more important to them than obtaining pleasure. They were deeply moved by recognizing the negativity of pleasure and the positivity of pain; therefore, with great consistency they did everything to avoid evil, but deemed it necessary to utterly and deliberately repudiate pleasures, since they regarded these as mere snares that deliver us up to pain.

Of course, as Schiller claims, we are all born in Arcadia;[c] that means we enter the world full of aspirations to happiness and pleasure and cherish the foolish hope of achieving them. However, usually fate soon comes along, seizes us rudely, and teaches us that nothing is *ours*, but everything belongs to *fate*, insofar as it has an undisputed right not only to all our possessions and earnings and wife and child, but even to arm and leg, eye and ear, indeed, to the nose in the middle of our face. In any case, after a while we gain experience and the insight that happiness and pleasure are a mirage,[d] which is visible only from afar and vanishes when we come closer; that, on the other hand, suffering and pain are real, are their own immediate representatives, and are neither in need of illusion nor of expectation. If this doctrine bears fruit, we will cease to chase after

435

---

[a] [*Elective Affinities*, Part 1, ch. 2, towards the end]
[b] ['The better is the enemy of the good', Voltaire, *La Bégueule. Conte moral* (*The Prude, a Moral Tale*), 1772; second line]
[c] [An allusion to Friedrich Schiller's poem 'Resignation' (1786)]   [d] *Fata Morgana*

happiness and enjoyment and will, on the contrary, be intent on barring pain and suffering as much as possible. We recognize then that the best that the world has to offer is a painless, quiet, tolerable existence and limit our aspirations to such an existence to achieve it the more securely. For the surest way not to become very unhappy is not to want to become very happy. *Merck*, the friend of Goethe's youth, also recognized this when he wrote: 'The indecent pretension to happiness, to the extent that we   436 dream of it, spoils everything in this world. Whoever is able to free himself from this and desires nothing but what is at hand can get along' (*Letters to and from Merck*, p. 100ᵃ). Therefore, it is advisable to reduce to moderate proportions our claims to pleasure, possessions, rank, honour, and so on, since it is precisely the pursuit and struggle for happiness, glamour, and enjoyment that lead to the greatest misfortunes. In any case, this is already wise and prudent for the simple reason that it is easy to be very unhappy, but not just difficult but quite impossible to be very happy. Therefore, the poet of the wisdom of life rightfully sings:

> Whoever chooses the golden mean,
> stays away from the sordidness of the old hut
> and modestly avoids the envied palace.
>
> The mighty pine tree sways in the strong gale;
> and soaring towers tumble in heavier falls;
> and lightning strikes mountain summits.ᵇ

But those who have fully absorbed the doctrine of my philosophy and, therefore, know that our entire existence is something that it were better should not be and that negating and rejecting it is the greatest wisdom, will not have great expectations of any thing or any condition, will not passionately strive for anything in the world, nor will they greatly lament the failure of some undertaking. Rather, they will be led by Plato's 'No human affair is worth great trouble' (*Republic* X, 604).ᶜ Readers should also see the motto of Sadi's *Gulistan*, translated by Graf:ᵈ

ᵃ [*Briefe an und von Johann Heinrich Merck: eine selbständige Folge der im Jahr 1835 erschienenen Briefe von J. H. Merck* (*Letters to and from Johann Heinrich Merck, following the Letters by J. H. Merck Published in 1835*), ed. Karl Wagner, Darmstadt: Diehl, 1838]

ᵇ *Auream quisquis mediocritatem/ Diliget, tutus caret obsoleti / Sordibus tecti, caret invidenda/ Sobrius aula. / Saevius [Saepius] ventis agitatus ingens / Pinus: et celsae graviore casu / Decidunt turres: feriuntque summos / Fulgura montes [montis].* [Horace, *Odes* II, 10, 5–12]

ᶜ οὔτε τι τῶν ἀνθρωπίνων ἄξιον μεγάλης σπουδῆς (X, 604b)

ᵈ [*Moslicheddin Sadi's Rosengarten*, trans. Karl Heinrich Graf, Leipzig: Brockhaus, 1846]

If you have lost possession of a world,
Be not aggrieved, for it is nought;
If you have gained possession of a world,
Do not rejoice, for it is nought.
Pains and pleasures will pass,
Pass by the world, for it is nought.   Anwari Soheili[a,55]

437
However, what makes achieving these beneficial insights especially difficult is the above-mentioned hypocrisy of the world, which we should,
therefore, reveal early to young people. Most splendours are mere semblance, just like theatre decorations; the essence of the thing is missing. For
example, ships festooned with pennants and wreaths, cannon salutes,
illuminations, drums beating and trumpets sounding, cheering and shout-
ing, and so on, all this is the advertisement, the suggestion, the hieroglyph of
joy; but joy is mostly not to be found here, it alone has declined to attend the
celebration. Where it actually turns up, it normally slips in uninvited and
unannounced, by itself, quietly, and without ceremony,[b] often at the most
unimportant, most trivial occasions, under the most mundane circumstances, indeed, anywhere but at glamorous or glorious events; it is, like
gold in Australia, scattered here and there, according to the vagaries of
chance, without rule or law, often only in tiny grains, and very rarely in large
quantities. In contrast, in all the things mentioned above, the sole purpose
is to make others believe that joy had arrived; this appearance[c] in the minds
of others is the goal. It is the same with sorrow as it is with joy. How
mournfully does that long and slow funeral procession move along! There is
no end to the rows of carriages. But just look inside; they are all empty, and
the deceased is actually escorted to the grave by all the coachmen of
the entire town. An eloquent illustration of the friendship and the esteem
of this world! This is the deceitfulness, hollowness, and hypocrisy of human
dealings.[d,56] – Another example is provided by the many invited guests in
festive garments, welcomed ceremoniously; they are the embodiment of
noble, elevated sociability. But instead of this, normally only affectation,
torment, and boredom have arrived; for where there are many guests, there
is much rabble – even if they all have medals on their breasts. For the
genuinely good society is everywhere and by necessity very small. But in
general, magnificent, glamorous celebrations and revelries always carry an
emptiness, even a jarring note inside of them, not the least since they noisily

---

[a] [*Anwar-I-Suhaili*, the Persian version by Ali Wai'z-Al-Kashifi of Sanskrit animal fables, better known
   in the Arabic version of *Kalilah and Dimnah*]
[b] *sans façon*   [c] *Schein*   [d] *Treibens*

contradict the misery and meagreness of our existence, and the contrast enhances the truth. However, seen from the outside, all this has its effects, and that was the purpose. Hence *Chamfort* makes the fine remark: 'Society, the circles, the salons, what is called the world, is a miserable play, a bad opera, without interest, barely sustained by the stage machines, the costumes, and the decorations.'[a] – Similarly, academies and philosophical lecterns are the flagship, the outward semblance of *wisdom*; but wisdom too has often declined to appear and is to be found somewhere else entirely. – Jingling bells, priests' costumes, pious attitudes and grotesque activities are the advertisements, the false semblance of devotion, and so forth. – Therefore, almost everything in the world can be called a hollow nut; the kernel in itself is rare, and even more rarely is it to be found in the shell. It must be sought in a completely different place and is often found only by chance.

(2) If we wish to assess the state of human beings, of their happiness, we should not ask what gives them pleasure, but what saddens them; for the more trivial the latter, taken in itself, the happier the person, because a state of well-being is required in order to be sensitive to trifles; when unhappy we do not feel them at all.[57]

(3) We should take care not to build the happiness of our life on a *broad foundation* by making many demands; for, resting on such a foundation, happiness collapses most easily, since this provides the opportunity for many more accidents, which are bound to happen. Therefore, the building of our happiness is, in this respect, the reverse of all other buildings, which rest most securely on a broad foundation. Consequently, lowering our aspirations in proportion to our means of every sort is the safest way to avoid great misfortune.

In general, it is one of the greatest and most frequent follies to make *copious arrangements* for life, in whatever way this might be done. For, first of all, we count on an entire, full human life, which, however, very few attain. Next, even if we live such a long life, it still proves too short for the plans that we have made, since their execution always requires more time than we had assumed. Furthermore, such plans, like all human affairs, are subject to so many failures and obstacles that they very seldom reach their completion. Finally, even if in the end everything is accomplished, the transformations that time produces in *ourselves* have not been taken into

438

439

---

[a] *La société, les cercles, les salons, ce qu'on appelle le monde, est une pièce misérable, un mauvais opéra, sans intérêt, qui se soutient un peu par les machines, les costumes, et les décorations* [Chamfort, *Maximes et pensées*, ch. 3] [See p. 123, n. e]

account, for we have not been mindful of the fact that our capacities do not last our whole life – neither for achieving nor for enjoying. As a result, we often work towards things that, when finally achieved, are no longer suitable for us; or, in preparing for a work, we spend those years that at the same time, unnoticed by us, rob us of the powers for its execution. Hence it frequently happens that we are no longer able to enjoy the wealth that we earned with so much effort and risk, so that we have laboured for others; or that we are no longer able to fill the position that we finally obtained after many years of striving; things have come too late for us. Or, conversely, we arrive too late with things, namely where services or productions are concerned; the taste of the times has changed; a new generation has grown up that takes no interest in these matters; others have got there first on a shorter path, and so forth. Horace has all that is mentioned here in mind when he says:

Why do you wear out your soul, which is too weak for eternal plans?[a]

The cause of this frequent blunder is the inevitable optical illusion of the mind's eye, by virtue of which life when seen from its beginning seems infinite, but when looking back from the end of its path seems very short. Of course this illusion has its advantages; for without it, hardly anything great would ever come to pass.

In any case, life treats us like a traveller for whom, as he advances, objects take on shapes different from those they showed from afar and are transformed, so to speak, as he approaches them. This is especially the case with our desires. Often we find something completely different and, in fact, better than we sought; and often we find what we are looking for on a path quite different from the one we had first taken in vain. Moreover, where we were seeking pleasure, happiness, and joy, we often find instead instruction, insight, and knowledge[b] – a lasting, veritable good instead of one that is transient and only apparent. This is also the idea that runs through *Wilhelm Meister*[c] like a ground bass,[d] since it is an intellectual novel and, therefore, of a higher order than all others, even those by Walter Scott, which are all merely ethical, i.e. understand human nature solely from the perspective of the will.[58] The same fundamental idea is symbolized in large, coarse lines – like those of stage decorations in the theatre – in *The Magic Flute*, that grotesque, but significant and ambiguous hieroglyph. In fact, it would be

440

---

[a] *quid aeternis minorem/ Consiliis animum fatigas?* [Horace, *Odes* II, 11, 11–12]   [b] *Erkenntniß*
[c] [Goethe's novel *Wilhelm Meister's Lehrjahre* (1795–6)]   [d] *Grundbaß* [*Basso ostinato* or *continuo*]

perfectly expressed, if in the end Tamino were cured of his desire to possess Tamina[a] and instead of her solely demanded and obtained initiation into the temple of wisdom, whereas his necessary counterpart, Papageno, would rightly receive his Papagena. – Excellent, noble human beings soon become aware of this education through fate and gratefully submit to being formed[b] by it; they realize that instruction, but not happiness is to be found in the world; hence they become accustomed and content to exchange hope for insight and in the end say with Petrarch:

> I have no delight other than learning.[c]

It can even happen that they only pretend to pursue their wishes and aspirations and merely toy with them, so to speak, but actually, in their heart of hearts, they expect only instruction, which then imbues them with a contemplative, ingenious, sublime touch. – In this sense, it can also be said that we are like alchemists who, while only searching for gold, discovered gunpowder, porcelain, medicines, and even laws of nature.

B. Concerning our attitude towards ourselves

(4) Just as the worker who helps raise a building either does not know the design of the whole or, at least, does not always bear it in mind, so, similarly, does a human being completing the individual days and hours of his life behave towards the totality of the course of his life and its character. The more worthy, significant, carefully planned, and individual this life is, the more necessary and beneficial it is that he visualize its minimized outline, the ground plan, from time to time. Of course, part of this is that he has made a small start in the 'Know thyself',[d] hence knows what he actually and primarily wants above all else, what is essential for his happiness, and also what occupies the second and third place after this. And it is also important that he knows what on the whole is his vocation and role in the world and his relation to it. Now if this relation is of a significant and grandiose kind, then the sight of the plan of his life, on a reduced scale, will more than anything else strengthen, uplift, encourage him to be active, and prevent him from going astray.

441

---

[a] [Pamina]   [b] *bildsam* [related to '*Bildung*' (education, formation)]
[c] *Altro diletto, che 'mparar, non provo* [Francesco Petrarca, *Trionfo d'Amore* (*Triumph of Love*), I, 21]
[d] γνῶθι σαυτόν

Just as the wanderer has a systematic overview of and recognizes the path that he has travelled in all its turns and bends only after he has reached the top of a hill, so we first recognize at the end of a period of our life, or even at the end of our entire life, the true interconnectedness of all our deeds, achievements, and works, their exact coherence and concatenation and, indeed, also their value. For as long as we are in the middle of it, we act only in accordance with the fixed qualities of our character, under the influence of motives and according to our abilities, hence with necessity throughout, insofar as at every moment we merely do what seems right and proper to us at the time. Only the result shows what has come out of this, and the retrospective view of the whole shows the how and where from. For this reason, while performing the greatest deeds and creating immortal works, we are not conscious of them as such, but merely as appropriate for our present purposes, corresponding to our present intentions, and so the right thing at the moment. But our character and abilities shine forth only afterwards, from the interconnected whole; and in its individual moments we then see how, as if happening through inspiration, we took the only right path out of a thousand wrong ones – guided by our genius.[a] All this applies to the theoretical as well as the practical, and conversely to the bad and misguided. – The significance of the present is seldom recognized immediately, but only much later.[59]

(5) An important aspect of the wisdom of life consists in the right proportion in which we focus our attention in part on the present and in part on the future, so that the one should not spoil the other. Many live too much in the present – those who are carefree. Others live too much in the future – those who are anxious and prone to worry. Rarely will someone find the right balance. Those who by means of striving and hoping live only in the future, who always look ahead and impatiently rush towards coming things – which are supposed to bring true happiness for the first time –, but who in the meantime let the present slip by without heeding or enjoying it, can be compared despite their precocious airs to those donkeys in Italy whose pace is quickened by a stick fastened to their head with a batch of straw hanging from it, so that they always see it right in front of them and hope to reach it. For they cheat themselves out of their entire existence by constantly living for the meantime[b] alone – until they are dead. Therefore, instead of always being exclusively occupied with the plans and worries for the future or abandoning ourselves to longing for the past, we should never forget that the present alone is real and certain. On the other hand, the

---

[a] *Genius*   [b] *ad interim*

future almost invariably turns out differently from what we expect and, in fact, even the past was different, and indeed, on the whole, both are of less consequence than it seems to us. For distance, which makes objects appear small to the eye, makes them appear larger to the mind. The present alone is true and real; it is actually filled time; and exclusively in this lies our existence. Therefore, we should always appreciate the present by accepting it cheerfully and, consequently, should consciously enjoy as such every tolerable hour free of immediate unpleasantness or pain, i.e. not tarnish it through sullen faces about failed hopes in the past or worries about the future. For it is definitely foolish to spurn or wilfully ruin a good present 443 hour because of annoyance about the past or anxiety about the future. Worry and, indeed, regret, should be granted some definite time; but afterwards we should think like this about what happened in the past:

> Despite my anguish I will beat it down
> the fury mounting inside me, down by force.[a]

And about the future:

> But all lies in the lap of the great gods.[b]

But about the present: 'Regard every single day as a single life'[c] (Seneca), and make this time, which alone is real, as pleasant as possible.

Only those future evils are entitled to upset us that are sure to come and whose date of arrival is assured as well. But these will be very few; for evils either are merely possible, or at most probable, or they may be certain, but the date of their occurrence is completely uncertain. Now if we surrender to these two kinds, we will no longer have a moment's peace. So, in order not to be deprived of all peace in our life through uncertain or indefinite evils, we must accustom ourselves to look at the former as never bound to happen and the latter as certainly happening not very soon.

However, the less our peace is disturbed by anxiety, the more we are troubled by wishes, desires, and aspirations. Goethe's popular song, 'I have set my heart upon nothing',[d] really says that only after we have been expelled from all potential aspirations and are reduced to a bare existence do we share in that peace of mind that is the foundation of human happiness, insofar as it is necessary for finding the present, and hence all

---

[a] Ἀλλὰ τὰ μὲν προτετύχθαι ἐάσομεν ἀχνύμενοί περ, / Θυμὸν ἐνὶ στήθεσσι φίλον δαμάσαντες ἀνάγκῃ [Homer, *Iliad* XVIII, 112f.]

[b] Ἤτοι ταῦτα θεῶν ἐν γούνασι κεῖται [Homer, *Iliad* XVII, 514; *Odyssey* I, 267]

[c] *singulas* [*singulos*] *dies singulas vitas puta* [Seneca, *Epistles*, 101, 10]

[d] [First line of the song 'Vanitas! Vanitatem vanitas!' from the series '*Gesellige Lieder*' (Sociable Songs)]

of life, enjoyable. To this end we should always bear in mind that today comes only once and never again. But we think that it happens again tomorrow; however, tomorrow is another day, which also happens only once. We forget that each day is an integral and hence irreplaceable part of life, and instead consider it as included under life just as individuals are under a common concept. – Likewise, we would better appreciate and enjoy the present if on good and healthy days we were always aware how during periods of illness or grief, memory recalls to us every hour free of pain and privation as infinitely enviable, a lost paradise, an unappreciated friend. But we spend our fine days without noticing them; only when the bad ones arrive do we wish for the others to come back. With sullen faces we let a thousand cheerful, pleasant hours slip by without enjoying them, only afterwards, during gloomy times, to mourn their passing, vainly longing for their return. Instead we should cherish every present moment that is tolerable, even the everyday present, which now we let go by with such indifference, even impatiently pushing it to pass – mindful of the fact that at this moment it is crossing over into that apotheosis of the past, where from now on, illuminated by the light of immortality, it is preserved by memory, in order to present itself as an object of our deepest longing when memory one day will lift the curtain, especially during dire times.

(6) *All limitation makes us happy.* The narrower our scope of vision, our sphere of influence, and our range of contact, the happier we are; the wider they are, the more often we feel tormented or frightened, since worries, desires, and fears multiply and increase along with them. For this reason, even blind people are not as unhappy as it must seem to us a priori; this is attested by the gentle, almost serene calm of their features. It is partly based on this rule that the second half of life turns out unhappier than the first. For during the course of our life the scope of our purposes and relations becomes ever wider. During childhood it is limited to the most immediate environment and narrowest circumstances; during youth it already extends considerably further; during adulthood[a] it comprises our entire course of life, in fact, often extends to the remotest circumstances, to states and peoples; and during old age it encompasses our descendants. – In contrast, any limitation, even of the mind, promotes our happiness. For the less stimulation of the will, the less suffering; and we know that suffering is positive and happiness is merely negative. Restricting our sphere of influence removes the external causes of stimulation from the will, restricting the mind to the internal ones. However, the latter has the disadvantage of

[a] *Mannesalter*

opening the door to boredom, which indirectly is the source of countless sufferings, insofar as we grasp at anything to banish it – seeking dissipation, society, luxury, gambling, drinking, etc., although they entail all kinds of harm, ruin, and unhappiness. 'Tranquillity in leisure is difficult.'[a] But how much *external* limitation is conducive, even necessary, to human happiness – as far as it is possible – is evident from the fact that the only poetic genre which attempts to portray happy human beings, the idyll, always depicts them essentially in a highly restricted position and environment. The feeling in this matter is also at the base of our delight in so-called genre-pictures. – Accordingly, the greatest possible *simplicity* of our circumstances and even the *monotony*[60] of our way of life, as long as it does not produce boredom, will make us happy. For they make us least feel life itself, and consequently the burden essentially connected with it; it flows by like a brook, without waves and vortices.

(7) What ultimately matters with respect to our weal and woe is what fills and occupies our consciousness. Here, every purely intellectual occupation will on the whole achieve much more for the mind capable of it than real life, with its constant alternation of success and failure together with its agitations and vexations. But of course predominant intellectual capabilities are required for this. In addition it must be noted that, just as the externally directed life dissipates and distracts us from our studies and deprives the mind of the requisite calm and collection, on the other hand persistent intellectual activity renders us more or less incapable of dealing with the hustle and bustle of real life. Hence it is advisable to suspend such activity completely for a while when circumstances arise that in some way demand energetic practical action.

(8) In order to live with perfect *mindfulness*[b] and draw from our own experience all the instruction that it contains, it is necessary that we often think back and recapitulate what we have experienced, done, learnt, and what our feelings were, and also compare our previous judgement with our present one, and our intents and aspirations with our success and the satisfaction produced by it. This is the repetition of the private instructions provided to everybody by experience. Moreover, our own experience can be considered the text, and reflection and knowledge the commentary on it. Much reflection and knowledge, combined with little experience, resemble those editions whose pages offer two lines of text and forty lines of commentary. A lot of experience, with little reflection and scanty knowledge,

446

---

[a] *Difficilis in otio quies*　[b] *Besonnenheit*

resemble the Bipont editions,[a] which have no notes and leave much that is
unintelligible.

Pythagoras' rule that in the evening, before going to sleep, we should
review what we have done during the day, aims at the same advice. Whoever
lives in the hurly-burly of business or pleasure without ever pondering the
past, but instead merely reels off his life, loses clear mindfulness; his mind
becomes a chaos, and a certain confusion enters his thoughts, to which the
abrupt, fragmentary, as it were, chopped quality of his conversation soon
bears witness. This is the more the case the greater the external commotion,
the larger the number of impressions, and the smaller the inner activity of
his mind.

Here it must be remarked that after a long time and after the circumstances and surroundings that affected us have passed, we are unable to
recall and renew the former mood and feeling that these had caused in us;
yet we can very well remember our own *utterances* prompted by them back
then. These are now their result, their expression, and their criterion.
Therefore, memory or paper should preserve these products of memorable
times. Diaries are very useful for this purpose.

(9) To fulfil ourselves,[b] to be everything to ourselves, and to be able to say
'All my possessions I carry with me',[c] is surely the quality most conducive to
our happiness. Hence Aristotle's statement, 'Happiness belongs to those
who suffice themselves',[d] cannot be asserted often enough. (This is essentially also the same idea in the extremely apt phrase by Chamfort, which I
prefixed as a motto to this treatise.)[61] For partly we cannot count on
anybody but ourselves with any certainty, and partly the complaints and
disadvantages, the dangers and vexations that society carries with it are
innumerable and inevitable.

No path to happiness is more mistaken than living it up in the big world
(high life[e]); for its purpose is to transform our miserable existence into a
succession of joy, indulgence, and pleasure, in which case disappointment
cannot fail to materialize, as it will likewise occur with its obligatory
accompaniment, mutual deception.[*,62]

---

* Just as our body is covered in clothes, so our mind is covered in lies. Our words, our actions, our entire
being are mendacious; and only through this cover can we sometimes guess our true way of thinking,
just as the shape of the body through the clothes.

[a] [See p. 36, n. d]   [b] *sich selber genügen*
[c] *omnia mea mecum porto* [Cicero, *Paradoxa Stoicorum* (*Stoic Paradoxes*), Paradoxon I, 8; also Seneca,
Epistles, 18 ('*omnia bona mea mecum sunt*')]
[d] ἡ εὐδαιμονία τῶν αὐτάρκων ἐστί (*felicitas sibi sufficientium est*; *Eudemian Ethics* 7, 2 [1238a12])
[e] [Original English]

First of all, every society requires mutual accommodation and a mutually agreeable temper; hence the larger it is, the duller. We can only be entirely *ourselves* as long as we are alone; therefore, whoever does not love solitude, also does not love freedom; for only when we are alone, are we free. Compulsion is the inseparable companion of every society; each one demands sacrifices, which are the more difficult, the greater our own individuality is. Accordingly, we will flee, tolerate, or love solitude in exact proportion to the value of our own self. In solitude the wretched person feels his whole wretchedness and the great mind the full extent of its greatness; in short, everyone becomes aware of himself as what he is. Furthermore, the higher someone ranks in the order of nature, the lonelier he is – essentially and inevitably. But then it is a blessing for him when physical solitude accords with intellectual solitude. Otherwise, being frequently surrounded by heterogeneous beings has a disturbing, even adverse effect on him, robs him of his self and has nothing to offer as compensation. Also, whereas nature has established the greatest moral and intellectual diversity between human beings, society, disregarding this diversity, treats them all as equal, or rather, sets up artificial differences and degrees of class and rank instead, which are often diametrically opposed to the ranking list 448 of nature. In this order, those whom nature has placed low are in a good position, but the few whom she has placed high miss out. Therefore, the latter are in the habit of withdrawing from society; and in every society the vulgar element predominates as soon as it is large in numbers. What spoils society for great minds is the equality of rights, hence of entitlements, despite the inequality of capabilities, hence (social) achievements, of others.[63] The so-called good society accepts all kinds of merits, except intellectual ones; these, in fact, are contraband. It obligates us to show infinite patience with every folly, stupidity, perversity, and dullness. In contrast, personal merits are supposed to beg for forgiveness or disguise themselves; for intellectual superiority offends by its mere existence, without any agency of the will. Accordingly, what we call good society not only has the disadvantage of presenting us with human beings whom we can neither praise nor love, but it also does not allow us to be ourselves in harmony with our nature. Rather, it compels us to shrink, or even disfigure ourselves, for the sake of harmony with others. Ingenious discourse or ideas only belong in ingenious society; in ordinary society they are positively loathed; for in order to please here, it is absolutely necessary to be platitudinous and narrow-minded.[64] In such a society, therefore, we have to give up three quarters of ourselves through great self-denial, in order to become like other people. In return, of course, we have the others. But the more a

person possesses his own worth, the more he will find that the gain does not
cover the loss and business turns out to his disadvantage, because usually
people are insolvent, i.e. their company has nothing that would compensate
for its boredom, arduousness, and disagreeableness and for the self-denial
that it imposes. Accordingly, most society is so constituted that whoever
exchanges it for solitude gets a good deal.[65] Furthermore, in order to replace
genuine, i.e. intellectual superiority, which it cannot bear and which is also
449   hard to find, society has arbitrarily adopted a false, conventional superiority,
based on arbitrary rules, traditionally inherited among the higher classes,
and, like a password, changeable. This is what is called *guter Ton, bon ton*,
fashionableness.[a] But its weakness becomes apparent once it collides with
genuine superiority. – Moreover, 'when good taste appears, common sense
retreats'.[b]

In general, people can be *in the most perfect harmony* only with themselves – not with their friends, not with their lovers; for the differences of
individuality and disposition[c] always lead to dissonance, even if only slight.
Therefore, genuine, profound peace of heart and perfect peace of mind,
these highest earthly goods after health, are to be found in solitude alone
and, as a permanent disposition, only in the deepest seclusion. And if our
own self is great and rich, we enjoy the happiest state that can be found on
this miserable earth. Indeed, let us be frank; as intimately as people may be
joined by friendship, love, and marriage, ultimately they are *absolutely honest*
only with themselves and maybe also with their child. – The less a person,
due to objective or subjective conditions, has to come in contact with other
people, the better off he is. *Solitude* and desolation let us survey their evils,
even if we cannot feel them all at once. Society, on the other hand, is
insidious; it conceals behind the appearance of diversion, communication,
sociable pleasures, and so on, great and often irremediable evils. One major
area of study for the young should be *learning to tolerate solitude*, because
it is a source of happiness and peace of mind.[66] – It follows from all this
that those are best off who have counted only on themselves and can be
everything to themselves. Even Cicero says: 'Whoever is completely on his
own and relies on himself, cannot but be perfectly happy' (Parodoxon II).[d]
Moreover, the more somebody has in himself, the less can others be to
him. It is a certain feeling of self-sufficiency that prevents people who

---

[a] [Original English, preceded by German and French expressions literally for 'good tone']
[b] *quand le bon ton arrive, le bon sens se retire*   [c] *Stimmung*
[d] *Nemo potest non beatissimus esse, qui est totus aptus ex sese, quique in se uno* [*sua*] *ponit omnia* [Cicero, *Paradoxa Stoicorum*, Paradoxon II, 17]

possess inner worth and riches from making the considerable sacrifices demanded by communion with others, let alone seeking such a communion through marked self-denial. The opposite of this makes ordinary people so sociable and accommodating, since it is easier for them to tolerate others than themselves. We must add to this that what has real value finds no esteem in the world, and what is esteemed is worth nothing. The seclusion of all worthy and excellent people is the proof and the result of this. As a result, one who has something valuable in himself possesses genuine wisdom of life, if in case that it is necessary, he restricts his needs in order to preserve or expand his freedom and, accordingly, makes his inevitable dealings with the world of humans as short as possible. 450

On the other hand, what makes human beings sociable is their inability to bear solitude, and within solitude themselves. It is inner emptiness and tedium that drive them to society, and also to foreign lands and travel. Their mind lacks the elastic force to impart its own movement; therefore, they seek to enhance it through wine, and many turn into alcoholics in this way. For the same reason they need constant excitement from outside, in fact the strongest excitement, i.e. that which comes from beings like themselves. Without this their mind collapses under its own weight and falls into an oppressive lethargy.*,[67] Also it might be said that every one of them is only a small fraction of the Idea of humanity, hence that he needs to be greatly supplemented by others so that a somewhat complete human consciousness comes out. In contrast, whoever is a complete human being, a human being par excellence, represents a unity and not a fraction and, therefore, has enough in himself. In this sense, we can compare ordinary society to that Russian horn music in which each horn plays only one note and music is produced solely by all the horns sounding together at the right moment. For the sense and mind of most people is as monotonous as such a one-note horn; in fact, many look as if they always had one and the same thought and were incapable of thinking anything else. This not only explains why they 451

---

* As is well known, evils are alleviated by bearing them collectively. Among these, people apparently count boredom, so they sit together in order to be bored together. Just as the love of life is at bottom only the fear of death, similarly the drive to sociability in humans is really not a direct one, since it is not based on the love of society, but on the fear of loneliness, in that it is not so much the charming presence of others that is sought, but rather the dreariness and anxiety of being alone, together with the monotony of one's own consciousness, that are to be escaped. In order to avoid these, people put up even with bad company and the annoyance and the constraint it necessarily brings with it. – On the other hand, if the revulsion against all this has won and if, as a result, a habit of solitude and the inurement against its immediate impact have arisen, so that it no longer produces the above-described effects, then we can continue to be alone with the greatest ease without longing for society, exactly because the need for it is not a direct one and, on the other hand, we are now accustomed to the beneficial qualities of solitude.

are so boring, but also why they are so sociable and prefer to move in a herd: the gregariousness of mankind.[a] It is the monotony of their own being that becomes unbearable to every one of them; – 'All stupidity suffers from weariness with itself'[b] – only together and conjointly are they anything at all, just like those horn players. In contrast, the intellectually brilliant person can be compared to a virtuoso who performs his concert *alone*; or to the piano. Just as the piano, in itself, is a small orchestra, he is a small world, and what all the others are only through collaboration, he represents in the unity of an individual consciousness. Like the piano, he is not part of a symphony, but suited for the solo and solitude. If he is supposed to work together with others, he can do so only as the principal voice with accompaniment, like the piano; or for setting the tone in vocal music, like the piano. – Meanwhile, whoever likes society can deduce from this simile the rule that what the people with whom he keeps company lack in quality, must to some extent be made up in quantity. In a single brilliant person he can find enough company. But if none but the ordinary sort are to be found, it is good to have a good many of them, so that something may come out of the diversity and collaboration – in analogy with horn music I mentioned – and may heaven grant him patience.

452

It is also due to that inner emptiness and insufficiency of human beings that, if once people of a better sort unite for the sake of realizing some noble, ideal end, the outcome is almost always the following: that from the plebs[c] of humankind – which in an innumerable mass fills and covers everything, like vermin, and is always ready to grab anything indiscriminately and fight its boredom with the help of it, or its lack under different circumstances – that out of this plebs a few sneak or push their way in; and soon they either destroy the whole project or change it in such a way that it becomes practically the opposite of the original intention. –

Incidentally, sociability can also be seen as a mutual mental warming of people, like the physical warming which they achieve by moving closely together when it is very cold. But whoever has much mental warmth himself needs no such aggregation. In the second volume of this work, in the last chapter, readers can find a fable I invented on this note. According to all this, everyone's sociability stands approximately in reverse proportion to his intellectual worth; and 'He is very unsociable' almost implies 'He is a man of great qualities'.

For solitude confers a twofold advantage on the intellectually superior person; first of all, being on his own, and the second, not being with others.

---

[a] [Original English]   [b] *omnis stultitia laborat fastidio sui* [Seneca, *Epistles*, 9, 22]   [c] *plebs*

The last we will value highly when we consider how much constraint, annoyance, and even danger, every social intercourse brings with it. 'All our evils come from our inability to be alone',[a] says La Bruyère. *Sociability* belongs to the most dangerous, even destructive inclinations, since it brings us into contact with beings the great majority of whom are morally bad and intellectually dull or perverted.[68] The unsociable person is one who does not need them. To possess in ourselves so much that we do not need society is already very fortunate, because almost all our suffering arises from society and because peace of mind, which, after health, constitutes the most essential element of our happiness, is jeopardized by every society and, therefore, cannot very well exist without a considerable amount of solitude.[69] In order to share in the happiness of peace of mind, the Cynics renounced all possessions; whoever renounces society with the same intention has chosen the wisest means. For what Bernardin de St Pierre says is as apt as it is beautiful: 'Abstention from food guarantees health of the body, and abstention from people guarantees tranquillity of the soul.'[b] Accordingly, whoever becomes friends with solitude from early on, indeed, comes to love it, has gained a goldmine. But not everybody is able to do this. For, just as need originally herds people together, so does boredom after need has been eliminated. Without these two, we all would probably remain alone, because only in solitude do our surroundings correspond to the exclusive importance, indeed uniqueness, which we all possess in our own eyes and which is reduced to nothing by the crush of the world, where at every step it receives a painful disclaimer. In this sense solitude is actually everybody's natural state; it reinstates us as the first Adam in the original happiness appropriate to our nature.

But Adam also had no father or mother! In another sense, therefore, solitude is not natural for human beings, namely insofar as when entering the world they find themselves not alone, but among parents and siblings, hence in a community. Accordingly, love of solitude cannot exist as an original tendency, but can develop only as a result of experience and reflection. And these happen in proportion to the development of our own mental powers, but at the same time together with our advancing age; so that, on the whole, everyone's sociable drive will be inversely proportional to his age. The small child starts to cry out of fear and misery

453

---

[a] *Tout notre mal vient de ne pouvoir être seuls* [Jean de La Bruyère, *Les Caractères, ou Les mœurs de ce siècle* (*The Characters, or the Manners of the Age*), ch. XI ('*De l'homme*')]
[b] *la diète des alimen[t]s nous rend la santé du corps, et celle des hommes la tranquillité de l'âme* [Jacques-Henri Bernardin de Saint-Pierre, *Études de la nature* (*Studies of Nature*), Étude huitième (Study 8), 1784 (first edn.)]

as soon as it is left alone just for a few minutes. For the boy, being alone is a great punishment. Young men easily associate with one another; only the more noble and high-minded among them seek solitude from time to time; but to spend an entire day on their own is still difficult for them. For the grown man, on the other hand, this is easy; he is able to be alone often, and the more the older he becomes. The old man, who alone remains of a vanished generation and, in addition, has grown out of or is dead to life's pleasures, finds in solitude his proper element. But in individuals, the increase in the inclination towards seclusion and loneliness will always happen in proportion to their intellectual worth. For, as mentioned before, it is not a purely natural inclination, directly caused by needs, but rather just an effect of experience and reflection on it, in particular the insight gained into the morally and intellectually miserable nature of the great majority of people. The worst aspect of this is that in the individual, the moral and intellectual defects conspire and work hand in hand, resulting in all kinds of extremely distasteful phenomena, which make social intercourse with most people unpalatable, in fact, insufferable. And so, although there are many things in this world that are thoroughly bad, the worst remains society; so that *Voltaire*, that sociable Frenchman, was compelled to say: 'The earth is covered with people who are not worth talking to.'[a] The same reason for this inclination is given by the gentle *Petrarch*, who loved solitude so strongly and consistently:

> I've often sought the solitary life
> (river-banks know it, and fields and woods)
> to escape these dull and clouded minds,
> who have lost the road to heaven.[b]

He treats the matter in the same way in his fine book, *The Life of Solitude*,[c] which seems to have been *Zimmermann's* model for his famous work on solitude.[d] Chamfort expresses this merely secondary and mediate origin of unsociability in his usual sarcastic manner when he says: 'It is sometimes said of a man who lives alone that he does not like society. That is often as if we were saying that a man does not like walking because he does

---

[a] *la terre est couverte de gens qui ne méritent pas qu'on leur parle* [Voltaire, Letter to Cardinal de Bernis, 26 June 1762]

[b] *Cercato ho sempre solitaria vita/* (*Le rive il sanno, e le campagne e i boschi*), / *Per fuggir quest'ingegni storti [sordi] e loschi*, / *Che la strada del ciel' hanno smarrita* [from *Il Canzoniere* (*Songbook*), sonnet 259] (according to the *Concordanze del Canzoniere de Francesco Petrarca*, Florence: Ufficio Lessicografico, 1971), trans. A. S. Kline]

[c] *de vita solitaria* [first version 1346, published 1366]

[d] [Johann Georg Zimmermann, *Ueber die Einsamkeit* (*On Solitude*), 1784–5]

not like walking in the evening in the forest of Bondy.'*,a,70 But also the   455
gentle Christian Angelus Silesius says the same in his own way using
mythical language:

> Herod is an enemy; Joseph is the mind,
> God makes known to it the danger in a dream (the spirit).
> The world is Bethlehem, Egypt is *solitude*:
> Flee, my soul! Flee, or else you will die of grief.b

Giordano Bruno speaks in the same way: 'Many who wished to taste a
heavenly life on earth, have cried with one voice: "Lo, then would I wander
far off, and remain in the wilderness."'c And similarly Sadi, the Persian, says
of himself in *Gulistan*: 'Weary of my friends in Damascus, I withdrew into
the desert near Jerusalem to seek the companionship of animals.'d In short,
all those have spoken in the same way whom Prometheus had formed of
better clay.e What pleasure could be afforded to them by their dealings with
beings to whom they can only relate in a way that establishes a communion
by means of the lowest and most ignoble elements in their own nature, that
which is ordinary, trivial, and common in it – beings who, since they are not
able to rise to their level, have no other choice but to drag them down to
their own, which hence becomes their goal? Accordingly, it is an aristocratic
feeling that nourishes the tendency to seclusion and solitude. All rascals are
sociable, pitifully so. But that a human being is of a nobler kind first shows
itself in the fact that he does not delight in others, but more and more
prefers solitude to their company and then gradually, over the course of
years, comes to understand71 that, apart from rare exceptions, there is only
one choice in the world, that between solitude and commonness. Even
Angelus Silesius, with his Christian meekness and love, could not leave this
unsaid, as tough as it sounds:

---

* In the same sense, Sadi says in *Gulistan*: 'Since this time we have renounced companionship and
chosen the path of seclusion; for safety is in solitude.' [See p. 174, n. c]

b *on dit quelquefois d'un homme qui vit seul, il n'aime pas la société. C'est souvent comme si on disait d'un
homme, quil [qu'il] n'aime pas la promenade, sous le prétexte qu'il ne se promène pas volontiers le soir dans
la forêt de Bondy* [a large forest near Paris with a bad reputation as a place for brigands] [Chamfort,
Maximes et Pensées, ch. 4]

c [Angelus Silesius (Johann Scheffler), *Cherubinischer Wandersmann* (*Cherubinic Wanderer*) (1674),
Book 3, no. 241]

d *tanti uomini, che in terra hanno voluto* [*volsuto*] *gustare vita celeste, dissero con una voce: 'ecce elongavi
fugiens, et mansi in solitudine'* [Psalms 55:7] [Giordano Bruno, *De gli eroici furori* (*The Heroic Frenzies*),
Part II, Dialogue 2]

e [See p. 174, n. c]

f [Compare Juvenal, *Satires* XIV, 34, where it says: '*quibus* (...) *meliore luto finxit praecordia Titan*'
(those whom the Titan had formed of a better clay)]

Solitude is necessary; only be not common;
So you can be in the desert everywhere.[a]

456   But with regard to the great minds, it is quite natural that these true
educators of the whole of humankind feel as little inclined to frequent
association with the others as the pedagogue to join in the games of the
children who noisily surround him. For the great minds, who have come
into the world to steer the others through the sea of errors towards the truth
and draw them out of the dark abyss of crudeness and commonness up into
the light, towards education and ennoblement – they must live among
them, but without actually belonging to them, and therefore, since their
youth, feel markedly different from the others, but only gradually, in the
course of years, come to a clear understanding of the matter. Afterwards
they will make sure that their mental alienation from the others is joined by
a physical one and nobody is allowed to come near them, unless he himself
is more or less exempt from the common vulgarity.[72]

And so it follows from all this that the love of solitude does not arise
directly as an original drive,[b] but develops indirectly, in particular in nobler
minds and only gradually, not without overcoming the natural drive for
sociability, indeed, with the occasional opposition of Mephistophelian
whispered insinuations:

Be done with nursing your despair,
Which, like a vulture, feeds upon your mind;
The very meanest company bids fair
To let you feel a man among mankind.[c]

Loneliness is the lot of all eminent minds, which at times they will
bemoan, but always choose as the lesser of two evils.[73] With increasing age,
'Dare to think'[d] in this part becomes easier and more natural, and in our
sixties the drive to solitude is actually natural, and in fact instinctive.[e] For now
everything unites to promote it. The strongest appeal for sociability, namely
the love of women and the sexual drive, no longer works, indeed, the
asexuality of old age lays the foundation for a certain self-sufficiency, which
gradually absorbs the sociable drive in general.[74] We have done away with a
457   thousand delusions and follies; the active life has for the most part ceased; we
have nothing left to expect, no more plans and intentions; the generation to
which we really belong no longer exists; surrounded by an alien generation,
we are objectively and essentially alone. Meanwhile, the flight of time has

---

[a] [*Cherubinischer Wandersmann*, Book 2, no. 117]   [b] *ursprünglicher Trieb*
[c] [Goethe, *Faust* I, 1635–8]   [d] *sapere aude*   [e] *naturgemäßer, ja, instinktartiger*

become more rapid, and intellectually we would still like to use it. For if the mind has retained its power, then the great amount of knowledge and experience we have acquired, the gradually perfected elaboration of all our thoughts and the great facility in the use of all our powers make studies of every kind more interesting and easier than ever. We see clearly in regard to a thousand things that before were as if in a fog; we reach results and feel our entire superiority. From long experience we have ceased to expect much from people, since, on the whole, they do not belong to those who gain in stature on closer acquaintance. Moreover, we know that, except for rare strokes of luck, we will find nothing but very deficient specimens of human nature, which are better left untouched. Therefore, we are no longer exposed to the usual deceptions, become aware who everyone is, and will seldom feel the desire to associate more closely with people. Finally, the habit of isolation and communion with ourselves has been added and become second nature, especially if we recognize in loneliness a friend of our youth. Accordingly, the love of solitude, which previously had first to be wrested from the sociable drive, is now quite natural and simple; we exist in it like fish in water. Therefore, every individuality that as a result of its eminence is unlike the rest, and hence stands on its own, feels depressed in its youth because of this isolation essential to it, but relieved in old age.

Of course, people share in this real advantage of old age only in proportion to their intellectual abilities, hence the eminent mind does so before all others, but perhaps everybody does to a lesser degree. Only extremely miserable and common natures will still be as sociable as ever in their old age; they are a burden to society, for which they are no longer suited, and at most manage to be tolerated, whereas before they had been sought after.   458

The inversely proportional relation we have described between our age and the degree of our sociability lets us also discover a teleological aspect. The younger people are, the more they have to learn in every respect; nature has referred them to the mutual instruction that we all receive when associating with our peers and which can be called a great Bell–Lancaster educational establishment,[a] since books and schools are artificial institutions removed from nature's plan. Very expediently, we attend this natural teaching institution the more assiduously, the younger we are.

'Nothing is altogether happy',[b] says Horace, and 'No lotus without a stem', is an Indian saying. Thus solitude, apart from its many advantages,

---

[a] [Referring to an educational method of mutual instruction among pupils independently developed by Andrew Bell (1753–1832) and Joseph Lancaster (1778–1838)]
[b] *Nihil est ab omni parte beatum* [*Odes* II, 16]

also has its small disadvantages and complaints, which, however, in comparison with those of society, are minor. Therefore, whoever possesses something worthy in himself will always find it easier to get along without rather than with other people. – Incidentally, among these disadvantages is one we do not become conscious of so easily as the others, namely that just as our body, by always staying at home, becomes so sensitive to external influences that every cool breeze affects it pathologically, similarly our mind becomes so sensitive due to its constant seclusion and loneliness that we feel worried or insulted or hurt by the most insignificant incidents, words, or even mere facial expressions, whereas those who are constantly in the thick of the fray do not even notice such things.

But someone who, particularly during his early years, is unable to endure for any length of time the barrenness of solitude, as often as the justified dislike of people may have driven him into it, this person I advise to become accustomed to carry a part of his loneliness with him in society, hence to learn even in society to be alone to a certain degree and not to tell others immediately what he is thinking and, on the other hand, not to take too literally what they are saying. Rather, he should, morally and intellectually, not expect much from what they say and hence, in regard to their opinions, strengthen that indifference within himself that is the surest way of always practising a laudable tolerance. Then he will be not quite in their company, although he is in their midst, but will behave in a more purely objective fashion towards them; this will protect him from too close a contact with society and hence from any contamination or even injury. We actually possess a dramatic description of this restricted or entrenched sociability, which is worth reading, in the comedy *La comedia nueva o El café*,[a] namely in the character of D. Pedro in the second and third scenes of the first act. In this sense, we can also compare society to a fire, at which the prudent person warms himself from a safe distance, but does not stick his hand inside, like the fool, who after scorching himself escapes into the cold of solitude and complains that the fire burns.

(10) *Envy* is natural to human beings; nonetheless it is a vice and a misfortune at the same time.[*,75] Therefore, we should regard it as the enemy of our happiness and try to smother it like an evil demon. *Seneca* guides us to do so with the beautiful words: 'Let us enjoy what is ours without

459

---

* People's envy shows how unhappy they feel; their constant attention to the doings of others how bored they are.

a [Leandro Fernández de Moratín (*The New Comedy or The Coffee*) (1792)]

comparing; no one will ever be happy if tormented by the fact that someone else is happier' (*On Anger* III, 30),[a] and again: 'When you see so many who are ahead of you, think of how many are behind you' (*Epistles*, 15);[b] so we should more often consider those worse off than ourselves than those who seem to be better off. Even when actual evils have occurred, considering greater suffering than ours will afford us the most effective consolation, although it flows from the same source as envy, and next association with those who are in the same situation as us, our fellows in misery.[c]

So much for the active side of envy. In regard to the passive side we should remember that no hatred is as implacable as envy; consequently, we should not incessantly and assiduously endeavour to excite it; rather, we would do better to deny ourselves this pleasure, like some others, because of its dangerous consequences.   460

There are three aristocracies: (1) that of birth and rank, (2) the aristocracy of money, and (3) the aristocracy of the mind. The last one is in fact the most distinguished and is also recognized as such, if we only give it time; for Frederick the Great already remarked: 'Privileged minds rank on a level with sovereigns',[d] which he said to his Lord Chamberlain, who took umbrage at the fact that while ministers and generals ate at the chamberlain's table, Voltaire was to be assigned a place at a table where only rulers and princes sat. – Each of these aristocracies is surrounded by a host of people envying them, who are secretly bitter against every one of its members and, if they do not have to fear him, try hard to let him know in various ways that 'you are not better than us!' But these very efforts betray their conviction to the contrary. The method to be deployed by those who are envied consists in keeping everyone belonging to this group at a distance and in avoiding any contact with them as much as possible, so that they remain separated by a wide gulf, and, where this is not possible, calmly bearing their efforts, whose source in fact neutralizes them – a method we see applied consistently. In contrast, the members of one aristocracy will for the most part get along very well with those of the other two without envy, because everyone puts his merit on the scales against that of the others.[76]

(11) A plan should be considered carefully and repeatedly before being implemented, and even after we have thoroughly deliberated everything, we should still make a concession to the inadequacy of all human cognition, as a result of which there can always occur circumstances that are impossible to

---

[a] *nostra nos sine comparatione delectent: numquam erit felix quem torquebit felicior* [*De ira* III, 30, 3]
[b] *quum adspexeris quot te antecedant, cogita quot sequantur* [*Epistles, 15, 10*]   [c] *sociis malorum*
[d] *les âmes privilégiées rangent à l'égal des souverains*

study or foresee and that can render the entire calculation inaccurate. This concern will always put a weight into the negative side of the scale and advise us not to move without need in important matters: 'Do not disturb what is at rest.'[a] But once we have come to a decision and started to act, so that everything now must run its course and we only have to wait for the outcome, then we should not alarm ourselves by constantly renewed reflection on what is already done and repeated concerns about potential danger. Instead, we should dismiss the matter completely, regard all thoughts of it as closed, and calm ourselves with the conviction that we had thought everything out carefully at the proper time. This advice is also given by an Italian proverb *legala bene, e poi lascia la andare*,[b] which Goethe translates as 'You, saddle well and ride with confidence'; – as, incidentally, a large part of the aphorisms he provides under the heading 'Proverbially'[c] are translations of Italian proverbs. – If nonetheless the outcome is bad, that is due to the fact that all human affairs are subject to chance and error. That *Socrates*, the wisest among human beings, needed a *genius*[d] cautioning him in order to do the right thing in his own, personal affairs, or at least to avoid missteps, proves that no human understanding is adequate for this purpose. Therefore, the dictum, supposedly coming from a pope, that for every misfortune that befalls us we ourselves are to blame, at least in some respect, is not unconditionally and in all cases true, although it is so in the majority of cases. In fact, this feeling seems to have a large share in the fact that people try to conceal their misfortune as much as possible and, as far as they can manage, put on a happy face. They worry that we might infer guilt from the suffering.

(12) When something unfortunate has already occurred and cannot be changed any longer, we should not permit ourselves to think that it could have been different, and even less so by what means it could have been prevented; for then the pain increases until it is unbearable, so that we become a self-punisher.[e] Rather, we should imitate King David, who, as long as his son was lying sick in bed, besieged Jehovah relentlessly with pleas and entreaties, but shrugged it off and no longer thought about it after he had died. But whoever is not lighthearted enough for this should seek refuge in the fatalistic standpoint by clarifying to himself that everything that happens, happens with necessity, and hence is inescapable.

---

[a] *quieta non movere* [*Stare decisis et non quieta movere* – 'Maintain what has been decided and do not alter what has been established'; legal principle]
[b] ['Tighten the saddle properly, then set out on your journey whole-heartedly']
[c] *Sprichwörtlich* [series of poems]   [d] *Dämonions*
[e] ἑαυτοντιμορούμενος, [after Terence's *Heautontimoroumenos*]

Nonetheless, this rule is one-sided. It may be suited for our immediate   462
relief and reassurance when facing misfortunes; but when, as is mostly the
case, our own negligence or recklessness is at least in part to blame, the
repeated, painful reflection on how this could have been prevented is a
wholesome self-chastisement for our instruction and improvement, that is,
for the future. And we should not, as we are used to doing, try to make
excuses or whitewash or belittle before ourselves mistakes that we have
obviously committed, but should acknowledge them to ourselves and bring
them clearly before our eyes in their entire magnitude, so that we can firmly
resolve to avoid them in the future. Of course, doing so means having to
inflict on ourselves the great pain of dissatisfaction with our own self;[77] but
'Whoever has not been tormented, has not been educated.'[a]

(13) In regard to everything that concerns our weal and woe we should
keep a tight rein on our imagination.[b] So first of all we should not build
castles in the air, because they are too costly, insofar as we have to tear them
down again with a sigh immediately afterwards. But to an even greater
extent we should beware of alarming our heart by imagining merely possible
misfortunes. For if these were completely plucked out of thin air, or at least
far-fetched, when waking up from such a dream we would immediately
realize that everything was mere deception and, therefore, rejoice the more
in the better reality and at most infer a warning against a quite remote,
though possible, misfortune. But our imagination does not play readily with
such things; quite leisurely, it builds at best bright castles in the air. The
material for its gloomy dreams are misfortunes that threaten us in a quite
real fashion, even if remotely; our imagination enlarges these, brings their
possibility much nearer than it actually is, and envisions them in the most
terrifying manner. Such a dream we cannot immediately shake off when
waking up, as we can a cheerful one; for the latter is soon refuted by reality
and leaves at most a faint hope in the womb of possibility. But when we
have surrendered to black thoughts[c] (blue devils[d]), they have brought
images close to us that do not vanish so easily. For the possibility of a
thing in general is certain, and we are not always able to measure the degree   463
of its likelihood; then possibility easily turns into probability, and we have
delivered ourselves up to anguish. Therefore, we should look at things that
concern our weal and woe only with the eyes of reason and judgement, and
operate with dry and cold deliberation, with mere concepts and in the
abstract.[e] We should leave the imagination out of this, for it cannot judge,

---

[a] ὁ μὴ δαρεὶς ἄνθρωπος οὐ παιδεύεται [Menander, *Monosticha* (*Aphorisms*), 422]   [b] *Phantasie*
[c] *schwarzen Phantasien*   [d] [Original English]   [e] *in abstracto*

but brings mere images before our eyes that agitate the mind in a useless and often very painful manner. This rule should be most strictly followed in the evening. For just as darkness makes us timid and lets us see dreadful figures everywhere, so obscurity of thought has an analogous effect, because every uncertainty gives rise to insecurity. Therefore in the evening, when fatigue has covered understanding and judgement with subjective darkness, when the intellect is tired and confused[a] and cannot get to the bottom of things, the objects of our meditation – when concerning our personal affairs – easily assume a dangerous air and become terrifying apparitions. Mostly this is the case at night, in bed, when the mind is completely relaxed and, therefore, the power of judgement is no longer up to its task, but the imagination is still active. Then the night paints everything black. Consequently, our thoughts before falling asleep or even when waking up in the middle of the night are often distortions and inversions of things that are almost as bad as dreams and moreover, when concerning personal affairs, usually pitch-dark and indeed horrible. In the morning such phantoms have vanished, just like dreams. This is the meaning of the Spanish proverb: 'noche tinta, blanco el dia' (the night is coloured, the day is white). But even in the evening, as soon as the lights burn, the understanding, like the eye, does not see as clearly as during the day; hence this time is not suited for meditating on serious, and especially unpleasant, affairs. For these, morning is the right time, as it is in general without exception for all efforts, mental as well as physical. For morning is the day's youth: everything is cheerful, fresh, and light; we feel strong, and all our faculties are at our complete disposal. We should not shorten it by getting up late, nor should we waste it with unworthy activities or conversations; instead we should regard it as the quintessence of life and, in a way, consider it sacred. On the other hand, evening is the day's old age; in the evening we are jaded, garrulous, and careless. Every day is a small life, for which waking up is its birth and which is concluded by sleep as its death. – Hence going to sleep is ultimately a daily death and each awakening is a rebirth. In fact, to complete this thought, we could regard the discomfort and difficulty of getting up as the birth pangs.[78]

In general, the state of health, sleep, nourishment, temperature, weather, environment, and many other external factors have a powerful influence on our mood, and this in turn on our thoughts. Therefore, just as our view of some matter is so much subject to time and even place, so is also our capacity for achievement as well. Hence

464

---

[a] θορυβούμενος

Appreciate the serious mood,
For it comes so rarely.   Goethe[a]

Not only do we have to wait to see whether and when objective conceptions
and original thoughts occur at their convenience, but even the thorough
deliberation of a personal affair does not always succeed at the time we have
determined in advance and when we have sat down for it. It too chooses
itself its own time, when the proper train of thought becomes active of its
own accord and we follow it with undivided interest.

To rein in the imagination, as recommended, it is also important that we
do not allow it to represent and picture previously suffered wrong, harm,
loss, insults, affronts, humiliations, and so on, because by doing so we re-
ignite the long-dormant indignation, rage, and all the hateful passions,
which pollute our mind. For, according to a beautiful simile told by the
Neoplatonist Proclus, just as in every city apart from the noble and
distinguished people all sorts of rabble (*ochlos*) also live, so there exists in   465
every human being, even the most noble and illustrious, the disposition to
the utterly base and common elements of human, indeed animal, nature.
This mob must not be excited to riot, neither should it be permitted to look
out of the window, for it looks ugly; but the figments of the imagination we
have described are its demagogues. Also relevant here is the fact that the
smallest offence that comes from people or things, when constantly brooded
over, enlarged and painted in shrill colours, can puff up into a monster
about which we get greatly upset. Instead, we should adopt an extremely
prosaic and sober perspective on everything unpleasant, so that we can take
it as lightly as possible.

Just as small objects, held close to the eyes and restricting our range of
vision, conceal the world – similarly people and things in our *immediate
surroundings*, as completely insignificant and indifferent as they may be, will
often unduly occupy our attention and thoughts, which they do in a
disagreeable manner, and block out important thoughts and affairs. We
should counteract this tendency.[79]

(14) When looking at things we do not possess, the idea can easily arise in
us: 'How about this being mine?', which makes us feel the privation.
Instead, we should more often ask: 'How about this *not* being mine?' By
this I mean that we should sometimes try looking at what we own in the way
we would remember it after losing it, and indeed everything, whatever it
may be: possessions, health, friends, lover, wife, child, horse, and dog; for

[a] [From Goethe's poem '*Generalbeichte*' (General Confession), which is part of the series '*Gesellige
Lieder*' (Sociable Songs)]

most of the time, only losing things teaches us their value. On the other hand, as a result of this recommended way of looking at things, firstly, their possession will immediately make us happier than before and, secondly, we will prevent their loss in every possible way, that is, not endanger possessions, not offend our friends, not tempt a wife's faithfulness, watch over the children's health, and so on. – Often we seek to brighten the gloom of the present by speculating about favourable possibilities and concocting all kinds of chimerical hopes, each of which is pregnant with disappointment, which will not fail to happen when the hope is dashed by harsh reality. It would be better to make the many bad possibilities the objects of our speculation, which would in part occasion provisions for defending against them, and in part pleasant surprises when they do not come to pass. For after living through some anxiety we are always noticeably more cheerful. In fact, it is even beneficial from time to time to envision great misfortunes that might possibly affect us, in order to endure more easily the much smaller ones that actually befall us by consoling ourselves in looking back to those great ones which did not happen.[80] But the previous rule should not be neglected over this present one.

(15) Since the affairs and events that concern us occur in confused fashion, without any order and connection to one another, in glaring contrast, and with nothing more in common than that they are our affairs, our thinking and caring about them must be equally abrupt so as to correspond to them. – Accordingly, when attending to one matter, we have to abstract from and disregard everything else, in order to attend to, enjoy, and endure each matter at its proper time, wholly unconcerned about anything else. Hence we must have drawers for our thoughts, as it were, one of which we open while all the others remain shut. In this way we avoid having a heavily oppressive worry spoil every little present pleasure and deprive us of all peace; we make sure that one consideration does not displace another, and that concern about important affairs does not lead to the neglect of many smaller ones, and so on. In particular, whoever is capable of elevated and noble considerations should not let his mind be so completely occupied and filled by personal affairs and lowly concerns that they prevent the former from entering; for that would really mean 'to ruin life's purpose in order to live'.[a] – Of course, self-restraint is required for this control and diversion of ourselves, as for so much else; but we should be encouraged to this by the consideration that every human being has to endure a great deal of severe constraint from outside, without which no life

---

[a] *propter vitam vivendi perdere causas* [Juvenal, *Satires* VIII, 84]

is possible. Yet a little self-restraint, applied in the right place, afterwards   467
prevents a lot of coercion from outside, just as a small segment of the circle
close to the centre corresponds to one a hundred times larger at the
periphery. Nothing helps us evade constraint from outside as much as
self-restraint; that is what Seneca's dictum says: 'If you want to subject
everything to yourself, subject yourself to reason' (*Epistles*, 37).[a] Also, self-
restraint is always in our power, and if worst comes to worst or it affects our
most sensitive spot, we can ease it a little. Coercion from outside, on the
other hand, is inconsiderate, unsparing, and merciless. Therefore, it is wise
to pre-empt the latter through the former.

(16) To set a goal for our wishes, to rein in our desires, to tame our anger,
always mindful that the individual can only achieve an infinitely small part
of all that is desirable, but that many evils must befall everyone, hence, in a
word, to 'abstain and endure'[b] – this is a rule without whose observance
neither wealth nor power can prevent us from feeling miserable. Horace
aims at this in the following remark:

> Amid all this, read and question the learned
> How you may be able to live your life in tranquillity;
> So that you are not agitated and tormented by every needy desire,
> Of fear and hope for things of little use.[c]

(17) 'Life consists in movement',[d] says Aristotle, obviously with justification; and just as our physical life consists in and persists through continuous movement, so also our inner, mental life constantly demands
occupation, occupation with anything, through action and thought; one
proof of this is people who have nothing to do or to think about and who
resort to drumming with their fingers or some implement. For our existence
is essentially restless; therefore, complete inactivity soon becomes unbearable for us in bringing about the most dreadful boredom. We ought to
regulate this drive so as to satisfy it methodically, and hence better.
Consequently,[81] activity, doing, possibly making something, but at least
learning something, are vital for the happiness of human beings; their
powers demand to be used and they want somehow to perceive the result   468
of this. However, the greatest satisfaction in this respect is provided by

---

[a] *si vis tibi omnia subjicere, te subjice rationi* [*Epistles*, 37, 4]

[b] ἀπέχειν καὶ ἀνέχειν, *abstinere et sustinere* [Epictetus' motto, as quoted in Aulus Gellius, *Noctes Atticae* (*Attic Nights*) XVII, 19]

[c] *Inter cuncta leges, et percontabere doctos / Qua ratione queas traducere leniter aevum; / Ne [Num] te semper inops agitet vexetque cupido, / Ne [Num] pavor, et rerum mediocriter utilium spes* [Horace, *Epistles* I, 18, 96–9]

[d] ὁ βίος ἐν τῇ κινήσει ἐστί (*vita motu constat*) [See p. 284, n. a]

making, producing something, be it a basket or a book; seeing a work of our own hands grow daily and finally reach its completion makes us immediately happy. A work of art, a text, even a mere handicraft achieve this; of course, the nobler the sort of work, the greater the pleasure. In this respect those are happiest who are conscious of their ability to produce significant, great, and coherent works. This imbues their whole existence with an interest of a higher order and imparts a flavour to it that is lacking in the lives of others, which in comparison, accordingly, are dull. For these people life and world have, apart from the material interest which is common to all, a second, higher, formal interest in containing the material to their works, which they are busily engaged in collecting throughout their life as soon as personal need allows them to breathe at all. Also their intellect is in a way a double one; one for ordinary relationships (matters of the will) like that of everybody else; and one for the purely objective comprehension of things. So their lives are twofold as well; they are spectators and at the same time actors, whereas the others are merely actors. – Meanwhile, we should all do something in proportion to our abilities. For we realize the extent to which we are adversely affected by a lack of systematic activity, of some kind of work, on long pleasure trips, when we feel quite unhappy from time to time, because, lacking an actual occupation, we are, as it were, torn out of our natural elements. To labour and fight against resistance is a human need, as digging is for moles. The stagnation produced by the contentment of a lasting pleasure would be unbearable to us. Overcoming obstacles means the full enjoyment of our existence; they might be of a material nature, as in acting and doing, or of an intellectual nature, as in learning and investigating; struggling with them and winning make us happy. If the opportunity to do so is lacking, we create it as best we can. Depending on the nature of

469   people's individuality, a person will hunt, or play ring and pin,[a] or, guided by an unconscious aspect of his nature, pick a quarrel, hatch a plot, or get himself involved in fraud and all sorts of depravities, only to put an end to the unbearable state of peace. 'Tranquillity in leisure is difficult.'[b]

(18) We should not take *images of the imagination* as the guiding star of our efforts, but clearly thought-out *concepts*. Yet most of the time the opposite happens. For, after closer inspection, we will find that what ultimately tips the balance in our decisions are mostly not concepts and judgements, but an image of the imagination which represents one of the alternatives. I do not remember in which novel by Voltaire or Diderot virtue always presented itself to the hero – when he was young and a Hercules at

---

[a] *Bilboquet*   [b] *Difficilis in otio quies*

the crossroad – in the shape of his old tutor, the tobacco tin in his left hand, the pinch of snuff in the right, and moralizing; vice, on the other hand, appeared in the shape of his mother's chambermaid. – Especially when we are young, the goal of our happiness is fixed in the form of some images that are present in our mind and often remain through half or even our entire life. They are actually taunting spectres; for when we have attained them, they dissolve into nothing, because we learn from experience that they achieve none of what they promised. Of this kind are individual scenes of domestic, civil, social, and rural life, images of the residence, surroundings, badges of honour, attestations of respect, and so forth; 'every fool has his cap';[a] also the image of the beloved often belongs here. It is probably natural that we fare in this way; for what is intuitively perceived,[b] because it is immediate, also has a more immediate effect on our will than the concept, the abstract thought, which only gives the universal without the particular; but it is the particular that contains reality. And yet it is only the concept that keeps its word; therefore, to be educated is to rely on it alone. Of course, it sometimes needs elucidating and paraphrasing by a few pictures, yet only with a grain of salt.[c]

(19) The previous rule can be subsumed under the more universal rule that we should everywhere control the impression of the present and intuitive in general. Compared to what is merely thought and known, this impression is disproportionately strong, not by virtue of its matter and content, which are often very small, but by virtue of its form, of intuitiveness and immediacy, which intrudes into the mind and disturbs its peace or shakes its resolutions. For what is present, intuitive, since it is easily taken in, always takes effect with all its force. Thoughts and reasons, on the other hand, require time and quiet to be thought through step by step; therefore, we are not able to have them completely present at every moment. Accordingly, the pleasant, which we have renounced as a result of reflection, tempts us nonetheless when we see it. Similarly, a judgement whose utter incompetence we realize offends us; an insult whose contemptible nature is clear to us enrages us; and similarly ten reasons against the existence of a danger are outweighed by the false illusion of its actual presence, and so forth. In all of this the original irrationality of our essence asserts itself. Women will often succumb to such an impression, and there are few men in whom reason predominates to such an extent that they do not have to suffer from the effects of it. Whenever we are unable to overcome such an impression by means of mere thoughts, it is best to neutralize

470

---

[a] *chaque fou a sa marotte*   [b] *das Anschauliche*   [c] *cum grano salis*

it with the help of its opposite, for example, the impression of an insult by seeking those who hold us in great esteem; or the impression of an imminent danger by actually contemplating what thwarts it. The Italian whom Leibniz mentions (in his *New Essays*,[a] Book I, ch. 2, §11) could withstand the pain of torture, while it happened, by not allowing the picture of the gallows to vanish from his imagination for one moment, as he had resolved to do, for that is where he would have ended up had he confessed. That is why he shouted 'I see you'[b] from time to time, words he later explained. – For the very reason we are considering here it is difficult, when all the people around us have a different opinion than ours and behave accordingly, not to be swayed by them, even if we are convinced of their error. For a fugitive king who is persecuted and travels strictly incognito, 471 the ceremonial subservience of his trusted companion, observed while they are alone, has to be an almost necessary cordial lest in the end he should doubt himself.

(20) Already in the second chapter[82] I have stressed the great value of *health*, which is the primary and most important ingredient of our happiness, and I wish here to mention a few quite general instructions for strengthening and maintaining it.

We should harden ourselves by imposing on the body – as a whole as well as each part – quite a lot of effort and exertion as long as we are healthy, and get used to withstanding all sorts of adverse influences. However, as soon as some sickness, of the whole or a part, shows itself, we should immediately take the opposite course and let the sick body, or a part of it, rest and nurse it in all possible ways; for what is ailing and weakened is incapable of being hardened.

Muscles are strengthened by vigorous use; nerves, on the other hand, are weakened by it. Hence we should exercise our muscles through appropriate exertion, but save the nerves from it. Accordingly, we should protect the eyes from light that is too bright, especially reflected light, from any straining in twilight conditions, and also from prolonged looking at objects that are too small. We should also protect the ears from too loud a noise, but in particular the brain from forced, persistent, or ill-timed effort; hence we should let it rest during digestion, because then the same vital force that produces thoughts in the brain is hard at work in the stomach and intestines making chyme and chyle; and also during or after strenuous muscular exercise. For the motor nerves are similar to the sensory ones, and just as the pain that we feel in injured limbs has its true seat in the brain, so also it is

---

[a] [*New Essays Concerning Human Understanding* (1704)]   [b] *io ti vedo*

actually not the arms and legs that work and walk but, in fact, the brain, that part of it which, by means of the medulla oblongata and the spinal cord, stimulates their nerves and thereby sets them in motion. Accordingly, the fatigue that we feel in the arms and the legs has its real seat in the brain;   472
which is why only *those* muscles get tired whose movement is voluntary, i.e. starts out from the brain, whereas the ones that work involuntarily, like the heart, do not. Obviously the brain is impaired when we force it to produce strong muscle activity and mental exertion at the same time, or even just in quick succession. This is not contradicted by the fact that at the beginning of a walk, or in general during short errands, we often feel a heightened mental activity; for at that point no fatigue of the parts of the brain just mentioned has occurred and, on the other hand, such a light activity of the muscles and the respiration, which is increased because of it, promote the rising of arterial, and hence better oxidized, blood to the brain.[83] – But we should in particular give the brain the full measure of sleep necessary to refresh it; for sleep is for the entire human being what winding up is for a clock. (See *The World as Will and Representation*, vol. 2, p. 217.[a]) This measure will be the greater, the more developed and active the brain is. However, to exceed it would be a mere waste of time, since the sleep would then lose in intensity what it gains in extension. (See *The World as Will and Representation*, vol. 2, p. 247.[b])*,[84] In general, we need to understand that our thinking is nothing but the organic function of the brain and, accordingly, behaves analogously to all other organic activities in regard to exertion and rest. Just as excessive exertion ruins the eyes, so it ruins the brain. It has rightly been said: The brain thinks, just as the stomach digests. The delusion of an immaterial, simple, essentially and constantly thinking soul that is indefatigable and dwells in the brain, having no need for anything in the world, has misled quite a few people to senseless practices and weakening of their mental powers; for example, Frederick the Great once tried to give up sleep completely. The philosophy professors would do well not to   473
encourage such a delusion, which is practically pernicious, through their spinning-wheel philosophy[c] that strives to accommodate the Christian catechism. – We should accustom ourselves to regard our mental powers

---

* Sleep is a piece of *death* that we borrow *anticipando* [in anticipation] and in exchange get back and renew our life, which was exhausted by the day. *Le sommeil est un emprunt fait à la mort* [Sleep is a loan from death]. Sleep borrows from death for the sustenance of life. Or: It is the *temporary interest* of death, which itself is the paying off of the principal. The higher the interest and the more regularly it is paid, the later it is called in.

[a] [Hübscher *SW* 3, 239f.]   [b] [Hübscher *SW* 3, 274f.]   [c] *Rocken-Philosophie*

definitely as physiological functions, in order to treat them accordingly, to take care of them, exert them, and so forth, and to keep in mind that every physical suffering, complaint, or disorder, in whichever part it might occur, affects the mind. It is Cabanis' *Relations of the Physical and the Moral in Man*[a] that best enables us to do so.

Neglect of the advice given here is the reason why some great minds, and also great scholars, have become feeble-minded, childish, and even insane in their old age. For example, that the celebrated English poets of this century, like *Walter Scott*, *Wordsworth*, *Southey*, and others, in their old age, even already in the sixties, have become intellectually blunted and inept, indeed, have lapsed into imbecility, can doubtless be explained by the fact that, seduced by high remuneration, they all conducted writing as a trade and wrote for the money. This leads to unnatural exertion, and whoever puts the harness on his Pegasus and drives his Muse with a whip, will pay for it in a similar way as the one who has done compulsive service to Venus. I suspect that *Kant* too, during his last years, after having finally become famous, overdid things and thus brought on the second childhood of his last four years. In contrast, the gentlemen of the Weimar Court, Goethe, Wieland, and Knebel, remained intellectually strong and active into their great old age, because they were not paid hacks; the same goes for Voltaire.

Every month of the year has a particular, immediate and weather-independent influence on our health, our bodily states in general, and in fact also on our mental states.[85]

C.   Concerning our attitude towards others

(21) To get through life, it is useful to bring along a large supply of *foresight* and *forbearance*;[b] the former protects us against harm and loss, the latter from disputes and quarrels.[86]

474

Whoever has to live among human beings is not allowed to reject any individuality absolutely, not even the worst, most deplorable, or most ridiculous, insofar as it is after all posited and given by nature. Rather, we have to accept individuality as something unalterable that, as a result of an eternal and metaphysical principle, is bound to be the way it is; and in bad cases we should think: 'It takes all kinds of folks.'[c] If we act otherwise, we do

---

[a] *Rapports du physique et du moral de l'homme* [1802]
[b] *Vorsicht und Nachsicht* [*Vorsicht* normally means 'caution', but Schopenhauer plays on the verbal parallelism between the two terms]
[c] [Goethe, *Faust* I, 3483]

an injustice and challenge the other to a fight to the death. For no one can change his actual individuality, i.e. his moral character, his cognitive powers, his temperament, his physiognomy, and so forth. If we condemn his being completely and utterly, nothing remains for him but to fight us as a mortal enemy; for we wish to grant him the right to exist only under the condition that he become a different person than he irreversibly is. Therefore, in order to be able to live among people, we must accept everybody's given individuality, in whatever way it might have turned out. We are only allowed the intention to use it in a manner permitted by its nature and constitution, but we are not to hope for it to change, nor simply to condemn it for what it is. This is the true meaning of the saying: 'Live and let live.' However, the task is not as easy as it is just; and we should deem those lucky who are allowed to avoid many an individuality for good. – Meanwhile, in order to learn to tolerate people, we should practise our patience on inanimate objects that stubbornly resist our actions by virtue of mechanical or else physical necessity, for which daily opportunities exist. Afterwards we learn how to transfer the patience thus acquired on to people by getting accustomed to thinking that, wherever they stand in our way, they too must do so by virtue of a strict necessity that follows from their nature, just like that with which inanimate objects act. Therefore, it is equally foolish to be full of indignation about their actions as it is to be about a stone that gets in our way. In regard to some people, it is most prudent to think: 'I will not change him; hence I shall make use of him.'

(22) It is astonishing how easily and quickly homogeneity or heterogeneity of mind and temper between people makes itself known in conversation; it is noticeable in every trifle. Even if the conversation refers to the most alien, indifferent matters, between essentially heterogeneous people nearly every sentence of the one will more or less displease the other, and not a few will actually annoy him. Homogeneous people, on the other hand, immediately feel a certain accordance in everything, which in the case of great homogeneity flows into a perfect harmony and even unison. This primarily explains why quite ordinary people are so sociable and easily find good company everywhere – such decent, amiable, stout people. With extraordinary people it is the other way around, and the more so, the more brilliant they are; so that, in their seclusion, they can really be delighted at times to find in someone else just some chord that is in tune with themselves, and be it ever so small! For each one can be to the other only as much as the other is to him. Really great minds live in an aerie, like eagles, high up, alone. – Secondly, this explains how the like-minded find one another so quickly, as if they were drawn to one another with magnetic force – kindred

475

souls greet each other from afar. Of course, we will have the opportunity to observe this most frequently in those with a vulgar disposition or inferior talents, but only because they exist in abundance and better and excellent natures are rare and also called such. Accordingly, in a large community intent on practical purposes, for example, two downright scoundrels will recognize each other as quickly as if they wore a standard, and will at once join forces to plot abuse or treachery. The same would happen if, as is actually impossible,[a] we imagine a large society consisting entirely of really intelligent and ingenious people, except for two dunces who are also present. These will feel drawn to each other by sympathy, and soon each one of them will rejoice in his heart to have come across at least one sensible man. It is really curious to witness how two people, especially of the morally and intellectually inferior sort, recognize each other at first sight, eagerly try to move closer to each other and, while greeting each other cordially and happily, rush towards each other like old friends. It is so remarkable that we are tempted to assume, in accordance with the Buddhist doctrine of metempsychosis, that they had already been friends in a previous life.[87]

476

But what separates people even in the case of great accord, and produces temporary disharmony between them, is the diversity of their present mood, which is almost always different for each person, in accordance with their present position, occupation, environment, physical state, momentary train of thought, and so on. This leads to discord between the most harmonizing personalities. To be able to make the correction needed for removing such a disturbance and to establish an equal temper[b] would be an achievement of the highest culture. How much the uniformity of mood achieves for a social group, can be inferred from the fact that even a large society is roused to lively communication and honest concern, amidst universal contentment, as soon as something objective, be it a danger, or a hope, or some news, or a rare spectacle, a play, music, or something else, affects all simultaneously and in the same manner. By defeating all private interests, it creates a universal harmony of spirits. Lacking such an objective influence, usually a subjective one is chosen;[88] and bottles are the ordinary means of bringing about such a common mood in a gathering. Even tea and coffee serve this purpose.

However, the disharmony that the difference in momentary temper produces in every community in part explains the fact that in memory, when it is freed from this and all similar influences however transitory, everybody presents himself in an idealized or even glorified way. Memory

---

[a] *per impossibile*   [b] *gleichschwebende Temperatur*

acts like the collecting lens in the *camera obscura*; it pulls everything together and thereby generates a much more beautiful picture than the original. In part we already secure the advantage of being seen in this way through every absence. For although the idealizing recollection needs some time to com-   477 plete its work, the work is begun at once. Therefore, it is wise to see our acquaintances and good friends only after considerable periods of time; when meeting them again, we notice that memory has already been at work.

(23) Nobody can see *beyond himself*.[a] By this I mean: Everyone sees in the other only as much as he is himself; for[89] he can only grasp and comprehend in accordance with his own intelligence. And if this is of the lowest kind, all intellectual talents, even the greatest, will fail to have an effect on him, and he will perceive nothing in the person who possesses them but what is lowest in his individuality, hence merely all his weaknesses and defects of temperament and character; from his point of view, these make that person up. The higher mental abilities exist as little for him as colour for someone who is blind. For all minds are invisible to those who have none themselves; and every appreciation is a product of the value of the assessed and the cognitive range[b] of the assessor. From this it follows that we reduce ourselves to the level of any person with whom we speak, insofar as every advantage that we can have over him disappears, and even the necessary self-denial remains completely unrecognized. If we now consider how utterly base the disposition of most people is and how little talent they have, hence how thoroughly *common* they are, we will realize that is it impossible to talk to them without during that time becoming *common* ourselves (by analogy with electrical distribution); then we will thoroughly understand the actual meaning and the appropriateness of the expression 'to lower oneself',[c] but also gladly avoid any company with which we can only communicate by means of the shameful part[d] of our nature. We will also understand that in regard to dunces and fools there is only *one* way to demonstrate sense,[e] and that is not to talk to them. But of course quite a few people will feel in society like a dancer who attends a ball with only lame people; with whom should he dance?

(24) That rare human being gains my respect who, when having to wait   478 for something, and so sitting around with nothing to do, does not immediately beat time or rattle with anything he happens to have at hand, like his stick, or knife and fork, or anything else. Probably he is thinking about something. In contrast, we recognize in many people that for them seeing

---

[a] *über sich*   [b] *Erkenntnißsphäre*
[c] *sich gemein machen* [*gemein* is otherwise translated as 'common']   [d] *partie honteuse*   [e] *Verstand*

has completely taken the place of thinking; they seek to become conscious of their existence through rattling, if in fact no cigar is at hand, which would serve the same purpose. For this reason, they are constantly all eyes and ears for everything that goes on around them.

(25) *La Rochefoucauld* has fittingly observed that it is difficult to hold somebody in high esteem and to love him very much. Accordingly, we would have the choice whether we want to gain people's love or their respect. Their love is always selfish, although in very different ways. Moreover, the means by which we earn it are not always suited to make ourselves proud of it. Mainly, someone will be popular to the degree that he keeps his demands on the mind and heart of others low, and indeed does so in earnest and without dissimulation, and also not from that kind of forbearance that is rooted in contempt. If we now recall the very true dictum of Helvétius: 'The degree of intelligence necessary to please us is a fairly exact measure of the degree of intelligence that we possess',[a] then the conclusion follows from these premises. – But the opposite is the case in regard to people's veneration; it is extorted from them only against their will and is also mostly concealed for this reason. Hence it affords us, internally, a much greater satisfaction; it depends on our worth, which is not immediately the case with people's love; for this is subjective, veneration objective. Of course, love is more useful to us.

(26) Most people are so subjective that effectively nothing interests them except they themselves. It follows from this that with everything that is said, they immediately think of themselves and every accidental relation, however remote, to something personal completely occupies their attention. Consequently, they have no capacity left for comprehending the objective content that is discussed; in addition, no grounds have any validity for them as soon as their interest or their vanity opposes them. Hence they are so easily distracted, so easily hurt, insulted, or offended that, whatever it is that we are objectively discussing with them, we cannot be careful enough to avoid any possible, perhaps unfavourable relation of what is said to their worthy and delicate self, which we have before us. For that alone is what they care about, nothing else, and whereas they have no sense or feeling for the true and fitting aspects, or the beautiful, fine, and witty aspects of what is said, they have the most subtle susceptibility for anything that could hurt their petty vanity even in the most remote and indirect way or reflect somehow unfavourably on their extremely precious self. Consequently, in

479

---

[a] *le degré d'esprit nécessaire pour nous plaire, est une mesure assez exacte du degré d'esprit que nous avons* [*On Mind* 2, 10 n.1]

their vulnerability they resemble small dogs on whose paws we step so easily by accident and whose squeaking we then have to endure. Or we could compare them to a sick person covered with sores and boils, whom we must carefully avoid touching at all. With some the matter goes so far that they feel literally insulted by any intellect and understanding that is shown, or not sufficiently concealed, in conversation with them, although they hide such a feeling for the time being. Afterwards the inexperienced person will ponder in vain how in the world he could have brought their resentment and hatred upon himself. By virtue of the same subjectivity they are also easily flattered and won over.[90] Therefore, their judgement is often corrupt and merely an expression in favour of a party or class, but not an objective and fair one. All this depends on the fact that in them the will by far outweighs cognition, and their meagre intellect is entirely in the service of the will, from which it cannot free itself even for a short while.

Astrology provides a brilliant proof of the miserable *subjectivity* of human beings, as a result of which they relate everything to themselves and go from every thought in a straight line immediately back to themselves. It relates the course of the great celestial bodies to the pathetic I, as it also connects the comets in the sky with earthly quarrels and shabby tricks. But this has always happened and already did in ancient times. (See, for example, Stobaeus, *Eclogues* I,[a] 22, 9, p. 478.)[91]

(27) We should not despair over every absurdity that is uttered in public or in society or written in literature and well received, or at least not refuted, and think that this is the end of the matter. On the contrary, we should know and be confident that the matter will gradually be pondered, illuminated, deliberated, weighed, discussed, and in the end often judged correctly; so that, after a period appropriate to the difficulty of the matter, almost all people will comprehend what the clear mind had seen at once. Meanwhile we have to be patient. For a person possessing the correct insight among those who are deceived resembles the one whose watch is right in a town where all the church clocks are set incorrectly. He alone knows the correct time; but of what use is that to him? All the others go by the wrong clocks of the town, even those who know that his watch alone gives the right time.

(28) People resemble children in that they become naughty when we spoil them; therefore, we should not be too lenient and nice to anybody. Just as we will normally not lose a friend by refusing him a loan, but very easily by granting it to him; in the same way, we will not easily lose a friend

480

---

[a] [See p. 39, n. a]

by behaving proudly and a little bit negligently, but will often do so as a result of too much friendliness and accommodation, which make him arrogant and unbearable, thus leading to the break. But it is especially the idea that we need them that people cannot stomach at all; cockiness and insolence are the inevitable result. In some these arise, to a certain extent, just because we might often have dealings with them or speak to them in private. Soon they assume that we ought to put up with anything from them and will try to extend the limits of civility. Consequently, so few are suited for any kind of more intimate acquaintance, and we should be on our guard not to become familiar with vulgar natures. But if someone should have the idea that I need him much more than he needs me, he will at once feel as if I had robbed him of something; and he will try to avenge himself and get it back. *Superiority* in dealing with others arises solely from the fact that we need the others in no way at all and make this known.[92] Therefore, it is advisable to let everybody, man or woman, feel from time to time that we can very well do without them; that strengthens a friendship. Indeed, with most people there is no harm in letting a grain of contempt slip in every now and then. They will appreciate our friendship all the more: '*chi non estima vien stimato*' (Who does not respect will be respected) says a fine Italian proverb. But if we value someone very highly, we must conceal this as if it were a crime. That is not very pleasant, but it is true. Dogs can hardly tolerate too much kindness, let alone humans.

(29) That people of a nobler sort and greater talent often betray a striking lack of knowledge of human nature and worldly wisdom, especially in their youth, and, therefore, can be easily deceived or otherwise misled, whereas vulgar natures are much faster and better at getting on in the world, is due to the fact that, when we lack experience, we have to judge a priori, and that no experience in general matches the a priori. For this a priori provides ordinary people with their own self, but not the noble and excellent; they are, as such, very different from the others. Therefore, when they appraise the thoughts and actions of others according to their own, their calculation proves incorrect.

But when such a person has finally learned a posteriori, from instruction by others and his own experience, what is to be expected from human beings as a whole, namely that from a moral or intellectual perspective five-sixths are constituted in such a way that whoever does not come into contact with them through circumstances, is better advised to avoid them from the start and, as far as possible, have no contact with them at all – then this person will still hardly ever obtain a *sufficient* notion of their pettiness and wretchedness. Instead he will have to continually expand and complete it as long as he lives, while at the same time he often miscalculates to his own detriment. And then again, once he has really taken to heart the instruction received, it will happen to him nonetheless that, in the company of people unknown to him, he has to wonder how, according to their words and gestures, they all appear quite reasonable, honest, sincere, honourable, and virtuous, and also intelligent and witty. But that should not deceive him; for this is merely due to the fact that nature does not behave like bad poets who, when presenting a scoundrel or fool, proceed so clumsily and with such intent that at once we see the poet behind every character, disavowing their attitude and speech and calling out as a warning: 'This is a villain, this is a fool; do not attach any value to what he says.' Nature, on the other hand, acts like Shakespeare or Goethe, in whose works every person, and be it the devil himself, is right while standing before us and speaking. The persons are conceived so objectively that we are drawn into their interests and forced to sympathize with them, because the characters are, like the works of nature, developed from an inner principle, in virtue of which their speaking and doing occur naturally, hence with necessity. – Therefore, whoever expects devils to walk around in the world with horns and fools with bells will always be their prey or their plaything. In addition, in their dealings with others, people behave like the moon and the hunchback in always showing only one side, and everyone has an inborn talent, through mimicking, to rework his physiognomy into a mask, which portrays precisely what he is actually *supposed* to be and which, since it is exclusively calculated for his individuality, fits him so closely that its effect is extremely deceptive. He puts it on whenever he needs to ingratiate himself. We should think as much of it as if it were made from wax cloth,[a] mindful of the splendid Italian saying: '*non è si tristo cane, che non meni la coda*' (No dog is so evil that it does not wag its tail).

In any case, we should take care not to form a very favourable opinion   483
of any new acquaintance; otherwise we will in almost all cases be disappointed, to our own shame or even detriment. – Here also a saying by Seneca deserves to be taken into consideration: 'We can take proofs of moral character also from the smallest matters' (*Epistles*, 52).[b] People reveal their character especially in little things, in which they do not check themselves, and often we can conveniently observe in insignificant actions, mere mannerisms, the boundless egoism that does not know the smallest

---

[a] [Probably referring to wax cloth as a material for making masks for the theatre, for example in the Italian *Commedia dell'Arte*]
[b] *argumenta [argumentum] morum ex minimis quoque licet capere* [*Epistles*, 52, 12]

consideration for others and which afterwards does not disown itself in matters of importance, albeit in disguise. And we should not miss such an opportunity. When someone proceeds ruthlessly and seeks only his own advantage or convenience, to the detriment of others, in the small daily instances and circumstances of life, in matters to which the principle applies that 'The law does not concern itself with trifles';[a] when he usurps what is there for everybody, and so on; then we should convince ourselves that there is no justice in his heart, but that he would also be a scoundrel in larger matters, as soon as law and authority do not tie his hands, and we should not trust him an inch. In fact, whoever breaks the laws of his club without shame, will also break those of the state as soon as he can do so without risk.[*,93]

To forgive and forget means throwing precious experiences out of the window.[94] If someone with whom we have relations or dealings has shown something unpleasant or annoying, we just have to ask ourselves whether he is so valuable to us that we would want to put up with the same thing repeatedly and more frequently – and in stronger form too. If he has so much value to us, there is not much to say, since talking helps little; hence we have to let the matter go, with or without reprimand, but should realize that in doing so we are asking for the same thing again. On the other hand, if we answer the question in the negative, we must break with this worthy friend immediately and for good or, if it is a servant, dismiss him. For it is inevitable that in a given situation he will do the same thing, or something completely analogous, even if now he faithfully promises the opposite. Someone can forget everything, everything, but not himself, his own essence.[95] For character is positively incorrigible, because all actions of a person flow from an inner principle by virtue of which, under the same circumstances, he must always do the same and cannot do otherwise. Readers should consult my essay on the so-called freedom of the will and free themselves from the delusion. Therefore, to make up with a friend with whom we had broken off is a weakness for which we shall atone when, at the first opportunity, he repeats the same thing that led to the breach and, indeed, does so with even greater impudence, being secretly aware of his indispensability. The same is the case with dismissed servants whom we take on again.[96] Just as little, and for the same reason, can we expect that someone will do the same as before under *changed* circumstances. Rather,

484

---

* If in human beings, as they usually are, the good outweighed the bad, it would be more advisable to rely on their justice, fairness, gratitude, loyalty, love or compassion, than their fear. But since the reverse is the case, the opposite is advisable.

[a] *de minimis lex non curat* [a principle of Roman law]

people change their attitudes and behaviours as rapidly as their interests change; in fact, their intentionality[a] draws its bills on such a short term that we ourselves would have to be even more shortsighted not to dispute them.

Accordingly, supposing that we wanted to know, for instance, how someone will act in a position in which we intend to place him, we must not rely on his promises and assurances. For, even assuming that he spoke honestly, he speaks of a matter that he does not know. Therefore, we have to calculate his actions solely on the basis of weighing the circumstances that he will have to face and their conflict with his character.

In general, to arrive at the absolutely necessary, clear and thorough understanding of the true and very sad nature of human beings as they mostly are, it is extremely instructive to use their behaviours and attitudes in literature as a commentary on their behaviours and attitudes in practical life, and vice versa. This is very helpful in order not to doubt ourselves or others. However, no trait of particular meanness or stupidity that strikes us in life or in literature should ever become the object of annoyance or anger, but only of knowledge, in that we see in it a new contribution to the characterization of humanity and keep it in mind as such. Then we shall look at it in much the same way as the mineralogist who encounters a characteristic specimen of a mineral.[97] – Exceptions exist, in fact, ones so great that they are beyond belief, and the diversity of individualities is enormous; but on the whole the world is in a sorry state, as has been said long ago; the savages eat one another, and the civilized ones deceive one another, and that we call the course of the world. What are the states, with all their artificial, externally and internally directed machinery and their measures of force, other than precautions to limit the boundless injustice of humans? Do we not see, in the whole of history, every king, as soon as he is firmly established and his country enjoys some degree of prosperity, use these to attack the neighbouring states with his army, as with a band of robbers? Are not all wars basically plundering raids? In early antiquity, as also in part during the Middle Ages, the conquered became the slaves of the victors, meaning effectively that they had to work for them. The same goes for those who pay war contributions; for they surrender the proceeds of previous work. 'In all wars, the objective is nothing but stealing',[b] says Voltaire, and the Germans should take heed.[98]

485

---

[a] *Absichtlichkeit*

[b] *Dans toutes les guerres* [. . .] *il ne s'agit que de voler* [Voltaire, *Dieu et les hommes, par le docteur Obern. Œuvre théologique, mais raisonnable* (*God and Men, for Doctor Obern. A Theological, albeit Rational Work*) (1769), ch. 1]

(30) No character is such that it should be left to its own devices and be allowed to let itself go, but each needs guidance through concepts and maxims. But if we want to go far in this, namely as far as a character that has arisen not from our inborn nature, but is actually acquired and artificial, arisen merely from rational deliberation, then we will soon find these words confirmed:

Expel nature with a pitchfork, it will still come back.[a]

For we can well appreciate a rule for behaving towards others, indeed, discover and fittingly express it, and will nonetheless soon afterwards break it in real life. Yet we should not let ourselves be discouraged and think that it is impossible in our worldly existence to conduct our behaviour according to abstract rules and maxims and that, consequently, it is best to just let ourselves go. Rather it is the same as with all theoretical prescriptions and instructions for the practical: first we must understand the rule, then we must learn to comply with it. The former is achieved all at once through reason, the latter gradually through practice. We show the pupil the fingering on the instrument and the parries and thrusts with the rapier. He fails immediately, despite his best intentions, and now thinks that to follow them is nearly impossible due to the speed with which he reads the score and the heat of the fight. Yet he learns it gradually through practice by stumbling, falling, and getting up again. It is the same with the grammatical rules in Latin writing and speaking. There is no other way for the boor to become a courtier, the hothead a distinguished man of the world, the frank person reserved, the noble ironic. However, such a self-conditioning, achieved through long habit, will always act as a constraint coming from the outside, which nature never quite ceases to resist and occasionally breaches unexpectedly. For all acting according to abstract maxims relates to acting from original, inborn inclination in the same way that a human artefact,[b] like a watch, where form and movement are forced upon the material alien to them, relates to a living organism, in which form and material permeate each other and are one. Therefore, this relation between acquired and inborn character affirms the words of Emperor Napoleon: 'All that is not natural is imperfect',[c] which generally is a rule applicable to everything, be it physical or moral, and whose sole exception that I can think of is the natural

---

[a] *Naturam expelles furca, tamen usque recurret* [Horace, *Epistles* I, 10, 24]

[b] *Kunstwerk* [In the sense of 'artificially made']

[c] *tout ce qui n'est pas naturel est imparfait* [*n'est jamais parfait*] [(Frédéric Lullin de Châteauvieux) *Manuscrit venu de St. Hélène d'une manière inconnue* (*Manuscript Having Come from St. Helena in an Unknown Manner*), London: Murray, 1817; Napoleon was almost certainly not the author of this text]

aventurine,[a] known to mineralogists, which cannot compete with the artificial one.

Therefore, we should beware of any form of *affectation*. It always arouses contempt: first of all as a fraud, which as such is cowardly, since it is based on fear; and secondly as self-condemnation, in that we want to appear as something that we are not and hence be regarded as better than we actually are. The affectation of a quality, bragging about it, is a confession that we do not have it. Be it courage, or learning, or intellect, or wit, or success with women, or wealth, or genteel position, or anything else of which a person boasts, we can conclude that it is precisely in this that he is lacking something; for it would not occur to someone who actually possesses a quality to its full extent to parade or affect it; instead he is completely assured in its possession. This is also the meaning of the Spanish saying: '*herradura que chacolotea clavo le falta*' (the clattering horseshoe lacks a nail). Admittedly, as mentioned in the beginning, nobody is allowed to loosen the reins and show himself the way he is, because all the bad and bestial elements of our nature need to be concealed; but this only justifies the negative, dissimulation, not the positive, simulation. – We should also realize that affectation is recognized even before it becomes clear what is affected. And finally, it does not hold good for long, but the mask falls off eventually. 'Nobody can wear a mask for long; dissemblance quickly returns to its own nature' (Seneca, *On Mercy* I, 1).[b],[99] 487

(31) Just as we carry the weight of our own body without feeling it in the way we feel another body that we want to move, we do not notice our own faults and vices, but only those of others. – Instead, we all possess a mirror in others, in whom we can clearly see our own vices, faults, bad habits, and distasteful traits of every kind. But most of the time, we are like a dog that barks at the mirror, because it does not know that it is seeing itself, but thinks it is seeing another dog. Whoever finds fault with others, works on his own self-improvement. Hence those who have the inclination and the habit quietly, by themselves, to subject the external behaviour and, generally, the doings of others, to thoughtful and *sharp criticism* work for their own improvement and perfection; for they will possess either justice or enough pride and vanity to avoid themselves what they severely reprove. The opposite is true of tolerant people: 'We grant this freedom and claim it in turn',[c] is 488

---

[a] *Aventurino* [a form of quartz]

[b] *Nemo [enim] potest personam diu ferre [fictam]: ficta in natura, suam recidunt, de Clementia* [I, 1, 6]

[c] *hanc veniam damus petimusque vicissim* [Horace, *The Art of Poetry*, 11; *hanc veniam petimusque damusque vicissim* ('We claim this freedom and grant it in turn')]

their motto. The Gospel moralizes aptly about the mote in the other's and the beam in our own eye,[a] but the nature of the eye brings with it that it looks outward and does not see itself; therefore, noticing and rebuking our mistakes in others is a very useful means of becoming aware of them in ourselves. We need a mirror in order to improve.

The same rule also applies in regard to style and manner of writing: Whoever admires a new folly in them instead of censuring it is going to imitate it. Hence each spreads so quickly in Germany. The Germans are very tolerant; that is obvious. 'We grant this freedom and claim it in turn' is their motto.[100]

(32) Human beings of nobler sort believe in their youth that the essential and decisive relations and resulting connections between people are the *ideal* ones, i.e. those that are based on similarity of attitude, way of thinking, taste, mental powers, and so on; but they later realize that it is the *real* ones, i.e. those resting upon some material interest. These are at the basis of almost all connections; in fact, the majority of humans have no notion of different relations. Therefore, everybody is treated according to his office, or business, or nation, or family, hence in general according to the position and role assigned to him by convention; as a consequence, he is sorted and treated like a manufactured good.[b] In contrast, what he is in and for himself, as a human being, comes up only by chance and hence only by way of exception, and is set aside and ignored by everybody as soon as it is convenient, which is most of the time. But the more significant someone is as a human being, the less he will appreciate this arrangement; hence he will try to evade it. However, it is based on the fact that in this world of want and need, the means for meeting these are everywhere what is essential and therefore prevalent.

(33) Just as it is paper money, and not silver, that circulates in the world, so instead of genuine respect and true friendship, there are external demonstrations and gestures, copying them as naturally as possible. On the other hand, we can also ask whether there are people who really deserve true respect and friendship. In any event, I attach more value to the tail-wagging of an honest dog than to a hundred such demonstrations and gestures.[101]

True, genuine friendship presupposes a strong, purely objective and entirely disinterested concern for another's weal and woe and this, in turn, real identification with the friend. The egoism of human nature is so much opposed to this that true friendship belongs to the things of which we do not know whether they are fictitious or actually exist somewhere, just like those enormous sea-serpents. Meanwhile, there are all sorts of

---

[a] [See Matthew 7:1–5]   [b] *fabrikmäßig behandelt*

associations between people – of course, chiefly based on hidden egoistic motives of the most diverse kinds – that nonetheless possess a grain of that true and genuine friendship, whereby they are so ennobled that they are allowed to bear the name of friendship with some justification in this world of imperfections. They stand far above ordinary liaisons, which are rather such that we would stop talking to most of our close acquaintances if we heard what they say about us in our absence.

Next to cases where we need serious help and significant sacrifice, the best opportunity to put the genuineness of a friend to the test is at the moment when we tell him about a misfortune that has just befallen us. For then his features either express true, sincere, and unalloyed sadness, or they confirm through their calm composure, or some other fleeting feature, the well-known saying by *La Rochefoucauld*: 'In the misfortune of our best friends, we always find something that does not displease us.'ᵃ The usual so-called friends, on these occasions, are often barely able to suppress the twitch of a faint, complacent smile. – There are few things that put people in a good mood with such certainty as when we tell them about a serious misfortune which has befallen us recently or some personal weakness that we unashamedly reveal to them. – How characteristic!¹⁰²

Distance and long absence harm all friendship, however grudgingly 490 we admit it. For people whom we do not see, even if they are our most beloved friends, gradually wither into abstract concepts during the course of the years, and our concern for them more and more turns into a merely rational, indeed traditional concern; lively and deeply felt sympathy is reserved for those who are before our very eyes, even if they are merely beloved animals. So sensuous is human nature. Hence Goethe's dictum proves itself here:

The present is a mighty goddess. (*Tasso*, Act IV, scene 4)ᵇ

House friends are often rightly called thus, insofar as they are more the friends of the house than the master, and hence are more like cats than dogs.¹⁰³

Friends call themselves honest; enemies are honest; therefore, we should make use of the latter's reproach for the sake of self-knowledge,ᶜ as a bitter medicine. –

ᵃ *dans l'adversité de nos meilleurs amis, nous trouvons toujours quelque chose qui ne nous déplait pas* [François La Rochefoucauld, *Réflexions ou Sentences et Maximes morales* (*Reflections or Moral Aphorisms and Maxims*) (1664–5); 1.99, withdrawn after first edn.]
ᵇ [*Torquato Tasso*]   ᶜ *Selbsterkenntniß*

Are friends in need really so rare? – On the contrary! No sooner have we become friends with someone than he is already in need and wants to borrow money. –

(34) What a novice is the one who imagines that to show intellect and understanding is a means to become popular in society! On the contrary, they excite in the incalculable majority a hatred and resentment that are all the more bitter, as the one experiencing them has no right to denounce what caused them, in fact, hides it from himself. What exactly happens is this: when someone notices and senses a great intellectual superiority in the one he is speaking with, he concludes, quietly and without distinct consciousness, that the other notices and senses his inferiority and limitation to the same extent. This enthymeme[a] arouses his bitter hatred, resentment, and anger. (See *The World as Will and Representation*, vol. 2, third edn., p. 256,[b] the quotes by *Dr Johnson* and *Merck*, the friend of Goethe's youth.) Hence Gracián rightly says: 'The only way to be popular for us is to wear the skin of the most stupid animal.' (See *The Oracle, a Manual of the Art of Discretion*,[c] 240, *Works*, Amberes, 1702, Part II, p. 287.)[104] For to display intellect and understanding is only an indirect way of reproaching all others for their incompetence and stupidity. Moreover, ordinary nature is in an uproar when catching sight of its opposite, and the secret instigator of the uproar is envy. For the satisfaction of their vanity, as we can observe daily, is a pleasure that people value above all else, but which is only possible by means of comparing themselves to others. And there are no merits of which people are as proud as the intellectual ones, since on these alone rests their superiority over the animals.[*,105] Hence to show people our own decisive superiority in this respect, especially in the presence of witnesses, is extremely audacious. They feel provoked by it to seek revenge and will often look for an opportunity to achieve this by means of insult, thereby passing from the realm of intelligence to that of the will, in which respect we are all equal. Therefore, whereas rank and wealth can always count on deference in society, intellectual merits cannot expect it at all; at best they are ignored; otherwise they are seen as a kind of impertinence or something

---

* The *will*, we might say, people have given themselves; for the will equals themselves. But the *intellect* is a feature that they have received from heaven – i.e. from eternal, mysterious fate and its necessity, whose mere instrument was their mother.

[a] [Formal argument in which one line is missing, either a premise or the conclusion]
[b] [Hübscher *SW* 3, 255f.]
[c] *Oráculo manual, y arte de prudencia* [Baltasar Gracián (1647); '240' refers to the number of the aphorism. Schopenhauer translated this work into German under the title '*Hand-Orakel und Kunst der Weltklugheit*' (Pocket Oracle and the Art of Worldly Wisdom). See *HN* 4/ii, 131–267]

that their owner has come by without permission and now dares to flaunt. Hence everybody quietly plans to humiliate him in some other way and only waits for an opportunity to do so. The most humble demeanour will barely succeed in obtaining forgiveness for intellectual superiority. Sadi says in *Gulistan* (p. 146 of the translation by Graf): 'We ought to realize that the ignorant person feels a hundred times more aversion to the intelligent than the intelligent feels distaste of the ignorant.'[a,106] – Intellectual *inferiority*, on the other hand, works as a true recommendation. For what warmth is for the body, the pleasant feeling of superiority is for the spirit; so everyone moves closer to the object that promises it to him, as instinctively as we move towards the stove or sunshine. This object is solely that person who is decidedly inferior, to men in regard to intellectual qualities and to women in regard to beauty. Of course, to show unfeigned inferiority towards some people is not easy. In contrast, we should observe the greatly affectionate friendship with which a fair looking girl approaches an incredibly ugly one. Bodily assets are not very important in men, although we feel more comfortable next to a shorter than to a taller man. Consequently, among men the dumb and ignorant are generally popular and sought after, among women the ugly ones; they easily acquire the reputation of an extremely good heart, because everyone needs a pretext for her fondness, in front of herself and of others. For this reason, any kind of intellectual superiority is a very isolating quality; people shun and hate it and attribute all kinds of faults to its owner.*[,107] It is the same with beauty among women; very beautiful girls find no friend of the same sex, not even a companion. They are better off never to apply for positions as lady's companions; for already when presenting themselves the face of the prospective new mistress darkens, who has no use for such a foil, be it for herself or her daughters. – The opposite is true in regard to advantages of rank, because these do not act, like the personal advantages, through contrast and distance, but through reflection, like the colours of the surroundings that are reflected on the face.

492

---

* Friendship and camaraderie are by far the chief means of *advancing in the world*. Now, great *abilities* always make us *proud* and hence little suited to flatter those who only have meagre abilities, indeed, from whom we are, therefore, supposed to conceal and deny the great ones. Awareness of small abilities acts in the opposite way; it gets along splendidly with humility, affability, good will, and respect for the bad, and hence procures friends and benefactors.

    What has been said applies not only to public service, but also to honourable positions, distinctions, and even fame in the scholarly world, so that, for example, in the academies dear mediocrity is always at the top, people of merit enter late or never, and so it is with everything.

[a] [See p. 174, n. c]

(35) Very often inertia, selfishness, and vanity play the greatest role in our trust in others; inertia when we prefer to trust somebody else, in order not to investigate, be vigilant, or act ourselves; selfishness when the desire to speak about our own affairs tempts us to confide in someone else; vanity when it concerns something that we are proud of. Nevertheless, we demand that people honour our trust.

On the other hand, we should not become angry about distrust; for it contains a compliment for honesty, namely the frank acknowledgement of its great rarity, as a result of which it belongs to those things whose existence we doubt.

(36) For *politeness*, this cardinal virtue of the Chinese, I have provided one reason in my work on morals, p. 201.[a] The second one is the following. It is a tacit agreement to mutually ignore our morally and intellectually miserable nature and not to blame one another – with the result that, to our mutual advantage, it comes to light less readily.

Politeness is prudence; consequently, impoliteness is stupidity; to make enemies by being unnecessarily and intentionally rude is mad, as if we set our house on fire. For politeness, like a marker, is obviously a false coin; to spend it sparingly shows lack of understanding,[b] to spend it generously, understanding. All nations close a letter with *très-humble serviteur* – your most obedient servant[c] – *suo devotissimo servo*; only the Germans hold back the 'servant', because it is, of course, not true! But whoever practises courtesy to the point of sacrificing actual interests resembles one who would give out genuine gold coins instead of markers. – Just as wax, by nature hard and brittle, becomes so malleable by means of a little warmth that it assumes any desired shape, we can make even stubborn and hostile people pliable and accommodating with the help of a little politeness and friendliness. Accordingly, politeness is for human beings what warmth is for wax.

However, politeness is a difficult task, insofar as it requires that we pay the greatest respect to all people, whereas the majority do not deserve it; it also requires that we feign the most lively interest in them, whereas we must be glad to have none. – To combine politeness and pride is something worthy of a master.[d] –

We would be much less upset about insults, which actually always consist in expressions of disrespect, if we had not, on the one hand, a quite exaggerated idea of our great worth and dignity, hence nourished an inappropriate pride, and, on the other, had made it clear to ourselves

---

[a] [*BM*, 191 (Hübscher *SW* 4, 198)]   [b] *Unverstand*   [c] [Original English]   [d] *ein Meisterstück*

what everybody in his heart usually thinks of the other. What glaring contrast there is between the sensitivity of most people about the slightest hint at a rebuke aimed at them and what they would hear if they could listen in on the conversations of their acquaintances about them! – Instead, we should keep in mind that ordinary politeness is only a grinning mask; then we would not cry murder when it shifts a little or is taken off for a moment. But when somebody becomes outright rude, then it is as if he had thrown off his clothes and stood there naked.[a] Of course, he would look bad then, like most people in this state.

(37) We ought not to take someone else as our model in our doings, because position, circumstances, and relations are never the same and also the difference of character colours the action differently, so that 'when two do the same thing, it is not the same'.[b] We must, after careful deliberation and keen reflection, act according to our own character. Hence originality is indispensable also in regard to the practical; otherwise what we do does not fit what we are.

(38) We should not dispute someone's opinion, but take into consideration that, if we wanted to talk him out of all the absurdities that he believes, we might grow as old as Methuselah without finishing the task.

We should also refrain from correcting people during conversation, however well-intentioned our remarks may be; for it is easy to offend people; to improve them is difficult, if not impossible.

When the absurdities of a conversation that we happen to overhear start to annoy us, we should imagine that it is a scene in a comedy between two fools. This is well-tried.[c] – Anyone who has entered the world to *instruct* it seriously in regard to the most important matters can count himself lucky to escape unscathed.[108]

(39) Whoever wants his judgement to be believed, should pronounce it coolly and without passion. For all vehemence springs from the will. Consequently, we ascribe the judgement to the *will* and not cognition, which by its nature is cold. Since the will is what is radical in human beings, cognition being merely secondary and additional, we shall more readily believe that the judgement has sprung from the excited will than that the excitement of the will has arisen merely from the judgement.

(40) Even if fully justified in doing so, we should not be tempted to praise ourselves. For vanity is such an ordinary and merit such an extraordinary thing that, as often as we seem to praise ourselves, even if only indirectly, everybody will bet a hundred to one that it is vanity that speaks through us

---

[a] *in puris naturalibus*   [b] *duo cum faciunt idem, non est idem*   [c] *Probatum est*

495

and lacks the sense to appreciate the preposterousness of the matter. – However, despite all this, Bacon might not be completely wrong when he says that the saying that 'something always sticks'[a] is true not only of slander, but also of self-praise, and hence recommends it in small doses. (See *On the Dignity and Advancement of Learning*,[b] Book 8, p. 228.)

(41) If we suspect that somebody is lying, we should pretend to believe him; then he becomes bold, lies more brazenly, and is unmasked. On the other hand, if we notice that a truth that he wants to conceal in part slips out, we should pretend not to believe him, so that, provoked by the contradiction, he lets the rearguard of the whole truth advance.

(42) We must consider all our personal affairs secret and must remain complete strangers to people with whom we are well acquainted beyond what they see with their own eyes. For their knowledge of the most innocent matters can, in the course of time and changed circumstances, be disadvantageous to us. – Generally speaking, it is more advisable to demonstrate our understanding by what we keep secret than by what we say. The former is a matter of prudence, the latter one of vanity. The opportunities for both happen with equal frequency; but we often prefer the fleeting satisfaction afforded by the latter over the permanent utility of the former. We should even deny ourselves the emotional relief of talking aloud to ourselves once in a while, as happens to lively people, so that it does not become a habit, because in this way thought and speech become such close friends that talking to others turns into thinking aloud too. However, prudence demands that we maintain a wide gulf between thinking and speaking.

At times we imagine that others cannot possibly believe a thing that is of concern to us, whereas it does not occur to them at all to doubt it; but if we alert them to it, then they are really no longer able to believe it. We often betray ourselves, because we think it impossible for people not to notice – just like throwing ourselves from a height through vertigo, i.e. because of the idea that it is impossible to stand here firmly, while the torment of standing here is so great that it is better to cut it short: this delusion is called vertigo.

On the other hand, we should know that people, even those who otherwise do not betray any particular acumen, are great experts in the algebra of other people's personal affairs, in which, by means of a single given quantity, they solve the most complicated problems. For example, if

---

[a] *semper aliqid haeret*
[b] *de augmentis scient[iarum]* [i.e. *De Dignitate et Augmentis Scientiarum* (*The Great Instauration*, Part I), Book 8, ch. 2, Explication to Parable 34]

we tell them about a previous incident, without mentioning any names or other descriptions of persons, we should beware of introducing a single positive, individual circumstance, be it ever so insignificant, as for instance a place, a point in time, or the name of a subordinate character, or something else only indirectly connected to it. Because then they immediately have a positively given quantity with the help of which their algebraic acumen solves everything else. The excitement of curiosity is so great here that, by means of it, the will spurs on the intellect, which now is driven to achieve the remotest results. For as insusceptible and indifferent people are to *universal* truths, as keen are they to attain particular truths.

In accordance with all this, reticence has been most urgently commended by all teachers of worldly wisdom for a variety of reasons; therefore, I can let the matter rest with what has already been said. I will merely mention a few Arab maxims that are especially forceful and little known. 'Do not tell your friend what your enemy is not to know.' – 'If I keep my secret, it is my prisoner; if I reveal it, I am its prisoner.' – 'In the tree of silence hangs its fruit – peace.'

(43) No money is spent more profitably than that out of which we let ourselves be cheated; for we have exchanged it directly for prudence.

(44) If possible, we should feel no animosity towards anyone, but should remember everyone's actions[a] in order to determine their value, at least in regard to ourselves, and adjust our attitude and behaviour towards them accordingly – always convinced of the invariability of character; to ever forget someone's bad trait is like throwing away hard-earned money. But in this way we protect ourselves against foolish confidence and foolish friendship. –

'Neither love nor hate' contains half of worldly wisdom, 'say nothing and believe nothing' the other half. Of course, we shall be only too glad to turn our back on a world that makes rules like these and the subsequent ones necessary.

(45) To show rage or hatred in words or gestures is useless, dangerous, imprudent, ridiculous, and common. Hence we must never show rage or hatred except through deeds. The latter we will be able to do the more perfectly, the more completely we have avoided the former. – The cold-blooded animals alone are the poisonous ones.

(46) 'Speaking without emphasis':[b] this old rule of worldly-wise people intends to leave it to the understanding of others to find out what we have said; this understanding is slow, and before it is finished we are gone. 498

---

[a] *procédés* [b] *parler sans accent*

On the other hand, 'speaking with emphasis'[a] means speaking to the feelings, where everything turns out upside down. Gesturing politely and speaking in a friendly tone, we can truly insult quite a few people without immediate danger.[109]

D.   Concerning our attitude towards the course of the world and fate

(47) Whatever form human life may take, it has always the same elements and, therefore, it is essentially the same everywhere, whether it is lived in a hut, at court, in a monastery, or in the army.[110] As varied as its events, adventures, fortunes and misfortunes may be, it is with life as it is with confectionery. There are a variety of different crinkly and colourful shapes; but all are kneaded from the same dough; and what has happened to one person is much more similar to what has befallen another than the latter imagines when he hears it told. Moreover, the events in our life resemble the images in a kaleidoscope, where we see something different with every turn, but actually have the same thing before our eyes.

(48) An ancient writer remarks very aptly that there are three forces in the world: σύνεσις, κράτος καὶ τύχη – prudence, strength, and luck. I believe the last to be the most powerful. For the path of our life is comparable to that of a ship. Fate, τύχη, favourable or adverse fortune,[b] plays the role of the wind by quickly speeding us far ahead or casting us far back; against this our own efforts can achieve little. These play the role of the oars. If they have carried us forward some distance through long hours of work, a sudden gust of wind throws us back just as far. If the wind is favourable, on the other hand, it advances us so much that we do not need the oars. This power of luck is unsurpassably expressed by a Spanish proverb: '*da ventura a tu hijo, y echa lo en el mar*' (Give your son luck and cast him into the sea).

Chance may be an evil force, to which we should leave as little as possible. Yet who, among all the providers, is the only one that, while giving, most clearly shows us that we are not entitled to its gifts, that we do not have our worthiness to thank for them, but solely chance's benevolence and grace, and that we can joyfully set our hope on humbly receiving many an undeserved gift in the future? – It is chance, the one that understands the royal art of making it clear that all merit is powerless and counts for nothing compared to its favour and grace.

499

---

[a] *parler avec accent*   [b] *secunda aut adversa fortuna*

When looking back at our path of life, surveying its 'labyrinthine and erratic gait',[a] and having to see many a case of failed luck and of misfortune that we attracted, we can easily go too far in reproaching ourselves. For our course of life is by no means simply our own doing, but the product of two factors, namely the series of events and the series of our decisions, which constantly intertwine and modify each other. In addition, in regard to both our horizon is always severely limited, insofar as we cannot predict our decisions far in advance and can foresee future events even less; of both, we really only know well those that are present. Therefore, as long as our goal is still remote, we cannot even head for it in a straight line, but steer in its direction only approximately and by conjecture, and often have to change course and veer. All that we are able to do is to make our decisions in accordance with present circumstances, hoping to bring us closer to the main goal. Hence the events and our main purposes are mostly comparable to two forces pulling in different directions, and the resulting diagonal is our course of life. – Terence has said: 'The life of man is just like playing dice: if what you most want to throw does not show up, what turns up by chance you must correct by art',[b] where he must have had a kind of backgammon[c] in mind. More succinctly we can say: Fate shuffles the cards and we play. But for expressing my present reflection, the following simile would be the most suited. Life is like a game of chess: we draw up a plan; but it remains dependent on what in the game the opponent, and in life fate, see fit to do. The modifications that our plan sustains in the process are mostly so great that, when executed, it is hardly recognizable on the basis of a few fundamental features.

Incidentally, there is something in our course of life that exceeds all this. For it is a trivial truth, confirmed all too frequently, that we are often more foolish than we think. In contrast, the fact that we are often wiser than we ourselves imagine is a discovery made only by those to whom this applies and who even then make it only late. There is something wiser within us than the mind.[III] For when it comes to large moves, the chief steps in the course of our life, we act not only according to the clear knowledge[d] of what is right, but also according to an inner impulse,[e] one might say instinct, which arises from the deepest ground of our essence. Afterwards we find

---

[a] [Goethe, *Faust* I, 14]

[b] *in vita est hominum quasi cum ludas tesseris: si illud, quod maxime opus est jactu, non cadit, illud quod cecidit forte, id arte ut corrigas* [P. Terentius Afer (Terence), *Adelphi* (The Brothers) Act IV, scene 7]

[c] *Triktrak* [also '*Tricktrack*' or '*Ticktack*', a game similar to backgammon known in Germany since the Middle Ages]

[d] *Erkenntniß*　　[e] *Impuls*

fault with what we have done according to clear concepts that are, however, also sketchy, acquired, even borrowed, according to general rules, other people's examples, etc., without sufficiently weighing the maxim 'One thing does not suit all'.[a] In doing so, we easily do injustice to ourselves. But in the end, it becomes clear who was right; and only a happily reached old age is capable of judging the matter subjectively and objectively.

Perhaps that inner impulse is unconsciously guided by prophetic dreams, forgotten after waking up, which furnish our life with an evenness of tone and dramatic unity that the wavering and erring, easily altered, consciousness of our brain[b] could not give it, and as a result of which one called to achieve great things of a certain kind secretly feels this within himself and works towards it from the time of his youth, just like bees building their hive. But for everyone it is what *Baltasar Gracián* calls 'the great synderesis':[c] the instinctive great care of ourselves, without which we would perish. – It is difficult to act according to *abstract principles*; it is successful only after a lot of practice, and even then not every time; and often these principles are not sufficient. On the other hand, each of us possesses certain innate concrete principles that are in his blood,[d] in that they result from his thought, feeling, and willing. Most of the time he does not know them abstractly,[e] but only in looking back on his life becomes aware that he has always followed them and was drawn by them as if by an invisible thread. Depending on their nature, they will lead him to happiness or unhappiness.[112]

(49) We should constantly have the effect of time and the mutability of things before our eyes and, therefore, with everything that is happening now we should immediately imagine the opposite; accordingly, we should vividly picture unhappiness in happiness, enmity in friendship, bad in fine weather, hatred in love, betrayal and regret in trust and openness, and vice versa. This would provide a lasting source of true worldly wisdom, in that we would always remain prudent and not be deceived so easily. For the most part, we would then have anticipated the effect of time. – But perhaps to no other knowledge is experience as indispensable as the correct appreciation of the volatility and mutability of things, because for the time of its duration every condition exists with necessity and, therefore, with good reason, every year, every month, and every day looks as if it shall ultimately be proven right for all

---

[a] [A line from Goethe's poem '*Beherzigung*' (Taking to Heart) from the cycle *Lieder* (*Songs*)]
[b] *Gehirnbewußtsein*
[c] *la gran sindéresis* [Aphorism 96 of Gracián's *Oracle* (see p. 404, n. c); German: '*Synteresis*' – guarding, preserving; in Catholic theology the conscience as that which is divine in human beings, an innate knowledge of moral truth]
[d] *Blut und Saft*   [e] *in abstracto*

eternity. But none is so proven, and change alone persists. That one is prudent who is not deceived by apparent stability and even foresees the direction that change will immediately take.*,[113] On the other hand, that people usually think of the temporary state of affairs, or the direction of events, as permanent, is due to the fact that they have the effects before their eyes, and do not understand the causes; but it is the latter that bear the seed of future changes within themselves, whereas the effect, which alone exists for them, contains none of it. They stick to the effect and assume that the causes, which are unknown to them and which were able to bring about the effect, will also be able to sustain it. In this, they have the advantage that, if they err, they always do so in unison;[a] therefore, the calamity that befalls them as a result is always a universal one; however, when the thinker has made a mistake, he is alone as well. – Incidentally, this is a confirmation of my dictum that error always arises when drawing a conclusion from the consequent to the ground. See *The World as Will and Representation*, vol. 1, p. 90.[b]

502

But we should *anticipate time* only theoretically and by foreseeing its effect, not practically, namely in such a way that we forestall it by demanding *ahead* of time what only time can bring about. For whoever does so will discover that there is no worse, no more unyielding usurer than time, and that, when forced to give advances, it demands higher interest than any Jew. For example, it is possible, by means of quicklime and heat, to force a tree to grow leaves, blossoms, and fruits within a few days; but afterwards it will die. – If a youth already wants to exercise the procreative power of a man, even if only for a few weeks, and achieve at nineteen what he could do very well at thirty, time will at most grant an advance, but part of the powers of his future years, in fact, part of his life itself, will be the interest. – There are diseases of which we can only be properly and thoroughly cured by letting them run their natural course, after which they disappear by themselves without leaving a trace. But if we insist on becoming healthy immediately at this very moment, here too time must provide an advance; the disease is expelled, but the interest is weakness and chronic complaints for the rest of our life. – If in times of war or unrest we need money, and need it immediately, at this very

---

* *Chance* has such a great leeway in all human affairs that when seeking through sacrifices to prevent a danger threatening from afar, this danger often vanishes due to an unexpected turn of events, and now not only the sacrifices that were made are lost, but with the altered state of affairs the change that they have brought about proves a clear disadvantage. Therefore, we should not reach too far into the future with the precautions that we take, but should take chance into account and boldly face many dangers, hoping that it will pass like many a dark thundercloud.

[a] *unisono*   [b] [*WWR* 1, 104–5 (Hübscher *SW* 2, 90)]

moment, we are compelled to sell properties or government stocks for a third or less of their value, which we would receive in full, if we had given time its due and waited for a few years; but we force it to give an advance. – Or we need a sum of money for a long journey; within one year or two we could set it aside from our income. But we do not wish to wait; so we borrow it or take it out of the capital, meaning, time has to advance the money. Its interest then spreads disorder in our accounts, a permanent and growing deficit, which we can no longer cast off. – This then is the usury of time; all those who cannot wait are its victims. Wanting to speed up the measured pace of time is the most costly undertaking. Consequently, we should take care not to owe interest to time.

(50) A characteristic difference between ordinary and intelligent minds that frequently makes its mark in everyday life, is that the former, in their deliberation and assessment of potential dangers, always only ask and consider what *has already occurred* that is of a similar nature. On the other hand, the latter also think about what *might possibly occur*, and in doing so take into consideration that, as a Spanish proverb says, '*lo que no acaece en un año, acaece en un rato*' (what does not happen within a year, happens within a few minutes). Of course, the difference in question is natural, since taking in what *might* happen requires understanding, what *has* happened, merely the senses.

Our maxim, however, should be: Sacrifice to the evil demons! That means, we should not shy away from spending a certain amount of effort, time, or money and putting up with inconvenience, complications, or privation in order to shut the door on the possibility of misfortune; and the greater the misfortune might be, the smaller, remoter, and less probable the possibility might be. The clearest example of this rule is the insurance premium. It is a public sacrifice offered by all on the altar of evil demons.

(51) We should neither erupt in joy nor break into lamentations about any incident, in part because of the changeability of all things, which can transform it at any moment, and in part because of the deceptiveness of our judgement concerning what is beneficial and what is detrimental for us, as a result of which almost everybody has at one time moaned about something that afterwards turned out to be his true good, or rejoiced about a thing that later became the source of his greatest sufferings. Shakespeare has aptly expressed the attitude recommended to counter this:

I have felt so many quirks of joy and grief,
That the first face of neither, on the start,
Can woman me unto it.*   (*All's Well*, Act III, scene 2)[a]

In general, the person who stays calm during all accidents shows that he knows how immense and thousandfold the possible evils in life are. Therefore, he looks at the one that has happened right now as a very small part of what might have happened. This is the Stoic attitude, in accordance with which we should never forget the human condition,[b] but should always remember what a sad and miserable lot human existence is in general, and how innumerable the evils are to which it is exposed. To refresh this insight, we just need to look around; wherever we are, we will soon have it before our eyes, this struggling and floundering and toiling for the miserable, barren existence that yields us nothing. Accordingly, we will scale down our aspirations, learn to acquiesce in the imperfection of all things and affairs, and always expect accidents, in order to avoid them or to endure them.[114] For accidents, large or small, are the element of our life; this we should always keep in mind. But we should not, as a discontented person,[c] lament with Beresford and pull faces about the hourly *Miseries of Human Life*,[d] and even less should we 'invoke God for every flea bite'.[e] Instead, as a prudent person,[f] we should take the practice of caution in anticipating and preventing accidents – whether they are caused by people or by things – to such lengths and become so sophisticated in doing so that, like a clever fox, we neatly get out of the way of every great or small misfortune (which most of the time is merely clumsiness in disguise).

That it is less difficult to endure a misfortune, if we have regarded it as 505 possible in advance and, as people say, have braced ourselves for it, might chiefly depend on the fact that, if we calmly think through a case before it happens, we clearly take in the extent of the misfortune in all its aspects and, therefore, recognize it as finite and manageable. As a result, if it actually

---

* I have felt so many bouts of joy and grief that I shall never again let myself like a woman be carried away to either at the first sight of the occasion. [In his footnote Schopenhauer offers a German translation that has been rendered into English here]

[a] [*All's Well That Ends Well*]
[b] *conditionis humanae oblitus* [reminiscent of Seneca, *Epistles*, 15, 11 ('*oblitus fragilitatis humanae congeram*')]
[c] δύσκολος
[d] [James Beresford, *The Miseries of Human Life; or the Groans of Timothy Testy and Samuel Sensitive; with a few Supplementary Sighs from Mrs Testy. In Twelve Dialogues* (1806)]
[e] *in pulicis morsu Deum invocare* [Erasmus, *Adages* III, 4, 4, which goes back to a fable by Aesop, 'The Man, the Flea, and Heracles']
[f] εὐλαβής

strikes, it cannot affect us with more than its true severity. But if we have not done so and are hit unprepared, at the first moment the frightened mind is unable to gauge the magnitude of the misfortune; it is then incalculable and, therefore, easily presents itself as immense, or at least much greater than it actually is. In the same way, darkness and uncertainty make every danger appear greater. Of course, there is the additional aspect that, together with the misfortune anticipated as possible, we have also thought about grounds for solace and relief, or at least have got used to imagining them.

But nothing will enable us to calmly endure the misfortunes that befall us better than the conviction of the truth that, in my *Prize Essay on the Freedom of the Will*, I have deduced and established from ultimate grounds, namely as it says there on p. 62: 'Everything that happens, from the greatest to the smallest, happens necessarily.'[a] For human beings are soon able to acquiesce in what is inevitably necessary, and this knowledge[b] lets them regard everything as necessary, even what has been brought about by the strangest coincidences as much as what happens according to the most well-known rules and complete anticipation. I refer here to what I have said about the calming effect of knowledge of the inevitable and necessary (*The World as Will and Representation*, vol. 1, pp. 345–6[c]). Whoever is imbued with it, will first willingly[115] do what he can, but then willingly suffer what he has to.

We may regard the small accidents that vex us hourly as meant to keep us in practice, so that the strength to endure the great ones does not slacken while we are lucky. In the face of the daily troubles, small frictions in human intercourse, insignificant offences and indecencies of others, their gossiping, and so on, we have to be a Siegfried, bearing horns on his head, i.e. not feel them at all, let alone take them to heart and brood over them. On the contrary, we must not let all of this affect us, but kick it away, like small stones that lie in our path, and not take it up into our innermost deliberations and ruminations.[116]

(52) However, what people commonly call fate is mostly only their own stupid pranks. Consequently, we cannot take heed enough of the fine passage in Homer (*Iliad* XXIII, 313ff.), where he commends *mêtis*,[d] i.e. prudent reflection. For even if evil pranks are atoned for only in the next world, stupid ones are atoned for in this, although once in a while mercy may be put before justice.

---

[a] [*FW*, 79 (Hübscher *SW* 4, 60)]   [b] *Erkenntniß*   [c] [*WWR* 1, 332–3 (Hübscher *SW* 2, 361)]
[d] μῆτις

Not the person who looks furious, but the one who looks intelligent appears terrible and dangerous – as certainly as the human brain is a more terrible weapon than the lion's claw. –

The perfect man of the world would be the one who was never irresolute and never precipitous in his actions.

(53) Next to prudence, courage is an absolutely essential quality for our happiness. Certainly, we can give ourselves neither the one nor the other, but inherit the former from our mother and the latter from our father; but with resolution and practice, we can assist what is present of these qualities. To this world, where 'the dice fall like iron',[a] we need an iron mind,[b] armoured against fate and armed against human beings. For life is a battle, each one of our steps is challenged, and Voltaire says rightfully: 'We succeed in this world only with the sword drawn, and we die with the weapons in our hand.'[c] Therefore, it is a cowardly soul that shrinks, laments, and wants to give up hope as soon as clouds gather or even just appear on the horizon. Instead, our motto should be:

Never bow to suffering, go and face it.[d]

As long as the outcome of a dangerous matter is still doubtful, as long as the possibility still exists that it will be a happy one, we should not consider hesitating, but only resisting, just as we should not despair of the weather as long as there still is a blue patch in the sky. Indeed, we should go as far as saying:

507

Even if the world will break apart,
the ruins would strike a fearless one.[e]

The whole of life itself, let alone its goods, are not worth the cowardly trembling and shrivelling of the heart:

Therefore, live forcefully,
and bravely turn your breast against misfortunes.[f]

But even here excess is possible; for courage can degenerate into recklessness. In fact, a certain amount of fearfulness is necessary for our existence in this world; cowardliness is merely its transgression. Bacon has fittingly

---

[a] [From Friedrich Schiller's poem 'In einer Bataille (Von einem Offizier)' (In a Battle [By an Officer])]
[b] *Sinn*   [c] *on ne réussit dans ce monde, qu'à la pointe de l'épée, et on meurt les armes à la main*
[d] *tu ne cede malis, sed contra audentior ito* [Virgil, *Aeneid* VI, 95; trans. Robert Fagles]
[e] *Si fractus illabatur* [*inlabatur*] *orbis, / Impavidum derient ruinae* [Horace, *Odes* III, 3, 7–8]
[f] *Quocirca vivite fortes, / Fortiaque adversis opponite pectora rebus* [Horace, *Satires* II, 2, 135–6]

expressed this in his etymological explanation of panic-stricken fear,[a] which leaves the older explanation by Plutarch (*Isis and Osiris*,[b] ch. 14) far behind. For he derives it from *Pan*, as personified nature, and says: 'For the nature of things has imbued all living beings with fear and terror as the preserver of their life and essence, avoiding and repelling evils that befall them. However, this same nature does not know how to practise moderation; but always admixes vain and empty fears with the beneficial ones, to the point where all beings (if their inside could be seen), especially the human ones, are full of panicky terror.'[c] Incidentally, it is characteristic of panicky terror that it is not clearly conscious of its reasons, but assumes them more than knows them, indeed, when in need, simply claims fear itself as the ground of fear.

---

[a] *terror Panicus*   [b] *de Iside et Osiride* [356d; part of Plutarch's *Moralia*]
[c] *Natura enim rerum omnibus viventibus indidit metum, ac formidinem, vitae atque essentiae suae conservatricem, ac mala ingruentia vitantem et depellentem. Verumtamen eadem natura modum tenere nescia est: sed timoribus salutaribus semper vanos et inanes admiscet; adeo ut omnia (si intus conspici darentur) Panicis terroribus plenissima sint, praesertim humana.* (*De sapientia veterum* [*On the Wisdom of the Ancients*] VI (*Pan, sive natura*)]

On the different stages of life

Voltaire has made the fine remark:

> Who has not the spirit of his age
> Has all the misfortune of his age.[a]

Therefore, it is appropriate that, at the end of these eudaemonological observations, we take a look at the changes produced in us by the different stages of life.

Throughout our entire life we are always aware only of the *present*, never more. What differentiates it is the fact that in the beginning we have a long future before us, but towards the end we see a long past behind us. Also our temperament, though not our character, undergoes some well-known changes, so that each time the present acquires a different hue. –

In my chief work, vol. 2, ch. 31, pp. 394ff.,[b] I have explained that and why in our *childhood* we behave much more as *cognitive* than as *willing* beings. This is exactly what the blissfulness[c] of the first quarter of our life is based upon, as a result of which afterwards this period lies behind us like a lost paradise. In childhood we have only few relationships and small needs, hence little stimulation of the will; therefore, the greater part of our essence is taken up by *cognition*. – The intellect, like the brain, which reaches its full size already in the seventh year, develops early, although it does not mature early, and incessantly seeks nourishment in a whole world of the existence that is still fresh, where absolutely everything is coloured with the charm of novelty. As a result, the years of our childhood are perpetual poetry. For the essence of poetry, like all art, consists in conceiving the Platonic Idea, i.e. what is essential in every particular and hence common to its *kind*,[d] so that each thing shows up as a representative of its genus[e] and *one* case stands for a

509

---

[a] *Qui n'a pas l'esprit de son âge, / De son âge a tout le malheur.* [Voltaire, *Stances à Madame du Châtelet* (1741)]
[b] [Third edn., pp. 449ff. (Hübscher *SW* 3, 450ff.)]   [c] *Glücksäligkeit*   [d] *Art*   [e] *Gattung*

thousand.[a] Although it seems that in the scenes of our childhood we are always merely occupied with the respective individual object or event, and only insofar as it interests our present willing, this is really not the case. For life in its entire significance stands before us so new, fresh, and without its impressions being deadened by repetition that, in the midst of our childish pursuits, we are always, secretly and without a clear intent, engaged in grasping the essence of life itself in the individual scenes and events, the fundamental types of its shapes and embodiments. We see all things and persons, as Spinoza expresses it, from the perspective of eternity.[b] The younger we are, the more each individual represents its entire genus. This continually decreases from year to year and makes for the great difference between impressions that things have on us in our youth and in old age.[117] Consequently, the experiences and acquaintances of childhood and youth afterwards become the fixed types and rubrics of all later knowledge[c] and experience, its categories, so to speak, under which we subsume everything that comes later, although we are not always clearly conscious of this.[*,118] Accordingly, the firm foundation of our view of the world already forms in childhood, and thus also its shallowness or depth; it is later elaborated and perfected, but in essence not changed. Therefore, as a result of this purely objective and hence poetic view that is essential to childhood and is supported by the fact that the will is still far from acting with its full energy, as children we behave far more as purely cognitive than as willing beings. Hence the serious, contemplative gaze of some children, which Raphael used with such happy results in his angels, especially those of the Sistine Madonna. For that very reason, the years of childhood are so blissful that their memory is always accompanied by longing. – Whereas at that time we are devoted to the first *intuitive* comprehension of things with such sincerity, education, on the other hand, is at pains to teach us *concepts*. However, concepts do not provide what is really essential; rather this lies, as the ground and genuine content of all our knowledge,[d] in the *intuitive* apprehension[e] of the world. But this we can only gain ourselves, it cannot be in any way *produced* in us. Therefore, our intellectual, just as our moral, worth does not come from the outside, but arises from the depth of our own essence, and no Pestalozzian pedagogics can form a thinking human being

510

---

* Oh, in childhood! when time still moves so slowly that things almost seem to stand still, in order to stay as they are in all eternity.

[a] [In his *Theory of Colours*, Goethe states about Galileo that he proves that 'for a genius, one case stands for a thousand' (Sect. 5, 17th century, 'Galileo Galilei')]

[b] *sub specie aeternitatis* [*Ethics* V, 31, schol.]   [c] *Erkenntniß*   [d] *Erkenntnisse*   [e] *Auffassung*

from a born fool: never! He is born a fool and must die a fool. – The deeply intimate apprehension of the first intuitive external world that we have described also explains why the environment and experiences of our childhood impress themselves so firmly on our memory. For we completely abandoned ourselves to them, nothing distracted us, and we looked at the things that were before us as if they were the only ones of their kind, indeed, the only ones existing. Later the quantity of things we then become acquainted with deprives us of courage and patience. – If readers will recall at this point what I have presented on pp. 372ff.[a] of the second volume of my chief work, namely that the *objective* existence of all things, i.e. their existence in mere *representation*, is a consistently pleasant one, whereas their *subjective* existence, which consists in *willing*, is strongly mixed with pain and sorrow, they will most probably also accept the following proposition as a brief account of the matter: All things are delightful to *see*, but terrible to *be*. According to what was said above, in childhood things are much better known to us from the perspective of *seeing*, hence of representation, objectivity, than from the perspective of *being*, which is that of the will. Whereas the former is the delightful side of things, and the subjective and horrible side still remains unknown to us, the young intellect considers all those shapes presented to it by reality and art as just as many blissful beings; it imagines that they are as beautiful to *be* as they are to look at, and even much more beautiful than that. Hence the world lies before it like an Eden; this is the Arcadia where we are all born.[b] Some time later the thirst for real life develops, the urge to act and to suffer, which drives us into the hurly-burly of the world. There we come to know the other side of things, that of being, i.e. of willing, which is frustrated at every step. Then the great disillusion gradually happens, and after it has made its appearance people say: 'The age of illusions is past';[c] yet it continues and becomes ever more complete. Consequently, we can say that in childhood life represents itself as a theatre setting seen from afar, in old age as the same, but seen from close up.

Finally, the following also contributes to the happiness of childhood. As at the beginning of spring all leaves have the same colour and almost the same shape, so we humans also all resemble one another in early childhood and hence harmonize admirably. But with puberty there begins divergence that becomes greater and greater, like the radii of a circle.

What dims the rest of the first half of life, the age of youth, which has so many advantages over the second half, indeed, renders it unhappy, is the

511

---

[a] [Hübscher *SW* 3, 424ff.]　　[b] [See p. 358, n. c]　　[c] *l'âge des illusions est passé*

hunt for happiness on the firm assumption that it exists in life. From this arises constantly deluded hope and from this in turn discontent. Deceptive images of a dreamed, vague happiness hover before us in capriciously chosen shapes, and we search in vain for their original. So in our youth we are mostly dissatisfied with our situation and environment, whatever they are, because we attribute to them what belongs to the vacuity and misery of human life everywhere, and with which we first become acquainted right now after having expected quite different things. – We would have gained much, if, through timely instruction, we were able to stamp out the delusion in young men that there is much to be achieved in the world.[119] But the opposite happens, because we often come to know about life through literature earlier than through reality. At the dawn of our own youth, the scenes described by the former hang resplendent before our eyes, and now we are tormented by the longing to see them realized – to touch the rainbow. The youth expects the course of his life to take the form of an interesting novel. Hence arises the deception which I have already described on p. 374[a] of the above-mentioned second volume. For what imparts the charm of all those images is just this, that they are mere images and not real and that, therefore, when looking at them,[b] we find ourselves in the calm and contentedness of pure cognition. To be realized means to be filled with willing, which leads to unavoidable pain. I also refer the sympathetic reader to p. 427[c] of the same volume.

Consequently, if the character of the first half of life is an unsatisfied longing for happiness, that of the second is dread of misfortune. For, with the second half, the recognition has more or less occurred that all happiness is chimerical, whereas suffering is real. Now the more rational characters at least will strive rather for mere freedom from pain and an undisturbed state than for pleasure. – When the door bell rang during the years of my youth, I was happy, since I thought that now it[d] was coming. But in later years my feeling on the same occasion rather resembled alarm: I thought, 'Here it comes'. – There are two contradictory feelings towards the human world for excellent and talented individuals, who as such do not quite belong to it and, consequently, live alone, more or less, according to the degree of their merits. During one's youth, one often has the feeling of being *abandoned* by the world; in later years, on the other hand, it is the feeling of having *escaped* from it. The former, an unpleasant one, rests on the lack of acquaintance with the world, the latter, a pleasant one, on being acquainted with it. – As a

---

[a] [*WWR* 2, Hübscher *SW* 3, 426f.]   [b] *bei ihrem Anschauen*   [c] [Hübscher *SW* 3, 487f.]
[d] [Happiness]

result, the second half of life contains, like the second half of a musical period, less striving, but more peace than the first. This depends on the fact 513 that in our youth we believe that lots of happiness and pleasure can be found in the world and are just hard to come by, whereas in old age we know that there is nothing to be gained, and so are perfectly reassured, enjoy a tolerable present, and take delight even in little things.[120] –

What the mature man has achieved through his life's experience and what makes him see the world differently from the youth and the boy is, first of all, *impartiality*.[a] First and foremost, he sees things quite simply and takes them for that they are, whereas for the boy and the young man the real world is hidden, or distorted, by a delusion, made up of self-made fancies, traditional prejudices, and strange fantasies. For the first thing that experience has to do is to free us from the phantoms and false concepts that ensued in our youth. Saving the youthful age from these would really be the best education, although only a negative one, but it is difficult. To this end, we would have to keep the child's horizon in the beginning as narrow as possible and within it teach it all clear and accurate concepts, and only after it had got to know everything within this horizon correctly would we gradually widen it, always taking care that nothing obscure and also nothing half or inappropiately understood remained. As a result, the child's concepts of things and human relations would be clear and accurate, though still limited and very simple, so that they always merely needed expansion, not correction; and so forth until the age of adolescence. This method requires in particular that we do not allow novels to be read, but substitute appropriate biographies like, for example, that by *Franklin*,[b] *Moritz's Anton Reiser*,[c] and many others. –

When we are young we imagine that the events and persons important for the course of our life will make their entrance with drums beating and trumpets sounding; in old age retrospective reflection shows that they all slipped in through the back door quietly and hardly noticed.[121]

Moreover, from the point of view so far considered, we can compare life 514 with a piece of embroidered material, of which we get to the see the top side in the first half of our life and the reverse side in the second half; the latter is not as beautiful, but more instructive, because it lets us see the connection of threads. –

---

[a] *Unbefangenheit*
[b] [Benjamin Franklin; a part of his autobiography was first published in French as *Mémoires de la vie privée* (1791), two years later in English as *The Private Life of the Late Benjamin Franklin*]
[c] [Karl Philipp Moritz, *Anton Reiser* (1785–90)]

Intellectual superiority, even the greatest, will assert its decisive dominance in conversation only after the fortieth year. For maturity of years and
fruit of experience can be exceeded in many ways, yet never replaced by it;
they provide even the most ordinary human being with a certain counterweight against the forces of the greatest intellect as long as it is young. I am
referring here to the personal, not to works. –

Every human being who is excellent in some respect, everyone who does
not belong to the five-sixths of humankind that are so miserably endowed
by nature, will hardly remain free of a certain touch of misanthropy after the
fortieth year. For as is natural, he had extrapolated from himself to others
and has slowly been disappointed; he has realized that, either in respect of
the mind or of the heart, and mostly both, they are far behind him and are
not his equals, which is why he likes to avoid getting involved with them; as
in general everybody, in accordance with his inner worth, will love or hate
solitude, i.e. his own company. *Kant* too deals with this kind of misanthropy in the *Critique of Judgement*, towards the end of the general remark
to §29 of the first part.[a]

In *young people* it is a bad sign from an intellectual and moral perspective,
if they *find their way* quite early in human affairs, are at once at home in
them, and join in them as if prepared; this indicates commonness. In
contrast, disconcerted, perplexed, awkward, and wrong behaviour points
to a nobler kind of nature.[122]

The cheerfulness and vital energy of our youth rests in part on the fact
that, going uphill, we do not see death, because it lies at the foot of the other
side of the mountain. But once we have crossed the summit, we will actually
catch sight of death, which so far we knew only through hearsay; and since
simultaneously our vital force begins to ebb, our vital spirit decreases as well,
so that now a gloomy seriousness replaces youthful high spirits and is also
imprinted on our face. People may tell us what they want, but as long as we
are young, we regard life as endless and use time accordingly. The older we
grow, the more we economize on it. For in old age every day that we have
lived produces a sensation related to the one that a delinquent has at every
step on his way to the gallows.[123]

Seen from the standpoint of youth, life is an infinitely long future; from
the standpoint of old age, it is a very short past, so that in the beginning it
looks like things we observe through the objective lens[b] of the opera glasses,
but in the end like things seen through the eyepiece.[c] We have to have
grown old, and hence have lived a long time, in order to recognize how short

---

[a] [A125/B126]   [b] *Objektivglas*   [c] *Okular*

life is. – In our youth time itself has a much slower pace; therefore, the first quarter of our life is not only the happiest, but also the longest, so that it leaves more memories behind and, when it comes down to it, everybody would be able to tell more about it than about two of the following quarters. And in the spring of life, similar to the spring season of the year, the days finally even become annoyingly long. In the autumn of both they grow shorter, but brighter and more constant.

When life draws to a close, we do not know where it has gone.[124] But why in old age do we see the life that we have lived as so short? Because we take it to be as short as its memory is. For everything insignificant and much that was unpleasant have been dropped, hence little is left. For as our intellect in general is very imperfect, so also is our memory; what we have learned must be practised, what has passed must be pondered, if both are not to sink gradually into the abyss of oblivion. But we usually do not brood over the insignificant and rarely the unpleasant, which would be necessary in order to preserve it in memory. And the insignificant grows in volume, since through frequent and ultimately countless recurrence many things that seemed significant in the beginning become unimportant; therefore, we remember the earlier better than the later years. The longer we live, the fewer are the events that seem important to us or significant enough to be pondered afterwards, which would be the only way to fix them in memory; so they are forgotten as soon as they are past. Hence time passes ever more without a trace. – Furthermore, we do not like to ponder the unpleasant, the least so if it wounds our vanity, which is most often the case, because few woes befall us for which we are entirely blameless. This is another reason why much of what is unpleasant is forgotten. It is due to both losses that our memory is so short, and proportionally ever shorter the longer the material. Just as the objects on the shore from which we are sailing away become ever smaller and more difficult to recognize and to distinguish, so also do our years past with their experiences and deeds. Moreover, memory and fantasy will sometimes have us envision a long past scene of our life as vividly as if it had been yesterday, and it then comes very close to us. This happens because it is impossible similarly to visualize the long interval of time that has elapsed between now and then, in that it cannot be conjured in one image and, in addition, because the events that are part of it are for the most part long forgotten, only a general, abstract[a] knowledge of it remaining, a mere concept, no intuition. Hence it is for this reason that what is long past appears so close when it comes to particular events, as if they had happened

516

---

[a] *in abstracto*

only yesterday, but the intervening time vanishes and our whole life presents itself as inconceivably short. Sometimes in old age the long past that is behind us and hence our own age might even appear almost incredible to us at times, which mainly happens because we first and foremost see the same stationary present before us. However, inner events of this nature are ultimately based on the fact that it is not our essence in itself, but only its appearance that is situated in time, and that the present is the meeting point between object and subject.[125] – And again, why in our youth do we see the life that is still before us as so immeasurably long? Because we must have space for the boundless hopes with which we populate it and for whose realization Methuselah would die too young. Also because we use as its criterion the few years that are already behind us and whose memory is always rich in material, and consequently long, with novelty making everything appear significant, which is why afterwards we ruminate about it, and often repeat it and so impress it on memory.

At times we think we long to return to a distant *place*, whereas it is actually the *time* that we long for, which we spent there when we were younger and fresher. Time then deceives us under the mask of space. If we travel to the place, we become aware of the deception. –

In order to reach a great age, there are, together with a sound constitution as a necessary condition,[a] two ways, which can be explained by the burning of two lamps: one burns for a long time, because it has little oil with a very thin wick; the other, because it has a lot of oil with a strong wick. The oil is the vital force, the wick its use in every conceivable fashion.[126]

In regard to the *vital force*,[b] until the thirty-sixth year we can be compared to those people who live off their interest; what is spent today comes back in tomorrow. But from that age, we are analogous to the man of private means who starts to spend his capital. In the beginning, he does not notice at all; the largest part of the expenditure is restored automatically, and he does not pay attention to a small deficit. But the latter grows gradually, becomes significant; and the increase itself grows larger every day. It spreads more and more; each today is poorer than yesterday, without hope for things coming to a standstill. The decrease accelerates more and more, like falling bodies – until finally nothing is left. It is a very sad case, if vital force and property, which are compared here, are actually both at the point of melting away together; hence the love of possessions grows with age. – In contrast, in the beginning, until we come of age and even for a while after that, in regard to the vital force we resemble those who add a little interest to their

---

[a] *conditio sine qua non*   [b] *Lebenskraft*

capital; not only is what has been spent recovered automatically, but the capital increases. And this too might be the case with money thanks to the care of an honest guardian. O happy youth! O sad old age! – Nevertheless, we should take care of the youthful powers. Aristotle remarks (*Politics*, last book, ch. 5[a]) that of the Olympic victors, only two or three had won as boys and then again as grown men, because through early exertion, which requires preparation, the powers were so greatly exhausted that afterwards, at the age of manhood, they were lacking. Just as this applies to muscular strength, so it does also to nervous strength, whose expression are all the intellectual achievements; consequently, the precocious geniuses,[b] the child prodigies, the fruits of a hothouse education, who excite our astonishment when they are boys, afterwards become very ordinary minds. Also the early, coerced exertion of learning the ancient languages might be to blame for the later lameness and lack of judgement in so many scholars. –

I have remarked that the character of almost everyone appears to be particularly appropriate for one period of life, so that it makes a more favourable impression during this time. Some are amiable when they are young, and then it is over; others are strong, active men, whom old age robs of their worth; some present themselves most advantageously in old age, when they are more gentle, because more experienced and equanimous; this is often the case with the French. This must be due to the fact that character itself possesses something youthful, manly, or elderly, which the respective age accords with or acts against as a corrective.

Just as when we are on a ship we notice our advance only through the objects on the shore, which recede and accordingly become smaller, we become aware of growing old and older through the fact that older people increasingly seem young to us.

I have already discussed above how and why everything that we see, do, and experience, leaves the fewer traces in our mind, the older we grow. In this sense it might be claimed that only in youth do we live with full consciousness; in old age, only with half. The older we become, the less consciously we live. Things rush by without leaving an impression, just as the work of art that we have seen a thousand times makes none. We do what we have to do, and afterwards do not know whether we have done it.[127] The more unconscious life becomes, the more it rushes towards the complete cessation of consciousness, the faster becomes its course. In childhood the novelty of all things and events makes us aware of each one; hence the day is immeasurably long. The same happens to us when we travel, when,

519

---

[a] [*Politics* VIII, 4 (rather than 5) (1339a)]   [b] *ingenia praecocia*

therefore, *one* month appears longer than four at home. However, the novelty of things does not prevent the longer-seeming time from often feeling really 'drawn out' to us in both cases, more than in old age and more than when being at home. But gradually, through the long habit of perceiving the same things, the intellect is ground down so far that more and more everything passes over it without effect, so that the days become more and more insignificant and thus shorter. The hours of a boy are longer than the days of an old man. Accordingly, our lifetime has an accelerated motion, like a ball that is rolling down; and just as on a rotating disk every point runs the faster, the farther away it is from the centre, time passes more and more quickly for us all in proportion to our distance from the beginning of life. Consequently, we can assume that in our mind's immediate appreciation the length of a year is inversely proportional to our age. For example, if the year is one-fifth of our age, it appears ten times as long as when it is only one-fiftieth of our age. The difference in the pace of time has the most decisive influence on the manner of our existence at every age. First, it causes childhood, although it only encompasses about fifteen years, to be the longest time of our life and, therefore, the one richest in memories.
520   Next, it makes us subject to boredom in reverse proportion to our age. Children constantly need diversions, be it play or work; when they stop, they are instantly seized by terrible boredom. Also youths are still very much amenable to boredom and look forward with disquiet to unfilled hours. In mature[a] age, boredom disappears more and more; and for old men, time is always too short and the days fly by as fast as arrows. It is clear that I speak of human beings and not of beasts[b] that have grown old.[128] Because of this acceleration of the course of time, in later years boredom often vanishes; and since the passions too, together with their torment, fall silent, the burden of life as a whole actually becomes lighter than in youth, if only one's health is preserved. Hence we call the period that precedes the beginning of weakness and afflictions of old age, 'the best years'. In regard to our well-being, that is what they might actually be. But the youthful years, when everything makes an impression and forcefully enters consciousness, retain the advantage of being the fruitful time for the mind, the spring that starts the blossoms. Profound truths can only be beheld, not calculated, that means, their first recognition[c] is immediate and brought about by the momentary impression; it can only occur as long as this impression is strong, vivid, and deep. Accordingly, in this respect everything depends on the use we make of the years of our youth. In later years we are more able to act on others, indeed,

---

[a] *männlichen*   [b] *Vieh*   [c] *Erkenntniß*

on the world, because we ourselves are complete and finished and no longer attached to the impression; but the world affects us less. These years, therefore, are the time of doing and achieving, but the former are those of original apprehension[a] and cognition.[b]

In youth intuition dominates, in old age thought; hence the former is the time of poetry, the latter that of philosophy. Also in a practical respect, in youth we let ourselves be determined by intuitions and their impressions, in old age only by thought. This depends in part on the fact that only in old age have a sufficient number of intuitive cases occurred and been subsumed under concepts in order to provide them with full meaning, content, and credit and to moderate the impression made by intuition through habit at the same time. In contrast, in youth the impression of the intuitive, hence also the external side of things, is so predominant, in particular on lively and imaginative minds, that they see the world as an image. Therefore, it is most important for them what kind of figure they cut and how they look – more than how they feel internally. This already shows itself in the personal vanity and fondness for dressing up of young men.

The greatest energy and highest exertion of our mental powers undoubtedly occur in youth, until the age of thirty-five at the latest; from then on they decrease, though very slowly. Yet the later years, even old age, are not without intellectual compensation. Only now have experience and erudition really become prolific; we have had time and opportunity to contemplate and consider things from all sides, have compared each one with every other and discovered their points of contact and connecting links, and so we are really able to understand them in their interconnectedness. Everything has become clear. Consequently, we know even more thoroughly what we already knew in our youth, since we have much more evidence for every concept. What we thought we knew in our youth, we really know in old age; moreover, we actually know much more and possess knowledge that is thought through from all sides and hence really interconnected, whereas in youth it is always sketchy and fragmentary. Only *someone who grows old* develops a complete and appropriate representation of life, in that he takes it in in its entirety and natural course and in particular not, like the others, merely from the side of entry, but also from that of departure, so that he especially recognizes its worthlessness,[c] while the others are always still caught in the delusion that the right thing is still to come.[129] In youth, on the other hand, there is more conception, so that we are able to make more out of the little that we know; but in old age, there is more judgement,

[a] *Auffassens*   [b] *Erkennens*   [c] *Nichtigkeit*

penetration, and thoroughness. A privileged mind already collects in his youth the material for his very own insights,[a] his original fundamental views, hence what he is destined to present to the world; but only in his late years does he become the master of his material. Accordingly, we will find most of the time that the great authors have delivered their masterworks around the age of fifty. Nonetheless, youth remains the root of the tree of knowledge, although only the top yields fruits. But just as every age, even the most miserable, thinks of itself as much wiser than its immediate predecessor, not to mention earlier ones, so does every stage of human life; however, both are often wrong. During the years of physical growth, when our mental powers and our knowledge also increase daily, it becomes a habit for the day to look down with contempt on yesterday. This habit takes root and remains even when the mental powers start to decrease and today should rather look up to yesterday with veneration. Consequently, we often underrate the achievements and the judgements of our early years.[*],[130]

In general, it needs to be said here that, although the intellect, or the mind, in its basic qualities is inborn, just like the character, or the heart, of a human being, nonetheless it by no means remains as unchanged as the former but is subject to quite a few changes, which even occur regularly on the whole, because they are partly grounded in the fact that the intellect has a physical basis and partly in the fact that it has an empirical material. Hence the intellect's own power grows gradually until it reaches its peak and then gradually declines into imbecility. On the other hand, the material that occupies all these powers and keeps them active, hence the content of thinking and knowing,[b] experience, knowledge, practice, and through them perfection of insight, is a steadily growing quantity, until for example a decisive weakness appears that drops everything. This fact that human beings consist of one absolutely unchangeable element and another that is regularly changing in a twofold and opposite manner explains the diversity of their appearance and worth at different stages of life.

In a wider sense we might say: The first forty years of our life provide the text, the following thirty the commentary to it, which first teaches us to understand the true meaning and connection of the text correctly, together with its moral and all the details.

---

[*] But most often in youth, when time is most precious, we spend it lavishly and only begin to be economical with it in old age.

[a] *Erkenntnisse*   [b] *Wissens*

But the end of life is like the end of a masked ball, when the masks are removed. Now we see who those with whom we came in contact during the course of our life have truly been. For the characters have come to light, the deeds have yielded fruits, the achievements have received their just evaluation, and all delusions have crumbled. Indeed, all of this needed time. – But it is most curious that even we ourselves really recognize and understand ourselves, our own goals and purposes, only towards the end of our life, especially in our relation to the world and to others. To be sure, often, but not always, we will have to assign a lower place to ourselves than we had previously expected; sometimes also a higher one, brought about by the fact that we had no sufficient concept[a] of the baseness of the world and, accordingly, had set our goal higher than the world did. We come to know incidentally what we have in ourselves.[131] –

It is customary to call youth the happy time of life, and old age the sad one. That would be true, if passions made us happy. Young people are torn hither and thither by them, with little joy and much pain. Cool old age is left in peace by them and soon assumes a contemplative air; for cognition becomes free and receives the upper hand. Since cognition in itself is painless, consciousness will be the happier, the more it prevails. In old age we are better able to prevent misfortunes, in youth we are better able to endure them.[132] We just have to consider that all pleasure is negative and all pain positive in order to understand that the passions cannot make us happy and that old age is not to be deplored, just because some pleasures are denied to it. For every pleasure is always merely the satisfaction of a need; and that with this need the pleasure too comes to an end is as little to be lamented as the fact that a person can no longer eat after a meal and must stay awake after a night's rest. Plato (at the beginning of the *Republic*[b]) much more correctly considers old age happy, insofar as it is finally rid of the sexual drive, which has incessantly troubled us until then. We might even assert that the diverse and endless whimsies that the sexual drive produces and the affects[c] that arise from it maintain a constant, moderate madness in people as long as they are under the influence of this drive, or devil, by which they are constantly possessed. Hence they would only become fully rational after it dies down. But it is certain that, in general and apart from all individual circumstances and conditions, a certain melancholy is characteristic of youth and a certain serenity of old age. And the reason for this is that youth is still under the domination, indeed, the compulsory service of that demon, who does not easily grant it a free hour and at the same time is the

524

---

[a] *Vorstellung*   [b] [329a–d]   [c] *Affekte*

immediate or mediate author of each and every calamity that befalls or threatens people. Old age, in contrast, possesses the serenity of somebody who is rid of a shackle that he has worn for a long time and now freely moves about. – On the other hand, it might be said that after the sexual drive is extinguished the true core of life has been consumed and only its shell is still present, in fact, that it resembles a comedy that, started by human beings, afterwards is finished by automata wearing their clothes.[133]

Be that as it may, youth is the time of unrest, old age that of repose; from this alone their mutual comfort could be inferred. Children covetously stretch their hands far out, after everything colourful and diverse that they see before them; they are attracted by it, because their senses are still so fresh and young. The same happens, with greater energy, to the youths. They too are attracted by the colourful world and its diverse shapes, and their fantasy immediately makes more of it than the world will ever be able to offer. Hence they are full of desire and longing for the undetermined, taking away their peace, without which there is no happiness. Accordingly, whereas the young believe that God knows what wonderful things can be had in the world, if only they could find out where, old people are infused with the Qohelethian 'All is vanity'[a] and know that all nuts are hollow, as much as they may be gilded.[134] For in old age, all this has ceased, in part because the blood has turned cooler and the excitability of the senses has decreased, in part because experience has clarified the value of things and the content of pleasures, by means of which we have gradually cast off the illusions, chimeras, and prejudices that previously concealed and distorted the free and pure view of things, so that now we recognize everything more accurately and clearly and take it for what it is and have also, more or less, come to the insight of the worthlessness of all earthly things. It is this that gives almost all old people, even those of very ordinary abilities, a certain air of wisdom, which distinguishes them from the young.[135] But primarily this all leads to peace of mind, which is a large component of happiness, in fact really its condition and essence.

Furthermore, we believe that sickness and boredom are the lot of old age. The former is not essential to old age, especially not if a great number of years is to be attained; for 'with increasing age, health and sickness increase'.[b] And as far as boredom is concerned, I have shown above why old age is even less exposed to it than youth. Moreover, boredom is by no means a necessary companion of solitude, to which age certainly leads us for reasons easily foreseen, but it is so only for those who have never known other than

---

[a] [Qoheleth (Ecclesiastes) 1:2]   [b] *crescente vita, crescit sanitas et morbus*

sensuous and social pleasures and have failed to enrich their mind and develop their powers. To be sure, at a greater age the mental powers decline; but where there was much, there will be enough left for fighting boredom. Also, as shown above, correct insight still increases through experience, knowledge, practice, and reflection, judgement sharpens it, and connections become clear; we gain more and more of a comprehensive overview of the whole in all matters. So our own innermost self-culture, by means of ever new combinations of accumulated knowledge and its occasional enrich- 526
ment, still advances in all its parts and occupies, satisfies, and rewards the mind. All of this compensates to a certain extent for the aforementioned decline. Moreover, as already pointed out, time passes more quickly in old age, which counteracts boredom. The decrease in physical strength hurts little, if we do not need it for earning a living. Poverty in old age is a great misfortune. If it is averted and health is sustained, old age can be a very tolerable part of life. Comfort and security are its main needs; therefore, when we are old we love money even more than before, because it compensates for the powers we lack. Deserted by Venus, we will gladly seek exhilaration in Bacchus. The need to teach and to speak has taken the place of the need to see, travel, and learn. But it is lucky when old people are still left with the love for study, also for music, theatre, and in general with a certain susceptibility for external things, as indeed in a few they last well into the oldest age.

Only at a later age do people really achieve Horace's 'admire nothing',[a] i.e. the immediate, honest, and firm conviction of the vanity of all things and the hollowness of all the splendours of the world; the chimeras have vanished. They no longer believe that somewhere, be it in a palace or a hut, a particular happiness dwells, greater than the one they essentially enjoy everywhere, if they are free of physical or mental pain. For them, the great and the small, the noble and the humble, according to the measure of the world, are no longer different. This bestows a special kind of peace of mind on old people, with which they look down smilingly on the artifices of the world. They are completely disillusioned and know that human life, what-ever we do to dress it up and adorn it, soon shines through in its paltriness and basically is the same everywhere, despite the paint and ornament – an existence whose true value can always only be determined by the absence of pain, not the presence of pleasures, and even less of pomp. (Horace, *Epistles* 527
I, 12, 1–4.)[b] The fundamental characteristic of old age is disillusionment; the illusions have vanished, which until then gave life its charm and spurred us to be active. We have recognized the vanity and emptiness of the splendours

---

[a] *nil admirari* [*Epistles* I, 6, 1]   [b] [Where Horace praises the advantages of health and a simple life]

of the world, especially of pageantry, glitter, and pretence of grandeur; we have come to know that there is little behind most desired things and longed-for pleasures, and hence have gradually gained insight into the great poverty and vacuity of our entire existence. Only in our seventieth year can we completely understand the first verse of Qoheleth. But it is this which gives a certain morose air to old age. – What somebody is to himself is of no greater benefit to him than in old age.[136]

However, most people, who were always dull, turn more and more into automata the older they grow; they think, say, and do always the same, and no external impression is able to change this any longer or elicit something new from them. Speaking to such old people is like writing in the sand; the impression is wiped out almost immediately. So an old age of this sort is, of course, merely the dead residue[a] of life. – Nature seems intent on symbolizing the entry of a second childhood in old age by the, albeit rare, appearance of third teeth.

The accelerated vanishing of all powers with increasing age is, of course, very sad; but it is necessary, even beneficial, because otherwise death, for which it prepares, would be too difficult. Therefore, the greatest benefit gained by a very great age is euthanasia,[b] an extremely easy death, not triggered by any illness, not accompanied by any convulsions, and not felt at all. Readers can find a description of this in vol. 2 of my chief work, ch. 41, p. 470.[*,c,137]

---

* Human life can actually be called neither long nor short, because it is basically the measure in accordance with which we evaluate all other lengths of time. – The *Upanishads* of the *Vedas* (Oupnek'hat, vol. 2, p. 53) states *the natural lifespan* as a hundred years. I think that is correct; for I have noticed that only those who live past ninety are blessed with *euthanasia*, meaning, they die without any illness, also without stroke, without convulsion, without the death rattle, in fact, sometimes without growing pale, often when seated, after a meal, or rather do not die, but simply cease to live. At any earlier age, we die merely of diseases, hence prematurely. – In the Old Testament (Psalm 90:10) the human lifespan is given as seventy, or at most eighty years and, what is more important, Herodotus ([*Histories*] I, 32 and III, 22) says the same. But it is nonetheless wrong and is merely the result of a crude and superficial comprehension of daily experience. For if the natural lifespan were seventy to eighty years, then people who die at that age would die *from old age*. But that is not the case; like younger people, they die *from illnesses*; but illness is essentially an abnormality; hence this is not the natural end. It is only between ninety and a hundred years that people die *from old age*, but then they do so as a rule without illness, without death struggle, without rattle, without convulsion, sometimes without turning pale, which is called *euthanasia*. Therefore, the *Upanishads* are correct in setting the natural lifespan at a hundred years.

a *caput mortuum* [Literally: 'head of the dead', in ancient chemistry, the dry residue of chemicals after heating them]
b *Euthanasie* [Obviously, Schopenhauer uses the expression in the literal sense of 'good death', not in the modern sense of mercy-killing]
c [Hübscher *SW* 3, 535f.]

For however long we might live, we are never aware of anything else but the indivisible present; but memory daily loses more than it gains by adding. – The older we grow, the smaller human matters all and sundry appear; life, which in youth stood firm and stable before us, now shows itself as a rapid flight of ephemeral appearances; the worthlessness of the whole emerges.[138] 528

The fundamental difference between youth and old age always remains that the former has life in sight and the latter death; accordingly, the former possesses a short past and a long future, the latter the reverse. Life during the *years of old age* resembles the fifth act of a tragedy; we know that a tragic end is near, but we do not yet know which one it will be.[139] Indeed, when old we only have death before us, and when young, life; and the question is which one is more precarious, and whether on the whole life is not an affair that it is better to have behind us than before us; for already Qoheleth says (7:2): 'The day of death is better than the day of one's birth.'[a] Desiring a very long life is in any event an audacious wish. For *quien larga vida vive mucho mal vive,*[b] says the Spanish proverb.[140] – 529

To be sure, the course of the individual's life is not indicated in the planets, the way astrology wants it to be; but the course of a human being's life in general is, insofar as one planet in turn corresponds to each stage of life and his life is successively dominated by all the planets. – In the tenth year, *Mercury* rules. Just like this planet, the person moves rapidly and easily in the most narrow circle; he can be persuaded by small things, but learns a lot and easily under the rule of the god of astuteness and eloquence. – At age twenty, the rule of *Venus* begins: Love and women take complete possession of him. In the thirtieth year, *Mars* rules: The person now is fierce, strong, brave, belligerent, and defiant. – In the fortieth year, the four planetoids are in control; accordingly, his life expands: he is frugal,[c] i.e. indulges in the useful, thanks to *Ceres*; he owns his own hearth by virtue of *Vesta*; he has learned what he needs to know thanks to *Pallas*; and the mistress of the house, his wife, rules as *Juno*.*[141] – At fifty, *Jupiter* rules. Already the person has outlived most others and feels superior to the present generation. Still in complete command of his powers, he is rich in experience and knowledge; he has (in accordance with his individuality and position) authority over all those around him. Therefore, he no longer wants to take orders, but give

---

* The approximately fifty planetoids that have been discovered since are an innovation that I do not accept. Therefore, I treat them the way I treat philosophy professors: I ignore them, because they do not suit my plans.

[a] [Rather, Qoheleth (Ecclesiastes) 7:1]   [b] ['whoever lives long, experiences much evil']   [c] *frugi*

them himself. Now he is most suited to be a ruler and sovereign in his sphere. Thus Jupiter is at his highest point and with him the fifty-year-old. – But, at sixty, *Saturn* follows and with him the heaviness, slowness, and tenacity of *lead*:

> But old folks, many feign as they were dead;
> Unwieldy, slow, heavy and pale as lead.
>
> *Romeo and Juliet*, Act II, scene 5[a]

530   At last comes *Uranus*; there we enter heaven, as people say. *Neptune* (as thoughtlessness unfortunately has called him) I cannot take into consideration here, because I am not allowed to call him by his true name, which is *Eros*. Otherwise I would show how the end is tied to the beginning, that is, how Eros is secretly connected to death, by virtue of which Orcus,[b] or Amenthes of the Egyptians (according to Plutarch, *Isis and Osiris*, ch. 29), is the 'one who receives and gives',[c] hence not only the taker, but also the giver, and death is the great reservoir of life.[142] For this very reason, everything comes from Orcus, and everything that is alive now has been there. – If we only were able to understand this conjurer's trick, in virtue of which everything happens, then it would all be clear.

---

[a] [Shakespeare. Schopenhauer provides his German translation in a footnote]   [b] [Underworld]
[c] λαμβάνων καὶ διδούς [29 (362e)]

Versions of Schopenhauer's text

Only one edition of *Parerga and Paralipomena* was published during Schopenhauer's lifetime. The first volume appeared as:

A   1851: *Parerga und Paralipomena: kleine philosophische Schriften, von Arthur Schopenhauer. Erster Band.* Berlin, Druck und Verlag von A. W. Hayn.

The present translation uses the text as edited by Arthur Hübscher, *Arthur Schopenhauers Sämtliche Werke* (Mannheim: F. A. Brockhaus, 1988), vol. 5. Hübscher's text is a confection based on A, but resulting from a substantial revision of it that includes numerous alterations and added material from handwritten sources. The majority of these come from Schopenhauer's own copy of A, in which he made extensive notes. Others come from passages in his manuscript remains. Working on the assumption that Schopenhauer was assembling revisions with a view to re-publication, in 1862, two years after Schopenhauer's death, Julius Frauenstädt incorporated many of these handwritten passages in a new edition, which he described as 'improved and considerably augmented':

> *Parerga und Paralipomena: kleine philosophische Schriften, von Arthur Schopenhauer. Zweite, verbesserte und beträchtlich vermehrte Auflage, aus dem handschriftlichen Nachlasse des Verfassers herausgegeben von Dr. Julius Frauenstädt. Erster Band. Berlin. Druck und Verlag von A. W. Hayn.*

Thereafter various revisions appeared in the versions of Schopenhauer's complete works under different editors, who have not agreed on the placing of all the handwritten passages. Here we simply follow Hübscher's decisions. (For a full account of the handwritten sources, editorial history and list of variations across the different editions, see Hübscher, *SW* 5, 531ff.)

The upshot of this process is that, although, almost without exception, all the words in the text we have translated are Schopenhauer's, he never saw a published German text that resembled the present edition very closely. Setting aside mere orthographical variations, the incorporated alterations to A, numbering well over four hundred, are of different kinds: some are small grammatical or lexical changes, some add emphasis to a point or give an extra bibliographical reference, some correct errors. Others insert substantial material amounting to whole paragraphs. In this translation we have been selective, noting only those changes to A that introduce significantly new material, or that have their source in the *Manuscript Remains*, in those manuscript books to which Schopenhauer gave the titles 'Senilia', 'Spicilegia', 'Philosophari', 'Adversaria' and 'Cogitata'. Information on the manuscript sources can be found in Hübscher *SW* 5, 531–2. (Manuscript passages adopted into published works are not included in Hübscher's *HN*.) We have not noted every insertion of clauses within sentences, or simple additions of bibliographical references. As a result many shorter insertions whose origin is in Schopenhauer's handwritten notes in A have passed unremarked.

PREFACE

1 Schopenhauer had drafted two earlier versions of a Preface for this work, both preserved in *HN*. The first is from p. 329 of the manuscript entitled *Spicilegia* (late 1845):

> It goes without saying that no one will make their first acquaintance with me through these subsidiary works, or indeed wish to assess me on the basis of them. They are written for those who have bestowed their appreciation on my previous, more important writings, which contain the system of my philosophy, to the extent that they welcome such specific expositions of subordinate matters and fragmentary allusions to those that are more important, albeit coming only from me. Accordingly, I have also presupposed familiarity with my philosophy, wherever the context demanded it, and speak throughout to readers who are already acquainted with me.
>
> It can be said on the whole that the first volume contains the *Parerga*, the second the *Paralipomena*, the greatest portion of which are to be regarded as supplements to my chief work. – This applies especially to Chapters I – [XIV] of the second volume. Thus these chapters presuppose knowledge of my philosophy, while the rest of the second volume, and the whole of the first, are comprehensible without such knowledge, although those who have become attached to my philosophy will recognize many connections to it everywhere, and indeed elucidations of it.

The second version is from early 1846, also in *Spicilegia*, p. 334:

> The title gives sufficient indication of what is to be expected here: these are subsidiary works, the fruit of later years, which for the most part do not belong essentially to the more serious and more important writings that expound my philosophical system, while at the same time they often throw light on them retrospectively, but also explicitly elucidate them. In general,

however, they are composed in the spirit of those writings and thus are directed towards a reader who is familiar with them. In this respect *Parerga* and *Paralipomena* can be more precisely distinguished in this work, in that the former, which are more self-standing, do not presuppose familiarity with my philosophy as much as the latter, which are in a way supplements to the supplements. On the other hand, anyone who wanted to get to know me for the first time through these late products of my labours would achieve his aim only incompletely. For here I speak as if to acquaintances, not as if to strangers.

Meanwhile, I have not wished to delay publication of these lesser works any longer; because, in accordance with the way of nature, the end of my life's course cannot be far off, or, more correctly, its beginning. For it is those who will think **with** me, and thus will really live **with** me, who will come close, and already enter into existence: my welcome is meant for them, my farewell to a species that has remained alien to me.

SKETCH OF A HISTORY OF THE DOCTRINE OF THE IDEAL AND THE REAL

1 'primarily and generally because ... more narrow sense': handwritten addition to A.

2 Five sentences 'Closely considered ... Med. II, p. 15.)' and the preceding clause 'and to pronounce the great truth ... truly and unconditionally *given*': handwritten additions to A.

3 Three sentences 'Incidentally, pre-established ... everything in God' and 'Thus Malebranche alone ... dispensed with the thing, for': handwritten addition to A.

4 Footnote: handwritten addition to A.

5 Three sentences 'He very often expresses ... only as they appear': handwritten addition to A.

6 Footnote: an addition to A. 'One should take away ... use another term': handwritten addition. 'The opposition between ... spiritualism.)': from *Senilia*, 88.

7 In the footnote, three sentences 'For that reason we should never ... the owl by day' are a handwritten addition to A.

8 'since I have solved the problem ... immediate and thus ultimate': handwritten addition to A.

9 'hence the moral significance of the world and of existence is more firmly established than ever': handwritten addition to A.

10 Four sentences 'In particular, he has used the natural science ... new departures': handwritten addition to A.

11 'a mere fantasy': handwritten revision. In A: 'a mere metaphysical fantasy'.

12 Two sentences 'The only reason why the professors ... really quite specific': handwritten addition to A.

FRAGMENTS FOR THE HISTORY OF PHILOSOPHY

1 Two sentences 'However, it may be the case ... p. 504)': handwritten addition to A.

2 'Egyptians, Pythagoreans, and Empedocles ... Pythagorean wisdom': handwritten addition to A.

3 A long passage across four paragraphs, 'He also took over his more important basic astronomical ... instructed by the Brahmans themselves': handwritten addition to A.

4 'for how should there be a god in heaven when there is no heaven?': handwritten addition to A.

5 Three sentences 'Sincere *theism* ... thus not believed in' and 'Accordingly, to the degree ... solemn prompting': handwritten addition to A.

6 Footnote is a handwritten addition to A.

7 Three sentences 'Therefore, *logos spermatikos* ... form into appearance': handwritten addition to A.

8 This paragraph 'A principal source ... writings of Seneca': handwritten addition to A.

9 'However, people now want to dispute ... Neoplatonist school': handwritten addition to A.

10 'after the animal spirits ... would be of no further use', and footnote: handwritten additions to A.

11 Six sentences 'This latter identification was really a mere method ... mystify his students.)': handwritten addition to A.

12 Three sentences 'So now a certain ambiguity ... "The cowl does not make the monk"': handwritten addition to A.

13 This paragraph 'The fact that Spinoza ... properly ventilated': handwritten addition to A.

14 The passage from the beginning of this paragraph '*Leibniz* also ...' to '... be that as it may' is a handwritten revision. In A: 'Leibniz for his part also had to do with substances, of which, however, he assumed a multiplicity, but they were such as to be now extended, now thinking, and also both at the same time, according to circumstances – called monads.'

15 'Leibniz, on the other hand ... he recalled': handwritten revision. In A: 'Leibniz, on the other hand, recalled'.

16 'Kant's as well as my own doctrine': handwritten revision. In A: 'my own doctrine'.

17 Two sentences 'For already underlying ... a positive *force*': handwritten addition to A.

18 This paragraph 'But in general we see ... "simplicity is the seal of truth"': handwritten addition to A.

19 This paragraph 'The *dianoiology* ... is interesting as a type': an addition to A, from *Spicilegia*, 437.

20 This paragraph 'As the motto ... all things"': handwritten addition to A.

21 Two sentences '*Transcendental* is that ... towards its origin': handwritten addition to A.

22 Footnote: handwritten addition to A.

23 Footnote is an addition to A. 'Just as it is our eye ... *matter*)' from *Spicilegia*, 444. 'My intuition ... together with x' from *Senilia*, 34.

24 'We should compare this ... this pseudo-philosopher': handwritten addition to A.

25 Footnote: handwritten addition to A.

26 Footnote: handwritten addition to A.

27 This paragraph 'In regard to the proofs ... apply them to the former': handwritten addition to A.

28 Footnote: addition to A, from *Senilia*, 68.

29 'One can find the ontological proof ... I refer to here': handwritten addition to A.

30 Two sentences 'Hence the theoretical ... not a straw's breadth further': handwritten addition to A.

31 Footnote: addition to A, similar to a passage in *Senilia*, 98.

32 'three hundred and seventy million': handwritten revision. In A: 'three hundred million'

33 'This is also confirmed ... one that wills with cognition': handwritten addition to A.

34 'Thus let us get rid of the jargon of the philosophy professors!': handwritten addition to A. 'There is no other God ... Joshua': added to A, from *Senilia*, 5. Footnote added to A, from *Senilia*, 94.

35 'Human beings prefer ... main pillars of theism': addition to A, from *Senilia*, 97. The preceding clause 'and also in regard to their eternal salvation' is a handwritten addition to A.

36 'In accordance with this ... from the new God': handwritten addition to A.

37 This paragraph 'Closely related to the true origin ... (Ibid., p. 432)': handwritten addition to A.

38 'Already Vauvenargues says ... p. 331.)': handwritten addition to A.

39 This long footnote is a composite from various handwritten sources: *Spicilegia*, 451, 445, 452; *Senilia*, 10.

40 'Obviously he portrays ... and Shiva their demise': handwritten addition to A.

41 'despised by all ... existence after death': handwritten revision. In A: 'held in low esteem'.

42 Two sentences 'The moral results ... turn to my philosophy': addition to A, from *Senilia*, 79.

43 Four sentences 'However, if one wanted to hold ... (*On Mind* IV, 7)': handwritten addition to A.

44 Final sentence 'But now the man ... which face now to put on': handwritten addition to A.

ON UNIVERSITY PHILOSOPHY

1 Footnote: addition to A. 'It is quite natural ... influence I work against' from *Senilia*, 47. 'I have sought truth ... more with time' from *Senilia*, 76.

2 Four sentences 'The private lecturer *Fischer* . . . making fun of philosophy professors': handwritten addition to A.

3 Seven sentences added to A. 'In and of itself . . . proved by *neo-Catholicism*': handwritten addition. 'For *German* or *neo-Catholicism* is nothing . . . vol. 3, 1856' from *Senilia*, 98.

4 Five sentences 'But it was these purposes of state . . . philistinism': handwritten addition to A.

5 Two sentences 'It never occurs to a philosophy professor . . . Afterwards he decides its fate': handwritten addition to A.

6 'Accordingly, the relation . . . and paid prostitutes': handwritten addition to A.

7 Three sentences with quotations from Stobaeus, Xenophon and Ulpian 'Stobaeus reports that the Stoics . . . *cognitione* 50, 13)': handwritten addition to A.

8 'For that reason, beards flourished . . . pains to imitate': addition to A, from *Senilia*, 53. Footnote: handwritten addition to A.

9 Footnote: addition to A, from *Spicilegia* (1848), 403.

10 'They are the ones who Giordano Bruno . . . vol. 2, p. 83)': handwritten addition to A.

11 'In executing this . . . between two stools' and footnote: handwritten additions to A.

12 'Every professor of philosophy . . . his principal and chief profession': handwritten addition to A.

13 'There is also a passage . . . can achieve nothing': editor's insertion. Schopenhauer's handwritten addition to A reads: 'Passage in Sadi, *Gulistan*, that whoever has to struggle for his livelihood can achieve nothing.'

14 'It is not necessary at all . . . rest of their lives': handwritten addition to A.

15 'Moreover, reading the original works . . . in its own way': handwritten addition to A.

TRANSCENDENT SPECULATION ON THE APPARENT DELIBERATENESS IN THE FATE OF THE INDIVIDUAL

1 Footnote: handwritten addition to A.

2 From previous sentence 'the same way that in tragedies . . .' to 'Herodotus, chs. 35–43': handwritten addition to A.

3 Footnote: handwritten addition to A.

4 'Indeed, reflecting . . . This transcendent fatalism has': handwritten revision. In A: 'and has'.

5 Footnote: addition to A, from *Senilia*, 12.

6 'From this point of view . . . which rules chance itself': handwritten addition to A.

7 Five sentences 'The ancients do not tire . . . superficial and false' and footnote: handwritten additions to A.

8 Four sentences 'At the end of the *Republic* . . . bound by necessity': handwritten addition to A.

9 Footnote: handwritten addition to A.

10 Footnote: handwritten addition to A.

11 Three sentences 'On this rests the accidental occurrence ... true type of the human form': handwritten addition to A.

12 'The ineradicable tendency of humans ... secret code': handwritten addition to A.

13 Footnote: handwritten addition to A.

14 Two sentences: 'It is a big dream ... compatible with one another': handwritten addition to A.

15 'by explaining the inevitability ... pass off an omen as a miracle': handwritten revision. In A: 'by demonstrating its natural and necessarily acting causes clearly; for no rational human being doubts these'.

16 'so that above all we should remind ... (*Hamlet*, Act I, scene 5)': handwritten addition to A.

ESSAY ON SPIRIT-SEEING AND RELATED ISSUES

1 Two sentences 'Our ability to represent ... choose the object of our dreams': addition to A, from *Spicilegia*, 274.

2 'The totally unexpected quality ... objectivity and reality': handwritten addition to A.

3 'The same omniscience ... with their character': handwritten addition to A.

4 'On the whole, the intuition ... to a small degree': addition to A, from *Spicilegia*, 435.

5 'it looks as if they had intentionally ... were thinking least' and 'Therefore': handwritten additions to A.

6 'indeed an object that is often so far-fetched ... by lot or dice': handwritten addition to A.

7 Footnote: handwritten addition to A.

8 Footnote: addition to A, from *Senilia*, 61.

9 'whereupon she dreams these objects ... pp. 449–52)': handwritten addition to A.

10 Footnote: addition to A, from *Senilia*, 16.

11 'Since we actually see in a dream ... Bipont edition)': handwritten addition to A.

12 'and in the whole of ancient history ... rare exceptions': handwritten revision. In A: 'nonetheless only as rare exceptions'

13 Thirteen sentences, recounting Schopenhauer's anecdote, 'I shall record it here ... p. 62)': handwritten addition to A.

14 Footnote: handwritten addition to A.

15 This paragraph 'Here then it is important ... Herodotus IV, 155': handwritten addition to A.

16 'If magnetism has ... towards the afflicted part': handwritten addition to A.

17 'clairvoyance': Schopenhauer uses *die Clairvoyance* in A, *das Hellsehn* in handwritten revision.

18 'Belief in ghosts ... completely free of it': handwritten addition to A.

19 'crudest': *roheste*, handwritten revision. In A: *pöbelhafteste*, 'most rabble-like'.

20 Footnote: handwritten addition to A.

21 Footnote: handwritten addition to A.

22 Three sentences 'For a "living" ... simony in the world': handwritten addition to A.

23 Four sentences 'Therefore, the influence of clerics ... ruled by parsons', and the preceding clause 'in accordance with the maxim "When good taste appears, common sense retreats"': handwritten addition to A.

24 'Even among the negroes of the Sahara ... London 1853)': handwritten addition to A.

25 'Merck's *Travel Reminiscences* ... deceased donor': handwritten addition to A.

26 'Here what one person dreams ... p. 561': handwritten addition to A.

27 Three sentences 'Owing to this dilemma ... more common with Protestants than Catholics': handwritten addition to A.

28 'That the Chinese share the same idea ... 1834': handwritten addition to A.

29 'Just as two people sometimes have ... objectively as a body': handwritten addition to A.

30 Two sentences 'As is well known, the highest degree ... is fast asleep': handwritten addition to A.

31 Three sentences 'The same is recounted by Ennemoser ... competent witnesses': Hübscher's editorial addition on the basis of Schopenhauer's handwritten note in A: 'The same is recounted by Ennemoser about a somnambulist, Kachler: on this a paper in *Philosophari* [from where Hübscher supplies Ennemoser's text]. In London too the same happened with the somnambulist Prudence Bernard in a public session and in the presence of selected, competent witnesses (Brewster's son): on this likewise a paper in *Philosophari.*' Schopenhauer uses the extract on Bernard at *WN*, 409 (see Hübscher *SW* 4, 104).

32 These two paragraphs 'In any case ... somebody deceased could do it', and 'Ultimately, in explaining ... messages from a deceased': handwritten additions to A.

APHORISMS ON THE WISDOM OF LIFE

1 Two sentences added to A. 'All the advantages of rank ... kings in real life' from *Senilia*, 53. 'Metrodorus ... *Opera Polemica*': handwritten addition.

2 'This becomes apparent ... great and beautiful': handwritten addition to A.

3 Four sentences 'On stage, one actor ... the role we play': handwritten addition to A.

4 Six sentences 'No one can escape his individuality... on an inborn capacity': handwritten addition to A.

5 This paragraph 'A person possessing ... not possess': handwritten addition to A.

6 Seven sentences 'Without proper daily exercise ... *eo magis motis*': handwritten addition to A.

7 'If the "hard-to-please" ... one success': handwritten addition to A.

8 Footnote: addition to A, from *Spicilegia*, 449.

9 Footnote: handwritten addition to A.

10 Seven sentences 'That limited minds are so much subject ... substitute for thoughts' added to A, from *Senilia*, 137. Preceding passages 'How utterly worthless ... *making use of* it': handwritten additions to A, except for the reference to Ariosto.

11 Three sentences 'But for that very reason ... of this every day': handwritten addition to A.

12 'Or as *Oliver Goldsmith* says' and quotation: handwritten addition to A.

13 'Hence it was a wise statement ... ch. 10)': handwritten addition to A.

14 Footnote: handwritten addition to A.

15 'It is a great folly ... to the other side': addition to A, from *Spicilegia*, 460.

16 'This Aristotelian doctrine ... any kind of excellence': handwritten addition to A.

17 Footnote: addition to A, from *Spicilegia*, 457.

18 Footnote: addition to A, from *Senilia*, 143.

19 'And such an intellectual life ...pernicious consequences': handwritten addition to A; following sentence revised, adding 'bad company and'.

20 'Our moral virtues ... objects of hate': handwritten addition to A.

21 'When somebody is destined to impress ... from doing so', and 'For the leisure of each person ... himself is worth': handwritten additions to A.

22 'The philosophers of the Old Testament ... Qoheleth, 1:18)': handwritten addition to A.

23 This paragraph 'A great affliction ... innocuous': addition to A, from *Spicilegia*, 436.

24 'Wealth resembles sea water ... true of fame': addition to A from *Senilia*, 52.

25 This paragraph 'Among a race so poor ... philosophy professors': addition to A, from *Spicilegia*, 468.

26 '*Existing assets* ... pleasures of the world': handwritten addition to A.

27 'On the other hand, Dr Johnson ... age 67)': handwritten addition to A.

28 'then is doubly endowed by fate and': handwritten addition to A.

29 'Innumerable people ... oppressed them': handwritten addition to A.

30 'As inevitably as a cat ... palpable lie': addition to A, from *Senilia*, 79.

31 Footnote: handwritten addition to A.

32 Footnote: handwritten addition to A.

33 'But vain people ... things to say': handwritten addition to A.

34 Two sentences 'Civic honour may take its name ... fail to appear': handwritten addition to A.

35 In A here: 'I have nothing to say about official honour, which is sufficiently familiar'. The next three paragraphs, to '... due to the office itself' are handwritten additions to A, from *Adversaria*, 114.

36 'Moreover, such a morganatic ... concede a thing': handwritten addition to A.

37 Four sentences 'Here we also find ... follow immediately': handwritten addition to A.

38 'Whatever stupid ... legitimize it': handwritten addition to A.

39 'And when, for example ... they leave in triumph': handwritten addition to A.

40 Footnote: addition to A, from *Adversaria*, 124.

41 'Stobaeus . . . rejected even that': handwritten addition to A.

42 'Seneca, in his . . . it had happened"': handwritten addition to A.

43 This footnote, and the one shortly above: handwritten additions to A.

44 Footnote: handwritten addition to A.

45 'which probably does not derive . . . "complaint"': handwritten addition to A.

46 'Since Cupid's quiver . . . between the sexes': handwritten revision. In A: 'It has brought a foreign, hostile, indeed diabolical element into the relation between the sexes'.

47 Six sentences 'To all intents and purposes . . . with their blood': handwritten addition to A.

48 'The noblest deed . . . for all times': handwritten addition to A.

49 Footnote: handwritten addition to A.

50 Footnote: addition to A, from *Spicilegia*, 449.

51 'And the incidental remark . . . with respect to him': handwritten addition to A.

52 'In old age there is . . . *together with* us': addition to A, from *Senilia*, 61.

53 'However, it is also in accordance . . . *Epistles* I, 11, 27)': handwritten addition to A (citation added by Frauenstädt).

54 'The Latin version . . . not enjoyment': handwritten addition to A.

55 This paragraph 'But those who have fully absorbed . . . Anwari Soheili': handwritten addition to A.

56 'often at the most unimportant, most trivial . . . in large quantities', and six sentences 'It is the same with sorrow . . . human dealings': handwritten additions to A.

57 This paragraph 'If we wish . . . them at all': handwritten addition to A.

58 'perspective of the will [*Willensseite*]': handwritten revision. In A: 'ethical perspective [*ethische Seite*]'.

59 This paragraph 'Just as the wanderer . . . but only much later': handwritten addition to A.

60 'Accordingly . . . even the *monotony*': handwritten revision. In A: 'Likewise, the *monotony*'.

61 '(This is essentially . . . motto to this treatise)': handwritten addition to A.

62 'No path to happiness . . . deception', handwritten addition to A. Footnote: addition to A, from *Spicilegia*, 441.

63 'What spoils society . . . of others': addition to A, from *Senilia*, 47.

64 'Ingenious discourse . . . and narrow-minded': handwritten addition to A.

65 'because usually people are insolvent . . . gets a good deal': handwritten addition to A.

66 'The less a person . . . the better off he is': addition to A, from *Spicilegia*, 463. '*Solitude* and desolation . . . peace of mind', from *Spicilegia*, 460.

67 Footnote: addition to A. First two sentences 'As is well known . . . together' handwritten addition to A. Remainder from *Spicilegia*, 468.

68 '*Sociability* belongs . . . dull or perverted': handwritten addition to A.

69 'and because peace of mind, which . . . solitude': handwritten addition to A.

70 Footnote: handwritten addition to A.

71 'But that a human being . . . comes to understand': handwritten revision. In A: 'But a human being of a nobler and more elevated kind comes, over the years, to understand'.

72 Two sentences 'For the great minds, who have come into the world . . . common vulgarity': handwritten addition to A.

73 'Loneliness . . . lesser of two evils': handwritten addition to A.

74 'indeed, the asexuality of old age . . . drive in general': handwritten addition to A.

75 Footnote: addition to A, from *Spicilegia* 460.

76 This paragraph 'There are three aristocracies . . . of the others': addition to A, from *Senilia*, 32, 33.

77 'And we should not . . . with our own self': handwritten addition to A.

78 'Every day is a small life . . . as the birth pangs': addition to A, from *Senilia*, 137.

79 This paragraph 'Just as small objects . . . tendency', and end of previous paragraph 'Also relevant here is the fact . . . as possible': handwritten additions to A.

80 'In fact, it is even beneficial . . . did not happen': handwritten addition to A.

81 '"Life consists in movement" . . . hence better' and 'Consequently': handwritten addition to A.

82 'in the second chapter': handwritten revision. In A: 'in the introduction'.

83 Four sentences 'For the motor nerves are . . . blood to the brain': handwritten addition to A.

84 'for sleep is for the entire human being . . . a clock', 'This measure . . . p. 247)': handwritten additions to A. Footnote: addition from *Senilia*, 51.

85 Two paragraphs 'Neglect of the advice . . . Voltaire', and 'Every month . . . our mental states', and part of preceding paragraph 'We should accustom ourselves to regard . . . to do so': handwritten additions to A.

86 This paragraph 'To get through life . . . disputes and quarrels': handwritten addition to A.

87 'It is really curious to witness . . . in a previous life': handwritten addition to A.

88 'Lacking such . . . subjective one is chosen' and the previous two sentences 'How much the uniformity . . . harmony of spirits': handwritten additions to A.

89 'Everyone sees in the other only as much as he is himself' and 'for': handwritten additions to A.

90 The seven sentences 'Hence they are so easily distracted . . . flattered and won over' are mostly a handwritten revision. In A: 'Hence they are so easily distracted, so easily insulted, or offended, and also so easily flattered and won over'. The final clause of this paragraph is also lacking in A, and there are numerous small handwritten revisions to A.

91 This paragraph '*Astrology* provides . . . p. 478)': addition to A, from *Senilia*, 86.

92 '*Superiority* in dealing . . . make this known': addition to A, from *Senilia*, 5.

93 Three sentences 'And we should not miss such an opportunity . . . without risk': handwritten addition to A. Footnote added from *Senilia*, 16.

94 'To forgive and forget means throwing precious experiences out of the window': handwritten addition to A.

95 'someone can forget everything, everything, but not himself, his own essence': handwritten addition to A.

96 Two sentences 'Therefore, to make up ... we take on again': handwritten addition to A.

97 Two sentences 'However, no trait ... mineral': addition to A, from *Spicilegia*, 456.

98 Four sentences 'Do we not see ... Germans should take heed': handwritten addition to A.

99 'And finally, it does not hold good ... *On Mercy*, I, 1)': handwritten addition to A.

100 This paragraph 'The same rule ... motto', and most of the preceding paragraph 'Whoever finds fault with others ... in order to improve': addition to A, from *Senilia*, 6.

101 'In any event, I attach more value to the tail-wagging ... gestures': handwritten addition to A.

102 'There are few things that put people ... How characteristic!': addition to A, from *Spicilegia*, 461.

103 'Hence Goethe's dictum ... scene 4)', and paragraph '*House friends* ... cats than dogs': handwritten additions to A.

104 'What exactly happens is this: ... p. 287)': handwritten addition to A. Parenthetical publication details added by Frauenstädt. Reference to *WWR* 2 above also added by Frauenstädt.

105 Footnote: addition to A, from *Senilia*, 105.

106 Four sentences 'Therefore, whereas rank and wealth ... distaste of the ignorant"': handwritten addition to A.

107 Footnote: addition to A, from *Spicilegia*, 465.

108 'Anyone who has entered ... unscathed': handwritten addition to A.

109 'Gesturing politely ... without immediate danger': handwritten addition to A.

110 'Whatever form human life ... in the army': handwritten addition to A.

111 'There is something wiser within us than the mind': handwritten addition to A.

112 'Perhaps that inner impulse ... we would perish': handwritten addition to A. 'It is difficult to act ... unhappiness': addition from *Senilia*, 10.

113 Footnote: addition to A, from *Cogitata*, 13.

114 Two sentences, and part of preceding sentence 'in accordance with which we should never forget ... endure them': handwritten addition to A.

115 'willingly': handwritten addition to A.

116 Two sentences 'In the face of the daily troubles ... ruminations': handwritten addition to A.

117 Three sentences 'We see all things and persons ... and in old age': handwritten addition to A.

118 Footnote: handwritten addition to A.

119 Two sentences 'So in our youth ... achieved in the world': handwritten addition to A. Beginning of the next sentence 'But the opposite happens, because': handwritten revision. In A: 'And it certainly contributes to this that'.

120 'This depends on the fact ... in little things': handwritten addition to A.

121 This paragraph 'When we are young ... hardly noticed': handwritten addition to A.

122 This paragraph 'In *young people* . . . of nature': addition to A, from *Senilia*, 61.

123 Three sentences 'People may tell us . . . to the gallows': handwritten addition to A.

124 'When life draws to a close, we do not know where it has gone': handwritten addition to A.

125 Five sentences 'Moreover, memory and fantasy . . . object and subject': handwritten addition to A.

126 This paragraph 'In order to reach a great age . . . fashion': handwritten addition to A.

127 Three sentences 'The older we become . . . whether we have done it': handwritten addition to A.

128 Seven sentences 'The difference in the pace of time . . . beasts that have grown old': handwritten addition to A.

129 'Only *someone who grows old* . . . still to come': addition to A, from *Spicilegia*, 442. Above in this paragraph 'Everything has become clear': handwritten addition to A; 'What we thought we knew in our youth, we really know in old age': addition, from *Spicilegia*, 437.

130 Footnote: handwritten addition to A.

131 'But it is most curious that . . . what we have in ourselves': handwritten addition to A.

132 'In old age we are better able . . . endure them': handwritten addition to A.

133 Six sentences 'We might even assert that . . . wearing their clothes': handwritten addition to A.

134 'Accordingly, whereas the young . . . may be gilded': handwritten addition to A.

135 'and have also, more or less, come to the insight . . . distinguishes them from the young': handwritten addition to A. In next sentence 'But primarily this all leads to peace of mind [*Geistesruhe*]': handwritten revision. In A: 'This all leads to peace [*Ruhe*]'.

136 This paragraph 'Only at a later age . . . benefit to him than in old age': handwritten addition to A.

137 Footnote: addition to A, from three sources. 'Human life . . . lengths of time' from *Senilia*, 133. 'The *Upanishads* . . . prematurely' from *Spicilegia*, 435. 'In the Old Testament . . . a hundred years' from *Senilia*, 24.

138 This paragraph 'For however long we might live . . . whole emerges': handwritten addition to A.

139 'Life during the years of old age . . . which one it will be': addition to A, from *Spicilegia*, 448.

140 'and whether on the whole life is not . . . says the Spanish proverb': handwritten addition to A.

141 In the footnote: 'fifty . . . discovered since' is a handwritten revision. In A: 'six . . . discovered recently'.

142 'and death is the great reservoir of life': handwritten addition to A.

Glossary of names

ADAM, figure from the Hebrew Bible, first man

ADRASTUS, son of Gordias, king of Phrygia, in Herodotus' story of Croesus

AELIAN (Aelianus), CLAUDIUS (*c*.175–*c*.235), Roman author and teacher of rhetoric

AHRIMAN, Middle Persian equivalent of Angra Mainyu, Zoroastrian evil spirit

ALEMÁN, Mateo (1547–1615), Spanish novelist, author of *Guzmán de Alfarache*

ALEXANDER THE GREAT (356–323 BC), king of Macedon, supreme military commander

ALTENSTEIN, KARL FREIHERR VOM STEIN ZUM (1770–1840), Prussian statesman

AMMONIUS SACCAS (175–242), Neoplatonist philosopher

ANAXAGORAS (*c*.500–428 BC), Presocratic Greek philosopher

ANAXIMENES (sixth century BC) Presocratic Greek philosopher

ANGELUS SILESIUS (Johannes Scheffler) (1624–77), German mystic and poet

ANSELM OF CANTERBURY, SAINT (1033–1109), philosopher, theologian and Archbishop of Canterbury, developer of the ontological proof

APOLLONIUS OF TYANA (*c*.15–*c*.100), neo-Pythagorean philosopher and preacher

APULEIUS, LUCIUS (second century), Roman writer

ARCESILAUS III (fl. sixth century BC), King of Cyrene, described in Herodotus' *Histories*

ARIOSTO, LUDOVICO (1474–1533), Italian poet

ARISTIPPUS (*c*.435–356 BC), follower of Socrates, founder of the Cyrenaic school of philosophy

ARISTOPHANES (446–386 BC), Greek comic playwright

450

ARISTOTLE (384–322 BC), the great and immensely influential Greek philosopher

ARRIAN (Lucius Flavius Arrianus) (*c.*86–160), philosopher, historian and military commander

ARTEMIDORUS DALDIANUS (or Ephesius) (second century), author of *Oneirocritica* (*Interpretation of Dreams*)

ASMUS, see Claudius, Matthias

ATTERBOM, PER DANIEL AMADEUS (1790–1855), poet, writer on Swedish legends

AUGUSTINE, SAINT (353–430), Church Father, Bishop of Hippo

BACCHUS (Dionysus), Graeco-Roman god of wine and madness

BACON [of Verulam], LORD FRANCIS (1591–1626), English philosopher, statesman, scientist, lawyer

BAYLE, PIERRE (1647–1706), French writer of the Enlightenment, author of *Dictionnaire Historique et Critique* (*Historical and Critical Dictionary*)

BEATTIE, JAMES (1735–1803), Scottish poet, author of 'The Minstrel, or the Progress of Genius'

BEAUMONT, JOHN (*c.*1650–1731), English physician and geologist, author of *Historical–physiological and Theological Treatise of Spirits, Apparitions, Witchcrafts, and Other Magical Practices* (1705)

BEETHOVEN, LUDWIG VAN (1770–1827), German composer

BELL, ANDREW (1753–1832), Scottish Episcopalian priest and educationalist

BENDSEN, BENDE (1787–1875), writer, practitioner of magnetism

BERESFORD, JAMES (1764–1840), writer and clergyman, author of *The Miseries of Human Life* (1806)

BERKELEY, GEORGE (1685–1753), Bishop, Irish philosopher and proponent of idealism

BERNARDIN DE SAINT-PIERRE, JACQUES-HENRI (1737–1814), leading figure of the late French Enlightenment

BOHLEN, PETER VON (1796–1840), orientalist and Bible critic, professor in Heidelberg

BÖHME, JAKOB (1575–1624), Lutheran mystic and theosophist born in Silesia

BOSWELL, JAMES (1740–95), lawyer, diarist, biographer of Samuel Johnson

BOTTOM, NICK, a weaver, character in Shakespeare's *A Midsummer Night's Dream*

BRAHMA, Hindu god of creation, one of the Trimurti

BREWSTER JR., DAVID, son of Sir David Brewster, author of *Briefe über natürliche Magie* (1831)

BRIERRE (Brière) DE BOISMONT, ALEXANDRE JACQUES FRANÇOIS (1797–1881), French physician and psychiatrist

BRUCKER, JOHANN JAKOB (1696–1770), German pastor and historian of philosophy

BRUNO, GIORDANO (1548–1600), Italian philosopher of nature, burned to death as a heretic

BRUTUS, MARCUS JUNIUS (85–42 BC), Roman politician, involved in assassination of Julius Caesar

BUCHANAN-HAMILTON, FRANCIS (1762–1829), Scottish physicist, author of 'On the religion and literature of the Burmas'

BUCHHOLZ, PAUL FERDINAND FRIEDRICH (1768–1843), writer, possible author of 'Cabinet of Berlin Characters'

BURDACH, KARL FRIEDRICH (1776–1847), physiologist and professor of anatomy and physiology in Königsberg

BÜRGER, GOTTFRIED AUGUST (1747–94), German jurist and poet, said to have created the German ballad

BYRON, LORD GEORGE GORDON (1788–1824), British Romantic poet

CABANIS, PIERRE JEAN GEORGES (1757–1808), French physiologist, proponent of materialist view of consciousness

CALDERÓN DE LA BARCA, DON PEDRO (1600–81), Spanish dramatist

CARDANUS, HIERONYMUS (Girolamo Cardano) (1501–76), Italian Renaissance mathematician, physician, astrologer, author of *De utilitate ex adversis capienda* (1561)

CASSIUS PARMENSIS, GAIUS (died 30 BC), Roman military tribune in the army of Brutus and Cassius

CASTOR, twin brother of Pollux in Greek and Roman mythology

CATO UTICENSIS, MARCUS PORCIUS (95–47 BC), Roman statesman, opponent of Julius Caesar, committed suicide

CAZOTTE, JACQUES (1719–92), French writer, follower of mysticism

CERVANTES, MIGUEL DE (Miguel de Cervantes Saavedra) (1547–1616), Spanish novelist, poet and playwright, author of *Don Quixote*

CHAMFORT, NICOLAS (1741–94), French aphorist

CHARLES V (1500–58), King of Spain, Holy Roman Emperor

CHEOPS (Khufu) (ruled *c.*2580 BC), Egyptian pharaoh

CHLODOWIG I (*c.*402–37), King of the Franks

CHRISTINA, QUEEN OF SWEDEN (1626–89), reigned 1632–54

CHRYSIPPUS (*c.*280–*c.*206 BC), Greek philosopher, head of the early Stoic school in Athens

CICERO, MARCUS TULLIUS (106–43 BC), pre-eminent Roman statesman and orator, who composed the first substantial body of philosophical work in Latin

CLAUDIUS, MATTHIAS (pen-name Asmus) (1740–1815), German poet

CLEANTHES (331–323 BC), Stoic philosopher and head of the Stoic school in Athens

CLEMENT OF ALEXANDRIA (*c.*150–215), Christian Platonist philosopher

COLEBROOKE, HENRY THOMAS (1765–1837), English Indologist, translator of the *Upanishads*

COLEMAN, CHARLES, author of *The Mythology of the Hindus* (1832)

COLERUS, JOHANN CHRISTOPH (1691–1736), biographer of Spinoza

COLUMBUS, CHRISTOPHER (Cristóbal Colón) (1451–1506), Genoese-born explorer who made discoveries in the Americas

CONDILLAC, ETIENNE BONNOT DE (1715–80), French philosopher of the Enlightenment period and popularizer of Locke's ideas in France

CONSTANTINE THE GREAT (Flavius Valerius Aurelius Constantinus) (*c.*274–337), Roman emperor

COPERNICUS, NICOLAUS (1473–1543), Polish astronomer whose theories revolutionized the study of the solar system

CORDIER, PIERRE LOUIS ANTOINE (1777–1861), French geologist and mineralogist

CORNEILLE, PIERRE (1606–84), French dramatist, one of the founders of French tragedy

CRATES OF THEBES (fl. fourth century BC), Cynic philosopher, a pupil of Diogenes

CROESUS (*c.*595–547 BC), King of Lydia, of legendary wealth, defeated by the Persians

CRUSOE, ROBINSON, character in the novel of the same name (1719) by Daniel Defoe

CUPID, Roman god of love

D'ALEMBERT, JEAN LE ROND (1717–83), French philosopher and mathematician

DANTE ALIGHIERI (1265–1321), Italian poet, author of the great trilogy *La Divina Commedia* (*The Divine Comedy*)

DAVID (*c.*1040–970 BC), biblical king of Israel

DELEUZE, JOSEPH PHILIPPE FRANÇOIS (1753–1835), natural scientist, writer on animal magnetism

DEMOCRITUS (*c.*460–370 BC), Presocratic philosopher, principal proponent of ancient atomism

DESCARTES, RENÉ (1596–1650), French philosopher, important early modern rationalist philosopher who maintained a dualism between mind and body

DIDEROT, DENIS (1713–84), French philosopher, critic, mathematician and poet of the Enlightenment

DIODORUS SICULUS (fl. first century BC), Greek historian in Sicily

DIOGENES LAERTIUS (*c.*300–50), Athenian historian of ancient philosophy, whose work *The Lives and Opinions of Eminent Philosophers* is a rich source of knowledge about earlier thinkers

DIOGENES OF SINOPE (*c.*412–323 BC), Greek philosopher, Cynic

DIONYSIUS THE AREOPAGITE (first century), Greek judge who converted to Christianity

DIONYSUS, Greek god of wine, pleasure and festivity; also called Bacchus

DODD, DR WILLIAM (1729–77), doctor of divinity, executed at Tyburn for forgery

DONATUS, AELIUS (fl. mid-fourth century AD), Roman grammarian and teacher of rhetoric, teacher of St Jerome

DORGUTH, FRIEDRICH ANDREAS LUDWIG (1776–1854), judge in the court of appeals in Magdeburg, one of Schopenhauer's first adherents; Schopenhauer recognized his allegiance but considered him a 'troglodyte of philosophy'

DUPOTET, BARON (Jules Denis du Potet de Sennevoy) (1796–1881), French exponent of animal magnetism

DUTENS, LOUIS (1730–1812), French writer, editor of Leibniz's works

ECCLESIASTES, book of the Old Testament traditionally attributed to Solomon

EHRMANN, professor, son-in-law of the poet Pfeffel

EKENDAHL, DANIEL GEORG VON (1792–1857), writer on Scandinavia

ELEATIC SCHOOL, Greek school of philosophers, followers of Parmenides of Elea (early to mid-fifth century BC), who argued against plurality and motion

EMPEDOCLES (*c.*495–*c.*435 BC), Greek philosopher, important for his cosmology

ENDOR, WITCH OF, a female sorcerer in the Hebrew Old Testament

ENNEMOSER, JOSEPH (1787–1854), Tyrolean physician, author of manual on mesmeric practice (1852)

EPICHARMUS (550–460 BC), Greek writer of comedies in Sicilian Doric dialect

EPICTETUS (*c.*55–*c.*135), Greek Stoic philosopher

EPICURUS (341–270 BC), Greek philosopher, founder of the important school of Epicureanism

ERASMUS OF ROTTERDAM, DESIDERIUS (1467?–1536), humanist of the Northern Renaissance

ERIGENA, JOHANNES SCOTUS (*c.*800–*c.*877), Christian Neoplatonist philosopher

EROS, Greek god of love

ESQUIROL, (JEAN-)ÉTIENNE (Dominique) (1772–1840), French psychiatrist, author of a treatise on mental illness (1838)

EUPHRATES (*c*.35–118), Stoic philosopher

EUSEBIUS OF CAESAREA (*c*.263–*c*.339), called Father of Church History

FABIUS, EVERARDUS, author of a treatise on dreams (1836)

FEDER, JOHANN GEORG HEINRICH (1740–1821), professor at Göttingen, critic of Kant

FEUERBACH, PAUL JOHANN ANSELM VON (1775–1833), lawyer, one of the founders of modern German criminal law

FICHTE, JOHANN GOTTLIEB (1762–1814), German philosopher, one of the chief figures in German Idealism in the period immediately after Kant, author of the *Wissenschaftslehre* (*Science of Knowledge*) and *System der Sittenlehre* (*System of Moral Philosophy*). Schopenhauer attended Fichte's lectures in 1811–13, but describes him as a pompous and inferior thinker

FICINO, MARSILIO (1433–99), philosopher of the Italian Renaissance

FISCHER, FRIEDRICH, author of work on sleepwalking, animal magnetism and clairvoyance (1839)

FLOURENS, MARIE JEAN PIERRE (1794–1867), French physiologist and brain scientist

FONTENELLE, BERNARD LE BOVIER DE (1657–1757), French scientist and man of letters

FORMEY, JEAN HENRI SAMUEL (1711–97), Protestant minister and teacher, became secretary of the Academy of Berlin

FOURIER, JEAN BAPTISTE JOSEPH, BARON DE (1768–1830), French mathematician and physicist

FRANCIS I (1494–1547), King of France

FRANKLIN, BENJAMIN (1706–90), American author, scientist, and statesman; notorious philanderer, drinker, and author of moral platitudes, given to flying kites in thunderstorms

FRAUENSTÄDT, JULIUS (1813–79), Schopenhauer's associate and editor of the first complete edition of his works in 1873

FREDERICK THE GREAT (Friedrich II) (1712–86), King of Prussia

FREINSHEIM, JOHANN (1608–60), historian and philologist, editor of Livy's *History*

FRIES, JAKOB FRIEDRICH (1773–1843), professor of philosophy at Heidelberg and Jena; author of *System der Logic, ein Handbuch für Lehrer und zum Selbstgebrauch* (1807, 1819)

GALEN[US], CLAUDIUS (*c*.129–200), Roman physician

GALILEI, GALILEO (1564–1642), Italian astronomer

GASSENDI, PIERRE (1592–1655), French philosopher, scientist and scholar

GEDICKE (Gedike), FRIEDRICH (1754–1803), historian of philosophy

GELLERT, CHRISTIAN FÜRCHTEGOTT (1715–69), poet, professor of poetry and rhetoric in Leipzig

GELLIUS, AULUS (*c*.130), Roman grammarian

GLEDITSCH, JOHANN GOTTLIEB (1714–86), professor of botany in Berlin

GOETHE, JOHANN WOLFGANG VON (1749–1832), poet, dramatist and scholar in many fields, Germany's greatest writer and prominent Enlightenment figure. Schopenhauer knew Goethe in the period 1813–14 and collaborated with him over his theory of colours

GOLDSMITH, OLIVER (1730–74), Anglo-Irish writer and poet

GORDIAN(US), MARCUS ANTONIUS (192–238), Roman emperor for a reign of one month

GRACIÁN, BALTASAR (1601–58), Spanish philosophical writer, author of *El criticón* (1651, 1657); Schopenhauer's translation of *Oráculo manual y arte de prudencia* (1647) was edited posthumously by Frauenstädt and published as *Gracians Hand-orakel und Kunst der Weltklugheit* (1862)

GREGORY THE GREAT (Pope Gregory I) (*c*.540–604), Saint, traditionally known as the Father of Christian Worship

GROHMANN, JOHANN CHRISTIAN AUGUST (1769–1847), professor of philosophy in Hamburg

HAHN, COUNCILLOR, of Ingelfingen, wrote an account of clairvoyance in 1808

HALL, MARSHALL (1790–1857), English physician and physiologist

HAUSER, CASPAR (1812–33), a foundling of controversial origin, who claimed to have spent his life in solitary confinement; one with whose fate Schopenhauer identified

HEEREN, ARNOLD HERMANN LUDWIG (1760–1842), German historian, professor in Göttingen, teacher of Schopenhauer

HEGEL, GEORG WILHELM FRIEDRICH (1770–1831), German philosopher, leading figure in the movement of German Idealism, author of *Phänomenologie des Geistes* (*Phenomenology of Spirit*) and *Enzyklopädie der Philosopischen Wissenschaften* (*Encyclopedia of Philosophical Sciences*), professor of philosophy in Berlin and dominant intellectual figure in the first four decades of the nineteenth century. Consistently critized and satirized by Schopenhauer as a charlatan

HEINEKEN, JOHANN (1761–1851), professor of anatomy in Bremen

HELMONT, JOHANN BAPTISTE VAN (1577–1644), Dutch physician and natural scientist

HELVÉTIUS, CLAUDE ADRIEN (1715–71), philosopher of the French Enlightenment

HENNINGS, JUSTUS CHRISTIAN, author of a book on spirit-seeing (1780)

HENRY VIII (1491–1547), King of England

HERA, Greek goddess of marriage, queen of the gods

HERACLITUS (*c.*535–475 BC), Greek Presocratic philosopher

HERBART, JOHANN FRIEDRICH (1776–1841), professor of philosophy in Göttingen and elsewhere, opponent of Schopenhauer who reviewed the first edition of *The World as Will and Representation*, irritating Schopenhauer by claiming that his philosophy was a development of those of Fichte and Schelling

HERCULES, legendary Greek hero of great strength and prowess

HERODOTUS OF HALICARNASSUS (*c.*484–*c.*425 BC), ancient Greek historian and perhaps the first European historian

HERSCHEL, SIR JOHN FREDERIC WILLIAM (1792–1871), British physicist and astronomer, author of *Treatise on Astronomy* (1833) and *Outlines of Astronomy* (1849)

HIBBERT (Hibbert-Ware), SAMUEL (1742–1848), author of *Sketches of the Philosophy of Apparitions* (1824)

HICETAS (*c.*400–335 BC), Greek Pythagorean philosopher

HIPPARCHUS (190–*c.*120 BC), Greek mathematician and astronomer

HIPPOCRATES (*c.*450–*c.*380 BC), Greek physician

HOBBES, THOMAS (1588–1679), English philosopher

HOMER (fl. *c.*700 BC), the early ancient Greek poet, author of the epic poems the *Iliad* and the *Odyssey*

HOOKE, ROBERT (1635–1703), English natural philosopher and mathematician

HORACE (Quintus Horatius Flaccus) (65–8 BC), Roman poet, frequently quoted by Schopenhauer

HORST, GEORG CONRAD (1767–1838), spiritual privy counsellor, author of *Deuteroskopie* (1830), editor of *Zauberbibliothek* (1820–26)

HUME, DAVID (1711–76), Scottish philosopher, essayist and historian, often considered the greatest philosopher to write in English

HUTH, CASPAR JACOB (1711–60), editor of Leibniz's works

IAMBLICHUS (*c.*242–327), Greek philosopher, who unified Neoplatonism with polytheistic folk religions

JEHOVAH, the God of Israel in the Hebrew Bible

JEREMIAH, prophet of the Hebrew Old Testament

JESUS BEN SIRACH (Joshua ben Sira, also Ecclesiasticus), author of a book of the Old Testament, generally in Roman Catholic and Orthodox versions, but not in the Hebrew Bible

JOHNSON, SAMUEL (1709–84), English man of letters, lexicographer and subject of famous biography by James Boswell

JOSIAH (*c*.649–609 BC), biblical King of Judah

JULIEN, STANISLAS AIGNAN (1799–1873), sinologist, translator of the *Tao te King. Le livre de la voie et de la vertu* (1842)

JULIUS II (1443–1513), pope

JUNG-STILLING (Johann Heinrich Jung; assumed name Heinrich Stilling) (1740–1817), physician and writer

JUVENAL (Decimus Junius Juvenalis) (*c*.58–138), Roman satirist

KACHLER, AUGUSTE, medium and somnambulist in Dresden

KAMPE, FRIEDRICH FERDINAND (1852–3), author of history of religious movements

KANT, IMMANUEL (1724–1804), German philosopher, commonly considered the greatest philosopher of modern times, a view Schopenhauer shares. Author of *Kritik der reinen Vernunft* (*Critique of Pure Reason*) (1781 and 1787), *Grundlegung zur Metaphysik der Sitten* (*Groundwork to the Metaphysics of Morals*) (1785) and *Kritik der praktischen Vernunft* (*Critique of Practical Reason*) (1788) among other works, Kant is the most important single influence on Schopenhauer, who especially admires his resolution of the problem of freedom and necessity and his idealist account of space and time, but is highly critical of many aspects of Kant's philosophy

KARL AUGUST (1757–1828), Grand Duke of Saxony-Weimar-Eisenach

KEPLER, JOHANNES (1571–1630), German mathematician and astronomer, key figure in the Scientific Revolution

KERNER, JUSTINUS ANDREAS CHRISTIAN (1786–1862), German poet and spiritualist writer

KIESER, DIETRICH GEORG (1779–1862), physician and botanist, professor of medicine; author of *System des Tellurismus oder thierischen Magnetismus* (1826); editor of *Archiv für thierischen Magnetismus*

KNEBEL, KARL LUDWIG VON (1744–1834), poet, translator and friend of Goethe

KOTZEBUE, AUGUST FRIEDRICH FERDINAND VON (1761–1819), dramatist and author

KRUG, WILHELM TRAUGOTT (1770–1842), philosopher, Kant's successor in Königsberg

LA ROCHEFOUCAULD, FRANÇOIS DE (1613–80), French writer, famous for his *Maxims*

LABRUYÈRE, JEAN (de La Bruyère) (1645–96), French satirist

LANCASTER, JOSEPH (1778–1838), English educationalist

LANGLÈS, LOUIS MATHIEU (1763–1824), author of work on Hindustan (1821)

LAPLACE, PIERRE-SIMON (1749–1827), French mathematician and astronomer

LARRA, MARIANO JOSÉ DE (pseudonym Figaro) (1809–37), Spanish man of letters

LAVATER, LUDWIG (1741–1801), Swiss poet and physiognomist

LAYARD, SIR AUSTEN HENRY (1817–94), English diplomat and archaeologist

LECOMTE, PIERRE, executed in 1846

LEIBNIZ, GOTTFRIED WILHELM (1646–1716), German-born philosopher and mathematician, a leading figure in seventeenth-century intellectual life, best known for his *Monadology* (1714) and *Essays on Theodicy* (1710)

LESSING, GOTTHOLD EPHRAIM (1729–81), German Enlightenment philosopher, dramatist and art critic

LEUCIPPUS (5th century BC), ancient atomist philosopher

LICHTENBERG, GEORG CHRISTOPH (1742–99), German satirical writer, professor of philosophy at the University of Göttingen

LIVY (Titus Livius) (59 BC–AD 17), Roman historian

LOCKE, JOHN (1632–1704), English philosopher, important empiricist, author of *An Essay concerning Human Understanding*; Schopenhauer saw his own philosophy as stemming from Locke's mediated by Kant

LUCIAN (Lukianos) (born *c.*120), author of Greek satiric dialogues

LUCIUS VERATIUS, brutal individual who appears in *Attic Nights* by Aulus Gellius

LUCRETIA (died *c.*508 BC), semi-legendary figure in Roman history, her rape and suicide were the immediate cause of the revolution that overthrew the monarchy

LUCRETIUS (Titus Lucretius Carus) (99–55 BC), Roman poet and philosopher

MACLAURIN, COLIN (1698–1746), mathematician; professor at Aberdeen and Edinburgh; author of *Account of Sir Isaac Newton's philosophical Discoveries in four books* (1850)

MALEBRANCHE, NICOLAS (1638–1715), French theologian and Cartesian philosopher, author of *De la recherche de la vérité* (1674–5) and *Entretiens sur la métaphysique et sur la religion* (1688)

MARIVAUX, PIERRE CARLET DE CHAMBLAIN DE (1688–1763), French novelist and dramatist

MAUPERTUIS, PIERRE LOUIS MOREAU DE (1698–1759), French physicist and mathematician, president of the Berlin Academy

MELESIPPUS, son of Diacritus, member of Spartan delegation to Athens in 431 BC

MELISSUS (fifth century BC), Greek philosopher of the Eleatic school

MENANDER (342–290 BC), Greek comic playwright

MERCATUS, MICHAEL, friend of Marsilio Ficino

MERCK, ERNST VON (1811–63), merchant and travel writer

MERCK, JOHANN HEINRICH (1741–91), German military adviser, correspondent with literary figures

MESMER, FRANZ ANTON (1734–1815), founder of Mesmerism, an early form of hypnosis

METRODORUS OF LAMPSACUS (331–277 BC), Greek philosopher and major proponent of Epicureanism

MEYER, JOHANN GEORG, schoolmaster who looked after Caspar Hauser in Ansbach

MILLINGEN, JOHN GIDEON (1782–1862), army surgeon and author of *The History of Duelling* (1819)

MITTLER, character in Goethe's novel *The Elective Affinities* (*Die Wahlverwandschaften*, 1809)

MONTI, VINCENZO (1754–1828), Italian poet and dramatist

MORITZ, KARL PHILIPP (1757–93), German academic, author of *Anton Reiser* (1785–90)

MOZART, WOLFGANG AMADEUS (1756–91), Austrian composer

MÜLLER, AUGUSTE, somnambulist from Karlsruhe, recorded by Meier, *Höchst Merkwürdige Geschichte der Magnetisch Hellsehenden Auguste Müller* (1818)

MURATORI, LODOVICO ANTONIO (1672–1750), Italian historian

MUSONIUS (Gaius Musonius Rufus) (first century), Roman Stoic philosopher

MYLITTA , in Babylonian and Assyrian mythology, the goddess of love and fertility and war

NAPOLEON BONAPARTE (1769–1821), the great French military and political leader

NASSE, CHRISTIAN FRIEDRICH (1778–1851), German physician and professor, editor of *Zeitschrift für Anthropologie*

NEBUCHADNEZZAR II (*c.*605–562 BC), King of Babylon

NEOPLATONISTS (third to seventh centuries), a school of philosophers in late antiquity influenced by Platonism

NEWTON, ISAAC (1632–1727), the great English mathematician, physicist and astronomer, author of *Philosophiae naturalis principia mathematica* (1687) and *Opticks* (1704)

NICOLAI, CHRISTOPH FRIEDRICH (1733–1811), writer and bookseller in Berlin

OEDIPUS, in ancient Greek myth, king of Thebes

OENOPIDES (fifth century BC), Greek natural philosopher and astronomer

ORELLI, JOHANN KONRAD (1770–1826), editor of collections of ancient texts

ORMUZD, Middle Persian equivalent of Ahura Mazda, Zoroastrian deity, the one uncreated Creator

OSORIUS, HIERONYMUS (Jerónimo Osório) (1506–80), Portuguese author of *De Gloria*

OVID (Publius Ovidius Naso) (43 BC–AD 17/18), Roman poet

PAMINA, character in Mozart's *The Magic Flute*

PANCRITIUS, ALBRECHT, author of *Hägringar: Reise durch Schweden, Lappland, Norwegen und Dänemark* (1852)

PAPAGENA, character in *The Magic Flute*, matched with Papageno

PAPAGENO, bird-catcher, character in Mozart's *The Magic Flute*

PARACELSUS (Philippus Aureolus Theophrastus Bombastus von Hohenheim) (1493–1541), Swiss physician and natural philosopher

PARMENIDES OF ELEA (fifth century BC), Greek Presocratic philosopher, first of the Eleatic school

PAUSANIAS (fl. *c.*150), Greek travel writer

PELAGIUS (fl. *c.*400), initiator of a movement in Christian thought that emphasized free will as opposed to divine grace

PERIPATETICS, ancient Greek school of philosophy dating from about 335 BC, founded by Aristotle

PESTALOZZI, JOHANN HEINRICH (1746–1827), Swiss pedagogue and educational reformer

PETRARCH (Petrarca), FRANCESCO (1304–74), Italian poet and scholar

PETRONIUS (Titus Petronius Arbiter) (*c.*27–66), Roman courtier, assumed to be the author of the *Satiricon*

PFEFFEL, GOTTLIEB KONRAD (1736–1809), German poet and teacher

PHILO (of Alexandria, Philo Judaeus) (20 BC–AD 50), Hellenistic Jewish biblical philosopher

PHILO OF BYBLOS (Herennius Philon) (*c*.64–141), Greek antiquarian writer chiefly known for his Phoenician history

PHILOLAUS (*c*.480–*c*.385 BC), Greek Pythagorean, Presocratic philosopher

PHILOPONUS, JOHN (*c*.490–570), Christian philosopher, scientist and theologian

PHOTIUS I (*c*.810–93), Patriarch of Constantinople, statesman and scholar

PLATNER, ERNST (1744–1818), physician, philosopher and aesthetician, professor of physiology and philosophy at Leipzig

PLATO (427–347 BC), the great Greek philosopher of immense influence on subsequent philosophy, and one of the most important influences on Schopenhauer

PLINY THE YOUNGER (Gaius Plinius Caecilius Secundus) (*c*.61–112), Roman statesman and author

PLOTINUS (204–70), Neoplatonist philosopher

PLUTARCH (46–125), Graeco-Roman statesman and historian

POLLUX, twin brother of Castor in Greek and Roman mythology

POMPONATIUS, PETRUS (Pietro Pompanazzi) (1462–1524), Renaissance neo-Aristotelian philosopher

POPE, ALEXANDER (1688–1744), English poet

PORPHYRY (Porphyrius) (*c*.233–304), Neoplatonist philosopher, student of Plotinus

POUILLET, CLAUDE-SERVAIS-MATTHIAS (1790–1868), French physicist, known for his work *Eléments de physique expérimentale et de météorologie* (1827)

PRELLER, LUDWIG (1809–61), historian of philosophy

PRIESTLEY, JOSEPH (1733–1804), English theologian, philosopher and scientist

PROCLUS (412–85), Greek Neoplatonist philosopher and commentator on Plato

PROPERTIUS (*c*.50–*c*.15 BC), Roman poet

PROTEUS, Greek mythological figure, early sea god

PSEUDO-SOLOMON (*c*. first century BC), unidentified author of the *Book of Wisdom* (*Wisdom of Solomon*) in the Septuagint Old Testament

PTOLEMY (*c*.100–70), leading ancient astronomer

PUBLILIUS SYRUS (first century), Latin mime writer

PYTHAGORAS (*c*.570–*c*.497 BC), early Greek sage, founder of Pythagorean tradition in philosophy

PYTHAGOREANS, Greek philosophers, mathematics and music theorists in the tradition founded by Pythagoras

PYTHIA, THE, in ancient Greece, the priestess at Apollo's oracle in Delphi

QOHELETH (Koheleth), main speaker in the book of Ecclesiastes

REGNARD, JEAN-FRANÇOIS (1655–1709), French comic dramatist and travel diarist

REIL, JOHANN CHRISTIAN (1759–1813), German medical scientist

REINHOLD, CARL LEONHARD (1757–1823), professor of philosophy in Jena and Kiel, Kant's first great popularizer

RICHARDSON, S. JAMES (1809–51), explorer, author of *Narrative of a Mission to Central Africa* (1853)

RITTER, HEINRICH (1791–1869), historian of philosophy, taught in Berlin and Göttingen; co-author of *Historia Philosophiae Graeco-Romanae ex fontium locis contexta* (1838)

ROMANUS, CARL FRIEDRICH, author of a work on apparitions (1703)

ROSENKRANZ, JOHANN CARL FRIEDRICH (1805–79), professor in Königsberg, editor of edition of Kant's works (1838–40)

ROUSSEAU, JEAN JACQUES (1712–78), French writer of the Enlightenment

SADI (Musharrif-uddin Sa'di) (*c.*1213–92), Persian poet and popular writer

SALAT, JACOB (1766–1851), theologian, philosopher, professor in Munich

SAMUEL, leader of ancient Israel in the Books of Samuel in the Hebrew Bible

SANCHONIATHON (thirteenth century BC?), purported author of three lost works originally in the Phoenician language, preserved only in fragments

SAUL (*c.*1079–1007 BC), the first king of the united kingdom of Israel, according to the the Hebrew bible and the Qur'an

SCHELLING, FRIEDRICH WILHELM JOSEPH VON (1775–1854), philosopher of German Idealism and Romanticism, much criticized by Schopenhauer, though with somewhat more respect than Hegel and Fichte

SCHILLER, JOHANN CHRISTOPH FRIEDRICH (1759–1805), German poet, dramatist and aesthetician

SCHLEIERMACHER, FRIEDRICH ERNST DANIEL (1768–1834), professor of philosophy and influential Protestant theologist; Schopenhauer attended one of his classes at the University of Berlin, 'History of Philosophy during the Period of Christianity', and was unimpressed

SCHMIDT, I. J. (Isaak Jacob) (1779–1847), German orientalist

SCHUBERT, GOTTHILF HEINRICH VON (1780–1860), doctor, scientist, writer on dreams, professor in Erlangen and Munich

SCHULZE, GOTTLOB ERNST (1761–1833), German professor, sceptical critic of Kant, and Schopenhauer's teacher at the University of Göttingen

SCOTT, WALTER (1771–1823), Scottish novelist

SCOTUS, see Erigena

SCOULER, JOHN (1804–71), Scottish naturalist and ethnographer

SENECA, LUCIUS ANNAEUS (4 BC–AD 65), Roman poet and Stoic thinker, committed suicide at the instigation of Nero

SEXTUS EMPIRICUS (fl. *c.*200), Greek sceptical philosopher

SHAKESPEARE, WILLIAM (1564–1616), the great English dramatist and poet

SHENSTONE, WILLIAM (1714–63), English poet and landscape gardener

SHIVA, Hindu god, the destroyer or transformer, one of the Trimurti

SINCLAIR, GEORGE (?–1696), professor of philosophy and mathematics in the University of Glasgow, author of *Satan's Invisible World Discovered* (1685)

SOCRATES (470–399 BC), Greek philosopher, teacher of Plato

SONNTAG, JOHANN MICHAEL, author of work on apparitions (1703)

SOPHOCLES (*c.*496–406 BC), Greek tragedian

SOUTHEY, ROBERT (1774–1843), English Romantic poet

SPINOZA, BENEDICT (Baruch) DE (1632–77), Dutch philosopher of Jewish origin

STANHOPE, LORD (Philip Henry, Earl of Stanhope) (1781–1855), English aristocrat who adopted Caspar Hauser

STAUNTON, SIR GEORGE (1781–1859), English traveller and orientalist

STILLINGFLEET, EDWARD (1635–99), English theologian and scholar, Bishop of Worcester

STOBAEUS, JOHN (Joannes) (fifth century), author of an anthology of excerpts from previous writers, valuable as a source book for ancient philosophy

STOICISM, school of Hellenistic philosophy dating from the early third century BC, founded by Zeno of Citium in Athens

STRAUSS, DAVID FRIEDRICH (1808–73), German theologian and writer, portrayed Jesus as a historical figure in *The Life of Jesus* (1835–6)

STURZ, FRIEDRICH WILHELM (1762–1832), German classicist, author of work on Empedocles

SUÁREZ, FRANCISCO (1548–1617), Spanish philosopher and transmitter of medieval thought

SUETONIUS (Gaius Suetonius Tranquillus) (*c.*69–*c.*122), Roman historian

SZÁPÁRY, COUNT FRANZ, Hungarian magnetist, author of *Ein Wort über animalischen Magnetismus, Seelenkörper und Lebensessenz* (1840)

TACITUS, CORNELIUS (*c.*55–117), historian of the Roman empire

TAMINO, character in Mozart's *The Magic Flute*

TANNER, JOHN (1732–1812), lived among Native Americans and wrote an account of them

TELLER, JOHANN FRIEDRICH, author of a book on ghosts, *Vom Wiederkommen, Wiedersehen und Erscheinen der unsrigen nach dem Tode* (1806)

TERENCE (Publius Terentius Afer) (*c.*195–159? BC), Roman comic dramatist

TEXTOR, JOHANN WOLFGANG (1693–1771), mayor of Frankfurt, and Goethe's grandfather

THALES OF MILETUS (*c.*624–545 BC), Presocratic Greek philosopher

THEMISTOCLES (*c.*524–459 BC), Athenian politician and general

THEOGNIS (fl. sixth century BC), Greek lyric poet of Megara

THEOPHRASTUS (*c.*371–*c.*287 BC), Greek philosopher, successor to Aristotle in the Peripatetic school

THOMASIUS, CHRISTIAN (1655–1728), instructor in jurisprudence und philosopher, predecessor of the Enlightenment, staunch opponent of witch-trials

THORWALDSEN (Thorvaldsen), BERTEL (1770–1844), Danish sculptor

THYRAEUS, PETRUS (1546–1601), German Jesuit theologian

TIMBS, JOHN (1801–75), English antiquary, author (under the name Horace Welby) of *Signs before Death, and Authenticated Apparitions* (1825)

TREVIRANUS, GOTTFRIED REINHOLD (1776–1835), German natural scientist and mathematician

ULPIAN (Domitius Ulpianus) (*c.*170–228), Roman jurist

VALERIUS MAXIMUS (first century AD), Roman historian and moralist

VANINI, LUCILIO (Giulio Cesare) (1584–1619), Italian Renaissance thinker, tortured and executed by the church

VARRO, MARCUS TERENTIUS (127–116 BC), Roman scholar and satirist

VAUVENARGUES, LUC DE GLAPIERS, MARQUIS DE (1715–47), French moralist

VIRGIL (Publius Vergilius Maro) (70–19 BC), leading Roman poet

VERGINIA (*c.*465–449 BC), daughter of the Roman soldier Lucius Verginius, who killed her to protect her honour

VERGINIUS, LUCIUS, *see* Verginia

VISHNU, Hindu god, the maintainer or preserver, one of the Trimurti

VOLTAIRE (François-Marie Arouet) (1694–1778), French thinker central to the Enlightenment

WÄCHTER, CARL GEORG VON (1797–1880), professor of jurisprudence in
Leipzig, author of *Beiträge zur Deutschen Geschichte* (1845)

WELBY, HORACE, see Timbs, John

WENZEL, GOTTFRIED IMMANUEL (1754–1809), professor of philosophy
in Linz, author of work on dreams and spirit-seeing (1800)

WERNSDORF, GOTTLIEB, author of work on metempsychosis (1780)

WESERMANN, H. M., author of *Der Magnetismus und die allgemeine
Weltsprache* (1822)

WIELAND, CHRISTOPH MARTIN (1733–1813), German poet and writer

WILLIS, THOMAS (1622–76), British anatomist

WIX, THOMAS, apprentice executed for murder in 1846

WOLF, FRIEDRICH AUGUST (1759–1824), classical philologist, professor in
Halle and Berlin

WOLFF, CHRISTIAN (1679–1754), German Enlightenment philosopher

WORCESTER, BISHOP OF, see Stillingfleet, Edward

WORDSWORTH, WILLIAM (1770–1850), English poet

XENOPHANES (sixth/fifth century BC), Presocratic Greek philosopher

XENOPHON (*c.*431–355 BC), Greek soldier and writer, friend and student of
Socrates

ZEIBICH, HEINRICH AUGUST (1729–87), philologist, author of *Gedanken
von der Erscheinung der Geister* (1776)

ZENO OF CITIUM (333–264 BC), Greek philosopher, founder of the Stoic
school

ZENO OF ELEA (*c.*490–*c.*430 BC), Presocratic Greek philosopher, famous
for his paradoxes

ZEUS, Greek mythological figure, ruler of the gods

ZIMMERMANN, JOHANN GEORG RITTER VON (1728–95), Swiss doctor
and philosopher

Index

Made in the USA
Monee, IL
13 September 2021